DATE DUE

AP 19 '96		
DE 18 '99		
OC 12 '05		

DOMESTIC TRANSPORTATION: PRACTICE, THEORY, AND POLICY

SIXTH EDITION

DOMESTIC TRANSPORTATION: PRACTICE, THEORY, AND POLICY

SIXTH EDITION

Roy J. Sampson
University of Oregon

Martin T. Farris
Arizona State University

David L. Shrock
Iowa State University

HOUGHTON MIFFLIN COMPANY   Boston
Dallas   Geneva, Illinois   Palo Alto   Princeton, New Jersey

Library of Congress Catalog Card Number: 89-80960

ISBN: 0-395-43363-0

BCDEFGHIJ-CS-99876543210

CONTENTS

PREFACE

Transportation is ever changing and dynamic. New developments and new approaches, as well as new institutional arrangements, are common. The most significant change has been the complete deregulation of air transportation and surface freight forwarding and the reform of the regulation of other modes of transportation (rail, motor, household goods, and intercity bus). Adjustment to these regulatory changes personifies the 1980s and will continue into the 1990s.

We have attempted to integrate the deregulation of transportation into all parts of this book. An entirely new chapter (Chapter 14, "Consequences of Deregulation") has been added which discusses the ramifications of regulatory reform up to the late 1980s. New chapters have been added in carrier management (Chapters 20 and 21) and in physical distribution management (Chapter 24, "The Logistics Function" and Chapter 25 "Logistics Interface"). Additionally, our readers will note considerable coverage of passenger transportation and its problems — both in specific chapters (Chapters 8 and 9) as well as blended into examples and applications in other chapters. Most students relate more directly to this aspect of transportation and therefore this approach assists in the learning process. Likewise, the order of the chapters has been revised to make a more teachable book and give earlier emphasis to deregulation and its consequences. Finally, all factual and statistical data and end-of-chapter readings have been carefully updated, some chapters have been substantially rewritten and almost every chapter has been revised to some extent. As transportation has changed and developed, each edition of this book has been updated to reflect these changes.

Still our basic approach remains the same. We continue to integrate and present the transportation industry as a whole rather than separating the problems and practices artificially into rail, motor, air, water, pipeline, forwarder, or shipper spheres. We feel that incorporating both applied and theoretical approaches to transportation will be valuable to both economics and business administration students. We have merged the traditional subfields of transportation economics and physical distribution/ business logistics, since both are essential to transportation majors and are obviously desirable for students in both economics and business. Rather than specializing in one area, we have favored a middle ground equally comfortable for business administration and economics students.

We have organized the text into eight parts. Part I establishes the importance of our domestic transportation system and portrays its historical background and evolution as well as societal concerns with transportation. Part II is a comprehensive overview of our present system and its general performance as well as the international, passenger, and geographic aspects of transportation. Part III deals with the regulatory structure and institutions within which transportation operates and stresses deregulation and its consequences. Part IV considers rates, both theory and practice, in the important area of transportation pricing where the interrelationships of demand, costs, rates and the location of economic activities come into play. Part V is composed of two chapters which consider the interesting area of carrier management while Part VI analyzes in detail physical distribution/business logistics or the user side of transportation. Part VII discusses transportation problems and policy that are part of the institutional environment. Finally, Part VIII, a single chapter, presents the authors' educated guesses concerning future transportation technology, regulation and public policy, and the future role of traffic management/physical distribution/business logistics. After studying these 30 chapters, potential transportation majors should be ready for advanced courses, and nonmajors should have at least the minimum transportation background necessary for most general business activity. An instructor's manual is again available.

We wish to acknowledge our indebtedness and grateful appreciation to our former transportation professors, the late Professor Stuart Daggett, University of California at Berkeley, and the late Professor Ralph L. Dewey, The Ohio State University, and Professor L.L. Waters, Indiana University. We also wish to thank the many professors and students in four-year colleges and universities, and community colleges, independent study groups, and transportation practitioners whose use of our previous editions encouraged us to make this revision.

In particular, we are extremely grateful to our many colleagues throughout the country and abroad who have suggested numerous improvements through formal reviews, private correspondence, and informal verbal communication over the years. Their names are far too numerous to list here, but we hope that this new edition continues to meet their needs and that they will continue to give us their suggestions.

R.J.S.   M.T.F.   D.L.S.

PART I

THE ROLE OF DOMESTIC TRANSPORTATION

In order to appreciate the complexities of the domestic transportation system of the United States, it is necessary to understand three things: (1) the significance of transportation, (2) its environmental impact, and (3) its development.

A grasp of the significance of transportation, and its general and specific environmental effects, prepares us to understand why the specifics of the system are meaningful. An understanding of the past as well as the development and evolution of our transportation system prepares us to appreciate the position of domestic transportation today and to gain insight into its problems.

The first three chapters of this book are written with these ideas in mind.

CHAPTER 1

THE SIGNIFICANCE OF TRANSPORTATION

Our American transportation system is so all-pervasive and so efficient that most of us rarely think about it unless we are inconvenienced by a breakdown of some of its parts. Instead, we tend to take transportation for granted. Our daily journeys to and from work, shopping centers, or university classrooms involve transportation. Every product we consume has been transported, usually several times, before it gets to us. Even the services we consume would be impossible without transportation of tools, repair parts, or other means of producing services.

In a more general way, transportation is an important part of our culture and heritage. It played a pivotal role in the discovery, settlement, and development of our nation. The westward movement, discussed by historians and immortalized by folk songs about steamboating, railroading, and long cattle drives, was a chapter in transportation development. The freedom and mobility of our people, literally a nation on wheels and a people ever curious to see new places and ever anxious to undertake new tasks, is based upon efficient transportation. Our lives are shaped by transportation much more than we realize.

This wonderfully complex and efficient transportation system, however, did not reach its present form without travail, nor does it operate without direction. Its past history is dwarfed only by its present immensity and its future prospects. Therefore some understanding of this system — its general significance and its specific uses, its internal workings and its external relationships, its origins and its future paths, its problems and its accomplishments — is a necessary part of the education of every person aspiring to play a significant part in the economic, business, or political life of our country.

GENERAL SIGNIFICANCE OF TRANSPORTATION

Much of our social and cultural unity is based upon the existence of adequate transportation. Society is a blend of many regional and local viewpoints and traditions growing out of differing heritages, environments, and problems. Interregional contacts through travel and the exchange of goods promote the interchange of ideas and the breakdown of parochialism, thus encouraging an upward uniformity in tastes, health, education, and way of life in general.

Likewise, efficient transportation makes it possible for large geographic areas to be politically unified. Cultural similarity, mutual understanding, and the economic interdependence brought about by large-scale interregional trade reduce tendencies toward isolationism, while the ability to communicate rapidly makes unification administratively feasible. Ancient Egypt was held together for many centuries by its Nile River and ancient Rome by its magnificent system of highways. Ancient Greece, on the other hand, with a terrain that hindered a well-developed system of internal transport, remained a group of independent and squabbling city-states until it fell victim to an outside conqueror.

One cause for our own country's secession from Britain, despite a common heritage, was the slow and inefficient transport that hampered political administration and mutual understanding. In more recent times, the United States government authorized and supported the building of the first transcontinental railroad partly to encourage California to remain within the Union during the Civil War. The first Canadian transcontinental railroad was likewise built to encourage the province of British Columbia to remain a political part of Canada. Australians built a railroad across the wide desert area of their continent to hold their country together politically. Railroads played a key role in Bismarck's unification of numerous small independent states and principalities into modern Germany during the late 1800s. Many other examples of this kind could be cited illustrating the cohesive force of transportation.

Good transportation is also vital to national defense. The ability to transport troops and materials quickly and to mobilize industrial power is essential both in actual war and in international political bargaining. Transportation is both a weapon and a deterrent, and its importance to defense has increased rather than diminished in this age of global conflict and potential push-button nuclear warfare.

ECONOMIC SIGNIFICANCE OF TRANSPORTATION

The economic significance of transportation can best be appreciated by considering transportation in five separate but interconnected roles. These are: (1) transportation and economic development, (2) transportation and production, (3) transportation and distribution, (4) transportation and prices, and (5) transportation and the economy. Each will be considered in turn.

Transportation and Economic Development

Several basic elements are necessary for substantial economic growth. Three of these are an adequate transportation system, an adequate system of communication, and a flexible source of energy or power. Our primary concern is with adequate transportation.

The transportation system is an integral part of production and distribution. Both large-scale production and mass distribution are necessary for economic development. Neither is possible without efficient and relatively cheap transportation. Transportation is the very foundation of economic development.

We are fortunate in possessing one of the most highly developed domestic transportation systems in the world. Our present transportation system, however, is the result of a great struggle over a period of many years. Much of it was financed by profit-seeking foreign capital as others helped us develop the foundations of economic growth. Now we are doing the same for other areas, although generally not for direct profit-making purposes.

But the point is that the first, and often overlooked, economic significance of transportation is that it provides a foundation upon which the economic growth of a nation progresses. Therefore, those who make decisions affecting transportation, whether private transport company managers, public officials, or users of transport services, have great social responsibilities.

Transportation and Production

Transportation is an integral part of the process of production. This can be seen from several points of view. One traditional view is to note that transportation creates both place and time utility.

Basically, transportation means changing the place or the location of an item. The classical economists noted that value could be created by this process of changing location; thus they called this *place utility,* or the creation of value by changing position or location. For productive purposes, raw materials or parts for assembly are of no value unless they are transported to the place where they are needed. Production usually calls for the change of location of many items, bringing them together in the right proportions to produce something. We rarely refer to place utility today, but the principle still exists. Transportation creates value by changing the location of things and people so that production may occur.

In addition, transportation takes time. Not only is movement itself time consuming, but the assembly of goods uses time. We generally think of delays in time as being costly and wasteful. Often they are, but under some conditions they can be profitable and economical. Large-scale production involves assembling many items from diverse sources. All do not arrive at the same time, and storage (delay) is often necessary. However, having the necessary item so that the productive process moves smoothly can be very valuable. Some delay through storage of necessary components at times may avoid the greater delay of shortages. The matter of delay over time and its effect on production was called *time utility* by the classical economists. Again, transportation creates value by time utility.

It is easy to see that large-scale production depends on time and place utility and hence upon transportation. Often large-scale production is considerably cheaper than production on a smaller scale. Yet the huge output of our productive system would be impossible without adequate transportation and assembly facilities to bring tremendous amounts of raw materials to the place of production and to hold them until the exact time they are needed. Of course, the dependence on transportation as a foundation for large-scale production varies according to the characteristics of the product. Some products, like steel, require that tremendous tonnages of raw materials be transported and stored for the production process. Other items such as electronic gear require very small tonnages of materials. In the case of steel, it is a problem of mass movement of great weights. The problem in electronics may be just as perplexing; while the tonnages are very small, the materials are highly valuable and sometimes very fragile. In both cases, however, transportation is necessary in order to facilitate production on a large scale.

When we consider the nation as a whole or the entire world, it is apparent that transportation stimulates regional specialization and division of labor. All areas and peoples are not equally endowed. Resources, climate, arts, and skills vary. Thus the productive process in one region may be different from that in another. With adequate transportation, each area is able to specialize in the production it does best. This is the principle of comparative advantage, which is studied in basic economics. But this principle can be operative only when transportation is possible. If it is not possible to obtain the specialized goods produced elsewhere or to send the fruits of one region's production to others, each area finds it must devote most of its effort to satisfying its own needs. Little specialization or regional division of labor can take place without transportation.

Because of this regional specialization and division of labor, and because transportation allows large-scale production, the transportation system becomes a determining factor in the location of production facilities. Chapter 9 will analyze this locational factor in detail. It is necessary here only to point out that transportation furthers the productive process, helps determine where production is likely to take place, and permits the large concentration of foodstuffs and raw materials necessary to support densely populated manufacturing areas.

Finally, it should be noted that transportation is one of the costs of production. Although transportation obviously creates value, it does so only at a cost. Everything one buys has a transportation cost within it. The amount varies, of course, according to the characteristic of the item and the productive process. Yet the cost of transportation is there because transportation is an integral part of the productive process.

Transportation and Distribution

Transportation is also an integral part of distribution. Again, time and place utility are involved. An item produced at one point has little value unless it is moved to the place where it is needed or demanded. Movement through space creates value. The timeliness of marketing is most important. Delay in time can often increase value by preventing a market glut that lowers value. Storage and delay allow us to enjoy production long after the physical production has ceased. Hence value is created by changes in time.

Large-scale production cannot exist in a vacuum. It is necessary to have mass distribution systems to move the items produced. The most efficient large-scale production plant cannot operate unless the things produced are sold. An adequate transportation system provides the means by which mass distribution takes place. Commonly, it is said that "transportation broadens the market." All that this means is that transportation allows mass distribution to operate. Hence transportation and distribution are closely interconnected.

Again, the results of regional specialization or division of labor are unavailable without transportation. By having an efficient transportation system, the availability of goods is greatly increased. Perishable items are now available in areas where they were unheard of a few years ago because of technological advances of transportation. The whole country, indeed the whole world, is now a market for production based on good transportation. Transportation provides the means to distribute the results of production and makes a multiplicity of goods available from all around the earth.

Just as transportation determines the location of production, it also determines the location of markets. If transportation costs are high, a protected market area exists for a few producers just as effectively as if import tariffs or quotas existed. Often the determining factor in the marketing decision is transportation.

Finally, transportation obviously is one of the costs of distribution. In this sense, it has a marked effect on the price of most items. Naturally, the amount of transportation costs involved in distribution varies with the characteristics of the item, but, on the whole, transportation is a major cost of distribution just as it is of production.

Transportation and Prices

Enough has been said to make it apparent that transportation costs make up a substantial share of the price of any item. Estimates vary, of course, and different physical characteristics of an item mean different amounts of transportation costs, but, on the average, more than 20 cents of every consumer dollar goes to transportation. The Interstate Commerce Commission (ICC) makes various studies from time to time of the ratio of transportation rates to wholesale prices. For some items such as sand and gravel, transportation makes up over half the price. On others such as business machines, the ratio is less than 1 percent. Most products, of course, fall somewhere between these ranges.

In addition to being a component of all prices, transportation plays other roles in price. One of the more important of these is price stability. If long-haul transportation were not available, each market would be dependent on the local production area for its supply. Most items are not produced equally during each month of the year. This is especially true of agricultural items that have a long production cycle culminating in a harvest period. Under circumstances of isolation and without adequate transportation, the price of an item would be low when available in large quantities and high when scarce.

However, transportation allows other areas to compete in a given market. Therefore, if local supplies are unavailable, the price usually does not rise greatly. Supplies may be shipped in to meet the need. Theoretically, the price in any market in time of shortage of local supplies should rise no more than the cost of transportation, processing, and storage. Actually, because of the regional specialization and division of labor noted above, prices may rise considerably less than this, since the supplying area often produces more cheaply than the local area owing to economies of specialization. A great deal of price stability therefore exists in most market areas because of transportation.

In addition to price stability and the leveling out of supplies, transportation also promotes lower prices. By allowing more producers to enter a given market, more price competition is possible. Areas with the lowest production costs *plus* transportation costs set the price. Others must meet this price or lose their share of the market. Since regional specialization is possible, this may mean that suppliers some distance from a market are actually setting the price. Without transportation and more competitors in a given market, the price could be higher. Generally, adequate transportation promotes competition and lowers prices.

Economists have long pointed out the relationship between transportation and the use and price of land. Good transportation allows land to be used in a number of ways. The value of land will depend on its productivity. This productivity may be a matter of location or a matter of location plus the value of the yield from the land use. In either case, location is merely a conceptualization of the transportation position of land in space, and the value of the yield from land is primarily dependent upon the price in a given market. Thus both of these factors are based upon transportation. The same principles are involved for the value of other natural resources.

Enough has been said to make the points that all prices have transportation costs involved in them, that transportation promotes price stability, that transportation promotes competition and usually lowers prices, and that transportation often determines the price of natural resources.

Transportation and the Economy

Few people are fully aware of the size of the job done by our transportation system in supporting our country's economy and standard of living. Perhaps we can better appreciate this by looking at it in simple and personal terms.

Our railroads each year haul more than 12,500 pounds of freight for an average of around 650 miles for every person in the country. Trucks haul more than 19,000 pounds for over 300 miles, water carriers haul over 8,000 pounds for more than 800 miles, air carriers haul more than 55 pounds for 1,200 miles, and oil pipelines carry around 1,100 gallons of oil over 600 miles for each of us. Further, the average American now travels approximately 7,600 intercity miles per year — 6,100 miles by auto, 1,350 miles by air, 90 miles by bus, and 50 miles by rail. These figures do not include local hauling or travel.

Tables 1.1 and 1.2 give an overview of our dependence upon transportation and show how this dependence has changed in magnitude and among modes of transport during the past generation. Clearly, both in ton-miles (one ton of freight hauled for one mile) and passenger-miles (one passenger traveling for one mile), our individual dependence upon transport increased substantially during the period shown.

Additionally, the responsibilities of transportation were increased by our population growth of more than 40 percent since 1950 and by our tripling of industrial output. In summary, our transport system has provided a constantly increasing amount of individual services for our continually growing population and economy. Another way to consider the economic significance of transportation is to relate the transportation industry to segments of the total economy. This can be done by considering seven points: (1) the nation's annual transportation bill, (2) the amount and earnings of persons employed in transportation and transportation-related fields, (3) the amount of capital invested in the national transportation plant, (4) the importance of public expenditures to aid the transportation system, (5) the tax role of transportation, (6) the pivotal role of the transportation industry as a buyer of the production of others, and (7) transportation as a user and mover of petroleum products. In all cases, we will be considering transportation in a rather broad context.

Table 1.1   U.S. Intercity Ton Miles Hauled per Capita, per Mode, for Selected Years.

Mode	1950	1960	1970	1987
Railroad	3,927	3,193	3,761	3,967
Trucks	1,138	1,574	2,010	2,337
Oil Pipelines	848	1,574	2,102	2,407
Domestic Water	1,078	1,215	1,556	1,794
Air	0.2	0.5	16.1	37.0

Source: Calculated by the authors from data in Transportation Association of America, *Transportation Facts and Trends,* 17th ed., Washington, 1981, and Transportation Policy Associates, *Transportation in America,* 6th ed., Washington, July 1988 Supplement.

Table 1.2   U.S. Intercity Passenger-Miles Traveled per Capita, per Mode, for Selected Years.

Mode	1950	1960	1970	1987
Automobile	2,883	3,901	5,005	6,362
Air	65	188	579	1,453
Bus	149	107	123	97
Railroad	214	119	53	52

Source: Calculated by the authors from data in Transportation Association of America, *Transportation Facts and Trends,* 17th ed., Washington, 1981, and Transportation Policy Associates, *Transportation in America,* 6th ed., Washington, July 1988 Supplement.

The Nation's Annual Transportation Bill

The Transportation Policy Associates periodically calculates the annual freight and passenger bills paid by the country as a whole. The latest figures show that the nation paid about $291 billion for freight transportation services and about $513 billion for passenger transportation during 1987. Note that this transportation bill is almost 18 percent of the gross national product ($4,488 billion in 1987). Figures 1.1 and 1.2 show how the nation's freight and passenger expenditures are distributed among the various modes of transportation.

The Amount and Earnings of Persons Employed in Transportation

Overall employment in transportation and transportation-related industries was more than 10 million persons in 1986. This amounts to about 10 percent of the total labor force in the United States. The Transportation Association of America studies show that this proportion of total employed has held fairly constant since 1940, even though there have been some changes in the numbers in various occupational classifications. The four subgroups involved in this 10-million figure are carrier personnel, transportation equipment manufacturing personnel, related industry personnel (which includes auto sales and service, highway construction, and truck drivers in general industry), and transportation employees of federal and state governments. Thus it should not be assumed from these figures that one out of every ten employed persons drives a truck, runs an engine, or flies a plane. Even so, all these people are directly related to domestic transportation; and it is therefore possible to say that transportation is one of the largest employers in the economy.

Additionally, the earnings of full-time employees working directly in transportation are highly competitive on the average. In 1986, full-time employees in the transportation industry earned an average annual wage of $25,628, or 16.8 percent over the national average of $21,935 for all industries. Of course, averages can be misleading, but the figures do tend to show that wages in transportation are superior to those in many fields.

Thus, not only is one out of every ten persons employed in transportation or transportation-related fields, but the direct transportation workers are paid a high average annual wage. Transportation makes a substantial contribution to the total economy in both number employed and income generated by wages.

Figure 1.1 The Nation's Estimated Freight Bill for 1987*
(in billion of dollars, rounded)

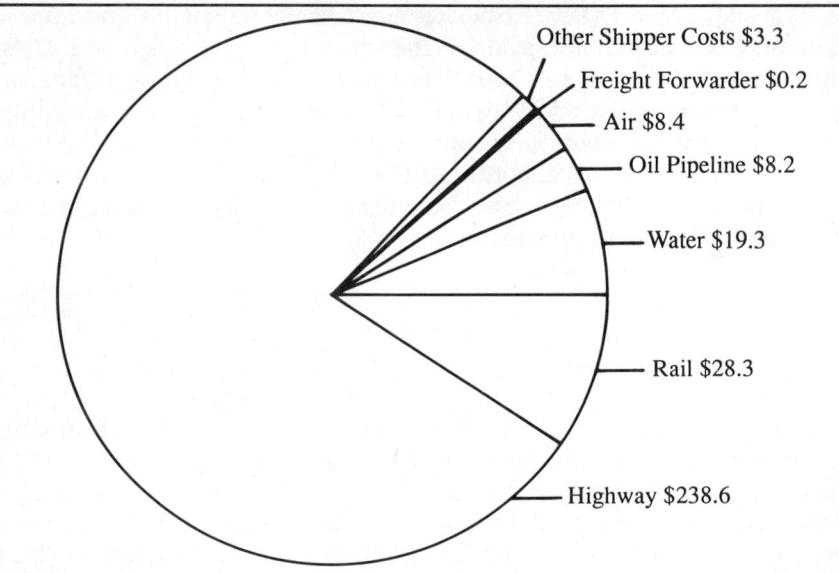

Other Shipper Costs $3.3
Freight Forwarder $0.2
Air $8.4
Oil Pipeline $8.2
Water $19.3
Rail $28.3
Highway $238.6

Figure 1.2 The Nation's Estimated Passenger Bill for 1987
(in billions of dollars, rounded)

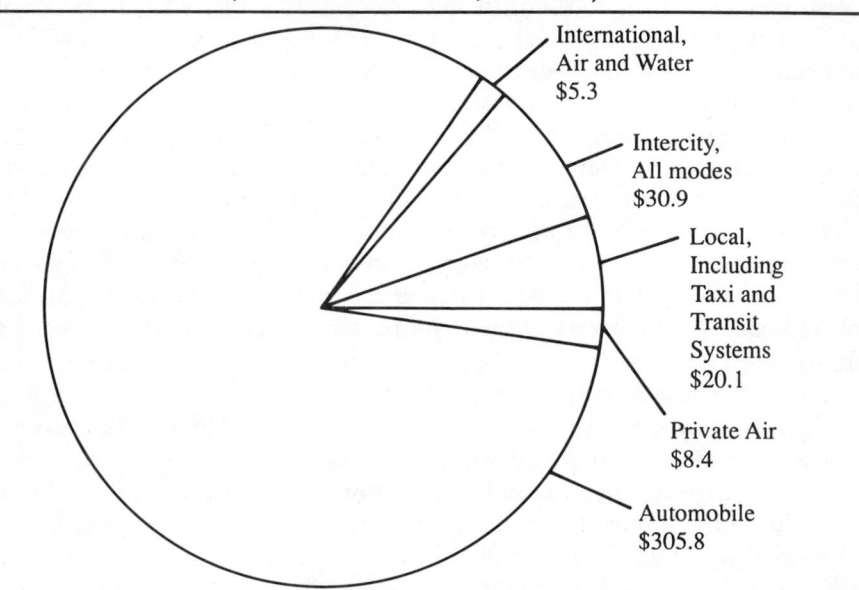

International,
Air and Water
$5.3

Intercity,
All modes
$30.9

Local,
Including
Taxi and
Transit
Systems
$20.1

Private Air
$8.4

Automobile
$305.8

*Figures include both regulated and nonregulated transportation, domestic as well as international.
**Includes loading and unloading of freight cars as well as the operation of traffic departments.
Source: Adapted from Transportation Policy Associates, *Transportation in America*, 6th ed., Washington, D.C., July 1988 Supplement. Copyright 1988. Used by permission of Eno Foundation for Transportation.

Capital Invested in Transportation

The fact that most types of transportation are heavy users of capital is fully developed later in this book. However, if one pauses to consider the tremendous amount of equipment, terminals, trucks, pipes, ships, and planes in our transportation system, it is readily apparent that the amount invested in transportation is substantial. The gross stock of fixed private capital invested in the transportation system was $584 billion in 1986. In that same year, business expenditures for new plant and equipment totaled $18.8 billion in this country.

Public Expenditures for Transportation Facilities

In addition to the tremendous sums privately invested in transportation facilities, large annual capital expenditures are made by federal, state, and local governments on transportation facilities, especially highways. While Chapter 26 will develop the background of these public aids and promotional undertakings, it can be noted here that the total amounts are large. For instance, in 1987 more than $75 billion was spent by federal, state, and local governments in building and administering domestic transportation facilities. It is clear that capital expenditures by the public through governmental projects are no small part of the governments' budgets each year. Again, transportation is seen as an important part of the economy.

The Tax Role of Transportation

But transportation does more than merely spend public funds on facilities; it collects and pays a rather significant share of the total tax bill for the various governments involved. Practically all highway expenditures are collected in the form of taxes on highway users, chiefly as gasoline taxes. Until the 1960s, both passenger tickets and freight bills included an excise tax to the federal government. In 1982, federal gas taxes increased from 4¢ per gallon to 9¢ per gallon, and in 1984, a 15.5¢ per gallon tax on diesel fuel was imposed. Airline tickets have included an 8 percent tax since 1970 as well as an air freight tax. In 1986, transportation accounted for over $15 billion in federal taxes. In regard to taxes collected by the states, over $24 billion was collected from transportation in 1986. In total, over $39 billion was paid to federal and state governments by transportation in 1986. Thus transportation plays a major role as a collector and payer of taxes in the economy.

Transportation as a User of Industrial Products

Finally, it should be noted that the transportation industry is a major consumer of the industrial production of the nation. When one considers that transportation in its broadest sense includes the assembly of automobiles and trucks, this is almost self-evident. Yet students are often surprised to learn that transportation uses 71 percent of all rubber produced, 66 percent of all petroleum refined, 72 percent of all lead, 24 percent of all zinc, 23 percent of all cement, 23 percent of all steel, 11 percent of all copper, and 16 percent of all aluminum. Certainly, transportation is one of the major buyers of the economy's industrial production.

Transportation and Petroleum Products

A close interrelationship exists between transportation and oil. About 66 percent of all petroleum refined in the United States is used in transportation. Highway uses account for about 81 percent of this, air transportation uses almost 8 percent, rail and water transportation consume about 3 and 7 percent, respectively, and lubricants for all modes of transport account for about 1 percent. But on the other hand, all petroleum and petroleum products are moved by transportation. During 1980, pipelines accounted for about 46 percent of this total movement, trucks for 27 percent, water carriers for 26 percent, and railroads for 1 percent in this country. During this period of concern over energy sources and shortages, the functions of transportation as both a user and a mover of petroleum products are of considerable significance.

Summary

There may well be other means of illustrating the economic significance of transportation to the total economy. However, by noting the nation's annual transportation bill amounting to 18 percent of the gross national product, the 10 percent of the labor force employed in transportation at high annual income levels, the large privately owned transportation plant, the large annual federal, state, and local government expenditures for transportation, the 14 percent of federal and 26 percent of state revenues attributable to transportation, the significant role of transportation as a buyer of industrial production, and the close connection between transportation and petroleum, one can readily appreciate the pivotal importance of transportation in our total economy.

Having considered the significance of transportation in a general as well as in an economic sense, we are ready to review briefly the role of transportation in business and as a mover of people.

TRANSPORTATION AND BUSINESS LOGISTICS

As indicated above, the provision of transportation services is itself one of our leading forms of private business enterprise. Many transportation companies have assets of more than $1 billion each, and several are in the $2 or $3 billion class, or higher. But the most important aspect of transportation is that it supplies essential business services to all other businesses.

Definition of Business Logistics or
Physical Distribution Management

During recent years, the terms *business logistics* and *physical distribution management* have become a part of our business vocabulary. These two terms often are used interchangeably, as they may be defined to include the same activities. Some persons do see differences in what these terms mean, but the authors prefer to think of them as being the same.

Business logistics, or physical distribution management, may be defined broadly as the management of the movement of goods through space (by transport) and through time (by warehousing, storage, production scheduling, and related activities) from their first origins as raw materials to their final destinations in consumers' hands.

The primary objective of physical distribution is the same as the overall objective of any privately owned business, namely, to optimize cost-value ratios. That is, it attempts to increase monetary values as much as possible, with the least relative increases in monetary costs. From the firm's viewpoint, this maximizes profits; from society's viewpoint, it increases economic efficiency. These two viewpoints do not necessarily conflict in a private enterprise economy.

Contrary to some, we do not view the physical distribution process as being a part of marketing. Rather, we prefer to think of marketing, as it is commonly conceived, as being part of a larger distribution process. This overall distribution process can be subdivided into institutional components and physical components. Institutional distribution — comprising various buying, selling, and related activities of wholesalers, jobbers, brokers, and retailers, as well as advertising, marketing, research, and the like — is what is known commonly as marketing. Physical distribution, on the other hand, includes such activities as the scheduling of purchasing, inventory control, storage, warehousing, and materials handling, some aspects of manufacturing or processing (as production scheduling and packaging), and, of course, transportation.

Average Costs of Physical Distribution

The aim of all economic activity involving goods is to transfer things from their present forms, places, and time references to more highly desired forms, places, and time references. That is, the objective is to increase values by increasing form utilities (by production) and space and time utilities (by physical distribution). Value increases, of course, are accompanied by cost increases. It is therefore worthwhile to consider the relative magnitudes of production and distribution costs.

Many marketing students agree that about 41¢ of the average consumer dollar spent for goods goes for production costs, and 59¢ for distribution costs. (These costs include profits, of course.) The authors' own studies indicate that at least 30¢ or more of the 59¢ distribution costs go for what we have defined as physical distribution, leaving 29¢ or less attributable to institutional distribution (marketing). Further, almost 16¢ of this 30¢ goes for transportation, leaving about 15¢ for the various other physical distribution costs.

This makes transportation costs the third largest single cost in the entire economic process of production and distribution. For the average business (although there are many exceptions, both upward and downward), transportation costs are exceeded only by the costs of labor and materials.

Business Management of Transportation
and Physical Distribution

As transportation and other physical distribution expenditures require such a large part of the revenues of the average firm, it is apparent that these expenditures must be well managed if the firm is to be most profitable.

Industrial traffic managers, who supervise the buying of their companys' transportation services, along with many other related transportation matters, have long been key figures in the activities of most large or medium-sized firms. They must be experts in transportation, as well as good managers. Their performance directly affects both company profits and company services.

Physical distribution managers (known by various titles, depending upon the preferences of individual companies) are relatively new on the business scene and are not yet as much a part of the scene as are traffic managers. Their function is to supervise all physical distribution activities (and sometimes even marketing activities) and to coordinate these with other company functions. They must have a good working knowledge of transportation but do not necessarily require the specialized knowledge of industrial traffic managers — they supervise traffic managers.

This book is concerned with basic transportation. It deals with the essential transport matters that every traffic manager and physical distribution manager must know and that every businessperson and well-informed citizen should know. It does not delve deeply into the advanced areas of traffic management and physical distribution management, although Part VI gives a general overview of these specialized fields of management. Those choosing careers in these fields can move from this beginning into more advanced topics or courses.

TRANSPORTATION AND PERSONAL MOBILITY

Table 1.2 shows that the United States is a mobile society. The importance of the movement of people from place to place cannot be overemphasized. This personal transportation may be within a city, from a city to its suburbs or the countryside, or between cities, states, regions, or even nations. But whatever the journey's length, passenger transportation is an integral part of our economy and society.

There are two distinct and competing forms of passenger transportation, private and for-hire. Private passenger transportation is primarily by automobile and usually involves relatively high costs per passenger-mile. For-hire passenger transportation, on the other hand, provides a basic day-to-day, hour-to-hour, regularly scheduled, convenient, and relatively inexpensive service essential to the needs of large numbers of persons. Each form of passenger transportation has a separate economic role to play. Our society would find it difficult to exist in its present form without both.

Although movements of goods and movements of people are distinct and separate transportation and economic functions, a close interrelationship does exist between people transport and things transport. Both use the same ways (highways, airways, railways, waterways), and both often are supplied by the same firm and even use the same vehicles. Thus a significant physical, operational, financial, and economic interface exists between freight and passenger transportation. Each is influenced by the other.

TRANSPORTATION AND CAREER OPPORTUNITIES

College graduates in nontechnical or nonscientific fields have a wide variety of occupational choices available in transportation and related areas. In addition to traffic or physical distribution management with commercial or industrial firms, mentioned above, careers are available with many federal, state, or local agencies involved with regulating, promoting, or operating transportation, or with purchasing transportation services.

Some are employed by consulting firms that deal with transport problems, and others by various private nonprofit organizations such as chambers of commerce, trade associations, shippers' associations, or other service groups. Still others work in firms supplying basic needs of the transportation industry — for example, financial institutions, transportation brokerage agencies, equipment manufacturers and dealers, and the like.

Transportation companies themselves have the same needs for a wide variety of personnel as do other businesses. These needs include almost all occupations, literally from accountants to zoologists. College students in business administration, economics, or liberal arts, with some academic background in transportation, are most likely to find entry-level positions with transportation firms in areas such as marketing, finance, computer or statistical applications, or terminal management. Some firms frequently hire graduates for special accelerated management trainee positions.

Altogether, several thousand professional and managerial positions, suitable for nontechnical college graduates, become vacant through attrition each year in the transportation industry itself. These do not include the additional positions created by economic growth, or positions closely related to, but not directly in, the transportation industry. There are other broad occupational fields with larger numbers of available positions, of course, but the number of job opportunities for college graduates in transportation and related fields still far exceeds the number of college students specializing in or doing substantial academic work in this area.

Until quite recently, entry into the managerial or professional levels in transportation was almost exclusively limited to white males. This is no longer so. Since the early 1970s, women and minority group members increasingly have been hired for challenging and upwardly mobile transportation positions.

ADDITIONAL READINGS

Bowersox, Donald J., Pat J. Calabro, and George D. Wagenheim, *Introduction to Transportation*, New York: Macmillan Publishing Co., 1981.
Chapter 2, "The Role of Transportation," pp. 14–28.
Coyle, John J., Edward J. Bardi, and Joseph L. Cavinato, *Transportation*, 2nd ed., St. Paul: West Publishing Co., 1986.
Chapter 1, "Transportation and the Economy," pp. 3–24.
Davis, Grant M., Martin T. Farris, and Jack J. Holder, Jr., *Management of Transportation Carriers*, New York: Praeger Publishers, 1975.
Chapter 1, "The Domestic Transportation System," pp. 3–20.
Farris, Martin T., and Forrest E. Harding, *Passenger Transportation*, Englewood Cliffs, N.J.: Prentice-Hall, 1976.
Chapter 1, "The Importance of Passenger Transportation," pp. 3–11.
Lieb, Robert C., *Transportation: The Domestic System*, 3rd ed., Reston, Va.: Reston Publishing Co., 1985.
Chapter 1, "Transportation and Its Role in Society," pp. 3–15.
Locklin, D. Philip, *Economics of Transportation*, 7th ed., Homewood, Ill.: Richard D. Irwin, 1972.
Chapter 1, "Economic Significance of Improved Transportation," pp. 1–18.
Pegrum, Dudley F., *Transportation: Economics and Public Policy*, 3rd ed., Homewood, Ill.: Richard D. Irwin, 1973.
Chapter 1, "Transportation and the Economy," pp. 1–37.
Stephenson, Frederick J., Jr., *Transportation USA*, Reading, Mass.: Addison Wesley Publishing Co., 1987.
Chapter 1, "The Relevance of Transportation," pp. 3–24.
Wood, Donald F., and James C. Johnson, *Contemporary Transportation*, 3rd ed., New York: Macmillan Publishing Co., 1989.
Chapter 1, "Transportation: An Overview," pp. 1–23.

CHAPTER 2

THE DEVELOPMENT OF TRANSPORTATION

The history of transportation development and growth in the United States is the history of the nation itself. In this respect, the necessity for an adequate domestic transportation system is aptly illustrated. This chapter will discuss the development of domestic transportation in this country and point out the economic and political effects of that development.

THE IMPORTANCE OF GEOGRAPHY AND TECHNOLOGY

It is hard to overemphasize the importance of geography in the development of domestic transportation. The United States is a huge land mass with a diversity of geographic forms. Some of these, such as mountains, prevent transportation systems from penetrating various areas. Others, such as rivers and lakes, promote transportation development with their natural ways or their relatively favorable grades. Additionally, the size of the country is both a deterrent and a stimulus to transportation development.

The continental land mass, with over 3 million square miles, held out a challenge to be conquered. More than 3,000 miles from coast to coast and 1,500 miles from the Gulf of Mexico to Canada, the United States presented a herculean task to our predecessors as they envisioned taming the virgin land. To meet the challenge and to settle and civilize such a vast area meant that transportation had to become a leading industry of the country, a necessary prerequisite, and a vehicle of history.

In any given area, land forms present a series of alternatives to the necessary transportation system. Often it is less expensive to go around a hill than to go over or through it, to go around a lake than to bridge it. Today's transportation network, reflecting these geographic alternatives, is not always based on the most direct line between two points. It was not until technology allowed us to travel in the air that transportation began to break the fetters of geography. And even here, the congestion of airways between some large cities (often located relative to geographic land forms such as rivers and harbors) again threatens to saddle transportation development with another barrier, space.

Technology, too, has been important. In order to develop necessary speeds and carry weights of economic significance, rail transportation had to await the development of the steel rail and the steam locomotive. To have adequate domestic motor transportation, improved highways were necessary. To move highway traffic in a flexible and expedient manner, adequate motive systems such as the internal combustion engine were necessary. Engines awaited advances in petroleum technology. And so it goes. Numerous examples and innovations could be cited. It is impossible at times to indicate which came first or which development caused what, but it is clear that technology and transportation have been closely tied together.

Thus as we trace the development of transportation, we must be alert to the forces of geography and the role of technology. Often a better understanding is gained by tracing development in terms of time. Hence the development of transportation as presented here is in more or less chronological order.

WATER TRANSPORTATION CAME FIRST

Water transportation came first in this country. While transportation by horse, on foot, by chariot and wagon had developed in early times, it was primarily the development of ocean-going vessels that led to real commerce among nations, states, and regions. Prior to the settlement of the New World by whites, ocean transportation had become quite highly developed in many areas of the world, and it was by means of ocean transportation that the New World was discovered.

When permanent settlement began in what is now the United States, the existing water transportation technology of Europe was imposed upon America. Parts of our coastline were indented by rivers, streams, and bays. Thus a most active water transportation system naturally evolved in America, particularly between the various settlements or colonies and Europe.

Overland travel was slow and tedious. Roads of colonial America were merely widened Indian trails which lacked bridges, wandered about the countryside in a haphazard manner, and were usually impassable in poor weather. The trip from Philadelphia to New York took three days by the fastest overland means and necessitated several transfers to different wagons and boats. It is little wonder, then, that water transportation was first developed and remained the main type of domestic transportation for many decades.

It was often easier for the earlier settlers to send their products to Europe than to trade with each other. Regular shipping routes between Europe and the colonies were well established. Markets in Europe were highly developed and organized. Good means for handling shipments were readily available. Most transportation, therefore, even as late as Revolutionary times, was between individual American points and Europe rather than between American ports.

With the many rivers on the American East Coast, it was only natural that water transportation would develop first. Settlement typically proceeded inland from the coastline. The successful tobacco plantation of early America always included its own dock and warehouse facilities at riverside. In the northern colonies where the fall line (upper limit of navigation because of rapids or falls) was closer to the coast, commercial ports or cities developed. In the middle and southern colonies where the rivers and bays were numerous and the geographical barrier somewhat more distant from the coast, fewer ports were developed as each settlement could generally accommodate trade by its own facilities.

In certain areas coastal traffic did develop, of course. Small boats could go farther upstream and hence tap more territory. These same boats could call at the numerous coastal points. With roads so dangerous and expensive, colonial America depended greatly on water transportation between its various settlements and colonies. Coastal water transportation was the accepted and in some cases the only domestic transportation available. For example, when General George Washington traveled to the then capital of our newly independent country (New York City) to be inaugurated as our first president, he traveled by boat from Virginia. Upon landing at the Battery on Manhattan Island, he paraded up Broadway on his stallion (which had also come by boat) to the capitol building on Wall Street (opposite the present site of the New York Stock Exchange).

Besides being naturally available and faster, coastal water transportation was generally cheaper than overland transportation. Even today water transportation remains one of the least expensive types of movement. The reason is quite simple. Less energy (hence less expense) is necessary to move a given weight on water than on land, provided that the movement is not at high speeds.

Above the fall line and on western rivers where the fall line was many miles inland, a very active raft and river traffic grew up. Various vessels were constructed to float with the current and provide efficient (although slow) transportation. It has been estimated, for example, that in 1790 over 150,000 bushels of grain were floated down the Susquehanna River to Philadelphia. Studies have shown that as late as 1818 some two-thirds of the market crops of the Piedmont plateau were raised within five miles of some river, and the remaining one-third not more than ten miles from navigable water. Commerce and economic activity were generally restricted to areas where transportation was adequate. In this case, inland water transportation was the key to settlement and development.

It was on the great rivers of the Midwest that inland water transportation achieved its zenith. Timber was close at hand to make rafts and boats. The Mississippi system extended almost across the entire continent and moved slowly to the sea. Here the flatboat was developed and played a significant role in the nation's development. These blunt-nosed boats with perpendicular sides were constructed of rough planks and propelled by the river current. Carrying large loads for that day and drawing but a foot or two of water, they were excellent vehicles for the movement of commodities from frontier farms to the markets of the world via the port of New Orleans. Often the boat was sold for lumber at the end of its journey. The boatman, who was often the farmer himself, merely walked back to his land. If the journey had been productive enough, however, or if a speedy return were urgent, the farmer would buy passage on one of the river steamers, a system of which had also developed on the Mississippi. This type of transportation was important for many decades. Students of history will recall that young Abe Lincoln made such a trip to New Orleans with cargo from Illinois.

This transportation was of considerable value to early America. A single flatboat might carry a cargo worth $2,000 or more. Such craft were readily constructed and required little skill to operate. A major share of the product of the Middle West was transported in this manner. The value of this transportation was large — one study estimates that $5,370,000 worth of cargoes floated down the Mississippi in 1807. By 1817 over 2,000 flatboats and barges a year were arriving at New Orleans, and that city had become the fourth most important seaport in the world. Unquestionably the flatboat provided one of the cheapest and most effective means of transportation in its day.

The application of the steam engine to transportation first took the form of steamboats. After Robert Fulton's first successful *Clermont* in New York in 1807, the steamboat provided upstream transportation on many of the country's rivers. Regular schedules were often established by the so-called packets, and the steamboat era commenced.

In the East, steamboats were principally used on the tidewater portions of rivers, with a few boats operating upstream on a few large rivers. It was principally in the West on the long Mississippi and Ohio rivers where steamboating reached its full development. As early as 1809 steamboats appeared on the Ohio River, and the first trip from New Orleans to

Pittsburgh was completed in 1811. It was not until 1814, however, that a distinctive type of shallow-draft boat was developed that could navigate in the shifting sand bars and silt of these great inland waterways.

Traffic developed rapidly, and along with flatboats and rafts, the steamboat made the Mississippi inland America's greatest transportation route of that time. This era continued for many years, and its romance is forever preserved in the writings of Samuel Clemens, who chose a bit of steamboat slang, "Mark Twain" (meaning a sounding of two measures), as his pseudonym.

Costs to shippers varied according to water conditions and according to competition. Speed was generally slow as we think of transportation today — six miles an hour upstream and ten to twelve miles an hour downstream. But the steamboat continued as the major transportation medium for many years. It was not until after the Civil War that it began to be displaced by the railroad as a leading mode of transportation. For half a century steamboating was the epitome of fast, efficient, and reliable transportation in America.

EARLY ROAD MOVEMENT

In colonial America, the provision of highways came very slowly. As noted above, early roads were merely the extension of primitive Indian trails, called *traces*. These early roads remained principally undeveloped because large amounts of capital and labor were necessary in constructing improved highways. Such large amounts of resources were not available for this type of internal improvement. Few roads worthy of the name were built prior to the end of the Revolutionary War.

Interestingly enough, the delivery of mail on so-called post roads was one of the first types of highway utilization. Even though the colonies had been developing for almost 150 years, the first post roads did not come until the 1770s. These were generally restricted to the coastline and connected major cities. Very few interior post roads were built. During the Revolutionary War, the lack of overland transportation was a definite deterrent to the maneuverability of military forces. It was generally recognized that the nation would have to be concerned with internal transportation improvements if it was to grow and develop.

Our first improved roads were primarily private enterprise undertakings. These took the form of turnpikes or toll roads. Beginning in the 1790s, this new era of inland transportation was inaugurated. These turnpikes were generally of a relatively high quality for that time. Tolls were charged for travel over them. These tolls typically were collected at a way station with a pole or gate extending across the road to bar the passage of persons who had not paid. Upon payment the pole was swung open and the traveler was permitted to proceed. Since the barrier was mounted on an upright, often called a pike, the derivation of the name *turnpike* is obvious.

The first and most famous privately owned turnpike in the new nation was constructed by the Philadelphia and Lancaster Company. Work began on this project, a distance of sixty-two miles between the cities of Philadelphia and Lancaster, Pennsylvania, in 1792. The road was completed in 1794, at a cost of almost a half-million dollars, and was a financial success almost immediately. The early success of the Lancaster Pike aroused the interest of other companies in this sort of development. By the early 1800s, there were hundreds of turnpike companies. Pennsylvania had chartered 86 companies which had completed 2,200 miles of turnpikes prior to the War of 1812; New York had 135 chartered companies and some 1,500 miles built during the same period. Most of these companies were joint stock companies, an organizational form developed somewhat earlier in England and the forerunner of modern corporations. This form of organization was necessary because of the difficulty of raising large sums of capital by any other private device.

It was soon recognized that the federal government would have to be involved in internal improvements, and in 1797 a project known as the National Pike was authorized by the United States Congress. Many statesmen such as Thomas Jefferson, John C. Calhoun, and Henry Clay were interested in the promotion of this type of national highway.

The National Pike, following the old Cumberland Road to the West, was envisioned as a connection to the frontier, which then lay just across the Appalachian Mountains. The first segment of the road, completed in 1818, extended to Wheeling, West Virginia, with its eastern terminus at Cumberland, Maryland. Additional extensions were made from year to year, with construction continuing for another twenty years.

Much of our present highway policy had its beginning with the National Pike. The road was of high quality and extended literally from border to border, since it was to have its western terminus at St. Louis on the Mississippi, the then western boundary of the United States. Additionally, it was to touch the major cities and centers of population as well as the capitals of the inland states. Hence it progressed through the old Northwest Territory, touching Columbus, Ohio, Indianapolis, Indiana, and Vandalia, Illinois, the then capital of that state. From 1806 to 1838, some $6.8 million was appropriated by Congress for its construction. An additional $1.6 million was appropriated for other federal highways during the period.

With the election of Andrew Jackson in 1832, the matter of the constitutionality of the federal government making internal improvements came to a head. Jackson, a champion of States' rights, felt strongly that the federal government should not spend money on national roads or other internal improvements. Consequently, during his administration the National Pike was abandoned as a federal project and turned over to the states through which it ran. The early road movement, which had accomplished so much in assisting the settlement of the West, came to a halt. The National Pike was never extended westward from Vandalia, Illinois, and thus never reached St. Louis.

With the growing interest in alternative means of transportation, principally canals and early railroads, there was little development of highways by the states after the Jackson administration. The remains of the National Pike are still to be seen in parts of the Midwest, and the role of the road was no small one. However, because of the question of its constitutionality and the development of other types of transportation, it was not until a later date that a revival of highway interest occurred.

CANALS

There was little more interesting and economically important to domestic transportation in the formative years of the United States than the canal. During the 1780s and 1790s, some short canals had been built around rapids in rivers to improve inland water transportation. It was not until around the 1820s, though, that the canal came into its own as an important mode of transportation. The advent of the famous Erie Canal, completed in 1825, brought on a period of expansion that lasted until 1837.

The importance of the Erie Canal, lying wholly within the state of New York, can hardly be overemphasized. This project connected the Hudson River in the East with the mammoth chain of freshwater lakes to the west and north of the nation — the Great Lakes. The canal was 364 miles long and cost approximately $7 million to construct, a gigantic sum in those days. However, the canal was well designed and proved to be an outstanding financial success.

The Erie Canal was a public works project of the state of New York. It was one of Governor De Witt Clinton's favorite projects, and he worked diligently to get New York to construct this expensive internal improvement. Indeed, for a period the project was referred to as "Clinton's Folly" by political opponents. Nevertheless, it quickly earned back all of its costs and proved a tremendous economic success to New York State.

Some historians believe that the development and the expansion of the port of New York City are directly connected with the success of the Erie Canal. It provided a cheap and efficient method of bringing the produce from the vast western area that bordered upon the Great Lakes to one of the finest natural harbors on the eastern seaboard. The area traversed by the Erie was relatively flat and was easily canalized. Upstate New York was one of the few places where the Allegheny barrier did not prevent easy transportation. In this sense, the Erie was fortunately located. Likewise, New York as a city became the leading port on the eastern seaboard after the construction of the Erie Canal. From a financial point of view, tolls collected in the first seven years covered the entire construction costs of the canal.

The need for relatively cheap transportation plus the financial success of the Erie led many other states to consider canals and similar inland waterway projects. One of the most famous, the Pennsylvania Public Works System, was designed to rival the Erie and draw westward-moving immigrants and eastward-moving produce through the port of Philadelphia. This project was a combination of canals and early rail transportation. The rail portion, necessary to cross the mountains, was made up of a series of inclined planes where canal boats were put upon wheels and drawn up and over the mountains by means of cables and stationary steam engines. The so-called main line of the Pennsylvania Public Works System from Philadelphia to Columbia on the Susquehanna River was completed in 1834 at a cost of $10 million. This was a rail section, since the topography of the area did not favor a canal. From this point, the Susquehanna was followed by a canal until the mountains were reached at Holidaysburg, where the portage railway took over the route. Across the mountains, another canal was built to the junction of the Allegheny and the Monongahela, at the then frontier town of Pittsburgh. This combination of rail and canal, however, did not prove to be a successful competitor with the Erie, although it probably did help Philadelphia to grow and develop. New York, having all-water transportation from the Great Lakes region, continued to draw the majority of the trade moving to the coast.

Other canals were attempted by other eastern seaboard areas. Two of these were the Chesapeake and Ohio Canal through Virginia and Maryland, which attempted to use part of the Potomac River and connect with the Ohio, and the James River Canal, which again attempted to bridge the mountains and tap the productive area to the west. The James Canal was abandoned after the expenditure of over $10 million, and the

Chesapeake and Ohio Canal never proved to be an outstanding financial success.

Inland, there was also an era of canal building in those states bordering upon either the Great Lakes or one of the large inland rivers. Canals connected Lake Erie to the Ohio River in several places, with the Miami and Erie Canal and the Ohio and Erie Canal being outstanding examples. Additionally, the Wabash and Erie Canal from Evansville on the Ohio River extended upward and through Indiana to join with the Miami and Erie Canal somewhat south of Toledo. Further, the Illinois and Michigan Canal connected Lake Michigan and Chicago with the Illinois River, thus making a continuous waterway from the Mississippi into the Great Lakes via Lake Michigan.

Evidence of the extent of canal construction that took place during the 1820s and 1830s may be seen in figures on state indebtedness for internal improvement. Between 1820 and 1840, over $200 million of debt was incurred by various states for canals. During the financial panic of 1837, this indebtedness proved to be too heavy for many states. Some found it necessary to default on interest payments on their bonds, and a few completely repudiated their debt.

While these early canals were rather crude affairs technologically as compared to modern systems, they were marvels of their time. Typically, they were rather shallow. For example, the Erie Canal was but four feet deep, with widths of twenty-eight at the bottom and forty feet at the water line. They served a flat-bottomed vessel able to carry substantial tonnage when propelled by mule power along the canal towpath. An adequate water supply and locks to overcome land elevations were among the greatest difficulties. In many cases, aqueducts had to be constructed, large lakes had to be created, and locks had to be designed with little use of modern materials such as steel and cement. It is a wonder that canals were able to carry as much traffic as they did.

Rather substantial amounts of tonnage moved over canals during the early days and up to relatively modern times. As late as 1870, there were as many as 7,000 canal boats on the Erie and allied systems in New York, causing a problem of congestion. Canal boats typically operated both day and night in continuous lines, one proceeding in one direction on the north bank and another proceeding in the other direction on the south. Historians have noted that it was possible to observe an almost con- tinuous line of lanterns or torches moving across the New York plains at the height of the glory of the Erie Canal. From a tonnage point of view, the Erie reached its peak of over 4.5 million tons annually in 1880 and declined thereafter. The economic importance of this is seen by the fact that New York State canals, including the Erie, collected tolls averaging more than $4 million per year from 1825 to 1870. Obviously, even after the financial panic of 1837 had brought the rapid construction of canals to a halt, the better located canals continued to be a factor in the country's transportation system. Even today inland waterways continue to be an important part of our domestic transportation.

Canals, however, passed from supremacy on the transportation scene, not only because more superior types of transportation became available, but also because of the inherent limitations of this type of transportation. The climatic factor was always a limiting one. Since many of the canals were in areas where water freezes during winter, they could be used only on a seasonal basis. Secondly, canals lacked the flexibility necessary to provide a complete transportation network. They could go only along water courses and more or less parallel to rivers. Likewise, in many cases, canals ran in the wrong direction. With the exception of the Erie and a few others, many of them tended to run in a north-south direction, whereas the economic expansion of the nation has always been predominantly in an east-west direction. Coupling these factors with excessive promotions and high costs of construction of some of the marginal projects, it is easy to see why canals, although important in young America, had definite limitations.

RAILROADS AND THE COMPETITIVE STRUGGLE

Beginning with the Baltimore and Ohio Railroad in 1830, a new type of transportation emerged. Its outstanding feature was flexibility. The railroads were not tied to the rivers like the early inland water transportation. However, the technological and economic advantages of rail transportation were not immediately apparent. Indeed, the railroads were subjected to a stringent competitive struggle for the first twenty to thirty years of their existence, and it was impossible to predict which mode of transportation would prove supreme — rail, canal, highway, or river.

Early tramways had been used in Great Britain during the 1700s, principally for the transportation of coal, and simple types of railways had been used in America to do special jobs such as carrying coal down to docks for loading onto canal boats. The Baltimore and Ohio Railroad, however, is generally considered the first of the many great American general-purpose carriers of freight. This company, chartered by the state of Maryland in 1827, began construction in 1828 and opened the first portion of its road in 1830. This date is therefore used to mark the beginning of the railroad era in the United States. A few English railroads had operated on a general freight basis a few years earlier.

Technology has always been important in transportation, and it is particularly important in rail transport. Although the development of the steam engine had come at a somewhat earlier date, its application to transportation was not immediately apparent. Indeed, the lack of locomotives held back the development of the railroad as a mode of transportation in its early days. When the Baltimore and Ohio Railroad opened in 1830, there were fewer than five locomotives in the United States and most of those were experimental. The famous Tom Thumb, constructed by Peter Cooper in New York during the 1820s, was an experimental model to demonstrate the practicability of locomotives and was used on the Baltimore and Ohio in 1830.

Early locomotives were primitive and developed such a small amount of horsepower that they were able to pull only extremely limited loads. The economic advantages inherent in railroad transportation had to await the development of better systems for converting energy into movement. Motive power technology has steadily increased over the years, and today's diesel-electric units represent a delicate balance between economy in fuel use, horsepower developed, and weight of unit.

Likewise, the development of steel rails was necessary before railroads could become a highly practical type of transportation. Early tramways using horses or mules for motive power often had wooden rails over which the wheels of vehicles moved. These were supplemented by straps of iron bolted to the wood. Iron-covered rails caused considerably less resistance to the iron wheel than did wood rails, and had a longer service life. These straps became loose when heavy loads were propelled at any speed, however, causing a safety problem when the metal straps were thrown up through the bottom of the cars (these were known as "snake-heads"). It was a natural step to substitute the all-metal rail. The iron T rail was later displaced by imported steel rails, and rail weights increased so as to carry heavier loads. As American industry developed, local steel of heavier and heavier weights was used until the heavy continuous welded steel rail of today represents the most modern development in rail technology. Certainly over time, technology both in rail and in types of motive power has played a most important role in the development of domestic rail transportation.

The development of the rail network of the United States in the nineteenth century can be compared to the development of the economy of the country. Each decade saw more and more trackage. New companies were formed, new areas opened up, and new economic developments undertaken. Table 2.1 illustrates the changes in total miles of railway.

Table 2.1 Total Miles of Railway Operated in the United States, Selected Years.

1830	23
1850	9,021
1870	52,922
1890	166,703
1910	240,831
1930	260,440
1950	223,265
1970	206,265
1980	184,500
1987	165,865

Source: Department of Commerce, *Historical Statistics of the United States for 1830 to 1890,* and Interstate Commerce Commission, various publications since 1900.

There was a marked growth of railroad mileage following 1830. Most of these early lines were local in character; however, they were often not interconnected and could scarcely be called a system. Most early rail expansion was confined to eastern states, with but a few small roads in the Middle West and South. To some degree, these early lines were considered supplemental to canals and rivers. Indeed, the vested interests of canal owners, operators, and workers involved in water transportation, plus the interests of persons concerned with highway transportation, caused great obstacles to early railway development. In some cases, legislatures required early railroads to invest part of their capital in canals or to build wooden fences where they paralleled canals so as not to frighten the tow animals. Also, some states required railroads to pay tolls to the state equivalent to what the freight hauled would have paid to state-owned canals.

But the flexibility of the railway and the economy that came with heavier rails, better motive power, and larger loads soon became evident. By 1850, the era of the trunk lines began; and by 1860, various systems had linked the East Coast to the Mississippi River and a substantial network of railroads covered the whole eastern half of the nation. While more will be said about consolidations and mergers in Chapter 26, it should be noted here that much of this expansion came by connecting numerous rail companies end to end. By the end of the 1860s, single-company service was available between New York and Chicago, and the basic trunk-line railroads had been established.

The Civil War and the tremendous economic advance of the 1860s provided a great impetus for railway expansion. The war proved the military and economic advantages of rail transportation. Some historians have given great weight to the role of the superior rail transportation network in the victory of the North. The war-accelerated business pace also led to more rail expansion; to secure California and the West to the Union, the first transcontinental railroad was started during the hostilities. While the Union Pacific built westward from Omaha, the Central Pacific built eastward from Sacramento. Although these lines were not joined together on the plains of Utah until 1869, this first rail link between the two coasts had been authorized and abundantly assisted by the federal government as a war project.

Settlement of the internal political problems of the nation and the advances in agricultural and industrial technology growing out of the war combined with the general war-born feeling for adventure and daring to spur the development of the West. Railroads shared and at times led in that development. The decades of the 1870s and 1880s witnessed the greatest increases in rail net expansion. Railway company agents actively promoted migration to the new western lands and in some cases roamed parts of Europe with advertisements noting the opportunities available in America and particularly in the American West. The role of the railroads in the settlement of the continent was an active one. The western railroad that did not employ a large staff of agricultural experts, promotional men, and land developers was rare.

More will be said about railroad promotion in Chapter 26. It should be noted, however, that the land grant policy of the 1850s to 1870s was partly responsible for much of this promotion. Beginning with sizable grants of land by Congress to the Illinois Central in 1850, the pattern of stimulating rail expansion by granting alternate sections of federal land continued until the final large grant was made in 1871 to the Texas and Pacific. More often than not, this land was wholly undeveloped and the building of the railroad made the remaining alternate sections of some value to the government. The general idea, however, was to settle the country, promote private ownership and development, and tame the continent. In this regard the policy was a success.

Additional aid by cities, states, and individuals was also substantial. Nearly every town wanted to be, indeed had to be, on a railroad. Cities offered free land, tax exemptions, guarantee of bonds, and public subscription of securities to entice railroads to build through their bounds. Substantial sums were involved. Unfortunately, some unscrupulous promoters took advantage of the desire for railroads to promote spurious ventures.

Even with these substantial aids, huge amounts of private capital were necessary. This led to two interesting aspects of nineteenth-century American business: the reliance on foreign capital and the development of the corporate form of enterprise. Many states borrowed abroad, only to default on their obligations during the periodic financial panics of the era. Large amounts of capital were also raised by private stock and bond sales in Europe. One expert estimates that during the 1880s more than $2 billion was raised in Europe by the sale of railroad securities. This often resulted in large blocks of stock under foreign ownership, in some cases more than 50 percent of the stock of a single railroad. Failure of promised profits to domestic security owners, foreign ownership and control, and delay of the envisioned economic development were important factors in the move to regulate railroads.

In order to gather the required capital, the corporate form of business organization was mandatory. A railroad was such a gigantic undertaking that the fortune of one man or a small group of men was insufficient for its construction. Hence the corporate form was used early in railroad development; and as successive issues of securities became necessary, this business form was further developed and refined. Indeed, one of the often overlooked benefits of the expansion of the domestic railway system was the acceptance and development of the modern corporation. Although some government-owned railroads were built, the expansion of the American rail network generally was a phenomenon of private ownership via the corporate form. It was, after all, a high period of the free enterprise, laissez-faire system. Many state governments had become over-involved in the canal era; and although they might be willing to aid in railroad construction, they generally avoided public ownership. The constitutional question of internal improvement remained from the Jackson and early highway era, so the federal government pursued a policy of promotion but not ownership. Thus the railroads typify the private-ownership, corporate form of business during the nineteenth century.

Excesses in railroad promotion and construction were common. Overcapitalization was prevalent. Many personal fortunes of some of the best-known financial names of America came out of abuses of railroad finance. Business ethics were at a low level, and there was little public concern over the excesses. The result often was to leave railroads with grossly overcapitalized corporate structures faced with tremendous pressures to pay bond interest and show profits on securities that frequently did not represent assets. Many of the financial and operating problems of later periods were a direct result of these abuses.

By 1900, the basic rail network had been laid. Although expansion continued even into the 1920s and a few remaining transcontinental connections were built between 1900 and 1910, the age of rail expansion was predominantly a nineteenth-century phenomenon. The building of branch lines and the filling in of railroad systems formed most of the expansion during the twentieth century. Finally, by 1930, the number of railroad miles began to decline. Uneconomical and unwise expansion could not sustain itself, particularly in the face of new competitive threats that characterized the twentieth century. The total number of railway miles has steadily declined since the 1920s as the railroads have attempted to readjust their plans to the needs of the nation.

Railroads developed in a romantic and significant period. Beginning with a competitive struggle, they proved their supremacy, knit the nation together, and triggered much of the development of the American economy. But new twentieth-century modes of transportation with other inherent advantages arose to share the glory of the railroad as the underlying basis of the American transport economy.

REVIVAL OF HIGHWAY TRANSPORTATION

Even while railroads were enjoying their greatest expansion, interest was reviving in highway transportation. Movement over roads had continued, of course, during the rail expansion, but it had been primarily local. During the 1890s, however, the concerted interest of three groups — the railroads, farmers, and bicyclists — led to a renewal of general concern for improved highways.

Railroads felt the need for improved roads primarily to provide local transportation from the point of production to the railroad. Farmers felt the need to get out of the mud, thus improving their mobility and enabling them to reach markets more readily. Cyclists saw the condition of the nation's roads as a positive deterrent to their sport and pleasure, and bicycle manufacturers heartily concurred. Collectively these groups sponsored the good roads movement, which led to the first modern attempts to improve our highway system.

With the advent of the internal combustion gasoline engine and its application to transportation via the early automobiles of the 1890s and early 1900s, a fourth group was added to the advocates of improved highways: automobile owners joined the growing pack and built upon early efforts to promote better roads.

During the 1890s, some states established aid systems in order to spur highway development. New Jersey was first in this area, establishing a state highway department to advise local officials and setting forth a formula by which landowners paid 10 percent, the county 60 percent, and the state 30 percent of the cost of highway improvements. Other states followed with similar plans; and in 1893, Congress created the Office of Public Road Inquiry within the Department of Agriculture. However, massive financial aid programs to governmental units owning the high-ways, usually state and county governments, did not come until the automobile became popular.

By 1915, forty-five states had enacted state aid laws, forty had established state highway departments, and twenty-four had designated state highway systems. Ownership, maintenance, and administration of highways remained primarily local and development was somewhat chaotic. Few road systems existed, most counties were able to improve but a small portion of their road mileage, and finances were inadequate. It remained for the two developments of federal aid and the state gasoline tax to launch the modern highway system.

The federal aid system was originated in 1916 when Congress appropriated $75 million to be expended over five years on highway improvement. The basic pattern of the domestic highway system was established in the 1916 act with (a) state ownership, construction, and maintenance of the highways; (b) a formula by which the federal govern-ment allocated fifty-fifty matching funds among states on the basis of population, area, and mileage; and (c) the provision of state highway departments to coordinate, engineer, designate, and contract for highway improvements. This pattern, or variations of it, has been followed ever since.

Two dimensions of highway improvement came during the 1920s. Congress recognized in the Highway Aid Act of 1921 that funds had to be concentrated upon a relatively few road systems if the enormous task of improving the nation's highways was to be accomplished. Hence the designation of a system of primary highways not to exceed 7 percent (later changed to 8 percent) of all state mileage was enacted. Although there have been subsequent variations, the principle of concentration has continued. The second factor was the broad adoption of the state gasoline tax, pioneered by Oregon in 1919, which proved to be the principal source of funds for highway improvement. Here the principle of user charges was adopted.

Following World War I, with the improvement of the highway system and the broad acceptance of the automobile, numerous persons went into the business of providing truck and bus transportation. Although there had been companies earlier, the system of improved and toll-free highways proved an impetus to individual enterprise. Many of the leading motor transportation companies of today date from this era of expansion. Likewise, the individualistic and competitive characteristic of motor transportation was firmly established by the public provision of the way and the ease of entry into this mode of transportation.

With the Great Depression of the 1930s, highway improvement was accelerated. Highway building was a favorite way of promoting employment and generating income. Although the road system expanded somewhat in total mileage, it was primarily the improvement of existing highways that occupied the attention of the nation. In many areas, the first large-scale building of hard-surfaced roads was a Depression phenomenon. Large sums were spent over a relatively short period, and the highway system was rapidly improved.

With the continued ease of entry into highway transportation, plus the provision of even more improved highways, the individualistic and competitive aspects of motor transportation intensified. Small truck and bus companies abounded, and many individuals attempted to sustain themselves by offering highway transport services for hire in a highly competitive market. These conditions of extreme competition played a prominent role in bringing about regulation of this mode of transportation, as will be shown in Chapter 11.

With the advent of World War II, the situation completely reversed itself. Little or no highway improvement took place, vehicles for commercial use were rarely available, gasoline was rationed, and travel was restricted. Much of the highway system and motor transportation equipment was dissipated with little or no replacement. This led to the need for tremendous postwar expansion in highways and motor transportation plants, ushering in perhaps one of the nation's greatest eras of highway and motor carrier expansion.

The principle of concentration of highway building funds was further refined in 1944 by the authorization of a system of high-speed, top-quality, limited-access highways known as the Interstate System. These plans were not implemented until 1956 when federal financing was put on a trust fund basis with the federal gas tax and other federal highway excise taxes, first imposed in 1917, directly linked to the construction of the Interstate System. This system, made up of 42,500 miles of the most densely traveled highways, connects most of the major cities and state capitals of the United States, and also connects with Canada and Mexico. The Interstate System is financed 90 percent by the federal government and 10 percent by state or local governments. This backbone of the nation's highway system is almost completed.

Much of the early Interstate System is now severely worn, however. The greatest highway problem for the remainder of this century is not one of building new roads. Rather, it is the repair and maintenance of the existing Interstate System and other federal and state highways and local roads and streets. This will require many billions of dollars annually. An additional federal gasoline tax of 5 cents per gallon for this job became effective in 1983.

With the improved highway system plus the accelerated business activity of the postwar years, the motor transportation industry has expanded tremendously. Railroads are limited by the location of their rails, but motor carriers have an almost unlimited flexibility. Streets and roads are everywhere, and motor carriers are equipped to give an extremely flexible and personalized transportation service. These characteristics will be further described in Chapter 4, but it is well to note here that motor transportation expanded very rapidly during the post–World War II period. From a relatively minor role of approximately 6 percent of the intercity ton-miles hauled during the war years, motor carriers are today the second most important type of transportation from a ton-mile viewpoint. To many cities and shippers, trucks are the sole means of freight transportation available.

Passenger transportation over streets and highways has an equally long and interesting history. Early urban systems, using primarily horse-drawn vehicles, were extremely important. Most large cities had systems of urban transportation early during their history, but the real development of the streetcar awaited the application of electricity. The generation from 1900 to 1930 saw the golden age of the trolley. After this, increased use of automobiles and more flexible buses put streetcars into a decline. Travel on both intracity and intercity buses grew steadily until World War II, but ultimately the convenience of the automobile and the speed of the airplane forced bus travel into a secondary role.

In the early 1970s, America again turned its attention to urban and intercity mass passenger transportation. Massive federal aid, a growing awareness of ecological problems, congestion, and fuel shortages all have created more concern about passenger transportation over streets and highways.

AIR TRANSPORTATION

Air transportation is the only truly twentieth-century mode of domestic transport. Beginning with the historic 1903 flight of heavier-than-air craft at Kitty Hawk, North Carolina, by the Wright brothers, this mode has reflected the astounding technological growth of the present century.

Air transportation has been interconnected with two great forces: war and government. It was not until World War I led to the training of numerous persons in the art of flying that travel by air was anything but an oddity. With many surplus warplanes readily available, former World War I pilots popularized the airplane by barnstorming all over the nation. The romance of war-born air aces was brought to practically every hamlet in America during the 1920s by these early flying pioneers. The adventurous had an opportunity to experience a new thrill, and the critic an opportunity to scoff.

The role of government in training pilots during World War I and in furnishing surplus "jennys" after the war is evident. However, its more important role of promoting air transportation by way of the U.S. mails is not as apparent. Experimentation with air mail service began in 1918, with the first transcontinental air mail service during 1919. By 1924, technology had developed to the point where continuous day and night service for transcontinental air mail could be established. These pioneering efforts were made by the federal government. It was not until 1925 that privately owned air transportation companies were given the opportunity to carry the mails.

The Kelly Act of 1925 authorized the U.S. Post Office to contract with air transportation companies to carry mail, but by 1927 the government had retired from the field. With the exception of a few months during 1934 when the government again carried air mail, privately owned air transportation has continued as the major form of air transport in this country. This has not been the case in other countries. The United States is unusual in having private air transportation companies promoted, but not owned, by the government.

Air transportation companies not only depended upon mail contracts in the early air age, but they also depended on government-provided airways. Federally maintained airways remain to this day. Locally owned and operated airports, with the exception of military or private fields, have also been provided, with nominal landing fees. The Air Commerce Act of 1926 prohibited the federal government from constructing or operating airfields and airports, but federal aid for airport building has been a part of domestic transportation promotion since 1933.

Throughout the 1930s, travel by air remained primarily emergency travel where speed was of utmost importance. Aircraft developed slowly, and air travel was expensive and uncomfortable by today's standards. Most airline companies were highly subsidized by air mail contracts and were more in the mail business than any other. It remained again for war to push air transportation forward.

Because of its outstanding characteristics of speed and flexibility, the airplane was widely used during World War II. Aircraft design was greatly accelerated, and many principles of aircraft construction were perfected under the stimulus of war. Additional thousands of persons were taught to fly, and the basic principles of handling air freight were developed. But perhaps more important was the fact that large numbers of military and civilian personnel were carried as passengers in wartime flights. Widespread knowledge about and the popularity of air transportation were established.

Following World War II, a tremendous expansion in air passenger traffic occurred. Flying became a common thing. Airline companies, applying war-developed techniques, offered frequent schedules and reliable equipment. Under competitive pressure from nonscheduled lines which sprang up after the war using surplus equipment and former military pilots, fares were driven down and service was greatly improved. By the late 1950s, air transportation was carrying more passengers than any other form of domestic transportation. The day of air travel had arrived.

With the coming of jet aircraft, air transportation matured into a speedy and reliable passenger transportation medium. By developing both trunk line services between major cities and feeder line services between smaller towns, air transportation routes blanketed the nation. Travel by air has continued to increase, and today it is the leading type of commercial passenger travel.

Air freight and air express have likewise grown, but remain relatively small in the total freight carriage picture. New jet equipment, however, provides unusual potentials for air freight, and this type of movement is gaining popularity in today's accelerated business-world activity.

A major problem facing air carriers today is how to maintain and replace an aging aircraft fleet. A growing number of accidents involving airframe failures in older aircraft have brought this problem to the forefront. Improved aircraft continue to become available; but the rapid growth in air passenger and freight transportation, narrowing carrier profits, and limited aircraft manufacturer capacities have made it impossible for carriers to obtain sufficient new equipment. This will continue to be a problem for most air carriers well into the 1990s.

REVIVAL OF WATER TRANSPORTATION

In any given period of time, several modes of transportation exist, and although one may seem to dominate, others are evolving. The distinguishing feature among various modes is rate of development. For example, transportation by water did not die out with the passing of the canal era or the steamboat's loss of supremacy to the railroad. It merely developed at a much slower pace. Water transportation persisted throughout the latter half of the nineteenth century, but more recent developments have led to increasing interest in, and emphasis on, this type of transport.

Domestic water transportation may be thought of in three divisions: (1) the Great Lakes, (2) inland rivers and canals, and (3) coastwise and intercoastal shipping. Each has distinctive characteristics and problems.

The Great Lakes, one of the outstanding inland waterways of the world, provided our country with a ready-made transportation route. Canals and locks connecting the various lakes were constructed as early as 1829, but it was not until the locks at Sault Sainte Marie (the Soo) were constructed in 1855 that the great inland water traffic developed on the lakes. The Soo locks plus the deepening of the river channel connecting Lake Huron and Lake Erie made available a magnificent waterway covering four lakes nearly a thousand miles in length and a natural channel spanning a third of the continent. Further work on the Welland Canal around Niagara Falls in 1916 plus a fourteen-foot channel down the St. Lawrence River (completed by Canada in 1903) allowed the Great Lakes to be used by some shallow-draft ocean vessels. The completion of the St. Lawrence Seaway in 1959 and the deepening of various lake channels have now made the Great Lakes, in effect, a part of the Atlantic Ocean and created what is popularly known as America's fourth seacoast.

Interest in further development of inland rivers and canals is also a twentieth-century phenomenon. Beginning with the $100 million conversion of the old Erie Canal into the New York Barge Canal by the state of New York during the early 1900s, new interest was stimulated in inland water transportation. The first conservation movement during the administration of Theodore Roosevelt also stimulated interest in waterways; and in 1907, Roosevelt appointed the Inland Waterways Commission to prepare plans for improving inland water transportation.

This revival of interest in inland water transportation was considerably more than a part of the conservation movement. A feeling that water transportation was inherently cheap and a vital resource was also involved. Perhaps even more important was the feeling that water transportation could be used as a competitive vehicle to keep railroad rates low. Furthermore, waterway improvements have always been looked upon with favor by Congress. Political advantage to congressional delegations can be gained by securing federal improvement of the waterways of the home district.

Rivers of the nation have always been owned and controlled by the federal government in the name of the people. Except for artificial waterways such as the successful schemes by New York and a few other states, developments in waterway improvements have always been a federal responsibility. As early as 1789, the federal government began improving harbors. The first of many rivers and harbors acts was passed in 1823, and, since 1866, Congress has made appropriations for waterway improvements almost annually. The question of who should provide the way has therefore rarely been a problem in water transportation.

Because of the political implications of waterway improvements, there has been a problem of coordination. Since Congress has favored spending funds as widely as possible in order to gain the greatest political advantage, improvements have rarely been planned to set up specific water transportation systems. Nevertheless, with a century of various aids plus the interest in planning generated during the early 1900s, and with a vastly improved technology, the inland waterways of the nation have developed into prime transportation media.

More will be said about the promotional problems of transportation in Chapter 26. It should be noted here, though, that considerable sums have been expended on waterways over the years. One of the Hoover commissions estimated that $1.6 billion had been spent by the federal government from 1824 to 1954 on waterways improvement, excluding the Great Lakes and seacoast projects. State and local governments have also spent large sums on waterways. The New York Barge Canal was said to have cost $177 million up to the 1930s. Illinois spent $99 million on the Illinois Waterway and the Chicago Sanitary Ship Canal, which connects the Illinois River to Lake Michigan. Many hundreds of millions of dollars have been invested in terminal facilities by local and state governments. As a result of these improvements and efforts, the United States has today a very active inland waterway transportation system.

Coastal canals are also important. Protected passage virtually from the Middle Atlantic states to the Mexican border is possible by way of a series of canals connecting bays and inlets. This waterway serves coastal as well as intercoastal traffic. During World War II, this protected passage was of great significance in view of the submarine menace off the Gulf and Atlantic coasts.

Coastal waterways, plus the many miles of inland rivers and canals, and the Great Lakes system, provide the domestic economy with a most significant transportation system. Ton-miles carried have greatly increased in recent years as improvements have allowed wider use of inland waterways.

PIPELINES: A MODERN GIANT

Almost every American has heard of the huge $8 billion Alaskan oil pipeline. This is said to be the largest privately financed construction project ever undertaken. Pipeline transportation, however, is not new in the American economy, although its importance in modern times has greatly increased. At present, pipelines are the third largest carriers of freight from a ton-mile viewpoint and constitute a most important part of our domestic transportation system.

The first pipelines were laid shortly after the first oil fields were developed in Pennsylvania. In 1865, a short two-inch line was laid as a means of providing cheaper transportation than that by teamsters. Prior to that time, crude oil had moved on large horse-drawn wagons mounted with heavy wooden tanks. The pipeline experiment was a success, and a new type of transportation was born.

Even though the first major pipeline (110 miles in length) was completed in 1879, pipelines were used primarily as local gathering agents and little long-distance transportation by pipeline was attempted for nearly half a century. Part of the reason for this slow development was the strong vested interests of railroads and teamsters. For example, railroads often refused to allow early pipelines to go under their tracks. Since the rail network was quite extensive by the latter part of the nineteenth century, this greatly restricted pipelines.

Pipeline transportation basically is a highly specialized type of carriage, the products hauled are limited to a few types, and the service is one way. The products carried must be able to flow; and because of the substantial amounts of the goods actually in the pipeline at one time and limited storage capacity at either end, there is no reversal of movement.

It is possible to distinguish two types of long-distance pipelines: the more numerous crude oil pipelines and the more recent product pipelines. Each specializes in a given group of commodities. The older crude oil pipelines are by far the most developed.

Pipeline transportation has been closely connected with two other factors: the development of the petroleum industry and the development of technology. It was only after the discovery of substantial petroleum fields following the turn of the century that pipeline transportation became important. Additionally, the market for petroleum products awaited widespread acceptance of the automobile and the widespread use of the internal combustion gasoline engine. Since these were primarily twentieth-century events, there was little real need for pipelines during earlier periods. The product pipeline was an even later development, the first movement of gasoline by pipeline occurring in 1930.

Heavy steel pipe of small size was used in early pipelines. Economy in pipe use awaited development of welded joints which solved earlier problems of leakage and corrosion. The submarine menace of World War II caused new experimentation with lighter-weight pipe, and the famous Big Inch (24-inch) pipeline and Little Big Inch lines were constructed. These federally constructed pipelines had a tremendous throughput and were laid safely inland away from the hazards of wartime water transportation. Experience gained from these projects proved that large-diameter, thin-walled pipe was practical. Since World War II, many miles of large-diameter pipeline have been laid.

Technology in pumping has likewise improved. Older pipelines used steam-driven reciprocal pumps spaced relatively close together. Diesel engines later replaced steam pumpers and allowed a reduction in manpower and energy. Since World War II, remarkable strides have been made in pumping by use of electrically driven centrifugal pumps which can be remotely controlled from a central dispatching point. The modern pipeline employs but a small fraction of the labor previously used in the many pumping stations on the pipeline. It is highly automated, with electronic controls turning the motors on and off, opening valves, and doing the mechanical tasks of pipeline operation, and it has far fewer pumping stations than were previously necessary. Indeed, pipeline transport is the most highly automated type of domestic transportation.

The pipeline system today is a large network of unseen yet highly important transportation routes. Most states have some pipelines within them, and it is said that no point in the forty-eight contiguous states today is more than 200 miles from a pipeline. Total throughput has steadily increased, and pipelines have successfully taken more and more crude and product petroleum movement from railroads and water carriers, their principal competitors. Today the invisible though ever-present pipeline is an essential carrier in our domestic transportation system.

THE POLITICAL AND ECONOMIC IMPACT OF TRANSPORTATION DEVELOPMENT

The political and economic impact of the development of domestic transportation has been significant. Because of improved means of moving about and getting goods to and from distant points, the whole nation has become less isolated and independent and a more unified body. Political unity has developed. Less need is felt for local governmental units, and some (such as the one-room school districts) have become almost a thing of the past because of transportation developments. Less provincialism prevails since goods and ideas can travel efficiently and rapidly over today's highly developed transportation system. Users of American domestic transportation services generally have a greater choice and flexibility and more options for trade-offs among transport modes and services than exist elsewhere in the world.

Although the economic, business, and political impact of transportation has been very great, it has not been without ramifications for the environmental-sociological aspects of our nation. Before studying the domestic transportation system in depth, we should be aware of some of these other effects. The following chapter considers some of the many environmental and sociological aspects of transportation.

ADDITIONAL READINGS

Bowersox, Donald J., Pat J. Calabro, and George D. Wagenheim, *Introduction to Transportation*, New York: Macmillan Publishing Co., 1981.
Chapter 3, "History of Freight Transportation," pp. 29–44.

Goodrich, Carter, *Government Promotion of American Canals and Railroads 1800–1890*, New York: Columbia University Press, 1960.
"Federal Debate and Decision," pp. 169–207.

Hazard, John L., *Transportation: Management, Economics, Policy*, Centersville, Md.: Cornell Maritime Press, 1977.
Chapter 1, "Transportation in National Development," pp. 1–33.

Levy, Lester S., and Roy J. Sampson, *American Economic Development*, Boston: Allyn & Bacon, 1962.
Chapter 11, "Establishing the Pattern of American Transportation and Trade," pp. 221–41.
Chapter 12, "America's Place in Twentieth-Century Transportation and Trade," pp. 243–62.

Locklin, D. Philip, *Economics of Transportation*, 7th ed., Homewood, Ill.: Richard D. Irwin, 1972.
Chapter 5, "Before Railroads," pp. 91–108.
Chapter 6, "The Era of Railroad Building," pp. 109–41.

McElhiney, Paul T., *Transportation for Marketing and Business Students*, Totowa, N.J.: Littlefield, Adams, 1975.
Chapter 3, "The Development of Transportation," pp. 30–42.

Morton, Stephen, "The Politics Behind the Route of the First Transcontinental Railroad in the United States," *I.C.C. Practitioner's Journal* (February 1963), 561–68.

Pegrum, Dudley F., *Transportation: Economics and Public Policy*, 3rd ed., Homewood, Ill.: Richard D. Irwin, 1973.
Chapter 3, "Development of Transportation in the United States," pp. 46–70.

Ransom, Roger L., "Canals and Development: A Discussion of the Issues," *American Economic Review* (May 1964), 365–76.

Segal, Harvey H., "Cycles of Canal Construction," and "Canals and Economic Development," in *Canals and Economic Development*, Ed. Goodrich, New York: Columbia University Press, 1961, pp. 169–249.

Taff, Charles A., *Commercial Motor Transportation*, 7th ed., Centersville, Md.: Cornell Maritime Press, 1986.
Chapter 2, "Highways," pp. 18–51.

Wicker, E. R., "Railroad Investment before the Civil War," in *Trends in the American Economy in the Nineteenth Century*, Princeton, N.J.: Princeton University Press, 1960, pp. 503–24.

CHAPTER 3
SOCIETAL CONCERNS WITH TRANSPORTATION

Transportation has been synonymous with progress in our country. The whistle of the train, the roar of the plane, the noise of the truck, have all been outward signs of progress to past generations and have typified the romance of transportation.

But recently we have begun to take a new look at progress. We have begun to realize that progress, like everything else, has costs. These costs may not always be easily measurable in dollars and cents, and they are not always individual in nature. They may be what the economist calls *social costs*. That is, the costs of some undertakings affect so many persons in such indirect or long-term ways that, in effect, all of society bears the burden of the activities. Even though widespread and hard to assess, these costs are very real and must be considered.

Before we examine the operation of our domestic transportation system and its regulatory, economic, and business environment, it is well to consider the environmental, sociological, and energy aspects of transportation.

ENVIRONMENTAL ASPECTS

One does not need to understand the details of the operation of our transportation system to see its environmental effects. Transportation is shaped by, and shapes, the physical environment. In this sense, it is closely interrelated to, and interacts with, the physical environment. Basically, this interaction is from two viewpoints: locational and operational.

Locational Interactions

The location of much transportation activity has already been established, but the system is not static. New activity and development take place, old activity diminishes and occasionally ceases. Thus the environmental aspects of transportation are really twofold, namely, the effects of present location of transport activities on the one hand, and the effects of new transportation activities on the other.

Present Location

The locations where transportation functions are presently performed have environmental effects on surrounding communities. For example, railroad tracks and superhighways divide towns and neighborhoods; location of interchanges affects the location of manufacturing, retailing, and distribution activities, and gives a character to a neighborhood or area of a city. Indeed, the existence of transportation facilities gives some cities their unique characters as the railroad town of old, the manufacturing or distribution center, or the port city. We will examine more completely the effects of transportation on the location of cities in Chapter 19.

There may be both positive and negative aspects of present transport locational effects. The positive aspects are the progress, development, and economic growth and activity arising from these historical locations. The negative aspects involve the character this locational effect brings with it. Examples are the rowdiness of a port, the transitory nature of the air terminal, the bleakness of a warehouse district, and the dirtiness of a railroad terminal. Some of these will also be considered below under sociological aspects, but the point here is that the location of transportation activities historically has affected and interacted with surrounding territory.

Location of New Transportation Activity

Although little can be done about present historical locations, much can be done about future developments. Transportation is so essential that it cannot be denied. But a community or neighborhood or region can decide whether the positive locational effects offset the negative locational effects. For example, in many major cities decisions concerning transportation changes needed to enhance progress and limit congestion are currently under consideration. In such cities, there is usually little disagreement on the need for infrastructure improvements. The problems arise when the needed changes disrupt a specific community or neighborhood. Does the community want the character that transport activity brings? Are the benefits worth the costs?

This is not an easy choice. The mechanics of decision making are not clear-cut. Political action and regulations are usually the ways in which society manifests its choices. Rarely are votes taken or such issues put to rational analysis. But that is the way of democracy. The majority must be convinced that the benefits of a new transportation activity outweigh the social costs, or the contrary. Then action is taken on these convictions.

Operational Interactions

A more important environmental interaction comes from the operation of transportation activities. Here also there are social costs. The beneficial operation of transportation brings with it the social costs associated with pollution, congestion, and ecological interaction. Each of these will be considered briefly in turn.

Pollution

Basically, three types of pollution arise from the operation of transportation facilities. To a considerable degree these are connected with the movement of people, particularly via private automobiles, but other means and modes of transportation contribute to pollution as well. Indeed, all economic activity adds to pollution in some way even though we do not always notice it. Transportation, since it is so universally visible as well as universally necessary, is more noticeable as a polluter than other activity.

The three types of pollution are air pollution, water pollution, and noise pollution. Each has separate aspects, causes, cures, and ramifications. This is not a text in ecology, and detailed analysis of each of these phenomena is not in order here. Yet we should be aware of each.

1. *Air pollution.* There is little doubt that transportation operations add to air pollution. Almost all transportation uses the internal combustion engine in one form or another. Internal combustion engines using gasoline produce four pollutants: carbon monoxide, gaseous hydrocarbons and benzene compounds, nitrogen oxide compounds, and nongases or heavier particles, the most important of which is lead. Additionally, there is a degree of thermal pollution involved when energy is converted into use by automobiles, trucks, planes, locomotives, or ships. All the chemical effects of these pollutants are not known, but their presence in the form of smog and haze cannot be denied.

From a technological viewpoint, progress is slowly being made in learning to control this problem. During the late 1960s, automobile manufacturers began to introduce emission control devices on vehicles. The federal government eventually established maximum emission standards. Many state and local governments have passed laws or instituted legal actions against transportation firms in an effort to abate pollution. A good example of the latter type of action is the numerous lawsuits filed by government against airlines polluting the air with exhaust emissions at major airports.

Many persons have suggested that the most effective answer to automobile pollution lies in the area of new power systems such as the electric-powered vehicle or the steam-powered car. Other persons are working on modifications to the internal combustion engine such as lower compression engines, the use of lead-free gasoline, the use of gasoline-alcohol fuel mixtures, and the use of hydrogen, LPG (liquefied petroleum gas), or natural gas as fuels.

Exhaust emissions can be controlled or abated and made less obnoxious. However, this can be done only at a cost. It is an open question as to who should pay the initial price of air pollution control. Ultimately the public will have to pay these social costs in the form of higher prices for automobiles and higher charges by for-hire transportation firms. The use of cleaner jet engines already has lessened air transport pollution.

2. *Water pollution.* Transportation activity also adds to water pollution. Ships must flush tanks, sanitary facilities on trains must be cleaned, automobiles and trucks must be washed, and so forth. It is often a matter of how these activities are done that is important. With proper precautions, water pollution can be controlled.

One of the visible and most publicized types of water pollution is the oil spill from ocean-going freighters or from offshore drilling accidents. Although these are not directly connected to the operation of domestic transportation, they are very closely related to our subject.

Here again social control takes the form of regulation and legal action. Both the federal and the state-local levels of government are involved. There is a cost to these controls, and this cost will be reflected in the price of the product or transportation service involved.

3. *Noise pollution.* Operation of transportation facilities creates noise. The neighborhood near an airport, subway, freight yard, or freeway knows this fact only too well. The din of the city, the jarring incessancy of airport activity, the ceaseless traffic of the freeway all affect the quality of life.

Technology is helping slowly. Buildings can be noise-proofed, schools can be relocated, jets and engines can be muffled. Abating or ameliorating noise pollution will be costly. Relocation of airports, freeways, and railways will be difficult and very costly.

Social action to control noise pollution has been a combination of local and federal activities. An example of local governmental action is the specification of airport operational patterns such as the prohibition of night takeoffs and landings, the prescription of glide paths, and the like. Control and location of truck routes are another example. Federal actions have come in the form of such things as maximum permissible noise levels for trucks and jet aircraft engines, and in freeway design. In all these and similar cases social costs are involved, and the methods of paying these costs are controversial.

Congestion

There are three types of congestion arising from the operational aspects of transportation: street congestion, highway congestion, and airway congestion. If walking is considered a mode of transportation, crowd or people congestion could also be added.

Congestion has many attributes. Perhaps its outstanding characteristic is variability. The degree of congestion varies with the size of the city or town, the location of the suburban area relative to the central business district, and the demographic distribution within the urban area.

There is also a time variable to transportation congestion. Traffic, both vehicular and pedestrian, varies by the time of day, the day of the week, and the season of the year. The daily peak traffic in the journey to and from work is easily observed. Weekend congestion on streets and highways leading to recreational attractions such as parks, beaches, and mountains presents more evidence of this time variability. Finally, the summer vacation peak presents a third easily observable variable transportation phenomenon.

Congestion costs time and money to all users of transportation facilities. The cost in efficiency of the carriers can be measured in terms of extra crew time and operational expenses for planes delayed in "stacks," or delivery trucks held up in traffic, or buses delayed in the five o'clock rush. But the time and value loss to the passengers of these transportation modes also is a very real cost, although difficult to measure. Also unmeasurable is the time value loss to individuals in their own vehicles as they are held up or delayed. A final subjective aspect of congestion is its effect on the quality of life. The frayed nerves, the indigestion, the disrupted routine caused by delay — these are costs to millions of users and operators. This is part of the cost of progress. Increasingly the question is asked: Is the cost worth the benefit?

Without answering that question here, one must note that street, highway, and airway congestion are facts of life. Technology can help somewhat by the use of computers to improve scheduling and thus reduce delay, by better traffic control systems, and by new alternative means of movement. Economics can also help by varying transportation prices to provide an incentive not to transport or travel during peak periods. There are many other possible ways to relieve a portion of this congestion, but they are beyond the scope of this book. However, the reader should be familiar with the existence of these problems.

Ecological Interaction

Mention must be made of one final aspect of the operational interactions of the transportation system. Transportation operation has varying effects on other ecological systems in nature. Many ecological situations evolve around delicately balanced systems of creation, birth, life, and death. Transportation may interrupt or alter portions of these systems. We do not always comprehend the complexities of ecology or appreciate that one action may affect a far-removed ecological subsystem. Examples of this are seen in the reported disastrous effects on the growth of Ponderosa pine trees in San Bernardino National Forest by vehicular emissions some eighty miles away on streets and highways in Los Angeles, the effects of oil spills on marine ecological systems in the Gulf coastal area and elsewhere, and the effects of water pollution from road-building projects on fish downstream.

Not all these ecological interactions can be predicted or even known, yet they exist. They too become a part of the natural and social cost of transportation. Study is necessary to correctly assess the various causes and effects. Indeed, sometimes they cannot be found. Yet they do exist, and we must be aware of them.

SOCIOLOGICAL ASPECTS

The sociological interactions of transportation activities are not as easily seen as are the environmental interactions. Yet they exist, and they provide materials for study by sociologists, cultural anthropologists, and others. It must also be mentioned that it is often transportation aspects in connection with a whole series of other factors that interact to cause sociological effects; rarely is it the transportation factors alone.

We do not intend to compile a complete list of sociological effects and interactions. But the point of sociological interactions can be emphasized by noting that transportation affects the character of neighborhoods, cities, and depressed areas, and acts as a status symbol. Other sociological effects also exist, of course.

Character of Neighborhoods

Transportation to some degree helps establish the distinct character of a neighborhood in an urban region. Some areas are bedroom communities, others are manufacturing districts, and still others are warehouse districts. Everyone is familiar with central business districts. The availability and means of transportation are pivotal factors in establishing the character of these districts or neighborhoods. Transportation makes the bedroom community possible; manufacturing and warehouse areas depend on transportation; and central business districts often exist because transportation allows many people to concentrate in one place during the working day. Regional amusement districts also depend on transportation. Sociologists, urbanologists, and others have many ways to classify the characters of neighborhoods. For our purposes, it is enough to note that transportation availability, the types of transportation, and the relative costs of transportation affect the character of neighborhoods.

Character of Cities

Whole cities may assume a sociological character. The port city, the distribution center, and the government city are examples of this sociological fact. The availability, type, and extent of transportation are an important attribute in city character, whether transportation is an artifact of design, as in the case of many railroad towns, or the result of a good natural harbor. Although many factors are involved, transportation is usually a factor of considerable importance.

Depressed Areas

There is some evidence that transportation plays an important role in depressed areas. When means of moving readily to and from work are denied or are not easily available, an area is likely to have lower than average per capita income. Sometimes depressed areas develop very close to transportation facilities where the location for living is less desirable than other areas. It is apparent that both the existence and the nonexistence of different types of transportation — mass transit or heavy freight transportation — have a role to play. However, for our purposes, it is enough to indicate that transportation, both the lack of and the nearness to, have a role to play in depressed area problems.

Status Symbols

Finally, it should be noted that transportation traditionally has provided sociological status symbols. Ownership of a spirited team of horses and a "surrey with a fringe on top" was a status symbol of a bygone age. Ownership of an automobile was once a status symbol. In modern society, multiple ownership of automobiles and ownership of certain brands or types of automobiles provide status symbols. In some parts of society, ownership of a boat is a status symbol, ownership of a private plane means status in other communities, and so forth. The point is that ownership of some preferred means of transportation is the focal point of one important type of status symbol. Many status symbols exist, but the ones relating to transportation are among the most common and readily recognizable ones.

ENERGY ASPECTS

Society also has a vital interest in the energy aspects of transportation. Transportation is a user and a distributor of fossil fuels, both of which aspects must be considered in terms of long-term and short-term impact.

Transport Fuel Use

Modern transport is uniquely dependent upon petroleum products. But the different modes require greatly differing amounts of petroleum to achieve a given amount of freight or passenger movement. These differing performance levels, under actual contemporary operating conditions rather than under some set of ideal or theoretical conditions, are indicated in Table 3.1. This means that actual load factors are used for freight and passenger transportation, rather than efficiencies for 100 percent utilization of carrier capacity. These figures do not take into account differences arising from varying trip characteristics or, in the case of freight transportation, the nature of the goods being transported. It should also be remembered that they reflect only fuel efficiency and not any other cost factors related to producing transportation services.

Table 3.1 Approximate Relative Fuel Efficiencies for Various Transport Modes under Current Operating Conditions

Mode	Freight Transport	Passenger Transport
Commercial air	1	1
Truck, long-haul	10	
Oil pipeline	15	
Domestic water	36	
Railroad	37	4
Automobile		1
Intercity bus		8

Explanation: 1 indicates least efficient; efficiencies of other modes expressed as multiples of this.
Source: Calculated by the authors from various published data.

This table shows that autos and commercial aircraft are about equally fuel-efficient in moving intercity passengers, but that railroads are four times and buses eight times as efficient as either. Likewise, long-haul trucks are about ten times and railroads about thirty-seven times as fuel-efficient as commercial aircraft in moving a given weight of freight for a given distance.

This does not mean, of course, that all transport should be, or can be, performed by the most fuel-efficient mode. Bus or rail service cannot be available for all potential passengers at all places and times. Also, the freight commodities hauled by the different modes frequently have quite different shipping characteristics and needs. Much of the freight moved by air simply would not move at all without air transport, for example. A variety of supply, demand, cost, and service factors must be considered in choosing the most appropriate mode of carriage. Sound economic or personal transport decisions cannot be made solely on the basis of fuel efficiency. Each mode is "best" for some specific needs, purposes, or circumstances.

The Short Term

As noted in Chapter 1, transportation accounts for about 66 percent of this country's petroleum usage. Much of this petroleum is imported, a fact particularly evident during the oil embargo and consequent fuel shortages of 1973–74. The temporary shortages drew much public attention to the energy aspects of transportation.

During the late 1970s Congress and the president created within the cabinet the Department of Energy and struggled to develop a comprehensive energy policy for the nation. They placed major emphasis on energy conservation. The new policy mandated some modifications of operating procedures by for-hire carriers, higher fuel taxes to discourage consumption, and maximum average fuel consumption levels for new automobiles. But little was done to provide alternatives to present passenger and freight transportation methods, or to increase fuel supplies.

Also there was little specific governmental recognition of the key role of transportation in moving fossil fuels (oil and coal). These fuels must be transported from their original sources to users by rail, barge, ship, pipeline, or truck. Our transportation system consumes a great deal of energy in simply distributing energy supplies among the rest of the economy's energy users.

The Long Term

Certainly transportation will continue to be a large user of energy and will continue to play a vital role in energy distribution. Perhaps transportation facilities and methods can be improved so that fuel can be used and transported more efficiently. Different types of vehicles may be developed, there may be more railroad electrification, and the movement of coal by pipelines (in the form of *coal slurry* — a mixture of crushed coal and water) will no doubt increase. Automobiles will be smaller and more efficient in energy consumption.

But although transportation improvements can increase the efficiency of fuel use and make existing fuel supplies last longer than would otherwise be true, the era of relatively low-priced fossil fuels has apparently ended. Barring unpredictable scientific or technological breakthroughs — the discovery of vast new energy sources or drastically more efficient methods of utilizing energy — we can expect energy prices to continue to increase within the foreseeable future. This, or course, will mean relatively higher transportation costs and changing transportation services.

ECONOMIC BENEFITS COMPARED
TO SOCIAL COSTS

The environmental, sociological, and energy aspects of transportation generally involve social costs of some type. To a marked degree, these aspects are related to urban developments and to the movement of people. But freight transportation also has environmental and social aspects. Recognition of these particular aspects as problems of transportation is relatively new. These features always have existed; it is only their recognition that is new.

When these aspects of the quality of life become problems and call forth changes to ameliorate these problems, an evaluation process is involved. Choices must be made. Decisions and actions to change or not to change these aspects must depend on a comparison of economic benefits to social costs. Few things are either all good or all bad. Thus both the good (economic benefits) and the bad (social costs) must be considered.

Two problems arise with any comparison of economic benefits to social costs. One of these is the problem of measurement. It is often most difficult to translate social costs and the environmental-sociological aspects of transportation into dollars and cents. It is nearly impossible to quantify the social costs of pollution, for example. It also may be difficult to measure carefully the economic benefits of transportation. Yet measurements of both costs and benefits somehow must be made.

The second problem is that the social decision-making process is inexact. When the whole of society is involved, and the function in question is as vital as transportation, it is not easy to get a clear decision on what to do or not to do. It is impossible to take a vote with all those affected voting their preferences. Hence much of the action, or inaction, takes place through political processes. The political process probably does not reflect the ideas of everyone in a completely satisfactory manner. Some political action is based more on emotion than on fact or on a careful weighing of economic benefits and social costs. But even though the decision-making mechanism is inexact, it provides virtually the only means for social action.

These problems of measurement and social decision making exist whether we are considering the environmental-sociological aspects or the regulatory-economic control aspects of transportation. The history and development of social action in the regulatory-economic control aspects of transportation are discussed in Part III. Perhaps the lessons already learned from economic regulatory experience will provide useful guidelines in dealing with these newer environmental-sociological problems.

SUMMARY

There are environmental-sociological-energy aspects of transportation just as there are historical and economic aspects. Sometimes these become social problems. These aspects are particularly difficult to measure in dollars-and-cents terms, yet they must be measured and evaluated in terms of economic benefits versus social costs. Broad social decisions must be made relative to the impacts of transportation, just as broad social decisions must be made relative to its regulatory-economic control aspects. In both instances, decisions may not always reflect adequate or careful analysis and will be political in nature. Yet by understanding these environmental-sociological aspects, regulatory-economic control aspects, and historical and developmental aspects, better decisions result.

Our domestic transportation system exists today as a balanced system. No one mode of transportation is supreme, as was true in the past. All forms have a role to play, and all possess separate economic characteristics and advantages. The next part of this book discusses these characteristics and advantages in some detail.

ADDITIONAL READINGS

Cheslow, Melvyn, "Improving Automobile Fuel Efficiency: The Impacts on Industry and the Economy," *Proceedings: Transportation Research Forum*, 16 (1975), 17–26.

Farris, Martin T., and Forrest E. Harding, *Passenger Transportation*, Englewood Cliffs, N.J.: Prentice-Hall, 1976.
  Chapter 7, "Passenger Transportation: The Social Benefits and Social Costs," pp. 219–34.

Farris, Martin T., and Paul T. McElhiney, eds., *Modern Transportation: Selected Readings*, Boston: Houghton Mifflin, 1973.
  Harper, Donald V., "The Dilemma of Aircraft Noise at Major Airports," pp. 145–64.

Foster, Jerry R., and Martin F. Schmidt, "Rail Terminals and the Urban Environment," *Transportation Journal* (Fall 1975), 21–28.

Heaver, Trevor D., and W. C. Waters, II, "An Economic Analysis of Controls on the Discharge of Oil at Sea," *Proceedings: Transportation Research Forum*, 15 (1974), pp. 571–81.

Lieb, Robert C., *Transportation: The Domestic System*, 3rd ed., Reston, Va:, Reston Publishing Co., 1985.
  Chapter 20, "Transportation/Energy Interrelationships," pp. 423–43.

Mehring, Joyce, "Potential Effect of Transport Price Increases on Energy Consumption," *Proceedings: Transportation Research Forum*, 17 (1976), 1–6.

Pegrum, Dudley F., *Transportation: Economics and Public Policy*, 3rd ed., Homewood, Ill.: Richard D. Irwin, 1973.
  Chapter 22, "The Urban Transportation Problem," pp. 534–66.

Smerk, George M., "The Environment and Transportation," *Transportation Journal* (Fall 1972), 40–49.

Steiner, Henry Malcolm, "Social Benefit Cost Analysis of Transport Proposals," *Proceedings: Transportation Research Forum*, 14 (1973), 673–81.

Talley, Wayne Kenneth, *Introduction to Transportation*, Cincinnati: South-Western Publishing Co., 1983.
  Chapter 8, "Energy and the Environment," pp. 141–56.

PART II

ECONOMIC CHARACTERISTICS AND PERFORMANCE OF DOMESTIC TRANSPORTATION

The physical transportation plant of the United States is composed of a variety of types of rights of way, terminal facilities, vehicles providing locomotive power and containing space for freight or passengers, communications equipment to facilitate centralized operational or managerial supervision or control over far-flung activities, and numerous forms of specialized accessorial equipment designed to make the transportation process more efficient or to cater to the needs of particular types of freight or passenger traffic.

The agencies of domestic transportation may be divided broadly into land carriers, water carriers, and air carriers. Land carriage includes transportation by railroad, highway (truck, bus, automobile), and pipeline. Air carriage today is confined to the airplane or to helicopters. Water carriage may be by oceangoing vessels between the East and West coasts of the United States (intercoastal) or between ports on a single coast (coastwise). Or it may be by barge and tugboat on inland waters, or by specialized steamers between ports on the Great Lakes. Superimposed upon these basic, or primary, modes of transport are such forms of secondary carriage as freight forwarders, express companies, and parcel post service, which use the facilities of one or more of the basic modes in providing transportation services.

Legally, we may think of carriers as being either for-hire or not-for-hire. The latter category frequently is referred to as private carriage; it is the situation in which persons (or firms) use their own vehicles to transport their own goods or personnel. The for-hire carrier, on the other hand, is in the business of hauling for others.

For-hire carriers, in general, are subject to some amount of federal or state economic regulation — federal if the carrier is engaged in interstate carriage, and state if it is operating in intrastate carriage. Private carriage, however, is not subject to this economic regulation but is regulated only in such matters as public safety, license fees, and taxes. In order to escape economic regulation, persons engaging in actual for-hire carriage have sometimes attempted by devious illegal means to disguise their activities by appearing to be engaging in private carriage.

For-hire carriers may be further classified legally as common carriers and contract carriers. A common carrier is one who makes a standing offer to serve the general public. This does not mean that the common carrier necessarily offers to haul anything anywhere at any time. Rather, it means that whatever product or products it offers to carry within an operating territory will be carried for anyone desiring its services. A contract carrier, on the other hand, hauls only for those with whom it has a specific formal contract of service and does not hold itself out to serve all comers. The difference between common and contract carriage, then, is in the general or the limited nature of the carrier's offer to serve — not in terms of what or where the carrier offers to haul, but in terms of whether or not it is offering to haul for everyone or only for a selected clientele. The legal duties, responsibilities, privileges, and regulations applicable to common and to contract carriage are quite different in many respects, as will be shown in Parts II and III. Thus the category into which a carrier is classified is of considerable importance to the carrier as well as to those who use its services.

Sometimes a carrier may be referred to as an exempt carrier, or a carrier may engage in exempt carriage. This means that the particular kind of service performed, or the product hauled, is such that the carrier is not subject to certain kinds of governmental regulations (usually rate or operating rights regulations) that in general apply to other for-hire carrier services. Exempt carriage may be either common or contract in form.

Although they may have some things in common, in general each mode and each legal type of carrier has its own service, operating, economic, and legal characteristics and problems. Many of these things affect the quality and quantity of available transportation services and facilities. It is therefore essential that the users of carrier services, as well as those in responsible carrier management or governmental regulatory positions, understand the differing features of various forms of transport; otherwise, intelligent decisions relating to carriage cannot be made. A primary purpose of this part is to describe, compare, contrast, and evaluate some of the most important features and problems of various forms of domestic carriage and to evaluate specific and overall performances of our transport system. Our approach in doing this will be mainly from the viewpoint of the users of transportation services.

Although concerned primarily with domestic freight transportation, this part also includes discussions of passenger and international freight transport. These forms differ from domestic freight transport in many ways, but are similar in others. Both, however, do interface closely with domestic freight transport in facilities and resource use, and in performing the essential overall functions of transportation.

CHAPTER 4
LAND CARRIERS

Intercity freight movements in the United States, excluding oceanborne coastwise and intercoastal movements, amounted to approximately 2,667 billion ton-miles in 1987 (the ton-mile, one ton moved one mile, is a recognized standard of measurement in freight transportation). Of this total, land carriers accounted for approximately 83 percent. Railroads lead in ton-mile volume with about 36 percent of the total ton mileage, followed by trucks and oil pipelines with about 25.1 and 21.9 percent. Waterways, including Great Lakes carriers but excluding deep-sea coastwise and intercoastal shipping, accounted for almost all of the remainder of the total volume handled (more than 16 percent), while air carriers moved just over 0.3 percent of the total. In addition, coastwise and intercoastal ocean movements, a large portion of which consisted of petroleum products, accounted for nearly 600 million ton-miles. It is evident that railroads, as they have been for a century, remain the backbone of our intercity freight movement. Other forms of carriage have been cutting deeply into rail dominance during recent years, however (see Table 4.1).

Table 4.1 Estimated Approximate Total Intercity Freight Ton Mileage and Percentage Moved by Each Mode of Transport for Selected Years

Year	Total Ton Mileage (billions)*	Rail	Highway	Inland Water	Oil Pipelines	Air
1946	944	68.0%	8.7%	13.1%	10.1%	0.01%
1956	1,376	49.2	18.1	16.0	16.7	0.04
1964	1,557	42.8	23.8	16.1	17.2	0.10
1977	2,331	35.6	24.1	16.1	24.0	0.18
1987	2,667	36.2	25.1	16.3	21.9	0.34

*Includes Great Lakes, but excludes coastwide and intercoastal deep-sea traffic.
Source: Data from Transportation Policy Associates, *Transportation in America*, various years. Copyright 1946, 1956, 1964, 1977, 1988. Used by permission of Eno Foundation for Transportation.

Intercity passenger mileage (one person for one mile and excluding strictly local movements) in the United States was approximately 1,859 billion passenger miles during 1987 (excluding private air travel and movement on inland waterways, such as ferry travel). Of this volume, apparently a little more than 80 percent moved by automobile. The remainder was divided among airlines, about 18 percent of total passenger mileage, intercity buses, over 1 percent, and railroads, under 1 percent. The characteristics of passenger transportation are covered more fully in Chapter 7.

RAILROADS

The railroad network of the United States consists of about 167,000 line miles. If double or multiple trackage, sidings, and yard trackage are added to this, the total track mileage exceeds 250,000. Rolling stock on these tracks is made up of approximately 20,000 locomotives, about 1,290,000 freight cars, not all railroad owned, and about 2,300 passenger-carrying cars (most of which are owned by Amtrak). Altogether, the book value of railroad investment in plant and equipment is in the neighborhood of $47 billion. Total railroad operating revenues recently have been about $26 billion, with net profits after taxes averaging around $2.7 billion (excluding Amtrak).

Operating this plant and equipment are about 18 Class I railroads (an ICC classification which includes railroads with average annual operating revenues of $50 millon or more — increased from $10 billion in 1978) and some 481 regional and local railroads. A labor force of around 250,000 employees, with a wage bill of $9.4 billion, was utilized in operating this system in 1987, compared with a labor force of 1,439,000 and a payroll of $3.9 billion required to operate the U.S. railroads in 1946.

There are nearly 500 railroads, and a large part of railroad operation is confined to a comparatively small number of firms. The 10 largest carriers, about 2 percent of the total, account for approximately 96 percent of revenue ton-miles, 94 percent of miles of road, and 98 percent of net operating income.

Although people sometimes tend to think of railroads as a prime example of big business, there is actually a considerable variation in the size of firms making up the industry, even among the large Class I railroads. They range from less than 500 route miles to over 20,000. Their revenues range from less than $100 million to several billion dollars.

At the other end, there are a number of small carriers operating as few as ten route miles, with one to three locomotives, and no owned rolling stock. These railroads, and many larger regional railroads, are the result of a trend toward spin-offs of trackage that has been unprofitable for a large unionized operation, but that may be profitable for a "mom and pop," nonunionized, low overhead version of the industry. In the last decade, the number of Class I railroads has declined by 62.5 percent, largely through mergers (discussed in Chapter 26), while the number of short-line and regional railroads has increased by over 22 percent.

Although fast freight trains moving on a main line may travel at speeds of 60 miles per hour or more, delays on sidings and in terminals reduce the railroads' average speed per car between origin and destination to around 20 miles per hour. This is an increase of about 25 percent over immediate post–World War II speeds, however. Because of fewer terminal and other delays, passenger train speed averages about twice that of freight trains. The average load moved in a freight car is about 67 tons; the average freight train hauls about 2,400 tons. The average length of haul per shipment is around 690 miles for the entire rail system. Average revenues received are less than 3 cents per ton-mile generated.

All U.S. railroad carriers are legally classified as common carriers. This means that the interstate activities of all railroads are regulated by the federal government and that their intrastate activities are subject to state regulation. As common carriers, members of the country's railway system are not required or equipped to haul anything anywhere at any time, but they come nearer this than does any other form of carriage.

As indicated above, a small proportion of leading railroads operate a relatively large proportion of our rail facilities and account for a substantial amount of the total freight traffic. Also, there are sizable geographic areas and a considerable number of communities, usually smaller towns, that are served by only one railroad. It is a mistake, however, to think of present-day railroads as monopolies, although for a considerable period during their earlier history railroads did have a virtual monopoly on long-distance transport in this country. Some critics of railroad regulation practices maintain that our regulatory laws and their administration, even today, reflect an earlier antimonopoly bias.

Competition, Costs, and Coverage

In the carriage of freight, railroads encounter keen competition from trucks for a large variety of commodities throughout the country. Pipeline and water carriers, although they are more specialized by product and geography, also have cut deeply into traffic formerly moving by rail, and in some instances they have almost completely taken over certain movements. Present indications are that these three alternate modes of transport will continue to compete effectively with rail carriers. Air movement of freight has not yet created any significant problem for the railroads.

Railroads also compete among themselves. Most large communities and many smaller ones are served by more than one railroad, often by several. In addition, the interchangeability of equipment, and thus of shipments among our various railroads (which is a unique characteristic of our railway system), provides an opportunity for numerous lines to compete for shipments that proceed beyond the line of the originating carrier. Even though a shipper may have only one railroad entering its town, it may have a choice between literally dozens of alternate railroads over which shipments may move before reaching a cross-country destination. Any industrial traffic manager or other person in a position to control the routing of large volumes of freight can testify to the steady stream of freight solicitors from competing railroads and other forms of carriage who are constantly attempting to sell their transportation services.

The cost structure of the railroad industry is such that railroads can be very competitive in their short-term pricing policies and in the pricing of particular services. Because of the very large investment in long-lived facilities — track rights of way, terminals, and rolling stock — a large portion of railroad costs are fixed or indirect in nature. During the life of these facilities, expenses of interest, depreciation, property taxation, maintenance, and similar costs do not vary with the amount of traffic handled. In addition, the usable life of much of the railroad plant is considerably longer in calendar years than is the life of most of the plant used by competing forms of carriage. Also, railroads have a large overhead expense in the form of executive, administrative, clerical, and other salaries that are not directly related to the volume of business handled. As a consequence, many railroad managers believe that perhaps as much as two-thirds of their total costs under usual operating conditions may be classified as fixed rather than variable (meaning varying with volume). This fixed expense, as a percentage of total expense, whatever it may actually be, apparently is higher for railroads than for other forms of transport, with the possible exception of pipelines.

Elementary economics students learn that in the short run (*short run* is the time less than that necessary for an investment to fully depreciate or be converted to other uses), it is necessary that a business cover only its variable costs to remain in operation. In other words, although it may be desirable that revenues exceed expenses, it is better to remain in operation under conditions that permit the direct or variable expenses to be covered and leave something to apply on fixed costs than to close down completely and be obligated for all the continuing fixed costs. By the same token, in the short run it pays to accept any particular traffic at a price that more than covers the direct costs associated with the particular movement. Railroad managements long ago learned these economic realities. Also, they learned that railroads, due to their heavy fixed, low variable cost structure, usually have a short-run pricing advantage over competitors with relatively higher variable costs, and that rate wars with competing modes, in the absence of restraining regulation, usually can be won by railroads. In the past, this cost structure has encouraged rate wars among railroads and between rails and other forms of carriage and the development of various kinds of discriminatory pricing policies. These matters will be discussed in more detail in Part IV.

Shippers, of course, are interested in what they get for their transportation expenditure. In addition to the actual freight rate, they may be concerned with such things as area coverage, frequency of departures, reliability of service, and speed of movement as well as special or accessorial services. some general comparative statements about these items may be made. It must be recognized, of course, that there usually are exceptions to broad generalizations.

Railroad freight rates between a given origin and destination are published in tariffs and usually are quoted in cents per 100 pounds. As in most pricing, a distinction is made between large and small quantities, with carload (CL) rates being lower than less-than-carload (LCL) rates. Very few railroads continue to haul LCL traffic. Also, as will be more fully explained in Part IV, rates may be *class* rates, which apply on all items moving from all origins to all destinations. Rates may also be *commodity* rates, which apply only to specifically named items moving between specified origins and destinations and usually requiring some designated routing or involving certain other restrictions. Typically, commodity rates are quoted on heavy-volume, bulky, low-value, long-haul goods; class rates apply on items with opposite transportation characteristics. Actually, although class rates are more generally applicable, most railroad traffic (perhaps 95 percent or more in terms of ton-miles) moves under commodity rates.

In general, rail freight rates are lower than truck rates on large shipments moving for long distances. Because of lower terminal handling costs and other cost features, however, this may not be true for small shipments or for some kinds of large shipments that move only for short distances. Long and short distances, of course, will vary by product and by physical conditions of transport such as terrain and traffic congestion. Depending upon the particular circumstances, a short distance in this connection might vary from 100 miles or less to 350 miles or more. Rail rates usually are higher than pipeline or water rates, although we must remember that these two forms of transport are specialized by product and geographical limitations.

On a national or regional basis, railroad area coverage is excellent. Not many areas or population centers are without rail transport. Some 3,000 U.S. counties, containing more than 99 percent of the country's population, are served by rail. Wide area coverage is made possible by highly developed railroad cooperation which permits rail cars to move with almost perfect freedom from the lines of one rail carrier to the lines of others. So far as the shipper is concerned, in effect, it is as if we had only one railroad serving the entire country. A shipper in the state of Washington deals with a local railroad, paying one rate (a joint rate) for a shipment perhaps destined to move over several rail lines (a through route) to a consignee in Florida. The details of this interline exchange and division of freight revenue are handled between the various railroads involved in the movement and are of no concern to the shipper. Although other forms of transport quote through routes and joint rates to a limited extent, no form begins to approach the extensive cooperation on a nationwide scale that is characteristic of the railroad industry.

Railroad cars, though, can go only where railroad tracks exist. Trucks, on the other hand, can go wherever roads are found and sometimes even where there are no roads. This means that goods destined for communities not served by railroads and individuals without direct access to rail tracks in rail-served communities must be delivered by truck. On the local scene, therefore, area coverage by rail is much less complete and less flexible than truck coverage, although railroads provide a more flexible and complete coverage nationally. Recent developments in piggyback or trailer-on-flatcar (TOFC) service, where truck trailers are brought to and loaded on rail cars for a line-haul movement and pulled from the destination terminal to the consignee's establishment by a truck tractor, are designed to combine the long-haul and national area coverage advantages of railroads with the local flexibility advantages of trucks.

Pipeline and water carrier area coverage is more restricted both nationally and locally than is rail carriage. Most shippers and consignees using these modes of carriage, however, ship or receive large volumes and are located and equipped to minimize the amount of necessary supplemental handling and transport.

Trains operate on timetable schedules which, in some respects, may be an advantage to shippers. This means, however, that departures from a given point are less frequent than those of a trucking company. A truck can leave a shipper's door at any time and can schedule its departure to arrive at the consignee's door at any desired time, whereas rail shipments are bound by timetables and sometimes by the necessity for building up a complete train before departure. In situations where a particular hour of arrival or departure is important, therefore, railroads frequently are at a competitive disadvantage compared to trucks. Railroad departures, however, are generally more frequent than are water carrier departures.

Reliability of traffic movements involves the on-time and undamaged delivery of the goods shipped, as well as the settlement of claims for damages or unusual delays en route. In areas of severe weather conditions such as heavy snow or rainfall, trains are more likely to run on schedule or be subject to fewer delays than are trucks. Storms and seasons also may affect water movements, and labor disputes may tie up any form of transportation. The loss or damage (L & D) to railroad carload shipments in general appears to be as favorable, if not more favorable, than for competing modes of transport. Common carriers by land, with certain exceptions, are held to fairly strict accountability for goods entrusted to their care (see Chapter 20), whereas the legal liabilities of water common carriers for lost or damaged goods are much less. Contract and exempt carriage reliability varies considerably, and owners themselves must be responsible for losses incurred in their own private carrier operations.

Shippers want their goods to reach their customers. Even though the shipper or the customer may eventually be reimbursed for losses or damages occurring en route, such occurrences may disrupt the orderly flow of production or merchandising and certainly do not win good will or contribute to good shipper-receiver or carrier-customer relations. Also, there is always the possibility that financial responsibility for losses cannot be proven. And small losses too insignificant to report and administrative and clerical expenses of claims must be considered. It is possible that shippers' loss experiences with different carriers of the same mode will vary more widely than their experiences between the different competitive modes, but, in any case, railroads in general appear to be at least as reliable from the loss and damage viewpoint as are any of the other modes.

With an average en route speed of approximately 20 miles per hour, railroad freight in general moves considerably faster than waterborne freight. On shorter hauls, truck transport usually is much faster than rail movements. On some long-haul runs, however, fast rail schedules have been established to compete effectively with the speed of trucks. Carload shipments, which do not have to remain in terminals for further loading and are not stopped en route for partial unloading, naturally may be expected to move at greater average speeds than less-than-carload shipments.

Financial Conditions and Outlook

The financial problems of railroads have been well publicized during recent years. Despite relatively prosperous economic conditions, the percentage rate of return on investment in the railway industry as a whole has reached as high as 4 percent only during a few years since World War II. Not all railroads have been characterized by low profits, of course. The economics of the industry are such that firms with high-density traffic (commonly measured in terms of tons moved per track mile per year) for relatively long hauls are more profitable. Also, it is less costly to operate a smaller number of long trains (100 or more rail cars per train) than to operate a larger number of short trains. These favorable conditions are more common in the southern and western portions than in the eastern portion of the country. Thus, southern and western railroads generally have been more profitable than eastern ones. But even the most profitable railroads have not had notably high profits for several decades.

The railroad financial situation is not only a problem for railroad management, investors, and employees, it is a concern of everyone. Shippers and businesspeople are concerned with the availability and quality of services and the levels of rates. Consumers, who ultimately bear the rate burden, are concerned about higher prices. Taxpayers have an interest from the viewpoint of possible subsidies or governmental ownership. Citizens in general also have a stake in the maintenance of adequate rail facilities for national defense.

Simply stated, the current railroad problem is that railroads are not taking in enough total revenues in proportion to their expenses. Many factors contribute to this. Much business has been lost to competing forms of transport. Automobiles, airlines, and buses have taken most of the passenger traffic. Freight has been lost (see Table 4.1), and much of this lost freight traffic has been in high-value and high revenue–producing movements.

Because of the long-lived nature of most of its large investment in plant and facilities, the railroad industry, with its decline in traffic, has been left holding excess fixed capacity. In the short-run period, which may actually extend for a long period of calendar time, the industry cannot adjust its capacity to the decreased demand for services and thus is stuck with its high fixed costs. To some extent, federal and state regulations have limited whatever flexibility railroads otherwise might have by requiring that portions of this excess capacity be maintained — that is, by forbidding the abandonment of certain services or runs even though they may be unprofitable or by opposing attempts to attain economies by consolidating duplicated facilities. Governmental regulations also have hampered price flexibility, both upward and downward, so that railroad managements have not been free to adjust to rapidly changing traffic conditions by what they think are appropriate price adjustments.

Railroad managements also blame obsolete union labor rules (the bases for which were established more than sixty years ago) for some of their financial difficulties. And railroads allege that their properties are over-taxed through assessments that are generally higher than assessments on other properties of similar value — for every dollar paid in railroad dividends during recent years, about three dollars have been paid in the form of federal, state, and local taxes. And railroad managements strongly object that their railroad tax dollars are being used to construct rights of way for, and to otherwise subsidize, their motor-, air-, and water-carrier competitors.

High fuel prices and fuel shortages emphasize the importance of railroads. More than three times as much freight tonnage can be moved per gallon of fuel by rail as can be moved by truck. Also, air pollution and number of workers required are reduced accordingly.

Under present technological conditions and within the foreseeable future, railroads will remain the backbone of our long-distance bulk commodity carriage. It is not possible to operate our economy as we know it without adequate and extensive railroad transport. Despite the unfavorable financial aspects of the railway industry, then, we are not faced with a choice between rail service and no rail service. Rather, the question is whether rail services will continue to be performed under our present form of private ownership and control or whether heavy subsidization or even governmental ownership may prevail in the future. The United States is the only major industrial nation with a completely privately owned railway system (one of Canada's two major railroads is privately owned and the other is owned by the government). Very few responsible persons in this country favor government ownership of railroads as such, but more and more persons fear that it is inevitable unless the present trends can be substantially improved.

By the early 1980s, many railroad managers were feeling more optimistic than they had for many years. The justification for this optimism can be seen in recent railroad operating trends. In 1987, the industry generated a 5.6 percent return on investment, one of the best years in railroad history. In addition, while overall carloadings decreased by about 11 percent between 1979 and 1987, intermodal carloadings nearly doubled. This is a strong indication of rail competitiveness for what traditionally has been truck traffic and of increased participation in the movement of containerized import and export traffic. In addition, railroad labor efficiency is improving. Between 1979 and 1987, railroad labor hours paid decreased by 47 percent while revenue ton-miles increased by over 4 percent.

TRUCKS

The U.S. highway system is made up of almost 3.9 million miles of roadway and streets. Almost 90 percent of rural roads and highways are paved. During the mid-1950s, construction and developments were started on a 42,500-mile system of interstate and defense superhighways designed to link all areas of the country. During the thirty years ending in 1980, federal, state, and local governments spent almost $350 billion on improving and maintaining our highway system. Currently highway expenditures are running in excess of $65 billion per year at all levels, more than triple the annual amount in 1970 and one and one-half as much as in 1980. About 1.7 million miles of our highways are identified as providing first class ride quality and having few, if any, visible signs of wear.

In addition to more than 135 million automobiles, more than 40 million trucks and buses of various kinds, including more than 1 million for-hire vehicles, operate over the vast highway network. Around 7 million persons are directly employed in various phases of trucking.

It is almost meaningless to speak of a "trucking industry" in any general sense. Actually, there are many trucking "industries." Almost all types of truckers do face some similar problems and have common interests with almost all other types. But differences among the various groups often are greater than are the similarities.

Unlike railroads, the for-hire trucking industry has always been made up of both common and contract carriers. Also, a sizable amount of exempt carriage (not subject to economic regulation) has always existed, as well as a large amount of private carriage. Not more than about one-third of truck ton-mileage (interstate) has ever been subject to federal economic regulation, with about another one-third (intrastate) subject to various individual state economic regulations.

Interstate truck carriers regulated by the ICC are classified by that body as Class I (annual gross operating revenues of more than $5 million per year), Class II ($1 to $5 million), and Class III (less than $1 million). Also, trucking firms are classified into about a dozen types, depending upon the nature of the services performed. Of these types, the General Freight Carriers probably are of most importance to most shippers, although other specialized types such as Household Goods Carriers, Automobile Carriers, Refrigerated Haulers, and various others are of particular importance to special shipping and receiving groups. Some General Freight Carriers specialize in hauling truckload (TL) shipments, others specialize in less-than-truckload (LTL), and still others actively seek both large and small shipments. Also, at least 100,000 owner-operators, usually one person owning and driving one truck, engage in exempt carriage (especially of agricultural products) on their own account or haul on contracts for larger for-hire carriers. Obviously, differing types and sizes of for-hire truckers have differing problems.

The for-hire trucking industry basically is made up of a large number of comparatively small firms, although there are notable exceptions. More than 32,000 intercity for-hire companies are subject to ICC regulation. Of these, more than 850 are Class I, 1,250 are Class II, and the remainder Class III carriers. In addition, of course, thousands of firms engage only in intrastate or exempt transportation, and over 35 million trucks are registered in the private (not-for-hire) category. Private, intrastate, and other exempt carriers, of course, frequently haul commodities that would have moved by regulated trucking firms or other forms of carriage. In 1987, almost 20 percent of for-hire tractors and 11 percent of trailers were operated by ICC carriers.

Private trucking grew rapidly during the 1960s and 1970s. By the early 1980s, there were at least around 500,000 private truck fleets with five or more vehicles each, plus an immense number of smaller private carriers. The federal Motor Carrier Act of 1980, along with favorable regulatory and court rulings, encouraged thousands of these private carriers, plus many new entrants, to engage in for-hire carriage. For example, within two years after the passage of this act, almost 1,000 large corporations with 10,000 subsidiary corporations were authorized to engage in previously prohibited Compensated Intercorporate Hauling (CIH); that is, one of a corporation's subsidiaries could haul on a for-hire basis for all the corporation's other subsidiaries.

In an industry with firms ranging in size from the single-vehicle owner-operator up to companies with assets of hundreds of millions of dollars each, industry averages must be viewed with reservations. Certain kinds of averages, however, do aid in understanding the nature of the trucking industry.

The overall trucking industry (that is, including private and all for-hire categories) essentially is characterized by short hauls. More than half of all truck trips are less than 5 miles one way and the average trip is about 11 miles. Only a little more than 1 percent of trips are more than 100 miles one way. These 100-miles-and-up trips, however, account for almost 25 percent of all vehicle mileage. Thus we get a picture of a large number of very short trips at one extreme and a smaller number of much longer trips at the other extreme.

The average length of haul by Class I intercity motor common carriers is around 490 miles. Some large carriers have average hauls of more than twice this distance. The average load carried by Class I and Class II carriers is about thirteen tons per vehicle, the average revenue received per vehicle mile is about $2.30, and per ton-mile approximately 18 cents. All of these averages have increased in recent years.

Performing its transportation services, our hypothetical average Class I motor carrier utilizes an average of 541 pieces of power equipment and 1,347 trailers, plus real estate, fixtures, and other facilities representing an average investment of around $7 million. It receives gross operating revenues of more than $18 million.

Costs, Competition, and Coverage

The trucking industry's cost structure differs drastically from that of the railroad industry in that variable or direct costs are very high in proportion to fixed or indirect costs. This is in large part due to the trucking industry's use of publicly owned rights of way and to its comparatively smaller investment in terminal facilities and vehicles. However, rapidly increasing fuel costs since 1973 have relatively favored railroads over trucks.

The wage bill alone including fringe benefits takes around 60 cents of every revenue dollar received by truck common and contract carriers. Viewed in another way, line-haul expenses typically account for more than one-half the revenue dollar; terminal expenses for around 13 cents; administrative, general, taxes, and licenses for another 13 cents; and depreciation and equipment maintenance require another 15 cents. The balance of the revenue dollar is spread over such items as traffic solicitation, insurance and safety, and profits. It is generally considered that a well-managed trucking firm can operate profitably with an operating ratio (percentage of operating income going for operating expenses) of 93; by contrast, railroads usually are in financial difficulties if operating ratios exceed the low or middle 70s.

It is easy to see why trucking costs vary much more directly in relation to the volume of traffic moved than do rail costs. And it follows, therefore, that the rates charged for trucking services even in a short-run period cannot fall very far below total costs. This gives railroads, which have a larger cushion of fixed costs, considerable pricing advantages in many short-run competitive situations (see Part III). Also, it must be remembered that owing to the nature of its investments, a short-run period for a railroad may include a much longer calendar time than it does for a trucking firm.

As indicated above, probably two-thirds of all intercity truck transportation has never been subject to economic regulation by the ICC. Some of this, however, is regulated by state agencies. Insofar as economic regulation applies, common carrier truck regulation is generally comparable, with a few exceptions, to the regulations applying on railroad carriage. Contract carriers are subjected to less regulation; private carriers generally are regulated only by state officials and in matters such as speed, safety, size and weight limits, and similar noneconomic aspects.

Truck carriage competes primarily with rail carriage for relatively high-class (that is, high value in relation to weight and bulk) traffic, particularly on shorter hauls. To a lesser extent, trucks compete with rail and water carriers for lower class traffic and on longer hauls, as well as with air freight carriers. Also, the various segments and firms in the trucking industry compete vigorously with one another. Common carriers compete with contract carriers, and both of them with exempt and private carriage. Most shippers using for-hire truck services have a variety of carriers to choose from. In addition, many shippers have found it advantageous to operate their own private trucks for all or some of their movements.

Like rail rates, truck rates usually are quoted in cents per 100 pounds. Also, generally there are differences between less-than-truckload (LTL) and truckload (TL) rates; in addition, volume (vol.) or any quantity (AQ) rates frequently are available. In comparing rail and truck rates, however, one must not forget that a shipment so small that it would not take a rail CL rate often may be large enough to qualify for a truck TL rate. Also, truck services often can be better tailored to individual shipper needs than can rail services. Shippers frequently are willing to pay more for what they consider to be better services. Transportation demand is service elastic as well as price elastic.

Because of the differing terminal and line-haul handling expense characteristics, truck rates generally are lower than rail rates on small shipments and on short hauls. It is harder to generalize on larger shipments subject to intermediate length or long-haul movements by rail class rates, but the rate differences between rail and truck on a considerable amount of such traffic are not great one way or the other. Truck lines, however, usually cannot quote rates competitive with the long-haul rail commodity rates that apply generally (but not exclusively) on heavy and bulky low-value goods moving in heavy volume.

Shippers may have to consider expenses other than rates, however. For example, packaging used for truck shipments may be less costly and weigh less than rail shipment packaging. Also, trucks usually furnish pickup and delivery services for small shipments and provide loading services for truckload movements, whereas rail carloads usually are loaded by the shippers themselves.

Up to fairly long distances, trucks (which do not have to become involved with congested terminals or be delayed on sidings) usually give much more rapid service than do rails. Even on very long hauls, truck speed generally is as good as fast rail freight. Trucks, too, are able to operate on a flexible time schedule, leaving and arriving according to the customer's wishes.

As pointed out above, local area coverage by trucks is excellent. On the national or even regional scene, however, area coverage is less complete owing to the restricted operating territories and scarcity of interchange agreements (through routes and joint rates) in the trucking industry. Where it is available, long-distance service generally is pinpoint in nature, that is, from one major center to another, with little or no coverage of intermediate or surrounding smaller communities. These weaknesses in trucking carriage are being improved steadily, however, as the industry becomes more mature.

Adverse weather affects truck schedules more than it does rail movements. As to loss and damage experience, it appears that there may not be any significant differences between rails and regulated truckers in general. Statistics on percentage loss and damage ratios are somewhat misleading because of the different inherent natures and values of the goods shipped and the kinds of packaging and protection used by the two modes.

Industry Outlook

For-hire truckers, in terms of profitability, stability, and growth, performed about the same as industry in general during the generation following World War II. But the future is not clear. The industry's basic problems are related to its achieving its proper place in the transportation scheme. Differences among common, contract, exempt, and private carriage, as well as other modes of transport, remain to be resolved. The kinds of commodities, the lengths of hauls, and the most efficient sizes of firms under various operating circumstances have not been determined. Much remains to be done in the area of interchange of shipments and equipment, not only between trucking firms, but also between other modes of transportation. These and similar problems can never be completely solved for all times and conditions, of course, but better solutions than those now in use can and will be reached.

The severe economic recession of the early 1980s hurt for-hire trucking, as well as other modes of transportation. More economic losses came from the Motor Carrier Act of 1980, which allowed a flood of new entries into an already depressed business and actively encouraged price cutting. The deregulation movement has significantly changed the motor carrier industry, increasing competition dramatically in many industry segments and decreasing the strength of the Teamsters Union (the number of trucking industry employees has dropped by more than 28 percent since 1978). In addition, larger carriers of general commodities have become an even more significant part of the industry. In 1978, the top twelve carriers (excluding United Parcel Service) generated 17 percent of all ICC carrier revenue. In 1987, this had risen to 30 percent. In the same time period, multiple-line carriage for Class I and Class II carriers decreased by almost three-fourths, from 10.8 percent of all traffic to 2.8 percent.

The results of these changes, and of higher fuel prices, remain to be seen. Many observers, though, predict continued rapid change for the industry. By its nature, trucking will retain its importance in the economy, as thousands of communities and destinations involving millions of shipments are not and cannot be completely serviced by other modes. In effect, the industry motto, "if you got it, a truck brought it," will continue to be true even if the performance and structure of the industry are altered considerably.

PIPELINES

Oil pipelines have surpassed inland water carriers in ton-mileage volume to become our third major form of carriage. These pipelines represent an investment of about $21 billion and operate more than 170,000 miles of pipeline. About three-fourths of pipeline of the more than 100 pipeline organizations were regulated by the ICC until September 1977. At that time their regulation was passed to the Federal Energy Regulatory Commission in the newly created cabinet-level Department of Energy. Regulated lines account for almost 90 percent of pipeline revenues.

The pipeline network consists of gathering, crude, and product lines. Gathering lines collect oil in the field and carry it to a certain distribution point. Crude lines then pump this unrefined oil to refineries. Product lines distribute the various refined products from refineries to consuming centers. About four-fifths of oil pipeline mileage is in the form of trunk lines carrying crude oil and refined petroleum products, with the remainder devoted to gathering activities. The average length of movement by crude lines (excluding gathering) is about 295 miles, and the average product movement is about 330 miles.

Most states contain some pipelines, but the geographical concentration of oil-producing centers and of consuming centers affects the concentration of pipelines. Texas alone contains one-fourth of the nation's pipeline mileage, and the next three leading states — Oklahoma, Kansas, and Illinois — contain another one-fourth. One-third of the states containing pipelines have less than 500 miles each. A glance at a map of our pipeline system, however, reveals that it consists in considerable part of an interconnected network similar to the railroad pattern.

Oil movements by pipeline amount to nearly 600 billion ton-miles annually. This figure includes more than 6 billion barrels of crude oil and over 4.5 billion barrels of refined products per year. This tremendous ton-mile movement is handled by something over 20,000 employees. Pipelines handle the vast majority of long-distance petroleum transportation, with water carriers a distant second and railroads an even more distant third. Motor carriers handle final distribution of most refined products and some relatively long-distance transportation of specialized products and service to areas not served adequately by other means.

Oil pipelines range in size from more than 10,000 to less than 10 miles, with one-third being less than 500 miles long. Although some are independent, most pipelines are affiliated with major oil companies as subsidiaries or pipeline departments, or through at least partial ownership. Several railroads have constructed pipelines during recent years.

Considerable pipeline mileage also is owned jointly by more than one pipeline organization through unique undivided interest contracts which are based upon each owner's investment in the project. One company usually builds and operates such an undivided interest line, dealing at arm's length with other participating organizations. It should be noted that such ventures legally are not corporations, partnerships, or shippers' associations.

Pipeline organizations are fond of pointing out the fact that their industry is the only form of transport that has never received any form of government subsidy. Pipelines, in general, may also claim to be the most profitable form of transportation. On gross revenues of more than $7 billion a year, they earn an overall return of more than 11 percent. Maximum earnings are limited by regulation and by a Justice Department consent decree signed by many companies as a result of a pre–World War II antitrust prosecution.

As common carriers, oil pipelines are obligated to transport on an equal basis for all customers making offerings (tenders) under defined conditions. Rates are published in tariffs on a cents per barrel (42 gallons) basis from point to point or zone to zone. On a ton-mile basis, rates average about 1.17 cents. The average revenue per barrel is around $1.40, which means that the pipeline transportation cost from oil field through refinery and to the consuming center, a distance of about 600 miles, is just over 3 cents per gallon.

A pipeline represents a comparatively large investment, but its operations are so highly mechanized and automated that very few employees are required for its operation. This means heavy fixed costs as compared to variable costs, and a low operating ratio (in the mid-50s, as compared to the low 90s for trucks or the mid-70s for railroads) is common.

Such cost characteristics, of course, require that a large and steady volume of oil be available for a considerable period of time in order that pipelines be feasible. With such conditions, though, pipeline transport is considerably less costly than rail or truck movements.

In general, bulk movements of oil by water transport are even less costly than pipeline movements, but water transport is more limited geographically and usually is much more circuitous. Historically, pipelines have been built mainly in areas not served by water transport or as feeders into or distributors out of ports. Pipeliners today, however, maintain that their large-diameter, or big-inch, pipe, 30 to 36 inches or larger in diameter, is competitive on a cost basis with water movements. It is only under very special conditions, however, that such large-diameter pipe is economically sound.

The efficiency of oil pipeline operations, coupled with rising costs for other forms of carriage, has stimulated interest in moving other commodities by pipeline. Coal, crushed and suspended in water, was first moved successfully for more than 100 miles in a commercial operation in 1957. This operation ceased in 1963, but since then serious consideration and some experimentation have been devoted to pipeline transport of such products as coal, ore, wood chips, and grain. The pipeline technique apparently is physically capable of being adapted to many commodities, but such innovations can be expected to come about only under unusual economic circumstances. One 273-mile coal slurry pipeline has been used in this country since 1970, and several others are being considered or planned.

ADDITIONAL READINGS

Bowersox, Donald J., Pat J. Calabro, and George D. Wagenheim, *Introduction to Transportation*, New York: Macmillan Publishing Co., 1981.
    Chapter 5, "Railroad Transportation," pp. 64–81.
    Chapter 6, "Truck Transportation," pp. 82–101.
    Chapter 7, "Pipeline Transportation," pp. 102–15.
Coyle, John J., Edward J. Bardi, and Joseph L. Cavinato, *Transportation*, 2nd ed., St. Paul: West Publishing Co., 1986.
    Chapter 3, "Railroads," pp. 47–73.
    Chapter 4, "Pipelines," pp. 75–94.
    Chapter 6, "Motor Carriers," pp. 115–35.
Hazard, John L., *Transportation: Management, Economics, Policy*, Centreville, Md.: Cornell Maritime Press, 1977.
    Chapter 4, "Functional Analysis of the Modes," pp. 96–126.
Lieb, Robert C., *Transportation: The Domestic System*, 3rd ed., Reston, Va.: Reston Publishing Co., 1985.
    Chapter 3, "The Railroad Industry," pp. 33–58.

Chapter 4, "The Highway System," pp. 61–86.
Chapter 5, "The Oil Pipeline and Water Carriage Industries," pp. 89–134.
Stephenson, Frederick J., Jr., *Transportation USA*, Reading, Mass.: Addison-Wesley Publishing Co., 1987.
Chapter 11, "Introduction to Highway Transportation," pp. 283–310.
Chapter 12, "General Commodity Trucking," pp. 312–37.
Chapter 13, "Specialized Trucking," pp. 339–60.
Taff, Charles A., *Commercial Motor Transportation*, 7th ed., Centresville, Md.: Cornell Maritime Press, 1986.
Chapter 5, "Types of Operations," pp. 97–120.
Chapter 6, "Local and Specialized Carriers," pp. 121–51.
Talley, Wayne Kenneth, *Introduction to Transportation*, Cincinnati: South-Western Publishing Co., 1983.
Chapter 9, "Freight Transportation: Railroads," pp. 159–83.
Chapter 10, "Freight Transportation: Truck Carriers," pp. 184–206.
Chapter 11, "Freight Transportation: Pipeline and Water Carriers," pp. 207–27.
Wood, Donald F., and James C. Johnson, *Contemporary Transportation*, 3rd ed., New York: Macmillan Publishing Co., 1989.
Chapter 5, "Highway Carriers," pp. 89–114.
Chapter 6, "Railroads," pp. 117–46.
Chapter 7, "Pipelines," pp. 151–77.

CHAPTER 5

WATER, AIR, AND
OTHER FORMS OF CARRIAGE

WATER CARRIAGE

Much of the United States is well-blessed with an excellent system of natural waterways. In addition to our Atlantic, Gulf, and Pacific seacoasts and their bays, we have the Great Lakes and a considerable number of important navigable rivers. Although various kinds of improvements and maintenance are necessary to make these waterways usable for modern commercial transportation and although large sections of the country are entirely without navigable waterways, our water transport system historically has played, and continues to play, an important role in our economy.

Excluding seacoasts and the Great Lakes routes, the United States contains about 29,000 miles of navigable waterways. More than 20,000 miles of these routes are in commercial use at present. Approximately 15,000 miles of these routes, with a standard operating depth of 9 feet or more, carry the great bulk of the nation's internal water traffic.

Internal Water Transport

About one-third of our internal navigable waterways are in the Mississippi Basin, made up of the Mississippi, Missouri, and Ohio rivers and several principal tributaries such as the Tennessee and Cumberland rivers. The Illinois River and the Illinois Barge Canal connect Chicago and Lake Michigan with the Mississippi above St. Louis (the Lakes-to-the-Gulf system); the New York State Barge Canal connects Lakes Erie and Ontario with the Hudson River above Albany.

Intracoastal waterways, including connecting rivers, canals, channels, and bays protected from the open seas, are found along most of the Atlantic and Gulf coasts. Except for a few short stretches, these waterways permit interconnected continuous navigation from New York to the mouth of the Rio Grande on the Texas-Mexico border. Numerous river systems, including the Mississippi and Hudson rivers, the Alabama-Tombigbee–Black Warrior system, and other smaller rivers (and canals) all along the Atlantic and Gulf coasts connect interior points with the *intracoastal* waterways.

In the Far West, internal waterways are limited mainly to the Columbia–Snake River system, San Francisco Bay, and Puget Sound and the rivers flowing into these great natural harbors, and a few small bays and their entering rivers on the Washington, Oregon, and California coasts. Other rivers west of the Mississippi Basin generally are unsuitable for commercial navigation under present conditions.

More than 1,800 companies with an investment of more than $2 billion operate tugboat (or towboat) and barge services on the nation's internal waterways. Of these 1,800 companies, about 1,400 perform for-hire services and the remainder are engaged in private transportation. Most of the for-hire operators are operating as exempt carriers, that is, they are not subject to ICC regulations. Fewer than 200 of these river and canal carriers are certificated as common carriers by the ICC, and fewer than 50 hold contract carriage permits.

Basically, as compared to railroads, most internal water carrier firms must be considered small businesses. Altogether, the 1,800 companies involved operate about 5,000 towboats or tugs and over 32,000 dry-cargo and liquid-cargo barges (over three-fourths moving dry cargo), and employ around 80,000 persons aboard their vessels. The revenues of the largest Mississippi River common carriers do not exceed one-tenth that of the largest railroads.

The barge and towboat operation has made rapid technological strides during the past thirty years, however, and under suitable circumstances it is very efficient. It accounts for more than 12 percent of the country's intercity ton mileage. During the mid-1930s, the typical towboat was around perhaps the 700-horsepower range. Today, 4,000 to 6,000 horsepower is quite common, and some giant tugs of 8,500 and 9,000 horsepower are in use.

A typical lower-Mississippi barge "tow" (actually a "push," as the tugboat is behind rather than in front of its barges) may be more than one-fourth mile in length and 200 feet wide. Such a tow will move at an average line-haul speed of 4 to 5 miles per hour and, under exceptionally favorable conditions, as rapidly as 8 to 15 miles per hour. One barge may carry as much tonnage as forty railroad cars, that is, 1,800 tons, and a single large towboat may push a string of forty barges or the cargo-capacity equivalent of sixteen 100-car freight trains. This cargo moves at an average cost to the shipper of less than 0.8 cents per ton mile, or at around one-fourth the average cost of railroad shipments.

Barge cargoes mainly consist of heavy, bulky, low-value-per-unit-of-weight mineral, petroleum, and agricultural products which can be rapidly loaded and unloaded by mechanical methods. Coal, petroleum products, and sand and gravel account for more than three-fourths of the Mississippi system's traffic. In some areas, especially in the Pacific Northwest, grain and lumber movements are important. Also, a variety of chemicals, iron and steel products, and manufactured items such as automobiles can be moved handily by barge.

Great Lakes Transport

The five Great Lakes, with an area of 95,000 square miles and a coastline of 8,300 miles, in effect form a fourth seacoast for a large portion of the United States. The eight states bordering these lakes contain about seventy commercial harbors, and products move for considerable distances to and from interior points in order to take advantage of cheap water transport. Highly specialized and efficient lake steamers, designed particularly for the mass transport of mineral products and grain, shuttle back and forth continuously during the eight-month ice-free navigation season to make the lakes the world's busiest, as well as largest, inland waterway. In addition to playing a tremendously important role in the early settlement and development of the Midwest, the Great Lakes waterways and their connecting transport arteries continue to support an inland industrial heartland without peer.

Many improvements were necessary to adapt the Great Lakes to modern commercial water transport, of course. The Welland Canal, around Niagara Falls, was opened in 1829 to connect Lake Ontario with Lake Erie and to tie the lakes system into the St. Lawrence River and the barge traffic of the Erie Canal–Hudson River system to the port of New York. The Soo Canal, connecting Lakes Superior and Huron around St. Mary's Falls and opened in 1855, today carries more freight tonnage than any other canal in the world, surpassing such noted international waterways as the Panama and Suez canals. Other improvements include the Detroit River Channel between Lakes Huron and Erie, and a host of smaller channel, canal, and harbor development projects.

Great Lakes eastbound traffic is dominated by iron ore and grain movements supplemented by pulpwood products and other semiprocessed or raw materials. Westbound, coal dominates, followed by petroleum products, limestone, and several less important industrial and manufactured items.

The Mesabi Range, west of Lake Superior, has long been the nation's principal source of iron ore. This ore has supplied the giant steel mills of the east lake areas with the raw materials necessary for U.S. steel leadership. Sufficient supplies are stocked during the busy summer navigation season to permit the mills to continue operations during the months when the lakes are icebound.

The continent's great grain-producing area, the states and Canadian provinces west of the Great Lakes, pours great quantities of wheat and smaller amounts of other grains into the U.S. ports at Duluth-Superior, Milwaukee, and Chicago, and into Canada's Fort William–Port Arthur area. This grain moves to eastern lake points for milling, transshipment by other forms of carriage, or export via the St. Lawrence.

On their westbound return, ore and grain steamers carry coal from Lake Erie ports to the great cities of the western lakes areas such as Detroit, Chicago, Milwaukee, and Duluth-Superior, and to smaller cities, as well as for land or barge transshipment to interior west lake areas. Also, petroleum products, automotive vehicles, iron and steel items, and similar manufactured commodities are moved in smaller volumes.

During the 1950s, the long-discussed St. Lawrence Seaway project was undertaken by the governments of the United States and Canada. In 1959, the Great Lakes finally were made accessible to large oceangoing ships via the St. Lawrence River. Although navigation of such vessels through the locks and channels of this project is somewhat tricky and many of the very largest ocean vessels cannot be accommodated at all, it is likely that at least three-fourths of the world's ocean merchant marine vessels now can pass into the Great Lakes. In no other place in the world does ocean transport penetrate so deeply into an interior industrial and agricultural complex equivalent to this.

Not all important lake ports have the necessary physical and institutional facilities for handling a large volume of oceanborne commerce, of course, and many areas of the lakes themselves are inaccessible to large ocean ships, but a rash of improvements was touched off along the lakes in expectation of a booming ocean commerce. The most rosy expectations were not realized, however, during the years immediately following the opening of the project's facilities, although ocean trade was greater than some opponents of the project had predicted. But the seaway has had a considerable influence upon previously established traffic patterns into and out of Atlantic Coast seaports and upon the rate structures of railroads and other forms of transport.

Coastwise and Intercoastal Transport

In addition to river, canal, intracoastal, and lake transport, our domestic water system includes coastwise and intercoastal ocean water transportation. Historically, from our beginning as a separate nation, coastwise and intercoastal shipping has been restricted to vessels built, owned, and operated by U.S. citizens. (The current expression of this principle of "cabotage" is in the so-called Jones Act, or Merchant Marine Act of 1920.) A considerable volume of coastwise water transport is by barge; the remainder, and the intercoastal traffic, is by regular ocean cargo ships. As late as the 1930s, these trades moved large tonnages of commodities such as lumber, canned goods, and iron and steel products.

During World War II, as a result of submarine attacks and government requisition and regulation of oceangoing vessels, coastwise and intercoastal water transport was drastically restricted. This traffic has not been healthy since the end of that war. Rate and service competition from other forms of carriage, especially rail, but also truck and pipeline, has prevented any great resurgence of intercoastal and coastwise ocean shipping of general cargoes. By the early 1960s, for example, intercoastal tonnage accounted for not much more than 2 percent of the nation's total water tonnage. (In comparison, tonnage in the Mississippi Basin amounted to almost 50 percent of the total water tonnage, the Great Lakes accounted for almost 20 percent, and the remainder was fairly evenly divided between the Pacific Coast on the one hand and the Atlantic-Gulf coasts on the other.) There is little basis for belief that oceanborne domestic tonnage will regain its former sphere of importance within the foreseeable future; actually, quite the contrary seems to be indicated at this writing.

Costs, Regulation, and Competition

Water carrier ton-mile costs under the best conditions probably are lower than the costs of any other form of carriage. Less power and fuel are needed to propel on water than on land. Rights of way and terminal facilities often are provided at no cost or at very little cost to the carrier. Also, as water cargoes typically involve large tonnages, the carrier's overhead costs are spread over many units with a resulting low per-unit cost of movement. The ratio of fixed to variable costs is fairly low. Fixed costs consist mostly of the costs of owning the vessels used; line-haul costs (as is true in the trucking industry) typically account for a considerable part of the water carrier's total costs.

It is difficult to generalize about operating ratios (see Chapter 4) in the water carrier industry as a whole owing to its many different types of equipment and trades. It appears, however, that a profitable level of operating ratio for most water carriers falls somewhere between what is considered adequate for trucks (93 to 95) and railroads (low 70s), that is, not higher than the low 80s.

There is another side to the water carrier cost issue, though. Some expenses of providing water transportation are borne by the general taxpayer. Improved rights of way (canals, channels, harbors, and various navigational aids) are costly, and insofar as the expenses of these facilities are not charged to carriers, they have to be supported out of general public funds. Also, substantial portions of terminal facilities and terminal costs often are levied against the public or shippers, or both.

In addition, even though the ton-mile costs of movement by water may be low, the actual ton mileage involved in moving a given cargo between specified points by water may be much greater than if the cargo were moved by land. Water routes often are long and winding rather than direct. For example, the water route over the lower Mississippi River is twice as long as the direct airline route, and the intercoastal water route is several times as long as the competing land routes. And a ton of freight moved five miles results in five times as much ton mileage as the same ton moved for only one mile!

The economic regulation of domestic water carriage has not been comparable to that of other major competing forms of carriage. Although water carriers are subject to ICC regulation, there are numerous exemptions and exceptions. Two of the most important of these exemptions exclude from regulation the carriage of liquid cargoes in bulk and the bulk carriage of three or fewer commodities. Many other less important exemptions apply. Private carriage, which is very important, is not regulated. The commission has estimated that not more than 12 percent of domestic water transportation is subject to its regulation, as contrasted to approximately one-third of truck transport and virtually 100 percent of rail and pipeline carriage.

Water carrier competition is mainly with railroads and with other water carriers. Actually, however, competition is not keen among water carriers themselves because usually there are not many carriers offering the same type of waterborne service between any two points. Some competition exists between trucks and water carriers, but this is not of great importance in most situations because of the specialized bulk nature of water carriage.

Competition between oil pipelines and water carriers of petroleum products has increased during recent years as larger pipe and more efficient pumping techniques have been developed (see Chapter 4). This competition is somewhat lessened, however, due to the fact that both pipelines and oil tankers frequently are owned or controlled by major oil producers. This in general has led to pipelines designed to supplement rather than to duplicate water capacity. When and if the pipeline techniques become more widely used for other bulk products such as coal, however, the competitive picture may be altered.

From the individual shipper's viewpoint, the principal advantage of using water transportation for domestic shipments in preference to land transport is low freight rates. Sometimes, in addition, water carrier facilities are more suitable for handling (loading and unloading) certain kinds of bulk commodities. A principal disadvantage, even for bulk shipments, is the generally slower and less frequently scheduled service available from water carriers. Goods in transit represent funds tied up in inventories — speed is money to the shipper. Also, slowness and less frequent departures and arrivals on the part of water carriers virtually preclude the filling of rush orders and sometimes require that shippers carefully plan their production and shipping schedules in advance. Then too, water carriage typically gives only pinpoint area coverage (see Chapter 4). Where it is available, water carriage generally serves only major points and bypasses many smaller intermediate communities. Also, delays due to adverse weather conditions frequently must be anticipated.

As previously explained, from the viewpoint of the economy as a whole, there are costs involved in water carriage not completely reflected in the costs of individual carriers. Likewise, from the shipper's individual viewpoint, rates alone do not always tell the complete story. Other costs, in addition to rates, may be of importance to shippers in comparing their total water transportation outlays with outlays for transportation by other modes of carriage.

For example, unless the shipper and the consignee are located directly adjacent to water facilities, goods must be transported to and from water by land carriers. This may involve extra handling expenses. That is, goods must be loaded onto a land carrier, hauled to the water carrier's dock, and reloaded onto the water carrier's vessel. At destination, the goods must be unloaded from the water carrier, hauled to the consignee's place of business, and again unloaded from the land vehicle. In addition to the extra handling charges, terminal fees of various kinds may also be incurred.

Another factor that water shippers must keep in mind is the generally limited liability of water carriers as contrasted with land carriers. Although no carrier is an absolute insurer of safe delivery of merchandise entrusted to its care, the responsibilities of water carriers for loss and damage to shipments are in general much less than the responsibilities of land carriers (see Chapter 20). For this reason, the shipper who wants cargo protection for a water shipment equivalent to the protection available on land movements frequently must purchase insurance.

Despite the above qualifications, however, from an individual shipper's viewpoint, water carriage may be the lowest-priced transport available (if it is available at all) under many circumstances, and it sometimes may be better tailored to individual service needs than are the other modes of transport. Water carriage by nature is particularly suited for movements of heavy, bulky, low-value-per-unit commodities that can be loaded and unloaded efficiently by mechanical means in situations where speed is not of primary importance, where the commodities shipped are not particularly susceptible to shipping damage or theft, and where accompanying land movements are unnecessary.

AIR CARRIAGE

U.S. scheduled commercial airlines now operate some 3,400 jet aircraft. These lines have an equipment investment of approximately $30 billion and employ more than 450,000 persons. Their total operating revenues are in the neighborhood of $50 billion annually and generally are increasing each year. These figures do not include commuter airlines and the general aviation fleet, which account for more than 275,000 smaller aircraft.

Passenger and Mixed Services

Air transportation is still primarily a passenger operation. Over four-fifths of the industry revenues come from this source. More than 11.5 percent of total airline revenues, on the other hand, come from freight and express services. Other revenues come from carrying mail, direct subsidies (public service revenues), excess baggage charges, and miscellaneous other sources. Direct subsidies, although much discussed, account for very little of the airline industry's total revenues.

Domestic intercity passenger miles handled by airlines at the beginning of World War II amounted to less than 1 percent of the nation's total for-hire carrier passenger mileage. By 1957, airlines had surpassed railroads as the leading common carrier of passengers. Not only has the number of passenger miles flown by airlines increased to more than 100 times the immediate pre–World War II level, but the average length per passenger trip (now more than 750 miles for domestic passengers) has increased by more than 100 percent.

During the same period, average scheduled airline fares have increased from a little more than 5 cents to around 121 cents per mile; railroad fares have gone from a little more than 2.3 cents to about 11 cents per mile. Lower-priced coach, tourist, or economy services have grown rapidly during recent years. The increased speed, convenience, and popularity of air travel seem to assure a continued growth of this service even if fares should increase substantially. However, air travel cannot be expected to increase as rapidly during the next twenty years as during the last twenty.

Although aggregate statistics and trends are useful in an overview of the airline industry, one must realize that the industry is made up of several types of carriers with different operating situations and problems. Airlines are classified in at least nine different groups. (There is, however, some overlapping; a carrier may be classed in one group for part of its service and in another group for a different kind of service.)

The most familiar group to most persons probably is the Domestic Trunk Lines which has permanent operating rights between principal population centers in the contiguous states. This group contains about ten carriers. About six Domestic Local Service Lines (sometimes called feeder lines) operate in and between areas of lesser traffic density and connect smaller population centers with major centers. Two firms make up the Intra-Hawaiian classification. Alaskan carriers are composed of six lines.

International Trunks, as indicated by the name of the group, operate between the United States and other countries, or over international waters. Some of these nine lines are merely extensions of other domestic carriers. Helicopter carriers provide airport-to-downtown services for passengers as well as for freight, express, and air mail in several of the country's larger cities. All-Cargo Lines, two in number, are authorized to carry only cargo — not passengers — between specified areas of the United States or between the United States and designated foreign countries. About two dozen other carriers perform mainly charter services and a limited number of individually ticketed flights. The miscellaneous category includes air taxi operators and air freight forwarders.

In addition, airline reporting classifications were changed in 1981 to reflect carrier size in terms of revenues. In 1987, using this classification, there were 14 majors ($1 billion or more in revenues), 20 nationals ($75 million to $1 billion), 32 large regionals ($10 million to $75 million), 27 medium regionals (less than $10 million), and 169 commuters, including medium regionals that operate planes with 60 or fewer seats and a cargo capacity of less than 18,000 pounds. This new classification system reflects both the service characteristics of commuters and the continuing overlap between the service characteristics of many former local feeder lines, as they have expanded their route authority, and the former trunk lines.

All major commercial airlines are common carriers, and their interstate passenger activities were subject to economic regulation by the Civil Aeronautics Board (CAB) from 1938 to 1978. In general, this regulation was comparable to that exercised over interstate land carriers by the ICC, although it differed in major respects. The Federal Aviation Administration (FAA) regulates safety matters and engages in promotional activities such as the development of airports and navigational facilities. Both the CAB and the FAA investigate accidents.

It is safe to say that historically the government's impact on commercial airlines has been much greater in the areas of safety and promotion, including direct and indirect subsidies such as airports, airways, experimentation, and development in connection with new types of aircraft and public service payments than in economic regulation as such. This has been justified on the grounds that air transport is a new mode in which the public has a vital peacetime commercial and wartime defense interest and that this newcomer would not be able to develop rapidly without subsidization if forced to compete on an equal basis with already well-established competitors.

Domestic airlines compete with railroads and buses as well as with private automobiles for passengers. They compete with both rails and trucks for freight. And, of course, they compete with one another. During the earlier years of CAB regulation, intramodal airline competition was limited. During more recent years, however, the CAB appears to have encouraged more airline versus airline competition, especially on the more dense traffic routes. Lessened regulations brought considerable additional competition, especially to dense traffic routes, and intensified competition.

Airline cost structures are more comparable to trucking industry cost structures than to railroad costs; the industry is one of relatively high variable costs in proportion to fixed costs. As airports and airway navigational aids are provided by the public, the principal fixed airline costs are those associated with aircraft ownership. And even though a fully equipped jet plane may cost many millions of dollars, only 6 or 7 percent of the industry's total costs are chargeable to such items as interest, depreciation, and amortization. In contrast, wages and salaries, fuel and oil, and various materials, supplies, and services account for more than four-fifths of total costs. A large part of these expenses and some other less important ones must be considered as variable in nature. It appears that a profitable industry operating ratio for airlines would be considerably higher than for the railroads, somewhat higher than for water carriers, but lower than for the trucking industry — perhaps in the high 80s.

This book is more concerned with the transportation of things than with the transportation of people. However, in air carriage particularly, the two are difficult to consider in isolation. Only the All-Cargo Lines carry freight exclusively. Other lines carry both passengers and freight, with passenger movements being of much greater relative importance. Freight haulage is increasing rapidly (even though from a small base) among the mixed carriers, however, and these carriers do compete with the All-Cargo group as well as with one another and with other forms of transport.

Two kinds of freight transport are offered. The more important in terms of volume is air freight. Except for high minimum charges on small shipments, this service is the most attractive in terms of rates, and it moves at fairly rapid speeds. Air parcel post is a U.S. mail service which has the lowest air rates for small shipments generally, but which loses some of the potential air speed advantages because of the lack of pickup and the slowness of delivery services.

For several years, a Greyhound air express service has been offered to areas isolated from major airports. Small shipments are carried by bus to connect with airlines. More recently, joint services have been worked out between trucking lines and airlines in some areas that provide for truck pickup and delivery and a line haul by air. One large freight company has successfully offered express overnight delivery of small shipments and parcels among most of the nation's major airports for several years. Recently, the U.S. Postal Service has entered this field with express mail service, as has United Parcel Service with "next day" air service.

Speed of movement is the primary advantage of air shipments, but terminal delays and congestion and out-of-town terminal location may considerably reduce this advantage unless air express is used. Frequency of departure is very high, and reliability of service (even in the face of adverse weather) is being rapidly improved. Coverage of service generally is limited to movements between major points on a single airline, and feeder service has not been notably efficient. Better area coverage is being developed by more interline cooperation, however, and especially by cooperation with bus lines and trucking companies.

A high rate level, of course, is the principal disadvantage of shipment by air. Average rates per ton-mile by air freight still are twelve or fifteen times as high as average rail ton-mile rates and two or three times as high as truck rates. Such averages must be used with caution, however. Many individual rail and truck rates are much higher and many air rates lower than the average. Also, airline distances typically are somewhat shorter than the routes usually followed by land carriers. In addition, the bulk of rail and even of truck carriage involves quite different products than those making up an air cargo. One would not normally expect to ship coal or lumber by air any more than one would expect to ship live lobsters, cut flowers, or high-style women's clothing long distances by rail.

Some airline managements recently have been attempting to change the frequently conceived picture of air freight as an expensive emergency service suitable only for high-value and highly perishable traffic. The industry spokespersons emphasize the speed advantages that may make it possible for distributors to reduce their overall costs (even though transportation costs may be increased) by carrying smaller inventories and eliminating far-flung warehouse services. New and more efficient aircraft that are being developed for air freight services may be expected to reduce service costs significantly.

Although the most optimistic predictions concerning the future of air freight may not be realized for a good many years, if ever, it seems certain that air freight movements will continue to increase for some time. More of the presently moving commodities will be handled and many items not moving in any appreciable quantity will be added. Even if the ton-mile volume of air freight doubles and redoubles several times, however, it still will not loom large in the overall ton-mile picture. But it may be extremely important (it is now, in fact) for some types of commodities and over some routes.

Industry Outlook

The widespread adoption of jet services greatly increased the speed, comfort, and convenience of air transport. These services, however, also increased the industry's capacity, caused heavy expenditures for the new aircraft, and forced many of the old craft into obsolescence. These factors, plus duplications of routes in many instances and other temporary cost-revenue relationships, brought the industry face to face with a severe financial situation in the early 1960s. The industry made a quick recovery, however, once the shock of transforming to jets had been absorbed. Business continued to increase; and by 1964, overall industry profits had approached the 10.5 percent considered to be fair and reasonable for the trunk lines by the CAB. By the late 1960s, however, airlines were again beginning to have financial difficulties. The introduction of jumbo jets and considerable route and schedule duplication, plus economic recession, increased airline problems in the 1970s.

By the early 1980s, the country's commercial airlines as a whole were in the worst financial situation of their history. A combination of overcapacity on many prime routes, permitted by lesser regulation, and a severe economic recession, which decreased travel, threatened insolvency for several airlines and hampered capital expansion for new equipment. Many observers believe that the return of overall national prosperity is not sufficient for airline prosperity. The industry may have to reorganize and rationalize its structure and services within the next decade. In addition, with its aging fleet, the airline industry is faced with a monumental need to upgrade its fleet (to ensure safety) at a time when profits are tight and manufacturer capacity is limited.

OTHER FORMS OF CARRIAGE
AND RELATED SERVICES

In addition to the five basic agencies or modes of transport discussed in this and the preceding chapter, several other organizational forms provide transport services. These forms, although they may operate equipment of their own, especially for pickup and delivery purposes, rely mainly on one or more of the five basic modes for line-haul services.

Freight Forwarders

Freight forwarders make up an important part of these secondary or indirect modes of transport. They may be classified according to the basic kinds of line-haul equipment utilized. Surface freight forwarders use the facilities of rail, motor, or domestic water carriers, whereas air freight forwarders use airline facilities in either (or both) domestic or foreign transport. (Also, foreign freight forwarders perform services somewhat different from domestic forwarders in connection with international water shipments, but this is outside the scope of this chapter.)

Domestic surface freight forwarders are regulated as common carriers in a way similar to railroads, motor carriers, and domestic water carriers under the Interstate Commerce Act. They deal directly with and are directly responsible to shippers and receivers. More than 100 forwarders are subject to some ICC regulation. The range of annual revenues of individual forwarder firms varies from more than $100 million down to less than $100,000.

The primary function of these forwarders is the consolidation of small shipments of several or numerous shippers into large shipments that move at lower rates. Forwarders sell their transportation services directly to a shipper. Then, in turn, they buy line-haul services from the basic modes (in effect, to use an analogy, they subcontract a part of the movement). Their operating expenses and profits are covered by the spread between rates on small shipments and rates on large shipments. Shippers pay no more (or perhaps less) than they otherwise would have to pay on a small-lot movement. In addition, they are relieved of the chores of dealing directly with the basic or primary carriers, and it is possible that they may receive better pickup and delivery services, a faster line-haul movement, and other distribution services.

As forwarders do not have equipment for line-haul movements, their investment is low in relation to revenues compared to the basic modes. With an investment of around $400 million, surface forwarders do a business bringing in gross revenues of approximately $2 billion. Almost three-fourths of these revenues are paid, in turn, to line-haul carriers. In performing their transportation services, these forwarders use motor vehicles for pickup and delivery and employ only a few thousand persons.

Although the volume of tonnage handled by freight forwarders is relatively small, typically something over 4 million tons annually for surface forwarders, the average length of haul is two to three times the average of all movements by primary surface modes. Also, the number of individual shipments handled is quite large — around 23 million during a recent year. This indicates an average weight per shipment of less than 600 pounds.

Some surface forwarders operate on a national basis, whereas others are regional. Generally the service is point to point between important commercial centers, but some forwarders do cover outlying areas for many miles with their pickup and delivery services. In many cases where these services are available, small shippers and even large shippers with occasional small shipments find them considerably more convenient, more efficient, and less expensive than regular small-lot shipment by the basic modes of transport. This, of course, is not always true.

About seventy-five air freight forwarders operate under the provisions of the Federal Aviation Act. These are about equally divided between domestic and international services, with some firms operating in both fields. Air freight forwarders have been less restricted in some regulatory aspects than are the surface forwarders.

Small Parcel Services

Since the bankruptcy and dissolution of REA Express during the mid-1970s, two major nationwide small parcel shipment services remain, in addition to limited air freight, forwarder, truck, Amtrak, and bus services. Surface and air parcel post services of the U.S. Postal Service are used extensively by mail-order houses and some other types of shippers of small parcels. Specific size and weight limitations apply on parcel post shipments, but within these limitations parcel post in general offers the widest possible geographical coverage and often the lowest available price. Somewhat offsetting these advantages, however, are several disadvantages. Parcel post may be relatively slow and inconvenient; for example, shipments generally must be taken to the post office and prepaid, and the customer may have to wait in line. Also, the service does not appear to be too reliable from the loss and damage viewpoint. Although payments for loss and damage are certain if the shipment is properly insured, damaged or nondelivered goods do not improve customer relations. And, in addition to this, it is often alleged that parcel post rates are low only because the service is subsidized by first-class mail or by the general taxpayer.

United Parcel Service (UPS), which is a privately owned organization, has expanded rapidly during the past few years, and it now serves every state. Many users find its small parcel services faster, more reliable, and sometimes less expensive than services of the U.S. Postal Service. United Parcel Service tonnage is now several times greater than parcel post tonnage.

Package Express Services

In addition to traditional small parcel services, a wide range of package express services is now available. These services generally rely on air transportation for line haul, usually in company-owned aircraft. Major package express companies include Emery Air Freight, Federal Express, Purolator, United Parcel Service, and the U.S. Postal Service. These and other firms provide guaranteed overnight delivery between U.S. points, and even some international points. While technically a part of the air transportation industry, their services are so unique as to require separate consideration. Overnight delivery between virtually all U.S. points would not be possible without high-speed air transportation and operation through central hubs that facilitate coordinated movement to and from a large number of diverse origins and destinations.

Brokers, Associations, and Private Cars

This survey of transportation agencies would not be complete without mention of various third-party transportation agencies, including brokers, shippers' associations, and private car lines.

Transportation brokers are intermediaries or middlemen who bring together shippers and carriers for a fee. They are not carriers and have no responsibilities in connection with the actual transportation or safe delivery of the goods concerned. (Special types of brokers also operate in international water transportation.) Since the movement toward deregulation in transportation began, there has been a major increase in the number of transportation brokers. In a less regulated environment, with many more carriers and greater price competition, brokers have come to serve a wider range of shippers. This trend should continue through the next decade.

Shippers' associations or cooperatives are nonprofit organizations, usually employing a small managerial and clerical staff designed to perform services similar to freight forwarder services for their members. They may be concerned with only one type of product (as an agricultural commodity) or a variety of products (as associations of retailers). They are not carriers, although investigations have sometimes revealed that particular associations are not bona fide cooperative organizations but in actuality have been operating illegally as freight forwarders.

A considerable number of rail cars are not owned by railroads themselves. Such cars, usually specialized in nature (as tank cars or refrigerator cars), may be owned by private shippers or by private car lines that make a business of leasing cars to others. The utilization of these cars and the charges made are determined by contractual arrangements and by special railroad tariffs. Approximately 180 companies own at least ten private cars each. The total ownership of this group is in the neighborhood of 325,000 cars. Equipment owned by such organizations as Pacific Fruit Express (refrigerator cars), General American Transportation Corporation (tank cars), and several smaller private car lines are common sights in every part of the country. Similar arrangements exist with semitrailer and container leasing operations.

A recent trend has involved the establishment of providers of a wide range of logistics services. These firms manage the materials and product flow for a company, arranging transportation, warehousing, and other services and serving as an agent of the firm.

INTERMODAL CARRIAGE

Although the various basic modes of transport have been considered separately in this and the preceding chapter, one should not suppose that a given shipment may not move over the facilities of more than one mode. Not only do separate carriers within the same mode cooperate in interchange of shipments, but separate modes frequently coordinate on the interchange of through movements. This intermodal coordination is permitted and sometimes required between some forms of carriage under certain circumstances by our transportation regulatory laws. Between 1978 and 1987, intermodal carloadings expanded from 8 percent to over 16 percent of total railroad carloadings. This trend has been a major reason behind the resurgence of railroad transportation in the last few years. Improved equipment with greater capacity, such as double stack container cars, and lighter empty weights, such as skeleton-type trailer-on-a-flatcar (TOFC) cars, has also contributed to this trend.

Coordinated transport of freight is found most often between rail and water, rail and truck, and truck and water. As has been mentioned above, there is some coordination between truck and air carriage, and bus and air. Also, there is coordination and cooperation between U.S. and foreign carriers. In the passenger transport field, also, a large amount of cooperation and coordination exists.

Although intercarrier coordination (and even intramodal cooperation in some cases) is far from complete, improvements are being made. One of the most successful recent efforts seems to be the trailer-on-a-flatcar (TOFC) or piggyback development.

Piggyback, the technique of carrying a loaded truck trailer on a rail flatcar for the line-haul portion of its journey, with pickup and delivery made by attaching a truck tractor, was revived during the early and middle 1950s. Since then it has grown very rapidly. More than 2 million piggyback cars now move as contrasted with fewer than 200,000 in 1955. Several piggyback plans are used. The trailers may be owned by shippers, railroad companies, or trucking companies. A few truckers have virtually abandoned line-haul runs, confining their operations to terminal areas. Piggyback car loadings, now exceeded only by coal car loadings, have been the fastest growing rail traffic component for several years.

Along with its obvious advantages in combining many of the best features of rail and truck transport, piggyback seems to be appreciated by the general public (with the exception, of course, of those who may stand to lose financially by the innovation). Not only does it demonstrate clearly that creative imagination still exists among railroad managements, but it removes many slow-moving trucks from already cluttered highways. Fuel shortages and prices greatly increased the demand for piggyback in 1973 and 1974 and since.

Fishyback (movement of truck trailers or rail cars on "roll-on, roll-off" water carriers) and birdyback (truck trailers via air transport) have not developed to any extensive degree as yet, although a number of companies are engaging in this form of coordination and others are considering it.

One of the most-discussed technological concepts today is containerization. A great deal of thought and experimentation is being given by both public and private agencies to the development of durable and standardized interchangeable containers. Ideally, a shipper should be able to load a cargo of small items into a container, lock it, take it by truck to a rail terminal, send it by rail to a seaport, by ocean carrier to a foreign port, and on to an inland destination by rail or truck. The development of such freely exchanged containers, of course, involves many problems other than technological ones. It has implications for intercarrier revenue division agreements, rate structures, and customs practices for foreign commerce as well as for loading and unloading methods and the obtaining of back-haul cargoes, among other things.

Several advantages of coordination in its various forms may be of great benefit to shippers. It may bring lower rates and better and more flexible services as well as wider area coverage. And the general consuming public stands to benefit by the more efficient use of transportation resources inherent in combining the most desirable features of all forms of transport into a tailored transportation package for each particular shipment or shipper. There is no doubt that the public itself will eventually force a much greater reliance upon coordinated transport even if some carrier managements are reluctant and some shippers are content with the status quo.

SUMMARY

This and the preceding chapter have discussed a remarkable diversity of domestic freight transportation alternatives. Nowhere else in the world do shippers have such a variety of choices among available modes, services, and prices. True, some shippers are limited to only one mode, or even to one carrier within a mode, owing to peculiar traffic, geographic, or other circumstances. But this is unusual.

Most shippers of most products in the United States may choose among at least two or three modes or some intermodal combination. Often, several carriers of a particular mode, especially trucks, may be available. Shippers frequently have the option of for-hire (either common or contract) or private carriage, or a combination of these. The physical distribution manager or traffic manager (see Part IV) can choose among many services and prices to satisfy company objectives or customer desires.

Also, the variety of alternatives helps assure the continuance of transportation even when some mode or carrier is not available because of strikes, a natural catastrophe, or some other cause. Further, variety increases competition, leading to better services and lower prices. Truly, its diversity is one of American domestic transportation's greatest strengths.

ADDITIONAL READINGS

Bowersox, Donald J., Pat J. Calabro, and George D. Wagenheim, *Introduction to Transportation*, New York: Macmillan Publishing Co., 1981.
  Chapter 4, "Water Transportation," pp. 47–63.
  Chapter 8, "Air Transportation," pp. 116–29.

Chapter 9, "Special Transportation Arrangements," pp. 130–42.

Coyle, John J., Edward J. Bardi, and Joseph L. Cavinato, *Transportation*, 2nd ed., St. Paul: West Publishing Co., 1986.

Chapter 5, "Domestic Water Carriers," pp. 97–113.

Chapter 7, "Air Carriers," pp. 137–54.

Chapter 9, "Third-party Transportation and Other Specialized Carrier Forms," pp. 157–73.

Lieb, Robert C., *Transportation: The Domestic System*, 3rd ed., Reston Va.: Reston Publishing Co., 1985.

Chapter 5, "The Oil Pipeline and Water Carrier Industries," pp. 89–111.

Chapter 6, "The Airline Industry," pp. 113–34.

Chapter 7, "Freight Forwarding, Specialized Small Shipment Carriers, and Intermodal Carriage," pp. 137–51.

McElhiney, Paul T., *Transportation for Marketing and Business Students*, Totowa, N.J.: Littlefield, Adams, 1975.

Chapter 7, "Water, Air and Pipeline Transport," pp. 95–116.

Stephenson, Frederick J., Jr., *Transportation USA*, Reading, Mass.: Addison-Wesley Publishing Co., 1987.

Chapter 8, "Domestic Water Transportation," pp. 193–221.

Chapter 10, "Pipeline Transportation," pp. 255–80.

Chapter 14, "U.S. Air Transportation," pp. 365–96.

Chapter 16, "Specialized Aviation Sectors: International Air Transportation and U.S. Air-Cargo Industry," pp. 435–59.

Talley, Wayne Kenneth, *Introduction to Transportation*, Cincinnati: South-Western Publishing Co., 1983.

Chapter 12, "Freight Transportation: Air, Forwarder, and Specialized Small-Shipment Carriers," pp. 228–48.

Wood, Donald F., and James C. Johnson, *Contemporary Transportation*, 3rd ed., New York: Macmillan Publishing Co., 1989.

Chapter 8, "Domestic Water Carriers," pp. 181–207.

Chapter 9, "Domestic Aviation," pp. 213–45.

Chapter 10, "Intermodal and Auxiliary Carriers," pp. 249–72.

CHAPTER 6

INTERNATIONAL TRANSPORTATION

This book is concerned primarily with U.S. domestic transportation, but there are significant interfaces, including both similarities and differences, between the country's domestic and international transportation. The two cannot be entirely separated, either physically or conceptually.

Almost all goods moving in international transportation, whether exports or imports, also move in domestic transportation by one or more of the carrier modes discussed in Chapters 4 and 5. Also, about one-fourth of the nation's international trade and transport is conducted with Canada and Mexico, mainly using the same carriers as are used in our domestic transportation. Further, our air carriers haul cargoes to and from all parts of the world. And often the same industrial traffic or physical distribution departments responsible for domestic shipments (discussed in Part VI) are also responsible for international shipments.

This chapter is not intended to give a comprehensive view of international transportation. That would require a separate book. Instead, the purpose simply is to emphasize the importance of this transportation to the United States, and compare and contrast it with domestic transport in several significant aspects.

THE U.S. ROLE IN INTERNATIONAL DISTRIBUTION

The United States is the world's leader, in monetary values, in international trade. This country, with about 4.6 percent of the world's population, accounts for 23 percent of the world's economy. Much of these goods and services enter international trade. U.S. exports of merchandise, $217.3 billion in 1986, and U.S. imports, $370 billion in 1986, amount to about 14 percent of the gross national product of the United States. In 1986, this meant monetary values of over one-half a trillion dollars annually, or in tonnage terms, a transportation movement of more than 1.5 billion tons (not ton-miles) during 1986 — or around 6.5 tons for every person in the country.

International Trade Values

U.S. exports and imports of merchandise have grown over the years. Table 6.1 notes the growth from 1970 to 1986 for selected years, as well as broad commodity groups. In dollar values, U.S. exports have increased from $42.7 billion in 1970 to $217.3 billion in 1986, a fivefold increase. On the other hand, U.S. imports in dollar values have increased from $40 billion in 1970 to $370 billion in 1986, more than a ninefold increase. Note in Table 6.1 that U.S. exports exceeded imports in 1970 and 1975 but the reverse was true for 1980 and 1986. During the late 1970s, merchandise exports and imports were close to being in balance, but in the 1980s merchandise imports have exceeded exports every year. The balance between the two is made up of capital movements and service payments, and illustrates the well-known foreign trade deficit.

Also note in Table 6.1 the variation over the years of dollar values of broad commodity groups. In exports, the dollar values of agricultural commodities has dropped from 1980 to 1986 while the other groups have steadily increased over the years. On the import side, petroleum has dropped in dollar values after the peak of petroleum prices in 1980 while both machinery and transportation equipment (mostly foreign-built automobiles) have increased very markedly from 1980 to 1986.

Irrespective of these dollar values, the point is that all imports and exports are transported — not only around port areas but many times to and from inland points at considerable distances and, of course, overseas or across U.S. borders. Thus, these data reflect the importance of transportation in international trade as well as the existence of a trade deficit or surplus.

Table 6.1 U.S. Exports and Imports of Merchandise, 1970, 1975, 1980, 1986 (in billions of dollars)

	1970	1975	1980	1986
Exports, total	42.7	107.7	220.6	217.3
Agricultural	7.2	21.9	41.3	26.1
Machinery	11.4	28.5	55.8	60.4
Transportation Equipment	6.5	17.2	28.8	34.9
Imports, total	40.0	98.5	244.9	370.0
Petroleum	2.8	24.8	77.6	34.1
Machinery	5.3	12.0	31.9	87.5
Transportation Equipment	5.9	12.2	28.6	74.0

Source: Statistical Abstract of the United States, 1988, p. 768.

Actually, a relatively small number of specific products accounts for a very large portion of world (and U. S.) international commodity distribution. For example, oil is by far the leading international commodity in terms of tonnage moved. For another example, grain accounts for about 30 percent of U.S. tonnage exports by water (but for only about 7 percent of total export monetary values). Although thousands of products constantly move from country to country, only a handful account for most of the tonnage and value.

Commodities in International Distribution

During recent years, machinery and transportation equipment have accounted for more than 46 percent of U.S. exports in monetary values. Various manufactured goods and chemicals have accounted for a little more than one-fourth of the total. This is not surprising for a major industrial nation. Some are surprised to find, though, that more than one-fifth of this country's exports consist of agricultural products, foodstuffs, various nonagricultural crude products, and mineral fuels. Table 6.2 shows the percentage of exports and imports in dollar values by commodity groups in 1986.

Actually, the United States exports more foodstuffs than all the rest of the world's nations combined. Among other specific products, this country originates three-fourths of the world's exported corn and soybeans, around 40 percent of all exported wheat and edible vegetable oils, 30 percent of exported rice, and substantial quantities of meat, fruits, vegetables, and nuts. Additionally, in the nonfood agricultural category, the United States accounts for 30 percent of the world's exported cotton and a sizable amount of tobacco.

In international distribution, the United States, unlike other industrial nations, is an agricultural giant as well as an industrial giant. Many other nations can supply large quantities of various industrial products to the world, but no nation is in the same class as the United States as a supplier of foodstuffs. For example, this country's wheat exports each year provide enough calories to supply the needs of more than 250 million persons. Efficient international and domestic freight transportation makes it possible for this country's farmers to feed foreign populations much larger than our domestic population.

In the mineral fuels category, coal is a large export item, most of which is carried to ports by railroads. Some refined petroleum products are also involved. In the machinery and transportation equipment group, new airplanes (the United States manufactures most of the world's aircraft) and luxury automobiles are important, as well as industrial equipment of all kinds.

On the import side, machinery and transportation equipment dominate. This group is weighted heavily by foreign-made automobiles as well as industrial equipment. Other manufactures is made up of a great variety of goods demanded by the U.S. consumer, with apparel and shoes being of some importance. The mineral fuels group is mostly crude oil and refined petroleum products. If the United States were self-sufficient in oil, the country would have less of a balance-of-trade problem. Food and crude materials make up a surprisingly small percentage of imports for such an industrial nation.

These categories of exports and imports suggest that most of the international trade of the United States is with developed or industrialized countries, rather than with developing countries, and this is so except for imported oil and some agricultural or food products. Developing or "poor" countries usually have little to sell abroad — this is one reason they are poor. And with little to sell abroad, such countries obviously do not have the funds (foreign exchange) to buy much abroad. Actually, 10 industrialized countries of more than 150 countries altogether (including the United States) with about 20 percent of the world's population account for about 60 percent of the world's international trade in monetary value terms.

Table 6.2 Percentage of Dollar Value of U.S. Exports and Imports by Commodity Groups, 1986

Exports	
Food and live animals	8.4
Beverages and tobacco	1.4
Inedible crude materials	8.4
Mineral fuels	3.9
Chemicals	11.0
Machinery and transportation equipment	46.2
Other manufactures	14.8
Imports	
Food and live animals	5.6
Beverages and tobacco	1.0
Inedible crude materials	2.8
Mineral fuels	10.1
Chemicals	4.1
Machinery and transportation equipment	43.7
Other manufactures	28.5

Source: *Statistical Abstract of the United States*, 1988, p. 775.

Origins and Destinations of U.S. Imports and Exports

In terms of major areas of the world, the most important U.S. international trade (values of combined exports and imports) is conducted with the Western Hemisphere (35 percent of exports and 29 percent of imports), Asia (29 percent of exports and 41 percent of imports), and Western Europe (29 percent of exports and 24 percent of imports). Table 6.3 shows merchandise exports and imports of the United States by areas and leading countries in 1986.

Canada and Mexico are important trading partners with the United States. This country exports more to Canada than any other country and imports more from Canada than any other country except Japan. Mexican imports are fourth after Japan, West Germany, and Taiwan, and exports to Mexico are second after Japan. Most of these Canadian and Mexican exports and imports are transported by rail, truck, and water (particularly on the Great Lakes) and some by pipeline.

Overseas exports and imports are dominated by Japan and other Southeast Asian countries, and Saudi Arabia and Israel in the Middle East are important trading partners. Imports from Asia are particularly large; Japan, Taiwan, and South Korea are leading import nations. Important Western European trading partners with the United States are the United Kingdom, West Germany, the Netherlands, and France (in that order) on the export side, and West Germany, the United Kingdom, Italy, and France on the import side. Additionally, Table 6.3 allows the student to determine with which countries the trade deficit is the greatest.

It should be noted, however, that many of the imports to the United States originate in plants and branches of U.S. firms owning productive plants abroad. But once more this illustrates the dimensions of transportation in international trade.

Another way to consider origins and destinations of U.S. international trade is to look at ports of entry and exit. The data in Table 6.4 show value by customs region by export and import. The New York region is most important, followed by the Chicago region (reflecting both ocean-borne trade and overland trade). The rest are San Francisco, Los Angeles, Boston, Miami, Houston, Baltimore, and New Orleans (ranked in that order). Also notice the balance or lack of balance between exports and imports in each region. Obviously, all these points of entry and exit must be served adequately by domestic transportation and must be located on international trade routes.

Table 6.3 Merchandise Exports and Imports of United States by Areas and Leading Countries, 1986 (in millions of dollars)

	Exports	Imports
Western Hemisphere	76,411	110,201
Canada	45,333	68,253
Mexico	121,392	17,302
Brazil	3,885	6,813
Venezuela	3,141	5,097
Colombia	1,319	1,874
Western Europe	61,642	89,825
West Germany	10,561	25,124
United Kingdom	11,418	15,396
Italy	4,838	10,607
France	7,216	10,129
Switzerland	2,977	5,253
Sweden	1,871	4,420
Netherlands	7,848	4,066
Communist Europe	1,989	2,001
Soviet Union	1,248	558
Asia and Middle East	64,532	153,869
Japan	26,882	81,911
Taiwan	5,524	19,791
South Korea	6,355	12,729
Hong Kong	3,030	8,891
Singapore	3,380	4,725
Saudi Arabia	3,449	3,612
Indonesia	946	3,312
Malaysia	1,730	2,421
Israel	2,239	2,418
India	1,536	2,283
Oceania	6,659	3,717
Australia	5,551	2,632
Africa	5,978	10,348
Nigeria	409	2,530
South Africa	1,159	2,365

Source: *Statistical Abstract of the United States*, 1988, pp. 771–73.

Table 6.4 U.S. Exports and Imports of Merchandise by Customs Regions, 1986 (in billions of dollars)

Region	Exports	Imports
Boston	18.3	40.3
New York	33.4	67.0
Baltimore	12.1	31.3
Miami	18.6	31.5
New Orleans	14.4	17.1
Houston	21.7	27.7
Los Angeles	22.2	53.1
San Francisco	32.1	44.1
Chicago	33.7	54.8
Total	217.3	368.7

Source: Statistical Abstract of the United States, 1988, p. 774.

MAJOR U.S. INTERNATIONAL TRADE ROUTES

The locations of international trade routes are influenced by a combination of economic, political, and geographic factors. Interactions of these factors are complex, but their basic features can be outlined rather briefly.

Simply stated, nations (or people) sell their surplus products in order to obtain funds to buy other things that are in short supply to them. Not all things can be produced in all areas. Even things that can be produced in many areas can be produced more efficiently (either absolutely or relatively) in some areas than in others. A variety of economic factors, including resources and technology, determine what a nation has for export and what it wants to import. Exports provide the financial means for imports.

In summary, for product X to move from country A to country B, the people of country A must have a surplus of X. The people of country B must want X and have the ability and willingness to pay A's asking price for it. Finally, B must be the most profitable market for A's disposal of its surplus X.

But international political or institutional conditions often intervene in this theoretically simple process. For various reasons, a nation may prohibit (embargo) certain kinds of products from being exported or imported, or may bar all exports or imports to or from certain other nations. Or quantity limitations (quotas) may be placed on certain kinds of imports or exports. Even if no embargoes or quotas exist, imports may be limited by protective or revenue tariffs (taxes) on imports. Conversely, exports may be stimulated by various kinds of direct or indirect subsidies. Often, political factors are at least as important as economic factors in determining what kinds and quantities of products move between what countries in international distribution.

A large portion of the world's international freight is transported over a small number of fairly well defined major traffic routes — perhaps a dozen or less, depending upon one's definition of a major route. These routes, of course, are not always the shortest distances between origin and destination points. Rather, they are significantly influenced by several geographic factors.

Three-fourths of the earth is covered by water (and about three-fourths of the world's international cargo tonnage moves by ships across this water). But this water-covered earth is split into four sections by two great land masses (North and South America; Europe, Asia, and Africa), which stretch virtually from North Polar to South Polar ice. There are only a few ways for ships to go around or through these land masses (Cape Horn, Cape of Good Hope, Panama Canal, Suez Canal). Thus, "great-circle" navigation routes (shortest distances on a globular earth) often are somewhat distorted.

Navigation routes also are influenced by weather, especially by floating ice, fog, winds, and currents. Weather factors are less important than formerly, but still frequently cause seasonal shifts in routes. The location of fueling stations, more important when steamships burned coal rather than oil, also influenced the locations of early routes. Some effects of this still remain.

Finally, water routes are significantly influenced by existing seaports, natural or artificial, and their facilities and services. These features include such things as water depths, loading and unloading equipment, storage facilities, inland resources and transportation facilities, and services a ship may need for its operations and maintenance.

Seven general routes or pathways carry the great bulk of water transport from and to the United States. These routes include:

North Atlantic: between Atlantic and Gulf Coast ports and Western European and Mediterranean ports; an extension goes into the Great Lakes via the Saint Lawrence Seaway, the Welland Canal, the Detroit River, and the Soo Canal, as far as western Lake Superior (2,000 miles from the Atlantic Ocean and 600 feet higher; nowhere else does ocean transport penetrate so far inland to such a heavily industrialized and grain-producing area).

South American: between Atlantic and Gulf Coast ports and eastern ports of Mexico, Central America, and South America (includes also various Caribbean island ports)

South African: between Atlantic and Gulf Coast ports and western and southern Africa; also extends around the Cape of Good Hope to include southeastern Africa, East Asia, Australia, and various Pacific islands

North Pacific: between Pacific Coast ports and Japan, the Philippines, and East Asia

South Pacific: between Pacific Coast ports and Australia, New Zealand, and Southwest Pacific islands

Suez Canal: between Atlantic and Gulf Coast ports and the Mideast, West Africa, Indian Ocean ports, East Asia, Australia, New Zealand, and Western Pacific islands

Panama Canal: between Atlantic and Gulf Coast ports and the west coast of South America, Australia, New Zealand, East Asia, and Western Pacific islands

International air freight generally moves over approximately the same major pathways as does international waterborne freight. Air carriers, of course, are not as much influenced by major geographic or weather factors as are water carriers. They can fly over obstacles and use great-circle navigation in many instances where ships cannot. But, like ships, their routes are influenced by the locations of people and products.

Land transportation between the United States and Canada and Mexico, and the so-called landbridge traffic across this country, are discussed below.

INTERNATIONAL CARRIERS

International freight (often called cargo, especially if moved by water carriage), like domestic freight, is moved by land, water, and air primary carriers. In contrast to domestic transportation, though, water carriage dominates. Also, there are some significant institutional and operating differences, as well as some similarities, between international and domestic carriage. Even the carrier equipment used differs in the case of water carriage.

Before discussing the specific similarities and the differences for various carrier modes, we should get some idea of the importance of each mode in U.S. international transportation. Table 6.5 shows exports and imports of the United States by method of transportation in 1970, 1980, and 1986. These data are in both dollar values and weight, and show that transportation by vessel is most important in both exports and imports.

However, note the substantial increase in the share of international air traffic in both exports and imports over the period 1970 to 1986. Purely from a weight point of view, vessels carry the majority of the international overseas cargo. Obviously, air freight is but a small portion of total cargo in the international trade of the United States, but it is made up of very valuable cargo in dollar terms and is growing at a much faster pace. International air cargo shipments are many times faster than shipments by vessel, and for high-value goods it is usually worthwhile to pay the higher air cargo rates and deliver the goods faster.

Table 6.5 Exports and Imports by Method of Transportation, 1970, 1980, 1986 (in billions of dollars and billions of pounds)

	Exports			Imports		
	1970	*1980*	*1986*	*1970*	*1980*	*1986*
All methods ($ value)	43.2	220.7	217.3	40.0	240.8	370.0
Land carriers ($ value)	12.5	53.7	63.8	11.8	47.7	86.4
Vessels ($ value)	24.6	120.9	90.1	24.8	165.1	221.6
Air ($ value)	6.1	46.1	63.4	3.4	28.9	62.0
Vessels (weight)	480.5	801.8	653.3	598.4	976.8	914.2
Air (weight)	.4	2.3	2.1	.6	1.3	2.8

Source: Statistical Abstract of the United States, 1988, p. 598 (land carriers value derived).

Water Carriers

Ocean water carriage differs from domestic water carriage (discussed in Chapter 5) in the variety and sizes of its equipment and in its services. Domestic water carriage, except for Great Lakes steamers, basically is barge carriage. These barges do differ in size, function, and degree of specialization, but not nearly as much as is found in ocean vessels equipment.

At least five distinct types of vessels are used in ocean freight transport. Each of these types may be further subdivided into several subtypes based on size, intended use, or extent of specialization. These types of equipment include breakbulk freighters, containerships, bulk freighters, tankers, and seagoing barges.

Breakbulk freighters are ships that primarily haul individually packaged or crated cargoes, that is, a variety of general cargoes are loaded, stowed, and unloaded one piece at a time. These vessels typically carry cargoes for dozens or hundreds of separate shippers on each voyage. Although they may be specialized to some extent (refrigeration for perishable cargoes, for example), breakbulk freighters are general cargo vehicles, comparable in function to railroad boxcars.

Containerships, to some extent, are substitutes for breakbulk freighters. Instead of handling each piece of cargo individually, several or many pieces are stowed into a container (as discussed under the head Inter-modal Carriage in Chapter 5). Containers are then individually loaded. Containerships function pretty much as do piggyback cars in railroading.

Stowing or "stuffing" of containers usually occurs at the shipper's place of business. They are then hauled to the seaport by rail or truck. Likewise, containers are distributed from destination seaports by other modes of carriage. Containers are not completely standardized in size, but usually they are 8 feet by 8 feet by either 20 or 40 feet — that is, they have a capacity of 1,280 or 2,560 cubic feet (which is equivalent to 32 or 64 tons of cargo in measurement tons of 40 cubic feet). Containerships may carry 1,500 or more such containers, although the newest containerships carry many more. Recently American President Lines placed an order for five containerships, built in West Germany, capable of carry 4,300 TEU (twenty-foot equivalent units) or 2,150 forty-foot containers. These fast ships (24 knots) are 903 feet long and 129 feet wide (20 feet too wide for the Panama Canal) and will be used in the transpacific trade. Obviously, deep channels and expensive specialized port facilities are required for handling, collecting, and dispersing containers.

Containerization is a relatively new development started by Malcolm McLain (Sealand Corp.) in 1956 in the Atlantic between U.S. ports and the Caribbean and followed in 1959 by Matson Navigation Company in the mainland to Hawaii service. Since that time, containerization has been widely adopted around the world and has been called the "container-ization revolution" in ocean shipping.

The various forms of containerization greatly reduce handling time and costs at seaports. This decreases the turnaround time of expensive ships. It also reduces losses through breakage and pilferage — which normally accompany handling operations — and consequently reduces cargo insurance costs. Moreover, containerization can considerably reduce the amount of time spent in transit.

Instead of simple boxes, some containerships carry wheeled containers, like trailers in highway trucking. This RORO (roll-on, roll-off) service facilitates loading and unloading activities through the use of tractors rather than cranes, and also facilitates movement between seaports and origin or destination inland points. Still other containerships engage in

LASH (lighter-aboard-ship) services, by hauling loaded barges between seaports.

Containers moving between East Asia and Western Europe often use the *landbridge* route across North America. This involves movement by containership to United States West Coast ports (or East Coast ports if from Europe), then movement by railroad to East Coast (or West Coast) ports, and then further movement by containership to Europe (or Asia). By bypassing the Panama Canal, this reduces the distance transported by several thousand miles. Time in transit also is reduced by several days — sometimes by as much as two weeks. Another important landbridge route operates across Canada, as well as a less important one across Mexico.

Recently, railroads have begun "double stack" service using special rail cars that stack containers two high on top of one another, accommodating four containers per car. This innovation has led to much more landbridge traffic. Some of the steamship lines have purchased these special double stack container rail cars and pay the railroads to haul them in expedited service. Other railroads own their own double stack cars and offer expedited service that does not stop in marshalling yards between the Pacific Coast and Gulf or East Coast points. These developments have allowed the railroads to become a larger partner in international transportation.

Containers bound for East Coast port areas from Asia, or West Coast port areas from Europe, frequently move from the West Coast (or from the East Coast if from Europe) by land transport. This is called *minibridge* traffic. *Microbridge* involves containerized movements between coastal and interior (noncoastal) points. Such movements always have been necessary, of course. The major differences in microbridge are that the cargoes are containerized and that more trucks are used than formerly.

These various kinds of intermodal "bridge" traffic are designed to make more efficient use of containerships and to decrease time in transit by taking advantage of the best features of both ocean and land transport. This traffic has increased substantially during the past few years, as it benefits both shippers and the participating carriers.

Bulk freighters are designed for loading and unloading nonpackaged dry cargoes by mechanical means, including gravity. They are used primarily for hauling such commodities as grain, coal, and ores. To continue the railroad analogy, bulk freighters are somewhat similar in use to gondola or hopper cars in rail transport. Unlike breakbulk vessels, they usually haul for only one shipper, or a few shippers, on any given voyage.

Tankers, like tank trucks and railroads tank cars, are built to haul liquid products. These products include crude or refined petroleum, liquefied (and refrigerated) gases, various chemicals, wine, molasses, and the like. Most tankers can haul different products on successive voyages.

Some even haul grain, which has flow characteristics similar to those of liquids. Tankers have increased rapidly in number, size, and speed during the past two or three decades.

Seagoing barges do not account for a large portion of the world's international freight tonnage. They are useful, however, in specialized situations involving small cargoes, short hauls, or routes with narrow or shallow channels. Seagoing barges generally are larger and more sturdily built than are river barges, and long tows (many barges in one tow) are seldom used. These barges usually are not highly specialized for one kind of traffic. They may haul bulk, breakbulk, containerized, or liquid cargoes.

Kinds of Services

Three basic types of services are available in international water transportation: liner (or berth) service, tramp (or charter) service, and industrial carriage. These correspond roughly to common, contract, and private carriage in land transport (discussed in Chapter 4).

Liner service provides regularly scheduled for-hire transportation of general commodities between named ports for previously announced freight rates. This service, equivalent to domestic common (public) carriage, generally is furnished by breakbulk freighters and containerships — and sometimes by seagoing barges.

Tramp service does not operate on a regularly scheduled time or route basis. Instead, ships literally "tramp" around the world, going wherever cargoes are available for transport — hence the name. Their freight rates are determined by individually bargained agreements with shippers. These agreements, called charters or charter parties, may be for one voyage between an origin and a destination port, or they may be for a designated period of time. This service employs most of the world's bulk freighters and often is provided by tankers and seagoing barges. Charter service is the international equivalent of contract carriage in domestic transportation.

Industrial carriage is the equivalent of domestic transportation's private carriage. That is, a shipper uses its own vessel to transport its own goods. Frequently, instead of buying or building its own vessel, a shipper may lease a vessel from someone else under a special long-run charter, thus obtaining in effect ownership control for operational purposes during the time period involved. Any type of vessel may be used for industrial carriage, of course, but tankers and bulk freighters are the types most commonly used.

The World Merchant Fleet

About 25,000 ships of all types (excluding seagoing barges and very small vessels) are engaged in hauling the world's international ocean commerce. Almost three-fifths of these vessels are primarily in the liner trades (breakbulk freighters or containerships). A little more than one-fifth are tankers, mainly in industrial carriage or tramp (charter) services, and almost one-fifth are bulk freighters (mainly tramps), with a small number as combination passenger/cargo ships. Table 6.6 shows merchant ships of the world (1,000 tons or more), by countries with fleets of over 450, for 1985. Combination passenger/cargo ships vary in size and are found in scheduled car ferry–cargo–passenger service in the Baltic, Mediterranean, and parts of Africa. Freighters (both breakbulk and a growing number of containerships) are found everywhere, as are bulk carriers (generally charters in tramp) and industrial ships.

Table 6.6 Merchant Fleets of the World, 1985 (over 450 ships of 1,000 gross tons or more)

	Total	Freighters	Bulk Carriers	Tankers	Pass/Cargo Combo.
World	25,555	13,937	5,787	5,456	375
United States	737	417	25	258	37
British Colonies	450	196	204	48	2
Mainland China	1,025	692	180	139	14
Cyprus	716	451	169	91	6
Greece	1,835	733	760	309	33
Italy	569	230	102	227	10
Japan	1,604	633	497	468	6
Liberia	1,852	386	764	694	8
Netherlands	464	363	28	69	4
Panama	3,620	2,068	952	565	35
Singapore	480	298	83	97	2
South Korea	487	240	176	71	0
Soviet Union	2,514	1,793	221	448	52
Spain	489	308	79	101	1
United Kingdom	541	206	96	227	12
West Germany	528	414	23	86	5
All others	7,644	4,509	1,428	1,558	148

Source: Statistical Abstract of the United States, 1988, p. 603.

Equivalent numbers of ships do not mean equivalent tonnage-carrying capacity, of course. Ships differ greatly in carrying capacity, both between vessels of different types and among vessels of the same type.

A typical bulk freighter, for example, may carry three to four times as much tonnage as a typical breakbulk freighter. And a typical tanker may carry 50 percent more tonnage than a typical bulk freighter. At the extremes, many breakbulk freighters carry less than 10,000 tons, whereas many tankers carry more than 100,000 tons — and some supertankers carry much more. Ships also differ significantly in speed and other performance characteristics, depending upon their age and design. New ships are likely to be faster and to operate with smaller crews and more efficiency than older ships.

Every merchant ship is registered in some country, its "flag" nation. The leading nations for numbers of ships registered, in order, are Panama, Soviet Union, Liberia, Greece, Japan, and Mainland China, as shown in Table 6.6. These six countries account for almost half of the world's total number of registered ships and more than one-third of the world's merchant marine tonnage.

U.S. registration accounts for less than 3 percent of the world's merchant fleet total, both in numbers and tonnage. Further, most of this country's flag ships are tankers or are in liner service, and generally they are older and less efficient ships. Further, 264 of U.S.-registered ships are governmentally owned, and 244 of these are laid up at three National Defense Reserve Fleet sites in California, Texas, and Virginia.

Reasons for the low numbers and tonnage of the American flag merchant fleet have been endlessly and inconclusively debated, but are beyond the scope of this discussion. The fact remains, however, that American-registered ships during recent years have carried only around 25 percent of this country's liner cargo, 7 percent of its tanker cargo, and about 1.5 percent of its bulk cargo. The world's leading international trading nation depends heavily on ships of other flag nations to transport its international ocean cargoes!

But many hundreds of ships owned by American citizens, especially tankers and bulk freighters, are registered in foreign countries, such as Liberia, Panama, Honduras, and others. This is called "flag of convenience" registration and is eagerly sought by some countries for registration fees or other accompanying revenues.

Estimates indicate that one-third or more of Liberian-registered ships and one-half of Panamanian ships actually are owned by Americans. The "convenience" to the American shipowners may be lower taxes, lower operational costs because of smaller or lower paid crews, less stringent safety standards, lower construction costs for foreign-built ships, and the like.

Around 25 percent or more of American international ocean cargoes are transported in American-owned vessels, including American-registered and flag of convenience ships. Actually, there is no economic reason why an American shipper should prefer a vessel of any one nationality over that of any other as long as the freight rates and services are equivalent. The smallness of the American merchant marine may be a cause for concern in case of war or other national emergency, and American merchant marine sailors and their unions deplore flag of convenience registration. But it is not at all certain that prohibiting flag of convenience registration by American shipowners would cause any sizable increase in the American-registered merchant fleet.

Flag of convenience registrations are not limited to American owners. Look again at Table 6.6 and note that three of the top six countries of registration are rather small nations (Panama, Greece, Liberia) without large amounts of foreign trade, as well as Cyprus, South Korea, the Netherlands, and Singapore. Part of this registration is also flag of convenience. Many of these ships are owned by citizens of other countries but registered in these countries because of low or no taxes, low registration fees, and little or no restriction allowing use of very cheap foreign crews. Also, ship registration provides an income to the registering nation.

A second interesting fact shows up in ship registration in the so-called traditional maritime nations: United Kingdom, the Netherlands, Denmark, Sweden, Norway, Finland, West Germany, and France. These are "cross traders" who traditionally haul cargo for many countries and thereby earn foreign exchange and provide employment for their citizens. These fleets generally exceed the needs of the international trade of their own country. A third factor is a political–foreign relations factor. It may be important to "show the flag" or help dominate some countries to have international trade carried in your own ships. This is certainly a factor in the large nationalized fleets of the Soviet Union and Mainland China.

We mentioned crew costs as a factor in flag of convenience registrations. U.S. merchant maritime wages are some of the highest in the world, and foreign crews are usually less expensive. Table 6.7 indicates the changes in maritime employment and compensation from 1970 to 1985. Many seamen in other countries, particularly Asian countries, are willing to go to sea for much lower wages. However, U.S. maritime law provides that U.S. flag ships must be manned by U.S. citizens. As noted above, a substantial number of flag of convenience ships are American-owned, manned by crews of non-U.S. citizenship. The footnotes in Table 6.7 indicate that these wages are in addition to room and board provided by the ship itself.

Table 6.7 Employment on U.S. Flag Merchant Vessels and Basic Monthly Wage, 1970, 1980, 1985

	1970	1980	1985
Employees	37,500	19,600	13,100
Wages[1]			
East Coast[2]	$470	$ 967	$1,419
West Coast[3]	652	1,414	2,069

[1] Over and above board and room but not including overtime.
[2] Five-day week.
[3] West Coast pays Saturday and Sunday while at sea.
Source: *Statistical Abstract of the United States*, 1988, p. 602.

The upshot of this wage pattern plus U.S. maritime policy (until the mid-1980s), which required U.S. flag ships to be built in U.S. shipyards, led to various subsidy programs which will be discussed in Chapter 28.

A final aspect of international water carriers is the passenger transportation business. At one time, passenger ships carried many people overseas on a scheduled basis with an emphasis on speed. In the postwar period, the intercontinental airline caused this type of transportation to cease. The only international passenger transportation by water affecting America today is the cruise business, an important form of tourism and a growing market.

Many cruise lines serve the United States and all except one, serving Hawaii, are of foreign registry; British, Greek, Dutch, Swedish, Norwegian, Italian, and French cruise lines are important. Some cruise companies have headquarters in the United States, particularly in Florida and San Francisco, but all use foreign ships and crews except for American Hawaiian Lines.

The market for cruising has a definite seasonal pattern. A cruise ship may sail on a full schedule in the summer to Alaska, northern Europe, or Japan-China; and in the winter in the Caribbean, the Mexican Riviera, South America, or Australia–New Zealand. Some cruise lines operate in the same market year-round; many Caribbean, Hawaiian, and Mediterranean cruises sail in both summer and winter. Sometimes discounted rates are used in off-season cruises for schedules such as summer Caribbean or Hawaiian cruises. Rates depend primarily on location of the stateroom, and sometimes discounts are offered for early booking, last-minute booking, and group booking. Travel agents are the primary marketers of cruises.

Cruising is like a luxury vacation, with cruise lines competing on the basis of service and amenities, shore excursions and ports of call, food and entertainment, even educational classes. The food is usually sumptuous, and cruise lines usually offer live entertainment, dancing, games, movies, gambling (when outside legal limits while at sea), shopping boutiques, sports (tennis, volleyball, shotgun target practice off the stern, table tennis, and swimming in both inside and outside pools), exercise facilities, beauty and barbershops, contests, and medical care. A cruise ship is like a luxury hotel with even greater amenities. Speed is not a factor in cruising — as a matter of fact, most cruise ships are quite slow as compared with the passenger liner of yesteryear.

An adjunct to the luxury cruise is the freighter cruise. Many freighters have accommodations for a few passengers (if there are more than twelve passengers, medical facilities and a doctor must be available) and supplement their revenue by offering a freighter cruise. Amenities are slight, although meals and cabin accommodations are usually quite good and the passenger may arrange shore excursions independently (if time permits). A freighter cruise may be quite adventurous and educational.

In 1987, Americans spent over $600 million for international water passenger transportation, mostly cruises.

Air Carriers

Domestic air carriers and air freight are discussed in Chapter 5. Most of the large U.S. domestic air carriers are also engaged in some international carriage. Actually, these carriers generate about one-fourth as many ton-miles in international freight as in domestic freight carriage. The same types of aircraft are used, and generally the same kinds of economic and operating conditions prevail in international and domestic air freight transport. As in domestic transportation, international air freight may move on passenger flights or on all-cargo flights.

Other nations' air carriers also participate in freight traffic from and to the United States, of course. Unlike American air carriers, though, most foreign airlines are owned wholly or partly by their governments. If these foreign airlines are more heavily subsidized by their governments than are their privately owned American competitors, it might be expected that America's airlines would be under considerable competitive rate or service pressure. For whatever reasons, however, American airlines do well in international competition.

The air freight market for international movements is hard to separate from the domestic air freight market. Also the air small package market operates both domestically and internationally. A typical analysis uses 70 pounds and under for the light weight market and over 70 pounds for the heavy weight market. One estimate of the world's air freight market is shown in Figure 6.1. Note that the U.S. domestic air freight market is estimated at $9.1 billion while the international air freight market is estimated at $12 billion.

Figure 6.1   World Air Freight Market (in billions of Dollars)

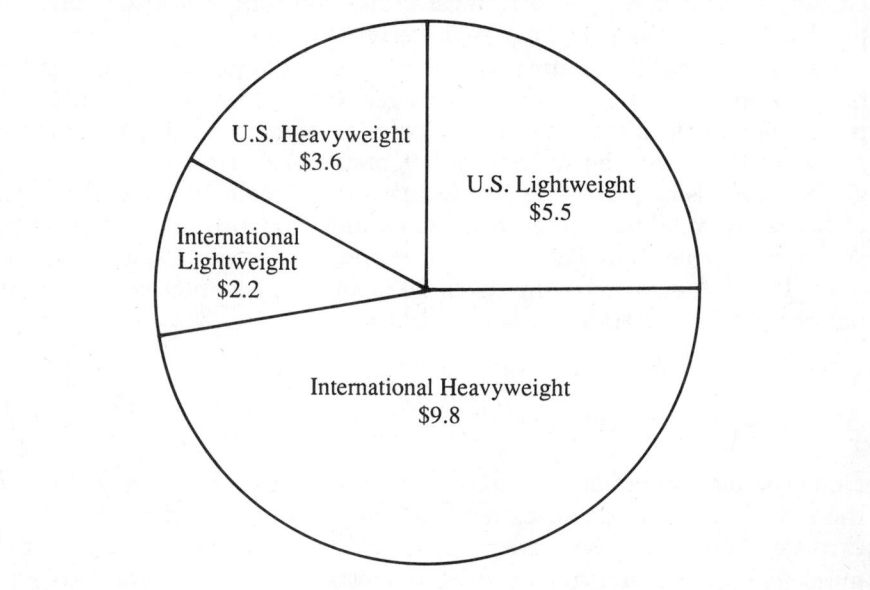

Source: Adapted from *Traffic World*, February 20, 1989, p. 29. Copyright 1989. Used by permission.

Further confusion between domestic and international air freight markets comes from recent expansions by some well-known domestic firms. In 1988, Federal Express, basically a domestic small package air express firm with overseas service to Japan and England, purchased Flying Tigers, basically an international air cargo firm with service to Southeast Asia, Australia, South America, England and Western Europe, and Saudi Arabia. Also in 1988, Consolidated Freightways, the second largest U.S. trucking firm that also owned a freight forwarding subsidiary in the international market, purchased Emery Worldwide. Other firms in the international air cargo market are DHL Worldwide Express, T.N.T. (an Australian carrier with many U.S. subsidiaries in trucking), and United

Parcel Service, particularly in the small package market. Additionally, a number of air freight forwarders generate business and use scheduled international flights on both domestic and foreign airlines.

In spite of the wide use of long-range planes such as 747s, DC-8s, and L-1011s in all cargo configurations, international air freight carriers compete little with ocean carriers. The largest all-cargo aircraft has a tonnage-carrying capacity of about 1 percent of the tonnage capacity of a small breakbulk ocean freighter. The aircraft can make a delivery within a few hours, or one or two days, however, whereas delivery by ocean carrier might require several weeks. International air freight usually involves small shipments of high-value products for intermediate or long distances, where quick delivery is important. Many of these products would not move at all without the availability of air carriage. However, there is a growing component of heavier air cargo movements internationally as shippers try to reduce transit times and inventories.

As Table 6.5 shows, this country's export tonnage by water carrier is about 310 times as much as that of air carriers, while water carriers import tonnage is 326 times greater than air carriers. Value figures are much different, though. In dollar terms, international air firms carry about 41 percent of the exports and about 22 percent of the imports. Obviously, international air carriers are important and specialize in high-value shipments that are time sensitive.

Land Carriers

International land freight transport occurs mainly between adjacent or nearby countries, where water transportation does not exist or is inconvenient. For the United States, this means a great deal of rail and truck traffic with Canada and Mexico.

Physically there could be a completely free flow of goods across and within the three countries, just as occurs among states within this country. Railroads and highways interconnect at various border points. Railroad track is the same gauge (width) in all three countries, and the rolling stock is similar and interchangeable. Likewise, highways and trucks are about the same.

Actually, free transborder traffic flow is impeded somewhat by institutional barriers. Customs requirements, including inspection of goods and perhaps import tariffs, must be met. Transborder carriers must have operating rights in each country. Some nationalistic restrictions exist to protect national producers and carriers. Generally, these protective barriers are greater for traffic entering Mexico than for traffic entering Canada from the United States. This is especially so for truck traffic.

Trucking inside Mexico can be performed only by Mexican firms, although a few Mexican firms have been given transborder operating rights in the United States. Still, however, most goods moving by truck across the U.S. border with Mexico, destined for interior areas, must be unloaded and reloaded at border points. Continuing negotiations between the two countries have led to some recent relaxation of institutional barriers to transborder trucking, but not very much.

Border crossings are considerably easier for trucking between the United States and Canada. There are literally hundreds of crossing points, as compared with only a handful on the Mexican border. Trucking firms in either the United States or Canada often have operating rights, at least limited ones, in the other country. Or goods may be turned over to subsidiary firms in the other country. Also, goods may easily proceed across the border in sealed vehicles for unloading and customs inspection at interior bonded warehouses, from where they are further distributed by national carriers.

There have been allegations by some U.S. truckers that authorities of some Canadian provinces have discriminated against them in the granting of Canadian operating rights. These allegations have not been supported by official U.S. investigations, however. But this country, in 1982, temporarily ceased granting new operating rights to Mexican truckers in the United States, on the grounds that U.S. truckers could not obtain similar operating rights in Mexico.

Except for customs requirements, there are no restrictions on rail movements between the United States and Canada or Mexico. Some rail traffic, especially piggyback movements, even move across the United States between Canada and Mexico. Unlike domestic rail transportation, though, a railroad in one nation cannot keep a car from another nation's railroad temporarily or indefinitely for its own use. Unloaded cars must be routed directly back to the home nation.

INTERNATIONAL CARRIER LIABILITY

A domestic carrier's liability for loss of or damage to the goods entrusted to it — the "duty of delivery" — is discussed in Chapter 20. Generally, that discussion is also applicable for land transport between the United States and Canada or Mexico. The carriers and the applicable laws are the same. The situation is very different for international water carriers, however.

An ocean carrier is legally obligated to exercise "due diligence" in providing a "seaworthy" vessel, and to proceed with "reasonable dispatch" to destination. Seaworthiness relates to a ship's physical condition, as well as its fuel and other supplies, its loading, and the quality of its officers and crew. The ship should be capable of performing its announced voyage under the conditions likely to be encountered. Reasonable dispatch means that a vessel should not go to unannounced places, except for emergency reasons or to save life or property at sea. The longer a voyage continues, the more likely it is that something will go wrong and cause a loss.

If an ocean carrier meets these two responsibilities, it is not responsible to shippers for cargo losses from such causes as shipwrecks or sinkings, collisions, fires, storms, and even errors in judgment in navigating and managing the vessel. Further, in the unlikely event that the carrier is liable for losses, the maximum amount that a shipper can recover is quite limited per package of cargo and for the overall cargo. If a ship and its cargo are lost at sea, as typically happens several hundred times each year, shippers usually cannot recover anything from the carrier. This is very different from domestic land carriage (see Chapter 20), where a high and strict degree of carrier liability exists.

This means that, unlike land carriage, almost all ocean shipments are or should be insured. Marine insurance is available in many forms and is a complicated subject beyond the scope of this discussion. In short, though, it is an essential requirement for ocean shippers. It provides protection for losses for which the carrier is not liable or for which the carrier may not have to pay even if it is liable. Also, insurance payments are prompt, whereas carrier payments — even if the carrier is liable and does pay — may be delayed by months or years of negotiation or litigation.

Marine insurance contracts, along with a commercial invoice and a bill of lading (transportation contract) showing that the goods have been loaded aboard a vessel, frequently are used to collect for goods sold by discounting with a bank while the goods are enroute. The buyer (or discounter) certainly would not be inclined to pay for goods somewhere on the high seas without proof that the goods are protected against loss by marine insurance.

Air cargo liability laws and insurance are fairly recent developments. In fact, they appear to be still rapidly evolving. In some respects, they are similar to those found in water carriage; in others, they differ.

An air carrier is responsible for furnishing an "airworthy" craft and for operating it with a "high degree of care." If the carrier proves that it has met these responsibilities, it may claim freedom from losses due to "perils of the air" and several other exemptions similar to those of water carriers. And an accident does not necessarily mean that the aircraft was not airworthy or was not operated with a high degree of care! Further, if a carrier is liable for losses, its liability is limited to a maximum amount per unit of cargo — usually much less than the actual value of the lost goods.

As air cargoes typically are quite valuable, air cargo insurance is as essential as marine insurance on international shipments. Air cargo insurance, like its marine counterpart, is too complex to be discussed here. It should be noted, though, that this insurance usually is limited to a maximum amount per *plane* and per *catastrophe*. Airlines, like truck movers of household goods, usually are in a position to help shippers acquire suitable insurance.

SHIPPER DOCUMENTATION AND ORGANIZATION

Domestic freight shipments typically involve only the shipper, a carrier, and the receiver. Documentation is relatively simple, consisting mainly of a few copies of the shipper's invoice and the carrier's bill of lading. The situation is very different for international shipments, however.

In addition to the shipper and the receiver, a typical international shipment may involve more than one carrier (domestic and international), as well as banks, insurance firms, port authorities, and several agencies of both the exporting and importing governments. Often, dozens of copies of each of dozens of documents are required for a single shipment.

A U.S. Department of Transportation study, a few years ago, found that thirty-six person-hours were required to prepare all the documents necessary for an average export shipment, and twenty-seven person-hours were needed for the average import shipment. The department's study indicated that about one-half of this clerical labor was duplicative or unnecessary. Efforts are being made to reduce the paperwork burden for international shipments, but the burden and its cost still are high. This burden and the lack of information about required documentation and related procedures certainly restrict American international trade, especially for smaller firms.

Large and frequent international shippers and receivers often perform all or most of the functions involved with acquiring the necessary transportation services, preparing documentation, and the like. This may be done by a separate export-import department within the firm, or it may be done by specialized personnel within the firm's industrial traffic department. Smaller or less frequent shippers, however, seldom have the personnel to perform all the necessary functions required in international transportation.

Fortunately, every major seaport and many inland points have organizations prepared to assist export sellers for a fee in all aspects of international trade and transportation. This complex of organizations includes international departments of banks, customhouse brokers, export merchants and commission houses, export managers and agents, ship brokers, marine insurance offices, international freight forwarders, and similar support agencies.

Many beginning or small shippers, at least until they become familiar with the procedures involved, rely wholly upon international freight forwarders to handle all aspects of their transactions. There are at least 1,000 of these forwarders doing business in this country. Also, assistance and helpful advice may be obtained from U.S. governmental sources, especially the Department of Commerce.

Although the carrier modes and alternatives and the institutional environments differ considerably between domestic and international transportation, and the paperwork is more burdensome in the latter, more and more domestic shippers and receivers are entering into international trade. The prospects appear good for a lessening of the burden, a better understanding of the problem, and a further expansion of this country's international markets.

SUMMARY

The United States is the world's leading international trading nation. A wide variety of goods are bought from or sold to people in almost all parts of the world. This trade is increasing. And all these goods must be transported by water, air, or land carriage, or some combination of these.

Water transportation is important in international trade from a tonnage point of view, whereas international air transportation shares importance with oceanborne traffic from a value point of view. International transportation overland by rail, truck, water (Great Lakes), and pipeline is considerable between our northern neighbors in Canada and our southern neighbors in Mexico.

But the country's international trade and transportation is fairly small compared to its domestic distribution of goods. This means that most firms are entirely or mostly involved with the domestic scene. Many distribution or traffic departments, which may be well staffed to handle domestic operations, have little if any knowledge of how things are done in the international sphere. This is especially true of smaller firms. There is no doubt that this lack of international capabilities seriously limits this country's further expansion into international markets, even though such expansion might benefit this country, other countries, and the firms involved.

There is no reason, though, for domestic firms with otherwise valid marketing opportunities abroad to fear the details of international transportation. Carrier modes, services, and procedures may be less familiar to a firm's personnel than are their domestic counterparts. Carrier liability laws, also, are quite different, and documentation is more complex than that of domestic distribution. But readily available sources of helpful information do exist. Or a firm may hire outside experts, for relatively low fees, to handle any part or all parts of the international distribution process.

ADDITIONAL READINGS

Bess, H. David, and Martin T. Farris, "U.S. Maritime Policy: A Time for Reassessment," *Transportation Journal* (Summer 1982), 4–14.

_____, *U.S. Maritime Policy: History and Prospects*, New York: Praeger Press, 1981.

Coyle, John J., Edward J. Bardi, and Joseph L. Cavinato, *Transportation*, 2nd ed., St. Paul: West Publishing Co., 1986.
Chapter 11, "International Transportation," pp. 212–35.

Farris, Martin T., "The Efficacy of U.S. Maritime Policy," *International Journal of Physical Distribution and Materials Management*, 12, No. 6 (1982), 5–25.

Kendall, Lane C., *The Business of Shipping*, Centreville, Md.: Cornell Maritime Press, 1979.

Lieb, Robert C., *Transportation*, 3rd ed., Reston, Va.: Reston Publishing Co., 1985.
Chapter 8, "U.S. Participation in International Maritime and Aviation Industries," 153–77.

Neresian, Roy L., *Ships and Shipping*, Tulsa, Okla.: PennWell Books, 1981.

O'Loughlin, Carleen, *The Economics of Sea Transport*, London: Pergamon Press, 1967.

Stephenson, Frederick J., Jr., *Transportation USA*, Reading, Mass.: Addison-Wesley Publishing Co., 1987.
Chapter 9, "International Water Transportation," pp. 223–50.
Chapter 16, "Specialized Aviation Sectors: International Air Transportation and U.S. Air-Cargo Industry," pp. 435–59.

Talley, Wayne Kenneth, *Introduction to Transportation*, Cincinnati: South-Western Publishing Co., 1983.
Chapter 18, "International Transportation: Air and Water Carriage," pp. 343–60.

Thuong, Le T., "From Flags of Convenience to Captive Ship Registries," *Transportation Journal* (Winter 1987), 22–34.

Toh, Rex, and Henry Susilow Idjojo, "Flags of Convenience Shipping in the 80's: The American Perspective," *Transportation Journal* (Summer 1987), pp. 34–42.

Wood, Donald F., and James C. Johnson, *Contemporary Transportation*, 3rd ed., New York: Macmillan Publishing Co., 1989.
Chapter 18, "International Transportation," pp. 479–521.

CHAPTER 7
PASSENGER TRANSPORTATION

Passenger transportation can conveniently be divided into two segments: private passenger transportation (private automobile, private airplane, motorcycle, bicycle, moped) and for-hire passenger transportation (commercial airline, intercity bus, train, transit bus, trolley, subway). Each segment has different characteristics, costs, and problems. However, private passenger transportation and for-hire passenger transportation can often be substitutes for each other, and therefore, they compete under certain circumstances and conditions. For example, one can take a train, an airline, or an intercity bus, or drive one's own car on a vacation trip. Or one may drive one's own car, take a transit bus, or use a bicycle, motorcycle, or moped to travel to work.

Additionally, it is often difficult to separate the markets for passenger transportation, and one means of travel will have an impact upon another means of travel. For instance, intercity travel by car may cause a portion of urban street congestion, and intercity air travel contributes to congestion on streets serving airports. Further, the same vehicle, such as the private automobile, is sometimes used for both intercity and urban travel, and usually the same streets and highways are used for both intercity and urban travel. Finally, passenger transportation often takes place jointly with freight transportation in the same vehicle and on the same trip. Examples would be both air passengers and air freight service on the same flight, intercity buses carrying packages and small freight at the same time, and so forth.

In spite of these difficulties, it is possible to think of passenger transportation as a separate thing from freight transportation. And the implications here noted merely make the analysis and study of passenger transportation more challenging and interesting.

MEASUREMENT OF PASSENGER TRANSPORTATION

There are at least three ways to measure the importance of passenger transportation: revenues, passenger-miles, and number of passengers.

Other measures of passenger transportation also help to clarify the specific characteristics of the various modes of passenger transportation.

Revenue Measurement

The dollars-expended or revenue-received measurement of the importance of passenger transportation was shown in Figure 1.4, "The Nation's Estimated Passenger Bill." Table 7.1 shows the detail for that $513.5 billion figure. It should be noted that in 1987 this amount expended was 11.5 percent of the gross national product. These data are divided into two categories: private transportation and for-hire transportation — with for-hire broken down by markets (local, intercity, international) and private given by mode (automobile and private air). The characteristics of each vary as we shall see directly. Note, however that private passenger transportation expenditures include the cost of new and used cars and private aircraft. Although these are transportation expenditures to the users, one must be careful to separate operating expenditures from capital expenditures. Even so, from an expenditures viewpoint it is apparent that the private automobile dominates passenger transportation, and air transportation is the dominant means of for-hire passenger transportation.

Passenger-Miles

Another measure of the importance of passenger transportation is that of intercity passenger-miles. Just as freight transportation is often measured in ton-miles, passenger transportation is often measured in passenger-miles (one passenger carried one mile) (see Table 7.2). It should be noted that only intercity passenger-miles are involved in Table 7.2 since passenger-mile data on urban transit systems and private automobile usage inside cities are not available.

Transit systems are best measured in terms of vehicle-miles operated. However, this figure cannot be compared to passenger-miles, for many people get on and off a bus or other transit vehicle in a given mile. We shall note the characteristics of transit systems below. However, once more the private automobile predominates in terms of passenger-miles, and air dominates in for-hire passenger transportation in a passenger-mile measurement.

Table 7.1 The Nation's Estimated Passenger Transportation Bill, 1987 (in billions)

Private Transportation	
Automobile	
New and used cars	$147.6
Other vehicles[1]	36.7
Repairs/Parking/Rental/Leasing/Washing/Storage	64.0
Gasoline and oil	94.5
Tire, tubes, accessories	31.8
Interest on Debt	26.0
Insurance paid less claims	16.2
Registration/Permits	5.6
Tolls	1.7
	$424.1
Air	
Aircraft	$ 1.9
Operating costs	5.9
	$ 7.8
Total Private	$431.9
For-Hire Transportation	
Local: Bus and transit[2]	$ 15.7
Taxi	6.5
Railroad Commutation[2]	1.6
School Bus	6.4
	$ 30.2
Intercity: Air[3]	$ 39.3
Bus	1.8
Rail[2]	1.6
	$ 42.7
International: Air[3]	$ 8.1
Water	.6
	$ 8.7
Total For-Hire	$ 81.6
GRAND TOTAL	$513.5
Percent of GNP	11.5

[1] Small pickups, vans, RVs, mobile homes.
[2] Includes operating subsidies and capital grants.
[3] Includes ticket taxes, domestic and international.
Source: Data from Transportation Policy Associates, *Transportation in America*, 6th ed., Washington, D.C., July 1988 Supplement, p. 5. Copyright 1988. Used by permission of Eno Foundation for Transportation.

Table 7.2 Intercity Passenger-Miles by Modes, 1987 (Billions of Passenger-Miles)

Private Automobile	1,494.9	79.9%
Private Aircraft	12.4	0.7%
For-Hire Air (Domestic)	329.1	17.6%
Intercity Bus	22.8	1.2%
Rail	12.3	0.7%
	1,871.5	100.0%

Source: Data from Transportation Policy Associates, *Transportation in America*, 6th ed., Washington, D.C., July 1988 Supplement, p. 8. Copyright 1988. Used by permission of Eno Foundation for Transportation.

Number of Passengers

A third measure of passenger transportation is the number of passengers carried by for-hire modes. These numbers are found in Table 7.3 for both intercity and urban passenger transportation. Once again air passenger transportation is the leading mode in terms of intercity passengers carried. However, air transportation does not dominate in number of passengers carried as it does in passenger-miles. Both intercity bus and rail carry substantial numbers of passengers, but each journey is short as compared with air transportation, which is predominantly in the long-haul business (thereby generating many passenger-miles). In urban transportation, the motor bus is the leading carrier in terms of passengers carried. Although there is no comparative measure of passengers carried by private automobile, either intercity or urban, we know from our other measures that the private automobile accounts for a vast number of passenger-miles and thus probably dominates on the basis of number of passengers as well.

Other Measures

Considered from the viewpoint of average length of haul, in 1987 air transportation led with 779 miles, followed by Amtrak with 259 miles, intercity bus at 118, and commuter rail with 23 miles. For these trips, air transportation received an average revenue of 11.3 cents (11.0 cents coach and 15.7 cents first class) per passenger-mile, Amtrak 10.6 cents, and intercity bus 9.9 cents per passenger-mile. For urban transportation, the average fare for all urban transit systems in 1987 was 61.8 cents per trip and the average length of the trip was 4.7 miles.

Table 7.3 Number of Passengers Carried by For-Hire Modes, 1987 (in millions)

Intercity		
Air (domestic)	420.4	39.8%
Bus	324.0	30.7%
Rail (Commutation 290.0, Amtrak 20.7)	310.7	29.5%
	1,055.1	100.0%
Urban		
Light Rail	133.0	1.6%
Heavy Rail	2,402.0	28.4%
Trolley Coach	141.0	1.7%
Motor Bus	5633.0	66.6%
Demand Response	70.0	0.8%
Other	76.0	0.9%
	8,455.0	100.0%

Sources: Intercity data from Transportation Policy Associates, *Transportation in America*, 6th ed., Washington, D.C., July 1988 Supplement, p. 9. Copyright 1988. Used by permission of Eno Foundation for Transportation. Urban data from American Public Transit Association, *Transit Fact Book 1988*, Washington, D.C., 1988, p. 32. Copyright 1988. Used by permission.

UNIVERSALITY OF THE PRIVATE AUTOMOBILE

A reader noting these statistical measures must be struck by the fact that passenger transportation is dominated by the private automobile. Everyone's daily observations and experience confirm this universality. It is an undisputed fact that the private automobile is an important and prevailing part of our everyday lives.

Nationally there were 135.7 million passenger cars and 40.9 million trucks and buses registered in the United States in 1986 (176.6 million vehicles) and 158.6 million licensed drivers. The car is the basis of many sociological, ecological, and psychological problems, some of which are familiar to all of us. But from a passenger transportation viewpoint, the importance and universality of the car cannot be overemphasized.

Costs of the Private Automobile

The economic costs of owning and operating a private automobile are considerable, but most car owners rarely appreciate the size of these costs. When students are asked how much it costs to drive a car, they usually reply in terms of how much they pay for gasoline. Naturally this varies according to how many miles are driven, so a more realistic number is the operating costs per mile. On the other hand, there are a number of fixed costs to owning a car and these should be considered too. Table 7.4 shows the cost of owning and operating a car for 1988 and selected earlier years.

Table 7.4 Cost of Owning and Operating a Private Automobile, 1975, 1980, 1985, 1988

	1975	1980	1985	1988
Operating Costs Per Mile				
Gas & Oil	4.82¢	5.86¢	6.16¢	5.20¢
Maintenance	.97	1.12	1.23	1.60
Tires	.66	.64	.65	.80
Total	6.45	7.62	8.04	7.60
Annual Fixed Costs				
Insurance	$ 383	$ 490	$ 503	$ 573
License/Registration	30	82	115	139
Depreciation	773	1,038	1,253	1,784
Finance Charges	NA	423	570	565
Total	$1,186	$2,033	$2,441	$3,061
Total Cost Per Mile (at 10,000 annual miles)	18.31¢	27.95¢	32.45¢	38.21¢

Assumptions: Intermediate-sized car used 10,000 miles a year for six years.
Insurance: Fire & Theft, $50 deductible 1975, $100 deductible 1980–85–88; Collision, $100 deductible 1975, $250 deductible 1980–85–88; Liability, $100,000/$300,000.
Source: Motor Vehicle Manufacturers Association of the United States, Inc., *Motor Vehicle Facts and Figures*, Detroit, 1988, p. 44. Copyright 1988. Used by permission.

Note the importance of the assumptions at the bottom of Table 7.4. Any study of car costs obviously varies with the age of the car, its size, where it is driven (insurance costs and registration costs vary across the United States), and the finance charges. But based on these data (intermediate-sized car driven 10,000 miles a year over a six-year ownership cycle), it costs 38.2 cents per mile to drive a car! It is a surprise to many that the largest per-mile cost of a car is depreciation (17.8 cents per mile) followed by insurance (5.7 cents per mile), finance charges (5.6 cents per mile), and then gas and oil (5.2 cents per mile). One can calculate one's costs per mile by simply adjusting for the number of miles driven a year, the size of the car, insurance and registration fees, and the initial price divided by six (recent studies have shown most cars are owned an average of six years) for depreciation, plus the costs of gas, oil, maintenance, and tires divided by the miles driven per year. But the point is that the actual cost is surprisingly high on average (38.2 cents per mile), and depreciation (17.8 cents) is the biggest single per-mile item — not gas and oil!

It should be noted that these are per-mile costs, not per–passenger-mile costs. To compare passenger-mile costs of the private automobile with average revenues received by for-hire carriers (11.3 cents air, 10.6 cents Amtrak, 9.9 cents intercity bus for intercity trips, or 61.8 cents per trip on urban transit), the costs of owning and operating a private automobile would have to be divided by passengers carried. If one carries two passengers per trip in a private car, the cost per passenger-mile drops to 19.1 cents; four passengers carried means 9.55 cents per passenger-mile. Herein lies the advantage of carpooling or vanpooling, which we shall discuss shortly, as well as the explanation of why the automobile is often the least expensive way for a family to travel on vacations.

Characteristics of the Private Automobile

Much of the reason for the predominance of the private automobile lies in the characteristics of this mode of travel: economy, comfort, convenience, speed, safety, and individualism.

Even though the economic costs are greater on a per-mile basis than any other means of for-hire passenger transportation, it should be noted that many of the costs of operating a car are what the economist calls fixed costs. Most outlays for insurance and taxes are paid once or twice a year. Sometimes parking costs are on the same schedule. Further, repair and maintenance expenses occur infrequently but are substantial when tires or a battery must be replaced or repairs made. Likewise, depreciation or loss of capital value is not always apparent until the vehicle itself is replaced. Rarely are these fixed costs thought of in terms of per-mile costs. Most people calculate the operating costs plus monthly payments on the car itself if they calculate at all. If these fixed costs are ignored, the gas and oil costs of operating a car compare favorably with for-hire transportation fares.

Besides the fixed-costs nature of the private car, the matter of alternatives is important. Once the car has been purchased, many of these fixed costs are incurred and will continue to be incurred whether the car is operated or not. Hence, it is probably rational to compare only gas and oil costs to for-hire fares, *once the car is purchased.* The only way to avoid the fixed costs is by not purchasing the car in the first place. Moreover, once the car is purchased, per-mile fixed costs drop when more miles are driven. In Table 7.4, for example, if the annual-miles-driven figure is doubled, the per-mile insurance, parking, and depreciation costs are halved. Thus, once the car is purchased, the rational alternative is to drive it.

Another characteristic of the private automobile is comfort. Although this will vary by model, by and large the private car is physically a very comfortable vehicle. None of the for-hire modes approach the comfort of the private automobile, which has been likened to an "extension of your living room" — soft seat, stereo or radio at your beck and call, ample leg and head room, relaxed atmosphere, pleasant surroundings, and so forth.

From an operational point of view, the private car is extremely convenient. First, the car awaits the driver at the door — no need to walk to a bus stop or train station in heat or rain or to take a limo to the airport. Second, the driver usually goes by the most direct route, whereas many trips by for-hire means do not follow the most direct route. Indeed, it would be quite a coincidence if the bus or train took the most direct route for everyone on board. Third, your car is ready to go when you are — no need to wait for a bus, train, or plane. In terms of convenience, the private car almost always surpasses for-hire transportation.

The fourth characteristic of the private automobile is speed. Of course, this is relative, but in intercity travel only the airplane is faster than the car, even given the wait at the airport. For-hire passenger transportation typically stops to pick up and deliver passengers, so the journey takes longer than when the private car is used. In urban travel, the ability to take a more direct route as well as to avoid intermediate stops makes the private automobile the fastest means available.

Even though the accident and fatality rates of the private automobile are much higher than for-hire means of travel, people feel "safe" in their own automobiles. That is, they perceive that they are safe whether they are or not. Surrounded by several tons of steel and glass, the driver has an impression of personal safety. Besides, he or she is in control, whereas in for-hire transportation someone else controls the vehicle. People are rarely mugged or attacked in their own cars, and they certainly feel less exposed to personal danger while in their automobiles. Regardless of accident and fatality statistics, the private car instills a feeling or perception of safety.

Finally, the private car has the characteristics of individualism. Almost endless options and combinations are available in colors, interior finish, sound systems, body styles, engine sizes, climatic controls, and even safety devices. Buyers can almost "tailor-make" their own cars. According to psychologists, the options and combinations can reflect the personality of the user. Literally, for some, their cars are extensions of their personalities. Also, many people feel that they lose their individuality when using for-hire transportation. The individual becomes just another person among many. The loss of individuality is furthered even more by constant references to "mass transit" or "public transportation."

These characteristics of economy, comfort, convenience, speed, personal safety, and individuality not only explain why the automobile is so widely used in spite of its costs but also provide a standard that for-hire means of passenger transportation must meet if people are expected to leave their cars at home and use an alternative mode of travel.

Trip Purpose and Average Length of Trip

Another illustration of the universality of the private car is found in trip purpose and length of trip. Various studies have been made from time to time and they show some interesting aspects of the private automobile.

First, most automobile trips are made with one or two people in the car. The average number of persons per trip will vary by purpose of the trip but on average in the United States there are 1.4 persons in a car per trip.

Second, while the purposes of automobile trips are many, when divided into broad classes on the basis of number of trips, personal business (shopping, visiting doctor, other personal business) makes up about 39 percent of all trips, work-related about 31 percent, and social/recreational/educational/miscellaneous about 28 percent. Table 7.5 shows these data by both number of trips and vehicle-miles traveled.

Third, most trips are relatively short — 7.8 miles each on average. These data are also in Table 7.5. Note that vacations and pleasure driving are longer trips, but since both are a small percentage of total trips, they do not increase the average greatly. The journey from home to work and back (8.5 miles average) and shopping (5.3 miles average) make up almost 48 percent of all trips by number and 43 percent of all trips by vehicle-mile. In any case, it is possible to say that the private automobile is used mostly for short trips.

Given all the above — registration numbers, cost characteristics, the comfort–convenience–speed–perceived safety–individualism of the car and usage characteristics (trip purpose, length of trip, and number of riders per trip), it is easy to see why the private automobile can be considered the universal means of passenger transportation.

Table 7.5 Motor Vehicle Trips, Travel, and Average Trip Length by Trip Purpose, 1983

Trip Purpose	Trips (%)	Travel (%)	Trip Length (Miles)
Earning a Living			
Home to Work	27.9	30.1	8.5
Work-Related	2.9	4.2	11.4
Subtotal	30.8	34.3	8.8
Family/Personal Business			
Shopping	20.0	13.4	5.3
Doctor/Dentist	1.2	1.5	9.7
Other	18.3	15.5	6.7
Subtotal	39.5	30.4	6.0
Civic, Educational, Religious	5.9	4.1	5.5
Social/Recreational			
Visiting Friends/Relatives	9.9	13.6	10.8
Pleasure Driving	0.3	1.0	22.7
Vacations	0.1	2.1	113.9
Other	12.2	13.3	8.7
Subtotal	22.5	30.0	10.6
Other/Unknown	1.3	1.2	7.2
Grand Total	100.0	100.0	7.8

Source: Motor Vehicle Manufacturers Association of the United States, Inc., *Motor Vehicle Facts and Figures*, Detroit, 1988, p. 51. Copyright 1988. Used by permission.

OTHER PRIVATE TRANSPORTATION SYSTEMS

There are four other types of private transportation, some of which are important in certain applications. These are motorcycles, bicycles, mopeds, and private aircraft.

There were over 5.4 million motorcycles registered in the United States in 1986, and they traveled over 9 million vehicle-miles. Retail sales of motorcycles were $1.045 million, with the majority of motorcycles being imported vehicles (550,000 with a dutiable value of $736,000). New registrations in 1986 were 631,000 (down from a yearly high of 838,000 in 1980). These vehicles are used in both intercity and urban transportation. The motorcycle is a very efficient user of fuel, averaging 50 miles per gallon. Unfortunately, the accident rate is high — 480,000 accidents in 1986, 4,342 of which were fatal. Also, motorcycles cause noise pollution, although the federal government has recently set noise standards that motorcycles must meet.

Bicycling has increased in popularity in recent years. Formerly considered primarily a recreational vehicle demanded mainly by teenagers, the bicycle came of age as a universal type of alternative passenger vehicle in the 1970s. Bicycle sales tripled from 5.6 million in 1965 to 15.3 million in 1973. Since sales peaked in 1973 during the Arab oil boycott, however, they dropped to about 6 million a year in 1976; nevertheless, sales have maintained a steady growth — about 6 percent a year — since then. Imports are also important in bicycles. In 1986 there were 5.3 million domestic shipments of bikes and 7.0 million imports for total sales of 12.3 million. It is a little-known fact that, in many years, sales of new bicycles are greater than sales of new automobiles.

For distances up to five miles, the bicycle is an alternative to the automobile. Sales of bicycles to adults were responsible for most of the remarkable increase in the early 1970s, and over 30 percent of current sales are to adults. An increasing number of adults ride bicycles to work or to classes or use them for personal business. In 1986 over 60 million adults rode bikes, according to government reports. In some areas of the country where climatic conditions are mild, bicycling is a year-round alternative to driving the family car.

Bicycle use would probably increase if more bike paths and bikeways were provided. Several programs of federal aid for bike paths have been tried over the past decade. The first was a $60 million program as part of the Land and Water Conservation Fund (Departments of Interior and Agriculture) for recreational bike facilities between 1969 and 1974. The 1973 Federal Aid to Highways Act allowed highway trust money — up to

$40 million per year coming primarily from the federal gas tax — to be used by the states for bike paths. In 1975 Congress allocated $6 million specifically for bikeway demonstration projects, and in the Surface Transportation Act of 1978, $40 million per year was made available for bikeway grants on a matching basis. The problem with these programs is that many states feel that all federal aid money available should go for highways; money for building bikeways, therefore, must compete with other highway projects.

Mopeds are a relatively recent development in the United States. Combining many of the features of the bicycle and the motorcycle, these vehicles are lightweight and relatively inexpensive (like the bicycle) but have a mechanical source of power (like the motorcycle), usually rather low horsepower. Many of them are imported; mopeds have been popular abroad for many years. There is disagreement over whether a moped is a bicycle or a motorcycle for purposes of registration, taxation, and safety regulation. Bicycles are under the jurisdiction of local governments, whereas motorcycles are registered, taxed, and regulated by state governments.

The final type of private passenger transportation is the private airplane. In 1986 there were over 275,700 civil aircraft in the United States, only 4,900 of which were commercial aircraft. The general aviation fleet amounted to 270,800 aircraft, the majority of which (164,600) were single-engine fixed-wing planes. Over 306,000 persons held private pilot licenses and 148,000 were certified as commercial pilots; only 8,700 were involved with airline transportation. Private business flying is an important subset of civil aviation, but personal use makes up the vast majority of civil flying. It is estimated that 12.4 billion passenger-miles were logged by private aircraft in 1987. Although this seems like a large amount, note in Table 7.2 that this composed less than 1 percent of the total intercity passenger-miles that year.

Unfortunately, the fatalities per million aircraft hours flown is high for general aviation at 1.53 as compared with .001 for air carriers, .01 for commuter air carriers, and 1.12 for air taxis. There were 2,568 accidents in general aviation in 1987 as compared with 22 for air carriers, 14 for commuter airlines, and 118 for air taxis. General aviation or private flying is not inexpensive and contributed $7.8 billion in 1987 to the Nation's Estimated Passenger Transportation Bill, as noted in Table 7.1. Aircraft sales were $1.9 billion and aircraft operating costs were $5.9 billion in 1987. Obviously, private air transportation is an important form of passenger transportation.

FOR-HIRE INTERCITY PASSENGER TRANSPORTATION

There are three modes of for-hire intercity passenger transportation systems: airlines, railroads, and intercity buses. Each has its own distinct characteristics as well as advantages and disadvantages. Within certain ranges, each competes with the other two as well as with the private automobile. But whereas the automobile has the characteristic of universality as we noted above, is a very personal type of transportation, is relatively expensive, and is used sporadically at the whim of the driver, for-hire passenger transportation displays a different set of characteristics. All three modes involve vehicles that are relatively intensively used on regular operating schedules with known costs to passengers (fares) that are relatively modest and using known routes on a continuous and fairly reliable basis. Because of these characteristics, the for-hire modes provide the "backbone" system of intercity passenger transportation for the nation.

Air Transportation: The Dominant For-Hire Mode

As noted in Table 7.2, air transportation is the leading mode of intercity travel, producing over 329 billion passenger-miles in 1987, which was almost 18 percent of total passenger-miles and far more than the 22 billion passenger-miles produced by intercity buses and the 12 billion passenger-miles produced by trains. However, this statistic may be somewhat misleading, since the average journey by air is rather long — 779 miles — and therefore each flight generates a large number of passenger-miles. We have already noted in Table 7.3 that on the basis of number of passengers, air transportation carries somewhat more than either buses or railroads. Even so, the nation possesses a very well developed and efficient passenger transportation system by air that is the envy of the world and that dominates the for-hire transportation modes.

Air transportation is big business. Commercial airlines in 1986 operated 3,799 aircraft, 3,282 of which were jets, 476 turboprop, and 101 piston powered. These lines have assets of over $13 billion and employ over 457,000 persons. Total operating revenues approach $34 billion a year.

The post–World War II period could easily be called the air age for passenger transportation in America. In 1940, air transportation produced only 1.2 billion passenger-miles, less than half of 1 percent of the total. It was not until 1950 that air passenger-miles reached 10 billion. By 1987, air produced an astounding 329 billion passenger-miles, some 17 percent of all U.S. passenger-miles (including the private automobile) and over 90 percent of all for-hire passenger-miles. By 1957, airlines had surpassed railroads as the leading for-hire carriers of people. Additionally, the average length of journey had increased during this air age from 474 in 1947 to 779 in 1987. Figure 7.1 illustrates this growth in the postwar period, as well as changes in the other modes.

During this same period, average scheduled airline fares increased from a little more than 5 cents to over 11.3 cents per passenger-mile, while railroad average fares increased from 2.1 cents to 10.6 cents per passenger-mile and average bus fares went from 1.7 cents to 9.9 cents per passenger-mile. Lower-priced coach, tourist, economy, excursion, discount, and group travel services have grown rapidly during recent years and now greatly exceed first-class travel in volume. The increased speed, convenience, and popularity of air travel seem to ensure the continued growth of this service even if fares should increase substantially. However, air travel cannot be expected to increase as rapidly in percentage terms during the next thirty years as during the last thirty without increases in the capacity of airports and airways.

Although aggregate statistics and trends are useful in an overview of the airline industry, one must realize that the industry is made up of several types of carriers with different operating situations and problems. Prior to deregulation of air transportation in 1977 and 1978, the Civil Aeronautics Board (CAB) classified airlines into nine groups. Since deregulation, the distinctions are much harder to draw, since airline companies are now free to move into almost every air market. However, from an equipment viewpoint, the Federal Aviation Administration (FAA), a division of the U.S. Department of Transportation, classified the 1986 U.S. civil air fleet as (a) 4,700 air carrier planes and (b) 270,800 general aviation planes (noted above under private air travel). Among the scheduled commercial carriers, there were 588 wide-body jets and 2,813 narrow-body jets in 1987, which generated 327 billion passenger-miles domestically and 76 billion passenger-miles in international service. Commuter carriers owned 1,841 planes in 1987 with an average seating capacity of 19.7 passengers and generated 5 billion passenger-miles. Additionally, cargo carriers owned 393 jets and 176 turboprop planes that carried over 8 billion ton-miles of freight and express cargo.

Another way to note the different types of carriers is by revenue generated. In 1981, the CAB began publishing statistical data in five new categories: majors, with revenue of more than $1 billion, of which there were 14 in 1987; nationals, with revenue of $75 million to $1 billion, of which there were 20 in 1987; large regionals, with revenue of $10 million

Figure 7.1 Intercity Passenger-Miles by Mode, 1940–1987

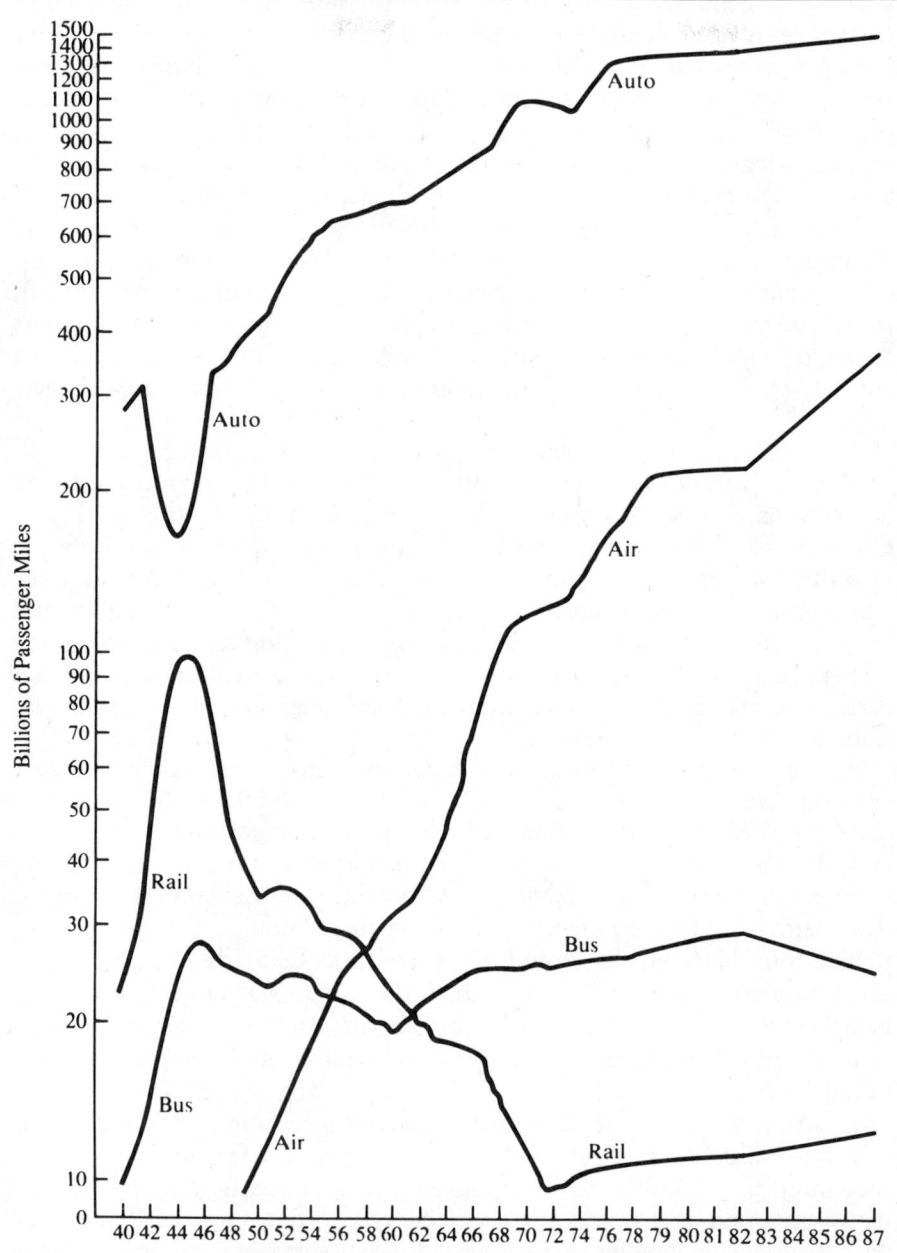

Source: Transportation Policy Associates, *Transportation in America*, 6th ed., Washington, D.C., March 1988, p. 8. Copyright 1988. Used by permission of Eno Foundation for Transportation.

to $75 million, of which there were 32 in 1987; medium regionals, with revenue below $10 million, of which there were 27 in 1987; and commuters, defined as medium regionals that operate planes with 60 or fewer seats and cargo capacity of less than 18,000 pounds, of which there were 169 in 1987. Among the majors are such well-known names as Alaska, America West, American, Braniff, Continental, Delta, Eastern, Northwest, Pan American, Piedmont, Southwest, Trans World, United, and U.S. Air. Basically, these carriers operate between the larger population centers with long-distance flights. Increasingly popular is the "hub-and-spoke" route structure wherein passengers from smaller population centers are flown on short or intermediate-length flights (spokes) into major airports (hubs), which are then connected by relatively frequent nonstop service. Mergers between majors and smaller airlines have led to greater concentration in airlines, with the top eight airlines flying over 85 percent of the passenger-miles.

The airline industry has been in a state of flux since deregulation, with many new entrants, many firms exiting the industry or being merged, and distinctions between operations blurred. We shall discuss this further in Chapter 14. Traditionally, the trunk-line carriers, now called majors, operated between major points and were known as "first-level" carriers. The second level was regional or feeder-type carriers operating in and between areas of lesser traffic density and connecting smaller population centers to major cities, while the third level was commuter and air taxi operations. Today these levels or distinctions have changed with deregulation, bankruptcies, and mergers.

All major commercial airlines are common carriers, and their interstate passenger activities were subject to economic regulation by the CAB from 1938 to 1978. In general, their regulation was comparable to that exercised by the Interstate Commerce Commission although there were major differences. The CAB also administered the direct-subsidy programs during that period. Since deregulation, economic regulation of the airlines was phased out between 1978 and 1985 and the CAB discontinued as a regulatory agency in 1985. We shall discuss this change in detail in Chapter 13. The FAA not only regulates safety matters but also engages in promotional activities such as the development of airports and navigational facilities.

It is safe to say that historically the government's impact on commercial airlines has been much greater in the areas of safety and promotion, including direct and indirect subsidies such as airports, airways, experimentation, and development in connection with new types of aircraft and public service payments. Direct-subsidy payments were made to trunk-line operators from 1938 to the mid-1950s but were discontinued at that time. Payments called public service revenues were made to the regional and local-service carriers until 1978. Since 1978 direct-subsidy payments called essential service payments have been made principally to local service–commuter operators in order to provide service to selected smaller communities. Additionally, an element of subsidy exists in the air mail contracts let by the government. These promotional activities, both direct and indirect subsidies, have been justified historically on the grounds that air transportation was a new mode in which the public had a vital peacetime commercial and wartime defense interest. Also, it was felt that this newcomer would not be able to develop rapidly without subsidization if forced to compete on an equal basis with already well-established competitors. Recent justifications for direct-subsidy payments to local service–commuter operators are that smaller towns cannot develop economically without airline service and the public should shoulder the burden of providing some level of essential service into smaller cities.

Domestic airlines of all varieties compete for passengers with railroads and buses and especially with private automobiles. And, of course, they compete with one another. During the earlier years of CAB regulation that began in 1938, intramodal competition was limited. Slowly the CAB allowed more and more competition among the airlines, especially on dense traffic routes. In the late 1970s, the CAB began to permit even greater levels of competition among carriers and actually played an active role in urging Congress to abolish all economic control over airlines. As noted above (and in Chapter 13 in greater detail), Congress moved to phase in deregulation in 1978; by the mid-1980s all economic regulation of airlines ceased. However, the FAA continues to regulate safety, investigate accidents, and operate the national airway system.

Airline cost structures are more comparable to those of the trucking industry than to railroad costs; the industry is one of relatively high variable costs in proportion to fixed costs. Airports typically are provided by local governments; the airlines pay landing fees and lease rents, which are variable costs. Navigational aids and the operation of the airways are provided by the FAA at no charge to the airline, although a federal 8 percent ticket tax provided funds both for upgrading airports via matching funds and for improving airways from 1970 to 1980. When the 8 percent ticket tax was extended in 1982, a portion of this revenue was allocated to pay for the FAA operation. These programs will be discussed in detail in Chapter 28.

Although it is true that modern jet aircraft are very expensive, costing millions of dollars, only 12 to 13 percent of the industry's total costs are chargeable to such items as interest, depreciation, and amortization. In contrast, wages and salaries, fuel and oil, and various materials, supplies, and services in the variable-cost category account for over four-fifths of total costs.

Costs of fuel (16 percent) and labor (37 percent) are particularly important in airline operation. When the price of fuel accelerated rapidly in the 1970s, airline earnings were greatly affected. Airlines began to shift to more fuel-efficient planes — although this took time. This shift plus a lowering of fuel costs in the 1980s helped airline profits. However, the increased competition coming with deregulation and the widespread discounting of fares in the 1980s offset cost savings from lower fuel prices. In 1987 at the height of fare discounting, some 92 percent of all passengers were traveling on discounts.

Air transportation employs many people — 456,349 in 1987, down some in recent years. Table 7.6 shows the number of employees in various job categories in that year. In 1986, average yearly compensation including fringe benefits in the airline industry was $40,418 — only railroads ($48,379) and pipelines ($44,000) were higher among the modes. This $40,418 figure compares with $31,219 for manufacturing, $30,338 for finance/insurance/real estate, and $26,301 for all industry.

Table 7.6 Number of Employees in the Airline Industry, 1987

Pilots and copilots	41,963
Other flight personnel	8,541
Flight attendants	76,662
Mechanics	51,223
Aircraft & traffic servicing personnel	194,927
Office employees	40,690
All others	43,333
Total Employees	457,339

Source: Traffic World, December 5, 1988, supplement, p. "c."

Safety has been of some concern in air transportation. However, as measured by fatalities, air carriers had only 22 fatalities in 1986 (at the rate of .001 per million miles), commuter carriers 14 (.01 per million miles), and air taxis 31 (1.12 per million miles). This compares with 46,056 people killed in motor vehicles in 1986. However, airline accidents are generally quite spectacular and make the evening news on TV. Some years have seen many fatalities on domestic airlines — 655 in 1977, 354 in 1979, 234 in 1982, nd 526 in 1985 — while many years have had few or no fatalities. It is generally agreed that commercial air transportation is the safest means of passenger transportation.

Air transportation faces many problems. The airline fleet is aging and there is some concern about safety and maintenance. The average age of nearly 3,000 airliners is about thirteen years, with half the planes in major airline fleets over fifteen years old. Several carriers have major re-equipment programs under way and others face the same capital-intensive task in the 1990s. There has been concern over decreased on-time service, some of this arising from the hub-and-spoke route system and some from increased airway congestion. The quality of cabin service is said to have decreased as well. Questions have arisen about adequate maintenance and upkeep. Antitrust concerns over increasing concentration in the industry are another problem. Finally, there is much concern over the need for new airports and enlargement of existing airports and airway capacity.

Many of these problems are short-term in nature and some arise from the adjustments and events brought on by deregulation. However, the comfort, speed, and convenience of air travel ensure a steady market growth and a more stable situation in the long run. The industry has successfully survived and adapted to several shocks previously, such as the shift to jets in the late 1950s, the coming of jumbo jets in the early 1970s, the fuel crisis, and the early adjustments to deregulation. The long-run outlook is for stability with continued steady growth in traffic and service, once the short-run problems have been solved.

Intercity Buses: Carrier of Many Passengers

The intercity bus industry consists of 3,594 operating companies of various sizes that offer service over the nation's highways between towns and cities. Transit motor buses, sometimes called city buses, are generally not considered part of the bus industry and will be discussed shortly under urban transportation service.

In 1987 intercity bus service generated $1.8 billion, as noted in Table 7.1, produced 22.8 billion passenger-miles (Table 7.2), and carried 324 million passengers (Table 7.3), the second largest number of passengers in intercity travel. Bus fares on average are lower (9.9 cents per passenger-mile in 1987) than air fares (11.3 cents per passenger-mile) or Amtrak fares (10.6 cents per passenger-mile). Buses serve most communities in the United States — far more than rail or air — and in the mid-1980s the American Bus Association boasted that buses served over 14,000 towns dependent solely on bus service (no competing rail or air service). Also it was said that buses served 96 percent of all towns with populations between 2,500 and 5,000, and all communities with populations over 5,000. The bus does indeed provide transportation to many and is probably the most universal type of for-hire passenger transportation.

As we have noted above, most bus trips are intermediate in length — 118 miles on average in 1987. Buses typically carry 45 passengers as well as packages and express. In 1987, the bus package business generated $179 million (about 10 percent of all bus revenue) while passenger service generated $1.777 billion. Package express by bus tends to be in small packages, under 100 pounds in size, and basically takes advantage of the widespread route structure of the bus system plus the relatively frequent bus service. One type of bus package freight of some importance is the delivery of the daily newspaper.

Essentially, the passenger side of bus service is broken down into three types of service: regular route, contract charter and special service, and local service. The traditional regular route service operates on a fixed route connecting cities and towns on a frequent scheduled basis with roadside "flag" service in some areas. Fares and schedules are published and usually regulated by state agencies. Prior to deregulation in 1982, the ICC regulated interstate bus fares and certificates.

The second type of bus service is contract charter and special service. This service has been growing in recent times. Here fares are not published and the bus company will offer a special customized service to and from specific points for groups of passengers. The bus company sells the tickets and usually requires a minimum load or the trip is cancelled. Often travel agents will charter a bus for a specific tour — say to the national parks in a given region, to a ski resort or a sporting event, to view the colorful leaves of autumn in New England, and so forth. The bus company furnishes the vehicle and the driver with the travel agent selling the tickets and taking the risk of falling short of a busload of passengers. In some instances, the bus company will let a contract to agents for customized journeys over a period of time — such as bus trips to Las Vegas or Atlantic City from points a few hundred miles away on a schedule such as four times a week. These contracts can be of any length but are usually for several months. In 1981 regular route service generated 125 million passengers while contract charter and special service produced 250 million passengers. Since that time, this portion of the intercity bus business has grown while regular service has decreased.

Local service refers to special bus runs from nearby cities into metropolitan centers. These are often intrastate in nature but sometimes are interstate, such as local service between Connecticut points and New York City. These local service runs are tailored to fit intercity commuting. Bus clubs have arisen in recent times — a number of businesspeople in a given smaller community join together to have bus service, sometimes with various amenities, to and from a place of work. This way the club members avoid driving their own cars or using commuter rail service while traveling in a customized service with a congenial group known to them.

Notice in Table 7.1 that school buses are an even larger contributor to the Nation's Estimated Passenger Transportation Bill ($6.4 billion in 1987). These are usually considered local transportation, although in many rural areas school bus routes are many miles in length. However, school buses are generally not considered a part of the intercity bus industry.

Buses are classified Class I and Class II by the ICC. Class I has a gross revenue of over $3 million a year and has fewer than 100 firms; Class II, gross revenue of under $3 million a year, has the vast majority of firms, most fairly small. Class I buses are dominated by two firms: Greyhound Lines and Trailways. These are the only nationwide bus systems and both have been owned by GLI Holdings since 1987.

Through a series of mergers in the 1920s and 1930s, two large bus systems emerged. Originally many railroads used buses as substitute service when they began cutting back on rail passenger schedules on less densely traveled routes. For a time, railroads owned a part of Greyhound Lines. The domination of these two firms is so complete that today 65 percent of all intercity bus passenger-miles are produced by either Greyhound Lines or Trailways — now having common ownership.

Many states began regulating buses for purposes of safety and protection of the highways in the 1920s. However, in 1935, intercity bus operations were brought under the regulation of the Interstate Commerce Commission through the Motor Carrier Act. This regulation was basically economic in character and dealt with entry, rates, and services. States continued to regulate buses as to safety and regulated the intrastate operations from an economic viewpoint. Abandonments of service have been of particular importance in state regulation. In 1982, Congress reformed the regulatory structure for buses, as we will note in Chapter 13. This was part of the recent deregulation movement, and much less economic regulation of buses exists today as compared with the past.

As to cost, buses use public highways and pay user taxes and licenses. Labor costs are a large portion of the expenses of operation: an ICC report in the mid-1970s determined that labor costs made up 57 percent of bus operating expenses. Other substantial cost items are fuel related. Between these three items — user charges and fuel and labor costs — it is readily apparent that the cost structure of the intercity bus is predominantly that of variable costs. In 1986, there were 36,000 employees in the intercity bus industry with average annual earnings (without fringes) of $21,958.

Intercity passenger traffic by bus has decreased in recent years (see Figure 7.1) after matching its wartime high of 27 billion passenger-miles in 1980. This has been due to three factors: bus deregulation, airline deregulation, and increasing use of the private car. Bus deregulation in

1982 made discontinuation of service much easier, and many smaller points lost service. Airline deregulation led to considerable price discounting by airlines to the point where the price of travel for 400–500 miles by air was often much less than the same journey by bus — and the journey was much faster. Private automobile ownership and use continues to increase, as we have noted above, and provides an excellent alternative to buses on short and intermediate-length journeys.

Studies have shown that the average bus passenger is in the lower income group and is either young or retired. The bus provides a good alternative for people on a limited budget or those who do not have ready access to a car. The fares are relatively low, the schedules are relatively frequent, and the coverage and network is good. Of course, buses compete with both trains and airplanes, but their greatest competition is with the private automobile. Even though transcontinental service is offered, the bus tends to specialize in the intermediate journey of about 118 miles. On long journeys, airplanes and trains tend to be faster and more comfortable even though sometimes more expensive. Therefore, it can be readily seen that the role of the intercity bus in the transportation system is apparently to carry a large number of passengers on an intermediate-length journey in a speedy, safe, and relatively efficient manner.

Rail Passenger Service: A Small Remnant of the Past

At one time practically all intercity travel in the United States was by railroad. Indeed, many of the early railroads were justified by and based upon their passenger-carrying capacity, not their ability to carry freight. Roads were crude and poorly developed, and the automobile, bus, and airplane were still part of the future. But even after the coming of these alternatives, trains remained the major mode of travel for many decades. As measured by passenger-miles, it was not until 1957 that airlines equaled and then surpassed trains as the major for-hire carrier.

Except for the World War II years when gasoline and rubber tires were rationed, the high point of passenger travel by trains came in the mid-1920s. As highways improved and automobile ownership broadened, more trips were taken by private automobile and all for-hire passenger transportation decreased. The introduction of reliable transcontinental bus systems also caused a decline in travel by train. By the 1930s, the trend in passenger travel by train was definitely downward, and some railroads were running losses on passenger service. After the war-induced traffic crunch, the downward trend in rail passenger traffic continued in the late 1940s. Two forces in the post–World War II period almost killed the passenger train: the rapid growth of airways for long-distance travel and the massive improvements in highways, particularly the Interstate System, which made the bus and the private automobile stronger competitors in the short- and intermediate-distance market (see Figure 7.1). By 1970, train travel was about one-tenth its size during World War II and one-fourth its 1920s size. Moreover, practically all railroads were losing money on passenger service. These relationships are noted in Table 7.7.

In 1970, Congress established the National Railroad Passenger Corporation (Amtrak) to provide a minimum amount of basic intercity rail passenger service through contracts with railroads (see Chapter 12). All rail passenger service over 75 miles in length was then taken over by this quasi-governmental organization. Existing railroads retained their commuter and short-haul operations. But with the coming of Conrail in 1976 (see Chapter 12), much of this commuter traffic too was taken over by another quasi-governmental organization. Several railroads still operated commuter lines, principally into the larger cities of the East Coast, Chicago, and San Francisco, from 1976 to 1981. In 1981 Congress allowed Conrail to transfer its commuter rail operations to Amtrak or regional authorities, and privately owned rail passenger service almost ceased.

In 1987 there were 6,083 rail passenger cars (as compared with 61,728 in 1929), most of which were owned by various public authorities and Amtrak. These cars carried 310.7 million passengers, over 290 million of whom were in commuter travel, and generated 12.3 billion passenger-miles, 6.9 billion of which were in commuter travel. The average length of journey for commuters was a bit over 23 miles, while Amtrak passengers traveled 259 miles on average. In 1987 there were twelve commuter railroad systems in operation using 4,656 rail cars and having 23,554 employees.

While commuter traffic tends to dominate the rail passenger statistics, this is not to say that all rail passenger traffic is short. Amtrak has a number of trains that run intermediate and long distances. Perhaps the most successful Amtrak operation is in the so-called northeast corridor (Washington to New York to Boston). The Railroad Revitalization and Regulatory Reform Act of 1976 (the 4-R Act) established the Northeast Corridor Project and allocated $1.75 billion to Amtrak to purchase track and equipment and upgrade its service. Under this act plus additional appropriations ($2.5 billion in 1981), Amtrak purchased 2,611 miles of its 24,000 route miles and operates a high-speed system in this corridor which is quite popular. Other corridors also are well patronized, such as Los Angeles to San Diego, Chicago to Detroit, Chicago to St. Louis, and Philadelphia to Pittsburgh. On routes outside the northeast corridor, Amtrak contracts with twenty-one railroads for the use of their track.

Table 7.7 Distribution of For-Hire Intercity Passenger-Miles (billions of passenger-miles)

	1926		1939		1944		1957		1970		1980		1987	
	Pass-Mile	Per-cent	Pass-Mile	Per-cent	Pass-Mile	Per-cent	Pass-Mile	Per-cent	Pass-Mile	Per-cent	Pass-Mile	Per-cent	Pass-Mile	Per-cent
Railroads	41.2	91	23.7	70	97.7	76	26.3	35	10.9	07	11.0*	04	12.3*	03
Buses	4.3	9	9.5	28	27.3	21	21.5	29	25.3	17	27.4	11	22.8	06
Airlines	nil	0	.8	02	2.9	02	26.3	35	109.5	75	204.4	85	329.1	90
Total	45.5	100	34.0	100	127.9	100	74.1	100	145.7	100	242.8	100	364.2	100

*Railroad passenger-miles in 1980 and 1987 can be subdivided into Amtrak and commutation:

	1980	1987
Amtrak	4.5	5.4
Commutation	6.5	6.9

Source: Data for 1926 from Transportation Association of America, Transportation: Facts and Trends, Washington, D.C. Data for 1939–1970 from Transportation Policy Associates, Transportation in America, 1st ed., Washington, D.C., March 1983, p. 13. Copyright 1983. Used by permission of Eno Foundation for Transportation. Data for 1980, 1987 from Transportation Policy Associates, Transportation in America, 6th ed., Washington, D.C., July 1988 Supplement, p. 8. Copyright 1988. Used by permission of Eno Foundation for Transportation.

The Amtrak Reorganization Act of 1979 changed the stated objective of Amtrak from its original "for profit" goal to that of "for service." It should be noted that in 1986 Amtrak served 491 cities in forty-four states and 94 of the points served had no airline service and 52 had no bus service. In 1987 Amtrak produced over 5 billion passenger-miles and has been slowly increasing its ridership over the years.

Amtrak's service has slowly improved but still runs at a loss. In the first seventeen years of operation (1971 to 1988) Congress invested over $4 billion in Amtrak — a part of which has been to cover operating deficits. In 1988, Amtrak fare revenue covered 65 percent of its operating costs (up from 48 percent in 1981). Almost every year during the Reagan administration, the president called for an end to subsidies for Amtrak. However, Congress continues to allocate funds to keep the "noble experiment in rail passenger service" alive. The Amtrak deficit in fiscal year 1987 was $602 million — down from $896 million in 1981 — and each year Amtrak comes closer to its goal of covering 100 percent of its costs. We will discuss Amtrak again in some detail in Chapter 12.

URBAN PASSENGER SYSTEMS

The movement of passengers within an urban context is a mix of both private and public for-hire transportation. Each individual urban area has its own transportation characteristics and its own mix. Therefore, generalizations are difficult and sometimes dangerous where urban passenger transportation is involved.

Likewise, urban passenger systems are multidimensional almost by definition. The problem is not simply that of moving or transporting people, for many social and environmental issues are also involved. A partial list would include: mobility for the less privileged, wider accessibility to employment, effect on urban development and redevelopment, access for the disabled, renewal of the central cities, control over street congestion, abatement of air and noise pollution, effect on quality of life, issues of city planning and zoning, effect on housing, the location of educational institutions, the effect on the criminal justice system, the ever-present lack of public funds at all levels of government, and the need to efficiently allocate public resources.

Additionally, many disciplines are involved in urban passenger transportation: the urbanologist, the traffic engineer, the city planner, the geographer and demographer, the sociologist, the social worker, the urban economist, the criminologist, the architect, the public administrator, and the transportation analyst. Given the high degree of urbanization of the

United States (over 75 percent of our population lives in urban places), almost every social problem involves urban passenger transportation in some way. The ramifications and interrelationships of urban passenger transportation are indeed widespread.

As a place to start, we will examine here the purely transportation elements of urban passenger systems, and will leave the broader implications and ramifications for the various specialists for Chapter 8.

A Mixed System with Joint Use

The first characteristic of urban passenger systems is that the system is a mix of both private and for-hire modes. The outstanding privately owned mode is the personal automobile. We have already noted the six outstanding characteristics of the private automobile: economy, comfort, convenience, speed, safety, and individualism. These characteristics mean that the private automobile predominates in the urban setting just as it does in the intercity setting. Other privately owned means such as bicycles, mopeds, and motorcycles are also important as alternatives in urban passenger systems.

However, side by side, there exists a series of for-hire modes that more or less compete with the privately owned modes. These are made up of transit bus systems; heavy-rail fixed-guide systems like subways, BART, MARTA, and Washington Metro; light-rail systems and streetcars, trolley coaches; taxis; and carpools and vanpools. The railroad commuter service discussed above is also a part of urban transportation systems in some areas.

The second characteristic is that many of these systems jointly use the public way. With the exception of the heavy-rail, commuter systems and a few parts of light-rail that are elevated or underground, all the rest depend on the public streets and roads for their guideways. Since the streets and roads are part of the social overhead or infrastructure provided by society as a whole, this joint use leads to the twin problems of who pays for what use of which public facility and who benefits from what use of which facility.

The Dominant Role of Governments

Not only is society involved in providing the way (streets and roads) but it is also involved in direct support of many of the urban passenger systems. Beginning in 1964, the federal government made a commitment of extensive grants for capital improvement of various urban systems (see

Chapter 12). In a 1974 act, the federal government added grants to assist in covering operating deficits of urban systems. These programs have grown over the years to the point where the most recent act (Federal Mass Transportation Act of 1987) allocated $16.5 billion over the five years 1987–1991 for various urban systems. We will discuss the details of these various federal acts in the next chapter.

But public aid to urban systems is not limited to the federal government. All levels of government are involved. State and local governments have played an increasing role and the federal government a somewhat smaller role. In 1987, for all systems, the farebox returned about 37 percent of operating revenues, state and local assistance grants about 51 percent (up from 32 percent in 1975), federal grants about 7 percent (down from 17 percent in 1980), and nontransportation revenues about 5 percent. The particular mix of revenues for operations varies by type of system and by locality, of course, but it is fair to say that on average somewhere between 50 and 60 percent of operating revenues in urban systems are derived from various levels of governments, not from users.

Turning to the capital side, the role of the federal government is even larger. In 1987, the federal government provided over 75 percent of all capital invested in the various systems; state governments, almost 10 percent; and local governments, about 15 percent. The federal capital assistance grant program, originally begun in 1964, continues to be the major source of money for improving and upgrading urban transportation systems.

Public Passenger System Characteristics

The transit bus dominates the industry. There were 2,672 motor bus systems in the United States in 1987. These bus systems used 57,687 vehicles (63 percent of total industry), generated 1.9 billion vehicle-miles (65 percent of total industry), carried 5.2 billion passengers (62 percent of total industry), and produced 19.7 billion passenger-miles (50 percent of total industry). Transit motor buses operate in cities of all sizes and almost everywhere in urban places in the country. Table 7.8 shows the total transit system by type of operation and illustrates the domination of the transit motor bus.

Demand response systems, commonly called dial-a-ride, are very numerous but produce relatively few vehicle-miles, passenger trips, or passenger-miles. Most of these are operated by public agencies or philanthropic groups like the Red Cross and carry a few passengers on short trips where transit is not readily available or cannot handle the disabled and so forth. Typically, the operation is in small vans or leased taxis and the user calls in ahead of time to arrange a ride. Dispatchers try to group several passengers going to the same area for shopping, doctors, or centers for the elderly. The fare often is subsidized and considered a social service in many dial-a-ride operations; in others, dial-a-ride may be an extension of a scheduled bus system where densities are low — picking up passengers and delivering them to a bus stop or distributing passengers from a bus stop.

Heavy-rail systems are found in Atlanta, Baltimore, Boston, Chicago, Cleveland, Miami, New York, Philadelphia, San Francisco, and Washington, D.C. These systems carry many passengers — about half as many as the 2,672 bus systems (see Table 7.8) — and generated 11.1 billion passenger-miles in 1987. Many are underground or elevated for a portion of their system.

Light-rail (mostly using the public street for its right of way) has been quite popular among the newer systems built in recent years. These systems are found in Boston, Buffalo, Cleveland, Detroit, Fort Worth, Newark, New Orleans, Philadelphia, Pittsburgh, Portland, Sacramento, San Diego, San Francisco, San Jose, and Seattle. Sometimes these are part of a multimodal system (for example, bus, heavy-rail, and light-rail) and sometimes a portion of these systems will be elevated or underground.

Commuter rail has already been noted above and is found in Boston, Chicago, Los Angeles, New York, Philadelphia, Pittsburgh, San Francisco, and Washington, D.C. These systems use regular rail tracks and produced 6.8 billion passenger-miles and carried 311 million passengers in 1987.

Another interesting characteristic is the matter of ownership. Some 1,435 of the 2,672 transit systems (29 percent) are publicly owned. However, these publicly owned systems own or lease 81 percent of the vehicles and generate 89 percent of the vehicle-miles and 96 percent of the passenger trips. Obviously there are many smaller privately owned transit systems, but public ownership tends to predominate in urban transit systems.

In 1987, about 70.6 percent of transit expenses were for labor (Table 7.8 shows there are 266,020 employees), materials and supplies make up 10.9 percent of expenses (all transit consumed 653 million gallons of diesel fuel, 57 million gallons of gasoline, and 4.7 million kilowatt hours of electricity in 1987), and other expenses include 4.3 percent casualty and liability costs, 3.7 percent utilities, 4.8 percent purchased transportation, 4.7 percent for services, and 1.0 percent other.

Average revenue per passenger was 61.8 cents in 1987, with the high adult fare being $2.75 and the low fare "free." Flat fares predominate — say 75 cents — but 30 percent of transit systems charge extra for a transfer, 8 percent have peak period surcharges, and 33 percent have zone fares. Total passenger revenue in 1987 was $5.9 billion (36.9 percent) and

Table 7.8 Transit Systems Characteristics, 1987

Type	Number	Vehicles	Employees	Vehicle-miles (millions)	Passenger trips (millions)	Passenger-miles (millions)
Motor bus	2,672	57,687	157,350	1,927	5,633	19,756
Demand response	2,569	16,059	24,498	305	70	421
Heavy-rail	12	10,168	51,334	490	2,402	11,198
Light-rail	14	766	3,818	18	133	405
Trolley bus	5	671	2,112	15	141	223
Commuter rail	12	4,656	23,554	189	311	6,819
Cable car	1	44	(a)	(a)	(a)	(a)
Automated guideway	4	88	(a)	(a)	(a)	(a)
Van pool	21	872	(a)	(a)	(a)	(a)
Ferry boat	25	92	2,806	2	44	211
Other	5	12	548	16	32	222
Total	5,048(b)	91,115	266,020	2,962	8,766	39,255

(a): Included in "other"
(b): Total is not sum of all modes, since many systems operate more than one mode.
Source: American Public Transit Association, *Transit Fact Book 1988*, Washington, D.C., 1988, Table 1, pp. 10–12. Copyright 1988. Used by permission.

$8 billion was provided in operating assistance from state, local, and federal governments. Total operating expenses (including depreciation and amortization) were $15.9 billion as compared with total revenues (including assistance) of $13.9 billion in 1987. Urban transit systems are rarely profitable and urban transit passengers rarely pay the full operating costs of the service.

Taxis, Carpools, and Vanpools

Taxis are not considered part of the transit industry, except where used in a dial-a-ride service. However, this service is an important part of for-hire public transportation and had a gross revenue of $6.5 billion in 1987. In 1986, 286,000 people were cab drivers or chauffeurs. There are two basic fare systems: a meter with a "drop charge" plus a per-mile fee, or zone fares and flat fares. Almost always fares are regulated by local or state governments. Taxis are organized three ways: employee-driver, lessee-driver, and owner-driver. An employee-driver operates a car owned by a company and is paid a commission, usually 43–50 percent of the fare. In a 1975 study, employee-drivers made up 71 percent of taxi operators. Lessee-drivers and owner-drivers are independent contractors. Lessee operations make up about 20 percent of total cabs and the drivers pay daily, weekly, or monthly fees to use the vehicle. Owner-drivers own their own vehicles, of course, and make up about 9 percent of the industry. Many taxicab firms are small (25 percent of the firms own fewer than 10 vehicles) and carry about 3 percent of the passengers. Firms with 10 to 24 cabs make up 38 percent of the industry and carry 15 percent of the passengers. Large firms (200 or more taxis) make up only 4 percent of the industry but carry 42 percent of the passengers. Cabs are routed on a point-to-point basis rather than regular routes and tend to be important to two groups of passengers: businesspeople and high-income passengers who use a cab because of its convenience, and low-income taxi-dependent people who don't own a car.

There are no good current data on carpools, yet we know this is an increasingly popular way to travel to and from work. In a 1975 survey, about 15.5 million of the over 80 million people in the work force used carpools, and 44.8 million, or 56 percent, used private automobiles. Both carpooling and vanpooling have increased in popularity since that date. Carpooling is often informally arranged among people working at the same location. The major motivation is economic, each person cutting his or her transportation bill markedly by pooling expenses. Look again at Table 7.4 and note the per-person per-mile costs of driving a private car if occupancy is four rather than one — 9.5 cents instead of 38.2 cents on an intermediate-sized car.

Vanpools are a growing alternative to the private car. The twenty-one vanpool systems in Table 7.8 are those which are part of transit systems. We know that many more vanpooling arrangements exist and are privately owned.

A number of firms and public agencies promote carpooling and vanpooling. One common device is for firms and agencies to furnish preferred parking for vehicles used in carpools and vanpools. Another popular device that has led to some of the more successful vanpooling operations has been that of the employer buying or leasing a van for multiple-occupancy travel to and from work. Often one employee is assigned to drive the vehicle and pay the operating expenses. A typical arrangement is a twelve-seat van with all expenses prorated by ten — the driver retaining the revenue from two seats as his or her pay and having use of the vehicle on weekends. Since the destination at work in the morning and origination at work in the evening is the same, these arrangements can be economical and sometimes pleasant and sociable. Studies by the U.S. Department of Transportation in the mid-1980s indicated that the cost of operating a twelve-passenger van was 33.2 cents per mile. Divide this by ten or twelve and it is apparent that per-person per-mile expenses are smaller (3 cents) in a vanpool operation than in any other mode. The firm or agency gains in several ways: required employee parking and security is much reduced (one parking space as compared to twelve), absenteeism seems to be less with group travel, employee stress and fatigue from commuting are less, and the firm or agency is making a social contribution by lessening congestion and pollution.

Outlook

Urban transportation systems will continue to present a challenge in the future. It is probable that problems will become greater, not less, as the nation continues to urbanize. During the Reagan administration, the role of the federal government in subsidizing operating costs was reduced, forcing state and local governments to play a greater role. If the federal role in providing capital costs should decrease in the future, a greater financial burden will be placed on the user of the service and on state and local governments, or service levels will have to be cut. Perhaps all three — less service, higher fares, and more state or local support — will be the result.

Urban transportation systems are an integral part of many social, economic, and ecological problems, as we shall discuss in the next chapter. American cities are fast running out of space to operate and park the multitude of private cars. A partial answer to the problem lies in multiple occupancy vehicles — an attribute of all the urban transportation systems discussed above. The 1990s will be a period of some uncertainty about urban transportation systems — not that the need or demand will diminish but rather where the funds will come from and how soon the urban population will embrace multiple occupancy systems.

SUMMARY

Passenger transportation will undoubtedly continue to be dominated by privately owned vehicles and publicly provided ways in the form of streets, highways, and airways. For-hire passenger transportation by various modes remains an alternative to and competes with the private automobile, and almost all of these, except rail commuter and heavy-rail fixed-guideway transit systems, will be joint users of the public streets, roads, and airways. The degree of public support for both capital and operations for roads, streets, airways, commuter rail, and transit systems will continue to be a challenging problem in the years ahead.

It is doubtful that America will abandon the private car in spite of its economic, social, and ecological costs. However, for some uses we may hope that multiple occupancy systems will help alleviate the problems in the urban setting. The next chapter will discuss some of the problems of passenger transportation.

ADDITIONAL READINGS

American Public Transit Association, *Transit Fact Book 1988*, Washington.

Coyle, John J., Edward J. Bardi, and Joseph L. Cavinato, *Transportation*, 2nd ed., St. Paul: West Publishing Co., 1986.
    Chapter 9, "Passenger Transportation and Tourism," pp. 176–90.

Fair, Marvin L., and Ernest W. Williams, Jr., *Transportation and Logistics*, Rev. ed., Plano, Texas: Business Publications, Inc., 1981.
    Chapter 7, "Intercity Passenger Logistics," pp. 102–20.
    Chapter 8, "Urban Logistics: Human and Goods," pp. 121–41.

Farris, Martin T., and Forrest E. Harding, *Passenger Transportation*, Englewood Cliffs, N.J.: Prentice-Hall, 1976.
    Chapter 2, "Economic and Physical Systems," pp. 17–62.
    Chapter 6, "Urban Transportation," pp. 183–216.

Gilbert, Gorman, and Robert E. Samuels, *The Taxicab: An Urban Transportation Survivor*, Chapel Hill, N.C.: The University of North Carolina Press, 1982.
Chapter 8, "The Economics of Taxicab Operations," pp. 103–22.
Hamer, Andrew M., *The Selling of Rapid Transit: A Critical Look at Urban Transportation Planning*, Lexington, Mass.: D. C. Heath, 1976.
Chapter 2, "Defining the Problem: Public Transportation Criteria and Rail Rapid Transit Mythology, " pp. 19–34.
Chapter 3, "Rail Versus Bus: The Art of Evaluating Alternative Modes," pp. 35–60.
Harper, Donald V., *Transportation in America: Users, Carriers, Government*, Englewood Cliffs, N.J.: Prentice-Hall, 1978.
Chapter 14, "Air Transportation," pp. 285–316.
Hazard, John L., *Transportation: Management, Economics, Policy*, Centreville, Md.: Cornell Maritime Press, 1977.
Chapter 9, "Air Transportation: Essential Characteristics," pp. 227–49.
Chapter 17, "Urban and Intermodal Transportation," pp. 488–526.
Lieb, Robert C., *Transportation*, 3rd ed., Reston, Va.: Reston Publishing Co., 1985.
Chapter 4, "The Highway System," pp. 61–86.
Chapter 6, "The Airline Industry," pp. 113–34.
Chapter 21, "Problems of Metropolitan Transportation," pp. 449–59.
Owen, Wilford, *Transportation for Cities*. Washington: The Brookings Institution, 1976.
Chapter 1, "Moving in the Metropolis," pp. 4–13.
Chapter 2, "Federal Aid and Key Policy Issues," pp. 17–21.
Smerk, George M., *Urban Mass Transportation: A Dozen Years of Federal Policy*, Bloomington, Ind.: Indiana University Press, 1974.
Chapter 1, "The Urban Transportation Crisis and the Growing Role of the Federal Government," pp. 5–89.
Stephenson, Frederick J., Jr., *Transportation USA*, Reading, Mass.: Addison-Wesley Publishing Co., 1987.
Chapter 7, "U.S. Intercity Passenger Train Transportation," pp. 172–88.
Chapter 17, "Personal Transportation Management, Strategy, and Decision Making," pp. 465–89.
Taff, Charles A., *Commercial Motor Transportation*, 7th ed., Centreville, Md.: Cornell Maritime Press, 1986.
Chapter 19, "Intercity Passenger Operations," pp. 388–402.
Chapter 20, "Urban Mass Transit," pp. 403–16.
Talley, Wayne K., *Introduction to Transportation*, Cincinnati, Ohio: South-West Publishing Co., 1983.
Chapter 13, "Passenger Transportation: Air Carriers," pp. 249–68.
Chapter 14, "Passenger Transportation: Surface Carriers," pp. 269–86.
U.S. Department of Transportation, *National Urban Mass Transportation Statistics*, Washington, May 1981.
Wood, Donald F., and James C. Johnson, *Contemporary Transportation*, 3rd ed., New York: Macmillan Publishing Co., 1989.
Chapter 5, "Highway Carriers," pp. 87–115.
Chapter 9, "Domestic Aviation," pp. 213–48.
Chapter 17, "Managing Transportation in the Public Sector," pp. 441–78.

CHAPTER 8

PASSENGER TRANSPORTATION PROBLEMS

Passenger transportation problems are of interest for three reasons. First, they are of interest in themselves since almost everyone participates in some way in passenger transportation. In our society, it has become an integral part of our lives, and therefore, its problems are experienced by all of us.

Second, freight and passenger transportation services are uniquely and closely interrelated. Often the two services are performed by the same for-hire firm, using the same ways and sometimes even the same vehicles, terminals, and personnel. Profits or losses made by such firms in one service may to some extent offset losses or profits in the other service. Also, public aids in constructing, maintaining, or operating ways, or other kinds of subsidies or taxes affect both freight and passenger services. Both private and for-hire transport of goods and people are intermingled on public ways. Clearly, what happens in passenger transportation may have significant effects on the costs and prices of freight services, as well as upon their quantities and qualities.

Finally, the transportation of people is a common element in many seemingly diverse problems such as urban redevelopment, pollution, congestion, energy availability, safety, budget priorities, bankruptcy, and diplomacy.

The purpose of this chapter is not to specify solutions to the problems of passenger transportation nor even to present a complete list of all its problems. Rather, the purpose is to point out a few of the ramifications of passenger transportation and to introduce the very frustrating but pervasive fact that passenger transportation is both a great economic benefit to society and the creator of a multitude of social ills and problems.

THE NATURE OF PASSENGER TRANSPORTATION

There are several distinctive aspects of passenger transportation that lead to problems in this area. These distinctive characteristics include the predominance of private carriage, the supremacy of air transportation for long-distance movements, by-product effects, the variability factor, the instantaneous and perishability factor, the substitutability factor, the investment cost factor, and the complexity of markets.

Predominance of Private Carriage

The private automobile provides far more passenger transportation than any other mode. The transportation of people is measured in passenger-miles, and automobiles currently produce almost 80 percent of all intercity passenger-miles.

Figure 7.1 in Chapter 7 shows intercity passenger-miles by mode and the changes from 1940 to 1987 and should be reviewed at this point. Note that the scale is logarithmic and that automobiles produced 1,495 billion passenger-miles in 1987; air, 329 billion; bus 23 billion; and rail, 12 billion.

Further, private automobiles account for by far the largest expenditure of funds for passenger transportation — $424 billion (83 percent) of the total dollars expended in 1987. The purchase of an automobile is a major expenditure for most people. The operating costs of fuel, repairs, depreciation, and the like are a major share of individual budgets. Some idea of the importance of this item can be gained by looking again at the nation's estimated passenger bill in Chapter 7. Most of this huge annual expenditure is for the purchase of new or used automobiles, tires, repairs, gasoline and oil, insurance, tolls, registration fees, and similar items by automobile owners. Although for-hire passenger transportation is important and provides valuable communications and cultural links among various areas, private carriage is the predominant form of passenger transportation. This characteristic leads to interesting problems.

First, very little public control exists for private carriage. Safety regulations and controls are well known, although regularly violated or abused. There is practically no price control for vehicles or operating costs. Individuals are on their own as to safety and price. Recently, society has begun to impose environmental controls in this area, but even here it is difficult to place and enforce restrictions on millions of car owners even though society as a whole might benefit.

Second, automobile owners tend to be ignorant of capital costs. The whole area of purchasing and financing private automobiles is one of bargaining and inexactness. Finance charges may be hidden, and equipment options on automobiles are such that no standard price or cost really exists. The trade-in situation is chaotic. Each purchase is an individual bargaining transaction.

Third, automobile owners tend to overlook operating costs. Purchases of gasoline and oil are small but frequent expenditures. Most drivers rarely calculate their operating costs per mile. Depreciation is a major operating expense overlooked by most. Fuel taxes and support of streets and highways are usually hidden in the price of gasoline or repairs. Review the breakdown of per-mile costs of owning and operating an automobile given in Chapter 7.

The result of consumer lack of knowledge of capital and operating costs is that most automobile owners have little idea of what it costs them to operate their cars, and without knowledge of those costs, it is impossible to make a rational choice among alternative means of travel. We know or can be quoted the bus, air, or rail fares between two points, but we have little idea of the auto "fare" between the same two points. Because of the private automobile's convenience, we often decide to travel by car. If we actually knew our costs, we might find that driving our car is two to three times as expensive as using for-hire transportation. As noted in Chapter 7, the Motor Vehicle Manufacturers Association estimates that it costs 38.2 cents per mile to own and operate an intermediate-sized car over 10,000 miles a year for a six-year cycle in 1988. The average revenue per passenger-mile in 1987 for air was 11.3 cents, for Amtrak 10.6 cents, and for intercity bus 9.9 cents — and average transit fares were 61.8 cents for an average trip of five miles. But Chapter 7 also noted the private automobile's characteristics of comfort, convenience, speed, perceived safety, and individuality which tend to overcome purely economic cost considerations. Further, since many costs of owning the private automobile are fixed or semifixed in nature, it is rational to drive the car more miles *once the car is purchased*, and perpassenger per-mile costs decrease with multiple occupancy. The result is that travel by private automobile continues to increase markedly, whereas passenger transportation by for-hire modes grows slowly.

However, a substantial portion of the transportation-related problems of society are directly connected to private automobiles. The environmental effects of transportation like congestion and pollution, noted in Chapter 3, are caused predominantly by motor vehicles. The difficulty of supporting and maintaining a healthy for-hire passenger transportation industry, whether publicly or privately owned, is directly related to the wide use of private automobiles. The sociological effects of transportation on neighborhoods, urban redevelopment, urban sprawl, and the like are also uniquely related to the private automobile.

The Supremacy of Air Transportation

Air transport has been the most important for-hire intercity passenger mode since the mid-1950s. Air transportation carries over 90 percent of all intercity for-hire passenger-miles in the nation. If one considers only the number of passengers, however, the situation is somewhat different, with air carrying 40 percent, bus 31 percent, and rail 29 percent. Since air travel typically is for long distances, air passenger-miles are of greater importance in intercity travel data.

Air travel is the most expensive type of for-hire passenger movement and the fastest. Capital costs and operating costs also are extremely high by air transport. Nevertheless, travel by air is only about one-third as expensive per passenger-mile in intercity travel as travel by private automobile.

If one considers commuter travel and movements within urban places, the picture changes again. The private automobile dominates with transit a poor second. Air transportation is predominantly an intercity or inter-continental mode of transportation. This has some implications, pointed out below, for market complications and the special problem of transit.

Many of the transportation problems of our society are related to air transportation. Congestion of airways, the condition of highways leading to airports, both air and noise pollution, the locational problems of airports, and controversies over the role of the public in support of air transportation are but a few of the policy problems in this area. Additionally, since air transport is the only mode of domestic transportation deeply involved in international transportation, it creates a variety of political and diplomatic problems.

By-Product Effects

Under certain circumstances, passenger transportation is a by-product of freight transportation. Under other circumstances, the transportation of goods is a by-product of the movement of people. Either way, a definite by-product effect is at work and causes policy problems.

In rail transportation, passenger business is a by-product of the much larger and more profitable freight transportation business. Indeed, most rail passenger service is now provided by either Amtrak or regional public authorities. Historically, it was often the other way around, with railroads being built into specific areas primarily as carriers of people into new territories. The development of freight transportation came only after settlement. In this sense, it is sometimes said that passenger transportation pioneers for freight transportation.

In motor transportation, the carriage of mail and passengers certainly preceded freight transportation. The same situation exists in air transportation, where passenger movement still is by far most important and is thought by many to be pioneering for a future heavy freight movement.

Regardless of which comes first, the by-product effect leads to problems. First, since much of the early development of transportation has been accomplished with public aid, the question arises as to whether it is the transportation of people or of freight that is being subsidized. Given the fact that the various modes of transport have grown up during different historical periods, it is likely that a developed or older mode will find itself in competition with a currently subsidized new mode.

Rail passenger transportation illustrates this problem. Much of our highway system development is justified on the basis of providing either easy and better travel for the general public or improved mail service. Passenger transportation thus provides a strong rationale for better roads. But improved highways are equally available for truck movements. Railroads pay property taxes, a portion of which go into improved highways, justified as necessary to move passengers, only to find that they are helping their competitors improve their capacities to move freight. Similarly, public aid to air transportation is justified on the basis of moving people and improving communications. Yet the capacity to move freight is a by-product of better air transportation.

A second problem exists in cost allocation and subsequent pricing. When two services, passenger movement and freight movement, are produced by the same capital and the same operators, what portion of the costs should be allocated to each? In air transportation, for example, it is difficult to ascertain completely how much of the total costs should be allocated to passengers and how much to freight. To be sure, some costs are incurred for only one specific service. Yet a large portion of common costs remain that are incurred for both services. What is a fair allocation?

The question takes on added significance when we remember that rates and fares are at least partially based on costs. Therefore, if the allocation of costs is incorrect, the fare structure probably is incorrect as well, and one service is subsidizing another.

The Variability Factor

Passenger transportation is characterized by extreme variability during the hours of the day, the days of the week, and the months of the year. Whereas freight tends to move continuously and at all hours, automobile traffic, commuter trains, intercity buses and transit buses, and planes do not. People move to and from work in a definite pattern. The weekend traffic jam is also evidence of this variability factor, and the Christmas holiday congestion on planes, buses, and trains illustrates the seasonal factor.

Facilities and labor in passenger transportation service tend to be used very intensively during peak movement periods. Indeed, to some travelers, the capital and labor committed seem inadequate at these times. Yet owing to the variability factor, this same labor and capital often remain idle for extended periods of low use or nonuse. The rates or fares for the services provided, though, must recoup the costs of this idleness as well as the costs of use.

This factor is particularly acute in urban passenger transportation. Commuter trains and buses are used intensively from 6 A.M. to 9 A.M. and from 4 P.M. to 7 P.M. Much of the rest of the day the crews, equipment, and capital facilities are idle or underused. It is not uncommon for one crew of operators to work the morning rush hours, and another crew to be hired for the evening rush hours.

The variability factor also is reflected in streets, highways, bridges, tunnels, and terminals. These facilities must be constructed with peak periods in mind, but resources for transportation are not unlimited. Allocations must be made, and the result often is inadequate facilities during peak periods. Many of the problems of urban transportation relate directly to this variability factor.

The variability factor also affects air transportation. Certain hours of departure and arrival are most popular with the traveling public. All airlines would prefer to make profits by serving the public at the most popular hours. The result has been a jamming of scheduled departures and arrivals at these hours. The result is inadequate gate space and inadequate runway capacity of airports and congestion of airways at certain times but underutilization at other times. This problem has increased to the point where the FAA has been forced to impose limits on the number of takeoffs and landings at certain hours at several of the country's busier airports. There is also a national debate over the allocation of "landing slots" and how to increase airway and airport capacity.

Price discounts may help partially in offsetting the variability factor. For some time airlines have offered lower fares during certain days of the week, during nighttime hours, and during certain seasons of the year. Rail passenger service has made some small use of the same device, and buses have attempted on occasion to shift passenger demand by use of price discounts. It is rare to find price discounts related to time of departure or arrival in freight transportation (with the exception of some differential rates, usually where circuitous routing is involved), but it is common in passenger transportation. The variability factor accounts for this peculiarity.

Instantaneous and Perishability Factor

The demand for passenger transportation also has the characteristic of being instantaneous and perishable. Although it its true that advance reservations are made for some kinds of passenger transportation, such as pleasure cruises, vacation trips by air, and Pullman travel by Amtrak, much passenger transportation occurs without much planning. People want to get on a bus, train, plane, subway, taxi, or car, and go immediately.

This causes a problem for for-hire carriers as well as for public planners. First, uncertainty of use is high. Past trends may help, but it is almost axiomatic in passenger transportation that actual use of equipment and facilities is hard to predict. Second, there is a tendency to overinvest and create excess capacity. Not knowing the demand, a supplier typically will provide more capacity than necessary. This tendency toward over-capacity is found in air, bus, rail, private automobile, and transit. Although some of this comes from the need to cover the peak period utilization (variability), much of its comes from the instantaneous nature of demand and the investment factors mentioned below.

To further complicate matters, passenger service is nonstorable and highly perishable. Overcapacity at some times would not be serious if output could be stored and brought out of inventory to meet peak or unexpected demands. But seat-miles cannot be stored for future use. Unfilled seats are output lost forever.

Substitutability Factor

A high degree of substitutability exists in passenger transportation. This is seen in four types of competition: intermodal, intramodal, interclass, and dollar competition.

Within limits, demand not served by one mode can quickly shift to another. A private car can substitute for a bus or a commuter train, an air carrier for an intercity passenger train, a cruise ship for an international air carrier, and the like. This modal substitutability is sometimes called *modal-split*. Many factors affect intermodal competition. These may include prices, availability, comfort, and convenience. Each market differs from others, and what is true for one area of passenger transportation may not be true in another. Yet demand can and does shift from one mode to another.

A second type of substitutability is intramodal. Air carriers compete with air carriers, buses with buses, trains with trains. Competition among firms of the same mode may be intense, and passengers can and do choose between competing carriers. Price usually is a significant factor in intramodal competition, but services or the amenities of travel certainly are important also. Some air travelers, for example, choose a carrier based upon the in-flight movie being shown, the amount of leg room provided, the equipment used, the schedule flown, or the destination reached. Time of departure and arrival is an important factor in business travel. The services provided by a given firm may have extreme importance and hence provide an explanation for carriers' efforts to focus on services through advertising and promotion.

Another type of substitutability is that between classes. Most products or services are produced as a single class or entity. Rarely would one find a steel company advertising first-class, second-class, and economy-class steel, or plumbers telling customers that they will give them first-class, second-class, or third-class service. But in passenger transportation, classes of service are common. A carrier literally may be competing with itself. This competition may be based on price or it may be based on the bundle of services, such as the free drink, free meal, greater leg room, or a combination of all these and other features. Whatever its base, interclass competition exists in almost all passenger transportation.

Dollar (income) competition leads to still another type of substitutability. This is particularly important in the pleasure travel market. After basic necessities are purchased, a consumer has only a certain amount of discretionary income left to spend on many competing things. A vacation trip competes with new furniture, a fur coat, a new automobile, the need to save for children's education, or just the desire to save because of future uncertainties. All goods and services compete for consumers' dollars, but in parts of passenger transportation, competition is for discretionary income. This may be a very intense type of competition. Such dollar competition helps explain why nontransportation factors may have a significant effect on passenger transportation demand at times. If the future looks good, demand for vacation travel may be high. But if the future looks questionable, passenger transportation may decline — even though it is cheaper, more intensively advertised, and offers more services than during a more prosperous period. Some parts of passenger transportation such as the journey to work, of course, are not so susceptible to this effect.

Investment Cost Factor

Passenger transportation, like other transportation, has high capital costs, large fixed obligations, low incremental costs, and long cycles of planning and production. These characteristics may lead to severe policy problems.

Passenger transportation can be provided only with large investments in vehicles and operating equipment, ways (highways, airways, railways, streets, and fixed guideways), and terminals. This imposes a high level of fixed costs on the firm or public entity providing these facilities. Hence capital investment is made only after much planning and tends to last for a long time. Even though demand can and does shift intermodally, intramodally, and interclass, a long-term commitment must be made. Often it takes many years for investment to adjust to demand, if it ever does, and capacity remains where it is not needed while other areas are short of facilities. This is true for all areas of passenger transportation.

There are several adverse effects of these high capital costs, long production cycles, and durable capital. First, there is a tendency to overinvest to ensure that sufficient facilities are available. Second, some facilities may be underutilized, while others are inadequate. Rapid shifts to match supply to demand are impossible or impractical. Third, extensive long-run planning is necessary if maladjustments are to be minimized. The complications of investment cost can become extreme in passenger transportation policy and may lead to considerable frustration on the part of users as well as carriers and planners.

Market Complexity

The market for all transportation is complex and has many diverse interrelationships. This is particularly so for the market for passenger transportation. There are at least three distinct general types of markets for passenger transportation — urban, intercity, and international or intercontinental. Different competitive relationships exist and different forces of supply and demand are at work in each.

The urban market is the most complex market for passenger transportation. More social and policy problems exist here, and more transportation modes are involved than in the other two types of markets. People can move within urban areas by private automobiles, city buses, streetcars, commuter trains, carpools or vanpools, taxicabs, subways, motorbikes, mopeds, bicycles, or walking. No one market encompasses all these modes, but it is common to have at least four or five ways of moving in an urban area.

Space for urban vehicular movement and for parking or temporary storage of vehicles when not in use is at a premium. Congestion and interference of one mode of movement with another are a further problem. Regulation and control of safety, prices and fares, service frequency, and service adequacy are still other problems found in urban transportation.

Ecological and sociological problems become acute in the urban market. Pollution, congestion, urban redevelopment, city planning, traffic engineering, effects on trips to work, effects on the characters of neighborhoods, and the like are examples of the social and ecological problems involved. Some of these effects are discussed below.

The intercity market for passenger movement involves air, private automobile, rail, and bus services. Distances traveled are much longer and motivation for travel differs from the urban market. Commuting is of much less importance, and business and pleasure travel are of primary importance. Sometimes it is useful to separate business travel from pleasure travel in the intercity passenger transportation market. Certainly different motivations for each exist, and the matter of economy, speed, luxury, and mobility for each class of travelers varies.

Since freight movement also tends to be intercity in nature, it is in this market that the question of one service subsidizing another becomes most important. The degree of public support of highways, railways, and airways is an important subsidy question. Variability factors cause problems here, but they are a somewhat different type than in urban transportation. Regulatory problems are of a different nature in intercity travel than in the urban market.

The intercontinental passenger transportation market is somewhat different from the intercity market and vastly different from the urban market. The modes involved here mainly are air and steamship. Motivations for travel are complex, involving vacations, educational travel, tours, business travel, diplomatic travel, and a variety of other reasons. This market responds differently from other markets to price variations and to the availability of facilities related to transportation such as hotels, restaurants, and recreational facilities.

In addition to the complexities of the three distinctive passenger markets, marketing institutions and approaches in passenger transportation differ from those in freight transportation. Basically, passenger transportation is retail oriented, whereas freight transportation is wholesale or producer oriented. In selling passenger services, many customers are involved and the service is usually sold quite frequently. In freight movements, relatively fewer customers are involved and sales contact may not be as frequent. Certainly in freight transportation, most units are large (carload, truckload, large air shipment), whereas in passenger transportation, units are small (a seat or reservation). The buyers of freight transportation tend to be more knowledgeable and specialized, whereas the buyers of passenger transportation are more casual and less informed, and the movement itself is more incidental to other occupations.

Sometimes these different institutions and approaches are not recognized clearly by for-hire carriers. The sales effort differs for each group, and what may appeal to an industrial traffic manager may not appeal to a vacation traveler. More intermediaries such as travel agents are involved in passenger transportation, and the matter of how the customer is served often becomes more important than price or other considerations. By and large, buyers of both freight and passenger transportation are concerned with both prices and service. But service to a shipper is quite a different matter from service to a traveler. Service for the latter is considerably more complex.

In summary, the distinctive characteristics of the predominance of private carriage, the for-hire supremacy of air transportation, the by-product effects, the variability effects, the instantaneous and perishability effects, the substitutability effects, the investment cost effects, and market complexities cause numerous problems in the area of passenger transportation, thus differentiating it from freight transportation. This causes many complex problems.

THE SPECIAL PROBLEM OF TRANSIT

Many of the above characteristics apply to urban transportation, but some do not. However, in the post–World War II period, there has been a special problem with passenger transportation within the cities. This can be called the special problem of transit.

Transit operations were originally privately owned and profit making. The streetcar or trolley had much to do with the shape and layout of American cities. People lived along the streetcar lines, and most commercial and manufacturing operations took place in the central business district (CBD). With the coming of the automobile, particularly in the 1920s, this pattern began to change. Autos provided more flexibility both for residency and for commercial undertakings. The streetcar was fixed to a track and was inflexible. Slowly it was replaced by the more flexible motor bus.

During the Depression of the 1930, even the motor bus was losing passengers because of both the automobile and the difficult economic times. With gas rationing and no new cars during the war, transit reached its high point in ridership at almost 28 billion passengers.

After the war, transit declined as automobiles took over urban travel. Suburbs grew more rapidly than the central cities. Shopping centers replaced the downtown shopping district, and many industries moved away from the contested CBD. Privately owned transit slowly began to be abandoned in the face of massive losses, and city after city took over the operation of transit systems. Today many transit operations are publicly owned (29 percent) and they carry the vast majority of the passengers (96 percent).

But a change in ownership did not improve things and transit continued to decline. By 1972, transit ridership had declined to 7.3 billion, about one-fourth its wartime peak. Figure 8.1 depicts these long-run changes.

As ridership declined in the 1950s and 1960s and losses mounted, service deteriorated. Equipment was not replaced, lesser-used routes were dropped, headways (time between buses) were lengthened — all in an attempt to stem losses. Political representatives of the cities cried out for federal aid and pointed out that all other means of passenger transportation received federal help.

Beginning in the 1960s, a federal aid program for transit was started. After a slow start, funding on the order of about $150 million a year was instituted. Grants were made primarily for capital — particularly equipment — on a two-thirds federal, one-third local basis. In the 1970s, society's concern deepened. For a time, the environmental aspects of transit were stressed. Buses carrying thirty to forty passengers helped alleviate congestion and pollution. Later in the 1970s, the beneficial energy aspects of transit were stressed. It took less scarce petroleum to move thirty to forty people in a bus than thirty to forty separate automobiles. Both these beneficial aspects remain today and will be discussed directly.

Federal aid was stepped up in the early 1970s to about $1 billion a year. In 1974, Congress appropriated about $2 billion a year for transit and began to allow money to be spent to subsidize operations as well as for capital. The matching ratios were changed to 80 percent federal and 20 percent local for capital and 50-50 for operations. By 1978, Congress had in place a program of spending almost $4 billion a year on transit aid. In 1982, this level of spending — $4 billion a year — was continued with a portion of the funds tied to the federal fuel tax increase (1 cent of the 5 cent increase — 4 cents to 9 cents per gallon — was for transit).

The latest five-year act was in 1987, when Congress appropriated $16.5 billion, over $3 billion a year. Portions of this ($6.2 billion) came out of the Highway Trust Fund (1 cent gas tax money) with a 75 percent federal and 25 percent local match for capital grants. The remaining $10.3 billion was in block grants with an 80 federal and 20 local match

Figure 8.1 Major Trends of Transit Ridership

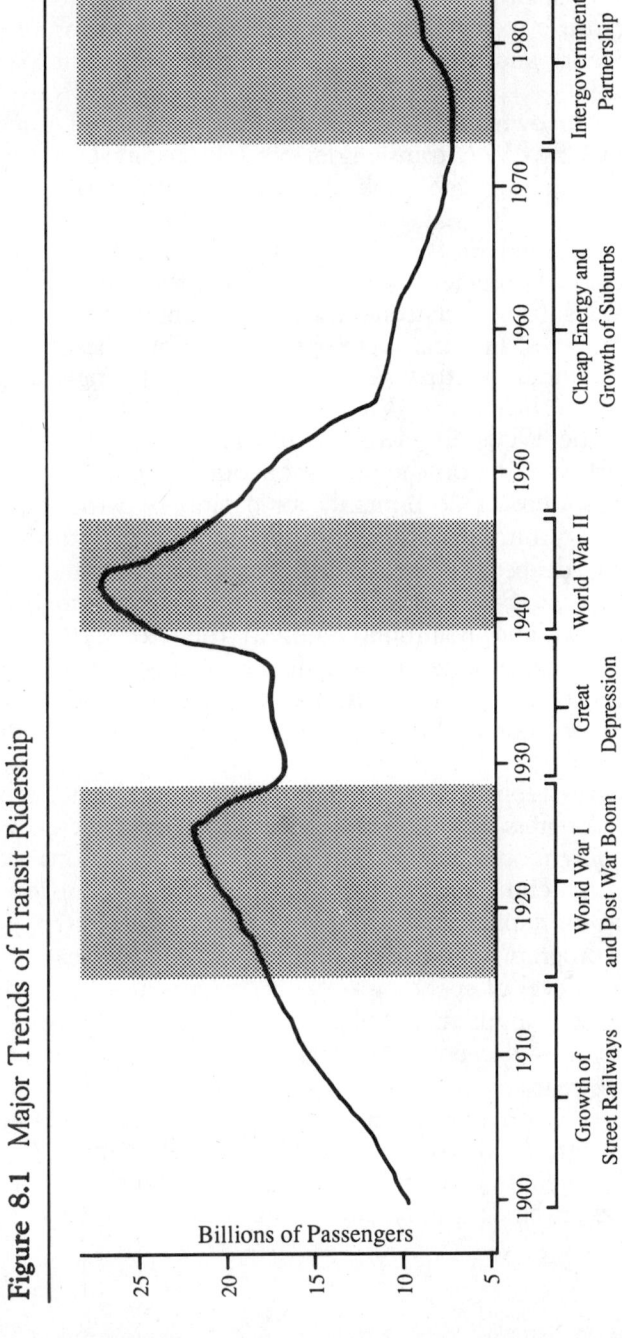

Source: American Public Transit Association, *Transit Fact Book 1988,* Washington, D. C., 1988, p. 31. Copyright 1988. Used by permission.

for capital and 50-50 for operating assistance. Most of the funds were directed toward cities over 200,000 in population and included various allocation formulas. An innovation in this act was "incentive grants" to systems which could show higher passenger-miles traveled per dollar of operating costs. Another innovation was the funding of ten regional research centers at universities. Table 8.1 gives the chronology of these social actions.

Table 8.1 Chronology of Federal Urban Transportation Policy

1961	Housing Act — Sets pattern of $25 million for demonstration projects on 2/3 federal, 1/3 local basis; $50 million for low-interest loans; administered by Housing and Home Finance Agency (later part of HUD).
1964	Urban Mass Transportation Act — First specific urban transportation act specifies $375 million for capital grants for three years on 2/3 - 1/3 basis; discretionary (Section 3) grants; also labor protection provisions (Section 13C).
1966	Amendments to 1964 Act — Congress appropriates $150 million for years 1967, 1968, 1969.
1968	Function transfer to DOT-UMTA moved from HUD to DOT.
1970	Urban Mass Transportation Assistance Act — Sets goal of $10 billion over twelve years in federal commitment; $3.1 billion committed for 1971.
1973	Highway Act — Allows diversion of funds from Highway Trust Fund, $780 million in 1974, $800 million in 1975 and 1976; cities allowed to substitute transit projects for Interstate Highway segments; $3 billion more under 1970 act; federal matching goes to 80 percent.
1974	National Mass Transportation Assistance Act — Second major act; $12 billion over six years program; $7.3 billion for Section 3 discretionary grants; $4 billion for formula grants (Section 5) based on population and population density; $.5 billion for rural transit; 80-20 match on capital grants; allows 50-50 operating grants for first time; half fares (or less) for elderly, students, disabled. One area recipient only and must have a five-year plan.

1978 Federal Public Transportation Act — Third major act; $15.2 billion for four years 1979–1983; $7.5 billion discretionary (Section 3) grants; $6.5 billion in formula grants (Section 5) broken into four tiers; basic tier: $3.5 billion (population and population density formula continuation of Section 5 of 1974 act), large-city tier: $1 billion (85 percent to cities over 750,000), rail-fixed guideway tier: $550 million (commuter systems based on train-miles and route-mile formula), bus tier: $1.425 billion (to purchase buses); $420 million rural assistance; $160 million for bus terminals; $120 million for intercity operations; continues 80-20 capital and 50-50 operating assistance match.

1982 Federal Public Transportation Act — Fourth major act; earmarks part of Highway Trust Fund for transit; $15.8 billion for four years 1983–1987; $4.2 billion from Highway Trust Fund (1 cent of 5 cent increase) to Section 3 discretionary grants but at 75-25 match; $1.2 billion Section 5 continuation for 1983 only; new Section 9 block grants, $9.5 billion for three years (88 percent to cities over 200,000, 8.5 percent to cities under 200,000, 3 percent to rural areas; formula on 88 percent = ½ bus revenue, ¼ population, ¼ population density plus portion reserved for rail).

1987 Federal Mass Transportation Act — Fifth major act; $16.5 billion for five years 1987–1991; $6.247 billion from Highway Trust Fund (1 cent gas tax) for capital in Section 3 discretionary grants at 75-25 match (40 percent for rail modernization, 40 percent for new fixed guideways, 10 percent for buses, and 10 percent at Secretary's discretion); $10.3 billion block grants in Sections 9 and 18, 80-20 match capital and 50-50 match operating assistance, $563 million per year to fixed guideway (population over 200,000 by formula), $2.5 million per year fixed guideway (incentive based on formula), $786 million per year for bus operations (areas over 200,000 by formula), $10.86 million per year bus incentive (based on formula), $17.2 million a year to urban areas under 200,000 (population based on formula), $5.86 million a year to rural areas plus percentage of Section 3 grants. New starts criteria, and $10 million per year to regional transportation research centers at universities.

Overall, the amount spent by the federal government to upgrade transit is not small. Spending and completing grants often lags appropriations. However, from 1965 to 1987 $34.8 billion has been spent in capital grants and $10.5 billion in operating grants. The amounts of federal grants per year are shown in Table 8.2.

Table 8.2 Federal Grants to Transit for Capital and Operations, 1965–1987 (in millions)

Year	Capital Grants	Operating Grants
1965–73	$ 2,256	—
1974	956	—
1975	1,287	143
1976	1,955	412
1977	1,724	572
1978	2,037	685
1979	2,102	869
1980	2,787	1,121
1981	2,946	1,230
1982	2,544	1,056
1983	3,162	888
1984	2,876	922
1985	2,510	881
1986	3,137	873
1987	2,476	820
Grand Total	$34,755	$10,472

Source: American Public Transit Association, *Transit Fact Book 1988*, Washington, D.C., 1988, pp. 57, 58. Copyright 1988. Used by permission.

In spite of these massive spending programs, transit ridership has increased very slowly. Note in Figure 8.1 that ridership increases slightly as transit systems are improved. Many fine new systems have been built in some cities, and most existing systems have been considerably improved. Many groups, such as the young, the elderly, the disabled, and the poor, were assisted by these improvements. Yet overall ridership has not gained as much as would be expected given the funds expended. Why?

The answer is complex but essentially turns on the American preference for the automobile and its inherent convenience and flexibility. Also, suburbanization of the population has made it difficult and expensive to maintain an efficient transit system. People still prefer to live in a spread-out manner and that means cars and streets and highways. Efficient transit operation depends on density of population, but the American dream is just the opposite. One of the great problems of passenger transportation is that viable public transportation with its many sociological, environmental, and energy benefits is contradictory to the American dream of a house in the suburbs with two cars in the garage.

SOCIAL AND ECONOMIC PROBLEMS

A number of problems arise from the distinctive characteristics of passenger transportation, in spite of the obvious economic benefits of an inexpensive, fast, and efficient system for moving people. Although not of equal importance, these problems fall into four groups: ecological, sociological, international, and energy considerations.

Ecological Problems

Our natural environment is a carefully balanced system of creation, life, and death. Ecology is the branch of biology that studies mutual inter-relationships among organisms and their environments. In recent years, the term has come to have a more specific popular meaning, however; it is currently used to refer to the study of the effects of the actions of human beings on the environmental balance and systems of nature. Passenger transportation is the cause of considerable ecological effects in this popular sense of the term.

As noted in Chapter 3, all transportation has ecological effects. However, because of the predominance of the private automobile and the supremacy of air transportation, the ecological effects of the movement of people are greater and more observable than the effects of transportation in general. These passenger transportation ecological effects are found principally in air and noise pollution and in the disturbing results associated with the construction of transportation facilities such as highways and airports.

There is little doubt that the gasoline-burning internal combustion engine emits a major part of the air pollutants found hovering over the urban areas of our nation. In the process of converting gasoline into energy, four classes of pollutants are manufactured. These are carbon monoxide, gaseous hydrocarbons and benzene compounds, nitrogen oxide compounds, and nongases or heavy particles such as lead. Through chemical reactions with sunlight and dirt and dust particles in the atmosphere, these compounds turn into the distressingly familiar smog which has come to be a sign of the concentrated presence of people. To a very marked degree, this type of pollution originates with the private automobile and to a smaller degree with airplanes.

Devices to control industrial pollutants are slowly being introduced and used. For a time, there was a tendency to blame air pollution almost solely upon industry and the visible pollution arising from the smoke-stacks of plants and industrial complexes. Slowly, though, the public learned that some pollutants are not easily visible to the naked eye and that the major offender is the private automobile. Although any one vehicle produces but a small amount of air pollution, in the aggregate, automobiles produce up to 90 percent of the air pollution in some locations. The knowledge that the total of many units, each producing but a little amount of pollution, actually is a serious problem was many years in coming.

During the late 1960s, the so-called environmental revolution led to great concern with the ecological effects of passenger transportation. Standards of allowable emissions from private automobiles were established, and goals for the 1970s were set. Various control devices were attempted with varying degrees of success. By and large, the establishment and enforcement of standards of allowable emissions are a governmental problem. Since each vehicle produces such a small increment to the total problem of air pollution, it is difficult to depend on individual action to solve the problem. Similarly, since air pollution does not respect the artificial boundaries of local governmental jurisdictions, an authority with very broad control is needed. Hence, federal standards were established for the 1970s.

One approach to the problem of air pollution from passenger transportation may be in developing new types of engines and fuels. Electric motors, steam-powered vehicles, internal combustion engines burning LPG or natural gas, and gasoline turbine engines are examples of attacking the problem by way of the propulsion system. All these systems have their advantages and disadvantages. But in all cases, these devices must compare favorably, economically and in performance, with the conventional internal combustion gasoline engine before they will have wide adoption.

The easiest and most direct way to handle the air pollution problem is at the manufacturing level. Equipping all new vehicles with pollution retarding devices at the time they are manufactured will go a long way toward solving the problem. Although devices are available for older vehicles, they must depend upon the individual actions of millions of car owners. Experience has shown that it is difficult to persuade large groups of individuals to act in concert on any social problem. Thus the solution to automobile air pollution will take a long time to work itself out.

Air pollution from airplanes is being solved in a more direct manner. After a series of lawsuits by local authorities during the late 1960s, airlines began to install pollution abatement devices on planes. Control was somewhat easier here, because local jurisdiction at airports is clear and the problem is localized to airports and to the landing and takeoff process. Air pollution arising during intercity flights is being solved by lesser-polluting engines.

Noise pollution caused by transportation also is a problem. Transportation by nature is noisy, and with the frequency of the movement of vehicles with small loads of passengers, passenger transportation is particularly noisy. The same problem of the aggregate as compared to the individual vehicle is found here. Although no one plane, bus, or car is very annoying, the total noise produced is a social problem. This problem can be very acute at areas located near airports and freeways, and therefore permissible noise standards were established during the 1970s.

Various devices and plans for muffling noise have been devised. Landscaping of airports and freeways can help. So can the redesign of engines. But perhaps the most hopeful approach is in the design of freeways and airports when they are originally built. Now that the problem of noise pollution is recognized, abatement often can be incorporated as part of the original design concept. Once again, though, the long-run situation seems brighter than that of the short run.

Control of noise pollution at existing locations is expensive and not entirely successful. It is necessary at times to move schools or places of residence and work away from the sources of noise. Sound conditioning is an expensive alternative that has been used in some instances. However, noise pollution from passenger transportation is an ever-present problem, and no quick solution appears possible.

Finally, the ecological effects of the construction of passenger transportation facilities is a serious problem. When highways and streets are constructed, atmospheric and water pollution occurs. Since airports require substantial land areas, they often are located outside of cities. As such features are imposed upon nature, they upset the ecological cycle in their countryside locations. The solution to this problem can only come in the twin areas of careful design with an eye to pollution causes and control of the construction processes.

Sociological Problems

Two broad sets of sociological problems arise out of transportation. These are the multiple effects of congestion and the effects on the quality of life. Passenger transportation with its variability factor, supremacy of air transportation, and reliance on the private automobile is a particular contributor to both of these problems.

There are three generally recognized types of congestion arising from passenger transportation — street, highway, and airway congestion. While congestion sometimes is absolute and related to the totality of the facilities available, the most common type of congestion arises out of the variability of passenger transportation. The rush hour crowd of vehicles and people is an excellent example of this type of congestion.

A portion of this congestion is caused by work habits and organizational structures. The habit of starting work at around 8 A.M. and quitting at around 5 P.M. is involved. Staggered shifts and variations of the nine-to-five pattern have proved helpful in some experiments. Too little has been attempted on a mass basis, however, and we remain creatures of habit causing our own twice-daily rush periods. In many employments, there is very little reason why the hours of work need to be tied to a nine-to-five pattern. Before the advent of electricity and when most jobs were outdoors, there was a real need to utilize the daylight hours. Today there is less need to continue this pattern. Society has it well within its means to at least minimize part of the congestion of streets and highways.

The same remarks apply to the weekly and seasonal congestion of passenger transportation facilities. The Monday-to-Friday workweek again is a product of a past era that evolved out of the rural workweek of six days. Part of this problem, of course, is based on religious institutions, but these may not be as dominant as they once were. Why should not some firms be closed on Wednesday and Thursday, or some other two days, rather than on Saturday and Sunday?

So too with seasonal congestion caused by summer vacations. It once was thought necessary to close schools so that the young might be employed in farm work during summer months. This tradition has persisted into modern times. Yet there is very little reason why schools could not operate on different schedules with vacations during different and varying months.

Seasonal, weekly, and daily congestion factors can be affected by price devices as well as by different institutional arrangements. Not enough off-peak pricing has been attempted in for-hire passenger transportation, although some modes such as air transportation have been active in this area. People respond to some degree to price incentives, and middle-of-the-week fares, off-season vacation rates, and off-peak daily discounts could be used more effectively.

Efficiency is another approach to congestion problems. This means moving masses of people with fewer vehicles and less space. The private automobile carries, on the average, fewer than two persons per trip, and highways use up lots of space. Various vehicles such as buses, subway trains, and mass transit cars carry far more people per vehicle and use far less space. The use of private automobiles may have to be banned in some areas in our larger cities in the near future. The problems of congestion and the social costs of providing adequate streets and sufficient parking may become so expensive that the adoption of a more efficient means of passenger transportation will become necessary. The technology and know-how to reduce a large part of the present street congestion are available. All that is lacking is the desire to use our technology and knowledge.

Airway congestion can be partially solved by better scheduling and more efficient methods of airway control. During the late 1960s, the congestion of airways and the matter of airway control became widely recognized problems. Congressional action to establish an airways and airports trust fund, tied to a variety of user taxes, was an attempt to solve this problem. Also, the actions of the FAA in restricting departures and arrivals at several major airports during certain hours was a late 1960s attempt to deal with this problem. FAA control of departures and arrivals was again necessary in the 1980s because of the effects of the air controllers' strike and the congestion of the air transportation system.

Street and highway congestion related to airport access is still another matter. Here the answer involves control of times of use of airports and more efficient means of access to and from airports. Plans to connect airports with downtown origination and destination areas by mass transit may have a pronounced effect on this problem.

The effects of passenger transportation on the quality of life are complex, and many suggested solutions are beyond the scope of this discussion. It is sufficient to note that both the presence of, and the lack of efficient and economical means of mass transit have effects on the sociological character of a city or part of a city. Neighborhoods take on a character that relates to their passenger transportation availability. The existence of a subway, bus system, or freeway affects the sociological and economic structure of a community. The lack of mass transportation may lead to an economically depressed area. The journey to work is so important that when means for it are not readily available work alternatives may be severely restricted.

Central business districts depend on low-priced and efficient passenger transportation, as do "bedroom" enclaves and suburbs. The automobile has helped bring urban sprawl to America, and the political and economic unity of our urban communities is affected by the existence of or lack of passenger transport. Analysis of all these sociological phenomena, and the many others that are related to passenger transportation, is not within the scope of this book. However, it should be emphasized that passenger transportation or its lack creates unique sociological effects and problems.

International Aspects

Although this book is concerned with domestic transportation, international matters are directly interrelated to some aspects of passenger transportation. Domestic airlines often have international operations, and even many that are solely domestic in route structure depend on international interchange of passengers for portions of their business. Although the various modes of land transportation also may interconnect with maritime service (or with Canadian or Mexican land carriers), the interconnection in air transportation is more direct.

Most of the world's airlines are government owned and operated. As such, they are agencies or arms of their own governments. U.S. airlines are privately owned and operated. This distinctive difference contributes to problems of fare determination, route awards, and international diplomacy.

As agencies of their respective governments, foreign airlines can be operated at a loss if the owning nations feel this is desirable policy. A foreign airline can penetrate a market in competition with a privately owned American airline with little thought of profit or loss. Problems of competitive relationships are obvious.

Some U.S. airlines feel they should be designated flag carriers and become instruments of U.S. foreign policy. In some instances, this almost has been the case in the past. Landing rights are negotiated between nations as bilateral agreements. The right of an airline to enter and serve a country is part of the overall international relations between the two nations involved. A landing right may come about because of some other type of concession such as a lower tariff, a changed import quota, or monetary or labor exchanges. Obviously, the privately owned airlines of the United States often find themselves at a bargaining disadvantage since they have no control over tariffs, quotas, labor exchanges, international loans, and the like.

It should be noted, however, that some of these potential international disadvantages have not been too severe. The United States provides such a desirable market as an originator of travelers to foreign points and as a destination for foreign travelers that the mutual exchange of landing rights generally has been accomplished with a minimum of friction. Most foreign governments are only too glad to allow U.S. carriers to land in their countries if they can land their own carriers in this country.

Some problems have arisen because of the technical efficiency of U.S. carriers. With the coming of jumbo jets, some nations attempted to restrict U.S. carriers on the number of serving flights. Their concern was that U.S. carriers would provide a superior service that would dominate air travel to the disadvantage of foreign government-owned carriers. Such restrictions are difficult to handle diplomatically.

International air fares are established at biannual meetings of the International Air Transport Association (IATA). Through this vehicle, all member airlines meet and bargain over changes in international air fares and procedures. Since no international regulatory agency such as the former domestic CAB or the FAA exists, IATA has considerable power in controlling international air transportation. In the late 1970s and early 1980s there was some concern over the conflicts between IATA and U.S. antitrust policy. Since that time, IATA membership is in two categories and U.S. airlines do not need to participate in IATA ratemaking, though some of them do. Also, all members of IATA do not embrace the "open competition" policy of airline deregulation found in the United States. As privately owned profit-seeking firms, U.S. airlines sometimes find themselves in unusual positions in working with their competitors who are, in effect, governmental agencies.

Finally, because the international air transportation market depends partly upon accommodations such as hotels, restaurants, tours, and recreational activities, air carriers often have constructed or acquired their own hotels and similar facilities. Several major U.S. air carriers have substantial investments in hotels and facilities abroad. This has both advantages and disadvantages. It is good business for the carriers and often stimulates travel and economic development in the country where the hotel is built. On the other hand, such activities provide competition for local hotels and facilities and sometimes do not improve the image of Americans abroad.

Energy Considerations

Another dimension was added to passenger transportation problems in the mid-1970s: energy considerations. The nation's use of all forms of energy continues to rise, but domestic energy supplies do not always keep pace. This is particularly true for petroleum.

Since transportation uses more than 63 percent' of all petroleum consumed in this country, the continuing domestic petroleum deficit had a major impact on transportation. Increasing amounts of petroleum were imported, and the extent of our dependency on foreign sources of petroleum was brought to our attention dramatically by the Arab oil boycott of 1973–74 and the shortages in 1977–78 arising from the Iran-Iraq war. After repeated efforts and much debate, Congress and the administration began to form a so-called national energy policy during the late 1970s. Part of this policy involved the creation of the new Department of Energy, part involved hotly debated actions related to energy conservation, and part involved efforts to find and develop new domestic energy sources.

Passenger transportation is a very large user of petroleum; hence, it is directly affected by the national energy policy. As already noted, the average load factor in American automobiles is only slightly more than one person per trip, whereas the load factor of for-hire means of transportation is usually 50 percent or more of the available seats filled. Automobiles are very inefficient users of energy, and move few people per barrel of petroleum compared with other modes. Table 8.3 shows not only petroleum demand by various modes but also transportation demand as compared with total domestic demand. Of course, all the demand noted in Table 8.3 is not for passenger transportation — a part is for moving freight and for highway construction. Even so, it is interesting to note that transportation uses about 64 percent of total petroleum (over 50 percent of which is imported from abroad) and that the highway mode uses about 83 percent and air transportation uses another 9 percent of the transport demand.

In addition to the large amount of petroleum imported, one must recognize that petroleum supplies are finite, and that although the prices paid for crude petroleum are a major factor in finding and developing new supplies, the specter of running out of oil at some future date is a possibility. Projections of future petroleum use, particularly by automobiles, seem to indicate that actions to conserve energy are necessary.

A number of approaches to energy use have been considered. One concrete action was a congressional mandate of energy performance standards (in average miles per gallon) for future automobiles. When these plans were instituted in the early 1970s, the average automobile got about 12 miles to the gallon. A goal of 27 miles per gallon for all automobiles by 1987 was projected. Each automobile manufacturer had to measure its "corporate fleet," that is, all vehicles of all sizes, and meet progressively higher yearly utilization rates or be fined. These were called CAFE (Corporate Average Fuel Efficiency) requirements. Thus, less efficient larger cars could be offset by more efficient smaller models. Also, estimates of fuel utilization had to be posted on all new cars. Although some conflicts existed between energy efficiency and ecological goals, compromises were necessary. Yet by 1987, the CAFE goals were met by automobile manufacturers by downsizing cars, using more plastic and light materials, and making more efficient engines. However, the total fleet of automobiles has continued to increase, and petroleum use by automobiles continues to dominate the energy picture.

Another approach turns on the provision of alternatives. More use of transit systems in urban areas, carpooling and vanpooling, use of such devices as motorcycles, mopeds, bicycles, and the like, can all help in meeting our energy problem. Still other approaches are to reduce the consumption of petroleum by raising prices through taxation, rationing or allocation schemes, and the like. A further approach is the development of vehicles using energy from nonpetroleum sources such as steam, electricity, hydrogen, and so forth. But whatever approach or combination of approaches is used, it seems certain that energy considerations will continue to be of great importance in future passenger transportation.

ECONOMIC AND POLICY CONSIDERATIONS

The distinctive characteristics and the ecological-sociological-international-energy aspects of passenger transportation give rise to major economic questions. Other economic considerations exist, but the following illustrate some of the complexities of passenger transportation policy decisions.

What is the most desirable form of urban passenger transportation? Assuming that a national urban passenger transportation goal of a low-priced, fast, and efficient system of movement is desirable, what physical form should this system take? Perhaps a combination of forms is needed. If so, what mix of forms is best?

Because the steel rail can move people rapidly and at a low expenditure of energy, some favor building more rail rapid transit systems. But these are very expensive and require high densities of population to be economically justifiable or energy efficient. Because intercity highways and intracity streets already provide busways that can be further utilized simply by adding more vehicles, some favor bus-related systems. These systems seem to be the best answer for areas where population densities are relatively lower and where improved streets or roads already exist. Still others look to new, exotic, or experimental systems such as monorails, tubes, and air-cushion vehicles.

Table 8.3 Transportation Demand for Petroleum, 1986

	Thousands of barrels	Percent of total demand
Highway		
Motor fuel	2,980,554	
Asphalt paving	162,795	
Road oils	818	
Total	3,144,167	82.9
Water		
Diesel and distillates	48,434	
Residual fuel oil	125,889	
Gasoline	26,912	
Total	201,235	5.3
Rail		
Diesel and distillates	73,800	
Residual fuel oil	14	
Total	73,814	1.9
Air [1]		
Aviation gasoline	9,002	
Jet fuel	336,894	
Total	345,896	9.1
All Modes		
Lubricants	29,000	0.8
Total Transport Demand	3,794,112	63.9
Total U.S. Domestic Demand	5,942,429	100.0

[1] Excluding military use.

Source: Transportation Policy Associates, *Transportation in America*, 6th ed., Washington, D.C., 1988, p. 15. Copyright 1988. Used by permission of Eno Foundation for Transportation.

All systems have advantages and disadvantages, and it is likely that most urban areas will develop a multimodal combination of passenger transport systems. The choice of how to mix the various forms of transport must be made as a series of trade-offs among cost, convenience, expediency, mobility, safety, energy, public acceptance, politics, and similar factors. But the initial step involves choosing whatever mix of forms seems most desirable under the given circumstances at the place and time of choice.

What degree of public support is desirable for urban passenger transportation? The federal government sponsored a number of experiments during the 1960s, and beginning in 1964 began to allocate millions of dollars yearly in grants to cities to upgrade urban passenger transportation services. This level of aid increased to billions with passage of the National Mass Transportation Act of 1974, $4 billion a year in the 1978 and 1982 acts and $3.3 billion a year in the 1987 act for the five years to 1991. As Table 8.2 notes, over $34.7 billion has been spent by the federal government for transit capital and $10.5 billion for operating assistance from 1965 to 1987, and since 1982 1 cent of the 9-cent federal gas tax has been earmarked for transit systems. In spite of these massive efforts, ridership has increased very slowly. The proper degree of public support is still an open question.

What is a desirable pattern of control and support for airways? Given the dominance of air transportation in intercity and intercontinental travel, plus the importance of safety, this question must be answered. The federal government owns and operates the airways, and local governments own and operate airports. For many years, air travel has increased faster than airports have been improved and than airway control has been developed. The result: increased airway and airport congestion and dangerous safety situations. Indeed, delays in airports and on the airways threaten to take away much of the natural advantage of speed possessed by air transportation.

During 1970, Congress passed the Airport and Airways Improvement Act, setting up the Aviation Trust Fund, which is financed by new and increased user taxes. This program was extended for another five years in 1982 with larger amounts going to airways. In 1987 this program was extended again for another five years, yet the situation in airway congestion and airport development seems as bad as ever as more people fly. Whether these programs will provide the needed improvements remains to be seen.

What is a desirable highway policy for the nation? The Highway Trust Fund was established in 1956, and the country embarked on a crash program of highway improvement. But completion of the Interstate System has been delayed because of inflation and lack of funds. As already noted, Congress raised the fuel tax in 1982 to 9 cents per gallon to provide funds to complete the Interstate System and rehabilitate the street and highway system, and in 1984 added a 15.5 cent per gallon tax on diesel fuel. However, many issues remain. If a strict user tax is desirable, should a portion of the Highway Trust Fund go to urban transit systems as it does under the 1982 act? How much user tax is too much? Are all classes of vehicles paying their proper share of the costs? Clearly, many highway policy questions exist, and all affect passenger transportation.

What is a desirable policy on rail passenger transportation for the nation? Railroad service is important in the commuter and intercity area of passenger transportation. The northeast corridor or megalopolis, a 400-mile strip from Boston to Washington, contains 30 percent of our nation's manufacturing and 21 percent of our retailing establishments and has almost 50 million people — all on some 1.4 percent of the nation's land area. The degree of urbanization in this megalopolis, exceeded in only a few places in the world, points up the problem of mass transportation. Urban and intercity rail passenger services exist here and are being vastly improved by the massive aid for high-speed rail passenger transportation provided by the 4-R Act. Should such high-speed rail intercity services be equally supported in other urbanized areas? If so, who should provide the support? And how?

Chapter 7 has described the creation of the National Railroad Passenger Corporation and Amtrak, and how this passenger transportation system has been given a goal of "for service" and not "for profit." Outside of the northeast corridor, Amtrak is primarily an intermediate and long-haul carrier — and piles up most of its deficit in such operations. Even with a "for service" goal, it is difficult to identify a specific national goal for intercity rail passenger transportation outside of a few corridors, and it is even more difficult to predict its success.

What is the most desirable set of priorities in public aids to passenger transportation? This final question encompasses the above questions, yet it is a separate policy problem in itself. Given that resources for transportation are limited and that choices must be made, what is the proper set of priorities for passenger transportation? Huge amounts have been allocated to highways and freeways during the years since World War II. In spite of this, congestion has increased. Indeed, some suggest that freeways merely accelerate the congestion problem by encouraging the greater use of automobiles and by funneling more vehicles into inadequate city streets and parking spaces.

Urban mass transportation finally was given massive federal aid in the late 1970s. Most of these funds, however, have been allocated to a few large cities. But small and medium-sized cities also have urban passenger transportation problems. Further, all the country is not urbanized, and rural areas likewise have passenger transport problems. The question of priorities for aid and resource allocation is an obvious one to raise, but not easy to answer. Although various imbalances are being reduced, we cannot be sure that our limited resources are being properly allocated.

It is clear that we have a tendency to segment the problem of passenger transportation and to consider urban transportation, highway policy, or airway policy in isolation from one another. There seems to be a built-in aversion to thinking about passenger transportation as a whole. As we have noted, this has led to a series of expensive crash programs designed to handle problems in specific areas. What we need most of all, perhaps, is some truly broad consideration of the whole of passenger transportation at the highest policy levels rather than segmented programs and proposals for specific modes.

SUMMARY

Passenger transportation is uniquely related to numerous ecological, sociological, international, and economic problems. This is partially because of the distinctive nature of passenger transportation, with its predominance of private carriage, supremacy of air transportation, by-product effects, variability effects, instantaneous and perishability effects, substitutability effects, investment cost effects, and market complexities. There is a special problem with transit in the cities. Numerous unanswered policy questions remain. There probably is greater need for policy determination in the area of passenger transportation than in any other transportation area. Great concern exists at various levels, the need for comprehensive and cooperative planning is apparent, and the opportunity for meaningful policy to achieve desirable results, once meaningful policy is established, is very great.

ADDITIONAL READING

Coyle, John J., Edward J. Bardi, and Joseph L. Cavinato, *Transportation*, 2nd ed., St. Paul: West Publishing Co., 1986.
   Chapter 10, "Urban Metropolitan Transportation," pp. 191–210.
Fair, Marvin L., and Ernest W. Williams, Jr., *Transportation and Logistics*, Rev. ed., Plano, Texas: Business Publications, 1981.
   Chapter 7, "Intercity Passenger Logistics," pp. 102–20.
   Chapter 8, "Urban Logistics: Human and Goods," pp. 121–41.

Farris, Martin T., and Forrest E. Harding, *Passenger Transportation*, Englewood Cliffs, N.J.: Prentice-Hall, 1976.
    Chapter 3, "Pricing Systems," pp. 65–102.
    Chapter 5, "The Marketing of Passenger Transportation Services," pp. 157–84.
    Chapter 6, "Urban Transportation," pp. 187–216.
    Chapter 8, "Policy Problems," pp. 237–53.
Fawcett, Stanley E., and Stanley A. Fawcett, "Congestion at Capacity-Constrained Airports: A Question of Economics and Realism," *Transportation Journal*, Vol. 27, No. 4 (Summer 1988) pp. 42–54.
Hamer, Andrew M., *The Selling of Rapid Transit: A Critical Look at Urban Transportation Planning*, Lexington, Mass.: D. C. Heath & Co., 1976.
    Chapter 2, "Defining the Problems: Public Transportation Criteria and Rail Transit Mythology," pp. 19–34.
    Chapter 3, "Rail versus Bus: The Art of Evaluating Alternative Modes," pp. 35–60.
Harper, Donald V., "The Continuing Dilemma of Aircraft Noise," *Transportation Journal*, Vol. 28, No. 2 (Winter 1988) pp. 33–42.
Hazard, John L., *Transportation: Management, Economics, Policy*, Centreville, Md.: Cornell Maritime Press, 1977.
    Chapter 17, "Urban and Intermodal Transportation," pp. 488–526.
Lieb, Robert C., *Transportation*, 3rd ed., Reston, Va.: Reston Publishing Co., 1985.
    Chapter 20, "Transportation/Energy Interrelationships," pp. 423–44.
    Chapter 21, "Problems of Metropolitan Transportation," pp. 449–59.
    Chapter 22, "Solving Metropolitan Transportation Problems," pp. 461–80.
Meyer, John R., and Jose A. Gomez-Ibanez, *Autos, Transit and Cities*, Cambridge, Mass.: Harvard University Press, 1981.
    Chapter 14, "The Role of Public Policy," pp. 277–96.
Miller, David R., ed. *Urban Transportation Policy: New Perspectives*, Lexington, Mass.: D. C. Heath & Co., 1972.
    Smerk, George M., "The Urban Transportation Problem: A Policy Vacuum?" pp. 5–19.
    Mertins, Herman, Jr., and David R. Miller, "Urban Transportation Policy: Fact or Fiction?" pp. 19–36.
Owen, Wilford, *Transportation for Cities*, Washington, D.C.: Brookings Institution, 1976.
    Chapter 6, "Energy and Federal Aid Strategy," pp. 50–59.
    Chapter 7, "Cost Implications of Alternative Federal Policies," pp. 60–70.
Pegrum, Dudley F., *Transportation: Economics and Public Policy*, 3rd ed., Homewood, Ill.: Richard D. Irwin, 1973.
    Chapter 23, "The Urban Transportation Problems," pp. 534–66.
Ruppenthal, Karl M., "Fuel Shortages and Passenger Transportation," *Proceedings: Transportation Research Forum*, 15 (1974), 561–70.
Schary, Philip, and Robert M. Williams, "Airline Fare Policy and Public Investment," *Transportation Journal* (Fall 1967), 41–49.
Smerk, George M., *Urban Transportation: A Dozen Years of Federal Policy*, Bloomington, Ind.: Indiana University Press, 1974.
    Chapter 1, "The Urban Transportation Crisis and the Growing Role of the Federal Government," pp. 5–89.
    Chapter 2, "Mass Transportation: Pro and Con," pp. 90–129.
    Chapter 4, "The Federal Demonstration Programs," pp. 183–217.
    Chapter 5, "The Federal Mass Transportation Programs," pp. 218–48.
_____, "The Urban Mass Transportation Act at Twenty: A Turning Point?" *Transportation Journal* (Summer 1985), pp. 52–75.
_____, "Update on Federal Mass Transportation Policy: The Surface Transportation Act of 1978," *Transportation Journal* (Spring 1979), 16–35.

Spychalski, John C., "The Diversion of Motor Vehicle-Related Tax Revenues to Urban Mass Transportation: A Critique of Its Economic Tenability," *Transportation Journal* (Spring 1970), 44–50.

Stephenson, Frederick J., Jr., *Transportation USA*, Reading, Mass.: Addison-Wesley Publishing Co., 1987.

Chapter 18, "Public Sector Transit Management, Strategy, and Decision Making," pp. 491–518.

Talley, Wayne Kenneth, *Introduction to Transportation*, Cincinnati, Ohio: South-Western Publishing Co., 1983.

Chapter 15, "Urban Transportation: Mass Transit," pp. 289–311.

Wood, Donald F., and James C. Johnson, *Contemporary Transportation*, 3rd ed., New York: Macmillan Publishing Co., 1989.

Chapter 17, "Managing Transportation in the Public Sector," pp. 441–78.

CHAPTER 9

FREIGHT TRANSPORTATION GEOGRAPHY: ROUTES AND COMMODITY MOVEMENTS

That wise Scotsman Adam Smith in the first portions of *The Wealth of Nations* set forth three leading propositions which may be summarized as follows: (1) the wealth of a nation is the product of its labor; (2) the greatest improvements in the product of labor result from the division of labor; (3) the division of labor is limited by the extent of the market.

With due humility we may add a fourth proposition, namely, "The extent of the market is controlled by the cost of transportation." In other words, transportation is not only a *necessary* factor in any organized economy, it also is a *limiting* factor in overall economic activity and development as well as that of a particular region, industry, or firm. The availability of adequate transportation does not necessarily ensure prosperity, but its absence guarantees economic stagnation.

Assuming that adequate physical transportation facilities exist, the pertinent limiting costs in for-hire transportation are the rates (prices) actually charged users by carriers. These rates may be more or less than the carriers' actual costs of performing services. (This distinction between "carriage rates" and "carriage costs" does not exist in private carriage, of course. Here the two are identical.) It has been said rightly that transportation geography is largely rate geography. This statement is based on the fact that rates (or costs from the users' viewpoint) often may be based as much or more upon economic or political considerations as upon geographical factors.

Freight rates will be more fully discussed in Part IV. It is only necessary at this time to point out that geography, inasmuch as it affects the location of transportation routes and the kinds and directions of commodity movements, does have a bearing on carrier transportation costs. To some extent, then, geography affects freight rates and thereby influences patterns of producer location, marketing areas, and routing practices, and sometimes even the availability of adequate transportation vehicles or rolling stock. At least a general knowledge of transportation geography, including available routes, and of the characteristics of commodity flows and their determinants is essential for any well-informed transportation student or practitioner.

THE LOCATION OF TRANSPORTATION ROUTES

Transportation routes are determined by a number of factors. These include physical geography (the way mountains impede and rivers facilitate transportation) and trade between regions and areas possessing different economic advantages (geographic division of labor and the market pull exhibited by major population centers). In addition, existing transportation systems tend to influence the location of economic activity. All of these factors have had an impact on the development of transportation in our nation.

Physical Geography and Transportation Development

Other things being equal, the ideal land transportation route between a fixed producing point and a given consuming center would be a straight line. This would minimize construction, maintenance, and movement costs. Other things are almost never equal, however. Numerous physical obstacles intervene. Often extensive detours are less costly than climbing, tunneling, or removing hills, bridging rivers or canyons, filling valleys, firming unstable soils, or draining swamps.

To detour or not to detour is both an engineering and an economic problem. Engineers can calculate the costs of going over, through, or around a mountain. The ultimate decision must be made on an economic basis, however.

It may be considerably more expensive to construct a route through an obstacle, but operating costs through the years ahead may be much lower over a direct than over a circuitous route. From the long-run viewpoint, it may be preferable to blast rather than to bypass. But builders, even if they recognize the long-run advantages of more expensive construction, may not have the necessary funds to undertake it. A cheaply built route with high operating costs may be chosen over more costly construction that could be utilized more cheaply, or there may be no choice.

Many thousands of miles of this country's highways and railways have been straightened or relocated to correct cheap building that could not have been avoided in the original construction because of lack of funds. But even in our affluent society, it is not economically practical to meet all geographic obstacles to transportation head-on. No one seriously proposes tunneling completely through the Rocky Mountains or bridging the broadest expanses of Lake Superior. Geography still severely limits the location of our transportation routes and forces up operating costs.

Many of our basic transportation routes were surveyed and laid out millenniums ago by migrating animals. Following the path of least resistance seems to be a basic principle of nature. This is as applicable in transportation as in other natural phenomena. Old-time woodsmen advised us never to go over anything that we can go around; animals also follow this principle and Indians followed the animals. Later, explorers, missionaries, hunters, trappers, and traders followed both. Then pioneer settlers followed the same ancient trails, and highways and railroads followed the pack trains and wagon tracks of settlers. Finally, trading posts, communities, and great cities crew up alongside these transportation routes and at points where routes intersect or change in form (as from water to land, or later from railway to highway). Even airways, physically the most flexible and obstacle-free of all routes, have tended to follow the same ancient paths in order to serve already existing communities located on or at the terminals of these routes. The general location and character of our internal waterways have been described in Chapter 5. Inland waterways are even more limited geographically than are land routes. Vessels can go only where there is enough water to float them. This completely excludes large areas of the country. River traffic must follow the often meandering courses of streams. Coastal, lake, and river navigation often is limited by the existence of promontories, shoals, dangerous rocks, adverse currents, and other natural obstacles as well as by the absence of suitable harbors.

Many natural hindrances to navigation have been overcome, of course, by canals, locks, and breakwaters, or by dredging, lighthouses, and similar aids. But these devices, like tunnels through mountains or bridges over streams, are expensive. As in land transportation route construction, what is possible from an engineering viewpoint often is not economically feasible.

Geographical Specialization and Division of Labor

Geographical factors other than natural obstacles also influence the location of all types of transportation routes. Some persons may have a desire for travel as such, but merchandise has no such desire. Long-distance transportation of goods grows principally out of trade between unlike regions — surpluses of one region are exchanged for surpluses of another.

Geographical specialization or division of labor, which exists in every nonprimitive economic society of any significant geographic size, is just as productive and just as essential as is personal specialization. Much of this regional specialization is based directly upon geographical factors such as climate, soils, or the location of particular kinds of natural resources (fuels, ores, timber, water, etc.). Some patterns of specialization, of course, may be attributed to historical accident or to a long evolutionary development from some now-forgotten first cause. Regardless of the original first cause, geography does at least set limits or boundaries around the kinds of production in which a given region may engage; geography therefore exercises a veto power.

Without delving too deeply into the subject matter of economic geography (which is another must for the well-informed transportation person), it is necessary that we point out that a definite pattern of regional specialization exists in the United States. Softwood lumber and other forest products, for example, come from the Pacific Northwest and the Southeast. Coal comes largely from Appalachian and western districts; citrus fruits from California, the Southwest, and Florida; iron ore from the Mesabi Range; corn from the Midwest; wheat from the plains states; and cotton from the Southeast, Southwest, and California. This illustrative list of geographically influenced or determined products could be greatly extended, of course.

Some type of manufacturing activity occurs in every metropolitan area. In this country, however, the region specializing most in manufacturing is the Northeast — roughly that area east of the Mississippi and north of the Ohio River. Geographical factors and historical evolution have given that region comparative advantages in many types of manufacturing which competing regions apparently have not yet been able to overcome. (Factors influencing the location of various kinds of economic activity will be considered in Chapter 19.)

Many cities also serve as distribution centers for their surrounding countrysides, and oceanborne foreign imports and exports are channeled mainly through several large seaport cities. Like sand moving through the center of an hourglass, commodities converge into and diverge out from these points. Inbound and outbound transportation routes, like spokes in a wheel, run to and from a common center. Such communities, which perform financial, storage, and other transport-accessory services, as well as the transshipment function, have a transportation role relatively much greater than the primary production and consumption roles of their populations. Usually some geographical advantage of location, present or past, accounts for the importance of such centers to transportation.

Sometimes, however, artificial economic or political favoritism such as unusually low freight rates or favorable transit privileges is responsible.

Existing Transportation Routes and Economic Activity

There is considerable interaction, of course, between existing transportation routes and the development of centers of population and economic activity. Nature apparently abhors a transportation vacuum as much as any other kind. It seems to be a principle of transportation that the creation of new routes, or the development of new types of facilities, or the expansion of existing facilities generally leads to a demand for their use. That is, supply precedes demand, and service demands tend to expand to fill service capacity — a kind of Parkinson's law of utilization or a Say's law of markets.

This principle of transport supply-pull development was demonstrated very clearly in the settlement of the American West after the building of western railways. Rail lines wandering across trackless wastes between nonexistent terminals soon attracted people, economic activities, and traffic. Numerous other historical and contemporary examples of this kind might be cited for all forms of transportation in this country and abroad.

After people, economic activity, and traffic agglomerate at various points on a transportation route, the mass tends to grow by its own internal activities and by attracting other people and activities. Eventually, economic activity at these points of agglomeration becomes so important to the route or to the transportation organizations operating over the route that it becomes economically impractical to abandon or substantially relocate the route. Likewise in laying out new routes today, the presence of now-thriving communities on the old routes cannot be ignored — they must be served even if this means costly circuity and higher construction and operating costs.

Practicing transportation and traffic personnel naturally are more concerned with existing routes than with the location of new ones. A detailed knowledge of what routes are available, what carriers operate over these routes, what time schedules and rates are in effect over various routes, and where interchanges between carriers can be made are among the indispensable tools of the traffic executive. Such knowledge is acquired only by long study and practice. Practical routing of shipments can be an extremely technical and complex affair. Not every existing natural route can be used without penalties of time or money. Obviously, a detailed discussion of these matters is beyond our present scope. It is possible, however, to make some general concluding statements within the framework of our present consideration of routes.

Major Interregional Transportation Routes

As a generalization, it is correct to say that the main long-distance routes of all our forms of transportation, and especially rail, highway, and air transport, tend to connect the same principal population centers and producing areas over the same major paths. This generalization holds for water transportation where it is available and (perhaps to a slightly lesser extent, because of its one-way movement) for pipeline transport. The routes of other modern carriers tend to follow roughly those laid down by the railroads, as the railroads are the oldest of our modern forms of carriage. Remember, however, that the rails themselves generally followed older pathways.

It is generally true, also, that interregional routes east of the Mississippi River tend to run in a north-south direction, whereas those west of the Mississippi are mainly east-west routes. In addition to numerous strictly local (intraregional) exceptions to this generalization, there are few major exceptions. These are found mainly on the Pacific Coast and in the Gulf area, and between the Great Lakes and North Atlantic seaboard cities.

Figure 9.1 pictures the principal long-distance land transportation routes of the United States. (These routes are general paths of transportation rather than the specific routes of individual carriers or highways.) As indicated above, air, water, and pipeline routes show a considerable tendency to conform to the prevailing basic rail-highway pattern. Comparison of this figure with a relief map of the United States showing mountains and mountain passes, rivers, valleys, and plains will greatly aid one in understanding why these routes are located as they are. Further comparison with a map showing population centers and densities and the kinds of commodities produced in various regions will complete the explanation. Although not consistently or centrally planned by some omnipotent governmental agency, the pattern is a logical one. Generally it has met, and continues to meet, our country's economic needs.

Ten major interregional routes are shown on Figure 9.1. An Atlantic Seaboard route parallels the East Coast, east of the Appalachians, connecting the Southeast with the North Atlantic area. An interior Southeastern route, connecting the Southeast with the Great Lakes, runs between the western side of the Appalachians and the valley of the Mississippi. A Mississippi Valley route parallels that river on the east, and a South Plains-Gulf route is found on the west. The Northeastern route joins the Great Lakes with the North Atlantic seaboard, and the North

Figure 9.1 Principal Land Transportation Routes of the United States

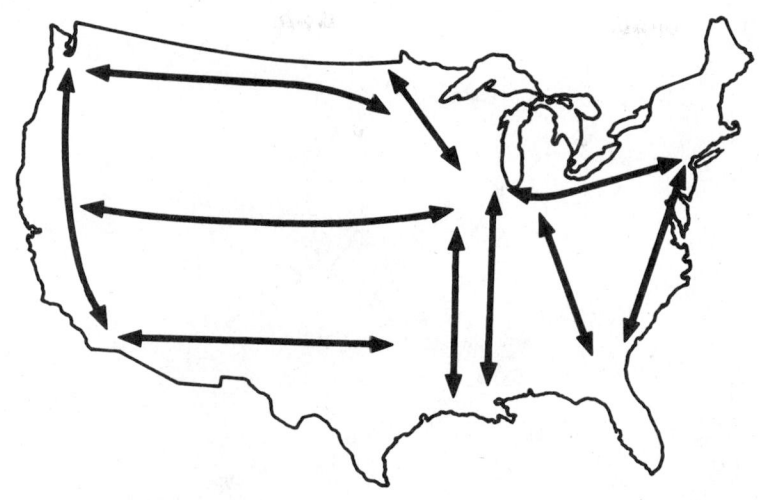

Plains-Great Lakes route runs somewhat northwest-southeast to connect those two areas.

Moving west, we find a Northern Transcontinental, a Central Transcontinental, and a Southern Transcontinental route. A substantial branch of the Central Transcontinental route, not shown, also runs into the Pacific Northwest, and an offshoot of the Southern Transcontinental route goes to the Gulf. Finally, we find the north-south Pacific Coast route connecting California and the Pacific Northwest.

We must re-emphasize the fact that Figure 9.1 shows only a composite skeleton of our system of transportation routes. Figures 9.2 through 9.6, covering railways, highways, waterways, and pipelines, put meat on the individual bones. Even these figures, however, cannot show all existing routes in detail.

Even a cursory glance at Figure 9.1, or at the more detailed maps of our transportation network, shows that most of the important routes run from and to the northeastern section of our country. This is no coincidence. Why it is so will be explained in the following section.

COMMODITY MOVEMENTS

Freight transportation differs from passenger transportation in at least two significant ways. First, the quantities of freight moving between points or

Figure 9.2 The Railroad Network of the United States

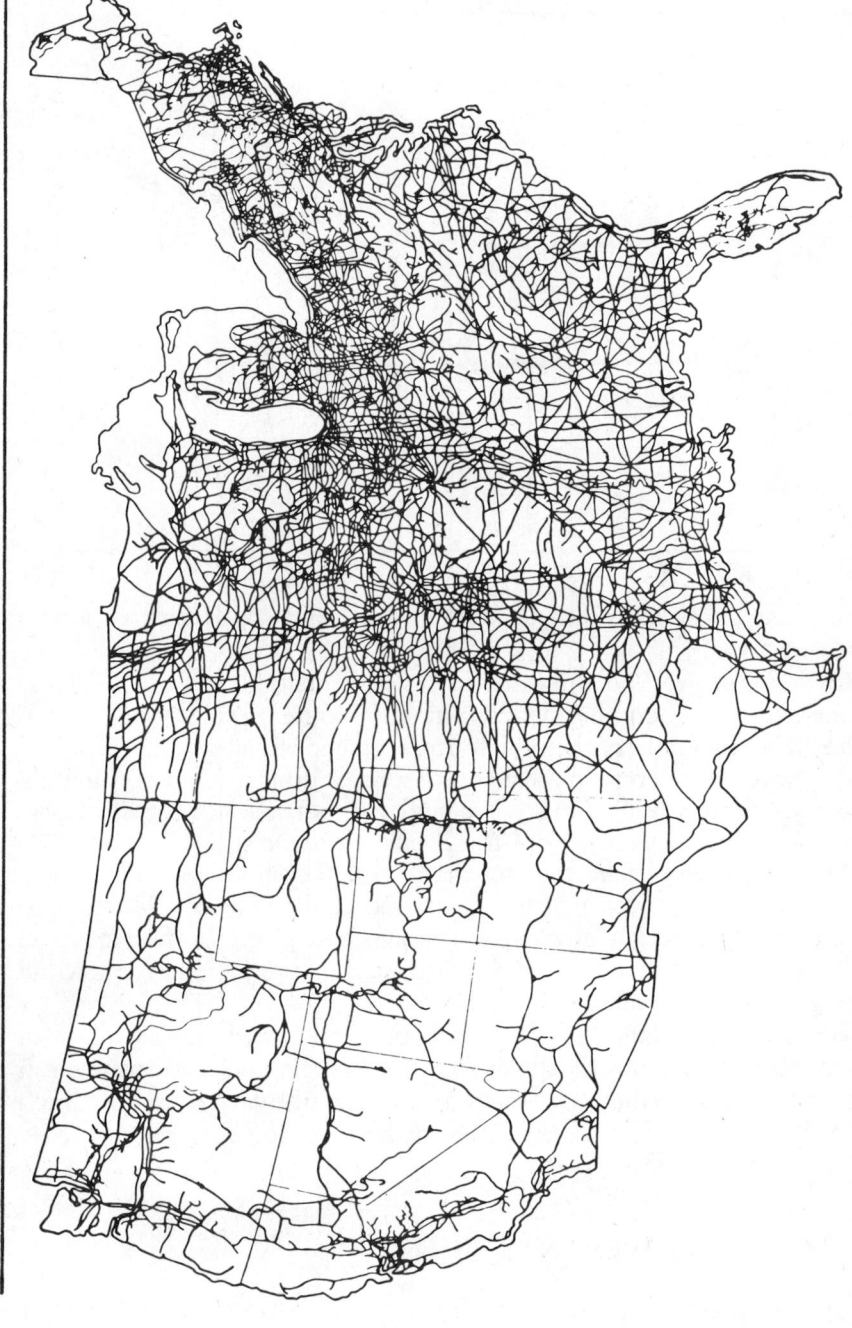

Source: Association of American Railroads. Used by permission.

Figure 9.3 The National System of Interstate and Defense Highways

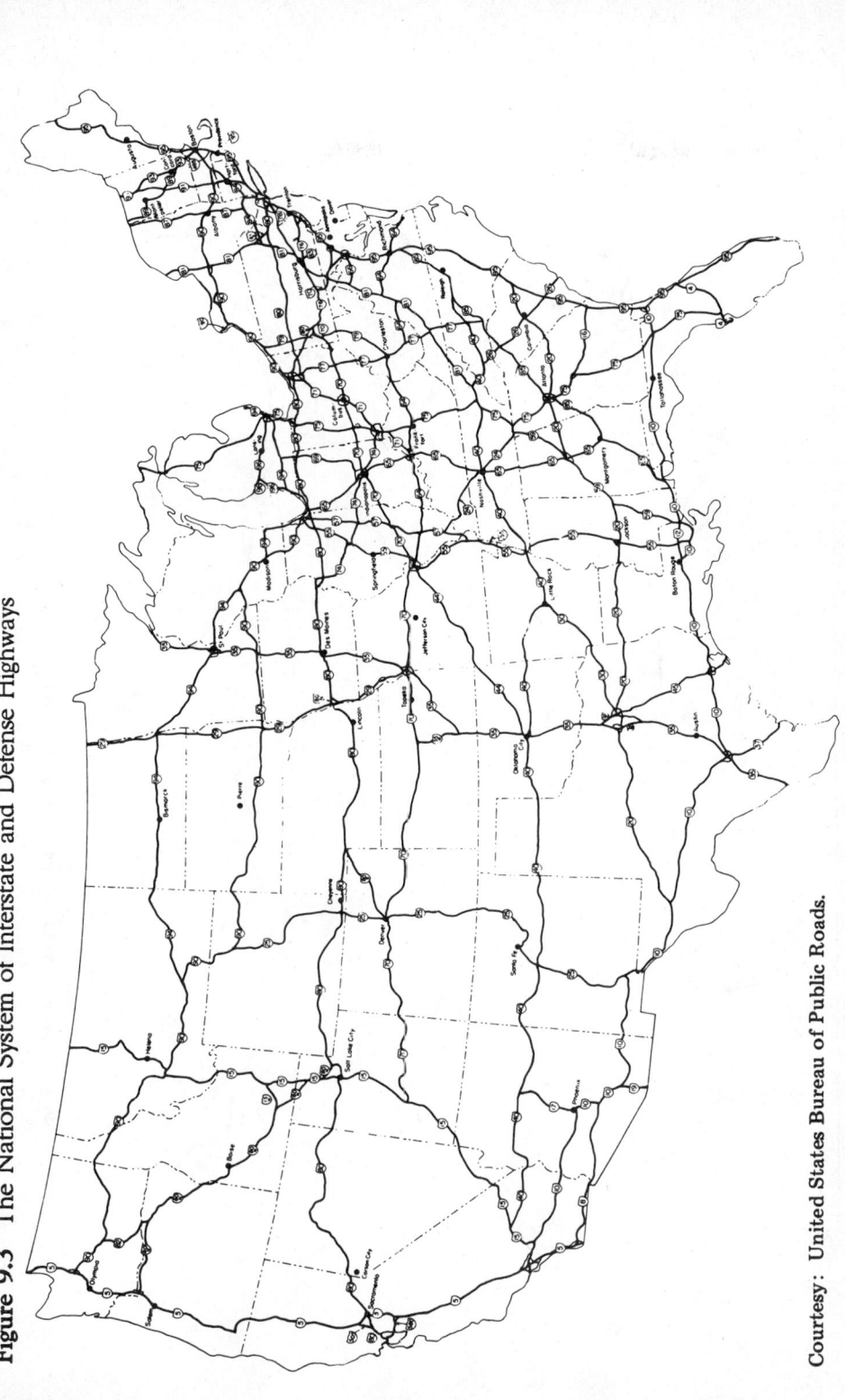

Courtesy: United States Bureau of Public Roads.

Figure 9.4 The Inland Waterways System of the United States

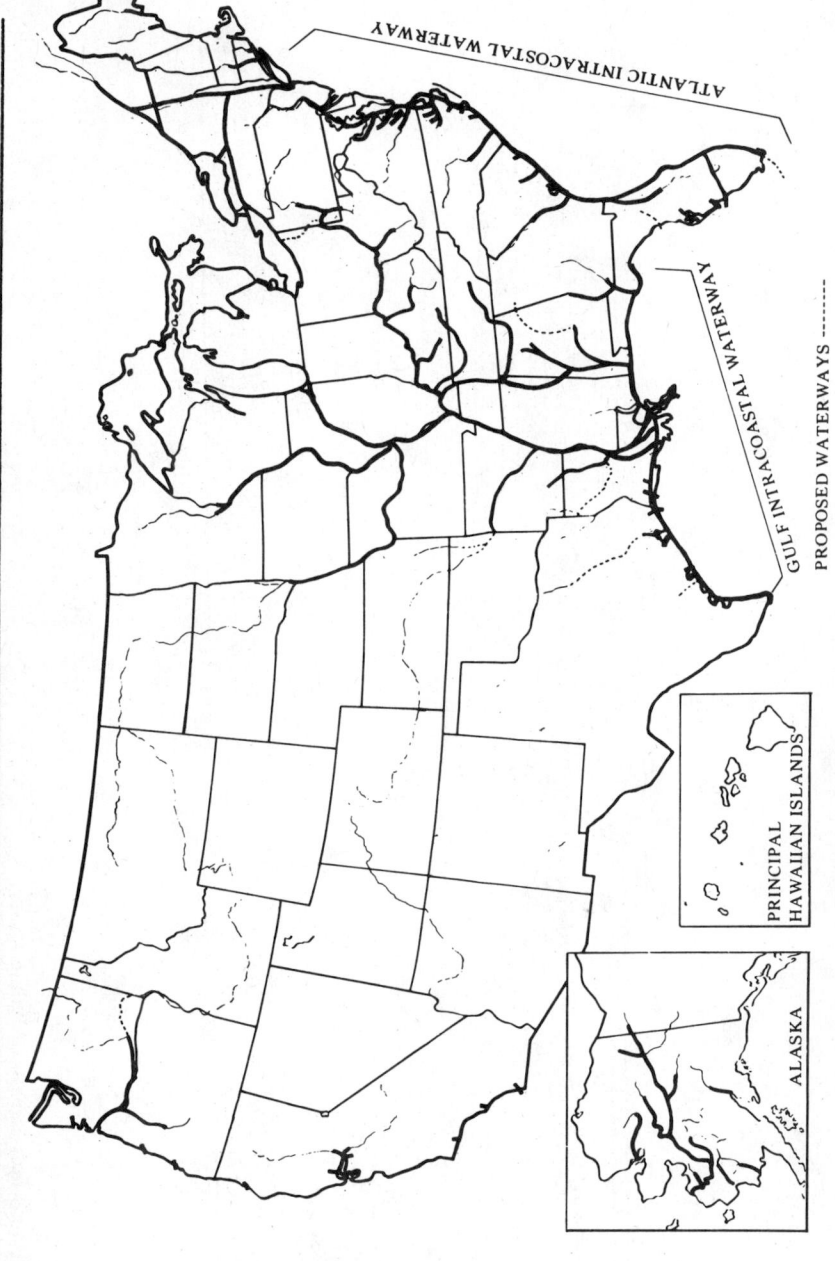

ATLANTIC INTRACOASTAL WATERWAY

GULF INTRACOASTAL WATERWAY

PROPOSED WATERWAYS ------

PRINCIPAL HAWAIIAN ISLANDS

ALASKA

Source: American Waterways Operators. Used by permission.

Figure 9.5 The Crude Oil Pipeline System of the Forty-eight Contiguous United States

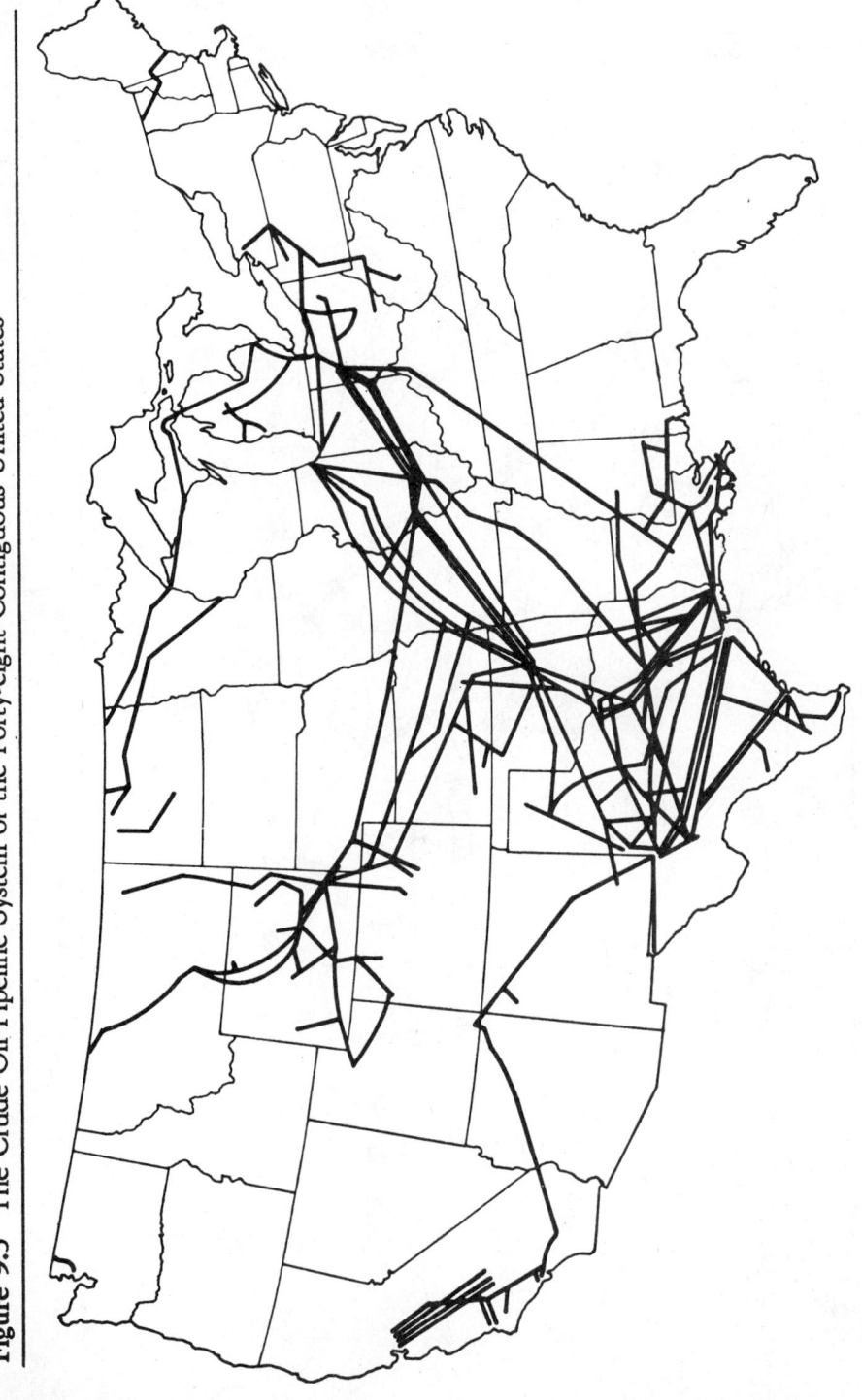

Source: Association of Oil Pipe Lines. Used by permission.

Figure 9.6 The Product Oil Pipeline System of the Forty-eight Contiguous United States

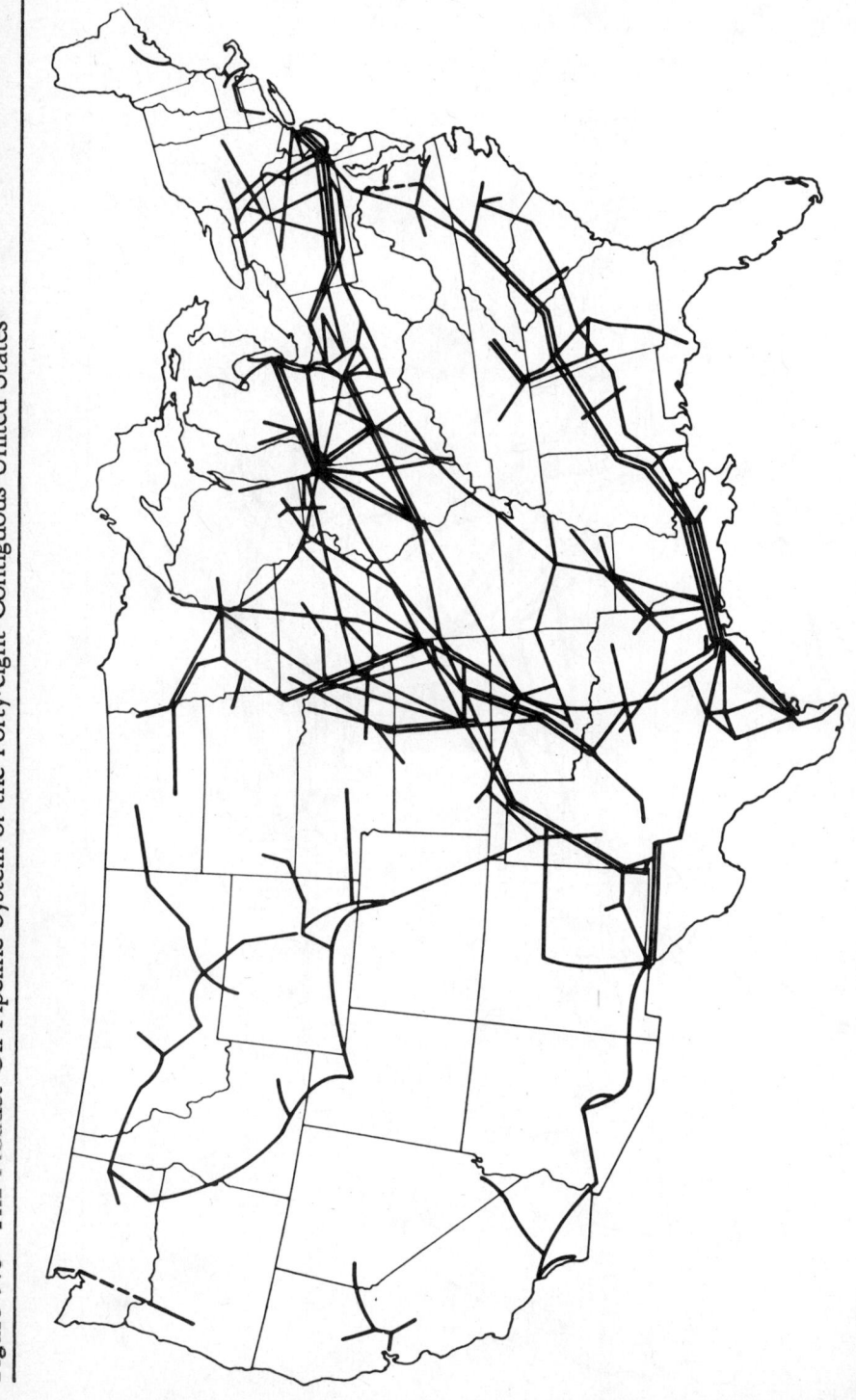

Source: Association of Oil Pipe Lines. Used by permission.

regions often are greatly unbalanced. Passengers are likely to go both from and to any given point in about equal numbers. Freight goes, but the same freight does not return. Geographic, resource, economic, and population factors determine how much of what is shipped and received at any point. Second, passenger traffic is likely to be fairly homogeneous. Basically, passenger transport sells a seat for a person. One seat is pretty much like another. Freight, on the other hand, may be very nonhomogeneous. It may differ greatly in size, weight, density, fragility, and other shipping characteristics. Thus, freight carriers are faced with quite different operating problems than are passenger carriers.

A principal environmental fact in the United States is that most people live in the northeastern section of the country. Population density per square mile in that section is about three times as great as in the Southeast and ten times as great as in the West. (There are smaller and scattered areas of dense population in both latter sections, of course.)

Necessarily, most consumption occurs where most people are. Likewise, since people make up the labor supply, most intensive forms of economic activity (manufacturing) also must take place in areas of concentrated population. Even if they wished to do so, inhabitants of a densely populated area could not engage in extensive forms of activity such as large-scale agriculture, cattle grazing, or timber growing. They do not have the necessary *space* resource, even if terrain, soil, and climatic conditions are otherwise suitable.

Aside from the factors of historic accident and evolution, then, this means that the densely populated northeastern portion of our country must be a manufacturing center. This region does have other locational advantages such as the proximity of coal and iron ore, good local transportation facilities, and a favorable location for access to European markets. Also, because of population density, it has a substantial home (intraregional) consumer market for its products.

The Southeast and West, on the other hand, are well suited for extensive forms of production. In addition to the necessary conditions of terrain, soil, and climate, they have space in considerable abundance. And, generally speaking, they do not have the Northeast's favorable conditions of labor supply, built-in home markets, and other desirable locational advantages. Their manufacturing activity is handicapped also by late arrival. Thus the economic destiny of these two areas has been, and is likely to be for some time, related to the production of foodstuffs and raw materials.

This economic environment forms the base for our long-distance commodity flow. As noted earlier, long-distance trade and its accompanying transportation is based upon the exchange of surpluses between unlike regions. This means that the predominant long-distance traffic movement in this country is a flow of foodstuffs and raw materials (including crude manufactures or semiprocessed items) from the West and the Southeast to the Northeast, and a backflow of manufactured or highly processed goods from the Northeast to the Southeast and West. In effect, the latter two areas are economic colonies of the Northeast in the same sense that the original American settlements were economic colonies of England, or that the pre–Civil War United States was an economic colony of Europe.

There are exceptions to this general picture, of course. Some foodstuffs are shipped out of the Northeast and some manufactured goods out of the West and Southeast. Also, there are significant areas of concentrated population, consumption, and manufacturing (which might be described as a pattern of subcolonization) within the colonial areas themselves. For example, the state of Oregon has been called an economic colony of California and Washington, and both of these Pacific Northwest states have been called economic colonies of California.

The word *colony* has acquired unpleasant moral and political connotations during recent years. It should be emphasized that the economic colonial pattern described above is not intended to carry such connotations. It may be bad or good, depending upon one's individual viewpoint. But actually it is nothing more than a logical geographical division of labor or specialization. Each of the described regions, like separate nations in foreign trade, has comparative or absolute advantages in certain types of production. Under our free enterprise system, it must be assumed that each region, like each individual, tends to engage in the kind of economic activity most profitable to it. Someone must grow trees, tomatoes, and tulips, just as someone must manufacture automobiles, anvils, and altimeters.

Such a pattern of interregional trade and transportation does create problems, however. Raw materials generally are heavier and bulkier than the manufactured items made from them, and consumed foodstuffs are completely removed from the stream of transportation. As the Northeast exchanges lighter manufactured goods for the heavier raw materials and foodstuffs of the West and Southeast, outbound freight tonnages of the latter regions are considerably in excess of inbound tonnages. Railroad cars and other freight vehicles that go to the Northeast fully loaded must return empty or only partially loaded to the West and Southeast.

An unbalanced freight movement creates problems for the management of transportation firms which naturally wish to operate with as little excess capacity as possible. It costs almost as much to move an empty vehicle, which brings in no revenue, as to move a fully loaded one. Such a situation does not encourage the enlargement of vehicle capacity. It also tends to shift vehicles into geographic areas where they will be more fully utilized both inbound and outbound.

These factors contribute to an almost chronic shortage of vehicle capacity, especially of the most desirable kinds of rail cars, during periods of peak seasonal demand for transportation. Unfortunately, many kinds of products tend to peak at the same time: lumber and plywood, wheat, tree fruits, and various kinds of fresh vegetables, for example. Often, during periods of shortages, rail cars must be allocated among various competing regions by the Association of American Railroads or even by the ICC.

In addition, as will be seen in Part IV, unbalanced freight movements tend to become reflected in the overall interregional freight rate structure and actually may contribute to a continuation of the imbalance.

Although we do have a definite pattern of broad regional specialization in this country, with direct and interconnecting transportation routes among these large regions, we must not forget that these broad regions themselves are made up of many smaller regions or subregional groups specializing in various types of production.

For example, different regions in the agricultural Southeast produce cotton, citrus fruits, and tobacco, and different parts of the agricultural West specialize in growing range cattle, apples, and melons. Likewise, various areas of the manufacturing Northeast specialize in automobiles, steel, and electronic devices. Also, as already noted, manufacturing areas do produce raw materials (coal in the Northeast, for example) and agricultural commodities, and raw materials or agricultural areas do engage in manufacturing activities of various kinds.

In reality, most transportation (even including that which may be classed as strictly local in nature) occurs as the result of exchanges among the specialized smaller regions within the larger regions we have been considering. Commodity-flow statistics for almost any one of our individual states, for example, will show that most out-of-state traffic comes from and goes to adjacent or nearby states. As indicated in Chapter 4, the average length of haul per shipment by railway, our basic form of long-haul transportation, is only about 650 miles. The average haul by Class I intercity truck common carriers, as you will also recall, is only about 500 miles. The average for all truck trips is about 11 miles.

The transport of almost any commodity tends to decrease with distance (or, more accurately, with shipping costs or freight-rate charges, which usually are in some way related to the distance moved). High transportation costs or charges cause distant consumers to search for usable substitute products or to engage in perhaps less efficient local production. A domestic freight charge in this respect has an economic effect similar to a protective tariff in international trade. Many essential or highly desired products without close substitutes do move in considerable quantities for long distances, of course. But even these commodities usually are aided in their movement by some kind of favorable freight-rate structure, and they usually are more heavily consumed in and near their producing area than in far-distant markets.

A comparatively small number of commodities account for most of the tonnage (and ton-miles) in long-distance transportation. This is more true for raw than for finished products, as one might imagine, but it is true even for manufactured goods. The annual railroad waybill statistics and publications of the ICC and the DOT (based on a 1 percent sample of all railway movements) dramatically illustrate this.

During a recent year, out of the 260 classifications into which the ICC grouped all commodities moving by rail, 17 classifications (a little more than 6 percent of the total) accounted for about 70 percent of all railroad tonnage originated.

During that particular year, out of 54 agricultural product classifications, the leading 5 (wheat, corn, flour, soybeans, and sugar beets) accounted for more than 57 percent of all originating railroad agricultural tonnage. Three mines products (coal and coke; sand, gravel, and stone; and iron ore) out of 24 classifications contributed 93 percent of the mines tonnage. Among 10 forest products classifications, 3 items (pulpwood; lumber, shingles, and lath; and logs, butts, and bolts) were responsible for 83 percent of the total volume. Fresh meats and cattle and calves made up 44 percent of the tonnage of 24 animal and animal product classifications. Manufactured and miscellaneous products were represented by 147 classifications out of which 4 (manufactured iron and steel; cement; scrap iron and scrap steel; and animal and poultry feed) accounted for 28 percent of the tonnage.

In the same year, incidentally, the total rail tonnage contributions of each of the five major commodity groups mentioned above was divided approximately as follows: products of mines, 54 percent; manufactured and miscellaneous, 28 percent; agricultural products, 9 percent; forest products, 6 percent; animals and animal products, 1 percent. (The total does not add up to 100 percent due to rounding.) The ten leading products shipped in order of tonnage volume were coal and coke; sand, gravel, and stone; iron ore; manufactured iron and steel; cement; pulpwood; wheat; scrap iron and scrap steel; lumber, shingles, and lath; and corn.

As indicated in Chapter 5, a high degree of product concentration exists in water carriage. Coal, petroleum products, and sand and gravel account for more than three-fourths of the tonnage moved by water in the Mississippi River system, and Great Lakes steamers specialize heavily in the carriage of mines products and grain. Pipeline traffic, of course, is the most specialized of all forms. Available statistics indicate that commodity concentration is not as pronounced in truck transportation as among these other major forms, but information on the actual composition of truck tonnage is somewhat scarce and unreliable. Air cargo, as you know, is only a statistically minute portion of the nation's overall freight tonnage.

CHANGES IN INTERREGIONAL RELATIONSHIPS

The output mix, or specialization, of all regions and subregions varies constantly over time. This variation usually is gradual in nature; but over a period of several years, it may have considerable cumulative effects upon interregional and intraregional commodity-flow patterns and upon the utilization of competing modes of carriage.

It is common knowledge that the northeastern portion of the United States has been declining in relative importance as a manufacturing center as industrialization has increased in the outlying colonial-type areas, for example. Figure 9.7 shows how this trend has affected various sections of the country over a thirty-year period.

As industrialization develops in an agricultural or raw materials–producing region, at least during the earlier stages of the process, the region's relative demand for long-haul transport is likely to decrease. The initial stages of industrialization will be based largely upon the manufacture or processing of locally produced raw materials. This has a double-barreled effect upon long-haul transportation. Not as much tonnage is sent to distant regions for manufacture, and not as much manufactured-goods tonnage is required from distant regions for local consumption. In other words, intraregional or short-haul transportation (for which trucks are well fitted) increases at the expense of interregional or long-haul transportation (in which railroads dominate).

It is not likely that all the new manufactured goods resulting from a region's developing industrialization will be consumed locally, however. Thus, such a region's demand for long-haul outbound transportation will not decline in direct proportion to its increased industrialization. Also, increased manufacturing activity, even though based primarily upon the utilization of locally produced raw materials, may require various kinds of subsidiary raw materials from outside areas.

After a region reaches a high level of industrialization, its local raw materials may no longer be sufficient to support its manufacturing activity, and its foodstuff production may be inadequate for the needs of its population. Then its dependence upon long-haul interregional trans-

Figure 9.7 Approximate Percentage of U.S. Mainufacturing Output (Values Added to Manufacturing) in Various Regions, Selected Years

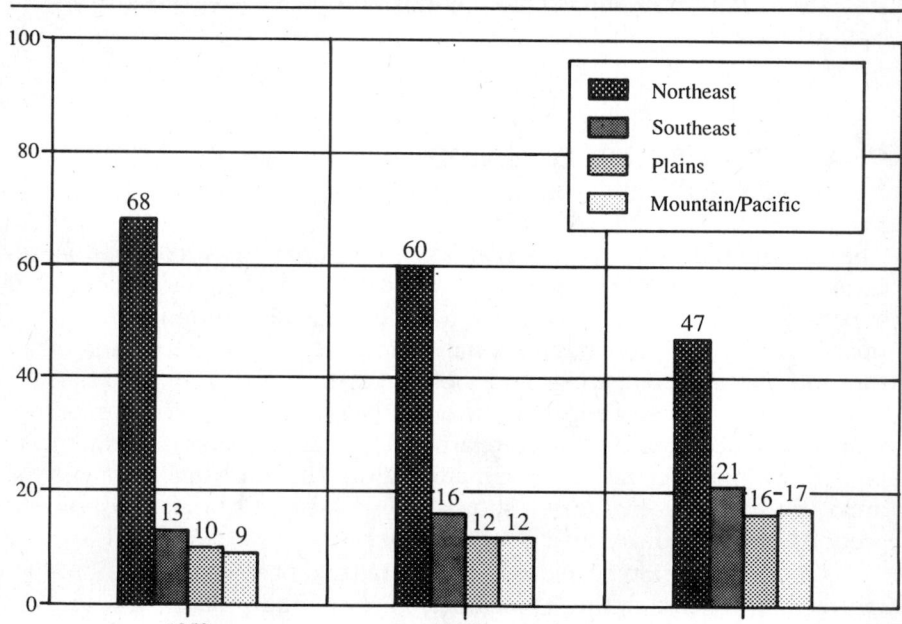

Source: Calculated and compiled by the authors from data published in *Statistical Abstract of the United States,* various years.

portation again increases. As will be explained in Part III, these various stages in regional industrial development, from the economic viewpoint of the individual region, may be greatly facilitated or hampered by the kind of interregional freight-rate structures in effect and may lead to regional producer pressures for modifications of existing rate structures.

EFFECTS OF INTERNATIONAL MARKET PATTERNS

While this text is devoted principally to domestic transportation, it is important to have an understanding of the impact of international markets on domestic transportation. The import and export of goods through specific ports has a tendency to alter domestic transportation patterns and their relative importance.

This can be seen to some extent by looking at changes in waterborne imports and exports from 1970 to 1986. In 1970, tonnage handled through Gulf Coast ports accounted for 14.5 percent and 38.0 percent of total import and export tonnages, respectively. In 1986, these figures had risen to 36.7 percent of total import tonnage and 39.7 percent of export tonnage.

While this may not change overall domestic traffic patterns, it does tend to change their relative importance as specific ports serve a greater or lesser role as magnets for export traffic or distribution centers for import traffic. Specific waterborne import/export tonnages are shown in Figure 9.8. In addition, operations such as those involved in landbridge intermodal transportation affect domestic traffic patterns.

Figure 9.8 Waterborne Imports and Exports by Coastal District, in Millions of Short Tons

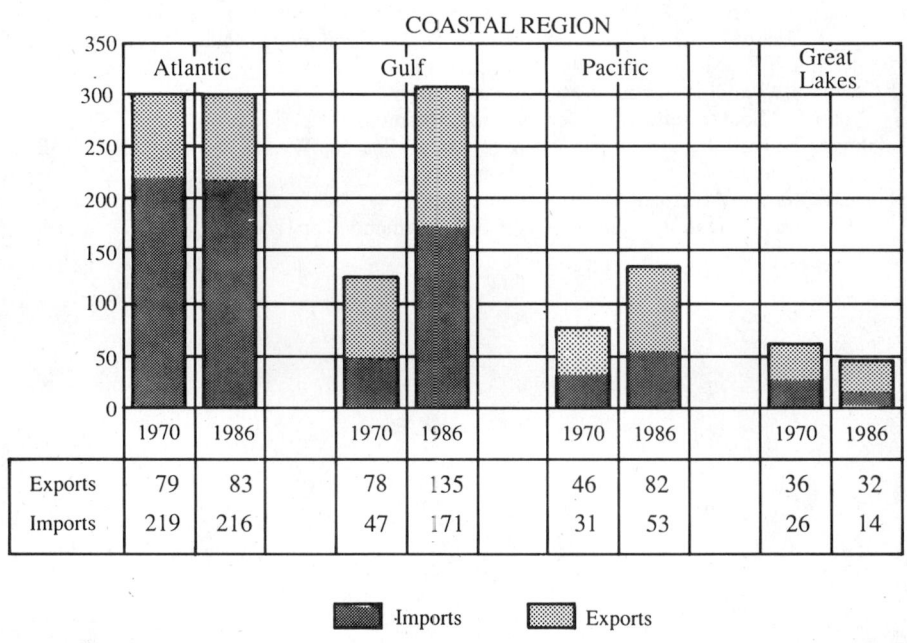

	Atlantic		Gulf		Pacific		Great Lakes	
	1970	1986	1970	1986	1970	1986	1970	1986
Exports	79	83	78	135	46	82	36	32
Imports	219	216	47	171	31	53	26	14

Imports   Exports

Source: Taken from data published in the *Statistical Abstract of the United States,* various years.

ADDITIONAL READINGS

Becht, K. Edwin, A Geography of Transportation and Business Logistics, Dubuque, Iowa: Wm. C. Brown, 1970.
  Chapter 1, "Introduction to Transportation Patterns," pp. 1–15.
  Chapter 2, "The Relative Decline in the Importance of Terrain and Climate in Shaping Transportation Patterns," pp. 6–16.
Daggett, Stuart, Principles of Inland Transportation, 4th ed., New York: Harper and Brothers, 1955.
  Part 3, "Transportation Geography," pp. 127–226.
Gilmore, Harlan W., Transportation and the Growth of Cities, Glencoe, Ill.: Free Press of Glencoe, 1953.
  Chapter 5, "Transportation Systems and Types of Communities," pp. 86–102.
Hay, William W., Introduction to Transportation Engineering, New York: John Wiley, 1961.
  Chapter 15, "Route Design and Location," pp. 432–54.
Pegrum, Dudley F., Transportation: Economics and Public Policy, 3rd ed., Homewood, Ill.: Richard D. Irwin, 1973.
  Chapter 4, "Transportation Geography," pp. 71–96.
Sampson, Roy J., "Another View of Comparative Regional Development," Land Economics (May 1960), 216–20.
  _____, Railroad Rates and Shipments from the Pacific Northwest, Eugene, Oregon: Bureau of Business Research, University of Oregon, 1961.
  Part 2, "Principal Rail Export Commodities and Their Destinations," pp. 5–32.
  _____, Railroad Rates and Shipments into the Pacific Northwest, Eugene, Oregon: Bureau of Business Research, University of Oregon, 1963.
  Part 2, "Principal Inbound Movements," pp. 6–19.
  Part 3, "Sources and Rates for Inbound Shipments," pp. 20–37.
Ulman, Edward L., American Commodity Flow, Seattle, Wash.: Washington University Press, 1957.
  Chapter 1, "American Internal Commodity Flow: Rail and Water Traffic," pp. 1–12.
  Chapter 4, "State-to-State Rail Freight Movements," pp. 28–169.

PART III

REGULATION/DEREGULATION OF DOMESTIC TRANSPORTATION

Transportation has been considered one of the regulated industries for many years, and regulation has an impact on all parts of transportation — carriers, shippers, and the general public. Only by understanding the regulatory framework within which transportation operates can one fully appreciate the complexities of transportation.

Transportation has always been regulated to some degree. The common-law obligations of carriers have existed for centuries (to be discussed more fully in Chapter 20). Comprehensive regulation of transportation by statute is built upon that common-law base and is of relatively recent origins historically. This part of the text will trace the growth and development of this comprehensive regulatory structure and the recent modifications generally known as deregulation. It will also introduce the reader to the regulatory institutions responsible for that regulatory structure.

Since the regulation of transportation is evolutionary, continuing to develop as conditions and society's ideas change, the first two chapters of this part are organized chronologically. One concerns the regulation of transportation monopoly and the other, the regulation of transportation competition. The next two chapters are concerned with regulatory developments since the late 1950s and particularly the so-called deregulation movement of the past few years. Then, after a discussion of the consequences of deregulation on the various modes, the final chapter on regulatory institutions is descriptive.

CHAPTER 10
REGULATION OF TRANSPORTATION MONOPOLY

The economic market for transportation has many facets. In some places and at some times it is extremely monopolistic. At other places and in other times it is quite competitive. Sometimes transportation operates simultaneously both as a monopolistic venture and as a competitive enterprise. An example of this would be competition at terminal points served by several carriers or modes, with monopoly at in-between locations served by only one carrier or mode.

Historically, transportation has tended toward monopoly. Where only one carrier serves a given location, monopolistic abuse is possible. This abuse may take many forms; and over time, society has become alert to many of these abusive actions. When a monopolistic firm charges extremely high rates or practices discrimination, it is quite likely that some sort of social control or regulation will be exercised. This chapter will discuss the steps taken by society to regulate monopolistic transportation markets which have developed in our economy.

THE EVOLUTIONARY NATURE OF
TRANSPORT REGULATION

Society provides the ground rules upon which business enterprise operates. These ground rules are never static. They may seem to be changing only slightly in any one period, but if viewed over long expanses of time, changes are apparent. The structure of regulation grows as a slow process, not by revolution. In transportation regulation, the change may be considered evolutionary. Our present regulatory structure evolved or developed out of the past and was modified as conditions changed over time.

The evolutionary nature of transportation regulation is most easily appreciated by tracing the building up of our regulatory structure. This structure reflects economic conditions and characteristics of the particular time period under question to a very marked degree. As conditions change because of technological advances or other new circumstances, regulations also change.

Change in transportation regulation was not always immediate or concurrent with changed conditions. A considerable lapse of time sometimes occurred between the two. Society needs strong evidence that a social structure is outdated and no longer provides satisfactory solutions before change takes place. This is known to social scientists as *social lag*.

Regulation During the Promotional Era

Early in the development of our nation, the necessity for adequate transportation was so great that society did little in the way of transportation regulation. Most transportation efforts were directed toward developing an adequate system. Although excesses did take place, as they inevitably do during the promotion of any undertaking, society was largely concerned with conquering the continent, acquiring transportation facilities, and providing the basis for economic growth. With such prodigious tasks, there was little concern for the niceties of protection against the abuses of monopoly.

There probably was little need to regulate during the pre–Civil War period. This was a period of struggle for supremacy among various modes of transportation. Infant railroads struggled against canals, teamsters and wagoners against riverboats, and they all competed against one another. Intermodal competition was the order of the day. There was little need to supplement the natural forces of the marketplace with regulatory laws and procedures.

This is not to say that regulation did not exist during the promotional period prior to the Civil War. The older areas were faced with the problems of social control while promotion was continuing farther west. Thus the promotional era was not always the same span of time for all regions. Indeed, as Chapter 2 points out, railroads continued to expand on mileage well into the twentieth century even though the second half of the nineteenth century is generally thought of as the time of greatest railroad competition.

The promotional period prior to the Civil War may be thought of as a period of experimentation with various types of social control. In those regions where problems arose, various types of solutions were attempted. These early attempts at transportation regulation took three forms: common law and judicial control, regulation by charter, and investigatory commissions.

Common Law and Judicial Control

Common law, which continues to exist today, is a body of rules and obligations based mainly on custom. Our common-law foundation came from England and serves as the basis for our whole legal system. It is largely based on precedent. One who wishes to consult the common law refers to past court decisions and jurists' opinions rather than a statute book or legislative enactment.

Common-law regulation of transportation has often been called regulation by lawsuit. Basically, rights and obligations under common law apply to individuals. Thus the right of the customer to reasonable service, at reasonable rates, and without unreasonable discrimination was the basis of some early lawsuits. The obligation of the common calling of certain industries was the basis of some rulemaking also. This obligation of common calling served as the legal basis for later statute law regulations of transportation.

Common law failed as an adequate method of regulating monopolistic abuses for several reasons. First, it was subject to judicial interpretation, and rarely did two jurists find the same precedent for, or make the same interpretation of, a similar situation. Second, the common law is inherently unsuited for regulation of a modern-day business monopoly. Under medieval conditions of individual redress for past wrongs, it was adequate. Under complex modern-day capitalistic business arrangements wherein a business enterprise deals with another business enterprise, it is inadequate. Specifically, common law lacks the ability to prevent abuses (it considers only abuses committed), to promote beneficial activity (it punishes but cannot promote), to have continuous regulation (each matter must be dealt with individually as the need arises), to control in the social interest (the common law is based on individual rights and cannot protect the rights of society as a whole), to expediently address itself to business abuses (lawsuits are very time consuming and expensive), and to deal with the specialized nature of commerce cases (judges often are not trained in the intricacies of business relationships and have to consider business cases melded with personal injury, murder, fraud, etc.). Modern-day circumstances called for social controls that were preventive, promotional, continuous, socially oriented, expedient, and specialized. The common law did not provide these.

Charter Regulation

Another device used during the promotional period was regulation by charter. As previously noted, popularity of turnpikes led to the development of joint stock companies. These early corporation-type organizations were also used to promote some canals and most early railroads. They were created as artificial persons by a special act of the legislature of the state. As the state granted this special privilege, the opportunity to specify rules and regulations arose. Early charters at times specified maximum rates that could be charged, sometimes maximum earnings on capital, and sometimes details of operations. Additionally, the right of eminent domain (right to take private property for public use) was often granted. Here again an opportunity to control was evident. Some early grants specified routes and controlled construction and extensions.

Often charters were without a term or had almost unlimited life (such as ninety-nine years). Uniformity was difficult since it was necessary to secure a charter in each state where the transportation firm operated and each charter was a special act of the legislature. Sometimes charters provided for tax exemptions or tax limitations as well as other valuable privileges such as the right to operate banks.

Charter regulation did not prove effective as a device of social control. Maximum rate control proved ineffective since conditions and costs changed. Maximum earnings control, usually in terms of returns on stock, could easily be subverted by issuing more stock. With a long or unlimited life on these charters, it was almost impossible to specify operating details or to foresee the need for future routes or extensions. Finally, after the Supreme Court ruled in the famous *Dartmouth College* case (4 Wheaton 518, 1819) that a charter was a contract that could not be changed by a subsequent legislature, the difficulty of regulation by charter was apparent. In spite of these difficulties, attempts were undertaken to regulate the various modes of transportation by charter.

Investigatory Commissions

Another type of regulation experiment was that of the commission with power to investigate only. In the latter part of the 1830s and the 1840s, such agencies were created, principally in New England, to investigate railroads. These commissions had no control over rates, but were given power to investigate and report upon the operation of the railroads and often to appraise the value of land when eminent-domain proceedings were involved. Occasionally they were given power to specify accounting systems and require statistical information. This type of regulation failed because it was powerless to protect the public, but the concept of a body of experts (a commission) meeting in continuous session was established.

State Regulation and the Emergence of Monopoly Controls

It was not until after the Civil War that positive control over monopoly abuses was instituted. Indeed, the immediate post–Civil War period was one in which much of the foundation of the present system of social control over all types of business was established. These controls were developed to deal principally with transportation and more specifically with railroad transportation.

Economic Conditions

Economic circumstances were such that the whole problem of social control came to a head during this period. Many social and economic changes had been caused by the war. Families had been broken up, the South was in devastation, many were restless, and the great surge of settlers into the open spaces of the West was about to begin. President Lincoln had signed the Homestead Act in 1863, opening up vast areas of the public domain to the stouthearted. Land grants had promoted railways in advance of settlement, and railroads were interested in settling people upon their land. Technological advances in agriculture had led to great increases in production, particularly in grain crops. Immigration only added to the large numbers of people opening new lands in the West. The result was an increasing agricultural surplus with plummeting agricultural prices.

New technology born of the urgency of the war was leading to rapid industrialization. Monetary problems from the war-born inflation added to the unrest. Business ethics were at a low ebb, and great fortunes were being made from the industrial revolution. Some investors felt they were being shortchanged in the resultant excesses of stock promotion and corporate manipulation. This was particularly true of railroad investors, many of whom were farmers or small businessmen who had invested personally or had urged cities, counties, and state governments to invest in order to construct transportation facilities.

The situation was particularly acute in the Midwest, the states of the old Northwest Territory. This area, one of the principal agricultural producers of the nation, found itself in dire competition with new areas of agricultural production to the West. Many agrarians of the region had invested in railroad promotions only to find that once the transportation system was operating, the rates were high, the service poor, discrimination rampant, and return on investment nil. These farmers were in a mood for action; something akin to an agrarian revolution was in the making.

The agriculturalists of Illinois, Iowa, Wisconsin, and Minnesota (the major states involved) did not understand the facts of supply and demand. Agricultural prices continued to decrease as excess production was generated on new western lands and as war-promoted demand ceased. Railroad and elevator rates went up as these businesses were able to exploit their new monopolistic positions. Farmers banded together in semifraternal organizations called *granges* (more properly known as Patrons of Husbandry) and struck out at their apparent enemies — the railroads and elevators. The tool of the agrarian revolt was the ballot box, and agricultural representatives to state legislatures were repeatedly elected in the late 1860s and early 1870s.

The Granger Acts

The reaction was the famous granger legislation or, as it is sometimes called, the granger movement. In the 1870s, legislatures of granger states passed stringent laws broadly regulating railroads and grain elevators. Typically, these laws had four parts: (1) establishment of maximum rates, (2) prohibition of local discrimination, (3) attempts to force competition by forbidding railroad mergers, and (4) prohibition of free passes to public officials.

In some states, the legislature specified maximum rates. But the matter of rate construction is complicated and requires trained personnel plus a great deal of information about costs and movement. Since the composition of the legislatures changed with each election and most legislators lacked the necessary knowledge to attack such a complicated task, this method of ratemaking was a failure. In some states, however, railroad commissions were established. Persons appointed to those bodies either had knowledge of the task or were able to learn its intricacies and stay in office over a span of time.

Local discrimination was regulated by prorate clauses which were much more stringent than the later long-haul/short-haul clauses. These regulations provided that a railroad could not charge the same or more for movement of a commodity over a short distance than it charged for movement of a similar commodity over a longer distance anywhere on its line. Although this was the basis of the long-and-short-haul regulation of today, it was necessary to modify prorate clauses so that branch lines had separate rate schedules and the hauls involved were over the same route in the same direction.

Railroad mergers were common. One of the means of securing a transportation monopoly was by consolidations and mergers. In prohibiting mergers, these early laws were merely reflecting the prevailing opinion of the day that competition was the most effective regulator. The impropriety of granting free passes to public officials, particularly judges, legislators, and others in authority, is obvious. Such actions were considered a form of bribery.

The reaction of the railroads was vigorous. A widespread educational campaign akin to modern-day public relations programs was undertaken. This campaign pointed out the injustices of the laws as well as their impracticability and their hasty passage. Railroads claimed they could not do business under such regulation. This claim was further backed up by the problems arising out of the Panic of 1873. The economy of the expanding nation experienced another of the brief, periodic, severe and sudden depressions which characterized the nineteenth century. Some railroads did go bankrupt, railroad construction did decrease, and many railroads suspended dividend and interest payments. Railroads claimed that many of their problems during this crisis were due to regulation. Faced with this "proof," plus the obviously unsound nature of some of the regulations, most states repealed or modified their granger laws in the middle and late 1870s. Illinois with its railroad commission remained the exception.

The Legal Basis of Regulation

Even though the granger laws were short-lived, they were of great significance in the evolution of transportation regulation. This was the first time our society had regulated a whole industry and had set up a structure of ground rules outside of the courts and the common law. The idea of regulation had been firmly implanted. Second, the granger laws served as the basis for later regulation of transportation. The similarity between the granger acts and the federal government's Act to Regulate Commerce of 1887 is not a coincidence. Finally, the granger laws provided a legal precedent for subsequent regulation of many other types of business.

In addition to the educational campaign and the results of the Panic of 1873, railroads challenged the legal right of states to regulate or control business. Court cases concerning constitutionality were instituted. While the question was being argued through the courts, many of the granger laws were repealed or modified. By 1877, however, the U.S. Supreme Court ruled that the states had indeed acted legally when they had regulated railroads and elevators.

Some six separate major cases were involved, but the most important decision (and the only case that was not a railroad case) was in *Munn* v. *Illinois* (94 U.S. 113, 1877). All the other so-called granger cases rested upon the opinion in this case, as does much of the legal foundation of regulation of other kinds of business.

Railroads and grain elevators claimed that they were private businesses and that setting their charges and rates by public enactment violated the

Fourteenth Amendment of the U.S. Constitution, which provides that a state cannot deprive a person of property without due process of law. The Fourteenth Amendment was new (1868) and somewhat untested. These cases, therefore, were also important as tests of this part of the Constitution.

The Court drew upon an opinion of Lord Chief Justice Hale in the 1600s which noted that common carriers had always been regulated in early societies. It noted that some businesses become "affected with the public interest" and are no longer private, but may be regulated in the public interest without necessarily violating the Constitution. Specifically, the Court stated in part:

> When . . . one devotes his property to a use in which the public has an interest, he . . . grants to the public an interest in that use, and must submit to be controlled by the public for the common good, to the extent of the interest he has thus created.

Struggle for Federal Control

The granger movement had not gone unheeded in Washington. Monopolistic abuses of railroads were nationwide. In 1872, President Grant sent a recommendation to Congress that an investigation of transportation be undertaken. The Senate set up a special committee, the Windom Committee, to investigate the possibility of cheaper transportation between the interior and the seaboard. This committee's report in 1874 began a long struggle that finally culminated in federal control in 1887.

The Windom Report, the first of many investigations and reports by congressional committees on transportation monopolies, concluded that the defects and abuses of the railroads were insufficient facilities, unfair discrimination, and extortionate charges. The report recognized that competition was the best regulator, but noted that private competition "invariably ends in combination." The solution recommended by the Windom Report was public competition by way of state or federally owned and operated railroads.

Partially as a result of the Windom Report, the House of Representatives passed a bill to regulate railroads in 1874. The Senate took no action and the bill died. Again in 1878 the House passed a regulatory bill. The Senate likewise acted and passed its own version of public regulation of railroads. The two approaches differed greatly, however, and the Senate and House became deadlocked over the matter. A special committee, the Cullom Committee, was appointed to make a thorough investigation of railroad monopoly abuses.

The Cullom Committee filed its report in 1886. It placed great emphasis upon the abuses of monopoly power by railroads. Many discriminatory practices of the railroads were investigated and highlighted. Discrimination among persons, places, and commodities was common. Stated rates were only a place for bargaining to begin for the large shipper, whereas the small shipper without bargaining power was forced to pay the quoted price. Rebates were common. The investigation disclosed that not only did the railroad monopoly exploit small shippers and noncompetitive points, but industrial monopolists in turn exploited railroads by demanding rebates. For instance, in 1885 the Marietta and Cincinnati (later part of the Baltimore and Ohio) charged the Standard Oil Company a rate of 10 cents per barrel for moving crude oil from Macksburg, Ohio, to Marietta while at the same time charging smaller shippers 35 cents. Then the railroad additionally rebated to Standard 25 cents a barrel for each barrel shipped by the small producers. The Cullom report did much to hasten federal regulation of railroads.

The final action leading to federal regulation was the decision in the *Wabash* case (118 U.S. 557), also in 1886. In the earlier *Munn* case, the U.S. Supreme Court had upheld state regulation of matters that obviously were interstate in nature, apparently on the grounds that Congress had taken no regulatory action. In the *Wabash* case, the Court decreed that the federal government alone had power to regulate interstate commerce.

The *Wabash* case grew out of the granger period and the Illinois regulatory law. The Wabash, St. Louis and Pacific Railway charged $39 for the carriage of goods from Peoria, Illinois (near the center of the state) to New York, whereas it charged $65 for the carriage of a like quantity from Gilman, Illinois (some 87 miles to the east) to New York. The reason for charging more for the shorter haul was the existence of competition at Peoria. This was a clear violation of the Illinois act, but the Supreme Court took careful note of the fact that the U.S. Constitution provided that Congress had the power to regulate interstate commerce. It thus held that a state could regulate commerce only within its borders (intrastate commerce). Since the destination here was New York, Illinois could not apply its law. Unless and until the federal government acted to regulate commerce, interstate movements could not be regulated. The *Wabash* case, coupled with the Cullom Report, forced a solution. A compromise was worked out between the House version of regulation and the Senate views. The result was the Act to Regulate Commerce of 1887. It should be noted that many provisions of this law were supported by railroads which often had been forced by economic circumstances and pressures to grant preferences that decreased their revenues. Now they could fall back on the law as a protection against requests for such preferences.

The Act to Regulate Commerce

The Act to Regulate Commerce, now know as the Interstate Commerce Act, became effective on April 5, 1887. This statute has been amended many times since. It presently contains separate parts covering all types of public transportation except air.

Basically the act was aimed at monopoly abuses. Control of discrimination was stressed in almost every section. Each of six principal sections of the act dealt with a different phase or abuse of monopoly power.

Section 1 required that all rates must be "just and reasonable" and that all "unjust and unreasonable rates" are unlawful. This provision applied to rates both for freight and for passengers. It was left up to the commission to determine what was just and reasonable. The idea of justness and reasonableness was merely a formalization of the common-law rule on charges of common carriers.

Section 2 dealt with personal discrimination. This section ordered the carriers to give equal treatment to shippers where transportation service was performed under similar circumstances and conditions. The law stated that it was unlawful for any carriers,

> directly or indirectly, by special rate, rebate, drawback, or other device, to charge, demand, collect, or receive from any person . . . greater or less compensation . . . than it receives from any other person . . . for doing . . . a like and contemporaneous service in transportation of a like kind of traffic under similar circumstances and conditions.

Exceptions were later allowed for freight and passengers of federal, state, and municipal governments, for charitable purposes, and for rail employees entitled to free passes.

The third section was a general discrimination clause. It contained a blanket prohibition of all "undue preference or prejudice" to any person, locality, or traffic either in rates or services. This clause appears to have been broad enough to cover both personal discrimination (Section 2) and long-and-short-haul discrimination (Section 4), but these types of discrimination were so prevalent that Congress decided to give them special treatment. It is well to note that all discrimination was not prohibited by Section 3, but only "undue" preference and prejudice. Again, the determination of "undue" was left up to the commission.

Section 4 contained the famous long-and-short-haul clause. This provided that it was unlawful for any common carrier

> to charge or receive any greater compensation . . . for the transportation of passengers or . . . property, under substantially similar circum-

stances and conditions, for a shorter than for a longer distance over the same line, in the same direction, the shorter being included within the longer distance.

The commission was authorized to make exceptions in special cases upon application by carriers. Further, it should be noted that the inclusion of the phrase "over the same line, in the same direction, the shorter being included in the longer" made this section considerably less stringent than corresponding earlier classes of the granger laws. Nevertheless, Congress felt strongly enough about this type of monopoly abuse to give it special treatment even though Section 3 probably would have been applicable.

The fifth section prohibited pooling agreements of various types, reflecting the popular opinion that enforced competition would protect the public. This provision was also directly related to the earlier prohibition of any consolidations or mergers by the granger laws.

Section 6 required that all rates and fares should be published and strictly observed. Because of the popular practice of suddenly changing rates after giving advance notice to but a few favored shippers (often called *midnight tariffs*), the act also ordered that specific public notice of any rate change be posted.

Finally, the act set up the ICC, originally consisting of five members appointed by the president with the consent of the Senate, and enumerated the powers and duties of this new type of governmental agency. The commission was patterned to a considerable degree on the investigatory-type commission of the promotional era and the strong granger commissions.

The commission was charged with administration of the act. It could hear complaints, take testimony, subpoena documents, and generally inquire into the business of common carriers. Upon adequate finding, it could issue cease-and-desist orders and determine awards of damages suffered because of violations. Penalties were to be imposed by courts of law, however. The commission had to go to court if carriers did not obey its orders. Finally, the commission was to report to Congress annually and recommend legislation it considered necessary.

Weaknesses and Early Regulatory Experience

It must be remembered that regulation by an administrative commission was a precedent-breaking step. The granger experience had been relatively short and limited. Earlier commissions in New England and the East had generally little power to enforce. All previous regulations had been on the basis of state jurisdiction. Now a whole industry across the entire nation was to be regulated by a quasi-judicial body of five men. Obviously, such a procedure was a step away from the laissez-faire philosophy of capitalism; just as obviously, the commission had to proceed slowly and lay the foundation for regulation as it progressed.

As the commission began its work, certain weaknesses in the act became evident. Basically, these were four in number: (1) testimony, (2) enforcing orders and review, (3) rate power, and (4) discrimination interpretations. All these involved court decisions and arose within the first ten years of the act's life. Perhaps the courts were jealous of this new body which had all the trappings of a court without all the formalities. Certainly the carriers were testing the act. Likewise, economic conditions played a role in that carriers did not feel entirely free to exercise monopolistic abuses during the depressed period up to the mid-1890s. With increased prosperity after 1895, violations became more numerous.

The matter of testimony came to a head early. In 1890 a shipper refused to divulge whether he had received a rebate, on the grounds that he might incriminate himself. When the Supreme Court held in favor of the shipper in 1892, Congress began a long series of remedial laws by passing the Compulsory Testimony Act in 1893. This act gave witnesses immunity with respect to their testimony and closed one of the basic weaknesses of the law.

The matter of enforcing orders was not so simple. Orders of the commission had to be enforced by a court order. Carriers automatically appealed commission orders to the court of jurisdiction (the lowest federal court). While the court considered the case, the carrier did not have to obey the commission's orders. Much time elapsed as the carrier pursued its appeal through successive levels of courts. Commission cases had no preference in crowded court dockets. Some cases dragged on as long as nine years after the commission had issued cease-and-desist orders.

In a series of cases in 1896 and 1897, the commission was shorn of all power to prescribe rates. The original act was quite clear that the commission could declare a rate to be unreasonable and unjust, but it did not specifically allow the commission to prescribe what was a just and reasonable rate. Up to 1896, the commission assumed this power, and in 68 out of 135 formal cases it had set maximum just and reasonable rates once it had found existing rates to be unjust and unreasonable. But in the *Social Circle* case (162 U.S. 184, 1896), the Supreme Court noted that no explicit power to set rates seemed to exist; and in the *Maximum Freight Rate* case (167 U.S. 497, 1897), the Court held that the commission was without power to set rates. These decisions were of great importance as they left the commission with little power. Once a finding of unreasonableness was made and orders issued to cease and desist, the carriers would appeal to a court. After a long lapse of time (while the carrier continued to charge the unjust rate), the court might uphold the commission. But since the commission could not specify the new rate, a very small change in the charge would necessitate the commission's going through the whole long and costly process again.

Another weakness was in court interpretation of Section 4. The phrase "under substantially similar circumstances and conditions" came under question. In the *Alabama Midlands* case (168 U.S. 144, 1897), the Supreme Court held that it was up to the carrier to determine whether or not conditions were similar and that competition at an end point and not at intermediate points created dissimilarity of conditions. This decision effectively destroyed the prohibition against local discrimination since it could nearly always be shown that differences in competition existed. Railroads rarely charged less for the longer hauls unless they were forced to do so by competition.

The effect of these court decisions and statutory weaknesses was to convert the ICC into little more than a fact-finding and reporting agency.

Strengthening Monopoly Regulation

Each of the weaknesses that had hampered the commission was dealt with between 1897 and 1910 in a series of separate statutes designed to strengthen the regulation over monopoly.

Congressional action to enforce testimony has already been noted. The matter of court review was partially dealt with when Congress passed the Expediting Act of 1903. This act allowed commission cases to be given priority over other cases upon certification by the attorney general that the matter was of public importance. This shortened the long lapse of time between commission deliberation and judicial review.

The Elkins Act, also in 1903, is often called the Anti-Rebate Act. Pressure on carriers to give rebates where competition existed was extreme. The railroads themselves recognized that the effect of rebates was cumulative and that shippers with competitive means of transportation were able to play one carrier off against another. Therefore they sponsored the Elkins Act which (1) made the receiving of a rebate unlawful, (2) made departure from the published rate a misdemeanor and adherence to the published tariffs enforceable by court injunction, (3) eliminated the imprisonment penalty for rebates while increasing the fine to $20,000, and (4) made the railroad corporation as well as the personnel of the carrier liable for violations.

After the turn of the century, another reform movement somewhat similar to the granger movement swept the country. Under President Theodore Roosevelt, attention was called to trusts and various other monopolistic abuses. Certainly the railroads, operating under extremely weak controls, were still guilty of abuses. Roosevelt called for new monopoly regulation over railroads in his messages of 1904, 1905, and 1906. The so-called Progressive movement was under way, and many new ground rules for the control of business were being born.

One result was the Hepburn Act of 1906 which has commonly been called the "rehabilitation of the ICC." This act, sponsored by Senator Hepburn of Iowa, erased two of the previous weaknesses of the original Act to Regulate Commerce and strengthened monopoly control in several areas. Commission orders became binding on carriers and had to be observed while appeal was being pursued in the courts. A fine was provided ($5,000 a day) for failure to comply with commission orders after not less than thirty days from the date of issue, and the order had to be observed for up to two years. The commission was given power to seek enforcement in court.

The second weakness erased was the matter of rate power. The commission was given authority to prescribe maximum rates once it had determined that a rate was unjust and unreasonable. The carrier could charge less than the maximum, but at least the commission had the power to establish how high a just and reasonable rate would be. It should be emphasized that the commission could exercise this power only after it had investigated and formally declared a rate to be unjust and unreasonable.

Regulatory powers were strengthened in several other ways. Jurisdiction of the commission was extended to include related and accessorial services such as express companies, sleeping-car companies, terminal services, and storage services. Privately owned rail cars came under commission jurisdiction. Oil pipelines were controlled. The domination of petroleum companies in the ownership of pipelines seems to have been the predominant reason for extending regulation into this area. This extension is extremely significant as it was the first step in the application of transportation regulation to nonrail carriage. Oil pipeline regulation was transferred from the ICC to the newly created Department of Energy in 1977.

Additionally, the commission's control over accounts and reports was strengthened. The original act had given the commission no power to enforce uniform accounting rules or to inspect the books of carriers or require reports. Many carriers had simply ignored this part of the law. Without adequate and correct information, effective regulation was impossible. The commission, therefore, was given power to inspect accounts, prescribe uniform accounting systems, and require reports.

Discrimination control was also strengthened. Regulations were authorized concerning the issuance of passes, the commodities clause was established, and the commission was given power to establish through routes and joint rates among participating carriers.

Under the commodities clause, Congress forced railroads to divest themselves of their noncarrier interests. Prior to this time, railroads had been producing many goods in competition with their shippers. This was particularly true of coal. By charging shippers high rates and charging themselves low or no rates, railroads were gaining a competitive advantage. Henceforth, rail carriers were prohibited from transporting articles in commerce that they produced or had an interest in, with the exception of lumber. They could produce commodities for their own use, but not transport them in commerce.

Additional strengthening took place with the passage of the Mann-Elkins Act (1910). This statute removed the phrase "under substantially similar circumstances and conditions" in Section 4, thereby restoring the long-and-short-haul clause which interpretation by the Supreme Court had virtually killed in 1896–97. Control over local discrimination was thereby re-established.

The Mann-Elkins Act strengthened further commission control by allowing the ICC to suspend a proposed rate change for 120 days while it investigated the reasonableness of the proposal. An additional 120 days were allowable if necessary to complete the investigation. Previously, a carrier might prepare a rate change and begin charging the new rate after 30 days. The commission might later find the new rate unreasonable and award reparations to the shipper. But this procedure was unsatisfactory because the shipper had usually already passed on the rate change to customers. Moreover, the act shifted the burden of proof of reasonableness to the carrier, whereas formerly the shipper had to contest and show that the changed rate was unreasonable.

Additionally, the commission was given power to control railroad classification procedures, its jurisdiction was extended to telegraph, telephone, and cable companies (this control was later shifted to the Federal Communications Commission), the president was given the power to set up a special commission to investigate railroad securities, and shippers were given the right to designate the route over which they preferred their shipments to move.

Certainly, in the period from 1903 to 1910, transportation regulation was strengthened and many previous weaknesses overcome. By the time of World War I, transportation regulation of monopoly seemed to be almost complete.

The Refinement of Monopoly Regulation

The basic structure of the control of monopoly in transportation seemed complete by 1910. However, the economy is never static and neither is transportation. Conditions change and under new circumstances, transportation regulation also needs changing. The outstanding refinements of monopoly regulation came out of the World War I years.

The basic philosophy of monopoly regulation had been to force railroads to compete vigorously with one another and, where competition was impossible, to substitute controls of the ICC. All carriers were forced to bid for the shipper's favor. Where there was but one carrier to a given destination, Section 4 was rigorously applied. The provisions of Section 3 (undue preference and prejudice) attempted to ensure that all areas, shippers, and types of traffic were treated on a parity. In case these controls failed, the commission had power to specify maximum rates where unreasonableness existed. From all points of view, regulation should have been most successful in protecting the public.

Unfortunately, regulation was not effective. A fundamental weakness was that it failed to provide for an adequate and healthy transportation system. This lack of positive control was pointed up by wartime transportation experiences where railroads were unable to provide adequate and coordinated service for the nation's needs.

Railroad credit was poor owing to overcapitalization. No financial controls had existed and many carriers were overburdened with excessive capitalization from an earlier period. Also, no control over the extension of rail lines existed; and in line with the idea of greater competition for the existing transportation demand, unwise and unneeded expansion of railroad plant had occurred. Little control over service standards existed since it was assumed that competition would naturally bring better service. Yet with rates and earnings restricted, the reaction of the carriers was to decrease the service level. Car shortages appeared, delays were common, and cooperation and coordination were very poor.

All these weaknesses became apparent under the strain of wartime transportation conditions. Although the United States did not enter the European conflict immediately, tremendous amounts of war material were produced in this country. Traffic increased greatly, placing a severe burden upon railroad plant which had not kept up owing to restrictive earnings and excessive competition. In 1917, the federal government, finding the railroads completely unable to offer the efficient service needed to pursue the war, seized the railroads. The carriers were so accustomed to competition, poor service, and individual action that they would not or could not offer a cooperative, efficient, and adequate transportation service in this time of need.

During the period of federal control, cooperation was forced upon the carriers. In an attempt to stem the inflationary pressures of a wartime situation, the government did not allow rate increases. Instead, railroad companies were guaranteed a profit while the government poured vast sums into updating and operating the railroad plant. Additionally, labor costs increased as the federal authorities granted railroad labor an eight-hour day in the Adamson Act. The result was a deficit, met out of the federal treasury, of more than $1.5 billion during the federal government's operation of the carriers. It should be noted, though, that this deficit was a deliberate governmental policy decision.

The Transportation Act of 1920 and the Recognition of Adequacy

After hostilities had ceased and against this background of inadequate service, Congress contemplated returning the carriers to private ownership. Extended debate as to what should be done about the railroads ensued. Out of all this deliberation emerged a new philosophy sometimes characterized as positive control.

It became apparent that controls based solely upon fostering competition and a commission charged with restrictive control where competition was impossible were not the answer. Instead, regulations aimed at increasing the financial health and adequacy of transportation became the key philosophy. In this sense, then, the Transportation Act of 1920 (the Esch-Cummins Act) marks the departure from reliance upon enforced competition and the substitution of increased emphasis on adequacy of transportation through positive controls.

The act of 1920 had many provisions aimed at positive controls. Basically, however, the changes in attitude are seen in the five areas of rates regulation, service regulation, regulations on combinations, security regulation, and labor regulation. Each will be considered in turn.

The new attitude of positive control was emphasized in the changes in rate control. Congress included the famous rule of ratemaking in Section 15a which mirrored these new goals. This section instructed the commission, in exercising its power to prescribe just and reasonable rates, to see to it that the railroads as a whole or in groups should earn a "fair return on a fair value." This phrase was taken from the pivotal 1898 case of *Smyth* v. *Ames* (169 U.S. 466) wherein the U.S. Supreme Court had prescribed a general level of compensation for regulated enterprises. The commission was authorized to determine what would be considered a fair return and was to ascertain aggregate fair value from time to time. But Congress set 5.5 percent as a fair return for the first two years of the application of the rule of ratemaking and allowed the commission to add another 0.5 percent for improvements and betterments. Thus the fair return became generally accepted at 6 percent.

It should be emphasized that the rule of ratemaking did not constitute a guarantee of a certain return. It was more of an aim or a goal upon which rate control was to be based. Since the return was to be based on the value of all assets in the industry or in a geographic segment of it, it was possible for some carriers to earn much less than the fair rate while others were earning more. The important thing was that Congress recognized the carriers' needs for adequate revenues and set a goal with this in mind.

The problem of some carriers earning more than 6 percent and some less was covered in the recapture clause. Since carriers competed with one another, it was necessary that they all charge a like rate. But all were not equally efficient or similarly capitalized. Congress therefore provided that one-half of all earnings in excess of 6 percent would be paid to the ICC and placed in a fund from which loans (at 6 percent interest) could be made to carriers earning less than the ideal. These loans were to assist weak carriers in updating their plant and increasing efficiency. The one-half of the excess not paid into the fund was to remain with the carrier as a type of incentive to be efficient. This carrier half, however, was to be placed in a reserve fund to be used by the carrier to offset possible low earnings in some years. When the reserve fund made up of the carrier's half exceeded 5 percent of the valuation of the particular carrier, it could be used for any purpose the carrier wished.

Besides the rule of ratemaking and the recapture clause, Congress gave the commission power to prescribe minimum rates. Maximum rate power had been exercised since the Hepburn Act; but prior to 1920, the commission had little control over how deeply rates might be cut in a competing situation. This new minimum rate power was very much in accord with the new philosophy of positive control in that Congress recognized the need for carriers to obtain adequate revenues.

The minimum-rate control power was coupled with new jurisdiction over the division of joint rates. The commission already had the power to prescribe the exact division of rates between carriers when they could not agree among themselves on the share of revenue each should receive from a joint haul. However, Congress directed the commission to consider the revenue needs of the carriers in future division. Again, the recognition of financial adequacy is apparent.

Finally, the commission was granted broader powers over the level of intrastate rates in order to remove discrimination against interstate rates. Several examples of state regulatory authorities forcing unusually low rates for the movement of goods within individual states had come before the courts. In effect, this type of discrimination caused the carrier to force interstate traffic to subsidize intrastate traffic by charging unduly low rates on intrastate movements. The Supreme Court had dealt with this problem in the *Shreveport* case (234 U.S. 342) in 1914. Congress now specifically allowed the commission to end intrastate discrimination against interstate rates by turning this court decision into statute law. Again Congress was concerned with adequate revenues.

Car shortages and poor service in time of seasonal movement had characterized rail operations under the philosophy of enforced competition. Powers over car service had been granted in the Esch Car Service Act of 1917, but the wartime seizure had intervened. Now Congress redefined service regulation powers and forced carriers to file their own regulations concerning service with the commission. The commission could change these rules so that better coordination and service could be offered to the shipping public. In case of emergencies, the commission was granted strong powers over the use of equipment.

Likewise, the commission was given the power to order the joint use of terminal facilities, with adequate compensation to owners. Previous to this, carriers with superior terminal facilities refused to allow carriers with terminals located less advantageously to use their facilities. Upon finding that the public was better served and that joint use would not impair the owner's ability to handle its own business, the commission could now order joint use.

Finally, the commission was given powers over carrier extensions and abandonments. This belated control was designed to prevent uneconomic expansion of trackage. The carrier now had to convince the commission of public need by securing a certificate of public convenience and necessity before extending its tracks. Abandonment control, which has been of more importance recently, was aimed at maintaining service on lines already established.

The new philosophy of positive control and the need for adequacy is again seen in the change of policy on carrier cooperation and combination. The act of 1920 allowed pooling agreements when they could be shown to be in the public interest. The act of 1887 had prohibited all types of pooling.

More important, however, was the new policy of allowing railroad consolidations and acquisitions of control. Regulations, almost from their beginnings, had forbidden carrier consolidation. During the granger period, it was considered proper to force the carriers apart and make them compete. The act of 1920, however, allowed consolidations and recognized that the public might be better served by financially healthy, larger railroad systems than by more numerous competing, near-bankrupt carriers.

Although this aspect of regulation will be further developed in Chapter 26, it is well to note here that Congress ordered the commission to draw up a master plan for a limited number of railroad systems that as fully as possible would preserve competition, maintain existing routes of commerce, and provide equal earning power for the consolidated systems. Consolidation was to be voluntary. Although the commission could approve those consolidations conforming to the master plan, it had no power to compel them.

Somewhat belatedly, Congress recognized that if the carriers were to serve the public adequately, they could not be allowed to issue securities indiscriminately. Much of the problem of inadequate earnings arose because of the gross overcapitalization of railroads in their earlier days. Pressure to pay interest and dividends often resulted in poor service and high rates. After 1920, railroads had to get approval of the ICC before issuing new securities or changing their financial structure.

Congress finally recognized that special treatment was necessary in the railroad labor field if the public was to be assured of consistent and adequate transportation. The problem of adequate labor legislation in the area of public service enterprises such as railroads has a long history. (More will be noted on this in Chapter 27 as well as in the next section of this chapter.) The Transportation Act of 1920 established the Railroad Labor Board, composed of nine members divided equally among carriers, labor unions, and the public. This board was to hear disputes that could not be settled by other means and recommend a solution, although its decisions were not binding. No antistrike provision was included. The significant aspect of the labor provision of the Transportation Act of 1920 is that it was a part of the pattern of recognition of the need for adequate service.

Results of the Act of 1920

The results of the Transportation Act of 1920 were disappointing. Although railroad credit was improved, great difficulties were encountered in administering the act. Carriers had been in a competitive struggle for so long that coordination and cooperation were quite alien to them. Likewise, resentment over increased regulation led to a series of court tests. By the time the Supreme Court had finished considering the provisions of the act, economic conditions had changed and the Great Depression was upon the nation. In a subsequent period and under changed economic conditions, many of the provisions of the Transportation Act of 1920 were modified or discontinued. The important thing about this act was not any specific provision, but the new philosophy of positive regulation and the recognition of the need for adequacy.

Labor and Bankruptcy Problems

The final phases of the regulation of transportation monopoly came in 1926 with the Railway Labor Act and in 1933 with amendments to the Bankruptcy Act. In these two pieces of social legislation, the Congress recognized the essential nature of rail transportation and the necessity for having a somewhat different set of values for an essential monopoly operating in a predominantly competitive economy.

The labor provisions of the Transportation Act of 1920 did not prevent a nationwide work stoppage on the railway system in 1922. It was obvious that the machinery of settlement of labor disputes without strikes was inadequate, and it was also obvious that work stoppages in the essential railway industry were intolerable. While the Railway Labor Act of 1926 did not prohibit work stoppages, its philosophy was that of making every effort to settle industrial disputes by every possible means short of compulsory arbitration. Many of the devices pioneered in this act were later adopted for labor disputes in general.

Disputes were to be settled, when possible, by conference between carriers and labor representatives. If this failed, a set of procedures involving the National Railroad Adjustment Board or the National Mediation Board was to be evoked. The composition and task of these boards, the procedures to be followed, and the alternative outcomes will be discussed in more detail in Chapter 27.

Amendments to the Bankruptcy Act in 1933 were designed with the same idea in mind, although in a different problem area. It had long been established that railroads could not be permitted to fail in the usual sense of businesses failing and going out of operation. The public depended upon their services too much to allow this to happen. But when a railroad was reorganized, it was handled under the common-law provisions on bankruptcy. Under these proceedings, several courts could be involved and all creditors had to agree to the reorganization, while the receivers operating the railroad might issue new securities or borrow money.

The new procedures attempted to simplify railroad reorganization by allowing but one court of jurisdiction and giving the ICC the right to approve reorganization plans as well as to approve court-appointed trustees. Additionally, only two-thirds of any creditor class needed to agree to a proposed plan. Trustees were generally disinterested third parties rather than creditor representatives. With but one court to satisfy, time in receivership was shortened; and by requiring ICC approval of reorganization plans, increased capitalization during bankruptcy became rare (whereas it had previously been common). The idea was to try to get the carrier back on its feet with a better, rather than a worse, financial position. Again, recognition of the need for financially stable and adequate transportation is evident.

THE ESSENCE OF MONOPOLY REGULATION

Although numerous other statutes were enacted during the period up to the 1930s, the major philosophy was that of regulating a monopoly. From the post–Civil War period, society had increasingly regulated and set up ground rules against transport monopoly. Although the emphasis had changed from time to time and various problems had been attacked as they occurred, the public was primarily concerned with the fact that the railroads, the transportation monopoly of the era, would abuse their economic power. By 1930, nearly all aspects of transportation monopoly had been controlled. The following summary illustrates this point and presents the essence of the regulation of transportation monopoly.

Elements of Transportation Monopoly Control

Rates and Discrimination Elements

1. All rates must be just and reasonable; all unjust and unreasonable rates are unlawful. The ICC has power to determine reasonableness and prescribe maximum and minimum rates.
2. All shippers must be treated equally if they have similar transportation circumstances and conditions (no personal discrimination).
3. All undue preference and prejudice to any person, locality, or type of traffic is illegal (broad discrimination prohibition).
4. A carrier may not charge more for a short haul than for a long haul where the short is included in the long haul over the same line and in the same direction. Exceptions allowed by petition.
5. Rates must be published and available to all. No deviation from the published rate is allowed under penalty of law. Rebates and passes are illegal (except for certain exemptions relative to passes).
6. The general level of rates for carriers as a group are to be so established as to allow the carrier to earn a fair rate of return on a fair value. Excessive individual carrier earnings are to be recaptured in part and made available as loans to carriers earning less than the determined fair level.
7. Rates may be suspended for a limited time while they are being investigated.

8. A carrier may not carry its own products in competition with other shippers (except lumber).
9. Commodity classification procedures may be controlled by the ICC.
10. Intrastate rates may be raised so as not to discriminate against interstate commerce.

Service Elements

1. Car service rules must be formulated, filed, and approved by the ICC. The commission may control car movement in emergencies.
2. The ICC may establish through routes and joint rates.
3. The commission may order joint use of terminals.
4. All abandonments and extensions must be approved by the ICC.
5. All pooling or combination must be approved by the ICC (after both were illegal *per se* for some time).
6. Labor disputes must progress through a complicated series of time-consuming administrative procedures in an effort to effect settlement of industrial conflict without work stoppage.

Security and Financial Elements

1. All accounts must be uniform and open for inspection.
2. Periodic and detailed financial reports must be rendered.
3. The ICC may divide revenues from joint rates with the needs of carriers as a standard.
4. All changes in capital structure and the issuance of securities must be approved by the commission.
5. All reorganization and bankruptcy must be approved by the ICC. A special procedure is established to facilitate restoration of the carrier to sound financial health.
6. All consolidations and mergers must fit a master plan and have ICC sanction (after being absolutely illegal for a period of time).

ADDITIONAL READINGS

Coyle, John J., Edward J. Bardi, and Joseph L. Cavinato, *Transportation*, 2nd ed., St. Paul, Minn.: West Publishing Co., 1986.
   Chapter 15, "Transportation Regulation: Background and Development," pp. 297–323.
Fair, Marvin L., and Ernest W. Williams, Jr., *Transportation and Logistics*, rev. ed., Plano, Texas: Business Publications, 1981.

Chapter 19, "Regulation of Transportation: Origin and Scope," pp. 348–86.
Guandolo, John, *Transportation Law*, 4th ed., Dubuque, Iowa: Wm. C. Brown Co., 1983.
    Chapter 1, "Regulation of Interstate and Foreign Commerce," pp. 1–30.
    Chapter 31, "Elkins Act," pp. 531–63.
Harper, Donald V., *Transportation in America: Users, Carriers, Government*, 2nd ed., Englewood Cliffs, N.J.: Prentice-Hall, 1982.
    Chapter 19, "Rationale of Government Regulation of Transportation," pp. 455–76.
Lieb, Robert C., *Transportation*, 3rd ed., Reston, Va.: Reston Publishing Co., 1985.
    Chapter 12, "Theory and Development of Early Transportation Regulation," pp. 235–52.
Locklin, D. Philip, *Economics of Transportation*, 7th ed., Homewood Ill.: Richard D. Irwin, 1972.
    Chapter 9, "Beginning of Railroad Regulation," pp. 211–21.
    Chapter 10, "Federal Legislation 1887–1920," pp. 222–39.
    Chapter 11, "The Transportation Act of 1920," pp. 240–54.
McElhiney, Paul T., *Transportation for Marketing and Business Students*, Totowa, N.J.: Littlefield Adams, 1975.
    Chapter 8, "Government Control and Regulation of Transportation," pp. 117–44.
Moore, Thomas Gale, *Freight Transportation Regulation*, Washington, D.C.: American Enterprise Institute for Public Policy Research, 1972.
    Chapter 1, "Background of Regulation," pp. 3–11.
    Chapter 2, "The Interstate Commerce Act," pp. 11–25.
Pegrum, Dudley F., *Transportation: Economics and Public Policy*, 3rd ed., Homewood, Ill.: Richard D. Irwin, 1973.
    Chapter 12, "The Foundations of Transport Regulation," pp. 268–89.
Wood, Donald F., and James C. Johnson, *Contemporary Transportation*, 3rd ed., New York: Macmillan Publishing Co., 1989.
    Chapter 2: "The Government's Role in Transportation," pp. 27–52.

CHAPTER 11

REGULATION OF INTERMODAL TRANSPORTATION COMPETITION

As we noted at the beginning of the previous chapter, the economic market for transportation has many facets. Transportation can operate both as a monopolistic venture and as a competitive enterprise at the same time. Whereas the previous chapter was concerned with the regulation of transportation monopolistic abuses, the present chapter will be concerned with the regulation of transportation competition.

THE NATURE OF TRANSPORTATION COMPETITION

The term *transportation competition* can have three meanings. It can mean the competition among firms of the same mode, as when railroads compete with one another for shippers' rail traffic. This is intramodal competition. A second meaning for transportation competition is when firms of different modes compete, such as the motor carriers competing with the rail carriers for a given type of traffic. This is generally referred to as intermodal competition. A third meaning is private versus for-hire competition. In this chapter, transportation competition will be discussed in all three senses, although primary stress will be placed on intermodal competition.

This is not to say that intramodal competition is unimportant or does not exist. Indeed, competition among the firms in each of the five modes of transportation not only exists but is of major importance, particularly to the shipper. Competition for consumers' business is, and always has been, one of the finest natural market regulators available to society. As a general rule, society depends upon it in most economic undertakings. However, there are some areas — transportation among them — where natural competition does not always work to the benefit of society.

Private versus for-hire likewise is an important type of transportation competition and appears to be increasing. With highways, waterways, and airways furnished by the public, shippers often operate their own vehicles to carry their own freight.

As noted in the previous chapter, where competition among carriers (intramodal) leads to a deterioration of service and an unstable financial situation, society's goals of an adequate transportation system go unfulfilled. Unnecessary and unwise duplication of plant may also be the result of uncontrolled intramodal competition. Where the resources used are small, the duplication and waste of competition may be tolerated and considered as the price paid for a market that better serves society's desires. But where investment is very large and service is inferior because none of the competitors is strong, duplication and waste of resources may be too high a price to pay for an end result that is not satisfactory.

Intramodal competition may also lead to unreliable service. Not only is duplication socially wasteful in some cases, but the spur of competition may bite too deeply and lead to unreliable service. The search for the cheapest method may lead to a poorer service level. The shipping public demands and expects a high level of performance from a transportation operation. This service should be available at all times when it is needed. Transportation agencies handle the goods of others and must have the highest degree of trustworthiness. Many times a search for the cheapest way brought on by competition among firms is not conducive to reliability, availability, and trustworthiness. To achieve high service standards, society has found it necessary to mitigate intramodal competition from time to time.

Where public safety is involved, intramodal competition does not always lead to a desirable goal. The desire to achieve the cheapest service in a competitive struggle may lead to lower standards of maintenance, unusual hours of work for operators with resultant accident hazards, and unsafe transportation vehicles which endanger either the users of the service or the innocent co-user of the facilities. These matters are of particular importance in air and motor transportation, and society has seen fit to regulate these agencies with the safety of the public at least partially in mind.

Intramodal competition, then, has both its desirable and undesirable aspects. Choice among the various firms providing a given type of transportation is highly desirable, but only to the extent that choice does not lead to unusual duplication and unusual waste of resources, inadequate service from the point of view of reliability, availability, and trustworthiness, and service that is unsafe for the public and the operator.

THE CHANGING CHARACTER OF THE TRANSPORTATION MARKET

Returning now to intermodal competition and to our historical or evolutionary approach to the subject of transportation regulation, the character of the transportation market in the 1930s must be noted. Although it may seem static at any given time, the transportation market is always changing and developing. The decade of the 1930s was perhaps the period of greatest change for transportation during the twentieth century. This period saw the emergence of keen intermodal competition in domestic transportation and the establishment of ready means for private versus for-hire competition.

As noted in Chapter 2, the domestic highway system dates its accelerated development to the Federal Aid Act of 1916 and the coming of the state gas (user) tax in 1919. The Highway Act of 1921 completed the institutional framework of matching federal and state funds, that is, concentration of expenditures on a limited number of miles, allocation of matching funds to states by formula, and coordination of planning and development by approved state highway departments. A great deal of money was spent on improving the nation's highways all through the 1920s. With the Depression of the 1930s, greatly accelerated spending on highways took place in an effort to combat unemployment. Public works, and especially highway improvement, were prime Depression-fighting weapons and Congress was liberal in its appropriations. The matching concept was temporarily abandoned and a new system (the Federal Aid Secondary System) of farm-to-market roads was authorized.

All this activity in the 1920s and particularly the 1930s provided better toll-free roads for the use of everyone. This naturally stimulated the development of motor carriage for hire. Highways were there to be used, capital requirements to enter the trucking business were small, legal barriers to entry were low, and the necessary level of skill or managerial ability was generally not high. Almost anyone could start a truck operation, and many did. With the extremely depressed conditions in the 1930s, this trend was greatly accelerated. Men without work and with little to lose could purchase vehicles with a very small (if any) equity from sales-hungry truck equipment firms. The number of small for-hire truck operators increased markedly. Intramodal competition was extreme and intermodal competition was prevalent as shippers, also seeking to reduce costs, were only too happy to shift their business to the numerous and battling truckers from the monopolistic and often haughty railroads. Intermodal competition was intense, and railroads found their traffic beginning to erode away.

Much the same story applies to water carriers. Following the renewal of interest in water transportation at the beginning of the twentieth century, increasing sums were spent by Congress on waterway improvement and development. Rivers and harbors appropriations have always had political importance. During a depressed period such as the 1930s, it became almost politically mandatory that each congressman get a rivers and harbors appropriation for his district. The waterways also were available. No user charges were levied, not even fuel taxes, to recover a portion of the cost of waterways improvement. Capital requirements were relatively low, and entry was easy. In areas served by waterways, therefore, barge competition also arose during the 1930s, although its impact was somewhat restricted owing to geographical factors.

To a lesser degree, the Depression period brought accelerated inter-modal competition between air and rail transportation. One phase of Depression spending concerned airports. Prior to 1933, airports were almost wholly financed by local governments; indeed the Air Commerce Act of 1926 had explicitly barred the federal government from airport construction and operation. But during the Depression, substantial sums were spent by the Civil Works Administration and Public Works Administration on airport improvements. It was not until after World War II, however, that a matching plan for airport construction was established.

In addition to relief expenditures on airports, the federal government began a program of improving airways in the 1930s. This program has continued.

Contracts to carry the mails stimulated the origination and growth of air carriers. The Air Mail Act of 1925 (Kelly Act) authorized the Post Office Department to award such contracts on the basis of competitive bids. There were no provisions that the bids must correspond to the cost of providing the service. Passenger fares, therefore, could be at a promotional level as long as a carrier retained its air mail contracts as a source of steady income. These contracts permitted intermodal competition between air and rail transportation on both passengers and freight.

One notable characteristic of the transportation market in the 1930s was the degree of social lag between regulation and transportation development. Although intermodal competition was growing and a new era of transportation was developing, social regulation continued in its monopoly-oriented cast. Only belatedly did regulation begin to catch up to the times, and even then it failed to appreciate fully that the whole structure of the transportation market had changed. Thus transportation regulation extended the rail pattern of monopolistic regulation to the newer competitive modes.

REGULATION OF MOTOR CARRIERS

Regulation of motor carriage exists on two levels: state control over intrastate commerce and federal control over interstate commerce. The same is true of all domestic transportation; but because of the characteristics of the motor carrier industry (see Chapter 4), the state level of control is more important in highway transportation than in other modes.

State Regulatory Attempts

Generally, control of highway transportation takes two forms. One is regulation of the use of the highways and the safety controls imposed upon operators; the other is economic regulation over the method of operation, the level of service, and the charges made.

State governments have always exercised their police power to regulate in the general welfare. Almost from the time that automobiles were introduced, speed limits were imposed and minimum levels of skills required of the vehicle operator were established. In the case of larger vehicles, regulations designed to protect the public as well as the operator extend to such matters as width and height limitations, length of vehicle or combinations of vehicle, brakes, and lights, and the existence and operation of various other safety devices. The public has every right to impose these types of controls, and the carrier must expect to conform. However, commerce may be impeded or restricted when such controls are so lacking in uniformity as to unduly restrict vehicles operating in one state from moving into or through another state.

In regulating the use of highways, state governments again are fully within their rights. This may be thought of as primarily protecting their investment in highways. Such regulations prescribe maximum weights of motor vehicles and the licensing of truck rigs. Weight limitations take many forms varying from simple overall gross-weight limitations to complicated axle-weight limitations — weight per inch of tire width, spacing of wheels beneath a load, and the like. Registration and licensing rules also take several forms. These various regulations are established according to the conditions and desires of each state. Unfortunately, the variety and lack of uniformity among the various states have often impeded the free flow of commerce across state lines. Sometimes competitive modes of transportation, particularly railroads, have viewed state weight limitations or safety controls as a means of limiting intermodal competition.

Economic regulation by states has been even more comprehensive in scope and has been partially designed to assure adequate service to the public. These controls predate federal economic regulations. In fact, some of the early state experimentation with economic controls established a pattern that was used when federal regulation was enacted in 1935.

Passenger service by bus was regulated shortly after World War I and existed in practically all states prior to 1930. This regulation apparently was designed to protect street and urban railroads. Regulation of truck lines was less widespread and had a varied history of experimentation at the state level. Basically, this state regulation imposed the obligations of common carriers upon all for-hire motor carrier operators. This required an operator to secure a certificate of public convenience and necessity by proving that the service to be offered was not only in the public interest, but also that the operator was fit, willing, and able to provide such service. Rates had to be published and adhered to, and discrimination was regulated to some degree. Insurance provisions to protect the public were sometimes included as well. Although these regulations did much to assure adequate service, it is interesting that railroads were very active both in proposing economic regulation of motor carriers on the state level and often in opposing the issuance of specific certificates of public convenience and necessity on the basis that they (the railroads) already adequately served the public. Without doubt one of the primary motives for regulation of motor carriage was the control of intermodal competition.

The legality of controlling all motor carriers as common carriers came under question during this period. That a state could regulate common carriers was not questioned, as the common-law doctrine of "common callings" applied. But in the 1925 *Duke* case (266 U.S. 570), the Supreme Court declared that a state could not make a contract carrier into a common carrier for purposes of regulation by simply passing a law. Texas got around this decision by requiring contract carriers to secure permits to operate. These permits had slightly less stringent requirements than the common-carrier certificates of public convenience and necessity. In the 1932 *Stephenson* case (287 U.S. 251), the Texas law was upheld by the Supreme Court. Hence, not only was the legality of state regulation firmly maintained, but the precedent of having several classes of carriers with different regulatory treatment was established. Even though all railroads were regulated as common carriers, federal regulatory law a few years later followed the *Stephenson* pattern. Most states changed their existing regulatory laws to conform to this pattern as well.

The matter of state control over interstate commerce proved more difficult. A state certainly has a constitutional right to regulate commerce within its own borders, but what about interstate commerce and the operators crossing state borders? In the *Duke* case previously noted, the Supreme Court held that a state could not deny a permit to an interstate operator. In the same year (1925), the Court held that the state of Washington could not deny an interstate bus operator a certificate of public convenience and necessity on the grounds that adequate service by rail and other bus lines already existed (*Buck* v. *Kuykendall*, 267 U.S. 307). The effect was the same as the earlier *Wabash* case in which a state attempted to control railroad interstate commerce. Only the federal government could regulate economic aspects of interstate commerce, regardless of the mode of transportation.

State regulation of motor carriage possessed the obvious weakness of being nonuniform. Indeed, it did not exist at all in some states. The additional limitation that state controls did not apply to interstate commerce only strengthened the demand for federal regulation.

Federal Regulation of Motor Carriers

After the *Duke* and *Buck* cases, there was a period of controversy over the desirability and the form of federal control over motor carriers. In 1925, the National Association of Railroad and Utilities Commissioners called for federal regulation. In 1928, the ICC recommended federal regulation of buses, and extended its recommendations to trucks in 1932. In 1934, the Federal Coordinator of Transportation (established under the Emergency Act of 1933) urged federal regulation of motor carriers.

Support for federal regulation came from both railroads and the larger existing motor carriers. Railroads felt that regulation would limit their competition and made the plea that since they were regulated, equity demanded that their competition also be regulated. The already existing motor carriers desired regulation to protect them from the less firmly established newcomers. Their case was one of mitigating a disorderly and unstable market and promoting reliable, safe, and responsible service. Most regulatory agencies supported regulation on the grounds of consistency. In all cases, support came not because of transportation monopoly and monopolistic abuses such as discrimination, as it had in rail transportation, but rather because of transportation competition, both intramodal and intermodal, and the excesses of a competitive transportation market.

Opposition to regulation was firmly expressed by agricultural groups who feared transportation monopoly and by some of the existing motor carriers, particularly contract carriers. However, with the continuation of the intense competition in trucking brought on by the Depression, federal regulation was established by Congress in 1935.

The Motor Carrier Act of 1935 was enacted as Part II of the Interstate Commerce Act. It brought control of motor carriers under the ICC and in no small way was an extension of the existing rail-monopoly type of regulation. The major provisions of the act may be summarized under the six headings of carrier classification, entry controls, rate controls, consolidation and merger regulation, securities and accounts provision, and regulatory innovations. Each of these will be considered in turn.

Carrier Classification

Previous state regulatory experience had shown that it was necessary to establish several classes of carriers. The number of firms is much larger in the motor carrier industry than in the rail industry, and the character of the firms varies considerably, as shown in Chapter 4. Although all railroads could be regulated as common carriers, the law had to recognize that only a portion of the motor carriers operated in this fashion. Therefore, five classes or groups of operators were defined in the law.

1. Common carriers that hold themselves out to serve the general public
2. Contract carriers that operate for hire under specific contract and special arrangements with a limited number of shippers.
3. Private carriers who own the goods they transport and do not directly serve the public
4. Brokers who sell and arrange transportation but do not actually perform transportation services
5. Exempt carriers not subject to the economic provisions of the law but still controlled as to safety, hours of work by employees, and standards of equipment

The very fact that several classes of carriers were established makes the regulation of motor carriers somewhat more complicated than the regulation of railroads.

Entry Controls

Common carriers in bona fide operation on June 1, 1935, and contract carriers in bona fide operation on July 1, 1935, were automatically granted the right to continue to operate in the same manner. No proof of public convenience and necessity or consistency with the public interest was necessary for these carriers. (This is known as a *grandfather clause*.) All new carriers entering the industry after that date had to secure certificates or permits from the commission.

In order to secure a certificate of public convenience and necessity, a common carrier must convince the commission that it is "fit, willing, and able" to perform the proposed service and that its service is required by present and future public convenience and necessity. Common carriers wishing to extend their right to serve additional territories or traffic must also meet these requirements. Certificates must specify the route served and the type of service to be rendered, including a commodity description.

A contract carrier must secure a permit. To do so, it too must show that it is fit, willing, and able to perform the service and that its proposed operation is consistent with the public interest and national transportation policy. Presumably, "consistent with the public interest" is a less rigorous requirement than showing "public convenience and necessity." Since the service of a contract carrier is more specialized and for a limited number of shippers who are presumed to be able to protect themselves, regulations over contract carriers are mainly designed to control their competition with common carriers.

Since the requirement of being "fit, willing, and able" generally means that a carrier wishing a certificate must demonstrate fitness by presenting a record of good operations and since operation is not possible without a certificate or permit, it is quite difficult to secure the right to operate. Additionally, it is necessary to show positively that the public convenience will be served or that the service is necessary by presenting evidence of lack of service on the part of existing carriers and the need for more competition. This is not an easy task. Even extensions of service of existing carriers must meet these same requirements. It seems obvious that the regulations in this regard are aimed at control of entry of new firms and the control of carrier competition.

Rate Controls

The Motor Carrier Act provided that all rates and fares must be just and reasonable, rates must be published and strictly observed, and adequate notice of proposed rate changes must be given. The ICC is empowered to determine the reasonableness and lawfulness of rates. Undue and unreasonable prejudice or preference in rates toward persons, places, and commodities is prohibited also, and the commission may suspend a proposed rate in order to carry on an investigation. All these provisions are the same as those found in Part I pertaining to rail transportation and clearly illustrate the application of the rail pattern of control to motor carriers.

The commission has the power to prescribe the maximum, minimum, or actual rate to be charged by common carriers if an existing rate is found unreasonable or unlawful. This also follows the rail pattern. The act originally provided that contract carriers file only minimum rate schedules with the commission and gave the commission authority to control only minimum rates. In 1957, this filing provision was changed to require filing of the actual rates charged rather than the minimum schedule. This came about largely because of common-carrier complaints that contract carriers had an unfair competitive advantage by knowing common-carrier rates although common carriers did not know the actual contract rates. These provisions further illustrate that the act was aimed at controlling transportation competition.

Consolidation and Merger Regulation

Use of the rail pattern of regulation is particularly evident in consolidation and merger regulation. The provisions of Part I (rail) of the Interstate Commerce Act were made applicable to motor carriers with but small changes. Consolidations, mergers, or unifications must be approved by the commission and be shown to be consistent with the public interest. An exception was made, however, because of the large number of small firms in the motor carrier industry. Any consolidation or merger involving fewer than twenty vehicles did not have to be approved (except that a railroad seeking control of a motor carrier had to obtain approval regardless of the number of vehicles). This twenty-vehicle exemption was changed in September 1965 to permit exempt mergers of motor carriers with aggregate gross revenues of not more than $300,000.

Securities and Accounts Provisions

The issuance of securities by common carriers in the motor carrier industry was also brought under the same controls as applied to railroads. Again an exception was made for small motor carriers. If the total par value of the securities outstanding and to be issued did not exceed $1 million or notes and debentures with a term of less than two years did not exceed $200,000, commission approval was unnecessary. The commission was given the same power to require, prescribe, and inspect the books and accounts of motor carriers that it had for rail carriers.

Regulatory Innovations

One cannot say that no new or different regulations were imposed by the Motor Carrier Act. Part II contained four areas of innovation by giving recognition to:

1. The competitive market structure of the motor carrier industry
2. The complexities of the industry
3. The existence of a well-developed state regulatory structure
4. The need to protect the safety of the traveling and shipping public

The Motor Carrier Act took cognizance of the more competitive market in motor transportation in three ways. Because of the existence of so many carriers, no provisions for the prescription of through routes and joint rates by the commission were included. It was assumed that the choice of the shipper would be so wide that such control was unnecessary. Likewise, no Section 4 or long-and-short-haul provisions existed. This type of discrimination by railroads is almost completely dependent on a monopoly structure and cannot exist when several firms operate in competition in a given locality. Finally, the ease of entry of new firms made control of abandonments unnecessary.

The complexities of motor carriers were also recognized in three ways. First, the very classification of carriers into five groups recognized that motor carriers differed and could not all be treated alike. Second, because of the possibilities of discrimination in favor of large shippers in a highly competitive market, dual operation as both a common carrier and a contract carrier by a single firm over the same route or in the same territory was prohibited. Finally and most importantly, eleven classes of carriers were exempted from economic regulation, although not from safety regulations. These fall into approximately the three categories of special groups, terminal operations, and local and contiguous groups.

For a variety of reasons, no doubt partially political, the act exempted from regulation the transportation of agricultural commodities and newspapers. The agricultural commodity exemption applies to vehicles owned and operated by farmers carrying products of farms and supplies to farms, vehicles operated and controlled by agricultural marketing cooperatives, and all vehicles carrying livestock, fish (including shellfish), and horticultural (added in 1952) or agricultural commodities, not including manufactured products thereof. This exemption, plus the exemption of vehicles carrying newspapers, was designed to allay the fears of some of the groups opposing motor carrier regulation. In the case of agricultural commodities, there was concern with the seasonal nature of the movement. This also simplified regulation since a tremendous number of vehicles are involved in these groups.

Vehicles owned and operated by railroads, water carriers, and freight forwarders in pickup and delivery service were exempted from economic regulation. Vehicles used exclusively in the transportation of persons and property when incidental to transportation by aircraft were added to this exemption in 1938. Service in most of these cases is part of a movement already controlled, and therefore regulation of this portion was felt unnecessary. This also decreased the number of vehicles covered and simplified regulation.

Carriers essentially local in character such as school buses, taxis, hotel vehicles, trolley buses, and vehicles under the control of the secretary of the interior and operated principally in national parks and monuments were exempted. Vehicles transporting passengers and property wholly within a municipality, between contiguous municipalities, or within a zone adjacent to and commercially contiguous to a municipality were also exempt. This cut down the scope of regulation and gave recognition to the fact that state regulatory procedures were quite highly developed.

The act gave recognition to the state regulatory structure in two ways. First, the ICC is explicitly denied jurisdiction over intrastate motor carrier rates providing that the carrier is operating legally under the jurisdiction of a state regulatory agency. (In rail regulation, the ICC was given power to order changes in intrastate rates under the act of 1920 under the so-called *Shreveport* rule.) Additionally, the act allowed the use of joint boards. Where a problem involves no more than three states, a joint board consisting of representatives of the regulatory agencies in the states involved may hear the matter and act in place of the ICC. Appeal to the ICC is possible, of course, but this innovation considerably simplified the work of the commission. It also recognized that since so many more firms are involved in motor transportation than in rail transportation and so many of the problems are regional rather than national in scope, a new approach is possible.

The final group of innovations concerns the regulation of safety standards and the necessity to protect the public by assuring adequate financial responsibility on the part of the carriers. First, it was recognized that motor carriers in using public highways should operate within a uniform set of safety standards. Rules governing the maximum hours of operator service, equipment safety standards, and other matters of safe operation are permitted under the act. These rules apply to all classes of carriers. Periodic inspection attempts to enforce these rules. Second, the commission may require carriers to purchase surety bonds and insurance to protect shippers and the general public or to show financial responsibility. No such rule was needed for railroads because they do not use public ways and because fewer financially irresponsible operators existed. Both of these provisions recognized the different character of motor transportation.

Problems in Federal Motor Carrier Regulation

A number of problems of interpretation, definition, and administration of the Motor Carrier Act have arisen. Over the years, the definition of the agricultural commodity exemption clause has been particularly troublesome. The problem of distinguishing between private and for-hire transportation has likewise been difficult.

Problems of definition of contract carriage in distinction from common carriage, problems of the scope of the rights issued under the grandfather clause, problems of applying consolidation and merger provisions (particularly where railroads apply to purchase motor carriers), problems of control over the rate level, problems of determining reasonableness and discrimination, and problems of control of entry of new firms and extensions of existing firms are all involved in the administration of the act. Wherever an industry as diverse and with as many separate firms as motor transportation is involved in regulation, administrative difficulties are bound to arise. Consideration of these interesting matters, however, is beyond the scope of a general book of this nature and properly belongs in a special treatise on motor transportation.

In conclusion, we can say that the changing character of the transportation market had forced society to look once more at its regulatory objectives. The structure of the regulation of transportation competition was established in the regulation of motor transportation and, with ICC interpretations, remained essentially the same for forty years.

REGULATION OF AIR TRANSPORTATION

Once transportation competition had been recognized as an emerging characteristic of the transportation market and the foundations of regulation of transportation competition had been established by the regulation of motor carriage, it was only a matter of time before the concepts were applied to other modes of transportation.

The second extension of regulation during the 1930s, the decade of transportation competition, came in 1938 with the regulation of air transportation. To a somewhat lesser degree than in motor carriage, the regulation of this developing mode of transportation reflected the changed character of the market into a more competitive one. Added to this were the national defense aspects of air transportation and the need to promote and develop this new mode.

This mixture of promotional and economic aspects of the regulation of air transportation is illustrated by the declaration of policy contained in the Civil Aeronautics Act. Congress directed that the regulatory body should consider the following as being in the public interest and in accordance with the public convenience and necessity:

1. The encouragement and development of an air transportation system properly adapted to the present and future needs of the foreign and

domestic commerce of the United States, of the Postal Service, and of the national defense

2. The regulation of air transportation in such a manner as to recognize and preserve the inherent advantages of, assure the highest degree of safety in, and foster sound economic conditions in such transportation

3. The promotion of adequate, economical, and efficient service by air carriers at reasonable charges, without unjust discrimination, undue preferences or advantages, or unfair or destructive competitive practices

4. Competition to the extent necessary to assure the sound development of an air transportation system properly adapted to the needs of the foreign and domestic commerce of the United States, of the Postal Service, and of the national defense

5. The regulation of air commerce in such a manner as to best promote its development and safety

6. The encouragement and development of civil aeronautics

It is readily apparent that the regulation of air transportation was to be both remedial and promotional. The promotional and safety aspects departed somewhat from the general scheme of regulation to protect the public from the excesses of competition as was the case in motor transportation.

Emergence of Air Transport Regulation

The regulatory structure in air transportation was developed during the mid-1920s and early 1930s. The background of regulation was principally on the federal level, as distinct from the emergence of the Motor Carrier Act out of state regulation. Also, air regulation developed faster in terms of time, as distinguished from the long history of attempts to regulate rail transportation. Comprehensive promotional and economic regulation of air transportation emerged out of four federal statutes, all dealing with air mail and airways. These four were the Kelly Act of 1925, the Air Commerce Act of 1926, the McNary-Watres Act of 1930, and the Air Mail Act of 1934.

The pivotal matter of the way in air transportation first involved the federal government when the Air Commerce Act of 1926 created the Bureau of Air Commerce (in the Department of Commerce) and directed it to establish, operate, and maintain all necessary air navigation facilities except airports. Air safety regulations were also allowed, and the bureau began to inspect and register aircraft and pilots, establish air traffic rules, and require minimum safety standards for airlines using federal airways.

Subsequent Depression spending in the 1930s and the removal of limitations on federal participation in airport development in 1938 brought the federal government into airport improvement on a federal-aid matching program.

As noted in Chapter 2, the Kelly Act of 1925 authorized the Post Office Department to contract with private companies for carriage of the mails. These contracts were let on competitive bids on a weight basis and thus provided an assured income base upon which investment and private development could proceed. The McNary-Watres Act of 1930 changed air mail payment provisions from weight to a space-mile concept. This formula was designed to stimulate the development of passenger carriage. With the government paying for the basic costs of operating the aircraft, any passenger fares collected were by-product income produced without additional costs to the operator. The Post Office Department was given power to "certify" routes, control consolidations and extensions, and prescribe a system of accounts.

Because of alleged air mail scandals in 1934, Congress attempted to impose the control of an independent regulatory group and to break up the close relationships between air operators and the postmaster general. This was done by giving the ICC authority to review the rates of air mail pay, to fix fair and reasonable rates for each route, and to prevent mergers and holding-company control. The overlapping and confused situation relative to air mail contracts, subsidies, and regulation under the Air Mail Act of 1934 hastened more comprehensive regulation in 1938.

Civil Aeronautics Act of 1938 and Revisions

With the passage of the Civil Aeronautics Act in June 1938, a new pattern of regulation was established. Prior to that time, all regulation over both transportation monopoly and transportation competition came under the ICC. Now a new regulatory authority was created, and while its organization, powers, and procedures were patterned after the existing regulatory authority, it had different goals and was given a somewhat different mission. After long legislative debate and discussion, some of which finally overcame President Roosevelt's initial desire to regulate air transportation under the ICC, a separate regulatory structure was established with both remedial and promotional roles. These dual roles are illustrated in the declaration of policy previously noted.

The regulation of air transportation had three main elements: control of entry and service competition, control of rates and earnings, and safety and miscellaneous controls. Although these elements parallel the controls over motor transportation to a great degree, the dual-role mission gave them a distinctive setting.

Air carriers in bona fide operation on May 14, 1938, were automatically granted the right to continue to operate in the same manner under the familiar grandfather-clause type of regulation used in motor transportation. No proof of public convenience and necessity was required of these existing carriers, but new carriers or extensions of operating rights of existing carriers had to show the CAB that the applicant was fit, willing, and able to serve and that a public need existed. Since the postmaster general had previously certified carriers to carry the mails, this provision merely validated these permits and utilized the already existing pattern of routes. However, owing to the pioneering state of aircraft technology as well as the substantial capital requirements necessary to provide air mail service, the number of carriers certified by the postmaster general and under the grandfather provisions was quite small. This was a contrast to the grandfather-rights problem in motor transportation where the number of initial firms granted rights was considerably larger.

Since new entrants and extensions of the operating authority of existing firms required certificates from the CAB, effective control over service competition was possible. By withholding certificates on a given route, competition could be restricted. By issuing certificates to new entrants or extending the rights of existing firms on given routes or between given points, competition could be increased. Although much has been written as to the actual policy followed by the CAB on certificates, the board generally tried to avoid the wasteful duplication, overexpansion, and poor service that could easily arise from transportation competition.

The ability to closely regulate competition in air transportation is a very real one. Since federal regulation appeared at a very early stage in the development of the mode, effective regulation was possible. The problems of measuring demand and potential growth of given air transportation markets, choosing among the several carriers that might apply to extend their service, and establishing the type of service to be offered were not easy. Additionally, CAB route decisions affected other agencies of the government (by way of air mail contracts, subsidy payments, and the necessity for providing more control over air safety and the airways, for example).

Following the intent of Congress to build up an adequate and well-rounded national air transportation system, the CAB had to establish a pattern of route competition and a number of operating criteria. The evolution of the so-called one-carrier principle of through service, the local or feeder system of regional carriers complementing through service, the concept of direct competition where demand warranted, the problem of balancing carrier systems to equalize competition, and the postwar struggle to resolve the nonscheduled carrier and supplemental carrier problem were all involved in administering the act. Discussion of these interesting administrative problems properly belongs in a more specialized treatise on air transportation. The point, for our purposes, is that the CAB had the ability to control transportation competition in the air.

An integral part of the control of competition in air transportation was the control of rates and thereby the earnings of air carriers. It is impossible to have adequate service without adequate earnings. Promotional elements and safety factors are also involved for financially weak carriers who can rarely promote, use, and afford the degree of safety demanded by the public.

Recognition of the important role of rates and earnings control was shown by a rule of ratemaking similar in philosophy to that laid down in the Transportation Act of 1920 and in the Motor Carrier Act of 1935. Specifically, the air carrier rule required that the regulatory body in setting rates consider the following:

1. The effect of such rates upon the movement of traffic
2. The need in the public interest for adequate and efficient transportation of persons and property by air carriers at the lowest cost consistent with the furnishing of such service
3. Such standards respecting the character and quality of service to be rendered by air carriers as may be prescribed by or pursuant to law
4. The inherent advantages of transportation by aircraft
5. The need of each air carrier for revenue sufficient to enable such air carrier, under honest, economical, and efficient management, to provide adequate and efficient air carrier service

This policy statement was implemented by granting approximately the same degree of rate control to the CAB that the ICC possessed. Rates and fares had to be published and observed. Changes in rates required notice, and the CAB had power to suspend rate changes while it investigated. All must be just and reasonable; and upon finding a rate to be unreasonable, the CAB had power to determine minimum, maximum, or exact rates. Undue discrimination was prohibited, but no long-and-short-haul provision was included nor was the *Shreveport* principle incorporated, since intrastate air service was minor. The main problems of rates centered about the adequacy of earnings and the promotion of air transportation.

Lack of adequacy of earnings by air carriers led the CAB to institute a direct subsidy plan. All carriers received cash subsidies from the time of regulation until the mid-1950s. At that time, subsidies for the larger trunk line carriers were phased out but subsidies in the form of "public service revenues" continued for the smaller regional carriers until 1978. The concept of paying subsidies to help promote air transportation remains and is a part of the Airline Passenger Deregulation Act of 1978.

The final element of control involved public safety and various miscellaneous controls. First, the miscellaneous group of controls involved power over consolidations and mergers, accounts (but not securities), authority to issue permits for foreign and domestic carriers to engage in overseas air commerce where the continental limits of the United States are involved (although the executive department has the ultimate authority in overseas air commerce), and power to exempt carriers not engaged in scheduled air transportation from economic regulations.

Second, the control of safety is such an important part of air transportation that a new approach was used and a separate regulatory board was established to oversee this aspect of the industry. It will be recalled that control over air safety actually predates the economic regulation of the 1938 act as it was included as a part of the Air Commerce Act of 1926. Under the 1926 act, the Bureau of Air Commerce was established in the Department of Commerce to inspect and certify aircraft, pilots, air schools, and equipment as well as to set up traffic rules and establish and operate airways.

Initially, the safety function in the 1938 act was split between the Civil Aeronautics Administrator in the Department of Commerce and the Air Safety Board, an investigatory group concerned with aircraft accidents and recommendations concerning accident prevention. In 1940, a reorganization was effected that centralized safety and airways regulation and operation under the Civil Aeronautics Administrator. The total effect of the reorganization was to place air safety regulation in the Department of Commerce under the CAA while maintaining economic regulation under the independent CAB. The matter was further clarified and refined in the Federal Aviation Act of 1958 when the Federal Aviation Agency was created and given comprehensive authority over air safety and the control of airspace. This agency was renamed the Federal Aviation Administration and became part of the Department of Transportation in 1966. Although safety regulation certainly has economic significance and is integrally connected to adequacy of earnings, its importance causes it to be controlled by a separate agency and to be considered apart from economic regulations.

In summary, the regulation of competition in air transportation rested upon the twin factors of control of entry and control of rates. Minor regulation came from various miscellaneous controls. The control of safety was emphasized both by effective separation from economic control and by the use of an entirely different agency established in the executive branch of the government. Economic control was administered by an independent regulatory body patterned upon, but separated from, the traditional regulatory group, the ICC. Finally, the CAB had a unique dual mission of both regulation and promotion of air transportation.

WATER TRANSPORTATION

During the decade of the 1930s, regulation had been extended to two major modes of transportation: motor and air. Coupled with prior regulation of railroads and pipelines, regulation of almost all modes of for-hire transportation and their competitive relationships was complete. Only water carriers and freight forwarders remained unregulated after 1938. Freight forwarders will be considered shortly. This section will discuss the regulation of water transportation.

The act of 1887 allowed the ICC to exercise partial control over water transportation if the movement was a joint rail-water move. Additionally, under the Panama Canal Act of 1912, the ICC was given control over rail-owned water operations. Regulation of other aspects of domestic water transportation (if it existed at all), however, was under the United States Shipping Board and its successor, the United States Maritime Commission. Until 1940, there was no separation of matters of ocean transportation from domestic water transportation.

The regulation of domestic water transportation is an excellent example of the regulation of transportation competition. There were few shipper complaints of abusive practices by water carriers. Almost all the interest in regulation stemmed from railroads, which were interested in bringing their competitors under control and placing some limits on intermodal competition. The regulation of water transportation as it finally evolved illustrates this concern.

Transportation Act of 1940

The Transportation Act of 1940 covered several areas of transportation. For our present purposes, its importance is that it established ICC control over domestic water transportation.

This regulation was very much in the rail pattern developed earlier, with certain modifications to fit water transportation. Actually, the regulation of water transportation is contained in Part III of the Interstate

Commerce Act (Part II being the Motor Carrier Act) and provides that some sections of Part I (rail-pipeline and general provisions) are applicable to water transportation. Section 4 (long-and-short-haul) from Part I was extended to water transportation; pooling agreements (Section 5) were prohibited; mergers and consolidations were subject to ICC approval under Part I; and free passes and the Elkins Act provisions were extended to water carriers. The regulation of domestic water transportation has three main elements: rates and certificates, exemptions, and miscellaneous provisions.

The 1920 provisions requiring rail carriers to obtain certificates of public convenience and necessity had been used as a pivotal element in the control of motor and air transportation. The same principle was used in 1940 in the control of domestic water transportation. Existing carriers were protected by grandfather-clause provisions if they were in bona fide operation on January 1, 1940. New carriers had to secure certificates by showing that the public convenience would be served and that they were fit, willing, and able to perform the proposed service. The same provisions applied to the extension of existing common-carrier certificates, just as in motor and air regulation. Contract carriers were required to secure permits upon showing that their proposed service was consistent with the public interest, as in motor transportation. In effect, this gave the ICC control over route competition and the number of firms entering the industry, thereby facilitating a major objective of the act — the control of intermodal competition.

Rates were controlled in the usual fashion. All charges had to be published and observed. A change in rates could be made only after due notice. Rates were to be just and reasonable. Upon a finding of unreasonableness, the commission could establish maximums, minimums, or exact rates. Undue discrimination or preference among persons, ports, localities, regions, or types of traffic was prohibited. Carriers had to establish through routes and joint rates, and the commission could establish these joint relationships and divide revenues among carriers if it desired. No *Shreveport* principle existed, since intrastate water transportation was of little importance, although Section 4 did apply as noted previously. Contract carriers had to publish minimum rates only, and a rule of ratemaking similar to the rail Section 15a was included.

As in motor transportation, several exemptions from economic regulation in addition to private transport were allowed. Commodities shipped in bulk were exempt where no more than three commodities make up the cargo, as were bulk liquid cargoes in tank vessels. Owing to the economic characteristics of water transportation, as noted in Chapter 5, this effectively freed the greater part of domestic water transportation from regulation. Also, miscellaneous water transportation, such as ferries, vessels used in a single harbor, small craft of less than 100 tons capacity, vessels used incidental to movement by rail, motor, or express companies or for lighterage, towage, floatage, or car ferries, was exempt.

A unique feature of the exemptions under Part III illustrates the goal of control of intermodal competition. Congress provided for the exclusion of "transportation by contract carriers by water which, by reason of the inherent nature of the commodities transported, their requirement of special equipment, or their shipment in bulk, *is not actually and substantially competitive with transportation by any common carrier. . . .*" (54 Stat. 948, emphasis added). Contract carriers must apply for this exemption and show that the service is noncompetitive, however.

Dual operations as both a common and contract carrier were prohibited, although the ICC could grant exceptions to this rule. Abandonment of service was not controlled, nor were water carriers subject to financial regulations.

In summary, it seems quite clear that control over domestic water transportation was primarily aimed at the intermodal competition that existed between rail and water transportation. Maximum rate cases have never been important under the act, few charges of discrimination have been lodged by shippers, and the public has rarely charged that water carriers have abused their privileges. Clearly, water transportation was controlled because of its competitive effect on other transportation.

NATIONAL TRANSPORTATION POLICY AND INHERENT ADVANTAGE

Perhaps nothing conceptualized the idea of transportation competition better than the Declaration of National Transportation Policy which was added as a preamble to the Interstate Commerce Act by the Transportation Act of 1940. For the first time, Congress attempted to set down in one general statement the transportation policy of the nation. This policy statement is as follows:

> It is hereby declared to be the national transportation policy of the Congress to provide for fair and impartial regulation of all modes of transportation subject to the provisions of the act, so administered as to recognize and preserve the inherent advantage of each; to promote safe, adequate, economical and efficient service and foster sound

economic conditions in transportation and among the several carriers; to encourage the establishment and maintenance of reasonable charges for transportation services, without unjust discriminations, undue preferences, or advantages, or unfair or destructive competitive practices; to cooperate with the several States, and the duly authorized officials thereof; and to encourage fair wages and equitable working conditions — all to the end of *developing, coordinating,* and *preserving a national transportation system* by water, highway, and rail as well as other means, adequate to meet the needs of the commerce of the United States, of the Postal Service, and of the national defense. All of the provisions of this act shall be administered and enforced with a view to carrying out the above declaration of policy. (54 Stat. 899, emphasis added)

It should be noted that the language of this declaration of policy encompassed all modes of transportation subject to the act. With the addition of water transportation, nearly all modes were regulated at this point. The terms "safe, adequate, economical, and efficient service" and "sound economic conditions" are recognition of the need for adequate earnings and regulation of competition that might lead to unsafe or inadequate service. The declaration not only repeats the policy of avoiding discrimination and preference, but also calls for the avoidance of "unfair or destructive competitive practices." Without doubt, the Declaration of National Transportation Policy was a recognition of the changed market in transportation, and it clearly is aimed at transportation competition, not transportation monopoly.

This recognition of transportation competition is based primarily on the new idea that each mode is part of a system of transportation and has certain peculiar and inherent advantages. Each mode does certain tasks better than the other modes. Each mode has a place in a transportation system of several modes. Although all modes should compete where they are competitive, the national policy should also be to preserve the inherent advantage possessed by each. The policy Congress was aiming at, therefore, was an *integrated transportation system* based upon *inherent advantage* of each mode with *controlled competition.* The implementation of these policy objectives was not as easy as stating the policy. Translating policy aims and declarations into direct action — interpretation and controls — is a complicated task.

The Transportation Act of 1940 contained several specific provisions aimed at implementing the Declaration of National Transportation Policy and at correcting or updating regulatory procedure and approach. Those intended to implement the declaration of policy were the creation of a

Board of Investigation and Research, changes in the burden of proof, and changes in the rule of ratemaking. Two provisions apparently aimed at updating regulation were the discontinuance of land-grant railroad rate provisions and modification of the consolidation and merger provisions.

Although the Board of Investigation and Research was temporary and ceased to exist in 1944, it indicated tangible recognition by Congress that the central regulatory problem was the regulation of transportation competition and the determination of inherent advantage. This three-man board was to investigate in depth and report upon three matters: the "relative economy and fitness" of rail, motor, and water carriers; the "subsidy question"; and the extent to which taxes were imposed on rail, motor, and water transport. If transportation was to be treated as a system with intermodal competition between its parts, some idea of the relative fitness and economy of each part obviously was necessary. If each part has peculiar inherent advantages which should be preserved, the degree to which one part was subsidized or taxed in preference or in prejudice to another was necessary. This was the task of the BIR.

Prior to 1940, the burden of proof in hearings involving rate increases was on the carriers, whereas the burden of proof involving rate decreases was on the commission. Hereafter, the carriers had to prove that rate decreases were just and reasonable or not unduly preferential or prejudicial when proposed. Since intermodal competition most typically takes the form of rate decreases, this procedural change both recognized that the central problem was intermodal competition and strengthened the commission's powers to control it. A final change giving recognition to intermodal competition was the amendment to Section 15a (rule of ratemaking) which directed the commission to give due consideration to the "effect of rates on the movement of traffic by carriers for which the rates are prescribed." The purpose here was to prevent the commission from prescribing rates designed to protect the traffic of another mode of transportation, that is, keeping rail rates high to protect water traffic.

The abandonment of land-grant rates was long overdue. Rail carriers had been forced to carry government freight and passengers at reduced rates for nearly a hundred years and had thereby more than adequately repaid the federal government for its grants of land. These obligations, which were contained in the land grants made between 1850 and 1871, were lifted for all nonmilitary traffic in 1940. In 1945 they were abandoned for military traffic as well.

Merger and consolidation provisions were modified in recognition of the actual pressures of intermodal competition. These changes will be further discussed in Chapter 24.

Without question, the major accomplishment of the provisions of the Transportation Act of 1940 was formal recognition that the problem facing transportation was one of intermodal competition, not monopoly. The recognition and attempted response to the changed transportation market was contained not only in the regulation of water transportation, but in the declaration policy and the modification of specific regulatory provisions.

Although the Transportation Act of 1940 established the general tone of the regulation of transportation competition, various later refinements and adjustments were necessary with the passage of time. Although a number of adjustments have been made over the years since 1940, three refinements seem important enough to warrant mention here. These are the regulation of freight forwarders in 1942, the Reed-Bulwinkle Act of 1948, and the Transportation Act of 1958.

FREIGHT FORWARDERS

Freight forwarders were the final mode of for-hire transportation to be regulated. As explained in Chapter 5, forwarders are important secondary or indirect carriers that consolidate or combine may small shipments (LCL or LTL) into larger lots (TL or CL) and use the services of line-haul carriers. The forwarder deals directly with both shippers and carriers and provides a necessary service to the small shipper.

In May 1942, this part of the transportation system was regulated by the addition of Part IV of the Interstate Commerce Act. The rail pattern was applied to forwarders in virtually the same manner as to the other modes; the usual entry, rate, and service controls were applied. Forwarders had to secure permits to operate and had to file rates that were open to inspection, just and reasonable, and not unduly discriminatory. A rule of ratemaking similar to that contained in Parts I, II, and III of the act was also included.

One unique feature of the Freight Forwarder Act was that forwarders could not own or control any carriers regulated under Parts I, II, or III of the Interstate Commerce Act, but those carriers might own and control freight forwarders. Forwarders also had to utilize common carriers in their line-haul operations and could not set up or utilize contract carriers. Forwarders themselves were specifically declared to be common carriers under a 1950 amendment to the act even though they are, in effect, also shippers.

THE REED-BULWINKLE ACT

As a result of a Supreme Court decision in 1945 (*Georgia* v. *Pennsylvania Railroad*, 324 U.S. 439), Congress enacted the Reed-Bulwinkle Amendment to the Interstate Commerce Act in 1948. This amendment legalizes conferences or bureau ratemaking in which the carriers decide among themselves what rate changes they will propose. The commission was given power to control the procedures, rules, and regulations of rate bureaus, to require periodic reports, and to inspect records, accounts, files, and memoranda.

The Reed-Bulwinkle Act also provided that the right of independent action on the part of any carrier or group of carriers must be allowed. Thus, although rate bureaus do serve a most useful purpose, they cannot impose their will upon all carriers. A carrier may publish its own rates if it desires. Hence, one of the more objectionable aspects of joint action is eliminated.

The Reed-Bulwinkle Act (now Section 5a of the basic act) is an important refinement of the regulation of transportation competition. It allows the commission to supervise the ratemaking function and thus to have a degree of control over intramodal competition. At the same time, it recognizes the competitive nature of transportation and preserves the right of an individual carrier to pursue a course of independent action.

THE TRANSPORTATION ACT OF 1958

Another refinement of the regulation of transportation competition is contained in the Transportation Act of 1958. This act basically affected rail transportation and the relative position of the railroads in the intermodal struggle, even though two of the six major provisions of the act deal with motor carrier regulatory problems. The six major provisions of the act of 1958 were: (1) temporary loan guarantees to railroads, (2) amendment and liberalization of the *Shreveport* rule of control over intrastate rail rates, (3) amendment of the discontinuation of service provisions, (4) amendment of Section 15a (the rule of ratemaking), (5) interpretation of the agricultural commodities exemption clause in motor carrier regulation, and (6) clarification of the distinction between private and for-hire motor carriers.

The loan guarantee program for railroads, designated as Part V of the Interstate Commerce Act, was explicit recognition of the problem of railroad credit. In place of direct federal aid, the government guaranteed payment of interest and principal to private lenders to railroads much as the FHA guarantees home loans. The program established in 1958 was short-lived, but it did establish a pattern of loan guarantees that was used in later years. Liberalization of commission control over intrastate rates and federal (in place of state) control over rail passenger service discontinuances indicated the increasing role of the federal government in transportation matters.

Perhaps the most significant part of the Transportation Act of 1958 was its attempt to ensure more intermodal competition in rates by further amending the rule of ratemaking by adding the phrase, "Rates of a carrier shall not be held up to a particular level to protect the traffic of any other mode." Even though Section 15a had directed in 1940 that the commission "give due consideration to the effect of rates on the movement of traffic by the carrier or carriers for which the rates are prescribed," it was believed that the commission had often prevented railroad rate decreases to meet intermodal competition and "preserve the inherent advantages" of the competitors. The addition of the new phrase was designed to prevent this from occurring. Clearly Congress was calling for more intermodal competition.

Clarification of the distinction between private and for-hire carriers and further interpretation of the agricultural exemption were both refinements of the Motor Carrier Act (Part II of the Interstate Commerce Act). In effect these were attempts to plug loopholes that had developed out of interpretations (particularly court interpretations) of the original act.

In summary, virtually all provisions of the Transportation Act of 1958 were aimed at promoting or clarifying the control of intermodal transportation.

THE ESSENCE OF INTERMODAL COMPETITION REGULATION

Changing conditions of the transportation market caused a changed emphasis on regulation of transportation after 1930. Realization of the new market condition came slowly. Nevertheless, by the decade of the 1940s and 1950s, Congress had recognized that intermodal competition and not monopoly by a single mode was the prevailing market condition.

Even though the rail pattern was utilized in the regulation of intermodal transportation competition, several facets of monopoly regulation were not used in the control of competition. Specifically excluded were the long-and-short-haul clause, the *Shreveport* principle, the commodity clause, and the service elements except extensions. Most of these controls came about because of monopolistic control of the transportation market.

On the other hand, the elements stressed in the control of transportation competition were entry, minimum rate control, inherent advantage, exemptions, carrier classification, safety, and liability. It should not be assumed that all these elements are necessarily consistent with one another.

In order to more clearly see the differences between monopoly regulation and regulation of transport competition, readers should compare and contrast the following summary with that at the end of Chapter 19.

Elements of Transportation Competition Control

Entry Controls

1. Entry is controlled to preserve competitive relationships, ensure safe operation, and guarantee adequate financial health of carriers.
2. Established firms at the date of regulation are preserved by grandfather clauses.
3. New firms must secure certificates of public convenience and necessity, or permits.
4. New carriers, or those desiring to extend their services, must prove they are "fit, willing, and able" to serve and that the public interest will be served by their entry.
5. Carriers may operate only over specified routes and carry specified commodities.

Minimum Rate Control and Inherent Advantage

1. Minimum rates are controlled with the goal of limiting intramodal competition.
2. Minimum rates are controlled with the goal of limiting intermodal competition and preserving the inherent advantage of each mode.
3. Minimum rates of one carrier cannot be held up to a particular level to protect the traffic of any other mode.

Exemptions and Carrier Classification

1. For-hire carriers are classified in numerous ways according to operating characteristics, as common, contract, supplementary, or non-scheduled.

2. Numerous carriers are exempt according to type of commodity hauled, such as agricultural commodities, bulk movement by water, or newspaper haulers.
3. Numerous carriers are exempt according to geographic operating characteristics, such as carriers wholly within one or contiguous municipalities, movement incidental to other transportation, or carriers operating in national parks and monuments.
4. Private carriers moving their own goods where the primary business is other than transportation are exempt.

Safety and Liability Controls

1. Control over motor vehicle condition, hours of labor of drivers, and safety devices is allowed.
2. Control over aircraft, pilot training, and pilot qualifications is provided.
3. Mandatory insurance provisions to protect shippers and the public are included.

Rates and Discrimination Controls

1. All rates must be just and reasonable. Regulatory bodies may suspend rates, determine reasonableness, and prescribe maximum and minimum rates.
2. Shippers must be treated equally if they have similar transportation circumstances and conditions. Undue preference and prejudice are prohibited.
3. Rates must be published and available to all. Public notice of rate changes is required. No deviation from published rates is allowed and rebates are illegal.

Security and Financial Controls

1. All accounts must be uniform and open for inspection.
2. Periodic and detailed financial reports must be rendered (although some classes of carriers are exempt from this requirement).
3. Changes in capital structure and the issuance of securities must be approved by regulatory authorities (with some exemptions).
4. Consolidations and mergers must be approved by regulatory authorities.

ADDITIONAL READINGS

Coyle, John J., Edward J. Bardi, and Joseph L. Cavinato, *Transportation*, 2nd ed., St. Paul, Minn.: West Publishing Co., 1986.
Chapter 15, "Transportation Regulation: Background and Development," pp. 297–323.

Fair, Marvin L., and Ernest W. Williams, Jr., *Transportation and Logistics*, rev. ed., Plano, Texas: Business Publications, 1981.
Chapter 19, "Regulation of Transportation: Origin and Scope," pp. 348–86.

Frederick, John H., *Commercial Air Transportation*, 5th ed., Homewood, Ill.: Richard D. Irwin, 1961.
Chapter 4, "Regulatory Legislation," pp. 107–25.
Chapter 6, "Civil Aeronautics Board Policy — Competition," pp. 152–62.
Chapter 7, "Civil Aeronautics Board Policy — Competition" (continued), pp. 163–97.

Fruhan, William E., *The Fight for Competitive Advantage: A Study of the United States Domestic Truck Air Carriers*, Boston: Graduate School of Business, Harvard University, 1972.
Chapter 3, "The Fight for Competitive Advantage — Fares," pp. 69–109.
Chapter 4, "The Fight for Competitive Advantage — Routes," pp. 110–23.
Chapter 5, "The Fight for Competitive Advantage — Capacity and Equipment Purchases," pp. 124–52.

Harper, Donald V., *Transportation in America: Users, Carriers, Government*, 2nd ed., Englewood Cliffs, N.J.: Prentice-Hall, 1982.
Chapter 22, "Government Economic Regulation of Highway Transportation," pp. 525–56.
Chapter 23, "Government Economic Regulation of Water, Oil Pipeline, and Air Transportation," pp. 557–93.

Hilton, George W., *The Transportation Act of 1958: A Decade of Experience*, Bloomington: Indiana University Press, 1969.

Johnson, James C., *Trucking Mergers: A Regulatory Viewpoint*, Lexington, Mass.: D. C. Heath, 1973.
Chapter 3, "The Development of Economic Regulation in the Trucking Industry," pp. 23–54.

Lieb, Robert C., *Transportation*, 3rd ed., Reston, Va.: Reston Publishing Co., 1985.
Chapter 13, "Intermodal Competition and the Expansion of Federal Regulation," pp. 255–74.

Locklin, D. Philip., *Economics of Transportation*, 7th ed., Homewood, Ill.: Richard D. Irwin, 1972.
Chapter 29, "Development of Motor-Carrier Regulation," pp. 666–84.
Chapter 32, "Regulation of Water Transportation," pp. 722–44.
Chapter 34, "Development of Air Transport Regulation," pp. 797–810.

Pegrum, Dudley F., *Transportation: Economics and Public Policy*, 3rd ed., Homewood, Ill.: Richard D. Irwin, 1973.
Chapter 14, "The Regulation of Motor Transport," pp. 310–35.
Chapter 15, "Regulation of Air, Water, and Pipeline Transportation," pp. 336–65.

Richmond, Samuel B., *Regulation and Competition in Air Transportation*, New York: Columbia University Press, 1961.

Spychalski, John C., "On the Nonutility of Domestic Water Transport Regulation," *I.C.C. Practitioners' Journal* (November-December 1969), 7–20.

Taff, Charles A., *Commercial Motor Transportation*, 7th ed., Centreville, Md.: Cornell Maritime Press, 1986.
Chapter 17, "Regulation and Transport Policy," pp. 374–87.

Taneja, Nawal K., *The Commercial Airline Industry*, Lexington, Mass.: Lexington Books, D. C. Heath and Co., 1976.

Chapter 1, "A Review of the Historical Developments," pp. 1–20.

Chapter 10, "The Regulatory Aspects of Airline Route Development," pp. 153–87.

Chapter 11, "Domestic Passenger Fare and Freight Rate Policy Decisions," pp. 189–223.

Wood, Donald F., and James C. Johnson, *Contemporary Transportation*, 3rd ed., New York: Macmillan Publishing Co., 1989.

Chapter 2, "The Government's Role in Transportation," pp. 27–52.

CHAPTER 12

NATIONAL TRANSPORTATION PLANNING

In the late 1950s, a series of congressional actions changed the regulatory picture and affected the whole structure of the transportation sector, indicating that the United States had entered an era of national transportation planning. Most of these changes in regulatory policy had four characteristics.

First, all called for direct congressional action. The previous pattern had been for Congress to outline broad policies and allow administrative commissions to implement its directives. During this period, however, Congress became directly involved in transportation planning and modified its role of purely policy determination.

Second, almost all these actions have attempted to solve specific transportation problems. Governmental action has frequently been triggered by specific crises, but in recent times congressional legislation has been geared to remedying specific problems in transportation more than ever before.

Third, tenacious adherence to the philosophy of private ownership wherever possible was a characteristic of all these transportation actions. Although the opportunity for nationalization has always been present, private ownership has generally prevailed.

Fourth, massive federal aid involved in transportation problem solving in the past thirty years has usually involved local and user participation. Although there are some exceptions, local involvement and user participation is prevalent enough to be considered a distinct characteristic.

These four characteristics are found in five separate areas: transportation system development, transportation administration and planning, passenger transportation, regional railroad viability, and environmental and energy concerns.

TRANSPORTATION SYSTEM DEVELOPMENT

The fact that the highway system, the airway system, and maritime capabilities had not advanced as rapidly as had the transportation demands of the nation brought about several crash programs. The first of these was the Interstate Highway program, started in 1956. The second was the airport and airways improvement program of the 1970s. The third was the maritime improvement program of the 1970s. The common purpose of these three programs was to update transportation systems.

Interstate Highway Program

Recognizing that the nation's highway system was deficient, Congress authorized the selection of pre-existing roads for the National System of Interstate Highways in the Federal-Aid Highway Act of 1944. This system was to be made up of a maximum of 40,000 miles of the most intensively used roads and was to be built to the highest engineering specifications. It was to reach from border to border, serve all principal metropolitan areas, and connect as many state capitals as possible.

This concept was not implemented until 1956. After much controversy, specific revenue sources were earmarked for a special Highway Trust Fund. This is the concept of linkage mentioned earlier. Funds collected from taxes were to be spent for highway improvement, and general revenue funds were no longer to be used for this purpose. A federal fuel tax of 4 cents per gallon, a weight tax of $3 per 1,000 pounds gross weight on larger vehicles, and excise taxes on heavy motor vehicles, tires, tubes, and retread rubber were enacted. These "user taxes" were increased to 9 cents per gallon on gasoline plus a larger weight tax on heavy vehicles in 1982, and a special 15.1 cent per gallon tax on diesel fuel in 1984.

In the years since 1956, tremendous sums have passed through the Highway Trust Fund. In the late 1980s, more that $11 billion per year was collected from these special transportation taxes. The concept of linkage has a unique cumulative feature. Taxes are based on use. The more highways are used, the more money is collected. The more money is collected and spent on highways the more the highways are used — hence, even more is collected for further spending.

The building program of the Interstate System was originally designed on a crash basis. Construction was to be completed between 1956 and 1972. Cost increases, design changes, expansion of the system (to 42,500 miles), and other factors have delayed completion. It is now estimated that the program will not be completed before the 1990s.

Local participation was provided by way of state ownership of the highways, state contracting of the construction, and state maintenance. Also, states provided up to 10 percent of the construction funds. Since

1973 other federal-aid highways have also shared in the trust fund, but the major annual expenditures have been for the Interstate System.

The highway program began to encounter difficulties in the late 1970s because of three factors. First, inflation had greatly accelerated the cost of completing the Interstate System and maintaining the other federal-aid highways. Second, in response to the energy program started in the 1970s (to be discussed below), both smaller cars and increased fuel efficiency led to a leveling out of the funds available in the Highway Trust Fund. Finally, many of the parts of the Interstate System constructed earlier were in need of repair and rehabilitation. Congress responded in late 1982 by raising the federal fuel tax by 5 cents per gallon (for a total of 9 cents) and other user taxes and again confirmed the goal of combating the deficiencies in the highway system. The special 15.1 cent per gallon diesel fuel tax was added in 1984.

One recent problem has been that the balance in the Highway Trust Fund has been growing as Congress appropriates less for expenditures than the receipts of the fund. For instance, in 1987 only 79.6 percent of the taxes collected were expended and the balance in the fund was over $13.6 billion. Some people claim that this fund "surplus" was created in order to make the federal deficit seem lower.

By and large the program has been successful. The Interstate System of divided lanes and limited access roads, built to the highest specifications on the most densely used routes, has provided the United States with one of the finest systems of advanced highways in the world.

Airport and Airways Improvement

The airport and airways improvement program was undertaken during the 1970s. The airlines adopted wide-bodied jumbo jets (747, DC-10, L-1011) as the second generation of jet aircraft. Airports and airways were unprepared for this innovation, however. Development of support facilities had lagged badly, and with the new jets and the rapid increase in air travel, deficiencies of airports and airways became obvious.

Airway congestion was common. Control facilities were unable to keep pace with the increased use of airways. Airports were unable to cope with the new generation of aircraft. Finally, there was increasing concern over the small contributions being made by airway users to the costs of providing airway control.

All this led to the Airport and Airways Improvement Act of 1970. In this act, Congress adopted the concept of the Highway Trust Fund and created an Aviation Trust Fund. Six specific taxes were earmarked for airways and airport improvement: an 8 percent tax on passenger tickets, a 5 percent tax on air freight, a $3 head tax on overseas passengers, a $25 yearly registration fee on aircraft, a 3.5 cent per pound registration fee on jet aircraft and a 2 cent per pound fee on piston planes, and a 7 cent per gallon tax on fuel used in noncommercial aviation. The largest revenue source is the passenger ticket excise tax.

Funds for airways improvement were to be set at an established level, but airport funds are made available in the form of grants to cities and local governments by a formula stressing use and population. The Air Commerce Act of 1926 prohibits federal ownership of airports except in the nation's capital, but local government grants for airports have been part of our transportation policy since the 1930s. The distinctions made in the 1970 act were that a specific source of revenue for these grants was earmarked, massive sums were involved, airport users were directly assessed a portion of the costs, and a special Aviation Trust Fund was created.

Grants are generally on a 75-25 matching basis, and the funds must be used for the operational aspects of airports, not for subsidiary purposes such as parking lots.

The initial act expired in 1981, and after a year, Congress reinstituted the program in September 1982 for five years. The use tax structure remained essentially the same with the added provision that a portion of the Aviation Trust Fund will be used by the FAA for operating the airways. In December 1987, Congress extended the Aviation Trust Fund for another five years. The 8 percent tax on passenger tickets continues to provide by far the largest amount of revenue for the fund. However, like the Highway Trust Fund, a "surplus" has been allowed to accumulate and stood at $5.7 billion in late 1987.

This example of transportation system development has many similarities to the Interstate Highway program and illustrates once more the characteristics of national transportation planning: direct congressional action, specific problem orientation, adherence to private ownership, and massive aid with local and user participation.

Maritime Improvement Program

The new maritime improvement program, which began in 1970, is another example of social policy concerned with transportation system development.

Again, a portion of the transportation system seemed to lag behind the nation's needs. American flag vessels declined from 1,145 in 1950 to 700 in 1970, with two-thirds of these being twenty-five years old or older. Whereas 42 percent of the nation's foreign commerce was carried in

American ships in 1950, only 5.6 percent was carried by American flag ships in 1970. In a special message dealing with these declines, President Richard M. Nixon in 1969 proposed a crash program to improve the maritime fleet. Congress responded by passing the Merchant Marine Act of 1970.

This act called for 300 new vessels of advanced design to be built over a ten-year period with federal assistance. The existing program of operating and construction subsidies was liberalized, income tax changes were made, and a government guarantee of $3 billion in construction and mortgage loans was instituted. Although this program was generally unsuccessful in attaining its goals, it does provide another example of massive federal aid, direct congressional action, and preference for private ownership.

TRANSPORTATION ADMINISTRATION AND PLANNING

Transportation administration and planning have been another area of concern during the last two decades. Examples of this concern include the short-lived reorganization of the federal airways function in 1958 and the creation of the Department of Transportation in 1966.

Reorganization of Federal Airway Functions

Congress enacted the Federal Aviation Act in August 1958. Although later actions have changed the situation somewhat, this action was another manifestation of congressional concern over transportation administration and planning.

The 1958 act created an independent administrative and planning body, the Federal Aviation Agency, which assumed the mission of the older Civil Aeronautics Administration. The FAA was given broad powers to manage, operate, and develop the nation's airspace. It existed as an independent agency from 1958 to 1966.

The FAA was given authority to prescribe traffic rules for navigable airspace, make safety rules for aircraft and their personnel, conduct examinations and investigations, engage in research and development designed to improve air transport, and approve airport expenditures involving federal funds. Congress also gave the agency the task of planning a national airport system. In short, the FAA has a major operational as well as administrative role in its physical operation of the nation's airways.

The independent status of the FAA lasted for only eight years. In 1966 it became part of the newly created Department of Transportation, with a slight name change, but with essentially the same role in air transportation.

The Department of Transportation

Creation of the U.S. Department of Transportation (DOT) is an outstanding example of concern with administration and planning in transportation. A proposal for the new department was contained in a special transportation message delivered early in 1966 by President Johnson, which dealt with safety, technological research, and internal federal reorganization and regrouping of existing transportation agencies. This was not a new proposal. Similar suggestions had been made in the 1870s, and at least nine similar recommendations had been made during the previous thirty years. This time, however, Congress acted and created a new cabinet department.

The creation of DOT did two things. First, it initially brought together under one cabinet official all or part of eleven major agencies or functions, and about twenty less important ones, primarily concerned with research, promotional, safety, or administrative aspects of transportation. Subsequent action has added other operating agencies such as the Urban Mass Transit Administration in 1968, but it should be noted that the vast majority of the parts of DOT came from already existing agencies (see Figure 12.1). Hence the first major task of the new department was to coordinate the executive functions of these many agencies of the government dealing with transportation and related matters.

The second major task of DOT is a planning, research, and recommendation function. Section 2 of the Department of Transportation Act of 1966 set forth several objectives in this connection. The department is charged not only to "assure the coordinated, effective administration of the transportation programs of the Federal government," but also "to facilitate the development and improvement of coordinated, effective transportation service, to be provided by private enterprise to the maximum extent feasible," "to encourage cooperation of Federal, State and local governments, carriers, labor, and other interested parties toward the achievement of national transportation objectives," "to stimulate technological advances in transportation," "to provide general leadership in the identification and solution of transportation problems," and "to develop and recommend to the President and the Congress for approval national

Figure 12.1   Origin Chart, Department of Transportation

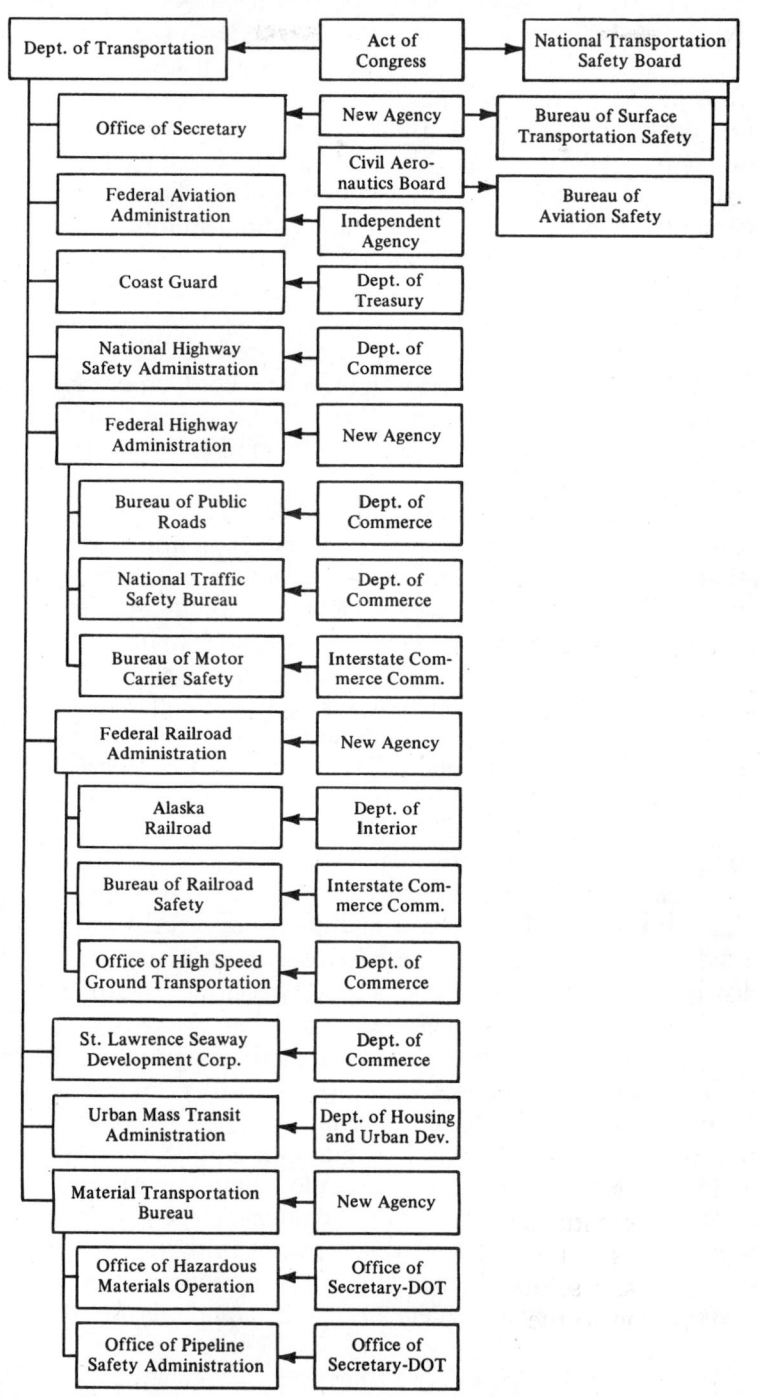

transportation policies and programs to accomplish these objectives with full and appropriate consideration of the needs of the public, users, carriers, industry, labor and the national defense" (see Public Law 89-670, October 15, 1966). The planning, research, and recommendation functions of DOT are apparent.

The department is organized into nine operating divisions and seven administrative divisions, plus the office of the secretary. DOT has assistant secretaries for policy and international affairs, budget and programs, governmental affairs, public affairs, and administration, as well as an Office of Inspector General and a general counsel. The operating divisions are the U.S. Coast Guard, Federal Aviation Administration, Federal Highway Administration, Federal Railroad Administration, National Highway Traffic Safety Administration, Urban Mass Transportation Administration, Saint Lawrence Seaway Development Corporation, Maritime Administration, and Research and Special Programs Administration (see Figure 12.2). Many of the operating divisions have bureaus and offices devoted to specific purposes.

Very few new powers were given to DOT. Rather, its formation brought many existing scattered powers and programs together into one organization under a single head where, it was hoped, better coordination and more effective results could be obtained. To a considerable extent, the actual effectiveness of the department depends upon its head — upon his or her ability to bring about coordination among diverse interest groups of federal and state officials, carriers, and shippers, as well as to obtain firm backing from the president and to sell the department's (administration's) transportation proposals to Congress. It may be expected, of course, that additional powers, either new or presently existing in other agencies, will be given the department by legislation or reorganization from time to time.

Most persons come into contact with DOT at the operational level. Anyone who flies on commercial aircraft hears a flight attendant recite FAA safety instructions, and the FAA operation of the airways became familiar to most during the PATCO (airway controllers) strike in the early 1980s. Most automobile drivers are somewhat aware that the Federal Highway Administration administers the matching grants of the Highway Trust Fund and sets standards for design, construction, and maintenance of the nation's highways. Most shippers realize that the Federal Railroad Administration administers safety programs and standards in rail transportation. Most users of urban transportation have heard that the Urban Mass Transportation Administration administers the matching grants to cities and other governments for development in that area. The National Highway Traffic Safety Administration is best known for its 55-miles-per-hour speed limit program, safety and wear standards for tires, fuel-use

Figure 12.2 Organization of the Department of Transportation

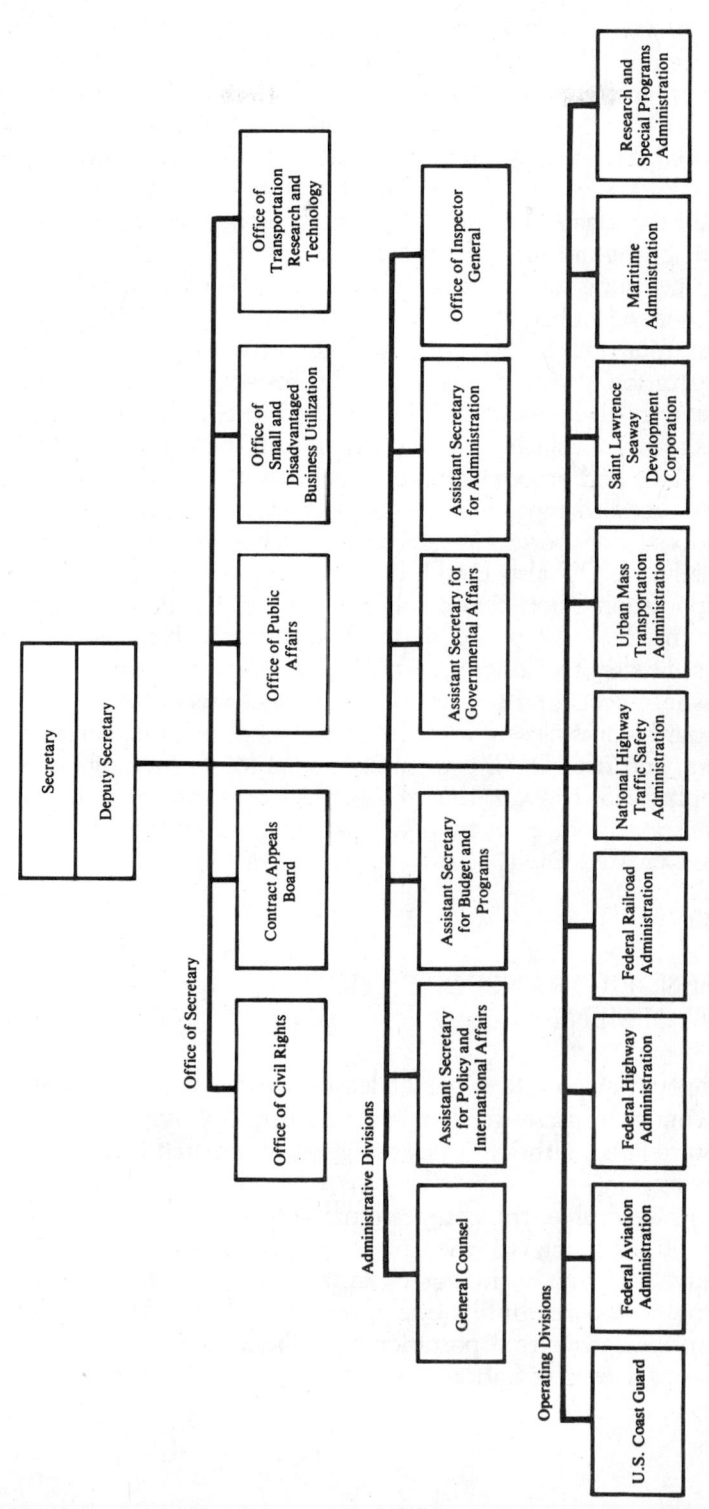

limits on vehicles (miles-per-gallon standards), and the mandatory seat belt program. The Coast Guard may be known to some for its boating safety programs, search and rescue missions, and work in ports and harbors as well as in the Great Lakes. The Saint Lawrence Seaway Development Corporation is involved with what is known as "America's fourth seacoast," the Great Lakes system. Finally, the Research and Special Programs Administration is probably best known for its administration of the hazardous materials standards.

The planning functions of DOT are less well known and less apparent to the general public. Anyone who follows transportation news, however, realizes that DOT has been actively involved in proposing national transportation policy, in planning the restructuring of the northeastern railroads, in dealing with the fuel crisis of the 1970s, in upgrading urban transportation facilities, and in putting forth the administration's transportation plans and proposals for future changes. The responsibilities of DOT will be discussed more fully in Chapter 15.

National transportation safety has become an important issue. The act establishing DOT also established an autonomous agency, the National Transportation Safety Board (NTSB). This five-person independent board is appointed by the president (each member with a five-year term) and reports directly to Congress. The NTSB has the authority to investigate and issue reports and to continually review safety in all transport modes. The board works closely with the Department of Transportation on safety matters, and uses DOT personnel in some of its investigations. It should be emphasized, though, that the board is separate from the Department of Transportation, even though it was created by the same congressional act that created DOT.

PASSENGER TRANSPORTATION
DEVELOPMENTS

Passenger transportation has at least two major problem areas of public concern: urban passenger problems and intercity passenger problems. Both are interrelated, although they are generally treated as separate aspects of transportation.

To some degree, the congressional actions noted above have provided a partial approach to the intercity problem found in the interstate highway and the upgrading of airway and airport systems. The most startling omissions, until quite recently, were the lack of concern with intercity passenger transportation by railroad and with the urban aspects of passenger transportation.

During the last three decades, there has been slow recognition that these two kinds of passenger transportation have been neglected. As the improved highway system began to draw increasing numbers of vehicles into already congested city streets and as the more efficient airway and airport system began to load up the access systems to and from airports, it became obvious that yet another portion of the transportation system was deficient.

Concern with the overall passenger transportation system can be conceptualized from two viewpoints — intercity rail passenger transportation and increased programs for urban passenger transportation.

Intercity Rail Passenger Transportation

Rail passenger service has been unprofitable in most instances since World War II. Alternative means of intercity travel have expanded greatly and have proven popular with travelers. The airplane's speed and the convenience of the automobile are difficult competition for railroads in long-distance travel markets. The speed and frequency of low-cost buses and the convenience of automobiles have taken away almost all but commuter traffic from railroads over short and intermediate distances. Improvements in highways and air transport have accelerated these trends.

Faced with a declining market and considerably liberalized rules allowing passenger train discontinuances after the Transportation Act of 1958, many railroads hastened to get out of the unprofitable intercity passenger business. Rail passenger service discontinuances accelerated greatly all through the 1960s, and the quality of service decreased as some carriers apparently attempted to discourage patronage. There was considerable question whether any intercity rail passenger service would survive into the next decade.

At the same time, it became apparent that there was a continuing need for rail passenger service in some geographic areas and that a demand for passenger trains existed among some groups. Many persons could not afford automobiles or preferred not to travel by air. An alternative means of passenger transportation was needed for the less affluent, older or retired persons, budget-conscious youth, and others. Congress became alarmed with the decline in rail passenger service, and portions of society continued to demand its restoration.

The first actions taken by Congress were the creation in 1965 of an Office of High Speed Ground Transportation in the Department of Commerce and the appropriation of funds for experimentation and demonstration. Appropriations of $20 million were made in 1966 and $35 million in 1967 and 1968; other appropriations were made until 1971. In

1966, the office became part of the new Department of Transportation, and its program became known as the Northeast Corridor Transportation Project. This program, which involved joint investment by the federal government and the Penn Central Railroad, led to the early Metroliners. But because of its limitations in geographic scope and operations, only a part of the overall problem of passenger transportation was involved.

In a more far-reaching action, Congress passed the Railway Passenger Service Act of 1970. This act created a semipublic corporation, the National Railroad Passenger Corporation (NRPC, originally called Railpax), with the specific mission of preserving and upgrading a basic system of intercity rail passenger service. The idea was not to maintain all existing service but to decide what essential service was needed, to improve the quality of service retained, and to arrive at a much improved (although less extensive) rail passenger service for the nation. Commuter services, for distances of less than fifty miles, were excluded.

Railroads with existing passenger trains were offered the opportunity to join the corporation and receive common stock in NRPC. Those not joining were required to maintain the existing level of passenger service until January 1975. Joining railroads were allowed to abandon all their existing passenger services and turn over passenger equipment, personnel, and cash to the new corporation. The experiment was projected to be profitable in two years. When it went into operation in April 1971 (after selection of the basic system by DOT), it was known as Amtrak (*Am* for American, *tr* for travel, and *ak* for track).

Amtrak contracts with railroads for necessary service and facilities and uses existing privately owned rail tracks. It originally purchased 1,200 passenger cars from railroads, operated over the essential routes selected by DOT between fourteen major cities, and reimbursed participating railroads on a cost-plus-5-percent basis.

Initial funding of Amtrak was $337 million. Of this, $40 million came directly from the federal government as subsidy, and $100 million in loan guarantees. Approximately $200 million came from joining railroads, according to their prior losses on passenger services. The NRPC has seventeen directors. Nine of these are appointed by the president with consent of the Senate, three are elected by common stockholders (participating railroads), and three are elected by preferred stockholders. The corporation was authorized to raise additional capital by borrowing or selling preferred stock (which it has never done), and its major source of funding to date has been additional federal money.

The Amtrak experiment was extended, and Congress has allocated additional funds to it periodically. Amtrak's major problems have centered on upgrading quality and retaining an essential core of rail passenger service. Its beginning rail passenger equipment was old and in a poor state of repair, the inertia of past unprofitable operations was difficult to overcome, and conditions of the track and roadbeds prevented speedy on-time services.

In the first seventeen years of operation (1971–1988) over $4 billion has been invested by Congress in upgrading and operating Amtrak. Passenger use has increased markedly and reached 5 billion passenger-miles in 1987, making Amtrak the sixth largest passenger carrier in the country. Amtrak operates 210 trains per day serving 525 cities in forty-four states with 24,000 miles of routes and has a work force of 23,100.

Amtrak has had considerable success in the northeast corridor, particularly with its Metroliner service between New York and Washington, D.C. The fuel shortages of 1973 added to the demand for its services and demonstrated the need for an alternative means of travel. But all parts of Amtrak are not equally used and are not profitable.

In the Amtrak Reorganization Act of 1979, Congress established standards for Amtrak losses. No route was to sustain losses of more than 7 cents per mile and no route was to be continued that did not carry 150 passengers per mile. Additionally, the stated goal was changed from "for profit" to "for service." By 1982 Amtrak was to achieve a revenue-cost ratio of 50 percent (revenues covered only 38 percent of costs in 1978). The prior system mileage was reduced about 16 percent under these standards. In 1988 Amtrak revenues covered 65 percent of its total costs (up from 48 percent in 1981), so governmental operating grants continue to be necessary.

In the heavily populated northeast where Amtrak has been relatively successful, a high-speed rail passenger system is being developed. In the Railroad Revitalization and Regulatory Reform Act of 1976 (the 4-R Act), Congress allocated $1.75 billion for Amtrak to purchase and upgrade its track. Another $880 million was allocated in the Amtrak Improvement Act of 1981, bringing the Northeast Corridor Project to a cost of $2.5 billion. In that corridor, 2,611 route miles are now owned by Amtrak. Expected operating times between Boston, New York, and Washington, D.C., also were prescribed by Congress. This is the only rail track that Amtrak is allowed to own. Elsewhere, it continues to contract with twenty-one other railroads for the use of their tracks.

In still another significant change, the Northeast Rail Service Act of 1981 allowed Conrail (to be discussed below) to transfer its inherited rail commuter passenger operations to Amtrak. A new organization, Amtrak Commuter Service Corporation, was created to operate those commuter rail operations in New York, Connecticut, New Jersey, Pennsylvania, and Maryland that formerly contracted with Conrail for service if they so chose. Some $50 million was appropriated for this transfer.

Presently, Amtrak continues to operate with large losses. However, it is relatively successful in corridor operations, such as the northeast corridor and that between Los Angeles and San Diego. Congress is repeatedly being asked to finance Amtrak's continuance, but considerable doubt remains concerning its future, especially in routes outside its corridor operations.

Urban Passenger Transportation Developments

Growing concern over urban transportation problems has stemmed from four interrelated urban factors: growth, deterioration of the central cities, ecological and sociological awareness, and scarcity of energy.

This country has experienced considerable urban population growth during recent years. Between 1970 and 1980, total population increased 11.4 percent but urban population increased 21.5 percent. We are an urban nation. In 1970, 58 percent of our population occupied 1 percent of the nation's land area, and in 1980, 74.8 percent of our population resided in 334 SMSAs (Standard Metropolitan Statistical Areas — a county with a central city of over 50,000 population). These facts stress the importance of urban transportation in America.

Deterioration of central business districts and of urban transit systems has accompanied rapid growth in many cities. The tendency for growth at the fringes of cities has been pronounced, and the character of downtown areas has been changing. Rail and bus transit systems have not always kept up with these changes. In many places, rail transit is old and designed to service a city with a different character. Further, when growth became pronounced, more emphasis was laid on private automobiles, and the alternatives of public passenger transportation were neglected.

An increasing awareness of the ecological and sociological effects of passenger transportation began to develop during the late 1960s. Smog, street congestion, noise pollution, traffic jams, changing sociological characters of neighborhoods, jangled nerves, and a lowered quality of life became all too familiar. Eventually, there was concerted social pressure for solutions.

The fuel shortage of the 1970s added to the problem. It became increasingly apparent that effective public transportation was less wasteful of scarce resources than was the one-person, one-car situation.

All these factors did not appear at once nor did they lead to a single massive program. Rather, action on urban passenger transport problems came slowly until the middle 1960s. Since that time, increasing discussion and debate have brought a series of progressively larger programs of federal aid.

The Urban Mass Transportation Act of 1964 was the real beginning of a federal policy in mass transit. The Housing Act of 1961 had provided federal funds for up to two-thirds of the cost of mass transit demonstration projects as part of a housing program. But the 1964 act was the first solely urban transportation program undertaken. This act provided for *discretionary grants* for up to two-thirds of the cost of equipment and facilities to cities qualifying for grants. The act authorized $25 million for 1965, $150 million per year for the period from 1966 to 1969, and $190 million for 1970. Less than the authorized amounts were spent, though, because concern over federal fiscal matters caused some spending postponements.

When the Urban Mass Transportation Administration was shifted into the Department of Transportation in 1968, more recognition was given to the problem's urgency. In 1970, Congress amended the 1964 act and committed a considerably larger sum to federal grants for facilities — $3.1 billion for the years 1970 through 1975. During the early 1970s, large sums were spent to assist cities in upgrading transit systems. In 1973, for example, more than $2 billion was appropriated for transit problems.

A significant policy change in 1973 authorized a portion of the Highway Trust Fund to be diverted to urban transportation systems. Considerable controversy accompanied this move, but Congress finally agreed to the diversion of $800 million in fiscal year 1974 for urban transportation equipment grants. Increasing amounts, with fewer restrictions, were allowed in future years as some cities opted to use federal funds for transit projects rather than urban highway construction.

In 1974 the National Mass Transportation Assistance Act allocated $12 billion in urban transport grants for the years 1974 to 1980. Part of these funds had previously been appropriated, but the important factor was that grants to cities were in terms of billions of dollars yearly in the late 1970s rather than the millions of the 1960s.

The 1974 act contained several significant policy changes. First, a substantial portion of the aid was allocated for the first time on the basis of population and population density. These *formula grants* went only to the largest cities, as Congress began to concentrate assistance to big urban areas. Second, the former two-thirds matching formula was changed to 80 percent for capital grants (that is, 80 percent federal, 20 percent local). Third, provisions were made for 50-50 matching grants to subsidize operating expenses of urban transit systems, another innovation. Fourth, only one designated grant recipient was allowed in each area — Congress thereby forced sometimes quarreling adjacent communities into areawide planning. Finally, specific recognition was given to the needs of the handicapped, youths, and the elderly, with special one-half fares applicable to these groups when certain kinds of grants are made. Also, grants were authorized for experiments with free transit, dial-a-ride systems, management training and development, and research and development.

The Federal Public Transportation Act was passed in 1978 as a part of the $31 billion Surface Transportation Act of that year. This act covered highway transportation along with urban transportation as well as highway safety and beautification and was the first such integrated transportation act. As far as urban transportation was concerned, the act authorized $13.5 billion for programs for the four-year period 1979 to 1983 — somewhat over $3 billion a year.

The 1978 act continued the 80-20 matching on capital grants and 50-50 matching on operating grants. However, the trend toward concentration of spending in larger cities was accelerated, and the preference for capital projects was continued. Although a substantial portion of the money continued to be discretionary and allocated by application by the cities to UMTA, a new program of four tiers was devised in place of the formula grants in the 1974 act. The basic tier was patterned on the formula grants of the earlier act and allocated funds on the basis of population and population density. The second, or large cities, tier reserved substantial sums for cities over 750,000 in population. The third, or rail–fixed guideway tier, allocated funds only to urban rail systems on the basis of mileage and miles operated. The final tier was a massive bus purchase program.

The Federal Public Transportation Act of 1982 was a four-year program, 1983–1986, involving an appropriation of $15.8 billion, or almost $4 billion a year. Some $4.2 billion of this comes from the Highway Trust Fund since a portion of the increase in federal fuel taxes (1 cent of the 5 cent increase) was specifically earmarked for urban transit systems. After 1983, the gas tax money — approximately $1.1 billion a year — goes to fund Section 3 discretionary grants but at a new 75-25 matching ratio. The four-tier approach in the 1978 act was phased out in favor of a *block grant* program of $9.5 billion over three years after 1983. Eighty-eight percent of this money goes to cities of over 200,000 on a formula based on vehicle-miles, population, and population density. Cities may use these funds as they wish for capital grants (80-20 matching) or operating assistance (50-50 matching).

The most recent act is the Federal Mass Transportation Act of 1987, part of the $65.5 billion Surface Transportation and Uniform Relocation Assistance Act of 1987. Some $16.5 billion was appropriated for the five years 1987 to 1991 — about $3.3 billion a year, which was somewhat less than the approximately $4 billion a year in the 1982 act. *Discretionary grants* for capital at 75-25 federal-local match continue at $6.247 billion out of the 1 cent gas tax funds, and $10.3 billion was appropriated for *block grants* with 80-20 capital match and 50-50 operating assistance match. Innovations included new "incentive grants" for systems in cities over 200,000 population where some funds are allocated on the basis of passenger-miles traveled per dollar of operating costs. In addition to funds for rural passenger transportation, $10 million per year was appropriated to establish ten regional university transportation research centers.

With the concern over federal spending by the Reagan administration in the 1980s, doubts as to the efficacy of these federal aid programs arose. Many of these doubts centered on the operating grants in which the federal government provided operating funds on a 50-50 matching formula. In order to get more efficiency in operations, the incentive grant program was begun in a small way in 1987. Urban transit seems to be destined to operate at a loss. If ridership cannot be increased or operating efficiency increased, the goal of phasing down federal operating grants would mean higher fares for urban users or states and cities furnishing a larger portion of the cost.

Irrespective of the outcome, the federal action in the urban passenger area illustrates the characteristics of direct congressional action, crash programs to solve pressing problems, massive amounts of federal aid, and local participation via matching funds.

REGIONAL RAILROAD TRANSPORTATION VIABILITY

The railroad situation in the northeastern portion of the country is another area of social action in the era of national transportation planning. The railroad sector of the transportation industry has been in a period of slow readjustment since 1930. This readjustment has not been easy, however, nor has the amount been the same in all geographic regions. In the Northeast, the adjustment has been so difficult that a problem of regional rail transportation viability surfaced in the 1970s.

There were many causes of this crisis. Shifts in population and industry left some parts of the Northeast with excessive railroad trackage and facilities. Much of the traffic is short-haul or less-than-carload lots of manufactured goods, more suitable for truck than for rail transport. Substantial portions of railroad revenues formerly came from passenger services, which were lost to other modes. In short, much of the inherent advantage of railroads in carrying unit loads of bulk freight over long distances simply no longer exists in the Northeast.

Also, the inability of railroad managements to control costs, partly because of labor contracts, and the inability to borrow for needed capital improvement because of long-continued low earnings, led to higher freight rates. This only drove more traffic to trucks and made the problem worse. Finally, severe storms and continued adverse weather caused repeated disruptions of service, loss of facilities, and loss of revenues at a critical time in the railroads' struggle for financial solvency.

During the late 1960s, several railroads slipped into bankruptcy. In June 1970, the giant Penn Central filed for receivership and five smaller railroads followed. These six railroads, encompassing much of the railroad system for seventeen northeastern states, were in receivership. It had been hoped that merger and consolidation would help solve the deteriorating northeastern railroad situation, and several mergers had been approved after much debate and delay. However, the mergers came too late. Simply combining rail systems already excessive to the region's needs was not the answer.

Receivership previously had been a device to attain financial health. Even though the process was traumatic and time consuming, a healthy railroad company usually emerged. Under receivership, a carrier continues to operate under the supervision of court-appointed trustees, while recapitalization is worked out. Certain fixed expenses are forgone during the process. This usually allows a carrier to operate and cover expenses while reorganization proceeds. Unfortunately, this did not prove to be the case for the Penn Central. In 1973, the court overseeing its bankruptcy stated its intention to cease the railroad's operations. Congress was jolted into action with the realization that the largest railroad in the country, which carried 20 percent of the nation's freight and passengers, was about to close down. The result was the Regional Rail Reorganization Act of 1973, known as the 3-R Act.

This act created a new planning and financing agency — the United States Railway Association — charged with restructuring the bankrupt railroads in the Northeast. It also created a semipublic company, the Consolidated Rail Corporation, to operate the restructured railroad system. Interim operating subsidies to maintain service while restructuring occurred, provisions for employee protection, and funds to begin rehabilitation of the railroad plant in the seventeen states involved were also included.

After considerable debate and testimony, the Final System Plan evolved. This designated 17,000 miles to be operated by the Consolidated Rail Corporation, popularly known as Conrail. This involved the abandonment of more than 6,000 miles of track, a part of which may be kept in service by local or state governments with federal assistance. The goal was to have Conrail emerge as a somewhat smaller but efficient and profitable rail system in place of the six bankrupt railroads.

One of the major provisions of the Railroad Revitalization and Regulatory Reform Act of 1976, the 4-R Act, dealt with Conrail and the plans made under the 3-R Act of 1973. Congress allocated more than $2 billion in debentures and preferred stock for Conrail to purchase northeastern regional rail facilities from their owners; established a Railroad Rehabilitation and Improvement Fund with $275 million to upgrade Conrail; gave $250 million for employee protection payments; and provided $360 million for five years for local rail service assistance on a sliding scale (federal share 100 percent in the first year, dropping to 70 percent in five years) to keep local rail service where local interests are willing to support those parts of the bankrupt northeastern railroads not included in Conrail.

Additionally, in an innovative program designed to assist in nationwide railroad rehabilitation, a fund of $1 billion in loan guarantees and $600 million in redeemable preference shares was established. Under this plan, any railroad is entitled to government assistance in upgrading its track and equipment by selling special redeemable preference stock (at very low dividend rates) to the Railroad Rehabilitation and Improvement Fund, or it can secure loan guarantees when borrowing privately.

Another portion of the 4-R Act of 1976 called for rail system planning. Each state was ordered to draw up a rail plan and designate lightly used rail mileage. Each railroad had to submit to the ICC a diagram of its system and identify any lines subject to future abandonment. Substantial rail mileage has been abandoned under these provisions, particularly in the Midwest where excess mileage was prevalent. Other provisions of the 4-R Act deal with funds for Amtrak, as noted above, with regulatory and rate reforms, discussed in Chapter 13, and with changes in merger and consolidation procedures, discussed in Chapter 26.

Conrail began operations April 1, 1976, and incurred heavy losses initially. Under the Final System Plan, Conrail was to become profitable by 1979, but it lost $221 million that year and $244 million in 1980. From 1976 to 1980, Conrail lost about $1.8 billion, and Congress had to come to Conrail's rescue with an additional $1.2 billion appropriation in 1978. In 1981, Congress allowed Conrail to transfer its commuter passenger operations to Amtrak and regional authorities. This move helped decrease the losses, and in 1981 the expenditures to modernize Conrail began to pay off — a small profit was earned for a short period before the 1982 recession. Since 1982 Conrail has earned a small profit.

Under the Northeast Rail Service Act of 1981, which allowed Conrail to get out of the rail passenger business, Congress provided for the privatization of Conrail under certain circumstances. The United States Railway Association created under the 3-R Act was to ascertain the profitability of Conrail and evaluate it long-term viability by June 1983. If the USRA determined that Conrail was profitable and had good prospects of operating as a private corporation, it was to be sold as a whole system.

If Conrail could not operate profitably in private hands, the secretary of transportation was to dispose of Conrail in a piecemeal manner after June 1984.

The USRA determined that Conrail was profitable and could be operated as a whole system. The federal government owned 85 percent of the common stock of Conrail (15 percent was owned by Conrail employees under an employee stock ownership plan), and bids were taken for this stock in 1984. A number of groups submitted bids, including two other railroads. The secretary of transportation was to determine which privatization plan best served the public, and considerable controversy arose over the various proposals to take Conrail private. Congress finally acted in October 1986, overriding the determination by the secretary of transportation to sell Conrail to the Norfolk and Southern Railway, by passing the Conrail Privatization Act, which provided for the sale to the general public of the government's 85 percent of Conrail stock.

On March 26, 1987, Conrail stock (58,750,000 shares) was sold to the public in one of the largest single stock offerings to that date. Some $1.645 billion was paid (at $28 a share) to the government. Over $7 billion had been appropriated in federal funds to rehabilitate Conrail and keep it in operation from 1975 to 1985. Today Conrail is a privately owned railroad with 13,300 route miles covering fourteen states in the Northeast. This is the core of the approximately 24,000 miles of railroad that had gone into receivership in 1970. The remaining miles were either abandoned, sold to other lines, or operated under various agencies under the Local Rail Assistance Program. The Conrail experience is another example of national transportation planning.

ENVIRONMENTAL AND ENERGY CONCERNS

As noted in Chapter 3, transportation has many important environmental and energy aspects. Public concern over these areas generally has not been directed explicitly at transportation (except automobiles), but many of the congressional actions concerning the environment and energy also affect transportation. Although much congressional action was directed toward the private automobile, various safety, emission, and noise standards were mandated for other forms of transport, especially for trucks and aircraft. Some of these mandates came from various operating divisions of the Department of Transportation.

The oil embargo and shortages of 1973 and 1974 awakened the nation to the so-called energy crisis. Congress reacted, after considerable controversy, by establishing performance standards in miles-per-gallon for automobiles produced in the late 1970s and the 1980s. Targets for fuel efficiency were established, and compliance programs were drawn up. Various tax penalties were proposed for fuel conservation. A new cabinet office, the Department of Energy, was created, placing one administrative head over most of the federal agencies dealing with energy. The regulation of oil pipelines was moved from the ICC to this new department. All this was called an energy program, but it directly affected both passenger and freight transportation.

SUMMARY

The last two or three decades have seen an era of transportation planning. This has occurred in the five areas of (1) transportation system development (Interstate Highway program, airport and airway improvement, maritime improvement); (2) transportation administration and planning (reorganization of the federal airway function, Department of Transportation); (3) passenger transportation developments (Amtrak, Urban Mass Transportation Assistance programs); (4) regional railroad transportation planning (restructuring the northeastern railroads, Conrail, 4-R Act); and (5) environmental and energy concerns (impacts of congressional environmental actions on transport, the energy program).

In each of these areas, the programs involved generally have been characterized by direct congressional action, crash programs to solve pressing problems, avoidance of nationalization, and massive amounts of federal aid, with local participation wherever possible.

ADDITIONAL READINGS

Bess, H. David, and Martin T. Farris, "U.S. Maritime Policy: A Time for Reassessment," *Transportation Journal* (Summer 1982), 4–14.

Bowersox, Donald J., Pat J. Calabro, and George D. Wagenheim, *Introduction to Transportation*, New York: Macmillan Publishing Co., 1981.
   Chapter 11, "Transportation Law," pp. 160–84.

Coyle, John J., Edward J. Bardi, and Joseph L. Cavinato, *Transportation*, 2nd ed., St. Paul, Minn.: West Publishing Co., 1986.
   Chapter 15, "Transportation Regulation: Background and Development," pp. 297–323.

Davis, Grant M., *The Department of Transportation*, Lexington, Mass.: D. C. Heath, 1970.

Fair, Marvin L., and Ernest W. Williams, Jr., *Transportation and Logistics*, rev. ed., Plano, Texas: Business Publications, 1981.
   Chapter 19, "Regulation of Transportation: Origin and Scope," pp. 348–85.

Harper, Donald V., *Transportation in America: Users, Carriers, Government*, 2nd ed., Englewood Cliffs, N.J.: Prentice-Hall, 1982.
  Chapter 16, "Rationale of Government Promotion of Transportation; Government Promotion of Railroad and Highway Transportation," pp. 371–408.
Hazard, John L., "Government Railroading," *Transportation Journal* (Spring 1980), 38–50.
_____ , *Managing National Transportation Policy*, Westport, Conn.: The Eno Foundation for Transportation, Inc. 1988.
  Chapter 1, "Evolving Federal Role in Transportation," pp. 1–28.
_____ , *Transportation: Management, Economics, Policy*, Cambridge, Md.: Cornell Maritime Press, 1977.
  Chapter 18, "Urban and Intermodal Problems," pp. 527–51.
  Chapter 19, "Government Policy and Plans," pp. 552–81.
Hille, Stanley J., and Richard F. Poist, Jr., "Urban Transportation Problems," *Transportation: Principles and Perspectives*, Danville, Ill.: Interstate Printers and Publishers, 1974, pp. 336–63.
Johnson, James C., "Lessons from Amtrak and Conrail," *ICC Practitioners' Journal*, 49, No. 3 (March-April 1982), 247–56.
Lieb, Robert C., *Transportation*, 3rd ed., Reston, Va.: Reston Publishing Co., 1985.
  Chapter 14, "Evolution of Federal Regulation and Promotion," pp. 277–89.
Mertins, Herman, Jr., *National Transportation Policy in Transition*, Lexington, Mass.: D. C. Heath, 1972.
  Chapter 4, "Department of Transportation," pp. 77–106.
Moyer, R. Charles, and Harold Handerson, "A Critique of the Rationales for Present U.S. Maritime Programs," *Transportation Journal* (Winter 1974), 5–16.
Norton, Hugh S., "The Wheel: Should We Reinvent It?" *American Economic Review* (May 1974), 378–83.
Patton, Edwin P., "Amtrak in Perspective: Where Goest the Pointless Arrow?" *American Economic Review* (May 1974), 372–77.
Smerk, George M., "The Environment and Transportation," *Transportation Journal* (Fall 1972), 40–49.
_____ , "The Urban Mass Transportation Act at Twenty: A Turning Point?" *Transportation Journal* (Summer 1985), 52–75.
_____ , "Update on Federal Mass Transportation Policy: The Surface Transportation Act of 1978," *Transportation Journal* (Spring 1979), 16–35.
Spraggins, H. Barry, "Rationalization of Rail Line Abandonment Policy in the Midwest Under the Railroad Revitalization and Regulatory Reform Act of 1976," *Transportation Journal* (Fall 1978), 5–18.
Tobey, Laurence E., "Costs, Benefits, and the Future of Amtrak," *Transportation Law Journal*, 15 (1987), 245–303.
Wilson, George W., "Regulation, Public Policy, and Efficient Provision of Freight Transportation," *Transportation Journal* (Fall 1975), 5–20.

CHAPTER 13
THE ERA OF DEREGULATION

Since the late 1950s, two series of events or "eras" have been taking place. One was the series of direct actions by Congress aimed at solving specific transportation problems which we called national transportation planning. This was the subject of the last chapter. The other was the movement toward less regulation, sometimes called deregulation, which is the subject of the present chapter. Sometimes the movement toward deregulation became mixed up with national transportation planning — an example would be the Railroad Revitalization and Regulatory Reform Act (the so-called 4-R Act) of 1976 where state rail plans were mandated and where the United States Railway Association was charged with restructuring the bankrupt railroads of the Northeast. Sometimes deregulation was a separate subject of congressional action — an example would be the Airline Deregulation Act of 1978. Additionally, sometimes deregulation was furthered by the manner in which the regulatory agencies applied congressional policy and not by congressional action itself. This has been called administrative deregulation to distinguish it from congressional deregulation. But irrespective of the method, transportation entered a new era of deregulation in the late 1970s and early 1980s.

BACKGROUND OF THE
DEREGULATION MOVEMENT

In order to appreciate the meaning and extent of the changes in transportation regulation, one must understand the background of the deregulation movement. From the Motor Carrier Act of 1935 (Part II of the I.C. Act) through the Transportation Act of 1958, the major national policy concern was the regulation of *intermodal competition* in the freight market. This was clearly spelled out in the Declaration of National Transportation Policy in the Transportation Act of 1940. Here Congress emphasized that in dealing with modes of transportation, regulation should "recognize and *preserve* the *inherent advantages* of each, . . . *promote* safe, adequate, economical and efficient service and *foster sound economic conditions* in transportation and among the several carriers . . . all to the end of *developing, coordinating* and *preserving* a national transportation system by water, highway, and rail . . . *adequate to meet the needs* of the commerce of the United States, of the Postal Service, and of the national defense" (emphasis added; read again this important policy statement in Chapter 11).

Likewise, a declaration of policy was contained in the Civil Aeronautics Act of 1938 which clearly set forth a goal for the Civil Aeronautics Board (CAB) for "the *encouragement* and the *development* of an air transportation system properly adapted to the *present and future needs* of the foreign and domestic commerce of the United States, of the Postal Service, and of the national defense, . . . regulation of air transportation in such a manner as to recognize and *preserve* the *inherent advantage* of, assure the highest degree of safety in, and *foster* sound economic conditions in such transportation" (emphasis added).

The Three "Pillars" of Regulation

It is possible to summarize the regulatory structure in the 1970s by noting the three "pillars" of regulation. Essentially these evolved out of the policies established by Congress noted above and their administration and interpretation by the regulatory agencies (ICC and CAB) and the courts. The three pillars are (1) control of entry and exit, (2) control of rates and earnings, and (3) control of service.

Control of Entry and Exit

The degree of competition in the transportation industry was strictly controlled by regulation of entry and exit. Entry into the various modes was controlled by the use of the certificate of public convenience and necessity. Potential entrants had to prove to the satisfaction of the ICC or the CAB that their service was needed by the public and that they were "fit, willing, and able" to serve the public. A public hearing was held and existing carriers could oppose the issuance of any new certificates — and usually they did. As noted in Chapter 11, carriers at the time regulation started (1935 for motor, 1938 for air, 1940 for inland water, and 1942 for freight forwarders) were given "grandfather rights." These certificates allowed the carriers existing at the time of regulation to continue to operate in the same manner without the necessity of proving their services were needed by the public.

"Fit, willing, and able" was interpreted to mean that the potential entrant had to demonstrate that it had proper equipment, personnel, financial resources, and operating experience in the industry. This requirement practically excluded all new entrants, for there was no way to obtain a certificate without operating experience and no way to get operating experience without a certificate. The only exception to this "catch-22" situation was for motor carriers where an *intrastate* operator might be able to prove it was "fit, willing, and able" on the basis of its operations wholly within one state and thereby obtain an *interstate* certificate.

Further, both abandonment and mergers were regulated. With the sole exception of motor carriers, once service was begun it could not be abandoned without regulatory permission and a public hearing. It was particularly difficult to abandon or discontinue either rail or air service once begun. Likewise, mergers between carriers had to be approved — also at public hearings. Once more the regulatory agencies were concerned with controlling the degree of competition in each mode in order to fulfill congressional policy of preserving the inherent advantage of each mode and developing a system adequate to meet the needs of commerce, the postal system, and the national defense.

In air transportation, the CAB decided not to allow additional firms to enter air transportation, saying: "The number of air carriers now operating appears sufficient . . . there appears to be no inherent desirability of increasing the present number of carriers merely for the purpose of numerically enlarging the industry" (2 CAB 447, 489, 1941). Competition was allowed between "pairs of points" as the CAB deemed that more service was necessary. Significantly, when competition was allowed, it was inevitably between *existing* carriers. No new entrants were allowed in trunkline air transportation although a series of regional and local service carriers were certificated after World War II.

In freight transportation, the ICC struggled with "preserving the inherent advantage of each [mode]" and fostering "sound economic conditions in transportation among the several carriers." The number of motor carriers in the country decreased from around 35,000 to nearly 15,000 from 1935 to 1980 as mergers among existing carriers were permitted. As existing certificates of public convenience and necessity were combined and existing carriers allowed to expand as the economy grew, many restrictions were placed on motor carriers' legal operating rights — often designed to protect the previously existing carrier's operations. The result was that the level of competition was literally prescribed by the ICC, and some motor carriers, among other restrictions, found themselves legally able to carry freight in one direction but not the other, serve terminal points but not intermediate points, serve between some cities only on a circuitous route, and carry some goods but not others.

Owing to the exemption of bulk cargoes, inland water carriers were really not greatly affected by regulation. The railroad industry continued to grow — but at a slower pace than the other modes — under the previously developed policy of regulated monopoly, even though a rail monopoly had long ceased to exist. Railroad earnings suffered, and in the 1940s and 1950s the railroads experienced continuing financial difficulties. There had been few railway expansions since the pre–World War I days, so control of entry was not a problem. However, control of mergers and particularly abandonment and discontinuance of service was a problem for the railroad industry.

Control of Rates and Earnings

The second pillar, control of rates and earning, operated at two levels: rate levels or earnings, and rate structure or nondiscrimination. Total carrier earnings were to reflect earlier congressional policy for railroads of allowing a "fair return on a fair value" (this standard taken from a Supreme Court case, *Smyth* v. *Ames*, 169 U.S. 466, 1898) and the "adequacy" provisions of the Transportation Act of 1920 discussed in Chapter 10. Likewise, the policy goal to "foster sound economic conditions" in the Civil Aeronautics Act of 1938 and the National Transportation Policy Statement of 1940 (both noted above and in Chapter 11) called for earnings control of the other modes. If earnings were too low, they were deemed "unreasonable" and a general rate increase was allowed. Earnings could also be found to be "unreasonably high," which called for a lowering of rates in general. A public hearing on earnings was held with a view to establishing "reasonableness" of the rate level or earnings.

In air transportation, the CAB interpreted its charge in such a way that direct cash subsidies were paid from the late 1930s to the mid-1950s to all airlines to "encourage and develop, preserve inherent advantage, and foster sound economic conditions" in air transportation. Direct subsidies continued to the regional and local service airlines in the form of "public service revenues" right up to the 1978 deregulation act. In motor transportation a revenue standard was used — the operating ratio (operating expenses over operating revenue times 100), since so many carriers existed that finding a "fair return on a fair value" for each was unrealistic.

Note that these congressional policies called for "cost-based" rate levels. Hence, if costs were increased — say due to a new labor contract

— the carriers could ask for an increase in the general level of rates and fares. Also, accounting regulation was necessary with uniform accounts prescribed in order that comparisons could be made.

Individual rates were to be nondiscriminatory in all modes ("not unduly preferential or prejudicial"). This followed the earlier doctrine that all shippers and passengers were to be treated alike "under similar circumstances and conditions." Public hearings were also held on this aspect of specific rates. The point is that the ICC and the CAB had the power to deem rates and fares "reasonable or unreasonable" as to earnings, and "discriminatory or nondiscriminatory" as to application. If rates or fares were found to be unreasonable or discriminatory, the agency could prescribe the proper rate or fare.

Further, all rates and fares had to be published and followed absolutely. No deviation from a published rate or fare was allowed by either carrier or shipper. If deviation was discovered, overcharge or undercharge claims (to be discussed in Part VI) were to be filed and penalties assessed. Advance notice — usually thirty days — was required for any rate or fare change after a public hearing was held and protests allowed. Joint action by the carriers organized in rate bureaus was exempt from antitrust laws (Reed-Bulwinkle Act, 1948, noted in Chapter 11) except in air transportation where the number of carriers was small. Security controls with regulatory agencies' permission required to issue securities was necessary to control earnings, and liability controls and credit limits were imposed to assure avoidance of discrimination. Literally the whole price structure in transportation was regulated.

Control of Service

All three "pillars" of regulation were interdependent and complemented one another. Service levels of the carriers were controlled in various ways — by the provisions in the certificate of public convenience and necessity or by rulemaking by the regulatory agencies.

Typically certificates of public convenience and necessity specified routes and described commodities that could be hauled in motor transportation. Frequency of service was also specified. When an existing "grandfather" carrier extended its operation by merger or by winning a new certificate, various "restrictions" were commonly attached. These were designed to protect other operators from what was deemed undesirable or unnecessary competition. Hence a carrier operating A to B and desiring to serve C might be given a certificate to operate from B to C but not from C to B — it had to return empty on the backhaul. Or the same carrier might be allowed to serve C but only by a circuitous route, say by way of a "gateway" point at D. Or a carrier was allowed to serve A to C but not pick up or deliver freight at B. These and other restrictions were designed to "assure sound economic conditions" in transportation.

In air transportation, certificates specified frequency of service and routes with named points served. As larger planes developed, the issue of who could fly nonstop and who had to serve intermediate points developed. Additionally, the CAB became concerned with conditions of service and involved itself in ruling on such things as meals, drinks, private clubs, legroom, and the pitch of the seat, as well as the difference between first class/tourist/excursion fares. In rail transportation, the ICC ruled on car supply and service levels, joint use of terminals, interchange provisions, and joint rail-inland water service. Further, insurance provisions in all modes were specified.

As noted in Chapter 11, various exemptions were allowed by law — private carriage and the agricultural commodities exemption in motor, the bulk commodity exemption in inland water, and local service exemption in both motor and inland water. These exemptions led to problems of definition and caused Congress to add a provision to the Transportation Act of 1958 (primarily an act to assist railroads) attempting to define private motor carriage (primary business test) and agricultural commodities.

Self-Enforcement via Adversary Hearings

It should not be inferred from this that the ICC and CAB had large field staffs which literally looked over the shoulder of the carriers to be sure there was compliance. The system was self-enforcing once a ruling or decision was made. Individual shippers could and did enter complaints as to rates and service. Likewise, competitive carriers could and did enter complaints when they believed that competitors were violating provisions of their certificates or were not observing rate provisions. Cities could and did enter complaints relative to their service or proposed service to rival production or distribution points. Many chambers of commerce maintained a traffic department whose task was to protect the competitive advantage of a particular point. Also, associations of shippers or regions could and did enter complaints. Both the ICC and CAB would hold public hearings if the complaints seemed to have merit and often amended or changed rulings or decisions on the basis of these adversary proceedings. Lawyers, consultants, regulatory practitioners, traffic services, and various transportation specialists were in constant demand.

The Genesis of Deregulation

The regulatory structure discussed above had evolved over ninety years in rail and almost forty years in motor and air transportation. But in the 1970s increasing dissatisfaction with the system began to arise. This move toward deregulation was partially due to changing political philosophy, changing economic philosophy, and frustration over the complexity of the regulatory system.

The Kennedy Transportation Message

The deregulation era began with the presidential transportation message of John F. Kennedy in April 1962. President Kennedy set a new tone by calling for more competition in transportation, following a series of earlier reports suggesting its desirability. He noted that "a chaotic patchwork of inconsistent and often obsolete legislation and regulation has evolved. . . . transportation is subject to excessive, cumbersome, and time-consuming regulatory supervision that shackles and distorts managerial initiative." He ended his message by dramatically calling for "greater reliance on the forces of competition and less reliance on the restraints of regulation."

The importance of the Kennedy message did not rest upon any resultant congressional action, however, for in fact Congress failed to change transportation policy. Its importance, rather, lay in the fact that it set a new tone, establishing a new goal and a new approach to regulation.

When President Lyndon Johnson took office, his concern lay with governmental coordination and efficiency in the transportation field. Accordingly, his major accomplishment was the establishment of the Department of Transportation and the attempted coordination of existing administrative agencies concerned with transportation. This was detailed in the previous chapter. Hence, Congress laid aside the Kennedy call for more reliance on competition and less reliance on the restraints of regulation and turned to coordination and planning.

Dissatisfaction with Regulation in the Early 1970s

Intertwined in the late 1960s and early 1970s were three forces leading to questions about the effects of the transportation regulatory scheme. First, there was a marked concern for the consumer. This movement, often called consumerism, was associated with Ralph Nader and various investigations carried on by "Nader's Raiders." Both the ICC and the CAB came under attack in these studies, and a series of legal actions challenged regulatory rules, such as the bumping of air passengers. In general, the movement seemed to emphasize that regulation was administered more for the protection of the carriers than for the benefit of the public.

Second, a series of studies by well-known academicians attempted to measure the costs of regulation. Moore in motor transportation, Friedlaender in railroads, and Jordan in air transportation pointed out that this cost involved the misallocation of resources and subsequently large social costs. The budgets of the regulatory agencies were small in comparison to the social costs occasioned by the action of regulations, according to these critics. Although there was controversy over the numbers generated by these analyses and the inability to measure offsetting benefits of regulation, the importance was that the estimated social costs of regulation were repeated over and over again. It became almost conventional wisdom that regulation was leading to misallocation.

Finally, the deteriorating railroad situation, particularly in the populous Northeast, led to further questioning of the efficacy of regulation. After a much publicized merger of two large railroads, the Penn Central filed for receivership in June 1970. Five smaller railroads in the same area also slipped into receivership. Over 20 percent of the rail freight and passenger traffic of the nation was carried by these lines. "Over-regulation" of the railroads was widely blamed for these dire financial circumstances, and in 1973 when the bankruptcy court in charge of the receivership stated its intention to cease operations, a crisis arose. Congress responded with the 3-R Act in 1973, followed by the 4-R Act in 1976, as noted in the last chapter. The important point here is that regulation was generally blamed for the fact that, with the exception of two profitable systems, much of the railroad operation in seventeen northeastern states was bankrupt.

Thus, in the early 1970s, regulation was charged with neglecting the consumer, causing considerable social costs and misallocation, and bankrupting the railroads.

Energy Concerns

When the so-called energy crisis began in 1973 with the Arab oil embargo, another factor was added to these dissatisfactions with regulation. Temporary shortages of petroleum called attention to the fact that airlines were operating on many flights with less than half their seats occupied, that many trucks were running empty because of route and backhaul restrictions, and that the private automobile not only used tremendous amounts of petroleum-based fuel while carrying slightly over one passenger per trip but also polluted the atmosphere and congested the streets and highways. Thus, the public became concerned about the additional factor of energy consumption in transportation.

These newly found energy concerns were attacked on many fronts. For example, Congress passed the Clean Air Act, establishing emission standards and mandating performance standards in terms of miles per gallon to be met by automobile manufacturers in future years. Some modification of regulation now took place — for instance, airlines were allowed to cooperate in order to reduce competitive but half-empty flights. The administration of transportation regulation received a large share of the blame for energy inefficiency in for-hire transportation, and energy use became a permanent concern.

THE MOVE TO EASE RAILROAD REGULATION: THE 4-R ACT

In the previous chapter, we discussed the first half of the Railroad Revitalization and Regulatory Reform Act of 1976 — the 4-R Act. As we saw, the railroad revitalization section established Conrail. The second half, regulatory reform, was part of the era of deregulation; its importance here lay in the fact that it established, in part, a pattern followed in later deregulation acts.

During President Ford's administration, the Council of Economic Advisors advocated deregulation, specific deregulation bills were introduced in Congress, and a timetable for deregulation of the various transportation modes was announced. However, the method of deregulation and the efficiency of more competition became very controversial. The principal results of this debate were some changes in the regulatory process and rate controls enacted as part of the 4-R Act.

Essentially three reforms were involved. First, the railroads were allowed to raise or lower rates without ICC suspension within specific limits. Carriers were given the freedom to increase or decrease rates up to 7 percent a year for two years where "market dominance" did not exist. The idea of a zone of rate freedom was new and conceptualized the earlier Kennedy goal of "unshackling managerial initiative" and allowing "greater reliance on the forces of competition and less reliance on the restraints of regulation."

Second, regulation of rates was to be limited by the concept of "threshold costs" on the one hand and "market dominance" on the other. Two ideas are involved here, both minimum rate control and maximum rate control. Any rate equal to or greater than variable costs could not be found to be unjust or unreasonable on grounds that it was too low. This idea of relating reasonableness to a cost threshold was new and was a victory for the railroads who had lobbied for variable-cost-based minimum rate control for years. As to maximum rates, no rate could be declared to be too high unless the ICC determined that the carrier possessed "market dominance" over the traffic. Although controversy developed over the exact definition of market dominance, a compromise was reached in October 1976. The definition states that "market dominance" is the *absence of effective competition* where any one of three conditions prevail: (1) the carrier proposing the rate change has a market share of 70 percent of the traffic, (2) the proposed rate is equal to 160 percent of variable costs of the carrier, or (3) the shippers have made significant investment in rail facilities and are hence locked into rail shipments. These new concepts of "threshold costs" and "market dominance" were repeated in later deregulation acts.

The third area of reform specified speedier action by the ICC on several types of proceedings and by rate bureaus processing rate proposals. One important time limitation assigned the ICC was that rail merger proposals had to be handled in thirty-one months. Decisions in rate-making proposals before rate bureaus had to be completed in 120 days. Further, Congress reaffirmed the principle contained in the Transportation Act of 1958 that railroads' rates should not be held up to protect a carrier of another mode.

As we have noted, the 1976 regulatory reforms were not only important in themselves but were also important in setting a pattern for later deregulation changes. The ideas of a zone of rate freedom, threshold costs, market dominance, and reformed procedures appeared again in 1980 deregulation acts.

AIR TRANSPORTATION DEREGULATION

In addition to rail regulatory reforms, the major thrust of the deregulation movement concentrated on air transportation in the mid-1970s. Beginning in 1975, the emphasis on deregulation settled on the area of air transportation for five reasons. First, air passenger transportation was of direct concern to a wide public of consumers as it was the most popular and visible means of intercity travel. Although freight transportation was of considerable importance, the effects of regulation in carrying goods were indirect. In air transportation, the public was directly involved.

Second, the energy and efficiency aspects of air transportation were well known, adequately documented, and easily understood by the public. Empty backhauls and circuitous routing of trucks were harder to understand and visualize, but two half-empty planes on competitive flights departing at the same time could be readily understood as a waste of energy and lack of efficiency.

Third, air service was relatively independent of other carriers, so the aftershocks of deregulation would not spread throughout the entire transportation system as surface deregulation would.

Fourth, the air transportation industry was financially healthy and apparently well managed, safety was strictly controlled, and there was little concern that strong competition would physically endanger the public.

Finally, abandonment of service to smaller communities had a ready solution in the growing commuter airline segment, and employee resistance to deregulation was slight.

As noted above, the Ford administration expressed support for deregulation in 1975, and the Council of Economic Advisors was strongly critical of the CAB. Early in 1975, Senator Edward Kennedy opened oversight hearings on CAB practices and procedures which provided a forum for the critics of air transportation regulation. Four conclusions emerged from these hearings. One, CAB controls were so restrictive that airline management really had little managerial discretion. Two, the CAB had been overly protective and paternalistic of the airline industry. Not one new trunk-line certificate had been granted out of over eighty applications to enter the industry from 1938 to 1970. Three, more competition and less regulation would lower fares to the consumers as evidenced by experience in the intrastate airline markets in California and Texas. And finally, owing to elasticity of demand, lower fares would be beneficial to the carriers themselves by stimulating increases in the numbers of passengers.

Although the deregulation bills proposed by the Ford administration did not pass Congress, another significant event did take place. President Ford appointed John Robson as chairman of the CAB, and he announced that henceforth the CAB would experiment with less control over fares and routes. Thus, administrative deregulation began as the CAB modified its interpretation of the law. Upon the election of President Carter, Robson was replaced by Dr. Alfred Kahn as chairman. Kahn, a well-known academic advocate of deregulation, not only set a goal of continuing experimentation and administrative deregulation but actively lobbied Congress and publicly campaigned for an end to airline regulation (and an end to his own agency, the CAB). Finally, in 1977, Senator Howard Cannon began hearings on an air transportation regulatory reform act which ultimately became the Airline Deregulation Act of 1978.

Air Cargo Deregulation, 1977

While the Cannon-Kennedy proposals were working their way through the legislative process, Congress passed and President Carter signed an act amending the Federal Aviation Act of 1958 (P.L. 95-163, 91 Stat. 1285, Nov. 9, 1977) which deregulated the air freight industry. This, the first of the specific deregulation acts of the late 1970s and early 1980s, essentially freed all-cargo aircraft operations from CAB regulation.

In brief, the act changed three things: entry controls, size restrictions, and rate controls. First, as to entry, any carrier (outside of Hawaii and Alaska) who had air cargo service in 1977 was granted a grandfather right to that service. In November 1978, any firm could apply for all-cargo certificates whether it had previously served or not. Fitness was to be the sole criterion for denial. Some seventy-four firms applied for all-cargo grandfather certificates, and when entry was opened in 1978, ten more firms were certificated as all-cargo carriers.

Second, the act removed restrictions on the size of aircraft used in air cargo service, which helped smaller commuter airlines as well as Federal Express. Third, all-cargo operators could establish any rate they chose as long as they avoided discrimination; after March 1979, the operators were relieved from filing freight tariffs with the CAB.

A number of smaller firms entered the industry, and service generally improved. However, freight rates increased about 10 percent, and the operators reduced the amount of liability coverage from $9 a pound to 50 cents a pound, much to the distress of shippers.

Airline Deregulation Act of 1978

In addition to appointing Kahn chairman of the CAB, President Carter sent a special message to Congress in March 1977 requesting air deregulation. The president listed six objectives for Congress. First, to the maximum possible extent, domestic airlines should be governed by competitive forces. Second, restrictions preventing entry into the industry should be eased. Third, carriers should be allowed to expand routes without obtaining CAB approval. Fourth, after a phase-in period, carriers should be free to set competitive prices with regulation retained only over predatory pricing. Fifth, carriers should be allowed to leave markets without prolonged hearings or onerous restrictions. Sixth, small communities should be protected from loss of service. After some employee protection provisions were added, the Senate passed an act more or less based on these objectives in April 1978 and the House acted in September 1978. President Carter signed the Airline Deregulation Act (P.L. 95-504, 92

Stat. 1705, Oct. 24, 1978), popularly known as the Kennedy-Cannon Act, and air passenger deregulation was a fact.

The scheme to deregulate air passenger transportation adopted a phased approach and can be summarized in six major provisions. First, through 1981, existing carriers could add service to one entirely new market each year and could protect one route each year from competition. Routes were defined as city-pairs. Two, airlines were permitted to expand into dormant routes if the carriers could demonstrate readiness and ability to serve. Dormant routes existed where a carrier which had previously been granted certification had not provided service five times a week for at least thirteen weeks of any twenty-six week period. It was estimated that over 22,000 dormant route miles existed. This provision caused an immediate rush by existing carriers to expand service and to rationalize their route structure by applying for dormant routes of other carriers. The CAB awarded 248 dormant routes to twenty-two carriers under this provision.

Third, airline fares could be decreased by 50 percent or increased by 5 percent per year without CAB approval. This was the same zone of rate freedom concept found in the 4-R Act but with different limits. The CAB could allow even greater rate cuts upon application or even greater rate increases if necessary to keep current with inflation. This provision was to be in force until January 1983.

Fourth, in order to protect small communities from loss of service, all cities served at the time of the act were guaranteed essential service for ten years after passage of the act. Although abandonment was considerably easier, the federal government assumed the obligation of either subsidizing noncompensatory operations or finding a substitute carrier to maintain "essential service" to small communities. The subsidy scheme was based on the needs of the communities for service and the appropriate use of aircraft for each market. Carriers proposing to reduce service below the level of "essential service" had to give ninety days' notice, and if a new carrier could not be found, the carrier could be required to continue service for thirty days with the government compensating for any loss. Additionally, a loan guarantee program was instituted to help smaller airlines purchase new planes (under fifty-passenger capacity).

Fifth, in an innovative provision, the whole program was to cease, that is, "sunset" on a prearranged schedule. In December 1981, the CAB was no longer to have control over routes and after that date any carrier could operate any route as long as FAA safety requirements were met. In January 1983, the CAB was to lose control over airline rates and airline mergers. By January 1984, the CAB was to submit a report to Congress with its recommendations on its future role, and unless Congress acted to the contrary, the CAB itself was to cease to exist by January 1985.

Sixth, nonmanagerial employees were protected if they were terminated because of the act. Should total employment decrease by 7.5 percent in any one year, a percentage of employees' wages would be paid for up to six years with the federal government assuming this obligation.

Another feature was the modification of the controversial "mutual aid pact" designed to lessen the possibility of a prolonged strike. Restrictions on equipment size that afforded exemption from the act were increased to planes with capacities of less than fifty-six passengers or 18,000 pounds of cargo. "Fill-up" rights were allowable, and the powers of the president to disallow grants of operating authority in international air service cases were restricted. Former functions of the CAB were to be transferred to other governmental agencies after 1985: control of mergers to the Department of Justice, determination of air mail contract rates to the Postal Service, and authority over foreign air transportation and compensation for "essential service" to the Department of Transportation.

ADMINISTRATIVE DEREGULATION

The criticisms of the regulatory scheme during the Ford administration and the actions of CAB Chairman Kahn were not entirely lost on the ICC. In 1977, the commission released a staff task force report calling for thirty-nine recommended changes in regulation and held extensive hearings on these proposals. Chairman Daniel O'Neil was committed to a more liberal interpretation of the act, and President Carter also emphasized administrative deregulation through two actions. One, as resignations occurred and terms of commissioners expired, the president appointed only commissioners pledged to deregulation. Second, because a full complement of commissioners was not appointed, the commission decreased in size to seven members, and the voting power of those committed to deregulation increased. Under these circumstances favorable to deregulation, the ICC became increasingly liberal in its interpretation of the regulatory statutes, and many modifications of the old rules were accomplished. In the area of railroad regulation, the ICC modified its existing rules and allowed contract rates between carriers and shippers in order to save fuel and improve car utilization. In 1979, the commission exempted rail movement of fresh fruits and vegetables in order to match the long-standing exemption of truck movements of this freight. In trucking, gateway restrictions were eased to increase fuel efficiency, commercial zones were enlarged, contract carriers' rules were eased, private carriers were allowed to apply for certificates or permits for backhauling (under the *ToTo* decision of the ICC), and so on. But it was probably in the interpretation of entry rules that administrative deregulation reached its peak — in 1979, some 98 percent of all applications for new authority were approved!

The more liberal interpretation of statutes and administrative deregulation by the ICC came to a head in the fall of 1979 when Senator Cannon and Representative "Buzz" Johnson, chairmen of the congressional committees dealing with transportation, wrote the ICC to cease setting policy until Congress acted on pending motor carrier deregulation proposals. This congressional reaction to administrative deregulation explains some of the unusual provisions in the Motor Carrier Act of 1980 — for example, oversight hearings.

MOTOR CARRIER ACT OF 1980

After extensive hearings, Congress enacted the Motor Carrier Act late in the spring of 1980, and the new bill was signed by President Carter in July 1980 (P.L. 96-296). The approach and tone of the act is contained in the congressional findings, which stated:

> Congress hereby finds that a safe, sound competition and fuel efficient motor carrier system is vital to the maintenance of a strong national economy and strong national defense. . . . the current statutes are . . . outdated and must be revised to reflect transportation needs and realities of the 1980s. . . . historically the existing regulatory structure has tended . . . to inhibit market entry, carrier growth, maximum utilization of equipment and energy resources and opportunities for minorities and others to enter the trucking industry; . . . protective regulation has resulted in operating inefficiencies [and] anticompetitive pricing; in order to reduce uncertainty . . . the ICC should be given explicit directions for regulation of the motor carrier industry and well defined parameters within which it may act; . . . the ICC should not attempt to go beyond the powers vested in it; . . . changes should be implemented with the least amount of disruption to the transportation system; . . . appropriate committees of Congress shall conduct oversight hearings on the effects of this legislation no less than annually for the first five years following the date of enactment . . . to insure that this Act is being implemented according to Congressional intent and purpose.

Two elements of these findings are noteworthy: the concern over administrative deregulation and the concern over fuel and energy resource use and operating efficiencies.

The act itself can be summarized under six headings: amendment to national transportation policy, entry regulatory changes, removal of operating restrictions, rate reforms, rate bureau changes, and miscellaneous changes.

First, an amendment was added to the Declaration of National Transportation Policy relative to motor carriers of property only. This amendment states it is the new national policy to promote competitive and efficient motor transportation in order to

(A) meet the needs of shippers, receivers, and consumers; (B) allow a variety of quality and price options to meet the changing market demands and diverse requirements of the shipping public; (C) allow the most productive use of equipment and energy resources; (D) enable efficient and well-managed carriers to earn adequate profits, attract capital, and maintain fair wages and working conditions; (E) provide and maintain service to small communities and small shippers; (F) improve and maintain a sound, safe, and competitive privately-owned motor carrier system; (G) promote greater participation by minorities in the motor carrier system; and, (H) promote intermodal transportation.

It is significant that hereafter a separate portion of the Declaration of National Transportation Policy is devoted solely to motor carriers. Up to 1980, the declaration applied to all surface modes of transportation with none singled out for special attention. Further, concern with both increased competition and resource use, especially energy use, now becomes our national policy in trucking. Likewise, opportunities for minorities, promotion of intermodal transportation, concern over small communities and small shippers, and adequacy of carrier profits are also part of national policy. In the long run, these amendments may be the major significant changes emerging from the act, depending on how some of the seemingly conflicting goals are attained.

Entry regulations were changed to make it easier for new carriers to enter the motor carrier market. A new entrant now must show merely that a "useful public purpose" will be served; formerly a prospective entrant had to show "public convenience and necessity." Existing carriers must now show that a new entrant is not needed, whereas before, a new entrant had to prove that more competition was needed. Master certificates in limited cases are now available.

Previous restrictions in operating certificates were to be removed in 180 days. Hence, the ICC was ordered to remove gateway restrictions and circuitous route limitations, broaden service to intermediate points, and allow round-trip authority where only one-way authority had existed previously. Broader descriptions of traffic were covered, and the ICC was told to "eliminate any other unreasonable restrictions that the Commission deems to be wasteful of fuel, inefficient or contrary to the public interest." Removal of these restrictions went a long way toward blunting earlier criticism of overregulation.

Under rate reform, the now familiar zone of rate freedom was used again. A carrier was allowed to increase or decrease rates 10 percent for two years without ICC suspension. The ICC could allow an additional 5 percent if it deemed it to be desirable. After two years, changes in the limits of the zone of rate freedom were to be tied to the producers' price index. Additionally, released rates were allowable whereby a carrier could limit its liability in return for a lower rate. Significantly, the commission was now given the power to order through and joint rates between motor carriers and between motor and inland water carriers. Further, a new rule of ratemaking was prescribed, based on revenue and capital needs of the carriers.

Significant changes were ordered in rate bureau operation and procedures. After January 1981, only carriers able to participate in a rate could vote; after January 1984, rate bureaus could no longer consider single-line rates (local rates), and antitrust immunity was to be withdrawn under certain circumstances. A Rate-Making Study Commission was established (three senators, three representatives, four public members) to investigate the question of continuing antitrust immunity, for rate bureaus. The commission was to report by January 1983, and it subsequently recommended removal of antitrust immunity, but Congress never acted on this recommendation.

A number of miscellaneous changes were also made by the act. A study was authorized to look into small-community service, and the "rule of eight" definition of contract carriers was modified. Several specific movements were added to the exempt list (including all movement incidental to air transportation), and more commodities were included under the agricultural commodities exemption clause. Private carriers were allowed to haul for their subsidiaries on a compensated basis, lumping was prohibited, and agricultural cooperatives were permitted to haul up to 25 percent regulated traffic and still be exempt. In addition, certain solicitation expenses were allowed, TOFC rules were lessened, recyclable commodities could be hauled free, discriminatory state property taxes on carriers were prohibited, procedures were shortened on merger proposals, and a series of financial changes were allowed.

STAGGERS RAIL ACT OF 1980

On October 14, 1980, the president signed P.L. 96-448, the Staggers Rail Act. This act, named for Congressman Harley Staggers of West Virginia, is generally considered to be a deregulation act even though it takes a somewhat different approach than other regulatory reform acts of 1977, 1978, and 1980. Whereas the air deregulation acts seemed to be primarily aimed at assisting the consumer (both the air freight shipper and the traveling public) and the goal of the Motor Carrier Act seemed to be that of improving energy and equipment efficiency, the Staggers Act was clearly aimed at improving the financial situation of rail carriers.

This concern over the financial position of the railroads is apparent both in President Carter's call for railroad deregulation and in the goals of the Staggers Act (Section 3). When President Carter proposed rail deregulation in May 1979, he stated:

> Deregulation presents the only viable option to either massive increases in federal subsidies to the railroads or increased government intervention in their operation — both of which are highly undesirable.

This theme was picked up by Congress, and in the findings in Section 2 of the act, much was made of poor railroad earnings and a projected capital shortfall of between $16 and $20 billion by 1985. In Section 3, Congress states, "The purpose of this Act is to provide for the restoration, maintenance, and improvement of the physical facilities and financial stability of the rail system of the United States."

Most of the Staggers Act, therefore, dealt with rate reforms. The act can be summarized under six headings: minimum and maximum rate control, zone of rate freedom, contract rates and other rate reforms, rate bureau reform, procedural changes, and miscellaneous changes.

Railroads now have considerable latitude in establishing rates without ICC permission. In effect, the ICC retains two types of controls: minimum rate control and maximum rate control. On the lower level, all rates must exceed variable cost as a minimum and contribute to the "going concern value" of the railroad or be deemed unreasonable and hence illegal. On the other hand, the ICC may not control maximum rates unless market dominance exists. The idea of market dominance came out of the earlier 4-R Act, but in the Staggers Act, market dominance is specifically defined in terms of revenue-cost ratios. Hence, a cost threshold for what is market dominance is built into the controls. Beginning in September 1981, market dominance was to be 160 percent of variable costs for one year and was to be increased by 5 percent a year until October 1984; it was not to exceed 180 percent nor be less than 170 percent of variable cost, depending on ICC cost formulas.

Additionally, rate freedom was also provided with a zone of rate flexibility somewhat like the zones of rate freedom in the air passenger and motor carrier acts. If a rate did not fall under the minimum controls (variable cost) or meet market dominance, it could be increased by an amount equal to a cost recovery index (inflation) plus 6 percent for four years with a maximum allowable increase of 18 percent. After October 1984, rates may be increased by 4 percent a year above the inflation rate unless the carrier was found to have adequate revenues. General rate increases were to cease after January 1984, and in effect rail rates were to be tied to the rate of inflation in the economy with a cost recovery index.

Other rate reforms include the legalization of contract rates by railroads. In effect, railroads may now become contract carriers up to 40 percent of their capacity as measured by major car types. Carriers may also enter into separate service contracts. Contracts must be filed and approved by the ICC. Further, railroads may enter into released value rates and agreements if they so desire — a repetition of the provisions of the Motor Carrier Act — and new rules were established concerning protests on grounds of unreasonableness of rates.

Rate bureau reforms also parallel the Motor Carrier Act passed earlier in 1980. Carriers must be able to participate in a joint rate in order to vote, and single-line rates may no longer be discussed. Rate bureaus may continue as publishing agents with antitrust immunity, but procedures for decisions are specified with more open public records, time limits, and participation.

Several noteworthy procedural changes involved a reduction in notice of rate changes from thirty days to twenty days for a rate increase and ten days for a rate decrease. The ICC must act within five months instead of seven months after a rate has been suspended. The ICC also must end merger hearings in twenty-four months and reach a decision in 180 days after hearings. On abandonments, procedure was shortened to 330 days overall.

A series of miscellaneous changes was involved: the long-and-short-haul clause was repealed, certain solicitation expenses were allowed, modification of state control over intrastate rates was specified, a cost accounting board was established, the redeemable preference share program was extended, recyclables could be hauled at low rates, labor protective provisions for the Rock Island and Milwaukee bankruptcies were provided, demand sensitive rates were repealed, elaborate rules governing surcharges were included, Conrail appropriations were involved, and special provisions concerning San Antonio Coal rates were specified.

In general, the Staggers Act provided greater flexibility to rail carrier management and limited the ability of the ICC to control the railroads.

HOUSEHOLD GOODS TRANSPORTATION ACT OF 1980

Shortly after the Staggers Rail Act was passed, Congress also changed the regulation of the household goods moving industry in P.L. 96-454. The Motor Carrier Act of 1980, passed in June, had not covered this area of transportation but many of the provisions of the earlier act were applied here, such as the congressional oversight hearings for five years, the goal of providing a variety of quality and price options, and the goal of more market competition.

Most of the changes in the Household Goods Transportation Act concerned problems that had surfaced in the post–World War II period. The act provided that written and binding estimates as well as guaranteed pickup and delivery contracts may be offered to the moving public at an additional charge. Carrier performance standards may be established by the ICC, and an arbitration procedure is established to settle consumer complaints. Practices such as weight bumping are declared illegal and carriers' control over their agents is regulated.

BUS REGULATORY REFORM ACT OF 1982

Congress passed P.L. 97-261, the Bus Regulatory Reform Act, which was signed by President Reagan on September 20, 1982. According to the American Bus Association, this new law "makes obsolete over 90 percent of what was heretofore written on economic regulation of the bus industry."

Much of P.L. 97-261 builds on and amends the Motor Carrier Act of 1980 to include buses. For example, congressional findings, the statement of national transportation policy, congressional oversight hearings for five years, the rule of ratemaking, removal of operating restrictions, new rules for rate bureaus, provisions for temporary and emergency authority, and prohibition of state tax discrimination are all repeated from the 1980 act and amended to include the motor bus industry. The major changes contained in the act can be summarized under four points: liberalized entry and exit controls, rate controls, pre-emption of state authority, and miscellaneous changes.

Barriers to entry and exit in the bus industry are drastically lowered. Proof of safety fitness and insurance coverage is all that is necessary on unsubsidized charter and special operations, contract carriers, and new or substitute service for discontinued air and rail service. Proof of "public interest" on all other proposed entry is much easier and anyone protesting bears the burden of proof that more service is not necessary. On the question of exit, bus service may be discontinued if revenue does not cover variable costs, and if a state refuses to allow discontinuance of service between points within the state on an interstate route, the ICC takes jurisdiction and may allow the exit.

Under rate controls, zone of rate freedom is used for three years for regular route service. In the first year, rates may increase 10 percent or decrease 20 percent, in the second year, they may increase 15 percent or decrease 25 percent, and in the third year, rates may change upward 20 percent or downward 30 percent, all without fear of ICC suspension. After three years, the ICC loses all jurisdiction over rates unless they are predatory or discriminatory. The ICC loses control over charter and special transportation rates (again unless predatory or discriminatory), and rates may be changed with ten days' notice rather than thirty days.

In perhaps the most startling reform, the ICC pre-empts regulation by the states on rates and schedules. As noted above, if a state refuses to allow discontinuances, the ICC may do so. Additionally, the ICC assumes jurisdiction over all rate and schedule changes in intrastate passenger service and express fares on interstate routes. Of course, state control over solely intrastate carriers continues.

Under miscellaneous changes, increased insurance and financial responsibility minimums are specified, control of securities passes from the ICC to the SEC, the Rate Making Study Commission (from the Motor Carrier Act of 1980) is extended to buses and charged with studying service to rural and small communities and to the elderly. Also, a bus terminal study is authorized as well as a study of the use of CB radios by carriers, and a moratorium of two years is ordered on granting authority to Canadian and Mexican carriers (both bus and truck). Further, carriers are allowed to mix charter and regular passengers on the same bus, and a modest employee protection plan is authorized.

In general, the Bus Regulatory Reform Act of 1982 allows almost complete deregulation of the motor bus industry.

SURFACE FREIGHT FORWARDERS
DEREGULATION ACT OF 1986

Congress essentially completed its deregulation efforts by passing the Surface Freight Forwarders Deregulation Act (P.L. 99-521), which was signed October 22, 1986. Air freight forwarders had been deregulated in 1977 and now deregulation was extended to surface freight forwarders (motor and rail). This act completely deregulated the freight forwarder business and was the final deregulation act. Interestingly, freight forwarders were the last to be regulated in 1942 and the last to be deregulated forty-four years later.

NATIONAL TRANSPORTATION POLICY
STUDY COMMISSION

The final element of the era of deregulation was the establishment in 1976 of a National Transportation Policy Study Commission. This eighteen-member commission made up of eleven congressional representatives and seven public members was charged with the task of investigating the transportation needs, resources, and requirements of the economy up to the year 2000. Several studies were undertaken and eighty recommendations were made in the final report of the commission in 1979. Although the commission did not deal directly with deregulation, many of its findings called attention to the dramatic projected growth of transportation by the year 2000, the need for massive investments of capital — $4 trillion between 1976 and 2000 — and the need to modify the regulatory structure. Perhaps the greatest significance of the work of the commission was its focusing of attention on the future needs of transportation.

SUMMARY

Transportation entered the era of deregulation in 1962 when President John F. Kennedy called for "greater reliance on the forces of competition and less reliance on the restraints of regulation." In administering the various regulatory acts of Congress, the ICC and CAB had imposed rules and regulations that tended to stifle the use of the market mechanism in transportation. Beginning in about 1970, various groups increasingly pointed out that regulation seemed to be aimed more at protecting the carriers than protecting the public, that misallocations and social costs came from regulation, and that some carriers (notably the railroads) seemed to be in dire financial straits because of regulation. The energy crisis of the 1970s added a further dimension to the concern over the efficacy of regulation.

After prolonged public debate, Congress passed a series of acts to reform the regulatory structure. Some, like the Air Cargo Deregulation amendments to the Federal Aviation Act of 1958, the Airline Deregulation Act of 1978, and the Surface Freight Forwarder Deregulation Act of 1986 completely removed public economic regulation. Others, such as the 4-R Act of 1976, the Motor Carrier Act of 1980, the Staggers Rail Act of 1980, the Household Goods Transportation Act of 1980, and the Bus Regulatory Reform Act of 1982, modified and changed transportation regulation in varying degrees. In the case of these last four acts, regulation remains but in a considerably different manner. This has led some groups to reject the term *deregulation* for these acts, preferring to call them *reregulation*. Regardless of the term used, however, the regulatory environment of all transportation has changed markedly since 1976.

Although the effects of these new acts and new philosophy of more reliance on market competition are still being worked out, the next chapter will consider the consequences of the deregulation movement.

ADDITIONAL READINGS

Coyle, John J., Edward J. Bardi, and Joseph L. Cavinato, *Transportation*, 2nd ed., St. Paul, Minn.: West Publishing Co., 1986.
    Chapter 16, "Changing Direction of Regulation," pp. 325–47.
Davis, Grant M., ed., *Transportation Regulation: A Pragmatic Assessment*, Danville, Ill.: Interstate Printers and Publishers, 1976.
Fair, Marvin L., and Ernest W. Williams, Jr., *Transportation and Logistics*, rev. ed., Plano, Texas: Business Publications, 1981.
    Chapter 19, "Regulation of Transportation: Origin and Scope," pp. 348–85.
Farris, Martin T. "The Case Against Radical Deregulation of Transportation, Communications, and Power," *ICC Practitioners' Journal*, 45, No. 3 (March-April 1978), 306–32.
_____ , "The Multiple Meanings and Goals of Deregulation: A Commentary," *Transportation Journal*, 21, No. 2 (Winter 1982), 44–50.
Farris, Martin T., and Norman E. Daniel, "Bus Regulatory Reform Act of 1982," *Transportation Journal*, 23, No. 1 (Fall 1983), 4–15.
Friedlaender, Ann F., *The Dilemma of Freight Transportation Regulation*, Washington, D.C.: Brookings Institution, 1969.
Fruhan, William E., *The Fight for Competitive Advantage: A Study of the United States Domestic Trunk Air Carriers*, Boston: Graduate School of Business, Harvard University, 1972.
Harper, Donald V., "The Federal Motor Carrier Act of 1980: Review and Analysis," *Transportation Journal*, 20, No. 2 (Winter 1980), 5–33.

Hazard, John L., "Transitional Administration of National Transportation Policy," *Transportation Journal*, 20, No. 3 (Spring 1981), 5–22.

Jordan, William A., *Airline Regulation in America*, Baltimore: Johns Hopkins Press, 1970.

Lieb, Robert C., *Transportation*, 3rd ed., Reston, Va.: Reston Publishing Co., 1985.
Chapter 15, "The Regulatory Reform Movement," pp. 291–329.

MacAvoy, Paul W., and John W. Snow, eds., *Regulation of Entry and Pricing in Truck Transportation*, Washington, D.C.: American Enterprise Institute for Public Policy, 1977.

Moore, Thomas Gale, *Freight Transportation Regulation*, Washington, D.C.: American Enterprise Institute for Public Policy, 1972.

Morash, Edward A., "A Critique of the Household Goods Transportation Act of 1980," *Transportation Journal* (Winter 1981), 16–27.

Rakowski, James P., "The Trucking Industry in the United States: A Study of Transportation Policy in Transition," *Traffic Quarterly*, 35, No. 4 (October 1981), 623–37.

Rakowski, James P., and James C. Johnson, "Airline Deregulation: Problems and Prospects," *Quarterly Review of Economics and Business*, 19, No. 4 (Winter 1979), 65–78.

Stephenson, Frederick J., and Frederick J. Beiers, "The Effects of Airline Deregulation on Air Service to Small Communities," *Transportation Journal*, 20, No. 4 (Summer 1981), 54–62.

Taneja, Nawal K., *Airlines in Transition*, Lexington, Mass.: Lexington Books, D. C. Heath & Co., 1981.
Chapter 5, "Economic Behavior," pp. 111–48.

U.S. National Transportation Policy Study Commission, *National Transportation Policies Through the Year 2000*, Washington, D.C.: U.S. Government Printing Office, 1979.

Williams, Ernest W., Jr., "The National Transportation Policy Study Commission and Its Final Report: A Review," *Transportation Journal*, 19, No. 3 (Spring 1980), 5–19.

———— , "A Critique of the Staggers Rail Act of 1980," *Transportation Journal*, 21, No. 3 (Spring 1982), 5–15.

Wood, Donald F., and James C. Johnson, *Contemporary Transportation*, 3rd ed., New York: Macmillan Publishing Co., 1989.
Chapter 5, "Highway Carriers," pp. 89–116.
Chapter 9, "Domestic Aviation," pp. 213–47.

CHAPTER 14

CONSEQUENCES OF DEREGULATION

Now that the changes in the regulatory environment have been analyzed, the question naturally arises: What have been the consequences of these changes? To be sure, the effects of these rather substantial changes are still being worked out and the impact of regulatory reform will continue into the future. Nevertheless, it is possible to indicate at this time (roughly a decade since deregulation and regulatory reform were put in place) some of the results of these changes. However, first we must summarize in a broad way the essence of deregulation.

ESSENCE OF DEREGULATION

Although each deregulation act had its own specific provisions, the deregulation movement can be summarized into three points: (1) less control of entry, (2) more flexibility in pricing, and (3) relaxation of regulatory rules.

Less Control of Entry

Reviewing the "three pillars of regulation" in Chapter 13, one will recall that control of entry and exit was discussed first. While the whole regulatory structure was interdependent, one of the important aspects of regulation was the control of entry by requiring that all carriers have a certificate of public convenience and necessity in order to offer service to the public. Railroads were by definition common carriers but even here a certificate was necessary to expand the system — and importantly, abandonment and discontinuance in rail was only by regulatory permission after hearings. In motor transportation, both of property and passengers, as well as air transportation, inland water transportation, and freight forwarding, a certificate of public convenience and necessity was required (except in certain exemptions such as private carriage, agricultural commodities by truck, bulk commodity service by inland water, local transportation, school buses, and passenger transportation in national parks and monuments). In order to make entry controls work, mergers and consolidations were regulated also. Further, new entrants had to prove in a public hearing that they were "fit, willing, and able," and existing carriers could protest. By controlling entry, the ICC and CAB were able to control the degree of competition between carriers in a given mode.

Under the air cargo deregulation provisions (1977), any carrier that was "fit" was granted entry after 1978. In the Airline Deregulation Act (1978), CAB entry control over passenger routes was phased out over time; after December 1981 the CAB lost all control over routes and entry was completely deregulated. Airline mergers continued to be controlled by the CAB until it ceased to exist (by "sunset" provision) in January 1985. After that date, DOT had control of airline mergers until 1989 when the Department of Justice took jurisdiction under the antitrust laws.

In the Motor Carrier Act (1980) it was no longer necessary to prove public convenience and necessity — only that a "useful public purpose" was to be served. Importantly, the burden of proof was shifted, and after 1980 the existing carriers had to prove that the new service of the potential entrant *was not* needed — whereas before the potential entrant had to prove that its service *was* needed. While a certificate is still required, the major criterion for obtaining one is "fitness," not "fit, willing, and able," which required prior operating experience. Essentially this means that anyone can enter trucking if proper equipment, insurance, and safety inspection tests can be met. Similar provisions were included in the Bus Regulatory Reform Act (1982): proof of fitness, safety, and insurance, and the burden of proof that service is not needed shifted to protestants. Although a certificate is still required with practical free entry, merger controls in both bus service and trucking ceased to be important.

In rail transportation, entry costs have been so substantial that entry was not much of an issue. However, abandonment, discontinuance, and merger controls were important under regulation. The Staggers Rail Act (1980) modified control over these matters and generally required the ICC to act on merger or abandonment proposals in a specific time period.

Under the Surface Freight Forwarder Deregulation Act (1986) entry is completely uncontrolled, just as under the Airline Deregulation Act (1978).

Therefore, even though certificates are still necessary in motor transportation and control is on the basis of fitness, insurance, and safety, entry is essentially open in transportation under deregulation.

More Flexibility in Pricing

The second "pillar" of regulation mentioned in Chapter 13 was control of rates and earnings. Two levels were involved: rate levels or earnings and rate structure or nondiscrimination. Rate levels were to be high enough to allow a "fair return on fair value" and "adequate earnings" in order to "foster sound economic conditions," while specific rates were regulated so as to avoid "undue preference or prejudice" under similar circumstances and conditions. Rates could be either "unreasonably high" — too high an earnings level, or "unreasonably low" — too low an earnings level. Specific rates could not unduly discriminate (preferential or prejudicial) between shippers, classes of freight, districts, points, port areas, regions, and so forth. The carriers typically "set a rate" (often by way of rate bureaus which were exempt from antitrust laws) and the ICC and CAB either approved or disapproved the rates after hearings. Further, all rates had to be published and filed with regulatory bodies, could not be changed without thirty days' notice, and had to be absolutely adhered to (charging more than the published rate led to overcharge claims, charging less led to undercharge claims).

Under the air cargo deregulation provisions, carriers were required to avoid discrimination but were free to set any price or rate they desired without regulatory approval, and after March 1979 carriers were no longer required to file freight tariffs with the CAB.

In airline passenger fares, a zone of rate freedom somewhat like the zone of rate freedom for railroads contained in the 1976 4-R Act was used. Airline fares could decrease by 50 percent or increase by 5 percent from 1978 to 1983 without CAB approval. After 1983, airlines were completely free to set any fare they wished and free market competition was to prevail in air transportation.

Under the amendments to the Declaration of National Transportation Policy contained in the Motor Carrier Act of 1980, Congress specified that in motor transportation the ICC must "allow a variety of quality and price options to meet the changing market demands and diverse requirements of the shipping public," as noted in Chapter 13. The same policy provision was repeated in the Bus Regulatory Reform Act of 1982 with the words "traveling public" in place of "shipping public." This policy provision was implemented by allowing a zone of rate freedom for both truckers and buses. In trucking, rates could increase or decrease 10 percent a year for two years (with the ICC allowed to add another 5 percent a year, which they did) without ICC approval. Thus a "zone" of approximately 32 percent on either side of the published rate was created, within which the trucker could set its rates without ICC approval. After two years the upper and lower limits were tied to the producer price index (formerly known as the wholesale price index). In motor transportation of passengers, the zone of rate freedom was a bit more complicated: increases of 10 percent or decreases of 20 percent in the first year (1982), increases of 15 percent or decreases of 25 percent in the second year, increases of 20 percent or decreases of 30 percent in the third year, and the ICC to lose all fare jurisdiction in 1985. Notice of rate changes was shortened in both trucking and bus transportation.

As to earnings, the same amendments to the Declaration of National Transportation Policy provided that earnings should "enable efficient and well managed carriers to earn adequate profits, attract capital, and maintain fair wages and working conditions." However, with entry practically open plus wide limits on the zone of rate freedom, there was little chance that carrier rate levels would be unreasonably high.

Additionally, "released value" rates were allowed in trucking for the first time (previously they were found only in household goods movement), whereby the carrier could limit its liability in return for a lower rate. Further, the rate setting procedure was reformed so that rate bureaus could no longer consider single-line (local) rates, a carrier had to be able to participate in joint rates to vote, and more disclosure provisions were added.

Under the Staggers Rail Act of 1980, more flexibility in pricing was also allowed. Once again a zone of rate freedom was prescribed — this time an increase or decrease of 6 percent a year for four years with a maximum of 18 percent increase or decrease from the published rate with an adjustment for a cost recovery index. After October 1984 rates could increase by 4 percent over the rate of inflation until railroads attained "revenue adequacy." Released value rates were allowed as well as rail contract rates — special specific contracts with a given shipper to be filed with the ICC but kept confidential, allowing for service or price concessions in return for specific volumes of movement. Also, rates below variable cost that did not contribute to railroad "going concern value" were illegal *per se* on the minimum side. On the maximum side, the ICC was to retain rate control where "market dominance" existed, which was defined as 180 percent of variable costs after October 1984 with adjustments allowed for a "cost recovery index." Rate bureau reforms were specified along the same lines as the Motor Carrier Act — no rate bureau action on single-line (local) rates, carriers must be able to participate in order to vote on joint rates, and more open public records must be kept. Administratively, the ICC exempted rate control over rail fruit and vegetable rates and over TOFC/COFC rates. Notice of rate change was lowered to twenty days for a rate increase and ten days for a rate decrease.

Note that in both rail and trucking, rates must still be filed even though considerable latitude exists within the various zones of rate freedom for the carrier to set its own rates without ICC jurisdiction. Also, rate discounts must be filed, as well as the confidential rail contracts. Therefore, some rate control continues to exist and the ICC continues to have legal jurisdiction where market dominance in rail rates exists or where rates exceed or drop below the zones of rate freedom. However, as a practical matter the ICC has not exercised its legal jurisdiction in rates exceeding or dropping below the limits of the zones of rate freedom except in the case of market dominance in rail rates.

The "bottom line" is that while rates must be filed with the ICC in rail and motor transportation, a great deal of flexibility exists for the carriers to set their own rates.

Relaxation of Regulatory Rules

All the deregulatory acts contained rule changes, generally modifying or outright abandoning prior regulatory rules but in a few cases adding other requirements. For example, prior to the air cargo deregulatory amendments to the Federal Aviation Act, there were size restrictions on air cargo planes. These were removed. In the Airline Deregulation Act of 1978 practically all regulation of service — the third pillar of regulation in Chapter 13 — ceased to exist. Also, the controversial "mutual aid pact" designed to prevent airline strikes was so modified as to make such arrangements useless. An added provision in the 1978 act immediately exempted aircraft carrying fifty-six or fewer passengers and cargo planes under 18,000 pounds. Both of these exemptions led to a rapid increase in commuter air service and more cargo service, as we shall see directly.

However, even though the philosophy of the Airline Deregulation Act was to allow as much market competition as possible, a provision for subsidies to small communities was included. Hence "essential air service" to small communities was to be supported by government payments for ten years (later extended for five more years), and a loan guarantee program for purchase of aircraft under fifty-passenger capacity was put in place. Likewise an employee protection plan was imposed.

Under the Motor Carrier Act of 1980, the amendment to the Declaration of National Transportation Policy specifically ordered the ICC (1) to promote greater participation by minorities in the motor carrier system, and (2) to promote intermodal transportation — both were new regulatory goals. However, all operating restrictions in certificates of public convenience and necessity and all commodity restrictions were to be removed in 180 days after the act. Rule changes for rate bureaus have been noted above. However, a small community service study was required and more commodities were added to the agricultural commodity exemption list. On the side of fewer rules, the definition of a contract carrier (the so-called "rule of eight" which said a carrier serving more than eight shippers was a common carrier) was abandoned, private carriers were allowed to haul for their subsidiaries on a compensated basis, and agricultural cooperatives were allowed to haul up to 25 percent regulated freight and still remain exempt. Rules on solicitation expenses were modified, recyclable commodities could be hauled free, discriminatory state property taxes were prohibited, and a number of financial rules were modified. Almost all of these changes meant less regulation.

Under the Staggers Rail Act of 1980, rate bureau rules were changed, advance notice of rate change was lowered, certain solicitation expenses were allowed, recyclable commodities could be hauled at low rates, demand-sensitive rates were abandoned and the long-haul, short-haul clause was modified, surcharges were allowed, and a cost accounting board was created. Several modifications were made to speed up merger and abandonment procedures as well as action on a suspended rate. Once more the thrust of most of these changes was relaxation of regulatory rules.

However, the Household Goods Transportation Act of 1980 tended to impose more regulatory requirements, not fewer. Written and binding estimates as well as guaranteed pickup and delivery contracts had to be offered. Carrier performance standards were to be specified by the ICC and an arbitration procedure was established. Weight bumping was declared illegal and carriers' control over agents was regulated. Indeed, the Household Goods Transportation Act, while called a deregulation act, actually increased regulatory rules.

Under the Bus Regulatory Reform Act of 1982, operating restrictions were to be abandoned, carriers could mix charter and regular passengers on the same bus, the ICC lost control over securities issued by bus companies (it passed to the SEC), rates could be changed with ten days' notice (previously thirty-day notice required), and the ICC lost control over charter and special bus rates unless they were predatory or discriminatory. However, some changes increased regulation and rules on buses. Specifically, the ICC was allowed to pre-empt state control of rates and schedules if a state failed to act on rates and schedules on intrastate service on interstate routes. A modified employee protection plan was mandated, studies of small-community and rural bus service and the use of CB radios were ordered, insurance provisions were increased, and a ratemaking study was required. Even so, on balance more rules were modified than increased as far as buses were concerned.

In general, then, regulatory rules were relaxed. This is the third part of the essence of deregulation (along with less control of entry and more flexibility in pricing).

IMPACT OF DEREGULATION ON AIR TRANSPORTATION

The impact of deregulation is most evident in air transportation for three reasons. First, air transportation was deregulated first in point of time (cargo 1977, passenger 1978), thus providing more time for the consequences of deregulation to be worked out. Second, the air passenger business is a retail business and more directly affects the public. That is, there are frequent purchases by the ultimate consumer of single quantities (a seat), often without professional assistance. Freight transportation is more like a wholesale business — purchases of large quantities of service by trained specialists which indirectly affect the price of the final goods. Almost everyone knows the effects of airline passenger deregulation while a smaller number sees the effects of freight transportation deregulation. Finally, air transportation was the only mode (until the Surface Freight Forwarder Act of 1986) to be wholly and completely deregulated. Under all other acts prior to 1986, regulation was modified and reformed but regulation remained in some degree. Therefore, we note the impact of deregulation on air passenger transportation first and then consider the various other modes.

First, open entry has meant more airlines. There were 11 trunk air carriers in 1978, 8 local carriers, 7 Hawaii/Alaska carriers, 3 all-cargo carriers, and 228 commuter carriers (total 257 carriers, of which 29 were not commuters). As noted previously, air carrier classifications were changed in 1981, so after that point air carriers were classified as majors ($1 billion gross revenue or more), nationals ($75 million to $1 billion revenue), large regionals ($10 million to $75 million revenue), medium regionals (under $10 million), and commuters (medium regionals operating planes with sixty or fewer seats and a cargo capacity of less than 18,000 pounds). In 1987, ten years after air deregulation, there were 14 majors, 20 nationals, 32 large regionals, 27 medium regionals, and 169 commuters (total 262 carriers, of which 93 were not commuters).

Another way to look at the change in the number of air carriers is to note changes since 1978, using the new classification, as in Table 14.1. Note that 121 new carriers entered the industry in the ten years since deregulation. Open entry certainly brought more carriers and more competition in general.

Table 14.1 Scheduled Air Carriers that Entered the Market, 1978–1987

	Entered	Exited	Still Operating	Others
Nationals	14	3	7	4 merged
Large Regionals	44	19	20	2 merged, 3 now operating as commuters
Medium Regionals	63	23	22	18 now operating as commuters
Total	121	45	49	

Source: From data in *FAA Aviation Forecasts, 1988–1989,* appendices A and B, used in "Focus: A Decade of Deregulation," *Traffic World,* vol. 216, no. 10, December 5, 1988, Supplement, p. A. Used by permission of Traffic World.

Second, free entry also meant free exit. Another result of deregulation has been more carriers leaving the market and more mergers. Looking again at Table 14.1, note that 45 of these 121 new entrants exited the market and only 49 were still operating in 1987. Note that 4 nationals and 2 large regionals have been merged out of existence and 3 large regionals and 18 medium regionals are now operating as commuters. Quite obviously, bankruptcies and mergers have also increased, as well as operational changes to commuters among the 121 new entrants since 1978.

Some of the new entrants were so-called "upstart airlines" — new operations offering discount fares such as People Express and America West. A few were so-called "niche-carriers," often firms attempting to offer premium-class service to a relatively few affluent passengers at a rather steep fare. Others were those formerly "local service" (in the earlier classification) which expanded into majors or nationals (under the new classification) once entry was open. Examples of these local service carriers prior to deregulation that expanded were Southwest Air, Allegheny (renamed U.S. Air), Pacific Southwest Air, Ozark, Republic, Piedmont, Alaska Air, and others. As noted above, excluding commuter lines, total scheduled carriers went from 29 in 1978 to 93 in 1987. However, as Table 14.1 shows, 45 of these new entrants went bankrupt or were merged in the first decade of air deregulation.

Third, the merger movement in air transportation really began accelerating in the mid-1980s, with 1986 the peak year. Major changes in ownership and operation in the first decade of deregulation are noted in Table 14.2

Table 14.2 Changes in Ownership and Operations in Scheduled Air Carriers, 1978 to 1987

1978	TWA eliminates all-cargo service
1979	North Central and Southern merge to become Republic Pan Am acquires National Allegheny changes name to U.S. Air
1980	Flying Tigers acquires SeaBoard World Republic acquires Hughes AirWest
1981	Texas International (later Texas Air) acquires Continental
1982	Braniff declares bankruptcy
1983	Continental declares bankruptcy
1984	Braniff re-enters as a national carrier American and United eliminate all-cargo service
1985	Piedmont acquires Empire People Express acquires Frontier
1986	Delta acquires Western Texas Air acquires Eastern and People Express Northwest acquires Republic United acquires Pan Am's Pacific Division Alaska acquires Jet America and Horizon Air TWA acquires Ozark
1987	U.S. Air acquires Pacific Southwest and Piedmont American acquires Air California

Source: From data in FAA Aviation Forecasts, 1988–1989, appendices A and B, used in "Focus: A Decade of Deregulation," Traffic World, vol. 216, no. 10, December 5, 1988, Supplement, p. A. Used by permission of Traffic World.

Fourth, operations were often changed into the "hub-and-spoke" configuration. Route structures were often modified from point-to-point service to hub-and-spoke — a central airport (hub) with service to outlying points (spokes) and through service between hubs. This allows greater efficiency in use of planes and emphasizes profitable routes. Sometimes service was increased to points not large enough for point-to-point service, but sometimes service by larger carriers was abandoned to the growing commuter carriers. Thus some towns received more "spoke" service and some less. Another impact was that passengers now generally fly to and between "hubs" with considerably less point-to-point service.

Fifth, concentration in the airline market was increased both by the hub-and-spoke configuration and the merger movement. According to a study by the Congressional Budget Office, the market share (measured in revenue passenger-miles) of the top four carriers increased from 57 percent in 1978 to 66 percent in 1987, and among the top eight carriers the increase was from 80 percent to almost 92 percent. This later comparison is most often quoted: 92 percent of all air passenger transportation is generated by the top eight carriers.

Further, due to mergers, concentration in some hubs has become extreme. Table 14.3 shows concentration in large hubs where one carrier enplaned 60 percent or more of the passengers. There had been some concern over this oligopolistic market structure, and obviously the degree of concentration has increased in air transportation.

Sixth, commuter airlines have expanded due to deregulation. While the number of commuter airline companies has decreased from 228 in 1978 to 169 in 1987, their role has increased markedly under the increased limits coming with deregulation and with the essential service (subsidy) program and government loan program for aircraft carrying sixty or fewer passengers. Measured in passenger-miles, commuter traffic rose from 1.280 billion in 1978 to 5 billion in 1987. Passengers carried grew from 11.3 million in 1978 to 31.8 million in 1987 (almost a threefold increase), and commuter aircraft increased from 1,047 planes in 1978 to 1,841 planes in 1987. Additionally, some commuter operations have been merged into major and national operations due to the hub-and-spoke configuration. Others have become "affiliated" with majors — an extension of major carrier operations by way of "code sharing." Under this system, the commuter or medium regional has its flights listed as that of a major carrier and makes connections with major carriers at hubs but serves less dense markets. Both the majors and the commuters benefit — the major carrier appears to serve many more points and have a wider market; the commuter can appear to be a much larger carrier than it actually is and can show a much wider service area because of its affiliation and connection via the major carrier.

Seventh, total air travel has increased due to more carriers and the hub-and-spoke system (as well as fare innovations described next). As previously noted in Part II, domestic passengers carried increased from 288 million in 1980 to 419 million in 1987. As measured by passenger-miles, the increase was from 204 billion in 1980 to 328 billion in 1987. Available seat-miles went from 345 billion in 1980 to 529 billion in 1987. Further, more seats were filled on average as measured by load factor (62.4 percent of seats filled in 1987 as compared with 55.9 percent in 1978).

Table 14.3 Single Carrier Enplaning Sixty Percent or More in Selected Hubs, 1987

Large Hubs	Carrier	Percent
Dallas/Ft. Worth	American	61
St. Louis	TWA	82
Pittsburgh	U.S. Air	85
Minneapolis/St. Paul	Northwest	79
Houston International	Texas Air	74
Detroit	Northwest	61
Charlotte	U.S. Air	90
Salt Lake City	Delta	77
Memphis	Northwest	85

Source: FAA Airport Activity Statistics, 1987.

Eighth, fare structures have changed. As we have already noted, many of the new entrants into air transportation used fare discounts to attract passengers. Soon all carriers instituted fare discount plans, usually with limitations such as reservation and/or payment in a given number of days before traveling, or staying over at destination over Saturday night, or other conditions. Fares were adjusted frequently since there was no longer the necessity of filing fares with a regulatory body. Hence some fares went up — particularly where the carrier had little competition, and some fares went down — particularly where competition was more intense. Many passengers who had a choice of times of departure and arrival, generally pleasure travelers, could find what seemed like bargains as compared with fares under regulation or even as compared with the usual published fare. However, other passengers who had less choice as to when to fly, typically business travelers, found fares increased. Fares varied by time of day, day of the week, season of the year, and so forth. Estimates made in 1987 after a decade of deregulation indicated that 92 percent of air passengers were traveling on discount fares and that the average discount from full fare was 62 percent.

Besides fare discounts, many airlines instituted promotional programs of various types. One of the most popular is the frequent flier program whereby the passenger earned mileage "points" by using a given carrier. After accumulation of a given number of miles or points, the traveler received free trips, upgrades from tourist to first class, and so on. Hotels and car rental firms also joined in such plans, and some passengers planned whole journeys around the number of points earned. The idea was to attract customers, of course, and instill loyalty to specific carriers, hotels, and car rental agencies. Carriers with service to well-known vacation destinations such as Hawaii advertised extensively about free trips "earned" by using their frequent flier program. Of course, substantial administrative costs were incurred in keeping track of the points or mileage earned. Also, a secondary market in frequent flier award arose, with brokers buying and selling awards. By the late 1980s there were concerns that so many free trips had been "earned" that there would be an adverse financial impact on carrier revenues.

In short, the pricing system was quite hectic, with frequent changes and numerous pricing options and innovations. Even so, it was commonly said that passenger fares in general were lower than they would have been under regulation. However, the Air Transport Association reported passenger yields per passenger-mile had increased from 8.67 cents in 1977 to 11.3 cents in 1987 (adjusted for inflation as measured by the consumer price index). Of course, a portion of these increased yields arose because of increased productivity in use of planes and labor.

Ninth, carrier earnings were unstable. In the early 1980s, a recession greatly affected carrier earnings (jet fuel selling for 39 cents a gallon in 1973 cost $1 a gallon in 1982). Also, fuel prices affected earnings. Some carriers went bankrupt because of too many discounts, rising fuel costs, and the extremes of competition. By the middle 1980s, mergers and acquisitions, as noted above, began to thin out the ranks of competitors and in some cases lower labor costs helped to keep some carriers in business. Net profit margin in 1977 for the airline industry was 3.8 percent; by 1987 it had dropped to 1.1 percent. Return on investment for the industry in 1977 was 10.2 percent but only 7.2 percent ten years later in 1987. Of course, some carriers did better than others but on average, deregulation, fare discounting, and promotional programs have led to lower industry earnings.

Tenth, deregulation increased the problem of capacity of the airway systems. A strike by federal air controllers and the subsequent dismissal of a larger number of controllers slowed the system and caused delays. Further, airport capacity, already behind at the time of deregulation, did not keep up to the increased passenger loads. The result was borne by the passenger in more congestion, less frequent on-time service, and numerous delays or even flight cancellations. Air travel was now readily available at a lower price to a more massive market but at a cost in delays, crowded planes and airports, and frustrations. A portion of all this was due to inadequate capacity in the airway system, inability of airline companies to purchase more equipment due to lower earnings, and the small growth in airports and runways.

Eleventh, it is generally agreed that the quality of service declined. On-time performance became a much publicized issue and the FAA began to publish monthly reports of late arrivals and departures (fifteen minutes from schedule, not due to mechanical failures). The reaction of the airlines was to lengthen published schedules to avoid an adverse on-time report. While the reported percentage of on-time flights therefore increased, the service in fact was less timely. Cabin service deteriorated. Food was not of the same quality as in the regulatory period, conditions in the cabin were often quite crowded, and luggage handling complaints increased.

Twelfth, labor problems seemed to increase in the air industry. In order to cut costs, many carriers instituted a "two-tier" wage system where new employees earned less in a given work category for a number of years until they reached the same level as more experienced workers. Labor unions objected to these schemes and there were some strikes and much bitter bargaining over labor contracts. In at least one instance, a carrier that was merged filed for bankruptcy in order to avoid fulfilling labor contract obligations. Employee stock ownership plans (called ESOPs) were supposed to help worker productivity and loyalty but led to bitter labor-management confrontations in many instances. We shall discuss the whole labor-management issue in more detail in Chapter 27.

Finally, as deregulation progressed there was increasing public concern with safety, maintenance, and age of aircraft. There was a marked increase in "near misses" and several headline-grabbing accidents caused public concern over maintenance and aircraft age. In spite of crashes, the total accident rate was down in the first decade of deregulation, as well as the fatality rate as measured in terms of 100,000 flight hours. Air transportation remains statistically the safest way to travel in spite of the headlines!

When the first ten years of deregulation was complete in 1987, there were numerous "evaluations" of the success or failure of deregulation. Opinions varied widely. Those claiming success pointed to the increase in passengers, lower fares, less restraint by government, and more choice by consumers. Those claiming failure pointed to poorer quality of service, lower earnings and bankruptcy of carriers, higher concentration and merger activity, safety and maintenance concerns, labor problems, customer dissatisfaction and frustrations, and instability in fares and discrimination. All of these claims are true to some degree and all — both pro and con — are the consequences of deregulation. While there were some calls for reregulation, on balance all seemed to agree that deregulation and wide open use of the free market were here to stay, and that air transportation would never be quite the same as it was under the forty years of regulation.

IMPACT OF DEREGULATION ON MOTOR TRANSPORTATION

In actual fact, there are many "motor transportation" industries. It is difficult to generalize about motor transportation since the firms vary tremendously in size and type of operation. For example, is a national over-the-road less-than-truckload carrier with terminals in all major cities of the United States the same as a local delivery carrier operating in one community, or a small bus line in a small town, or a household goods carrier operating in but one region of the United States, or a private carrier hauling goods of its owner, or a dump truck operator? All are motor transportation, yet each is different in operating and economic characteristics, and each has been affected by deregulation. Even so, some general analysis can be made about the impact of deregulation in this mode.

First, relatively free entry meant more carriers. As noted above, certificates of public convenience and necessity are still required, but "fitness" and a "useful public purpose" are all that is required to gain a certificate for the ICC under the Motor Carrier Act of 1980 (MCA 1980) and the Bus Regulatory Reform Act of 1982. However, as deregulation progressed, the ICC became more concerned with insurance and safety. Today a potential carrier must file proof of adequate insurance and a DOT safety inspection report to attain and to retain its certificate in regulated trucking.

As to the specific number of carriers in regulated trucking, like air transportation the classification system was changed during the deregulation period. Again using a ten-year span of time for analysis, some idea of the changes can be gained by considering 1978 as compared with 1987. (Given administrative deregulation as noted in Chapter 13, 1978 is a good starting date.) However, a Class I regulated motor carrier of property was defined as one with gross revenues of $3 million or more in 1978 but $5 million or more in 1987; Class II was gross revenues of $500,000 to $1 million in 1978 but $1 to $5 million in 1987; and Class III carriers were those with revenues under $500,000 in 1978 but under $1 million in 1987. Given these changes, Table 14.4 still shows the growth in total number of carriers during the ten-year period.

Table 14.4 Number of ICC-certificated Motor Carriers of Property and Percent by Class, 1978 and 1987

	1978	Percent	1987	Percent
Class I	1,045	6.0	856	2.3
Class II	2,929	17.0	1,266	3.4
Class III	12,900	76.0	35,505	94.0
Total	16,874	100.0	37,627	100.0

Source: From ICC data used in "Focus: A Decade of Deregulation," *Traffic World*, vol. 216, no. 10, December 5, 1988, Supplement, p. E. Used by permission of Traffic World.

As Table 14.4 shows, motor transportation has always had a large number of firms and has not been oligopolistic like air or rail. Under regulation there were over 16,000 regulated carriers in 1978, the vast majority of which were small in size (under $500,000 revenues or Class III). In the first three years of deregulation, 10,000 new firms were certificated and by 1987 there were 37,627 motor carrier firms with certificates — more than twice as many as under regulation. The vast majority are still small firms (under $1 million in gross revenue). It is possible to say, then, that the number of certificated truck lines more than doubled in the first decade of deregulation given easier entry requirements, and almost all were small businesses.

As we have repeatedly noted, all parts of motor transportation were never regulated. Local carriers, private carriers, trucking of agricultural commodities, and others were never regulated. Trucking which is purely intrastate in nature continues to be regulated by states in all but four states. Therefore, it is hard to really give a statistic for the total number of trucking firms, both regulated and nonregulated, and Table 14.4 is for the ICC-regulated sector only.

Some idea of the importance of the nonregulated trucking industry operating in intercity transportation can be gained by considering estimates of tons hauled and estimates of ton-miles produced. This is contained in Table 14.5, using data for the comparable period used in Table 14.4. Note that on the basis of tons, nonregulated intercity trucking has increased from 59 percent to 61 percent of total tons, and nonregulated ton-miles have increased from 56 percent to 58 percent of total ton-miles. In both instances, total tons and total ton-miles have increased between 1978 and 1987, making the percentage change in nonregulated even more important. Also, only intercity trucking is included here, and we know local carriers are important. Thus, we do not know how many firms are involved in nonregulated trucking.

Second, operating restrictions as to routes and commodities were essentially modified by MCA 1980 as far as the 16,874 carriers certificated in 1978 were concerned. Many of the new entrants asked for forty-eight-state authority; 11,586 new certificates for forty-eight-state authority were issued by the ICC from 1980 to 1987 for regulated trucking. Many carriers specializing in particular commodities or routes remain (there were 237 specialized Class I carriers in 1987, about one-fourth). But it is still possible to say that many regulated truck lines can now haul any type of freight just about anywhere in the United States. Competition has greatly increased.

Table 14.5 Estimates of Nonregulated Intercity Trucking Tons and Ton-Miles in 1978 and 1987

	1978	1987
Tons Carried		
Regulated	925 million	895 million
Nonregulated	1,335 million	1,430 million
Total	2,260 million	2,325 million
Percent Nonregulated	59 percent	61 percent
Ton-Miles Produced		
Regulated	265 billion	277 billion
Nonregulated	334 billion	389 billion
Total	599 billion	666 billion
Percent Nonregulated	56 percent	58 percent

Source: Derived from Transportation Policy Associates, *Transportation in America*, 6th ed., Washington, D.C., March 1988, pp. 6–7. Copyright 1988. Used by permission of Eno Foundation for Transportation.

Third, bankruptcies in trucking have increased markedly with deregulation. More carriers and more competition have led to a higher rate of failures (as well as rate discounting noted below). Bankruptcies can be measured in terms of how many per 10,000 companies. In 1978, trucking had about 20 failures per 10,000 companies — approximately the same as all business failures in the United States. In 1987, trucking had 150 failures per 10,000 companies as compared with 120 failures per 10,000 companies for all businesses. The peak year in trucking failures was 1985 when almost 190 failures per 10,000 occurred. One widely quoted study found six trucking fleets a day going bankrupt in 1985! And it should be added that some rather well known large nationwide carriers have been thrown into bankruptcy in the first ten years of regulatory reform.

Fourth, rate discounting has been rampant in motor transportation since 1980. The Motor Carrier Act of 1980 (MCA 1980) contained a zone of rate freedom as did the Bus Regulatory Reform Act of 1982. In MCA 1980 a zone of approximately 64 percent (32 percent above and 32 percent below the published rate) was established, within which the carrier could set a rate without ICC approval. In the Bus Regulatory Reform Act of 1982, the zone of rate freedom increased yearly for three years and in 1985 the ICC lost all control over bus fares. In both instances, rates still had to be published and filed with the ICC by common carriers — but the carriers had tremendous latitude as to the actual price charged. Given the ease of entry, many firms came into the market as price cutters and offered rates widely discounted from the published rates in order to secure business from existing carriers. In many cases in trucking, rate discounts exceeded the limits of the zone of rate freedom and it was common to find carriers offering 40 or 50 percent discounts from the published rate. Such deep discounting hastened the accelerated bankruptcy rates noted above.

Fifth, competition was intense in some motor carrier markets while concentration increased in others. In the bus industry there were many new firms, since entry was so easy. But concentration in the hands of one firm increased markedly in 1987 when the Greyhound Corporation sold Greyhound Lines to GLI Holdings, owners of Trailways. While both large firms continue to operate separately, one firm now dominates by generating 65 percent of the passenger-miles in the industry.

In for-hire trucking, competition has been intense in the full truckload sector. Entry is easy — certificates are easily attained and with no route or commodity restrictions as noted above. Further, the costs of entry are relatively low. All one really needs to get into the truckload business is a truck, a certificate (requiring safety inspection), and insurance. All are easily attainable, and with the bankruptcies noted above, used trucks and trailers are cheaply available.

On the other hand, competition is less and concentration is greater in the less-than-truckload (LTL) sector. Here entry costs are much higher. Terminals, either owned or leased, are necessary in most of the points served. A fleet of pickup and delivery vehicles is necessary to bring LTL freight to a terminal to be consolidated into unit loads for over-the-road hauling or to deliver from the terminal on incoming LTL freight. A sales force is usually required as well as an administrative staff to bill and collect, to pay license fees and insurance, to process claims, to administer payrolls, and so forth. Further, crews are necessary to load and unload, to sort out shipments, to drive local pickup and delivery trucks, and to maintain service vehicles. In truckload service, the owner-operator or the driver loads at the shipper's dock and unloads at the receiver's dock; in less-than-truckload service, the freight may go through several breakbulk points and be handled several times between origination and destination. While LTL rates are typically higher than TL rates, expenses of the LTL carrier are typically higher too. But the point is that the cost of entry into the LTL business is much higher than in the truckload business.

Various studies of motor carrier concentration have been done, but as noted above, trucking is made up of many, many small firms. Even so, considering only ICC certificated carriers, the top four generated 14 percent of all revenue in 1978 but 28 percent of all revenue in 1987. The top twelve generated 23 percent of all revenue in 1978 but 41 percent of all revenue in 1987. While concentration is less than in the airlines or railroads, there does seem to be a fairly high degree of concentration in the hands of relatively few certificated motor carriers (all LTL carriers) in an industry with over 37,000 firms. Most of this concentration is due to higher entry costs.

Sixth, private carriers (sometimes called "do it yourself" transportation) have become more important. MCA 1980 plus the *ToTo* decision mentioned in Chapter 13 allowed private carriers more latitude in their operation. Under *ToTo*, a private carrier could secure a common carrier certificate or contract carrier permit on its empty backhaul. MCA 1980 relaxed the prior stringent rules of private carriers hauling for corporate subsidiaries on a compensated basis. In the first year after MCA 1980, 719 corporations with 7,700 subsidiaries notified the ICC that they intended to undertake compensated intercorporate hauling. Also, the availability of backhaul authority has helped considerably in making private carriage a more viable option for the large shipper. Generally, private carriage does depend, among other things, on volume moved, so this growth has generally been limited to the large shipper of considerable volume.

Seventh, contract carriers and brokers have become more important in trucking. With removal of the so-called "rule of eight" (if a motor carrier had more than eight customers, it was a common carrier — or to put it another way, a contract carrier could not serve more than eight customers), the distinction between common and contract carriers is blurred. Many trucking firms have both common carrier certificates and contract carrier permits. This was called "dual operations" and was infrequently allowed under regulations, and the contract carrier operation was forbidden from competing with the common carrier operations of the same firm.

Today a trucker or a bus line is often both a common carrier and a contract carrier and buses are allowed to mix passengers (common carrier and contract carrier passengers on the same bus).

To get some idea of the importance of this, reports by Class I and II common carriers indicated that over 3 percent of their traffic was under contract in 1978 and 12 percent in 1987 — about four times as much in 1987. Another indication of the growth and importance of contract carriers is that in 1981, of the total ICC grants of authority, 82 percent were common carriers, 16 percent contract carriers, and 2 percent brokers. In 1987, only 29 percent of ICC grants of authority were to common carriers, 52 percent were to contract carriers, and 18 percent to brokers. We shall return to brokers momentarily.

Further, contract carriers are no longer required to file rates with the ICC. Hence, carriers with dual operations can use their contract carrier authority to offer very low rates to special customers, say a large shipper, while charging published common carrier rates to smaller shippers of the same freight. Also, since the rule of eight is gone, many smaller truckers find it easier to write a separate contract with each shipper and avoid the ICC and rate filing entirely. These are some of the reasons for the amazing growth of contract carriers under deregulation.

Brokers have also grown tremendously. A broker is a middleman who matches loads for a fee. Brokers have been regulated as part of motor transportation since 1935 but were not a very important sector of transportation except in the agricultural commodity area (which was exempt from economic regulation). With ease of entry, particularly in the truckload sector as noted above, there has been a substantial growth in commodity freight brokering. The broker offers his services to truckload carriers, having lined up a group of shippers using truckload services, and literally becomes the sales department of the truckload carrier. The broker is licensed by the ICC and must post a bond. The broker negotiates a price per truckload with the shipper and with the truckload operator, the difference in price being his commission. Thus, instead of maintaining a marketing staff and terminal in the point of destination, a truckload carrier uses a broker to secure a load at whatever price it can get in order to return toward its origination point with something on the truck. The rate charged is often lower than a published rate, depending on relative bargaining strength (how many empty trucks are available in a given day — the supply, and how many outbound truckloads are needed that day — the demand). The broker serves a useful purpose to the trucker (it gets a load without maintaining an office and sales force) as well as to the shipper (outbound shipment moves at a lower rate). Note, however, that brokering is mainly in the highly competitive truckload sector, not the less-than-truckload sector.

Eighth, earnings in motor transportation are down. Statistics do not exist for the vast majority of motor carriers (Class III carriers are not required to file revenue reports, and private or exempt carrier earnings are not a matter of public record). Considering Class I and Class II operating ratios (operating expenses divided by operating revenues times 100), general freight carriers had a 94.3 percent operating ratio in 1978 (expenses per ton-mile of 13.2 cents and revenues of 14 cents). In 1987 the operating ratio was 96.8 percent. Specialized Class I and Class II carriers had a 1978 operating ratio of 94.8 percent and a 1987 operating ratio of 97.2 percent. Of the top 100 carriers, only 13 had operating ratios under 90 percent in 1987 and 26 had operating ratios over 100 percent (expenses per ton-mile greater than revenue per ton-mile — operating at a loss). Net profit margins for all Class I and Class II general freight carriers was 1.4 percent in 1987 and 1.6 percent for all specialized Class I and Class II carriers. Margins have always been low in motor transportation but have become even lower since deregulation.

Ninth, the character of motor carrier operations has changed under deregulation. Prior to 1978, common carriers often "interlined" freight — a shipment would use two or more carriers operating in end-to-end configuration. In 1978 about 11 percent of freight was interlined. With relatively open entry and no route restrictions in certificates (note above that 11,588 certificates for all forty-eight contiguous states have been issued since 1980), in 1987 interlining was down to 2.7 percent of all freight. One-carrier service is now the rule in trucking.

The same is true to a degree in bus service. Contract and special bus service has grown markedly, as noted in Chapter 7, while regular route service has decreased. With deep discounting of airfares, it is now often cheaper to fly between many cities than to take the bus. Long-haul intercity bus service is down under deregulation due to airfare discounting and the comfort and convenience of the private car. The long bus journey is becoming a thing of the past except for tours and other contract operations.

Tenth, interestingly there has been a rise in "niche carriers" and some specialized carriers such as small package carriers. Some truck lines have become specialists on given routes or traffic lanes, Denver to Salt Lake City for example. These carriers do not try to serve all points — only a limited series of points with relatively efficient service. There are also some carriers specializing by commodities, not trying to carry everything for everybody. In the small package sector, the amazing growth of United Parcel Service (UPS) and Federal Express are well known. Both use motor transportation as well as air transportation. Indeed UPS has an extremely wide service territory domestically and abroad.

Eleventh, labor unions have become less powerful in motor transportation, both trucking and bus. Labor strife has been considerable, and two-tier wage structures are widely used in motor transportation just as in air transportation as noted above. The Teamsters Union claims to have lost 116,633 jobs since 1980 in spite of increased employment in for-hire trucking from 6.2 million in 1978 to 7.2 million in 1987.

Twelfth, there has been concern with service to small communities and with safety. Truck service to smaller communities seems to have dropped off but UPS seems to have stepped into the gap here — but often at a higher rate. There is definite concern with bus service to small communities and evidence seems to indicate it has decreased with deregulation.

Also, there has been concern with motor carrier safety. Yet the accident fatality rate per million vehicle-miles on large combination vehicles dropped from 7.66 in 1978 to 5.1 in 1987. Motor carrier accidents reported to the Department of Transportation decreased from 32,000 in 1978 to 26,000 in 1987 in spite of an increase in ton-miles during that period. Part of this exemplary safety record is due to more vehicle inspections (1 million in 1987 as compared with 150,000 in 1984), with more vehicles and drivers "out of service" for safety reasons. Also the ICC insistence on safety inspections as a prerequisite to issuing and retaining certificates or other authority to operate has been important.

In summary, motor transportation is obviously more competitive with more carriers, discount rates, fewer restrictions on routes and commodities carried, more bankruptcies, lower earnings, higher concentration in some markets, more private carriers, more contract carriers and brokers, changed character of operations (less interlining, more through service), less powerful labor unions, and concerns over service by truck and bus to small communities. Whether deregulation of motor transportation has been "good" or "bad" depends greatly on who's involved. The long-run consequences are still being worked out — but as with air transportation, motor transportation will never be quite the same as it was under forty years of regulation.

IMPACT OF DEREGULATION ON RAIL TRANSPORTATION

Recall from Chapter 13 that the aim of the Staggers Rail Act of 1980 was to restore the financial viability of the railroads. It is important to note this distinction and goal because the regulatory reforms in rail were distinctly aimed at assisting the carriers, not in providing more choice and free market competition for the customer as with air or with restoring efficiency and shipper options as with trucking. Therefore, most of the reforms dealt with rates and rules, not entry and competition. But, of course, deregulation affects all aspects of rail transportation.

First, the financial condition of the Class I railroads has indeed improved. During about the same comparison period we used above, profit margins increased from 4.98 percent in 1979 to 10.41 percent in 1987. Operating ratios improved from 95.0 percent in 1979 to 89.7 percent in 1987, and return on net investment increased from 2.93 percent in 1979 to 5.64 percent in 1987. Part of these improvements was due to lower labor costs, which were 49.5 percent of all expenses in 1979 and 42.2 percent in 1987, and a smaller labor force (482,962 in 1979 and 248,526 in 1987); part was due to increased capital expenditures — $13.9 billion in 1978 to 1982 and $17.5 billion in 1983 to 1987; part due to a smaller number of Class I railroads (to be discussed directly); and part due to higher levels of efficiency. And even though the rail share of total ton-miles of all transportation continued to decline slowly (37.5 percent of total ton-miles in 1980 to 36.3 percent in 1987), rail ton-miles increased from 932 million in 1980 to 968 million in 1987. Without a doubt, the carriers have benefited from regulatory reform.

Second, regulatory reform has allowed the railroads to better compete with the trucks and to generate new intermodal business. We can appreciate this development by considering TOFC (trailer on flatcar or piggyback) and COFC (container on flatcar) traffic. These are classified as "intermodal," and the railroads have been in this business — particularly TOFC — since the late 1950s. However, this type of rail transportation increased dramatically after being deregulated by the ICC. In 1979 only 8 percent of carloadings were TOFC/COFC, but in 1987 intermodal carloadings were 16.4 percent of all carloadings. Total intermodal trailers and containers loaded has gone up from 3.278 million a year in 1979 to 5.155 million a year in 1987, a 63 percent increase.

Third, the structure of the industry has changed. The number of Class I railroads with revenues of $50 million or more a year has always been fairly small. In 1979 there were forty-two Class I rail carriers but only eighteen in 1987, a decrease of twenty-four carriers. Part of this decrease came about due to consolidation and unification.

The Staggers Rail Act of 1980 had made mergers easier, and from 1980 to 1987 the ICC generally allowed any proposed merger. Table 14.6 gives some idea of this activity, which includes eighteen major mergers plus the privatization of Conrail. (Conrail itself was a merger of six railroads in the 1970s and had been owned by a governmental corporation, as discussed in Chapter 12.) Indeed, this period could be called the high point of railroad mergers, since more rail mergers took place from 1980 to 1987 than during almost any other comparable period in modern times.

Table 14.6 Class I Railroad Merger Activity, 1980 to 1988

1980   Detroit, Toledo, and Ironton merged into Grand Trunk Western
        St. Louis-San Francisco merged into Burlington Northern

1981   Detroit and Toledo Short Line merged into Grand Trunk Western
        Main Central merged into Guilford Transportation

1982   Colorado and Southern merged into Burlington Northern
        Ft. Worth and Denver merged into Burlington Northern
        Walla Walla Valley merged into Burlington Northern
        Spokane, Portland, and Seattle merged into Burlington Northern
        Missouri Pacific merged into Union Pacific
        Western Pacific merged into Union Pacific

1983   Family Lines merged into Chessie System (now CSX)
        Louisville and Nashville merged into Chessie System (now CSX)
        Cinchfield Seaboard System merged into Chessie System (now
          CSX)
        Boston and Main merged into Guilford Transportation

1984   Delaware and Hudson merged into Guilford Transportation

1985   Chicago, Milwaukee, St. Paul, and Pacific merged into SooLine

1987   Conrail privatization, ICC denies Santa Fe/Southern Pacific merger

1988   Southern Pacific merged into RioGrande Industries

Source: Adapted from "Focus: A Decade of Deregulation," *Traffic World,* vol. 216, no. 10, December 5, 1988, Supplement, p. K. Copyright 1988. Used by permission.

Fourth, mergers and a smaller number of carriers have led to a higher concentration and market share of the large carriers. As measured in ton-miles, the top three Class I rail carriers had 34.2 percent of the market in 1979 and 53.7 percent in 1987. The top seven carriers increased from 65.2 percent of ton-miles in 1979 to 88.6 percent in 1987. As measured in miles of railway, the top three increased from 32.4 percent in 1979 to 45.5 percent in 1987; the top seven from 58.1 percent of total miles in 1979 to 83.6 percent in 1987. This concentration in total miles is even greater since total miles decreased — total Class I mileage was 169,927 in 1979 but dropped to 132,220 miles in 1987, partially due to the rise of the small railroads (to be discussed directly) and abandonment of track.

Fifth, in addition to mergers, large rail carriers integrated by buying into other modes. In the regulatory days, the ICC generally did not allow railroads to own other modes (except motor carriers owned by railroads in 1935, and these were required to be "ancillary and auxiliary" — an extension of rail service and non-competitive with through motor carriers). After the Staggers Rail Act of 1980, the ICC allowed several large railroads to buy up and integrate carriers in other modes. The four most important examples were the purchase of American Commercial Barge Lines (1984) and Sealand (a maritime carrier, in 1986) by the Chessie System (now CSX), the purchase of North American Van Lines by Norfolk Southern (1985), and the purchase of Overnite Transportation, a large trucker, by the Union Pacific in 1987. Other railroads entered into this integration movement only to leave later on. For example, the Burlington Northern purchased three truck lines and Norfork and Western purchased a substantial share of Piedmont Airlines. As these other modes were integrated, there was talk of "megacarriers" — large transportation companies based on railroad ownership of several modes. We will discuss this concept in more detail in Chapter 26.

Sixth, deregulation led to the rise of small railroads. There have always been a number of smaller rail carriers (as noted in Chapter 4). In 1979 there were 393 regional and local railroads with 19,506 miles of track. By 1987 this number had increased to 481 regional and local railroads with 33,645 miles of track. "Small railroad" is really a misnomer, since some of these carriers are several hundred miles in length. The majority of these small railroads connect to Class I carriers and feed traffic into the larger through carriers.

As noted in Chapter 13, the 4-R Act allowed for state rail planning and the identification of rail lines with low density that were potential abandonments. Many of these portions of the total rail system were discontinued or abandoned with regulatory permission. In 1974 there were 200,916 miles of railway in the United States but only 147,064 in 1986. But not all of the less densely used track was abandoned. In many instances, regional or local railroads were created to own and operate these lines. Typically, the regional and local lines are nonunion, thus avoiding the expense and complicated work rules of the Class I railroads. Some of the so-called small railroads were agencies of other governments. For example, the state of South Dakota bought all of the track of the Milwaukee Road in that state in order to preserve rail service, and some counties purchased rail track in order to continue service in other states. In other instances, individual entrepreneurs (sometimes "railfans") took over trackage. Also, some industries dependent on rail service bought trackage. Finally, several sizable firms arose to specialize in owning and operating local and regional rail carriers. From 1978 to 1987, there were 207 small rail carriers started and 119 failures or bankruptcies. By 1987 some 481 local and regional rail carriers with 33,645 miles of track remained, as noted above. Obviously, there has been a marked increase in the local and regional railroad sector in recent times.

Sixth, contract rates became important. Prior to the Staggers Rail Act of 1980, special contracts with a given shipper were illegal — all shippers were to be treated equally under similar circumstances and conditions. Lower rates per 100 pounds were allowed for carload freight as compared with less-than-carload, some lower multiple car rates were published, and special commodity rates available for large shipments were published. But basically the common-law obligation to avoid undue preference or prejudice and treat all similar shippers alike was supreme. However, the Staggers Rail Act allowed for special individual contracts between carriers and shippers and now shippers could negotiate their own rates and service levels with the rail carriers. A substantial number of contracts were negotiated and filed with the ICC. Specific provisions of the contracts were confidential and not part of the public record. A 1986 ICC study disclosed that 41,021 contracts had been filed in the first five years after the Staggers Rail Act. Terms and provisions of these contracts are unknown except that they are generally with large volume shippers and a number were short term. Longer term contracts usually have escalation clauses (adjusting for inflation) and agreements for the shipper to share in productivity gains by the carrier. Under the Staggers Rail Act, contracts are to be limited to 40 percent of rail capacity as measured by major car types, but to date the ICC has never invoked this provision and some carriers have claimed in their annual reports that as much as 75 percent of revenues have come from special contracts. Allowing special contracts not only was one of the most startling changes in regulatory reform but had considerable consequences.

Seventh, aside from contracts, rail rates have varied. Recall that the Staggers Rail Act specified a zone of rate freedom within which rates can vary without ICC jurisdiction (a 6 percent increase or decrease a year from published rates for four years with a limit of 18 percent and limits increasing after 1984 by 4 percent a year above inflation until carriers reached "revenue adequacy"). Also, released value rates were allowed. The effect of these provisions is that some rail rates increased while others decreased. Rates still have to be published and adhered to but management has had considerably more latitude in what rates to offer.

Finally, there has been concern over "market dominance," and this concern has led to unsuccessful attempts by some groups to have parts of the Staggers Rail Act changed (generally called reregulation). Recall that when "market dominance" exists (defined as 180 percent of variable costs with inflation and cost recovery adjustments), the ICC has jurisdiction over rates. Some large "captive" shippers — mainly coal companies and public utilities — have been unhappy with the ICC administration of these provisions. The movement of coal is an important part of railroad freight (about 30 percent of carloadings in total and the major commodity moved by many railroads), and coal rates were quite low at the time of regulatory reform. Thus, coal rates did go up and coal shippers and their customers were generally "captive" (with no alternative economical means of shipping). However, the movement to reregulate has not prevailed in spite of these concerns over "market dominance."

In general, the impact of regulatory reform in railroads has been increased flexibility for carrier management, an improved financial condition of the railroads, increased productivity and lower labor costs, growth of intermodal traffic, more mergers and concentration, integration of transportation modes in some instances, the rise of the small railroad, special contract rates and services, and concern with market dominance. Even though railroads continue to be regulated, more freedom of market forces is the general impact of regulatory reform.

IMPACT OF DEREGULATION ON THE USER OF TRANSPORTATION

It is fitting to end the discussion of the consequences of deregulation by considering the impact on the user. This will vary according to which user one is talking about. First, in air transportation, passengers generally had more choice with lower fares for the pleasure traveler and higher fares for the business traveler who had less latitude in choosing when and where to fly. Some users in small communities had less service or commuter service in place of larger planes, while some users in small communities had air service where little or none existed prior to deregulation. Fliers between major points benefited by discount rates while fliers between small points and hubs often found higher fares. The vast majority of fliers had to use the hub-and-spoke system which was often more time consuming than point-to-point service and more congested. Air passengers were more concerned with safety and concentration of carriers with dominance of a single carrier (and sometimes higher fares) in some hubs. Overcrowding, delays, and poorer service seemed to affect all users.

Second, the impact on passengers in bus transportation was similar to the impact on those in air transportation. Small communities lost service. Users of contract bus carriers benefited. Given fare competition with air transportation, many bus fares were lowered, but there seems to be a definite shift from buses to air travel. Bus travel continued to decline overall and became quite local and regional in character.

Third, many trucking rates were lower where the shipper had bargaining power. Choice among carriers was greatly increased. Specific deals were possible with contract carriers. However, the small shipper generally did not benefit from rate discounting and sometimes found motor carriers uninterested in its business. Point-to-point service was common for truckload shippers and there was much more choice among carriers. Private transportation was more of an alternative for the large volume shipper and could be used in bargaining with truckload common and contract carriers. Small communities sometimes had poorer service or at least not better service than before. In general the impact on large volume shippers was the most favorable. Insofar as this helped decrease costs of production (or at least helped contain increase in prices), the consumer benefited. But the impact on prices was indirect and turned on the degree of producer competition, the ability of the shipper to bargain, and the degree of importance of transportation and logistics costs to total production costs.

Fourth, in railroad transportation, once more the large volume shipper benefited directly because contracts could be negotiated and various rate and service arrangements could be made. However, captive shippers in a "market dominance" situation apparently were in a less favorable situation. Once more lower rail costs indirectly affected prices and depended on transportation and logistics costs as a part of total costs, the degree of competition among producers as to whether lower costs were passed on in lower prices, and the ability of the shipper to bargain.

Finally, perhaps the biggest beneficiary from deregulation and regulatory reform was the person in charge of shipping or receiving in medium and large firms that generated a volume of freight. Titles varied (traffic manager, logistics manager, distribution manager), but these jobs now became more important to their employers, and their role in the corporate structure increased in importance. Although the transportation manager had always been able to affect costs by careful decision making, alternatives and options increased substantially with deregulation and regulatory reform. Now negotiation with the carriers became the most important task of those in charge of shipping and receiving, whereas previously the regulatory structure limited choices. The small shipper with small volumes usually did not have as much bargaining power over rates and service and so the impact of deregulation was less in this sector.

In Part VI, shipper management, we shall discuss in detail the role of the person in charge of transportation from the user viewpoint.

SUMMARY

In general, the consequences of deregulation have been that the whole structure of social control over transportation has been drastically changed and amended. In some modes such as air transportation the consequences have been prodigious. Both the carriers and the user have been markedly affected — some for the good and some for the bad, depending on conditions and circumstances. Certainly industry structure has changed with more bankruptcies and more concentration. In bus transportation, most of the consequences have been negative on the user and deregulation has accelerated·the downward trend in this industry. In trucking, consequences vary according to which area of trucking is involved, but generally the large shipper has lower rates and the ability to specify better service, the small shipper and small community have not benefited a great deal, and the industry structure has changed markedly with much more competition, bankruptcies, and, interestingly, more concentration in the LTL sector. In rail transportation, the consequences of regulatory reform have assisted the carriers, given large shippers more economic power, led to more concentration in an already highly concentrated market, and changed the industry structure with the rise of small carriers. Finally, for the user, the consequences again vary according to circumstance but generally the user has benefited. Certainly the biggest beneficiary has been the transportation manager in medium and large-sized firms with the greatest volume of freight to oversee.

The next chapter will analyze the regulatory institutions whose task is to oversee the transportation systems.

ADDITIONAL READINGS

Babcock, Michael, and H. Wade German, "The Impact of Deregulation on Rail TOFC Carloadings," *The Logistics and Transportation Review*, 20, No. 3 (September 1984), 205–11.

Bailey, Elizabeth E., David R. Graham, and Daniel P. Kaplan, *Deregulation of the Airlines*, Cambridge, Mass.: The MIT Press, 1985.

Beilock, Richard, and James Freeman, "Deregulated Motor Carrier Service to Small Communities," *Transportation Journal*, 23, No. 4 (Summer 1984), 71–82.

Brenner, Melvin A., James O. Leet, and Elihu Schott, *Airline Deregulation*, Westport, Conn.: Eno Foundation for Transportation, Inc., 1985.

Brown, Anthony E., *The Politics of Airline Deregulation*, Knoxville, Tenn.: University of Tennessee Press, 1987.

Corsi, Thomas M., Phillip Fanara, Jr., and Judith L. Jarrell, "Safety Performance of Pre–MCA Motor Carriers, 1977 vs 1984," *Transportation Journal*, 27, No. 3 (Spring 1988), 30–36.

Davis, Grant M., "Unresolved Issues in U.S. Trucking Regulatory Modernization Debate," *Transportation Practitioners Journal*, 54, No. 2 (Winter 1987), 163–76.

Fawcett, Stanley E., and Stanley A. Fawcett, "Congestion at Capacity-Constrained Airports: A Question of Economics and Realism," *Transportation Journal*, 27, No. 4 (Summer 1988), 31–45.

Glaskowsky, Nicholas A., *Effects of Deregulation on Motor Carriers*, Westport, Conn.: Eno Foundation for Transportation, Inc., 1986.

Harper, Donald V., "Consequences of Reform of Federal Economic Regulation of the Motor Trucking Industry," *Transportation Journal*, 21, No. 4 (Summer 1982), 35–58.

Hoover, Harward, Jr., "Pricing Behavior and Profitability in the Initial Phase of Deregulation: The Case of Motor Common Carriers," *Journal of Business Logistics*, 7, No. 2 (1986), 33–48.

Kahn, Alfred E., "Surprises of Airline Deregulation," *American Economic Review*, 78, No. 2 (May 1988), 316–22.

Kihl, Mary, "The Impact of Deregulation on Passenger Transportation in Small Towns," *Transportation Quarterly*, 42, No. 2 (April 1988), 243–68.

Kyle, Reuben III, and Lawrence T. Phillips, "Airline Deregulation: Did Economists Promise Too Much or Too Little?" *The Logistics and Transportation Review*, 21, No. 1 (March 1985), 3–20.

Meyer, John R., and Clinton V. Oster, Jr., *Deregulation and the Future of Intercity Passenger Travel*, Cambridge, Mass.: The MIT Press, 1987.

Morash, Edward A., and Charles R. Elis, "Motor Carrier Mergers, Mobility Barriers, and Regulatory Reform," *Transportation Journal*, 25, No. 1 (Fall 1985), 38–50.

Morrison, Steven A., and Clifford Winston, *The Economic Effects of Airline Deregulation*, Washington, D.C.: The Brookings Institution, 1986.

Oster, Clinton V., Jr., and C. Kurt Zoin, "Impacts of Regulatory Reform on Intercity Bus Service in the United States, *Transportation Journal*, 25, No. 3 (Spring 1986), 33–42,

Phillips, Lawrence T., "Structural Change in the Airline Industry: Carrier Concentration at Large Hub Airports and Its Implications for Competitive Behavior," *Transportation Journal*, 25, No. 2 (Winter 1985), 18–28.

Putsay, Michael W., "Reform of Entry into Motor Carrier Markets: Was the Motor Carrier Act 1980 Necessary?" *Transportation Journal*, 25, No. 1 (Fall 1985), 11–24.

Rakowski, James P., "Marketing Economies and Results of Trucking Deregulation in the Less-Than-Truckload Sector," *Transportation Journal*, 27, No. 3 (Spring 1988), 1–22.

Weiss, Leonard W., and Michael W. Kloss, Editors, *Regulatory Reform: What Actually Happened*, Boston: Little, Brown & Co., 1986.

CHAPTER 15

REGULATORY INSTITUTIONS

It is not enough to understand how the regulation of transportation has evolved and developed over time. One must also know something about how regulations are implemented. This involves the study of regulatory institutions and their structures, jurisdictions, and procedures.

The term *institution* may be used in various ways. When one uses it in conjunction with *economic* or *social*, it is usually taken to mean the rules of society. These rules include customs, laws, techniques, practices, and all sorts of ways in which the group or society organizes to gain its common goals. The last five chapters have explained the development of such transportation rules or institutions for transportation.

The person who speaks of a university, a court of law, or a governmental agency as an institution, however, is using the term to mean a specific thing, body, or device. Often this "thing" implements various economic or social rules or institutions. In this chapter, we shall be using the term *institution* principally in this second sense of a specific thing used to implement or put into practice social or economic rules or regulation.

In domestic transportation, there are four main regulatory institutions: commissions, courts, the legislature, and the executive. Each will be considered in turn.

COMMISSIONS

Although there is a great deal of overlapping and confusion among regulatory institutions, the most important of the group is the administrative commission. This particular institution has antecedents in the early attempts of society to regulate by way of investigation prior to the Civil War. These early commissions, mentioned in Chapter 2 and Chapter 10, were important particularly in New England. The investigatory commission was followed by granger commissions, sometimes called western commissions or strong commissions, which were established in the post–Civil War era of state regulation. These direct ancestors of the present-day regulatory commissions had great power under the law not only to investigate but also to enforce. Within the broad scope of jurisdiction set down by the legislature, these commissions became a law in themselves. Much of the organization, jurisdiction, approach, and procedure of these state granger commissions carried over into the federal regulatory commissions of modern times.

A commission as a regulatory institution is unique. If society wishes to lay down rules in other economies, it does so either by passing specific laws that directly govern the behavior of private enterprise or, more frequently, by instituting public enterprise and ownership. In the American economy, we have a tradition of maintaining private enterprise but regulating it through the medium of commissions created by the people through their legislature or assembly. The legislative process will be discussed more fully later, but it should be noted here that commissions are usually creations of legislatures and are granted broad policy limits within which they independently develop specific regulations and procedures.

In considering the various commissions involved in implementing transportation regulation, it should be clear that there are two levels of control — federal and state. This comes from our political structure as well as from the differentiation between interstate and intrastate commerce. Both levels have commissions, although with different jurisdictions. To a surprising degree, the procedures and approaches at each level are quite similar. Conflict between these levels, however, is not only possible, but leads to one of the ever-present difficulties of transportation regulation.

The Federal Level

Transportation regulatory institutions at the federal level are three in number: the Interstate Commerce Commission, the Federal Maritime Commission, and the Federal Energy Regulatory Commission. The first is the oldest of all federal commissions and regulates a number of modes of transportation. The others regulate maritime transportation and pipelines.

The Interstate Commerce Commission

As described in Chapter 10, the ICC was created by the Act to Regulate Commerce of 1887. As the first regulatory institution at the federal level, the ICC pioneered the development of regulation. Much of its procedure and approach has been used by subsequent boards and commissions.

Likewise, the structure, functions, and role of the ICC have served as a pattern for subsequent regulatory institutions at both the federal and state levels. Therefore, by examining the ICC in some detail, one can learn the basic elements of all similar regulatory institutions.

The ICC illustrates the usually preferred structure of a commission. It has an odd number of commissioners, divided in political affiliation, serving long-term staggered appointments. The five commissioners are appointed by the president with the consent and approval of the Senate for terms of seven years. No more than one commissioner is appointed to a term of office in any one year unless a commissioner resigns. The seven-year term makes it almost impossible for one president to appoint all the commissioners. Further, the law provides that no more than three of the five commissioners may be from the same political party. Since 1970, the president designates the chairperson of the commission. The size of the commission has varied over time; it once was as large as eleven and was made up of seven members in the early 1980s. In June 1986 the commission was officially reduced to five members, since the deregulation acts had made the commission workload less.

The function of a commission is to be an independent body of experts providing administration of the regulatory statutes. Its independence derives from the fact that it is usually created and directed in a broad policy sense by the legislature, but is appointed by the executive branch. The ICC reports to Congress and is not considered a part of the administration, even though the president has an opportunity to appoint its members. Removal of commissioners is difficult during their terms. They are protected much as judges are protected. The ICC has a good reputation for being composed of expert and highly qualified commissioners who are well acquainted with their tasks.

Legislatures and courts are ill-equipped to carry on continuous regulation of an expedient nature to promote the public welfare and prevent abuses. The legislature, meeting only periodically and made up of constantly changing personnel, is unable to act in an administrative fashion even if it should contain the desired degree of expertise. Courts cannot administer laws directly since they can act only on the issues brought before them. Further, they are extremely busy with many other matters and do not have the opportunity to become specialized in regulation. Commissions can act upon their own motion and do have the attributes of continuity, expediency, promotion, preventativeness, specialization, and concern with broad public welfare.

The role of the ICC basically is to administer the law. However, it has judicial and legislative functions as well. Indeed, students of administrative law have often pointed out that a commission exercises some of all the three roles of administrator, judge, and legislator.

By applying the general policy and enforcing the rules of the game as established by Congress, the commission acts in an executive capacity. The making of rules, the granting of operating authority, and the establishment of rates are examples of the commission's legislative function. The hearing of evidence, the determination of what is just and reasonable or unduly preferential or prejudicial are examples of its judicial function.

In order to accomplish its task, the ICC is divided into two divisions, both handling all three types of proceedings — finance, rates, and operating rights. Cases are assigned on an alternating basis and commissioner membership in the divisions is changed every six months. The divisions often act as appeal boards, after an initial decision has been made by one of the several employee boards of the commission. (Divisions are made up of appointed commissioners, whereas employee boards are staffed by certain categories of high-ranking civil service employees of the commission.) Decisions of these boards may be appealed to a division. Matters assigned to the boards do not involve taking testimony at public hearings. Matters the commission considers to be of general transportation importance are handled by the commission itself.

Proceedings before the commission can be either formal or informal. The informal complaint is usually handled entirely by mail and does not involve an appearance before the body. The formal complaint, on the other hand, is a carefully drawn document that is usually supported by evidence in a public hearing. Typically, formal complaints are heard by an administrative law judge who holds the hearing, collects evidence, "makes the record" on the matter, and renders a finding. If the finding is acceptable to both parties, the order recommended by the hearing examiner becomes a commission order. However, appeal to a division of the commission, and even to the full commission in cases of general transportation importance, is possible. Finally, orders of the commission may be appealed on certain grounds to a court of law (see Figure 15.1).

The commission maintains its own bar, specifying who may appear or practice before it. Persons desiring to take cases before the commission must have various educational and technical qualifications in order to be admitted to the commission bar. About 30 percent of those admitted to the bar of the ICC are nonlawyers who qualified on educational and technical grounds and passed a competitive national examination given by the commission twice a year.

The caseload of the commission is large. During 1985, for example, the commission handled 15,037 motor carrier matters and 1,231 rail carrier matters. The large number of motor carrier matters was a result of the Motor Carrier Act of 1980, discussed in the last chapter, and the easier entry requirements under the new deregulation law. This large formal caseload is in addition to numerous informal complaints.

Figure 15.1 Procedure and Appeal in Regulatory Matters Before the Interstate Commerce Commission

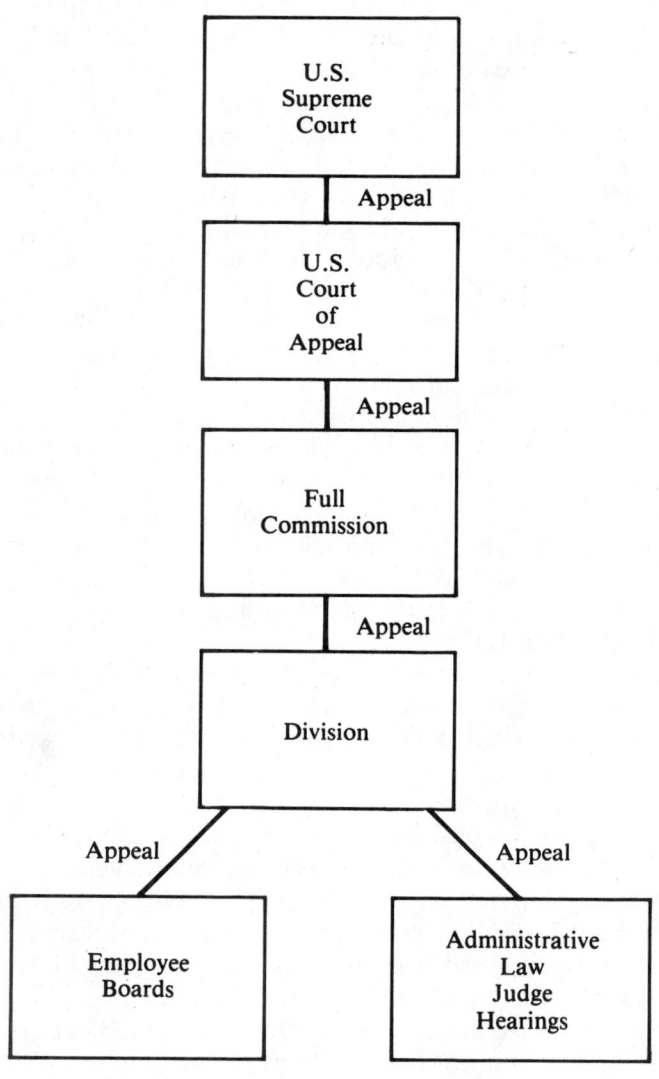

The commission has gone through an extensive reorganization during recent years in an attempt to streamline procedures and modernize its organization. The formation of the Department of Transportation also caused a shift of some of the work of the ICC to the new department.

Internally the commission is organized into seven staff offices and two bureaus under a managing director who is responsible for the day-to-day operations of the commission. Two offices report directly to the chairman: the Office of Government and Public Affairs, which is the ICC's liaison with Congress and a public information office, and the Office of Human Affairs, which is mainly concerned with personnel matters (see Figure 15.2).

The Office of Proceedings is responsible for docketing and publishing notices of hearings, the Office of General Counsel provides legal advice and defends the commission if challenged in court, and the Office of Hearings conducts formal oral hearings via administrative law judges mentioned above. The Office of Compliance and Consumer Assistance (with several regional offices) is the major contact that shippers, carriers, and the general public have with the commission. The Bureau of Accounts serves as the commission's principal financial advisor while the Office of Secretary issues the commission's decisions, orders, and opinions. The Office of Transportation Analysis, created in 1979, does policy planning and research, and the Bureau of Traffic advises the commission on rates and tariffs and prescribes rules in these matters. The Office of Public Assistance, originally created in 1980, is involved with consumer protection and represents the public in such matters as small shipments, problems with household goods movement, and adequacy of service.

In recent years, the commission has faced a reduced budget. In 1981 the commission budget was over $82 million but it dropped to $48 million in 1987. Likewise, the staff of the commission was reduced from 2,084 in 1977 to about 900 in 1987. A number of field offices have been closed or consolidated. All of this is due to the perception of Congress that the deregulatory acts have decreased the role of the ICC. Indeed, in recent years a number of bills have been introduced to abolish the ICC much in the same way the CAB was "sunsetted." However, none of these attempts has been successful.

The scope of authority and major functions of the ICC have been summarized by the Transportation Policy Associates as follows:

Regulates transportation carriers engaged in transportation in interstate commerce and in foreign commerce for portions within the U.S. Modes regulated include railroads, trucking companies, buslines, water carriers, and transportation brokers.

Figure 15.2 Organization of the Interstate Commerce Commission

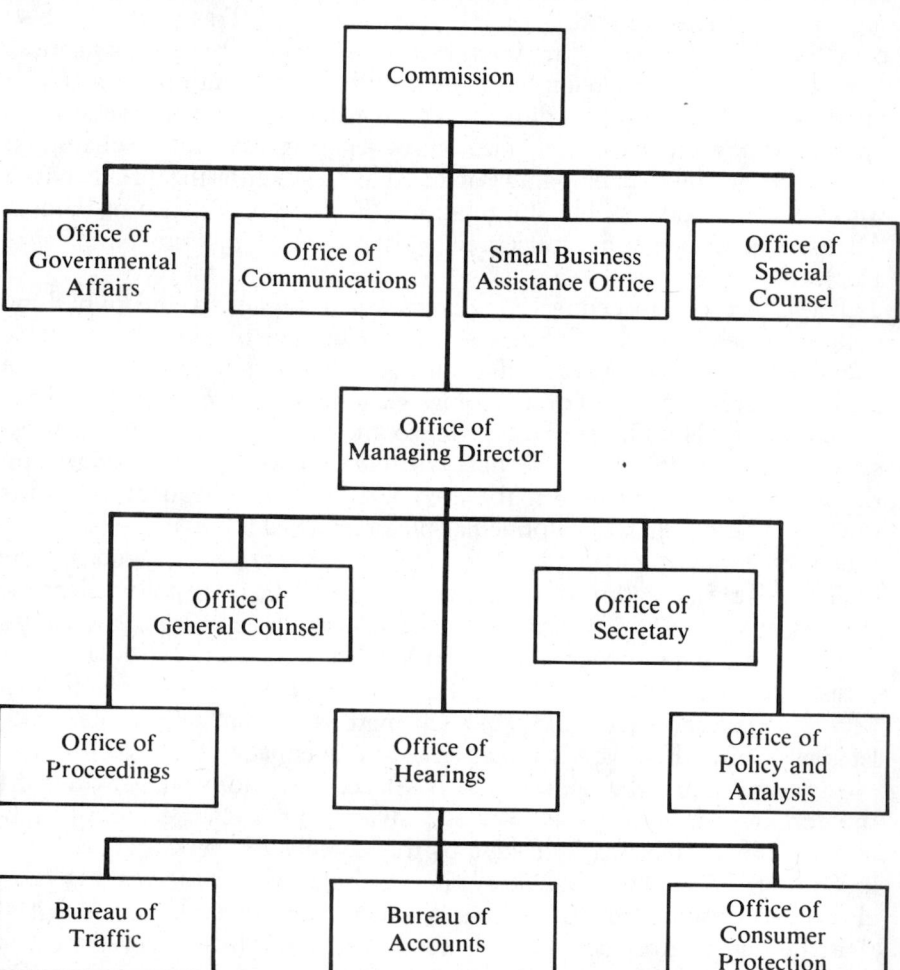

Major functions are settling controversies between carriers and users over rates and services. Prevents unlawful discrimination, destructive competition and rebating. Grants rights to operate to carriers and ensures their rates and services are fair and reasonable. Rules on mergers, acquisitions of control, sale of carriers, and issuance of securities. Prescribes accounting rules, awards reparations, approves rail abandonments, and recommends court action in rail bankruptcies. (Transportation Policy Associates, *Transportation in America*, 6th ed.,

Washington, D.C., March 1988, p. 32. Copyright 1988. Used by permission of Eno Foundation for Transportation.)

In addition, the ICC prescribes time zones under the Standard Time Act, determines reasonableness of parcel post rates, and performs several miscellaneous other duties in connection with surface transportation.

By noting these diverse and complicated duties, one can readily appreciate not only the great power and influence of the ICC on surface transportation but also the immense responsibility of the commission to the public and the carriers. Undoubtedly, the ICC is the most important regulatory institution in domestic transportation.

Federal Maritime Commission

The second major regulatory institution is the Federal Maritime Commission (FMC). This commission was established by Presidential Reorganization Plan 7 in 1961, but most of its regulatory powers are similar to those granted its predecessor agencies by the Shipping Act of 1916 and subsequent statutes. The FMC is composed of five members, each serving a four-year term and appointed by the president with the consent of the Senate. The president also names the chairman of the FMC.

The Federal Maritime Commission is organized internally into five administrative offices including the Office of Managing Director, which is responsible for the day-to-day operation of the commission. Under the managing director are six bureaus with the Bureau of Administration containing four offices and the Bureau of Investigation containing eight regional offices in various ports (see Figure 15.3).

The role of the FMC is to regulate waterborne foreign and domestic offshore commerce of the United States, ensure that U.S. international trade is open to all nations on fair and equitable terms, and protect against unauthorized, concerted activity in waterborne commerce of the United States. This is accomplished through maintaining surveillance over steamship conferences and common carriers by water; ensuring that only the rates on file with the commission are charged; approving agreements between persons subject to the Shipping Act of 1916; guaranteeing equal treatment of shippers, carriers, and other persons subject to the shipping statutes; and ensuring that adequate levels of financial responsibility are maintained for indemnification of passengers and cleaning up of oil and hazardous substance spills.

The Shipping Act of 1984 modified the authority of the FMC to permit the liner segment of the industry to compete more effectively with

Figure 15.3 Organization of the Federal Maritime Commission

FEDERAL MARITIME COMMISSION

Commissioner | Commissioner | Chairman | Commissioner | Commissioner

Office of the Managing Director

Office of Regulatory Policy and Planning

Office of the General Counsel

Office of Personnel

Office of Administrative Services

Office of Budget & Financial Management

Office of Management Evaluation & Review

Office of the Secretary

Office of Administrative Law Judges

Office of Energy & Environmental Impact

Office of Data Systems

Office of Consumer Affairs

Bureau of Agreements

Bureau of Tariffs

Bureau of Certification & Licensing

Bureau of Hearings and Field Operations

Field Offices

New York, N.Y.
Washington, D.C.
New Orleans, La.

San Francisco, Calif.
Chicago, Ill.
Puerto Rico

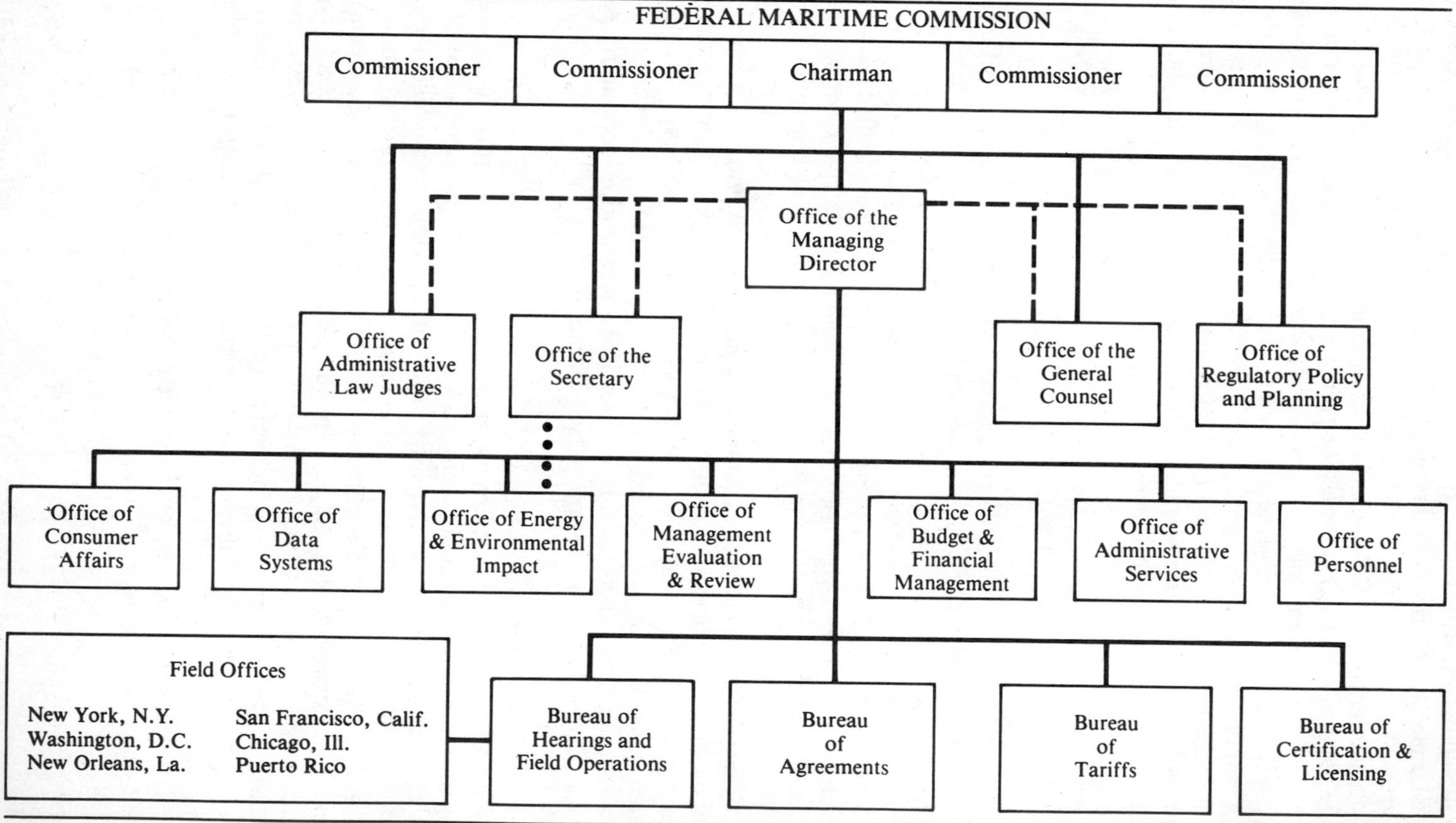

foreign carriers. This was accomplished by determining clearly that the FMC, not the Department of Justice, had jurisdiction over maritime transportation and by allowing confidential service contracts along with independent carrier rates. Formal and informal proceedings are used, much like those of the ICC, and agreements and ocean conference reports must be filed and monitored. Likewise, ocean tariffs must be filed with the FMC.

The workload of the FMC is large — for example, in 1986 over 645,000 pages of tariffs, 2,019 conference reports, and 692 agreements were filed. The budget of the FMC in 1986 was over $11 million.

Federal Energy Regulatory Commission

The Federal Energy Regulatory Commission (FERC) was created by the Department of Energy Organization Act of 1977 as a component of the Department of Energy but with independent regulatory powers. Its five members serve four-year terms and are appointed by the president with the consent of the Senate. The president also appoints the chairman of the commission.

Most of the powers of the Federal Energy Regulatory Commission deal with the transmission and sale of both natural gas and electric power in interstate commerce. Its predecessor agency was the Federal Power Commission. However, when it was created in 1977, the regulatory jurisdiction of the ICC over oil pipelines was transferred to the FERC. Therefore, the role of the Federal Energy Regulatory Commission as far as transportation is concerned is that it establishes rates and charges for the transportation of oil and petroleum products by pipeline as well as the valuation of such pipelines.

The Civil Aeronautics Board (1938–1985)

Before leaving the subject of federal commissions, mention should be made of the Civil Aeronautics Board (CAB). This board was created in 1938 with the passage of the Civil Aeronautics Act as discussed in Chapter 11. Between 1938 and 1978, the CAB had considerable regulatory power over the economic aspects of air transportation. (As noted in Chapter 12, the Federal Aviation Administration, a part of the Department of Transportation, regulates the safety aspects of air transportation.)

With the passage of the Airline Deregulation Act of 1978 (discussed in Chapter 13) the CAB progressively lost jurisdiction over airline transportation regulation. On January 1, 1985, the CAB ceased to exist (under the so-called "sunset provisions" of the 1978 act) and its remaining functions were transferred to other agencies. Jurisdiction over airline mergers went to the Department of Transportation until January 1989 when the Department of Justice took control, jurisdiction over air mail contracts went to the Postal Service, and jurisdiction over foreign air transportation and compensation for "essential air service" transferred to the Department of Transportation.

The State Level

As noted previously, regulation at the state level actually antedated federal regulation, and much of the state regulatory experience served as a testing ground for subsequent federal regulation.

Each state, as well as the District of Columbia, has a state regulatory commission or board. Because there are so many of these commissions, only broad statements can be made about their jurisdiction, organization, membership, and procedure. Each state commission is a study in itself. However, since the state level of control is quite important to some portions of domestic transportation, a general understanding of this regulation is essential. It should be noted at the outset, though, that transportation regulation is only a part of the control functions of state commissions. They also regulate various other businesses "affected with the public interest" (public utilities). In fact, in many state commissions, transport regulation plays a relatively minor role as compared to the regulation of these other industries.

Of the fifty-one state commissions, the typical size is a three-member group. Thirty-eight state commissions are made up of three persons, eight states have five-member commissions, two use seven-member commissions, two use one-member commissions, and one state has an eight-member commission. Commissioners usually serve for six years (in staggered terms), although a tenure of four years is also popular. Some serve as long as ten years, a few serve seven years, and in one case the term is three years. In thirty-five states, commissioners are appointed, usually by the governor with the approval or consent of the state senate (the house or assembly approves in some states rather than the senate). Fourteen states elect their commissioners by popular vote, and two states allow the legislature to elect the commission.

State regulatory commissions are especially important in the motor transportation field in two ways. First, it will be recalled that when the Motor Carrier Act was passed in 1935, Congress specifically denied the ICC jurisdiction over intrastate motor carriers operating legally under the jurisdiction of a state regulatory agency. It was also pointed out in Chapter 11 that the federal act to regulate motor carriers evolved out of a long struggle to control these carriers effectively at the state level. Thus state control was quite well developed in this area prior to federal control.

Most states require motor carriers of persons or property to secure certificates of public convenience and necessity if they are common carriers and permits if they are contract carriers. The procedure for showing that the carrier is fit, willing, and able is similar to federal procedures. Intrastate rates are likewise controlled, and various reports, accounting, and financial controls are often exercised. Insurance provisions are also common. It should be emphasized that state commissions control only the intrastate portion of carrier operations, although the line between interstate and intrastate is sometimes hard to draw. In recent times, a few states have followed the federal pattern and deregulated intrastate transportation. The first two states to deregulate were Arizona and Florida.

Second, state regulatory commissions are important in the motor carrier field because of joint boards. In recognition of state regulatory structures, as well as to simplify the federal regulatory task, the Motor Carrier Act of 1935 allowed these boards. It will be recalled from Chapter 11 that where a matter involves three states or less, a joint board composed of representatives of the state regulatory agencies in the states involved may act for the ICC. Appeal to the federal commission is allowed, of course, but in many matters the joint boards are quite important.

State regulatory commissions were very important in the past in the area of rail transportation and are still important where the movement is primarily intrastate in character. Since many bulky raw materials move primarily in intrastate commerce, many shippers and carriers find that they must appear before state commissions. In the railroad passenger field, especially in abandonments, state commissions have been most important until recently. They exercised principal jurisdiction over this aspect of service until the Transportation Act of 1958.

Since there is little intrastate commerce in air, water, or pipeline transportation, most state regulatory commissions have had but a minor role in the regulation of these modes. Occasionally, in large states such as California or Texas, intrastate air operations are important. Typically, however, state control of transportation has been in the motor and rail modes, with motor by far the most important.

ROLE OF THE COURTS

A second major regulatory institution is the courts, or the judicial process. Again there are two levels of control — federal and state. However, the distinction between the federal and state court levels is not as sharp as it is in the case of commissions. It is feasible, therefore, to consider both federal and state courts as a single regulatory institution. In a very real sense, courts may be considered partners of commissions in transportation regulation. A commission usually has no power to enforce its own orders and must rely on the courts for this. In this, the two institutions are partners. On the other hand, courts can and do review commission decisions (on certain grounds). Here the two institutions may be at variance with each other. Thus, in general the role of the courts is an independent one, which may or may not be in harmony with the commissions.

The role of the courts may be summarized under four main headings: constitutional interpretation, congressional interpretation, an enforcement role, and an adjudicative role.

Constitutional Interpretation

A primary role of the judicial process in our country is that of interpreting the Constitution. This is the principal function of the U.S. Supreme Court for all economic activity. The separation of powers between the executive and the legislative branches is one area in which the role of constitutional interpretation comes into play. Where conflict exists between the two branches, the courts are the final arbitrators of what the Constitution means. Administrative commissions, existing somewhere between (yet somewhat independent of) both administrative and legislative branches, are particularly involved here.

Provisions of the Fifth and Fourteenth Amendments protecting property are prime areas of constitutional interpretation where regulation is involved. An individual may not be deprived of property without due process of law under these amendments, and the courts decide when these amendments have been violated. The courts, therefore, are constantly called upon to interpret the Constitution and its application to the ever-changing social and economic scene. This is of particular importance when a commission is dealing with prices such as transportation rates.

Further, our governmental system is a dual one based on both federal and state levels. Congress has been given the power to regulate "commerce among the several states" under the Constitution (Article I, Section 8 [3]). Power to control commerce not included in that phrase normally resides with the states. The actual determination of what is to be considered interstate commerce (under federal control) and what is to be considered intrastate commerce (under state control) is a matter for judicial interpretation.

Congressional Interpretation

Even when Congress is quite explicit in its statutes, disagreement often arises when a law is applied. More often than not, this disagreement is over the exact meaning or interpretation of the law. Here again the courts have an important role to play. They determine the intent of Congress and settle disputes as to the meaning and application of laws. As far as transportation is concerned, it has been the courts over the years that have been the final arbitrators of the meaning of the Act to Regulate Commerce. The same may be said for the state courts in interpreting the meaning of state regulatory statutes.

At the federal level, for example, it was the courts that interpreted what was meant by an agricultural commodity under the exemption in the 1935 Motor Carrier Act. This interpretation defined the law, and in this particular case, Congress found it advisable to return to this question in the Transportation Act of 1958. This is an example of Congress becoming dissatisfied with the court's interpretation of congressional intent and redefining its terms. Nevertheless, the task of interpreting the law is a basic one for the courts.

Enforcement Role

As mentioned above, the ICC has no power to enforce its own orders. It must go before the courts and solicit a writ of injunction or writ of mandamus for enforcement. Likewise, the ICC cannot impose penalties for violations of the law. The Interstate Commerce Act specifically authorizes the courts to issue injunctions to prevent violations of commission orders. Similarly, the Elkins Act authorizes the courts to enforce observance of published tariffs. Fines for not heeding commission orders or for violating various acts are provided in the law. However, it is the courts that impose the prescribed penalties and enforce the law.

Adjudicative Role

The courts also have a primary role in dealing with litigation arising out of the application of regulatory statutes. Hearing cases on violations of the acts is a part of this role. However, it is well to remember that certain common-law obligations of carriers also exist. Here again, the courts act as adjudicator. Likewise, damages and reparations, both those awarded by the ICC and those granted under the common-law concept of liability, are matters for the courts to enforce and award.

Review of Commission Decisions

The role of the courts in reviewing commission decisions is a combination of interpretation and adjudication. As noted in Chapter 10, review of commission decisions shortly after the original Act to Regulate Commerce was passed made the law meaningless for a period of time. A major rationale of court review is to place a limit upon commissions. An administrative commission has very broad powers and could act in an arbitrary and unreasonable fashion. The courts protect against this possibility.

Originally, there was some concern over the delegation of the powers of Congress to control commerce to an administrative body. The Constitution specifically prohibits Congress from delegating its power to others. However, where adequate standards to guide the administrative commission have been set forth by the legislature, such a delegation of power has been held to be constitutional. These standards may be broad ones such as "rates must be just and reasonable" in the Interstate Commerce Act. But without "limitations of a prescribed standard," Congress cannot delegate its powers (*United States* v. *Milwaukee Railroad*, 282 U.S. 311, 1931).

Within these broad standards, though, the commission determines matters of fact. The ICC has primary jurisdiction to determine what is "just and reasonable" or what is "unduly prejudicial or preferential." The ICC has set up careful procedures and definitions of these terms. The courts on matters of review have generally accepted the commission determination of facts and have restricted themselves, at least in recent times, to matters of law.

But this does not mean that judicial review of commission findings is not possible. It merely means that the courts ordinarily will review a commission's decision only on certain limited grounds, primarily matters of law. These grounds for judicial interference can be summarized under the five headings of constitutionality, jurisdiction, procedure, evidence, and capricious and arbitrary actions.

The constitutionality of regulatory statutes is always a matter for judicial review. This ground for judicial interference, although it is often cited, has not been a generally successful one. The plea that a commission has exceeded its jurisdiction or has misinterpreted the law is more often used. Again, the exact meaning of a statute (a common ground for appeal) is a matter for the courts to decide.

Review because of incorrect procedure is also important. This involves such matters as proper notice, knowledge of alleged violations, right of counsel and a fair hearing, and other constitutional guarantees of individual rights. Likewise, a commission decision must be made upon substantial evidence and cannot be contrary to the finding of fact involved in the particular case. That is, a regulatory agency cannot act in an arbitrary or capricious fashion and must be able to sustain by fact the reason for its actions. Again, the limitation upon commission action is self-evident.

In summary, it may be said that the courts play a very important role as regulators of transportation. Not only do they act as a limitation upon commission action, but they also act as enforcers and give commission action its basic strength. In their interpretative role, they actually regulate carriers and shippers, whereas in their role of review, they attempt to set bounds beyond which the commission may not go. In general, they try to protect the rights of all parties. They are indeed a most important regulatory institution in domestic transportation.

THE LEGISLATIVE PROCESS

A third regulatory institution in domestic transportation is the legislature and the legislative process. It is essentially congressional acts with which we are concerned here, but the same concepts of the legislature as a regulatory institution apply equally at the state level.

Congress, or any legislature, acts as a regulatory institution in three ways. It is a promulgator of general transportation policy by way of statute enactment, a creator of commissions (and a delegator of authority to them), and an appropriator of funds to implement regulation. By its action or lack of action in each of these three functions, the legislature acts as a regulator.

General Policy

The transportation policy of the nation is promulgated initially by congressional action. What is and is not included in these regulatory acts sets the stage for commissions and the climate within which transportation operates. The development of transportation regulation described in the four previous chapters is an illustration of this legislative function.

Delegation of Authority

Congress creates the various commissions and boards that implement its regulatory laws. How these commissions are established, their jurisdiction and powers, and their organization and makeup are all part of the legislative process acting as a regulatory institution. The matter of delegation of authority has been mentioned above. Here again the standards or guidelines established in creating a commission are of primary importance. Commissions are creatures of the legislature, and it is from them that commission jurisdiction and authority are derived.

Appropriation of Funds

Once established, commissions must look to the legislature for financial support. Appropriations to operate commissions come principally from the legislature. Although fees may be charged (and may be an important source of financial support particularly for some state commissions), the major source of commission income is the annual legislative appropriation.

Procedures

Typically, legislatures act through committees. In the U.S. Congress, there are five standing committees having jurisdiction over transportation — two in the Senate (Committee on Commerce, Science, and Transportation and Committee on Environment and Public Works), and three in the House (Committee on Energy and Commerce, Committee on Public Works and Transportation, and Committee on Merchant Marine and Fisheries). Figure 15.4 shows these committees and indicates their respective roles.

New legislative proposals are referred to these committees, hearings are held to ascertain opinion on changes in the regulatory climate, and compromises are worked out. Committee members, especially where long service on the committee is involved, become expert on transportation matters, and new regulatory laws often carry the name of the chair of the Senate or House committee.

On some occasions, the congressional committees have sponsored special studies of transportation problems. Here the committee staff becomes important. The much-quoted Doyle report (*National Transportation Policy*, Report of the Commerce Committee of the U.S. Senate, Report No. 445, 87 Congress, 1961) is an example of a congressional committee study of the whole transportation system.

The process of writing regulatory statutes, creating commissions, granting them authority, appropriating funds to implement their operations, hearing proposals for new laws, and working out compromise solutions to current transportation problems is all an integral part of transportation regulation.

THE EXECUTIVE

The final regulatory institution is the executive, who may recommend legislation and administer or carry out the statutes set down by the legislature. In our economy, the executive branch of government has become more and more powerful as society has become more complex and interrelated.

As a regulatory institution, the executive exercises four important powers that affect transportation. These are the power of appointment, the power of enforcement, the power of investigation, and the power of recommendation.

Power of Appointment

The executive appoints members of the regulatory commissions. On the federal level, this gives the president the power to influence transportation regulation. (On the state level, this power does not exist in all states as we have already seen. However, in most of the states it does exist, and governors have the ability to influence state transportation regulation.) This power is not without limitation, however. Because of the organization of commissions, no one executive ordinarily can usually appoint all members of a commission. Even so, this power is a real and important one.

Presidential appointees to the ICC, FMC, or FERC can be quite important. Commissioners' background, knowledge, and qualifications affect regulation. Many appointees, particularly to the ICC, have been excellently qualified and have served long terms by way of reappointment. Unfortunately, politics has a role in commission appointments, and sometimes persons have been appointed not so much because of what they could contribute to effective regulation as because their appointment satisfied political debts or pressures. This unfortunate situation seems to have existed more at the state than at the federal level.

The power of appointment is further limited at the federal level by the provision that only a bare majority of the commissions can be from one

Figure 15.4 Standing Congressional Committees Having Jurisdiction over Transportation

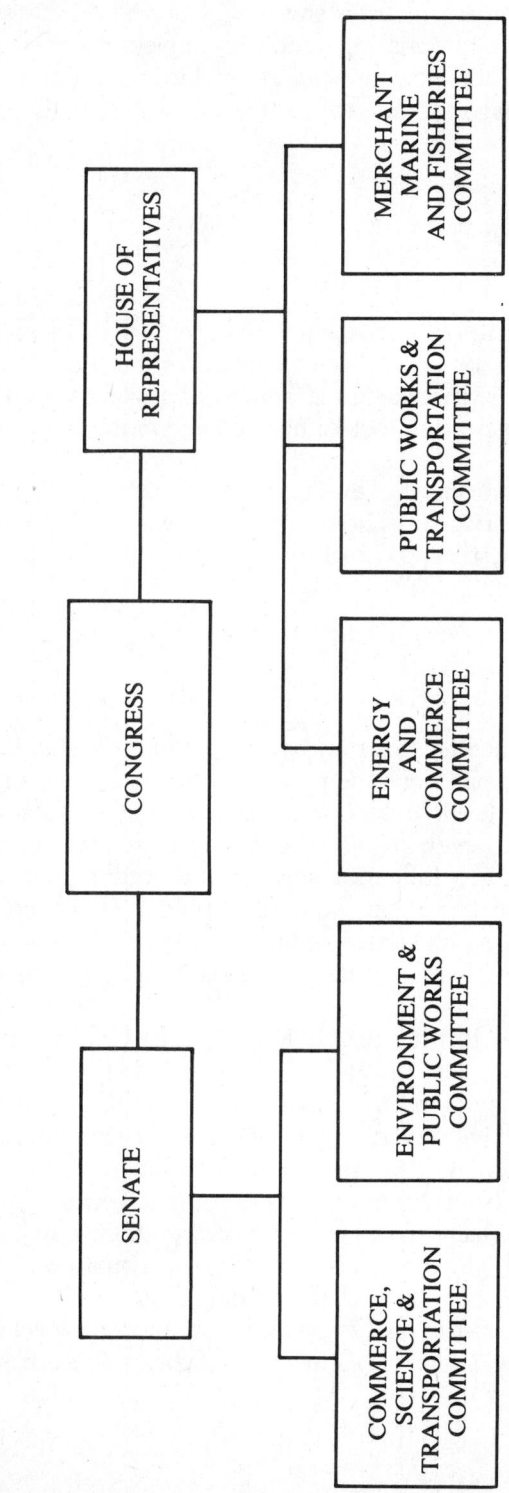

The present standing committee structure of Congress includes several committees which have both direct and indirect jurisdiction over policies affecting the transportation industry. The organizational chart above indicates the positions of these committees within the structure of the Congress. The table of functions on the opposite page points up the major areas of the transportation industry covered by the various committees, as well as the similarity of their respective jurisdiction.

SENATE COMMITTEES	HOUSE COMMITTEES
Commerce, Science, and Transportation Regulation of interstate common carriers, including railroads, buses, trucks, vessels, pipelines, and civil aviation; transportation in general; highway safety; inland waterways, except construction; Panama Canal and interoceanic canals generally; merchant marine and navigation; marine and ocean navigation, safety, and transportation; Coast Guard; interstate commerce; and transport R&D and technology matters. *Environment and Public Works* Construction and maintenance of highways; flood control and improvement of rivers, harbors, and environmental aspects of deepwater ports; noise/water/air pollution; and public works, bridges, and dams.	*Public Works and Transportation* Transportation, including civil aviation, but not railroads, railroad labor, and pensions; water transportation subject to ICC jurisdiction; highway construction, maintenance and safety; flood control and improvement of rivers and harbors; and waterway pollution. *Energy and Commerce* Oil and gas pipeline functions of Federal Energy Regulatory Commission; inland waterways; railroads, rail labor, and retirement; and travel and tourism. *Merchant Marine and Fisheries* Regulation of common carriers by water other than those under ICC; Coast Guard; merchant marine vessel inspections and navigation/safety equipment; navigation and pilotage; Panama Canal; registering and licensing of vessels and small boats; and U.S. Coast Guard and Merchant Marine Academies.

Source: Transportation Policy Associates, *Transportation in America*, 6th ed., Washington, D.C., March 1988, p. 33. Copyright 1988. Used by permission of Eno Foundation for Transportation.

political party. However, this is not too often an effective limitation since members of the opposite political party can usually be found who agree with a president.

Additionally, the power of appointment to various cabinet offices can be very important. Obviously, the secretary of transportation is the most important transportation appointment in the president's cabinet. However, other offices in the executive branch also may have an impact on transportation — some more directly than others. Figure 15.5 shows the cabinet offices with responsibility in the transportation area and notes briefly the role of each, with the exception of DOT.

The Department of Transportation (DOT) is undoubtedly the most important cabinet office in the executive branch as far as transportation is concerned. Chapter 12 discussed the creation of DOT in 1967 as part of the movement toward national transportation planning. At this point, it is important to note the various responsibilities and functions of DOT. Figure 15.6 contains a summary of the responsibilities of the nine operating divisions of DOT. Many of these executive agencies are well known to the general public and all affect transportation in a meaningful way. The president appoints the secretary of transportation and the upper levels of the management of DOT (deputy secretaries, assistant secretaries, general counsel, and operating division heads). The department has over 113,000 employees and over 3,000 field offices in the United States and abroad.

Power of Enforcement

As noted above, the orders of a commission must be enforced by a court. It is the Department of Justice that represents the commissions before the court to secure this enforcement. Likewise, it is the attorney general who must defend the commission in any legal action. Hence, the executive branch has the power to initiate enforcement, and how it proceeds can be very important to effective transportation regulation.

Power of Investigation

The executive's power of investigation has become of increasing importance during recent times. A series of studies and investigations by various departments or appointive groups of the executive branch has been made since World War II. The Sawyer report, the Weeks report, and the Mueller report — all named for the secretaries of commerce who supervised their preparation — are examples of this power of investigation.

The Landis report and the Hoover Commission reports are examples of the work of appointive groups from the executive branch who have investigated transportation regulation. Finally, the rather extensive investigations of both air and surface safety and the experiments in urban transportation and high-speed rail systems undertaken by the Department of Transportation are prime examples of the power of investigation.

Power of Recommendation

Another power exercised by the executive is that of recommendation to Congress. This takes two forms — budgetary and policy. Although Congress appropriates the funds to operate regulatory commissions, it is the executive branch that draws up the budget and recommends the appropriations. All the commissions are included within the federal budget and must submit their requests to the Bureau of the Budget. By action or lack of action within the general budgetary framework as laid down by the president, regulatory commissions may be affected.

The power of executive recommendation on the policy level has been of primary importance. One need only to recall that it was President Grant whose recommendations caused Congress to establish the Windom Committee and President Theodore Roosevelt who called for the Hepburn Act. In more recent times, President Kennedy's transportation message of April 1962 is an excellent example of the power of recommendation. In this instance, a special message was sent to Congress recommending substantial revisions in transportation regulation. This was the first time that a president had singled out transportation regulation for a special message (not embodied in his general message), and the practice has been followed since, with generally productive results. President Johnson's 1966 message led to the establishment of the Department of Transportation, President Nixon's 1969 message stimulated Congress to act on maritime improvement, and the 1974 Nixon message concerning urban mass transportation has been mentioned earlier. The roles of President Ford and President Carter in deregulation were noted in Chapter 13 as well as the recommendations of President Reagan relative to Amtrak and Conrail and urban transportation in Chapter 12.

SUMMARY

Transportation regulatory institutions are important at both the federal and state levels. In effect, these institutions create and implement the

Figure 15.5 Transport Responsibilities in the Executive Branch

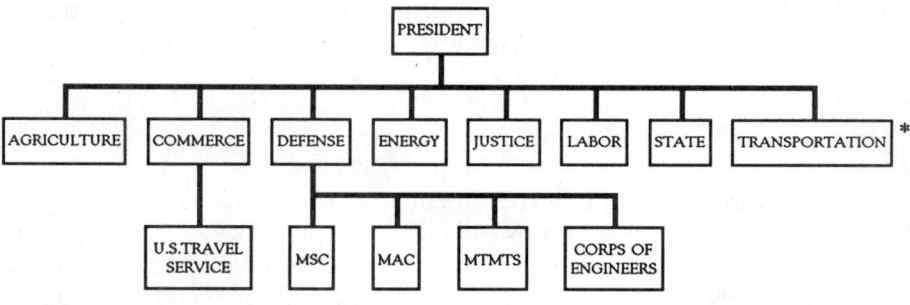

DESCRIPTION	RESPONSIBILITIES
President	Rules on matters relating to *international air transport* by U.S. and foreign carriers. Nominates (Senate confirms) members, and appoints the chairs of the FERC, FMC, and ICC.
Agriculture	*Office of Transportation* is responsible for developing USDA transport policies for agriculture and rural development and for representing their interests before federal and state regulatory agencies with respect to rates, charges, tariffs, and services of transport carriers.
Commerce	*U.S. Travel Service* plans and carries out a comprehensive program designed to stimulate and encourage travel to the United States by foreign residents. Accomplishes a quinquennial *census of transportation,* including "Truck Inventory and Use Survey" and "Commodity Transport Survey."
Defense	*Military Sealift Command* provides ocean transportation for DOD cargo and personnel and, as directed, for other U.S. agencies and departments; and operates ships in support of other U.S. agency programs.

*See Figure 15.6 for description of DOT functions.
Source: Transportation Policy Associates, *Transportation in America,* 6th ed., Washington, D.C., March 1988, p. 30. Copyright 1988. Used by permission of Eno Foundation for Transportation.

DEPARTMENT	RESPONSIBILITIES
Defense (continued)	*Military Airlift Command* provides air transportation for DOD cargo and personnel on a worldwide basis; and furnishes weather, rescue, and audiovisual services for the U.S. Air Force.
	Military Traffic Management and Terminal Service directs military traffic management, land transportation, and common-user ocean terminal service within the United States, and for worldwide traffic management of DOD's household goods moving and storage program. Provides for procurement of commercial freight and passenger transport services.
	Corps of Engineers constructs, improves, and maintains river, harbor, and port facilities; and administers laws for the protection and preservation of navigable waters and related wetlands. Compiles and publishes statistical data on domestic/foreign waterborne commerce.
Energy	Develops and implements national energy policies; administers petroleum and natural gas pricing, allocation, and import/export controls; assures energy supplies; and performs regulatory functions over oil and gas pipelines not assigned to FERC.
Justice	Performs a key role in ensuring strong competition in transportation under the U.S. free enterprise system, such responsibilities becoming more pronounced as a result of recent laws sharply reducing transportation regulation, especially as they relate to antitrust issues.
Labor	Administers and enforces laws relating to wage earners, their working conditions, and employment opportunities, including court actions under the Longshoremen's and Harbor Workers' Compensation Act and the Employee Retirement Income Security Act (ERISA).
State	Develops policy recommendations and approves broad policy programs concerning *international aviation and maritime transportation*, especially as they affect U.S.-foreign relations; e.g., bilateral pacts.

Figure 15.6 U.S. Department of Transportation Organization and Responsibilities

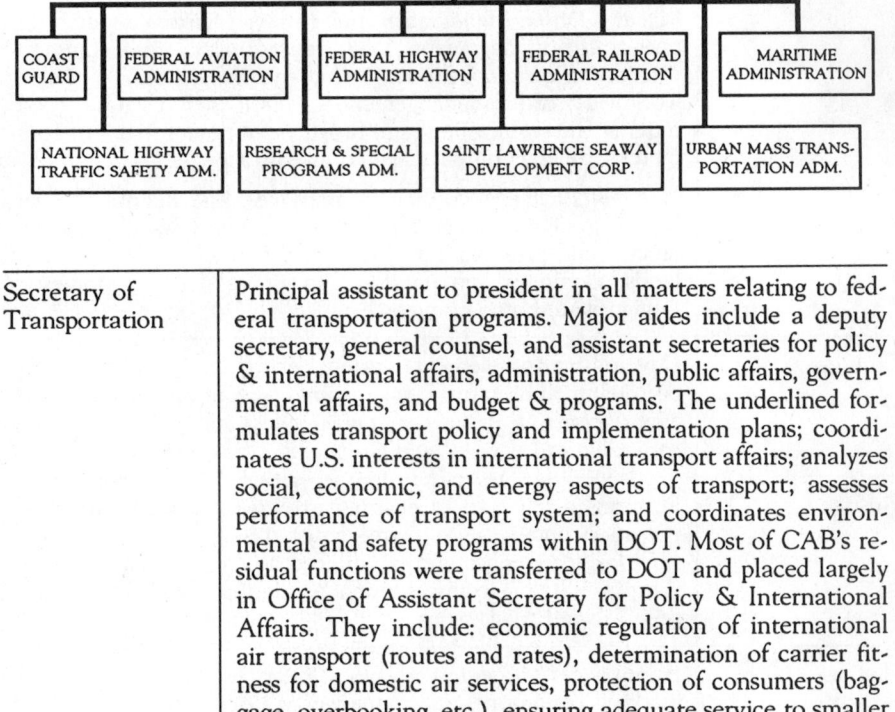

Secretary of Transportation	Principal assistant to president in all matters relating to federal transportation programs. Major aides include a deputy secretary, general counsel, and assistant secretaries for policy & international affairs, administration, public affairs, governmental affairs, and budget & programs. The underlined formulates transport policy and implementation plans; coordinates U.S. interests in international transport affairs; analyzes social, economic, and energy aspects of transport; assesses performance of transport system; and coordinates environmental and safety programs within DOT. Most of CAB's residual functions were transferred to DOT and placed largely in Office of Assistant Secretary for Policy & International Affairs. They include: economic regulation of international air transport (routes and rates), determination of carrier fitness for domestic air services, protection of consumers (baggage, overbooking, etc.), ensuring adequate service to smaller communities, grant of antitrust immunity, and protecting U.S. carriers against foreign actions.
Coast Guard	Maintains network of rescue vessels, aircraft, and communications facilities to protect lives and property on the high seas and navigable waters of United States. Enforces federal laws governing navigation, vessel inspection, port safety and security, marine environmental protection, and resource conservation. Sets ship construction and safety standards. Regulates Great Lakes' pilotage. Carries out R&D programs.
Federal Aviation Administration	Promotes civil aviation, including R&D programs; promulgates and enforces safety regulations; develops and operates nation's airways system; administers federal-aid airport programs; and certifies and registers aircraft and commercial/private pilots.

Source: Transportation Policy Associates, *Transportation in America*, 6th ed., Washington, D.C., March 1988, p. 31. Copyright 1988. Used by permission of Eno Foundation for Transportation.

Federal Highway Administration	Administers federal-aid highway program of financial aid to states for highway construction and rehabilitation. Develops and administers highway safety program, including aid to states and local communities. Coordinates and helps fund R&D programs. Its Office of Motor Carrier Safety regulates safety performance of interstate commercial motor carriers, including hazardous materials movements and cargo security/ noise abatement programs. Makes road checks, prosecutes violators. Develops highway data.
Federal Railroad Administration	Consolidates U.S. support and promotion of railroad transportation; administers and enforces rail safety regulations; administers rail financial-aid programs; and conducts R&D programs to improve railroad freight and passenger services and safety.
Maritime Administration	Promotes merchant marine; grants ship mortgage insurance; maintains National Defense Reserve Fleet; sponsors R&D for ship design, propulsion, and operations. Its Maritime Subsidy Board awards ship operating subsidies to liner carriers (ship construction subsidies have been discontinued) and determines scope of subsidized shipping services and routes — in line with MarAd's determination of ship requirements, services, and routes need for the U.S. foreign waterborne commerce.
National Highway Traffic Safety Administration	Implements motor vehicle safety programs and issues standards prescribing levels of safety needed; conducts test programs to assure compliance with standards and need for them; helps fund state/local safety programs; maintains national poor-driver register; sets fuel economy standards for autos with EPA and DOE; and assesses penalties for violators of its standards.
Research & Special Programs Administration	Serves as DOT's research, analysis, and technical development arm; and conducts special programs, with emphasis on: pipeline safety, movements of hazardous materials, cargo security, R&D, university research programs, and commercial air carrier data formerly collected, collated, and published by the CAB.
Saint Lawrence Seaway Development Corp.	Administers the operation and maintenance of the U.S. portion of the Saint Lawrence Seaway. Works closely with its Canadian counterpart to determine and set toll levels.
Urban Mass Transportation Administration	Develops comprehensive, coordinated mass transport systems for urban areas, including financial aid for equipment and operations; R&D and demonstration projects; aid for technical studies; planning, engineering, and designing.

social rules or regulations under which transportation operates. In this chapter we have discussed commissions at the federal level (ICC, FMC, FERC) and the state commissions. These are unique American institutions in transportation. We have also discussed the role of the courts as a regulatory institution. Here review, interpretation, adjudication, and enforcement are important. The legislative process as a regulatory institution has been noted in detail. Indeed, Chapters 10, 11, 12, and 13 have all given emphasis to the legislative process of setting transportation policy. In this chapter we have noted the various congressional committees (both in the Senate and the House of Representatives) as part of the process of regulation. Finally, the role of the executive branch with its power of appointment, power of enforcement, power of investigation, and power of recommendation was discussed. In the executive branch, the role of the Department of Transportation was stressed.

We have now completed Part III, Regulation/Deregulation of Domestic Transportation, and the next part, made up of four chapters, turns to transportation costs and rates.

ADDITIONAL READINGS

Bowersox, Donald J., Pat J. Calabro, and George D. Wagenheim, *Introduction to Transportation*, New York: Macmillan Publishing Co., 1981.
    Chapter 12, "Regulatory Institutions," pp. 185–216.
Davis, Grant M., *The Department of Transportation*, Lexington, Mass.: D. C. Heath, 1972.
Davis, Grant M., and Stephen W. Brown, *Logistics Management*, Lexington, Mass.: D. C. Heath, 1974.
    Chapter 13, "Federal Agencies Promoting and Regulating Transportation," pp. 301–20.
Harper, Donald V., *Transportation in America: Users, Carriers, Government*, 2nd ed., Englewood Cliffs, N.J.: Prentice-Hall, 1982.
    Chapter 20, "The Decision-Making Process in Government Economic Regulation of Transportation," pp. 477–96.
Hazard, John L., *Managing National Transportation Policy*, Westport, Conn.: The Eno Foundation for Transportation, 1988.
    Chapter 2, "The Federal Executive Setting," pp. 31–44.
    Chapter 3, "Administrative Performance of DOT," pp. 45–76.
Kneafsey, James T., *Transportation Economic Analysis*, Lexington, Mass.: D. C. Heath, 1975.
    Chapter 9, "Regulation of Transportation," pp. 81–99.
Lieb, Robert C., *Transportation*, 3rd ed., Reston, Va.: Reston Publishing Co., 1985.
    Chapter 16, "Federal Regulatory Agencies: Their Structure and Activities," pp. 331–52.
Locklin, D. Philip, *Economics of Transportation*, 7th ed., Homewood, Ill.: Richard D. Irwin, 1972.
    Chapter 13, "The Agencies of Control," pp. 282–310.

Norton, Hugh S., *Modern Transportation Economics*, 2nd ed., Columbus, Ohio: Charles E. Merrill, 1971.
    Chapter 17, "The Administrative Agencies of Control and Their Policy Making Role," pp. 303–30.
    Chapter 23, "Regulation in the Modern Economy, Problems, and Policy Issues," pp. 429–48.
Pegrum, Dudley F., *Transportation: Economics and Public Policy*, 3rd ed., Homewood, Ill.: Richard D. Irwin, 1973.
    Chapter 11, "The Agencies of Regulation," pp. 241–67.
    Chapter 21, "Regulation and Administration in Transport Policy," pp. 491–512.
Sampson, Roy J., "The Economic and Legal Environment of Domestic Transportation in the United States," *European Transport Law*, 3, No. 2 (1968), 294–317.
Stephenson, Frederick J., Jr., *Transportation USA*, Reading, Mass.: Addison-Wesley Publishing Co., 1987.
    Chapter 4, "Government Participation in U.S. Transportation," pp. 79–110.
Taff, Charles A., *Management of Physical Distribution and Transportation*, 6th ed., Homewood, Ill.: Richard D. Irwin, 1978.
    Chapter 20, "Institutional Aspects of Transport Policies and Programs," pp. 548–85.

PART IV

RATE THEORY AND PRACTICE IN DOMESTIC TRANSPORTATION

Expenditures for moving freight, with which we are concerned in this part, have hovered around 9 percent of GNP for many years. A substantial part of GNP, however, clearly well over 40 percent, is composed of expenditures for personal, business, and governmental services rather than the purchases of tangible goods. Freight charges are not paid on services. If we exclude the services portion of GNP, then, and apply the expenditures for freight movement only to the goods we buy, the average increases from around 9 percent to around 15 percent.

Until the recent move toward less governmental regulation (see Chapter 13), well over one-half of the total expenditures for freight movements in this country were directly regulated by the federal or state governments. Despite these changes, a sizable portion of for-hire freight charges still are subject to direct regulation. Also, where direct regulation has been removed, it has been replaced by the indirect "regulation" of antitrust laws.

As the costs of moving goods must be reflected in prices paid for goods, even average figures indicate how directly transport costs and for-hire freight rates affect all of us. These charges are much less than the 15 percent average for some products, but on others they range up to one-half or more of the prices paid by consumers. Cost and price elements of this magnitude affect sellers as well as buyers. Higher prices mean fewer sales; and in a competitive situation, those sellers with higher transport costs may find themselves relatively handicapped or even excluded from some markets because of the lower transport costs or freight rates of their competitors.

Literally, a freight-rate level or a rate structure may economically make or break an individual business, an industry, a community, or a large geographic region. Both the level of rates and the comparative rates paid by competitors are important to sellers of products. Freight rates may determine whether a business will be successful and whether its employees will continue to have jobs. Likewise, from the carriers' viewpoint, comparative rate levels may determine which mode or which carrier gets the bulk of the traffic and which goes into bankruptcy.

With the vital economic interests of consumers, producers and sellers, employees, carrier modes and individual carriers, and even entire industries, communities, or large sections of the country involved, it is easy to see why proposed freight rates or rate changes often lead to bitter controversy. Also, it is understandable why such controversy often results in the creation of more heat than light.

Unfortunately, the typical individual (even including the business-person whose transportation costs are quite important in operations) is woefully lacking in knowledge concerning freight rates. Such a person does not understand their economic and legal characteristics, their regulation, how they are made and changed, their application, their terminology, their structures, or their economic effects. Even one who realizes their importance as a cost factor is inclined to regard this as a necessary evil about which little can be done except complain and leave the details to that rather odd character surrounded by mountains of incomprehensible freight-rate tariffs in a corner of the shipping department.

This lack of general knowledge of freight rates and their effects is both unnecessary and undesirable. In this part, therefore, the authors propose to dissipate some of the clouds surrounding this subject.

CHAPTER 16

THE ECONOMIC AND LEGAL
BASIS OF RATES

Transportation rates are simply prices charged by carriers for performing their services. However, it is a mistake to assume that the subject of rates and ratemaking is a simple one. All major pricing systems are complex, and none more so than that used in transportation. Problems of supply and demand, or of costs and value of service, regulation and legal obligations, competition and capacity, and the forces of tradition are intricately interwoven into a pattern of chaos and confusion not unlike the Gordian knot. Those who would unravel this pattern, like Alexander, must cut directly into its heart.

One transportation practitioner, speaking to a nontransportation audience, compared freight rates to prices of bags of potatoes. This is a great oversimplification. To a consumer, any bag of potatoes (of a given weight and grade) is like every other bag. In transportation, however, each bag of freight services differs from almost every other bag in terms of content, grade, cost of production, and desirability in the consumer's eye. Every offer by every transportation company to every consumer for every specific piece of transportation service is a different bag.

To become an expert on rates, even for one form of carriage, requires lengthy study and practice (as well, perhaps, as a certain amount of talent along such lines). Despite their complexities, though, the principles of rates and rate structures, and their formation and effects, are not beyond the understanding of anyone with average intelligence and a basic grasp of the economics of pricing. The first step in this understanding is to comprehend what it is that rates are designed to do.

ECONOMIC FUNCTIONS OF RATES

Economically speaking, freight rates have two primary functions, one for the user and one for the carrier. These are (1) to permit freight to move, and (2) to compensate the carrier.

Whether a shipper uses a rate depends upon its level. If the rate is too high, that is, if it is higher than the value of the service to the shipper, goods will not move. Rates sometimes are set at high levels that are unusable for a variety of reasons. The carrier's cost of performing the service may be higher than the value of the service to the shipper; the carrier may believe its costs are at this level, which amounts to the same thing; or the carrier may overestimate the value of the service to the shipper.

Also, for some reason, a carrier may not wish to handle a particular traffic segment and thus may deliberately price itself out of a specific market. (In view of a common carrier's obligation to serve, discussed in Chapter 20, such a policy may have legal repercussions if proven. However, proof of such intent is difficult to obtain.) It has been alleged that some railroads have deliberately attempted to discourage business by overpricing in recent years. Trucking firms and airlines have also been accused of setting rates at levels that discourage the movement of traffic perceived as being less profitable, leaving such traffic for the railroads.

There is considerable debate about what constitutes a compensatory rate or rate level. In any case, rates in the aggregate must be high enough to compensate carriers for the costs they incur in performing such services as the public demands, including whatever profits are necessary to attract or retain sufficient capital investment for this purpose. The alternative ultimately is bankruptcy and cessation of service or some form of public subsidy that offsets carrier costs or adds to carrier revenues. It should be remembered, however, that it is not necessary that any particular rate be high enough to cover all costs or even the direct costs associated with it, nor that rates in the aggregate do this at all times. It is only necessary that *aggregate rates in the long run* cover all costs if services are to be continued. (See Chapters 4 and 5 for a discussion of fixed and variable costs, long-run and short-run periods, and operating ratios of the various forms of carriage.)

In the regulated public utility industries (which include transportation), there once was the belief, usually supported by law, that rate levels yielding an annual net return (accounting profit) of from 6 to 8 percent on investment in a well-managed company or group of companies were reasonable rates. If the yield was higher, there was a suspicion that the rates were too high and that the company or industry was enjoying monopoly profits. If, on the other hand, the yield was lower, assuming competent management and a normal level of demand for services, it was suspected that rates were too low and that the company or companies concerned were entitled to rate increases on the grounds of inadequate compensation.

Such an absolute earnings yardstick brings on problems of interpretation. What is a well-managed company? What is a normal level of demand? And, in particular, what is the investment base against which the yield is measured? Should investment be calculated at original cost of the assets used less accrued depreciation, at current replacement costs of assets, or by some other method? Should the allowable yield be measured against all assets, or should a distinction be made between firms with widely differing ratios of equity and debt financing? Many court cases have dealt with these and similar questions, but answers satisfactory to all parties involved have not been found.

Economists in particular have criticized absolute formulas of reasonableness. In the Hope Natural Gas case (*Federal Power Commission* v. *Hope Natural Gas Company*, 320 U.S. 591, 1944), the U.S. Supreme Court finally gave recognition to what economists had been saying for a long time. The decision in that case held, in effect, that a specific percentage rate of return on a specific evaluation of investment is not the most crucial test of reasonableness. Rather, the pertinent rate level is one that yields a rate of return sufficient to permit the firm to maintain its financial integrity — a yield that will permit a company to retain or attract whatever capital investment is necessary to provide the services expected from it by the public.

Certainly the *Hope* case formula more adequately meets the economic criterion of what constitutes a compensatory level of rates than does the more rigid fixed percentage of a fixed amount of investment. Even with the *Hope* formula, however, there are serious and unsolved problems. How are we to know whether a particular level of rates will permit a carrier or mode of carriage to maintain financial integrity? Testing in the marketplace over a period of time provides the only sure answer, but, if rates are too low, this may be devastating to carriers and result in disruption of desired transportation services. On the other hand, if rates are established at unnecessarily high levels, the result may be higher charges for the users of transportation services (the entire public) and a misallocation of economic resources. Clearly the *Hope* formula is no panacea, but it does shift the emphasis from a narrow legalistic definition into the economic arena where it belongs.

Measured against even such a flexible yardstick as the *Hope* formula, it is obvious that the rate of return of many carriers falls considerably short of reasonable over long periods of time. This is especially true among the railroads (see Chapter 4). Apparently pipelines as a group are not experiencing financial difficulties. Current airline problems dealing with acquisition of newer, more reliable equipment are less clear. Similarly, the picture in the water- and truck-transport industries is cloudy, with specific financial data not as readily available. It seems that these two modes of carriage are doing better than the railroads as a group, over time, although they are not doing as well as they would like.

In summary, one of the pressing transportation problems of our era is to devise a system of rates that in practice will allow traffic to move while adequately compensating carriers performing the desired services. Like most such problems, this one can never be solved for all time. Today's solution will be tomorrow's problem. In a dynamic world and an ever-changing economy, constant attention to major problems is essential to ensure even reasonably satisfactory results.

REGULATION AND REASONABLE RATES

English common law, which has been carried over into our statutory law, requires that common-carrier rates must be reasonable. As seen in Chapter 20, this is one of the historic duties of a common carrier. The obligation to charge reasonable rates originally was designed to prevent carrier exploitation of the public; it was aimed at unreasonably high rates in monopolistic situations. Today, however, it is interpreted to apply with equal force against unreasonably low rates. Also, the standards of reasonableness are as binding upon governmental regulatory agencies which approve, disapprove, or set rates as they are upon carriers.

Many thousands of pages have been written in attempts to define or describe just what is meant by an unreasonable rate. For our present purposes, however, it is sufficient to define an unreasonably high rate as one that allows a carrier to collect considerably more than is necessary under the circumstances to provide its service; in other words, to take advantage of some ability to exploit its public. An unreasonably low rate, on the other hand, is one that does not adequately compensate the carrier for its services. Obviously, both of these kinds of unreasonableness are in some way related to carrier costs, although other factors (such as demand, competition, and even public policy or public welfare) may enter into the picture.

The general prohibition of unreasonably high rates requires little discussion or justification at this point. Such rates are contrary to our long-established Anglo-American laws and ideas of economic justice and efficiency, just as are monopolistically exploitive prices in other areas of economic endeavor. The concept itself is not seriously questioned by many, although heated discussions may develop as to whether a particular rate or price does fall into the unreasonably high category.

The prohibition of unreasonably low rates, on the other hand, may require a little more discussion. Here, too, ideas of equity, efficiency, and allocation of economic resources are involved. If a particular rate does not adequately compensate a carrier for performing its services, one of two things must follow. Either the low-rate traffic is being subsidized by higher-than-necessary rates paid by shippers of other traffic, or the carrier (who has invested in the transportation business) is subsidizing the low-rate movement by receiving lower profits (or taking greater losses) than it otherwise would. If the aggregate rate level (rates in general) is unreasonably low, it follows that the capital value of the carrier or carriers concerned is being eroded; in other words, transportation investors as a group are subsidizing shippers and the general public as a group. Only those who are not opposed to one or some of the above results can support unreasonably low rates as such. But there may be a difference of opinion as to whether a particular rate or rate level is unreasonably low.

For some reason, a carrier may deliberately choose to charge an unusually low rate — one that it or others may believe to be less than adequate. This may, and very likely will, bring protests from other carriers or from producers of commodities competing with the low-rate traffic on the grounds that the carriers concerned or its shippers are thereby engaging in unfair or destructive competition. Shippers of noncompeting products may protest likewise on the grounds that unduly low rates to some mean unduly high rates to others. Even the general public, which has an interest in the maintenance of adequate facilities for desired transportation services, should be concerned about unduly low rates.

In the absence of convincing objections of this kind, many people would say that a carrier's decision to put even extremely low rates into effect on portions of its traffic is its own concern. If stockholders do not like to subsidize users or do not trust the decisions of their management, they can remove the managers.

It is quite a different matter, however, if a regulatory agency attempts to force carriers to put into effect or maintain particular rates or aggregate rate levels that are noncompensatory (however that may be defined). All courts have long held that such action by regulators constitutes "taking property without due process of law," which is a violation of the U.S. Constitution (the Fifth Amendment if done by federal action, and the Fourteenth Amendment if done by state regulatory agencies).

Inflation during the 1970s and early 1980s, combined with a significant lessening of regulation in the 1980s, increased rate volatility in many transportation markets. In an overall restructuring of relative rate levels, many rates were increased substantially, whereas others were significantly decreased. There may be grounds for questioning the economic judgment of some carriers in instituting many of these changes, both upward and downward, but there is little ground for questioning the legality of their having put such changes into effect. Legal reasonableness is largely based on a cost-revenue concept, a very short-range perspective, and may be quite different from economic reasonableness.

DEFINITIONS OF DEMAND AND SUPPLY

Demand is based on the purchaser's estimate of the value of a good or service; supply is based on the seller's estimate of the cost of making the good or service available. It is a commonly accepted truism that demand reacts with supply to determine prices, that demand establishes upper limits for prices, and that producers' costs (with a given demand situation) establish limits to the quantity that will be supplied. Since freight rates or passenger fares are prices for transportation services, these generalizations are as valid in transportation as in other forms of economic activity.

Like most truisms, however, those dealing with demand and supply describe only surface effects. To understand the workings of the described phenomena, it is necessary to probe into the depths. This and the following section will consider some deeper aspects of demand, and the final section of this chapter will more fully explore costs (supply) as related to the provision of transportation services.

First, it is necessary to have several definitions firmly in mind. The term *demand* as used by economists refers to the quantities of a good or service that would be purchased at all possible prices (just as *supply* means the quantities that would be offered for sale at all possible prices). An increase in demand, then, means that buyers are willing to purchase more than formerly at a given price or at all possible prices. Conversely, a decrease in demand means that buyers are no longer willing to purchase as much as before at any given price or prices. An example deals with the desirability of season tickets for a professional football team. As the team improves, there is a greater demand for season tickets at all prices. When the team's fortunes decline, there is less demand for tickets at all prices.

Sometimes one hears that "a decrease in price increases the demand, and visa versa." This is not correct, according to the above definitions. Actually, the correct statement should be that "a decrease (or increase) in price increases (or decreases) the quantity that people are willing to buy." Price changes as such do not increase or decrease demand.

Study of Figure 16.1 may further clarify these definitions and relationships. In that figure, the line SS is a supply curve or schedule showing how much sellers will be willing to provide at various prices, for example, two units at $2 and ten units at $4. The quantities that purchasers will buy at various prices are shown by the demand curve or schedule, line DD, ranging from two units at $7 to eight units at $2. The price that will just "clear the market" (where the quantity offered will equal the quantity purchasers are to buy) is at about $3.25. At this price, between six and seven units will be offered and bought. At lower prices, purchasers will be willing to buy more; but unless supply conditions change, sellers will not be willing to furnish more. Or at higher prices, sellers will make more available, but purchasers will not buy more.

Line D^1D^1 shows an increase in demand. Now, as can be seen, purchasers are willing to pay higher prices for the same quantities or to buy more at the original prices. A decrease in demand, which means that less can be sold at the original prices or that the original quantities can be sold only at lower prices, is shown by line D^2D^2. Changes in demand, increases or decreases, are caused basically either by changes in income levels (purchasing power) or by changes in consumer tastes or preferences, and these basic causes may be influenced by any number of factors.

Figure 16.1 Demand and Supply Schedules and Changes in Demand

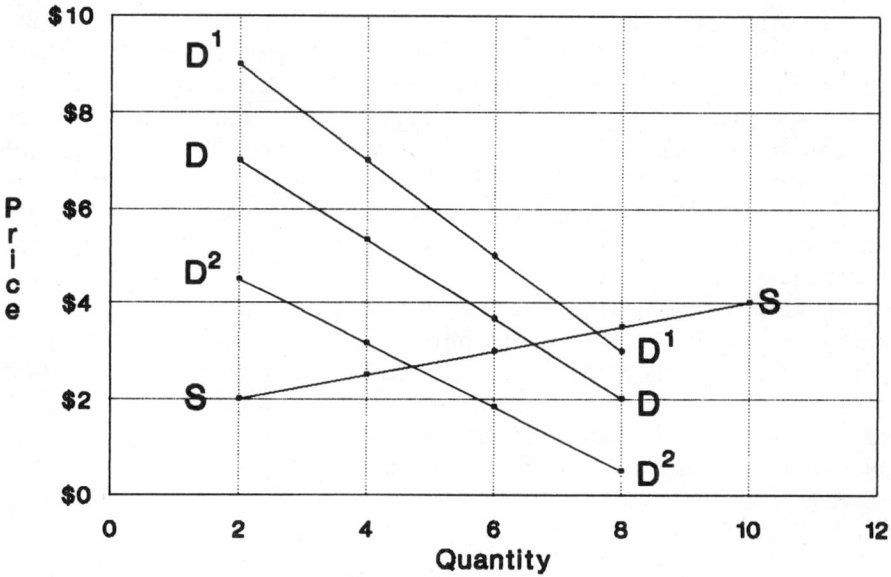

The incorrect statement to the effect that "demand varies with price" really recognizes, in a loose way, the important concepts economists label *elasticity* or *inelasticity* of demand. In normal pricing situations, it is almost always true (assuming that other things are equal or unchanged) that a price decrease encourages people to buy more and a price increase causes them to buy less.

Sellers usually are more interested in the effects of price changes on their revenues (and profits) than in the effects upon quantities sold as such. Sometimes a relatively small price decrease will generate so many additional sales that revenues will be substantially increased above their original level. Conversely, even a small price increase may reduce sales so much that revenues are significantly lowered. In these situations, it is said that demand is elastic. On the other hand, inelasticity of demand exists when a price increase results in increased total revenues or when a price decrease causes decreased revenues. Stated concisely, *total revenues vary inversely with price changes if demand is elastic, and directly with price changes if demand is inelastic.* Elasticity, unlike changes in demand itself, is purely a price phenomenon. Those who contemplate price changes should have some knowledge of the elasticity or inelasticity of demand for their product even if they are not acquainted with the economists' terminology.

Economists usually draw demand and supply curves as narrow lines as shown in Figure 16.1. This is convenient for exposition. In many situations, however, it may be more realistic to think of demand and supply curves as bands rather than narrow lines, as in Figure 16.2. For example, an individual who is willing to pay $4 for a given item also may be willing to buy the same item at $4.50 or $5. In other words, for each buyer there is a range of more or less equally acceptable prices that may or may not vary with conditions. These bands then create a zone of indeterminateness where the DD and SS schedules overlap. Within this zone, variations in price, production cost, or quantity have little or no effect on the other variables. The size of the zone will vary with products and marketing and cost conditions at any given time.

Before proceeding with a discussion of the nature of the demand for transportation, three other terms must be defined. *Aggregate demand* for transportation refers to the demand for services in general, that is, to the total of all of the individual demands for all services of all carriers. *Modal demand* means all demands for the services of a particular mode or form of carriage. *Particular demand* is used in referring to demands for the services of an individual carrier.

THE DEMAND FOR
TRANSPORTATION SERVICES

As already indicated, demand is related to value of service. But we might well ask, "value of service to whom?" There may be a social or community aggregate demand for transportation that is greater than the sum of the conscious individual demands; that is, all of us as a group may want more transportation facilities and services to be available than we are willing to pay for through our use of these services on an individual basis.

Figure 16.2 A "Zone" Concept of Demand and Supply

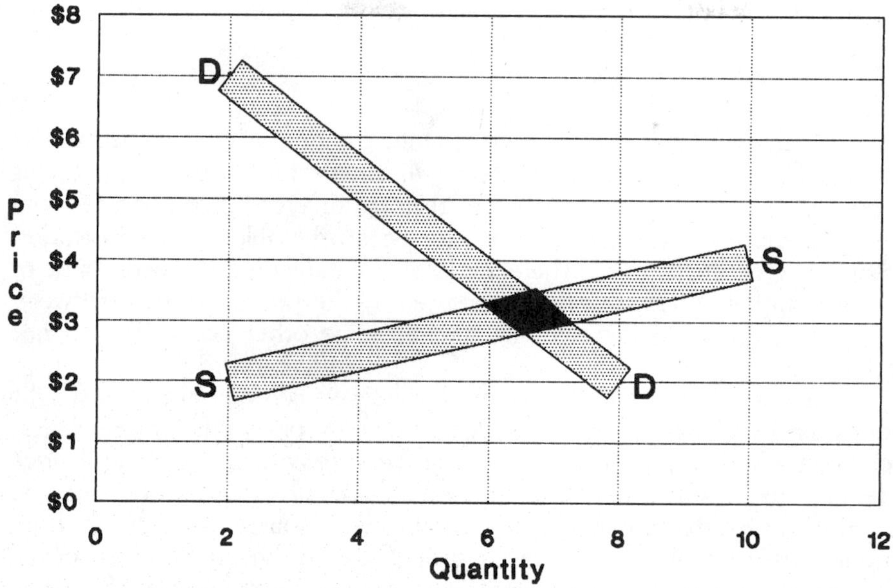

Demands of Society

The citizens of regions A and B may wish to have a highway or railway between their communities. For national defense or other reasons, a country may wish to maintain extensive commercial airline or merchant marine facilities. Or an underdeveloped nation, as our own country was a century ago, may desire expanded transport facilities to exploit latent natural resources or economic opportunities. But it may be that revenues from the actual or potential use of these facilities by private shippers or travelers is not sufficient to pay their costs. Still, society as a whole demands that these facilities and services be available, making the social demand higher than the sum of the individual user's demands.

If this social demand is to be met, the gap between what users are willing to pay for individual services and the revenues necessary to build, maintain, and operate the desired facilities must come from public subsidy. This may lead to at least a temporary excess of available services, or we might say that supply has outrun demand. Such a situation, in addition to creating a different allocation of resources than would exist in the absence of subsidy, may have a depressing effect on rates and revenues of unsubsidized forms of competing carriage. These effects are inevitable in meeting a social demand for excess capacity.

Demands of Individuals

Even from an individual user's viewpoint, it is not easy to determine the value of a transportation service. Long-distance transportation of goods is based primarily upon either inherent regional differences or upon regional specialization (which may or may not be attributable to transportation factors). One might think, therefore, that the individual shipper's value of transportation service could be measured by the price difference between its product at its point of origin and at some other point. This is not necessarily so.

Interregional price differences are as likely to be determined by freight rates as are freight rates to be determined by price differences. As an economist might say, "freight rates are both price determined and price determining." Many products sell at a standard price throughout the country even though freight rates from their points of origin to their numerous destinations may vary considerably. Much interregional cross-haulage of similar or identical products occurs between regions, often with few or no interregional price differences.

Strictly speaking, a shipper's value of service insofar as the transportation of a particular shipment is concerned is measured by the additional net revenue the shipper will receive if the shipment is made. Freight charges must be viewed alongside this revenue. If the freight charge is lower than the additional revenue, it will pay to make the shipment; if higher, it will not pay; if the two are identical, it becomes a matter of indifference.

Additional net revenue (or what economists sometimes call marginal revenue product or marginal value product) obviously is not the same as price times quantity, nor can it be precisely measured by calculations based upon interregional price differences (if any). Price is only a starting point. Additional net revenue from a shipment may be influenced by a shipper's (producer's) fixed versus variable cost situation, its existing inventory coupled with anticipated future market conditions, alternative opportunities for employing its resources, long-run considerations of customer good will and market development, and numerous other factors, all of which vary from shipper to shipper and over time. Even the shipper is not likely to know exactly how its additional net revenue will be affected by a given shipment. But as long as the shipper thinks it knows and acts accordingly, its demand for transportation is determined.

In view of the foregoing, it must be clear that a carrier, a group of carriers, or a regulatory agency cannot easily determine what freight rate or level of rates will maximize transportation revenues or attain any other objective. Factors determining the level and nature of the demand for transportation are complex and ever-changing. At best, only a reasonable approximation of an ideal rate structure can be expected. Nevertheless, it is possible to make some useful generalizations concerning the nature of transportation demand.

Determinants of the Degree of Elasticity

First, we must remember that the demand for freight transportation (and even for a considerable part of passenger transportation) is a *derived* demand; it is dependent upon or originates from the demand for the product being transported. No freight (and probably very few people) moves from place to place merely for the sake of movement. Thus, for products that are available or may be produced locally as well as brought in from more distant sources, it follows that the demand for transportation will be more elastic than the demand for the product itself. If the price of transporting a particular product is unduly high, or if its transportation rate is significantly increased, local sources of supply may be utilized even though production costs locally may be higher than in outside areas. Conversely, low or lowered rates may encourage outside shipments and discourage higher-cost local producers.

The aggregate demand for transportation, which grows out of the demands for all products, is closely related to the general level of economic activity. Thus it is relatively inelastic. Prosperity with high production, incomes, and purchasing power necessarily requires a great amount of transportation. Needs and demands for transport are not as great during depressed periods. Changes in general economic conditions, therefore, rather than changes in transportation prices as such, are of most importance in determining changes in the total quantity of transportation services used.

This does not mean that rate changes do not have some effects on aggregate transportation demand, during periods both of prosperity and of depression. As mentioned above, local production, which requires less transportation, may be stimulated by higher or discouraged by lower rates. But unless such rate changes are widespread and extreme in size, their impact on aggregate demand is likely to be minor.

The elasticity or inelasticity of modal demand is significantly affected by the availability, or the lack of availability, of other forms of carriage (in addition to the above-mentioned factors affecting aggregate demand). If only one form of carriage is available to, or suitable for, the transportation needs of a shipper, region, or type of traffic, we would expect to find a much greater degree of modal inelasticity than if alternate suitable modes of transport were available. Suitability is made up of many things, including type of equipment, routes, departure times and running time, reliability, pickup and delivery services, and other components of the transportation bundle.

The type and extent of intermodal competition faced may be quite important in shaping the rate structure of a given mode. For example, suppose that railroads are competing more keenly with trucks for short-haul than for long-haul traffic. Then if the railroads need additional revenues, it may be more practical from a demand viewpoint to make proportionately greater rate increases on long-haul than on short-haul movements. On the other hand, if transcontinental railroads are competing primarily with intercoastal water carriers, more of the additional revenues may have to be derived from short-haul or intermediate-haul traffic. This creates obvious problems for the railroads concerned if both kinds of competition exist!

The inelasticity or elasticity of a particular demand for transportation is influenced by the same factors that influence aggregate and modal demand. In addition, various kinds of business ties and arrangements and existing physical facilities of the shipper or its customer may be important. Such things may include purchasing reciprocity, particular kinds of loading and unloading docks and equipment, spur tracks, and similar items. Also, noncost or nonrational factors such as family ties, personal friendship, and even ignorance of alternate transportation facilities or shipper inertia often are important.

In review, it appears that of the three types of transportation demand we have considered, aggregate demand is least elastic (or more inelastic). Modal demand generally is next in order of elasticity, followed by particular demand, which is most elastic (or least inelastic) of the three. No doubt an informed observer can find exceptions to this generalization, as is true of all generalizations, but basically this seems to be the existing situation.

Several other general factors that contribute to the elasticity or inelasticity of all three types of demand should be mentioned. Demand is likely to be more inelastic (1) if the burden of increased rates (prices) can be passed on to an intermediate purchaser or final consumer (that is, if the demand for the product itself is extremely inelastic); (2) if the burden can be passed back to earlier production stages, as labor, or to the owners of land or natural resources; (3) if the shipper's or receiver's profit situation is such that higher rates can be absorbed easily; (4) when freight charges are only a small part of the total delivered cost (this condition may be found often with goods that are highly valuable in proportion to their bulk or weight); or (5) when freight rates are very low (demand usually is more elastic at higher than at lower price levels).

It is possible, also, because of tapering rate structures (see Chapter 17) which make the per-mile price of transportation significantly lower as the distance moved increases, that the demand for much long-haul transportation tends to be more inelastic than that for short-haul transport (again, because of a generally greater inelasticity at lower price levels). The evidence and logic are not quite as conclusive on this point as on the other five above-described situations. It may depend upon whether buyers think of transportation price increases or decreases in absolute dollars-and-cents terms or in terms of percentage increases or decreases in the total delivered price. It may be that this thinking varies among buyers and with the products concerned.

We have now looked at several factors that may contribute to inelasticity. Situations opposite those mentioned, of course, contribute to elasticity of demand.

It is difficult to develop empirical evidence of elasticity or inelasticity, and even more difficult to measure accurately the degree to which this condition exists in transportation. In the dynamic world of business and economics, a researcher cannot exclude alien elements as easily as can a chemist working with test tubes. The demand schedule itself may be shifting while rates are changing. There is a tendency for freight rates to increase during periods of high or rising levels of economic activity; thus aggregate traffic losses from price increases may be more than offset by a higher level of demand growing out of higher incomes and greater production. Also, rates of competing modes are likely to change in the same direction at about the same time, thereby minimizing the shift of traffic between modes as a result of rate changes.

Elasticity and inelasticity are more than matters of faith, although they are difficult to measure accurately. The nature of demand creates real problems for those involved with pricing carrier services, but its understanding also creates real opportunities. Demand stands on an equal footing with costs in determining what price level is economically sound.

TRANSPORTATION COSTS AND RATEMAKING

Everyone would agree that the costs of providing services determine an economically sound floor for rates. Costs are the underlying basis of the supply schedule described above. There is considerable disagreement, however, concerning just what costs are pertinent. Although it might seem at first that costs are more tangible and less controversial than demand, this is not always the case.

Fixed and Variable Costs

You will recall that a distinction between fixed or constant costs (those not varying with volume of output) and variable costs (which do vary with the quantity produced) was made in Chapter 4. This is a short-run distinction only, as all costs are variable in the long run. Chapters 4 and 5 discussed what is meant by short run and long run, as well as the differing fixed-variable cost relationships and operating ratios faced by each basic mode of transportation.

You know, too, that a firm that can cover its variable costs and have sufficient additional revenues to apply something toward its fixed costs will prefer to operate in this manner during the short run rather than cease operations entirely. In a competitive situation, then, this gives a short-run pricing advantage to firms having relatively high fixed costs as compared to some high variable-cost firms, assuming total costs are similar.

The following example demonstrates the short-run advantage falling to firms with high fixed costs. In this example, Firm A has a total fixed cost of $6,000 per month. These costs are related to such things as maintenance of its extensive and highly automated production facilities, service of its debt, and salaries for its management team. These costs must be covered if the firm is to continue to operate over the long run, but can be deferred or delayed in the short run. It is much like the case of periodic maintenance on your automobile — in the short run you can avoid periodic oil changes or wheel alignment, but in the long run these expenses (or alternates such as excessive engine repair or tire replacement) must be met. This firm has variable costs of $2 per unit of output it produces. These costs include such things as direct labor for manufacturing and the materials that make up each product. These costs must be covered in the short run, or operations will cease. Much the same thing will happen if you do not buy fuel for your automobile as you use it. When the firm produces 1,000 units of output in a month, it will incur total costs of $8,000 (fixed costs of $6,000 plus variable costs of $2,000).

The second firm, Firm B, has a very different cost structure. It is much less automated and incurs a fixed cost of only $2,000 per month. Its variable costs, possibly reflecting greater labor intensity, are much higher at $6 per unit. When this firm produces 1,000 units in a month, its total costs are also $8,000 (fixed costs of $2,000 and variable costs of $6,000).

Figure 16.3 graphically illustrates the cost characteristics of two firms. Firm A has a fixed cost (FC^1) of $6,000 and Firm B a fixed cost (FC^2) of only $2,000. Total variable costs for the two firms are represented by the areas between the total-cost lines (TC^1 and TC^2) and the fixed-cost lines. In the long run, each firm must generate $8,000 in revenues each month to cover its full costs for producing 1,000 units.

In the short run, however, Firm A has a distinct advantage. As long as it generates more than $2 per unit in revenue, it will be able to pay its laborers and purchase needed materials. Firm B, on the other hand, cannot afford to price its units at lower than $6 per unit to meet its short-run needs. This advantage can be seen more readily in the contribution approach cost curves shown in Figure 16.4. In this case, total variable costs are represented by lines VC^1 and VC^2. Total fixed costs make up the difference between the total-cost and variable-cost lines. It is easy to see that any revenue in excess of $2 per unit for Firm A and $6 per unit for Firm B will contribute to coverage of fixed costs.

Although accounting techniques often do not permit clear-cut distinctions between, or measures of, fixed and variable costs, there is little doubt that railroads (and pipelines) generally are characterized by high fixed costs as compared to motor, water, and air carriers. Also, as indicated in Chapter 4, railroad assets are long lived, giving that mode a long run of more calendar years than is found in other forms of carriage (again with the possible exception of pipelines). As many, perhaps most, competitive pricing decisions are made on a short-run basis, the implications are obvious.

Further, since the long run is made up of a series of short runs, it is equally obvious that price policies economically logical from a short-run viewpoint may never cover total costs, leading ultimately to bankruptcy or some form of subsidy. This is why regulatory agencies in establishing minimum rates sometimes say they are acting in the public's interest by protecting a carrier or mode of carriage from its own follies as well as protecting other carriers.

Out-of-Pocket Costs

Out-of-pocket costs is a term widely used in transportation circles often referring to the added costs incurred in performing an additional service. For example, it might be the cost added by increasing a 100-car freight train to a length of 101 cars, or of transporting another 100 pounds on a partially loaded truck. Economists would call this a marginal cost, but as generally used in the transportation industry, out-of-pocket cost is not as clearly defined as is the economists' term. Its meaning varies with the

Figure 16.3   Total Cost Curves for Two Firms

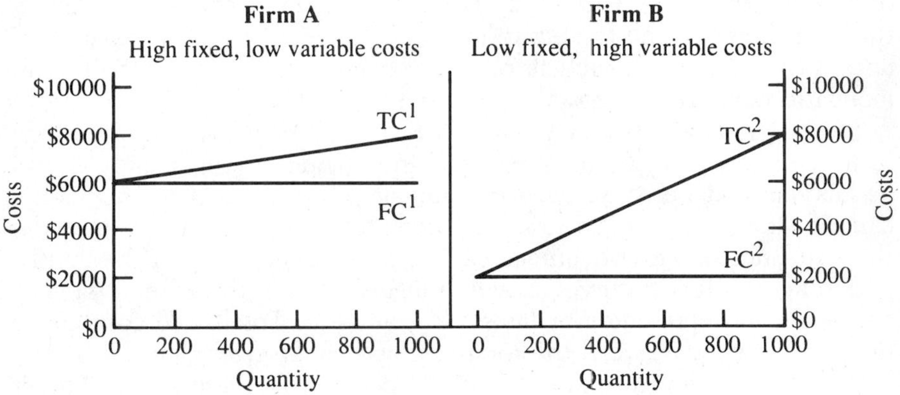

Firm A
High fixed, low variable costs

Firm B
Low fixed, high variable costs

speaker. It may actually mean marginal cost, average variable cost at some particular level of output, or one of those plus some additional arbitrary overhead amount to cover a portion of fixed costs.

Regardless of the meaning used, the analyses and arguments for and against out-of-pocket cost pricing are similar to those for variable-cost pricing discussed above. In the short run and with excess capacity, it does make sense to handle any additional traffic that does not increase direct costs as much as revenues. This type of pricing is best illustrated by the very low cost airline fares often introduced during off-peak travel periods. Any passengers enticed by these fares, and who would not be traveling otherwise, will contribute to overall carrier profitability. In the long run, however, it does not make much sense to replace capacity unless all costs associated with that capacity and its employment can be recovered.

Unallocable Costs

Common costs and joint costs arise out of situations in which two or more kinds of production or units of output are so interrelated that some costs cannot be allocated to either one on any rational economic basis. (As used by economists, common and joint costs are slightly different concepts — joint costs referring to a fixed proportion of by-product output — but their effects on costing decisions are the same.) Examples of unallocable costs include the line-haul costs related to transporting more than one type of product in a vehicle or the costs of hauling a

Figure 16.4   Contribution Approach Cost Curves

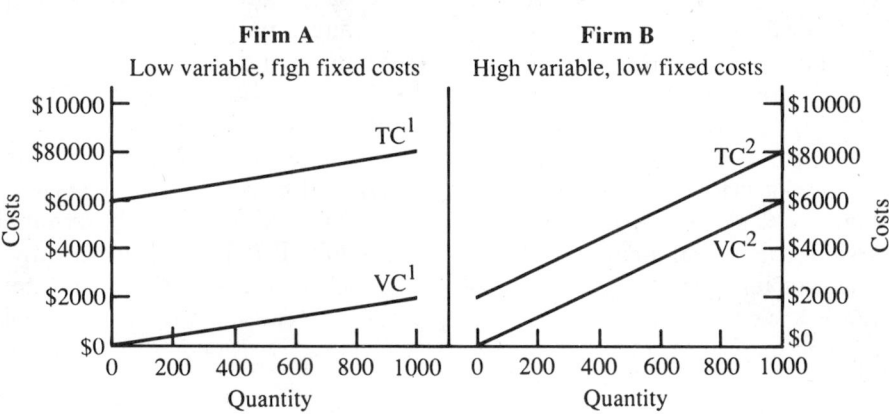

return load during a round-trip journey. The question lies in determining how much of the expense involved cannot be directly allocated to one product or movement.

Unfortunately, unallocable costs are very prevalent in transportation. When all costs of moving a particular shipment or type of traffic cannot be directly allocated to that traffic, however, it is not possible to base a price for this particular movement on its specific cost alone. The best that the rate maker can do is attempt to see that total revenues generated by all traffic involved in such common movements cover total costs. At worst, the rate maker must hope to cover the specifically allocable or direct costs.

Terminal and Line-Haul Costs

A carrier's operating costs are made up of terminal costs and line-haul costs, with elements of both fixed and variable costs in each. Terminal costs of a particular shipment, in addition to fixed costs, may include expenses for such operations as pickup, billing, and loading into a vehicle. Normally, terminal costs will be the same for a given shipment whether it moves for a long or a short distance. Line-haul costs, however, made up in considerable part of such variable items as wages and fuel costs, will be more or less proportionate to the distance hauled.

Terminal costs must be recovered quickly on short hauls, but they can be spread over many more miles on longer movements. This difference between long and short hauls frequently is reflected in tapering rate structures (see Chapter 17), that is, in higher per-mile rates on short than on long hauls. (Also, even though line-haul costs do increase with distance, they may or may not increase in direct proportion to mileage.) Further, even if line-haul costs are approximately the same, a carrier with high terminal costs will likely have higher rates on short hauls or a higher absolute minimum rate than a carrier with lower terminal costs.

Figure 16.5 illustrates the cost (and probable rate) structures of two firms, one with high and one with low terminal costs. Firm A is perhaps fairly typical of railroads, which generally have relatively high terminal costs, at least on small shipments, whereas firm B is more representative of lower terminal-cost motor carriers. This helps explain why trucks often have a significant pricing advantage over rail carriers in moving small shipments for short distances.

Cost of Service versus Value of Service

From the foregoing, it can be seen that costs are of equal importance with demand in establishing freight rates (or passenger fares) and that both are more complex than they appear at first. During recent years, there has been considerable controversy over the cost-of-service principle versus the value-of-service principle (sometimes called "charging what the traffic will bear") in ratemaking. During an earlier and less competitive era, value-of-service pricing was heavily favored by railroads. Losses on low-demand traffic could easily be offset by higher rates on high-demand movements. Today, though, when other forms of carriage are actively competing for the more valuable shipments, leaving commodities with a lower value of service for the rails, the value-of-service ratemaking concept is being questioned more and more.

The ICC has allowed competitive value-of-service rates, based on out-of-pocket or incremental costs, throughout most of its history. Sometimes this has resulted in traffic moving by rail (where out-of-pocket costs are relatively low) rather than by competing modes with lower total costs (including fixed costs) but higher out-of-pocket costs. The commission took a different stand, though, in the celebrated *Ingot Molds* case (*Ingot Molds, Pennsylvania to Steelton, Kentucky*, 323 ICC 758 and 326 ICC 77).

In that case, it was found that the total cost ("fully distributed cost," as defined by the commission) of the rail movement involved was higher than a combination water-truck movement cost, but that the out-of-pocket cost was lower. The full commission finally decided that the rail rate could not be lower than the total cost of the water-truck movement. This decision was upheld by the U.S. Supreme Court in 1968 (392 U.S. 571). This is an indication of how regulators have become much more cost-conscious in recent times.

Figure 16.5 Effects of Differing Terminal Costs

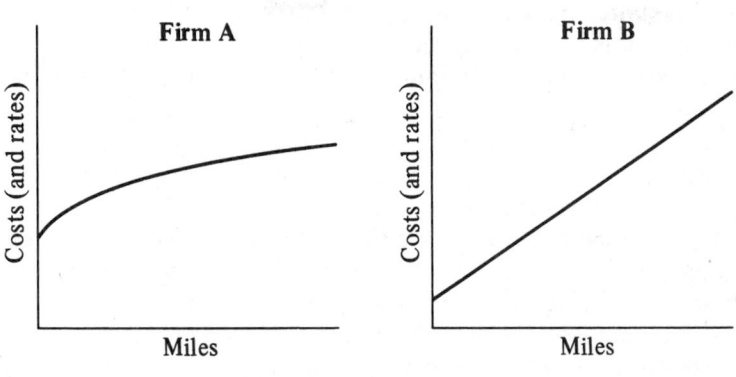

Total Cost versus Out-of-Pocket Cost

Carriers with relatively high variable and out-of-pocket costs (trucks, barge lines) tend to favor intermodal competitive rates based on total costs. Railroads, with relatively low variable and out-of-pocket costs, generally favor incremental cost pricing in intermodal competitive situations. Many economists, perhaps most, support the railroad position on the grounds that this leads to lower transportation prices. The U.S. Department of Transportation, almost since its formation, has advocated a more flexible ratemaking position for railroads (*flexible,* in this sense, means the ability to cut rates to meet or beat highway and waterway competition).

Certainly insofar as railroads have excess capacity and decreasing average per-unit costs with increasing traffic volume, rates based on out-of-pocket costs appear to be sound — at least until capacity adjustments can be made. This permits presently unused railroad capacity to be used at little additional cost and may increase railroad profits while lowering the nation's total freight bill considerably. Traffic diversion from trucks and barges might create temporary excess capacity in those modes, but both of these modes can adapt to capacity maladjustments more easily and quickly than can the railroads.

But the basic premise of railroad out-of-pocket cost pricing (excess capacity and decreasing costs) is at least questionable. Railroads do have overall excess track capacity, but much of this track is in very poor condition. And certainly no one would seriously argue that railroads have any general excess of freight cars, locomotives, centralized traffic controls, car location facilities, or modern freight yards and terminals. Can one rightly say, then, that an industry has excess capacity when expenditures of billions of dollars apparently are needed to enable it to handle its present volume of output satisfactorily?

It is quite possible that under present conditions the railroad industry is an increasing-cost industry rather than a decreasing-cost or a constant-cost industry. Much more unbiased empirical research, and less ax-grinding and opinion, is needed on this matter.

If railroads do not have excess capacity, the results of out-of-pocket cost competitive ratemaking are clear. Traffic moving at lower than total-cost rates must be subsidized — either by other (noncompetitive) traffic, government, or investors. But there may not be enough noncompetitive rail traffic to subsidize all the competitive traffic, and government subsidization is not compatible with a privately owned transportation system. Also, railroad investors as a group do not appear to be receiving handsome returns. It may be that too much out-of-pocket ratemaking, rather than too little, has contributed significantly to the sad financial state of many of the nation's railroads. What, then, can be done?

A few economists and others have advocated a gradual move toward *full-cost* pricing by railroads and other carriers. This means that a rate should include all the current direct or variable costs associated with a particular movement, plus all the indirect or fixed costs (including plant and equipment replacement costs) that will be incurred in the future as a result of the continuation of the movement.

This pricing concept emphasizes future investment costs rather than the historical costs of presently used plant and equipment. If all carriers priced on this basis, freight charges would reflect the true economic costs of transportation, and capital resources would be allocated optimally among carriers and carrier modes.

Such a full-cost pricing system does involve practical difficulties of cost estimation and allocation, and perhaps some elements of arbitrariness. But so does any other cost-based pricing system, present or proposed. This system is not more impractical or arbitrary than is the out-of-pocket cost system.

Conclusions on Cost-Based Rates

Neither value of service nor cost of service can be safely ignored in ratemaking, nor is it economically sound to overemphasize one at the expense of the other. Both demand and supply have a role in pricing. As stated earlier in this chapter, an economically practical freight rate is one that allows traffic to move (based on value of service), while at the same time covering the carrier's costs of movement (cost of service). If either of these criteria is not met, the carrier or the public, or both, may have a problem.

But whatever the relative role assigned to costs, there is still considerable dispute over what kind of cost is most appropriate for consideration in ratemaking. Many economists seem to have a fixation on marginal or out-of-pocket costs, carriers pursue their short-run traffic interests, shippers seek the lowest short-run freight charges, policy makers and regulators vary or are undecided, and the general public is indifferent or uninformed. There is general agreement that present transportation pricing methods could and should be improved. But major change always is difficult, especially when many conflicting viewpoints exist.

ADDITIONAL READINGS

Baumol, William J., et al., "The Role of Cost in the Minimum Pricing of Railroad Services," *Journal of Business* (October 1962), 1–10.
Bowersox, Donald J., Pat J. Calabro, and George D. Wagenheim, *Introduction to Transportation*, New York: Macmillan Publishing Co., 1981.
    Chapter 13, "Freight Rates," pp. 219–60.
Calmus, Thomas W., "Full Cost versus Incremental Cost: Again," *Transportation Journal* (Winter 1969), 31–36.
Coyle, John J., Edward J. Bardi, and Joseph L. Cavinato, *Transportation*, St. Paul: West Publishing Co., 1982.
    Chapter 12, "Cost and Pricing in Transportation," pp. 223–44.
Dean, Joel, "Competitive Pricing in Railroad Freight Rates," *Journal of Marketing* (April 1961), 22–27.
Fair, Marvin L., and Ernest W. Williams, *Transportation and Logistics*, Rev. ed., Plano, Texas: Business Publications, 1981.
    Chapter 16, "Principles of Rate Making," pp. 277–300.
Hazard, John L., *Transportation: Management, Economics, Policy*, Cambridge, Md.: Cornell Maritime Press, 1977.
    Chapter 2, "Transport Theory," pp. 34–64.
Jones, Eliot, *Principles of Railway Transportation*, New York: Macmillan Publishing Co., 1931.
    Chapter 4, "The Theory of Railroad Rates," pp. 34–64.
Lieb, Robert C., *Transportation*, 3rd ed., Reston, Va.: Reston Publishing Co., 1985.
    Chapter 9, "Cost and Demand in Intercity Transportation," pp. 181–99.
Locklin, D. Philip, *Economics of Transportation*, 7th ed., Homewood, Ill.: Richard D. Irwin, 1972.
    Chapter 7, "The Theory of Railroad Rates," pp. 142–70.
Nelson, James C., *Railroad Transportation and Public Policy*, Washington, D.C.: The Brookings Institution, 1959.
    Chapter 10, "Pricing Policies for Railroads," pp. 327–73.
Pegrum, Dudley F., *Transportation: Economics and Public Policy*, Homewood, Ill.: Richard D. Irwin, 1973.
    Chapter 10, "Theory of Pricing for Transport," pp. 164–85.

Roberts, Merrill J., "Railroad Maximum Rate and Discrimination Control," *Transportation Journal* (Spring 1983), 22–33.

Rose, Joseph R., "Limits on Marginal Cost Pricing," *Transportation Journal* (Winter 1964), 5–11.

Ruppenthal, Karl M., ed., *Issues in Transportation Economics*, Columbus, Ohio: Charles E. Merrill, 1965.

Section Six, "Transportation Pricing Theory," pp. 137–58.

Sampson, Roy J., "The Case for Full-Cost Ratemaking," *I.C.C. Practitioners' Journal* (March 1966), 49–62.

Waters, W. C. II., "Statistical Costing in Transportation," *Transportation Journal* (Spring 1976), 49–62.

Wood, Donald F., and James C. Johnson, *Contemporary Transportation*, 2nd ed., Tulsa, Okla.: PennWell Publishing Co., 1983.

Chapter 12, "Common Carrier Transportation Rates," pp. 535–70.

CHAPTER 17

RATEMAKING AND KINDS OF RATES

Despite their forbidding appearance, the transportation publications known as *classifications* and *tariffs* actually are simplifications. There may be as many as 2 million different kinds of commodities subject to transportation in the United States, and every one of these items conceivably is subject to transport between any two of thousands of origin and destination points. Further, in moving from origin to destination, an exceedingly large number of alternate routes may be used. For example, the House Committee on Interstate and Foreign Commerce once reported that there were more than 4,700,000 possible rail routes between Dallas, Texas, and Detroit, Michigan.

In selling their services, transportation companies must establish prices on all the items they carry between any of the points and by any of the routes served. If you calculate the astronomical number of individual prices required to do this and compare your findings with the relatively small number of items (at most, a few thousand) contained in the thickest classifications and tariffs, you will appreciate the tremendous simplification involved.

THE PREPARATION AND USE OF CLASSIFICATIONS

The first step in pricing a shipment is to determine what is to be shipped. This is the purpose of classification. Each of the hundreds of thousands of shippable commodities, from aardvarks to zymometers, is placed (classed or classified) in some one of a relatively small number of classes. Then, instead of shipping a commodity, in effect one ships a certain quantity of a certain class. In the basic railroad classification, all goods are reduced to about thirty-one classes. This might be compared to sorting potatoes. Every potato falling into a certain grade (that is, with similar characteristics) is placed in a bag with other like potatoes (the classification), and all the potatoes in a particular bag are priced alike.

Development and Present Status of Classifications

Classifications originally were developed by railroads, and rail classifications still are more extensive and comprehensive than those used by other modes of carriage. The following discussion will emphasize railroad classifications, pointing out the necessary differences between railway and other carrier practices.

Originally there were many railroad classifications in use, usually one for each major railroad. This was confusing. As rail transportation grew, however, these eventually were combined into one of three major classifications (Official or Eastern; Southern; and Western) based on the territories primarily served by the participating railroads, plus a few minor or special classifications. The Illinois Classification was one of the best known of the minor group. The same commodity often was classed differently, had different minimum weights distinguishing between CL (carload) and LCL (less than carload) shipments, and had differing rules for packaging in each of the several classifications.

Government operation of railroads during World War I clearly showed the need for and the benefits of more rail cooperation. The three major classifications were published together in one volume (the Consolidated Freight Classification) in 1919, and the Illinois Classification was added a few years later. This was a major step forward, and yet each of the separate classifications retained its own identity. Opposite the description of each commodity, the classification applicable in each of the respective classification territories was shown in separate columns. In 1952, after considerable pressure from the ICC, all railroads went over to the present Uniform Freight Classification, which applies the same classification to a commodity regardless of territory. The Uniform Classification Committee, with headquarters in Chicago, replaced the regional Official, Southern, and Western Classification committees in 1964.

The present uniform railroad classification is made up of thirty-one numbered classes, with the old first class of the Consolidated Classification now being class 100. Other classes are based on multiples or fractions of class 100, expressed in percentage terms, ranging from class 400 to class 13.

The format of the published classification consists of rules and regulations for its use and of the classes themselves. Commodities are listed alphabetically and described, and the pertinent class is shown with minimum weights. Class rates based on these classifications are higher or lower as the classifications go up or down numerically. (In the Consolidated Classification, however, lower numbers mean higher rates.)

The format and arrangement of motor carrier classifications are similar to that used by the rails. There is less uniformity in truck practices, however, as not all trucking companies use the National Motor Freight Classification. Ocean-water carriage rates usually are quoted on a "weight or space, whichever gives the highest charge" basis, whereas domestic water carriers often use the rail or motor carrier classifications. Pipelines that carry only one commodity have no classification problems. Classification practice is in its infancy in the air-freight business, with no generally used uniform national classifications. Freight forwarders use motor or rail classifications as appropriate to their mode of line-haul movement.

Classification Committee Procedures

Procedures employed by rail and motor carrier classification committees are approximately the same. Typically, a shipper (or a carrier) will propose that an existing commodity be reclassified or that a new product be brought into the classification. This proposal must be in the form specified by the rules of the committee. If it appears to be in order, it is docketed (scheduled for discussion). After adequate notice to the industry by publication in specified traffic journals and distribution of dockets to interested parties, a public hearing is held. Proponents and opponents of the proposal are heard, and the committee then votes. After a specified waiting period for objections to or appeals from the decision, the docket is closed. If the action taken results in a change in or an addition to the classification, the committee's publishing agent is notified and the revision is made.

Under some circumstances, a carrier or group of carriers serving a particular area will request permission to deviate from the established classification rate for some commodity or commodities. If approved, these deviations are published as exceptions to the classification for the carriers or areas.

What do the committees consider in establishing a classification for a particular commodity? Extensive lists of considerations have been developed, but four things are of most importance. First, the costs of transporting the good must be considered. This involves such characteristics as density (weight and size), shape, ease of handling, and susceptibility to loss or damage. The second consideration is the value of the service to the shipper, or what the traffic will bear. The third is the potential volume of the movement, as well as the direction and the origin and destination of the principal flow of traffic. Fourth is the competitive situation between carriers, modes of carriage, and intraregional and interregional producer and market competition. These factors and other considerations can be reduced to cost of service and value of service.

In 1983, the ICC ruled that only four factors can be considered in motor carrier freight classification. These are density, stowability (including unusual lengths or sizes), ease or difficulty of handling, and potential liability (damage to other goods, perishability, susceptibility to theft). The commission did not specify any relative weights or rankings for these four factors. This ruling seems to stress cost of service and de-emphasize value of service. Significantly, it does not allow different classifications based upon the quantity of goods shipped (TL versus LTL), although this may be recognized in the ratemaking process.

Many commodities are classified by comparison with commodities possessing similar transportation characteristics, that is, by analogy. In fact, pending the establishment of a specific classification, shippers may use the analogy rule for movements, and an unclassed article will be shipped at the class and rate applicable to some similar item.

Classification is a never-ending process, and classification committees and their publishing agents are quite busy. Shippers constantly demand lower classifications for their products in order to benefit from lower freight rates. Carriers want higher classifications for increased revenues (if they feel that demand is inelastic) or lower classifications to meet competition from other modes. Numerous new commodities are being developed each day, all of which eventually may require classification. A page from the railroad *Uniform Freight Classification* is shown in Figure 17.1.

As stated above, classification is merely the first step in establishing or determining the price for transporting a commodity. The classification tells only what is being shipped. In order to determine the price for moving it from one point to another, one must resort to a tariff.

KINDS OF TARIFFS AND THEIR USE

Simply speaking, a tariff is a price list. The word *tariff* was derived from an Arabic word meaning explanation or information. It explains or gives information on shipping prices (freight rates).

In the strict sense, any type of carrier publication having to do with prices or charges may properly be called a tariff. This would include classifications, passenger fare tables, routing guides, and similar publications. As commonly used, however, and as used in this book, the term *tariff* refers to publications quoting freight rates.

Basically, there are three kinds of freight tariffs: (1) class tariffs (and modifications of these called exceptions tariffs), (2) commodity tariffs, and (3) services tariffs. These will be discussed in this order. Then the general format and use of tariffs will be briefly described.

Figure 17.1   Page From the Uniform Freight Classification

Item	ARTICLES	Less Carload Ratings	Carload Minimum (Pounds)	Carload Ratings
2000	**ABRASIVES:**			
2010	Abrasive cloth or paper, including emery or sand paper, in packages	55	36,000	37½
2020	Corundum, emery or other natural or synthetic abrasive material consisting chiefly of aluminum oxide or silicon carbide:			
2030	Crude or lump, LCL, in bags, barrels or boxes; CL, in bulk or in packages	55	50,000	27½
2040	Flour or grain, in packages	55	36,000	35
2050	Refuse, including broken wheels, wheel stubs or wheel grindings, loose, see Note, Item 2051, or in packages	55	50,000	20
2051	Note.—LCL shipments may be loose only in lots of 10,000 lbs., subject to minimum charge as for 10,000 lbs.; shipments to be loaded by shipper and unloaded by consignee; shipper to furnish and install all dunnage and packing material; freight charges to be assessed on basis of gross weight of article and all dunnage or packing material.			
2060	Wheels, other than pulp grinding, in barrels, boxes or crates, or on skids if weighing each 300 lbs. or over; also CL, loose packed in packing material	55	30,000	40
2070	Wheels, pulp grinding, in boxes or crates, or on skids	55	30,000	40
2085	**ACIDS (see also Item 33800):**			
2090	Abietic, in barrels or in Package 84	55	40,000	22½
2100	Acetic, glacial or liquid:			
	In carboys, other than Package 800	100	30,000	45
	In glass in barrels or boxes or in Packages 514 or 800	77½	30,000	40
	In bulk in barrels or in Package 595; also CL, in tank cars, Rule 35	70	30,000	40
2110	Acetylsalicylic, in barrels, boxes or Package 1157	85	30,000	45
2120	Acids, noibn, dry:			
	In glass or in cans or cartons in barrels or boxes	92½	30,000	55
	In bulk in barrels, boxes, steel pails or 5-ply paper bags, or Benzoic acid or Fumaric acid in Package 1380	85	30,000	50
2130	Acids, noibn, liquid:			
	In carboys	100	30,000	60
	In glass in barrels, boxes or Package 514	92½	30,000	55
	In bulk in barrels; also CL, in tank cars, Rule 35	85	36,000	50
2135	Adipic, in bulk in barrels, boxes, steel pails or 5-ply multiple-wall paper bags, or Packages 1171, 1217 or 1380; also CL, in bulk in covered hopper cars, Rule 37, see Note, Item 2136	65	30,000	30
2136	Note.—Minimum weight on shipments in covered hopper cars will be marked capacity of the car, except when shipper certifies on bill of lading that car has been loaded to 90% of full visible capacity freight charges will be assessed on basis of actual weight.			
2140	Arsenic, fused, in barrels or boxes, or in bars wrapped in paraffined paper in wooden boxes only	70	36,000	37½
2150	Arsenic, other than fused:			
	In carboys	100	30,000	45
	In barrels; also CL, in tank cars, Rule 35	70	36,000	37½
2160	Azelaic, from animal or vegetable fats, in bags, barrels or boxes	65	30,000	30
2170	Boric (boracic)			
	In glass in barrels or boxes	85	30,000	45
	In cans or cartons in barrels or boxes, or in bulk in bags, barrels, boxes or steel pails; also CL, in double-wall paper bags or in bulk	70	36,000	35
2180	Carbolic (phenol):			
	In carboys	100	30,000	55
	In glass or in metal cans in barrels or boxes	77½	30,000	40
	In bulk in barrels, or in metal drums in barrels or boxes, or in Package 598; also CL, in tank cars, Rule 35	70	36,000	37½
2190	Chlorosulfonic, in bulk in barrels; also CL, in tank cars, Rule 35	60	36,000	35
2200	Chromic:			
	In glass or in metal cans in barrels or boxes, or in Package 800	85	30,000	45
	In bulk in steel barrels	70	36,000	37½
2205	Citric, dry:			
	In inner containers in barrels or boxes	85	30,000	45
	In bulk in barrels, in 5-ply multiple-wall paper bags or in Package 1388	70	30,000	40
2210	Cresylic (cresol):			
	In glass or in metal cans in barrels or boxes	77½	30,000	40
	In bulk in barrels; also CL, in tank cars, Rule 35	70	36,000	37½
2215	Decanedioic, in barrels, boxes, pails, or 5-ply multiple-wall paper bags	65	30,000	30
2220	Electrolyte, containing not to exceed 47% sulphuric acid:			
	In carboys, other than Package 800	100	30,000	45
	In inner containers in barrels or boxes, or in Package 800	70	30,000	40
	In lined barrels or rubber drums	60	30,000	35
2230	Fluophosphoric, in bulk in barrels; also CL, in tank cars, Rule 35	70	36,000	37½
2240	Formic:			
	In carboys, other than Package 800	100	30,000	35
	In glass in barrels or boxes or in Package 300	85	30,000	35
	In bulk in barrels; also CL, in tank cars, Rule 35	70	30,000	35
2250	Gluconic, liquid:			
	In carboys	100	30,000	60
	In bulk in barrels; also CL, in tank cars, Rule 35	85	36,000	50
2260	Hydrocyanic, in glass or metal cans in barrels or boxes, or in steel cylinders; also CL, in tank cars, Rule 35	85	30,000	45
2270	Hydrofluoric:			
	In containers in barrels or boxes, in steel jacketed lead carboys, or in Package 800	85	36,000	45
	In bulk in barrels or rubber drums, or in steel cylinders; also CL, in tank Rule 35	70	36,000	37½
2280	Hydrofluoric and sulphuric, mixed, in bulk, in metal barrels; also CL, in tank cars, Rule 35	70	36,000	35
2290	Hydrofluosilicic:			
	In carboys	100	36,000	45
	In containers in barrels or boxes	85	36,000	45
	In bulk in barrels or rubber drums; also CL, in tank cars, Rule 35	70	36,000	37½

Source: Uniform Classification Committee

Class Tariffs

The class tariff is the most basic type of freight-rate tariff in that it supposedly includes the price of shipping everything from and to everywhere (subject, of course, to the limitations of the geographical areas served by the carriers participating in the tariff and the kinds of commodities they offer to haul). It can only be used in conjunction with a classification; that is, one must first look up an item in the classification to determine its class. Then one must use the class tariff (which shows only the prices of moving classes, not named commodities) to determine the rate (usually given in cents per 100 pounds) for transporting items in this particular class from one point to another.

Since class tariffs typically cover shipments from and to a large number of specific points, some further simplification is necessary. Usually the points of origin and destination themselves are assembled into several groups which are identified by numerical or alphabetical symbols. Thus, instead of shipping widgets from the city of Mohawk to the city of Marcola, in effect one ships class 40 from group C-1 to group A-2. This grouping of points obviously greatly decreases the number of entries in a tariff, but makes its use somewhat more complex. A portion of a railroad class tariff is shown in Figure 17.2.

Class rates may properly be called distance-scale rates. Although they generally do not increase in direct proportion to the distance hauled, there is certainly a demonstrable relationship between rate level and distance. This tendency has become more pronounced during the past several decades.

Exceptions tariffs, as indicated above, are modified class tariffs. That is, although the classification still is used, certain specified items between specified points or in specifically named areas move at rates different from those shown in the basic class tariff. These modifications or exceptions usually are made for competitive reasons or for peculiar regional or local operating conditions.

Commodity Tariffs

Commodity tariffs differ from class tariffs in that they cover only the specific items and the specific movements named in the tariff. As items are listed by name and described in the commodity tariff, it is not necessary to use the classification in looking up a rate.

Commodity rates generally are established on products that move in large quantities between specific points. They do not necessarily apply in both directions; a commodity rate on widgets may exist from Mohawk to

Figure 17.2 Portions of a Railroad Class Tariff

SECTION 1—PART A—APPLICATION OF RATE BASES

Item	BETWEEN (See Item 110) AND Points on pages 123 to 203 in following Groups (See Item 110)	NORTH COAST TERRITORY (See Item 215)				SOUTH COAST TERRITORY (See Item 220)				
		NORTH COAST	CASCADE	PRAIRIE OR VALLEY	SPOKANE	SOUTH COAST	KELSO	SIERRA	NIPTON	LAS VEGAS OR RENO
		RATE BASES APPLICABLE (For rates, see Section 2)								
675	A............	995	956	915	878	995	956	936	915	878
	B............	912	875	840	805	912	875	858	840	805
	C, C-1......	870	836	801	768	870	836	819	801	768
	D............	829	796	763	731	829	796	780	763	731
	E............	787	756	725	695	787	756	741	725	695
	E-1..........	787	756	725	695	....				
	F............	746	717	686	658	746	717	702	686	658
	G............	705	677	649	622	705	677	663	649	622
	H............	829	796	763	731	705	677	663	649	622
	I............	663	636	611	585	③663	③636	624	③611	③585
	J............	639	613	588	563	③639	③613	601	③588	③563
	J-1..........	{①639 / ②705	613	588	563	....				
	J-E..........	{①590 / ②673	561	533	505	....				
	K, K-1......	995	956	915	878	995	956	936	915	878
	L............	912	875	840	805	912	875	858	840	805
	M............	870	836	801	768	870	836	819	801	768
	N............	779	748	718	686	....				

①Applies only from or to points in North Coast Territory in Washington and British Columbia; also points in Oregon named in National Rate Basis Tariff 1-A as taking Bonneville, Condon, Dike, Heppner, Kent, Portland, Rainier and The Dalles basis for rates.

②Applies from or to points in California and Oregon other than those included in "①" above.

③(a) Not applicable BETWEEN California and Nevada on the one hand AND New Mexico and Texas points on the other included in key groups shown in Items 700 to 979.

(b) Arbitraries referred to opposite the California points, pages 17 to 72 of this tariff, in Column headed "Basis Applicable" are NOT to be added to Items 700 to 979.

SECTION 2
CLASS RATES IN CENTS PER 100 POUNDS

RATE BASES NUMBERS	400	300	250	200	175	150	125	110	100	92½	85	77½	70	65	60	55
693..........	3172	2379	1983	1586	1388	1190	991	872	793	734	674	615	555	515	476	436
694..........	3176	2382	1985	1588	1390	1191	993	873	794	734	675	615	556	516	476	437
695..........	3180	2385	1988	1590	1391	1193	994	875	795	735	676	616	557	517	477	437
696..........	3188	2391	1993	1594	1395	1196	996	877	797	737	677	618	558	518	478	438
697..........	3192	2394	1995	1596	1397	1197	998	878	798	738	678	618	559	519	479	439
698..........	3196	2397	1998	1598	1398	1199	999	879	799	739	679	619	559	519	479	439
699..........	3200	2400	2000	1600	1400	1200	1000	880	800	740	680	620	560	520	480	440
700..........	3204	2403	2003	1602	1402	1202	1001	881	801	741	681	621	561	521	481	441
701..........	3208	2406	2005	1604	1404	1203	1003	882	802	742	682	622	561	521	481	441
702..........	3212	2409	2008	1606	1405	1205	1004	883	803	743	683	622	562	522	482	442
703..........	3216	2412	2010	1608	1407	1206	1005	884	804	744	683	623	563	523	482	442
704..........	3220	2415	2013	1610	1409	1208	1006	886	805	745	684	624	564	523	483	443
705..........	3228	2418	2018	1614	1412	1211	1009	888	807	746	686	625	565	525	484	444
706..........	3232	2424	2020	1616	1414	1212	1010	889	808	747	687	626	566	525	485	444
707..........	3236	2427	2023	1618	1416	1214	1011	890	809	748	688	627	566	526	485	445
708..........	3240	2430	2025	1620	1418	1215	1013	891	810	749	689	628	567	527	486	446
709..........	3244	2433	2028	1622	1419	1217	1014	892	811	750	689	629	568	527	487	446
710..........	3248	2436	2030	1624	1421	1218	1015	893	812	751	690	629	568	528	487	447
711..........	3252	2439	2033	1626	1423	1220	1016	894	813	752	691	630	569	528	488	447
712..........	3256	2442	2035	1628	1425	1221	1018	895	814	753	692	631	570	529	488	448
713..........	3264	2448	2040	1632	1428	1224	1020	898	816	755	694	632	571	530	490	449
714..........	3268	2451	2043	1634	1430	1226	1021	899	817	756	694	633	572	531	490	449
715..........	3272	2454	2045	1636	1432	1227	1023	900	818	757	695	634	573	532	491	450
716..........	3276	2457	2048	1638	1433	1229	1024	901	819	758	696	635	573	532	491	450
717..........	3280	2460	2050	1640	1435	1230	1025	902	820	759	697	636	574	533	492	451

Source: Trans-Continental Freight Bureau.

Marcola but not from Marcola to Mohawk. Also, specific named routings may be required. Like class tariffs, commodity tariffs often make extensive use of groupings of points of origin and destination and even of similar commodities. Sometimes the two forms of tariff are published together in a single volume as a class and commodity tariff, but usually commodity tariffs are separate publications. Often a separate commodity tariff will be published for a specific product such as coal or lumber, for example. Sometimes, though, commodity tariffs will include several types of products. These rates generally are less related to distance moved than are class rates. A page from a railroad commodity tariff is shown in Figure 17.3.

Since commodity rates are established for special movements, they usually are lower than and take precedence over class rates. (A shipper normally is legally entitled to use the lowest published rate for a movement regardless of where it is published.) In reality, however, it is somewhat misleading to think of commodity rates as special deviations from class rates. Actually, the great bulk of freight tonnage and ton-mileage both by rail and truck moves under commodity rates. (At one time perhaps more than 95 percent of rail tonnage in the country as a whole moved as commodity tonnage.) The commodity-rate tail wags the class-rate dog.

Services Tariffs

A considerable number of carrier services other than line-haul movement may be included in the transportation bundle (see Chapter 16). Some or all of these services may be included in the carrier's line-haul rate. On the other hand, additional charges may be made for various kinds of additional services such as switching, storage, icing, or diversion in transit. As all charges collected by a carrier must be based on published tariff rates, a variety of services tariffs are used for this purpose. Compared with rate tariffs, these services tariffs are fairly straightforward and easy to understand.

General Tariff Format and Use

General format of interstate tariffs is subject to ICC prescription or approval. Although this format varies in detail and complexity from tariff to tariff, in general all show in fairly uniform order such things as who issued the tariff; what tariff, if any, is replaced by it; what kinds of commodities and what geographical areas are included in its coverage; a

Figure 17.3 Page From a Railroad Commodity Tariff

SECTION 1—MISCELLANEOUS COMMODITY RATES				
ITEM	ARTICLES	FROM	TO	RATES In Cents per 100 lbs (Except as noted) / WESTERN GATEWAYS (See Item 9805)

ITEM	ARTICLES	FROM	TO	RATES In Cents per 100 lbs (Except as noted)	WESTERN GATEWAYS (See Item 9805)
962	Aluminum can stock, for can manufacture, not further processed than degreased, relubricated, coated, trimmed and sheared, not thinner than U. S. Standard Gauge 38 or thicker than U. S. Standard Gauge 24, in straight lengths not less than 20 inches, nor more than 40 inches in length or width, or in coils, commercially known as "Aluminum Can Stock", in packages or on platforms. ⓐMin CL wt 65,000 lbs. ⓑMin CL wt 80,000 lbs. ⓒMin CL wt 100,000 lbs.	Torrance......Cal. Trentwood....Wash.	Points taking following Group Rates (See Item 555): C (In Ky.), C-3,L, L-1,M,M-1 D,D-1,D-3,D-4,E, E-1,E-2,E-3,E-4, E-5,E-6,F,G,H,I, J,N K,K-2............ K-1..............	ⓐ149 ⓑ120 ⓒ187 ⓐ202 ⓑ187	Via Gateways shown opposite point of origin in TCFB Territorial Directory. (See Item 490)
963	Aluminum sheet, lengths of, semi-finished, in coils, requiring further rolling. Min CL wt 100,000 lbs. ⓐRates in cents per 2,000 lbs. ⓑThe provisions of Rule 24 of Uniform Classification or Exceptions thereto and Paragraph 2 of Part 1 of Item 545 do not apply. ⓒSubject to Item 9835.	Riverside......Cal. Torrance......Cal. Trentwood....Wash.	Points taking the following Group rates (See Item 555): B,B-1,C C-1,C-2,C-3,C-4,D, D-1,D-3,D-4, E,E-1,E-2,E-3, E-4,E-5,E-6,F, G,H,I,J,N	ⓐⓑ3412 ⓐ3412	Via Gateways shown opposite point of origin in TCFB Territorial Directory. (See Item 490)
		Points taking Rate Basis 1 or 4 rates (See Item 560)....	A,A-1......... K,K-2.........	ⓐⓑ3859 ⓐ3859	
965	(See Note 2) Aluminum or Aluminum Articles, viz.: Angles, Bars, Beams, Channels, Molding or Tees, Blanks, Stampings or Unfinished Shapes, flat, in packages, Extrusions, noibn, loose or in packages, Fittings, pipe, in crates, Forms, structural, noibn, fabricated from bars, plate or shapes ⅜ inch or thicker (See Note 4), Pipe (Subject to Note 1), Rods, in packages, Tubing (Subject to Note 1), Window and Window Frame Sections, unfinished. In straight or mixed carloads. Min CL wt 30,000 lbs. Note 1.—Shipments from Phoenix, Ariz., are entitled to storage-in-transit privileges as authorized in tariffs of individual lines, parties hereto and lawfully on file with the Interstate Commerce Commission. Note 2.—Shipments are entitled to partial unloading in transit privileges as authorized in tariffs of individual lines, parties hereto, and lawfully on file with the Interstate Commerce Commission.	Phoenix......Ariz. Spokane....Wash. Trentwood....Wash.	Points taking following Group rates (See Item 555): A A-1,ⓐK,ⓐK-2..... B,C,M-1 B-1,L,L-1,M C-1,C-4 C-2,C-3 D,D-1,D-3,D-4,E-1, E-2,N E,E-3,E-4,E-5,E-6.. F,G,I,J H .... K-1..............	289 281 257 ⓐ251 236 230 223 213 201 ⓐ223 ⓐ201 303	Via Gateways shown opposite point of origin in TCFB Territorial Directory. (See Item 490)
		Riverside......Cal. Torrance......Cal.	A A-1,ⓐK,ⓐK-2..... B,C,M-1 B-1,L,L-1,M C-1,C-4 C-2,C-3 D,D-1,D-3,D-4 E,E-3,E-4,E-5,E-6.. F,G,H,I,J K-1..............	311 303 279 ⓐ273 258 252 245 235 223 325	

Note 4.—Aluminum structural forms may be made partly from iron or steel not to exceed thirty percent by weight and not in excess of ten percent of the total weight may consist of bronze or brass bushings or shims.

ⓐApplies from Spokane and Trentwood, Wash.

ⓑApplies from Phoenix, Ariz.

ⓒSubject to Note 53, Item 9815.

Source: Trans-Continental Freight Bureau

table of contents; a list of participating carriers; indexes of the specific commodities and points included; explanations of the abbreviations and symbols used; rules for using the tariff; routing instructions and restrictions, if any; and the actual charges applicable.

As it is expensive and time consuming to publish a large tariff, but since the rate changes occur frequently, some provision must be made to keep tariffs up to date. This is handled by the publication of supplements as minor changes take place. These supplements must be checked by the tariff user in order to make certain that he or she is using the latest legal rate. Eventually, when an existing tariff is republished under a new number, all changes to date are incorporated in it.

One can understand what a tariff is, why it is necessary, and a little of how to use it by reading about the subject. For those actually using tariffs, however, there is no substitute for experience, and there are few if any short cuts. You know that in order to find the applicable rate on a particular movement it may be necessary to consult a commodity tariff, a classification, a class tariff, an exception tariff, and all current supplements. All these may appear to be formidable documents.

The novice tariff user should not become discouraged too easily, however. Anyone with a basic understanding of tariffs and average intelligence and reading ability can look up a rate. (It will take years to become an expert, however, and even the experts sometimes make mistakes.) For the beginner, a law of increasing returns seems to apply; as one uses a tariff more and more, it becomes increasingly easy to find new rates. Also one who has developed some proficiency in using one reasonably complex tariff can very quickly learn to use an entirely different one.

Fortunately, most shippers are concerned with a relatively small number of products, and these may move from one origin to only a few destinations. If this is so, the shipper can very easily reduce rate work to a routine by preparing a system of rate cards, rate sheets, or rate maps from the pertinent tariffs. Sometimes this is done by trade associations for their members or for branch plants by a headquarters traffic office.

One can always ask the carrier for rate information, of course. This is the procedure usually followed by those who ship infrequently. Large and frequent shippers like to have rate information at their fingertips, however, to aid in quoting customer prices quickly, to expedite paperwork connected with their shipments, and to eliminate the delays and inconveniences of continual calls to carrier rate clerks. Also, carriers, like shippers, sometimes make mistakes.

Carrier and shipper rate errors sometimes can amount to significant sums over a period of time. For this reason, many large companies maintain an internal staff of freight-rate auditors to look for overpayments and apply to carriers for refunds. Small shippers (and some large ones) often use the services of independent freight-rate audit bureaus or firms, which usually charge a percentage of the recovery, for the same purpose.

MAKING OR CHANGING RATES

Until recently, almost all common-carrier rates for railroads, trucks, and barges were mechanically handled and published for carriers by their rate bureaus (or traffic associations). These are carrier-maintained organizations for joining action in establishing prices within a specified geographic area or region. Such a joint pricing activity has been illegal for businesses in general under the antitrust laws since passage of the Sherman Antitrust Act in 1890. Carriers subject to ICC regulation, however, have generally been exempted from these laws under conditions prescribed by the commission. Intrastate traffic has likewise been exempted if subject to approved state regulatory agencies and procedures.

Bureau ratemaking received a severe blow from the regulatory reform acts of the late 1970s and the 1980s. Many of the antitrust exemptions for collective ratemaking were eliminated or tightened up, and all of them may eventually be eliminated. Without the antitrust exemptions, collective ratemaking is not possible because of the Sherman Act. Rate bureaus might remain in business as publishing agents for individual carriers, but their functions would be greatly altered.

Many more rates have been made by individual carriers since the early 1980s. Even today, most of the major rate bureaus (about ten railroad, a dozen truck, and a half-dozen water carrier bureaus) and numerous local bureaus still are in existence. Despite what may happen in the future, therefore, it is worthwhile to know how the bureau process has operated up until this time.

The internal organization of rate bureaus varies according to their charters and bylaws, but generally there are three levels of organization: (1) a standing rate committee of permanent staff employees of the bureau, headed by a permanent chairperson, does the necessary research and legwork on rate proposals, but has no vote; (2) a rate committee composed of the traffic managers (or their designates) of each of the participating carriers, which actually votes on rate proposals; and (3) an executive committee, usually made up of carrier vice presidents in charge of traffic, to whom appeals may be made by those dissatisfied with the results of rate committee votes. In some instances, appeals can be carried still higher, to a president's conference of the member carriers.

Any carrier in a given geographic area is entitled to participate in that area's rate bureau, and any participating carrier has the right of independent action either before or after a vote on a rate proposal. Votes generally are taken in closed session with no public announcement as to how individual carriers voted. Matters affecting more than one bureau, after being passed on by the originating bureau, often must be concurred in by the others affected.

What are the specific procedures involved in establishing a new rate or in changing an existing rate? Basically, rates are made by carriers through their bureaus, but several formal steps are involved. Let us suppose that you, a shipper, want to get a specific rate reduced.

The first step is to make your proposal to the appropriate rate bureau or, better yet, to persuade a carrier serving you (who is agreeable to your suggested lower rate) to make the proposal for you. The proposal should be supported by clear and concise evidence as to why the rate should be changed.

The rate bureau will study your proposal and docket it for a public hearing, probably after thirty or sixty days' notice to its member carriers and all other interested parties. At the hearing, your proposal should be supported as forcefully as possible with documentary evidence and verbal testimony from you, your supporting carrier, and anyone else with an interest in the matter whom you can persuade to appear. After considering all pro and con factors, the bureau's rate committee will vote on your proposal.

Let us assume that you have been successful in persuading the bureau to adopt your proposal. It will then file the new rate with the ICC (or with the appropriate state regulatory agency if the rate is strictly intrastate). The rate will be considered by the ICC or the state regulatory body, and if there are no serious objections to it from any source or if the matter is not considered to be of major transportation importance, it will probably be more or less automatically approved (approved by the absence of formal disapproval or suspension) and will become effective about thirty days after filing by the bureau.

This is a history of a typical routine rate change to which no one objects. The new rate may become effective within sixty to ninety days after your application. By far the largest percentage of rate changes (perhaps 90 percent) will come within this category.

Let us suppose, however, that your rate proposal is contested by one of your competitors. This protest, owing to the necessity for considering further evidence and possible appeals, will delay your proposal's processing through the rate bureau. Then if it is approved by the bureau, it likely will be suspended by the ICC or state regulatory body.

The regulatory body, in turn, will docket the proposal and hold public hearings on it after adequate notice to interested parties. The evidence for and against will again be considered. After a lapse of several months, your rate may finally be approved by the regulatory agency to go into effect after thirty days (or it may be disapproved, or approved only in part).

This does not necessarily end the process. Those who protest may appeal to the regulatory agency for reconsideration; and if they lose again, the matter may be appealed to the courts. Eventually the case may even reach the U.S. Supreme Court for settlement. The Court may uphold the commission's decision, or it may remand to that body for further action in line with the Court's views of its legality. In the meantime, many months or even years may have passed.

KINDS OF FREIGHT RATES

It is essential that anyone actively concerned with buying or selling transportation services understand the language of freight rates. Like other areas of buying and selling, this one has a professional jargon likely to be confusing or incomprehensible to outsiders. It is also highly desirable, both from the general information and the professional viewpoints, that businesspeople have some knowledge of the freight-rate structure — of how carriers quote prices for their transport services and how the different kinds of prices quoted relate to one another.

This section will explain some of the basic terminology of freight rates and describe some of the more common types of rate structures. Primary emphasis will be placed upon the rates of railroads and common-carrier trucking as these rate systems are more comprehensive as well as most important for most persons. Rates of other forms of carriage, which generally are closely related to rail and common-carrier truck rates, will be noted as appropriate.

The following discussion obviously does not purport to tell everything about the kinds of freight rates and their structures. To do this would require many volumes. Instead, it is the authors' intent to mention briefly the most important things about this topic that beginners in transportation ought to know. The next chapter will discuss in more detail some of the economic effects of various kinds of rates.

To better understand the terminology identifying particular kinds of rates, it is sometimes convenient to group these descriptive expressions together according to some similar characteristics. For example, we have distinguished between class tariffs and their exceptions and commodity tariffs. We can say, then, that class rates, or exception rates, and commodity rates are rates based on the kinds of things shipped. Other rates falling into this descriptive category are all-commodity or all-freight rates, where the rate quoted is applicable to any kind of product.

In addition to the above category, we may group rates into categories based upon the quantities shipped; route or routing characteristics; previous or future shipments of the product; agreements between carriers and shippers; and miscellaneous, that is, rates that do not clearly fall into any of these categories. The principal kinds of rates falling into each of these groups will be discussed in order. Contract and international rates are discussed separately.

Rates Based on Quantities Shipped

The most familiar of quantity rates are rail carload (CL) and truckload (TL) rates. As indicated in Chapter 4, CL and TL rates usually are considerably lower in cents per 100 pounds than are rates for smaller shipments of the same product.

A carload is generally understood to mean a single shipment from one consignor at one origin to one consignee at one destination, moving under a single bill of lading, at least meeting a minimum weight specified for the product, and loaded and unloaded by the consignor and consignee. Various tariff modifications, however, may permit stoppage en route for partial loading or unloading, deliveries to more than one party at destination (split deliveries), and carrier loading or unloading, or similar deviations. A carload may contain only one product or it may be a mixed car (two or more products). The same general specifications apply to truckload. Shipments not meeting the authorized tariff specifications cannot legally move at CL or TL rates.

In addition, truck carriers often quote volume (vol.) rates or any-quantity (AQ) rates. Volume rates customarily, but not always, are applied to shipments larger than truckload quantities and are lower than TL rates; they frequently are used to meet rail CL competition. Any-quantity rates may be applied to shipments either larger or smaller than truckload quantities.

In a limited number of instances, also, railroads quote trainload rates or multiple-car rates which may be considerably lower than CL rates. This kind of price quotation usually is defended by railroads on the grounds that it is necessary to meet competition from other forms of carriage and is justifiable on the basis of lower carrier costs incurred in handling large volumes regularly as contrasted with the costs of handling carload traffic. Such rates are not illegal as such, although they often have been discouraged by regulatory authorities and frowned upon by the general public because of their alleged discrimination against small shippers who do not ship enough to take advantage of them. The Anglo-American tradition tends to favor the small business over the large business, instead of the opposite.

During recent years, many railroads have been making extensive applications of incentive rates for some commodities. These are carload rates lower than the normal CL quotations and given to shippers who load considerably more into a car than the minimum quantity required for a CL rate. Railroads and shippers using these rates justify them on the grounds of lower shipper rates, lower costs (and consequently higher revenues per car and per unit of weight) for carriers, and better utilization of limited railroad resources. This last justification is particularly pertinent during the periods of rail-car shortage. Shippers who are not able to use incentive rates because of their own output characteristics or the quantity desires of their customers, however, as well as some competing carriers understandably oppose special incentive rates just as they oppose train-load or multiple-car rates.

Both railroad and truck carriers commonly impose minimum rates or charge for a minimum weight even though the actual shipment may weigh less than the minimum, or both. This type of rate is based upon the supposition that certain costs, especially those related to billing and other paperwork, do not differ greatly if at all in proportion to the weight handled or the distance moved. That is, the direct clerical expenses and various fixed-expense items may be as large for a 50-pound shipment moving only 50 miles as for a 5,000-pound shipment moving 500 miles.

Rates Based on Route or Routing Characteristics

A local rate is one covering a haul over the lines of only one carrier, whereas a joint rate is one involving a movement by two or more carriers. A through rate means one published rate from origin to destination in one tariff; these may be either local or joint in nature.

Combination rates are made up simply by adding one rate to another. For example, if the rate from A to B is 30 cents and the rate from B to C is 40 cents, the combination rate from A to C would be 70 cents. A combination rate differs from a proportional rate in that in the latter form only a part of one rate is added to another rate to get the total applicable rate. Using the above illustration, the proportional rate from A to C might be 30 cents (A to B) plus 60 percent of the rate from B to C (24 cents), or 54 cents. Combination or proportional rates may be either local or joint as well as through.

A differential rate is one in which some amount, a differential, is added to or subtracted from a standard rate. Differentials may be used over unusually circuitous or inferior routes, in connection with export and import shipments, or for various other reasons. An arbitrary rate adds an arbitrary to a standard rate. Arbitraries may be added to rates applying to major destination points for shipments that move beyond these points to outlying minor destinations, or they may be used on small shipments or on shipments with undesirable handling characteristics.

As one can imagine, there often are instances in which more than one rate may be found between given origins and destinations. Frequently this is not intended by, or even known to, the carriers concerned. As an illustration, a carrier may quote a rate of 90 cents per 100 pounds on some item from A to D in its tariff. An astute shipper's rate clerk, however, may find that the tariff provides for shipment of the same product from A to B for 30 cents, from B to C for 40 cents, and from C to D for 15 cents. In such cases, as shippers are legally entitled to use the lowest published rates, the shipper usually could use the rate of 85 cents rather than 90 cents. This is called the aggregate of intermediates rule; that is, the aggregate rate cannot exceed the sum of the published intermediate rates and is regulated under the Interstate Commerce Act.

Rates Based on Previous or Future Shipments of the Product

Rates based on previous or future shipments of a product are quoted in cases where a shipment stops in transit for some reason. This stoppage may be for processing, fabrication, or manufacture (as wheat into flour, logs into lumber into furniture, ore into metal, etc.), or for temporary storage. Such rates often are called transit rates (transit rate as used in this case should not be confused with the privilege of diversion or reconsignment, which also is sometimes loosely referred to as transit marketing).

The fiction or rationale behind such rates is that there is only one movement of the product involved from the first origin to a final destination despite its stopover and perhaps even a change in form. Thus, since rates in cents per 100 pounds or per ton-mile typically are lower proportionately on long hauls than on short hauls, advocates of this type of ratemaking maintain that shippers should not be forced to pay as much as the sum of two short-haul rates in getting their product to its final destination. Usually, if there is a rate difference between the inbound and the outbound form of the product, the higher of the two rates is considered the appropriate rate for the entire movement. An additional charge may or may not be made for the stopover privilege. Certainly the carriers' expenses are increased as a result of extra handling, paperwork, and necessary policing, but carriers sometimes prefer to absorb these extras in order to obtain or maintain business.

Transit rates are an important competitive device among carriers, shippers, and localities. As such, they are subject to abuse and require a considerable amount of policing. Carriers are not supposed to use them to discriminate between shippers or localities, a supposition that probably has not always been borne out by the facts. A carrier is not obligated to quote such rates; but once it does, they supposedly must be given to all who wish them under similar circumstances. But what are similar circumstances? And what if competing shippers are on the lines of another carrier that does not wish to quote such rates?

Shippers must also be policed by carriers or their agents to make sure that the transit-rate privilege is not violated. Careful records of incoming and outgoing tonnages must be kept and allowances made for wastage or accretion. Assume that a ton of corn can be milled into 1,200 pounds of edible cornmeal and 800 pounds of cattle feed (a 60-40 ratio). A miller who consistently brought in 1,000 tons of corn per month and shipped out 400 tons of cattle fee, but wanted to ship out 800 tons of cornmeal at reduced transit rates, would be suspect. Aside from the policing aspect, transit rates may involve a considerable amount of shipper and carrier bookkeeping.

The lower reshipping or transit-rate benefits may be applied either before or after stoppage, depending upon the pertinent carrier tariff. That is, a lower-than-standard inbound charge (floating in rate) may be applied on products that are to be reshipped later, or a lower-than-standard outbound charge (cutback rate) may be applied on shipments out of the transit point. Sometimes, too, the shipper pays a standard rate inbound and outbound and presents a claim to the carrier for a refund of the amount due under a particular transit-rate arrangement.

This discussion has only touched upon the essential elements of transit rates. This is an extremely complicated topic, involving at least several hundred commodities in many areas of the country and under a wide variety of operating arrangements and tariff rules. Transit rates, both in operation and in practical economic effect, are among the least understood of rates. Some additional comments will be made regarding the probable locational effects of transit rates in the following chapter, however.

Export and import rates are versions of reshipping rates in which the stoppage in transit is to permit loading onto an ocean carrier bound for a foreign destination or in which foreign-originated goods are transferred onto domestic carriers. These rates, although sometimes considerably lower than equivalent regular domestic rates for similar commodities moving over the same routes and by the same carriers to or from the same seaports, are usually not included in discussions of domestic transit rates.

Very few laypersons are even aware of the existence of export-import rates, and only a comparatively small number of shippers have occasion to use them. Further, it appears that most contemporary academic students of domestic transport consider these rates to be a proper subject for students of ocean transportation, whereas ocean transportation students apparently relegate them to the realm of domestic transport. The next chapter, dealing with rate structures, will further describe the structure of export and import rates as compared with other domestic rate structures.

Rates Based upon Shipper-Carrier Agreements

Under agreed rates, sometimes referred to as loyalty-incentive rates, a shipper enters into a formal agreement with a carrier or a group of carriers of the same mode to ship a certain volume, or in some cases a specified percentage of the total volume, by the particular carrier or group of carriers. In return, the shipper pays less than the standard published rate or receives a refund from the carrier for the difference between the standard rate and the agreed rate at the end of a named period of time. Under such agreements, the shipper normally is not under an absolute obligation to use the services of a given carrier or group of carriers; but a shipper who fails to live up to the agreed volume must pay the standard rate on all shipments.

Contract carrier rates (discussed separately below) are always agreed upon by the shipper and carrier by negotiation. These rates, however, are not generally included as agreed rates in the sense that the term is used here. Actually, in the United States, agreed rates between shippers and common carriers in domestic transportation generally have been considered unlawful. Such rates are widely used in Canada, Britain, and some other areas, however. Also, agreed rates are an integral part of ocean steamship conference rates, even for U.S. ocean carriers in foreign trade; if the steamship conference cannot supply needed vessel capacity, the shipper is allowed to use other lines without penalty.

Agreed rates have been frowned upon in this country's domestic transportation on several grounds. It is felt that this may be a form of discrimination between shippers, particularly between larger shippers who may be able to negotiate favorable agreements and smaller shippers who do not have as much bargaining power. This argument certainly may be valid if the agreement is based upon an absolute amount of tonnage. On the other hand, it is less sound if similar agreements are offered to all shippers on a percentage-of-total-tonnage basis.

Governmental agencies are permitted by the Interstate Commerce Act to negotiate with carriers for lower than standard rates. These lower rates are used extensively by the federal government because of its bargaining power resulting from a tremendous tonnage of shipments. Carriers are not particularly fond of this situation, as it permits government to play one carrier against another in bargaining and results in considerably lower carrier revenue on government freight. Many private shippers also oppose such rates as they feel that the resulting lower carrier revenues require higher rates from private shippers, which means, in effect, that private shippers are subsidizing government shipments. Various proposals have been made during recent years to amend the Interstate Commerce Act by eliminating this practice, with both railroad and shipper support.

Released-value rates may be considered as still another version of rates based upon agreements. Under these rates, the shipper, in return for considerably lower rates than otherwise would be applicable, agrees that in case of loss or damage to its goods, only an agreed-upon maximum loss or damage claim will be paid by the carrier. This kind of agreement is customarily used for passenger baggage and is widely used in shipping household furniture and personal effects by truck. Some other types of goods also usually move under released-value rates. The carriers' liability may be limited to a maximum absolute amount, as in baggage or ordinary livestock, or to a maximum amount per unit of weight, as in household furniture. The shipper can acquire the protection of full carrier liability by paying higher rates, but full-liability rates on such goods often are considerably higher than full-coverage transportation insurance purchased from an insurance company; the carrier itself may sell this insurance as an agent.

Miscellaneous Rates

Several kinds of rates do not fall clearly into any of the categories discussed above. For exposition purposes, therefore, the authors have grouped a number of these rates under the miscellaneous heading rather than enlarge the basic grouping of categories.

Piggyback rates, or trailer-on-flatcar (TOFC) rates, are rapidly increasing in importance as the piggyback movement continues to expand (see Chapter 5). Several versions or plans of piggyback services are offered, each with different rate-quotation methods.

Plan I. Railroads haul trailers, with or without wheels, for common-carrier truckers. The trucking company charges shippers rates from applicable motor carrier tariffs.

Plan II. Railroads offer a door-to-door service with their own trailers under their own rates.

Plan II ½. Railroads offer ramp-to-ramp service with their own trailers and under their own rates. Shippers, including motor carriers and freight forwarders, provide pickup and delivery services.

Plan III. Railroads haul trailers owned or leased by shippers or freight forwarders. This is a line-haul service without rail pickup or delivery, involving a flat charge regardless of the trailer's contents.

Plan IV. Railroads make a flat charge for moving flatcars and trailers, owned or controlled by forwarders or shippers, whether loaded or empty; that is, railroads supply only the right of way and motive power.

Plan V. Railroads and trucks publish joint through rates, with the carriers agreeing among themselves on such matters as trailer ownership, freight solicitation, revenue divisions, and similar matters.

Sometimes shippers are in no particular hurry to get shipments to their destinations and thus are willing to ship under lower *space-available* rates. This implies that the goods may not move promptly; rather, the movement will be made when higher priority freight is not available to utilize the carrier's full capacity. Shippers usually are promised that the goods will move not later than a specified date, however. This device is used most often in air and water carriage.

Some marketing businesses, especially those marketing fresh fruits and vegetables, lumber, and a few other items, specialize in selling or reselling carloads of commodities while they are en route to a general destination area. These brokers, wholesalers, or commission sellers, as they are variously called, make extensive use of diversion and reconsignment privileges (see Chapter 8). Even these devices sometimes do not give enough time for selling the commodity, however. Thus a need for slow transit or delay en route, especially on the part of Pacific Coast lumber wholesalers, has given rise to various proposals for *delayed* rates. Under these proposals, due to deliberate stoppages or delays en route, considerably more than the usual amount of time would be required for a given movement, thus giving the seller more time to make the sale. These proposals have not been sympathetically received by the ICC and have been opposed by many shippers and carriers primarily on the grounds that such delays would unduly tie up rail cars and contribute to car shortages, and perhaps decrease participating carrier revenues without corresponding benefits to the public in general.

Cube rates (rates based primarily upon the amount of cubic space occupied rather than upon weight) have been proposed recently. This concept has not been generally accepted, although it does not differ greatly
in principle from piggyback plans III and IV, some steamship rates, oil
pipeline rates, and even some air freight situations.

Opponents of a cube-rate system maintain that in addition to cubic
volume, some attention must be given to weight (as of feathers versus
lead, for example), susceptibility to loss and damage, value (at least insofar as this might affect loss and damage claims), handling characteristics,
the product's need for special accessorial services, and various other so-
called classification factors. It is not likely that pure cube rates will be
widely used by many carriers within the near future, but it is possible that
cubic volume may become relatively more important in classification and
ratemaking than it has been.

It should be re-emphasized at this point that all the above-mentioned
common-carrier rates, as well as various kinds not mentioned, are legally
required to be published in tariffs and thus fall into the categories of class,
exception, and commodity rates. For example, one might have a class or
a commodity CL rate that is joint, through, proportional, transit, released
value, incentive, and includes an arbitrary. Various other linkings of terminology may be encountered or imagined.

As indicated above, most of the foregoing discussion, except where
otherwise specified, has been in terms of rail rates or common-carrier
truck rates which originally were (and still largely are) patterned after the
already established rail rates. Some brief comment on the rates of other
forms of carriage now is necessary.

Freight forwarders often quote the line-haul rates of the common carriers used in their services or closely pattern their rates after those of the
common carriers. Domestic water carriers, as they are in direct competition with rail and truck carriers, often use the same tariffs as their competition or base their rates on them (usually somewhat lower, of course).

Air-carrier rates involve no particularly new terminology; these carriers
do, however, make extensive use of released value and considerable use
of space-available rates. Air-freight classification is not unduly complex.

The other major form of domestic carriage — oil pipelines — uses a
standard barrel as its pricing unit. This barrel is precisely defined not only
in terms of cubic volume (a form of cube rate) but with attention to such
variables as specific gravity and temperature which affect volume.

In addition to the above line-haul rates, any carrier may levy additional
surcharges or accessorial charges for the performance of special or non-
standard services in connection with a movement. Among others, such
services might include refrigeration or heating, transit, diversion or reconsignment, drayage, livestock feeding, special switching, and similar items.

Any such additional charges made by common carriers must be duly authorized and published in tariffs.

CONTRACT RATES

Contract carriage has existed in trucking and barge operations since the beginnings of these industries, but contract trucking has expanded considerably under the recent federal regulatory reform legislation. It appears that contract carriage may be replacing private truck carriage in many instances.

A limited amount of rail contract carriage was first allowed during the late 1970s. The Staggers Rail Act of 1980, however, has led to a great and increasing expansion of rail contracts. For some commodities and some individual firms, rail contract carriage now exceeds rail common carriage. But railroads are not allowed to allocate so much of their equipment to contract carriage that common carriage is impaired. This may be difficult to enforce during times of rail equipment shortages!

Contract rates are negotiated on a case-by-case basis between an individual shipper and an individual carrier and are governed by state law (not ICC regulation) once the contract is in force. In addition to rate levels, of course, contracts must contain many other provisions. Among other things, the contract must cover the amount of tonnage to be supplied by the shipper, the quantity and quality of carrier services to be furnished, the various other responsibilities and liabilities of both contracting parties, how contract disputes are to be settled, and the like.

In short, a "good" contract designed as a replacement for common carriage must be comprehensive enough, and specific enough, to cover all the possible circumstances that have previously been covered by hundreds of years of evolution of the common law and a century of U.S. statutory law regulating common carriage. Furthermore, it must avoid antitrust law violations — a new worry for carriers and shippers. Life has not been made less complex for shipper and carrier personnel involved with rate-making. Rather, the complexities merely have changed.

INTERNATIONAL RATES

As indicated in Chapter 6, this country's international transportation is conducted by ocean, land, and air carriage. Ocean carriage accounts for by far the greatest volume of this traffic.

Ocean Rates

Chapter 6 distinguishes between liner or berth services, used mainly for breakbulk cargo, and tramp services, used mainly for bulk and liquid cargo in international ocean for-hire carriage. Rates are made quite differently for these two kinds of services.

Tramp Rates

The tramp steamship business uses contract rates, called charter rates. These may be for a single voyage, priced at a specified amount per ton with a required minimum amount of tonnage (a "voyage" or "trip" charter). Or they may be included in a "time" charter, at a specified charge per day or other time period. Further, time charters may be either with a crew or without a crew (a "bare boat" or "demise" charter). Charters, obviously, can be lengthy and complex documents, although somewhat standardized forms are used for most of the important trades.

Charter rates are not regulated by anyone. Instead, they are determined by worldwide supply and demand conditions. Hundreds of private firms, located in all parts of the world and all together owning thousands of vessels, compete for the available business. The number of available ships is relatively fixed at any given time. Thus, if the demand for tonnage space is high, rates will be high. But a decrease in the demand for tonnage space will send rates quickly tumbling downward. It may be preferable for a ship owner to operate at some loss rather than to tie up a ship and receive no income from it at all. In competitive situations, a rate difference of a few cents per ton may determine which ship gets the cargo.

Charter rates, like other contract rates, are agreed upon by individual shippers and carriers. Most of the actual negotiations, though, usually are between ship brokers (representing carriers) and cargo brokers or agents (representing shippers). These representatives usually operate through the principal shipping exchanges, such as those in New York, London, or Tokyo, and have branch offices in numerous ports. They have excellent communications with one another throughout the world. It is not quite correct to say that the international charter market is a textbook example of pure competition, but it approaches this condition about as closely as does any other market.

Liner Rates

The liner trade is roughly equivalent to land common carriage. Its rates usually do not fluctuate as much as do tramp rates. Generally, rates are quoted at a specified amount per ton, varying with the kind of commodity to be transported. A "ton" may be based either on weight or on measurement at the carrier's option — that is, heavy, dense materials will be charged on a weight basis and light, bulky materials on a measurement basis. Further, depending on the particular trade, a weight "ton" may be a long ton (2,240 pounds) or a short ton (2,000 pounds). Likewise, a measurement ton may be 50 cubic feet or 40 cubic feet. Or the weights and measurements may be in metric tons or cubic meters. It is essential that a shipper, or a shipper's representative, know what kind of "ton" the carrier has in mind.

Liner rates usually include the stevedoring charges for loading and unloading vessels — that is, they are "ship's tackle to ship's tackle" rates. Sometimes these rates include the costs of moving goods from port storage areas to the ship's side, sometimes not. Port charges for storage and for the right to move across the port's wharves are paid separately by the shipper. Again, one must know what one is buying for a quoted rate.

Individual liner companies may make their own rates, but ratemaking usually is done through *steamship conferences*. These are carrier associations roughly equivalent to the domestic land-carrier rate bureaus described above. There are dozens of these conferences worldwide, covering all principal routes and trades. Not all liner carriers belong to conferences, but most do. Even ships owned by the Soviet Union have joined some conferences. If conference carriers cannot agree upon a rate level, an "open" rate may be declared — that is, each member carrier can charge what it wishes.

Unlike the practice in land carriage, steamship conferences often use a *dual-rate* system. This means that shippers who agree to ship all their goods aboard the vessels of a given conference for a specified period of time get rate reductions, typically 10 percent to 20 percent below the rates charged those who do not have such agreements.

Conference ratemaking and agreements are exempt from U.S. antitrust laws by special legislation. Agreements, rates, and tariffs involving movements from or to this country cannot be discriminatory to U.S. shippers and must be approved by the U.S. Federal Maritime Commission (FMC). As most of the conference carriers are not U.S. flag vessels, however, "approval" usually is routine and supervision and enforcement of anti-discrimination rules by the FMC is difficult.

Land and Air Rates

As noted in Chapter 6, a large amount of this country's international trade is with Canada and Mexico and mostly moves by land carriage. The carriers involved in this traffic are also domestic carriers, and their rate-making procedures and rates do not differ significantly from domestic procedures and rates. U.S. regulatory authorities (such as the ICC), however, have no jurisdiction over the foreign portions of these international rates.

International air-carrier rates resemble ocean-water rates in that they usually are airport to airport only and are quoted on a weight or measurement basis at the carrier's option. Rates usually are quoted on a per-pound basis, with 250 cubic inches (approximately 6 by 6 by 7 inches) being the equivalent of a pound. Larger shipments usually receive lower rates per pound-mile. Like domestic land carriers, air carriers have class and commodity rates, called *general commodity* and *specific commodity* rates, respectively. Specific commodity rates typically are as much as one-third lower than are general commodity rates.

Most international air carriers are members of the International Air Transport Association (IATA), a carrier association. IATA has divided the world into three major geographic areas with a freight-rate traffic conference for each. Members of these conferences make international air-freight rates for their respective areas in much the same way that steam-ship conferences and domestic rate bureaus do for their members. These rates are subject to approval by governments of countries from and to which they apply. If they are not approved or if the carriers themselves cannot agree on a rate, an open rate (as in steamship conferences) may be declared.

RATEMAKING IN TRANSITION

The Ratemaking Environment

The long-established procedures of common-carrier ratemaking presently are undergoing greater changes than have been seen since the early part of this century. Many more rates are being made or changed by individual carriers rather than through rate bureaus. Federal and state direct regulation is being lessened and in many cases eliminated altogether. Ratemaking certainly does not yet occur in a free market, but the present move is in that direction.

For example, the recent regulatory reform legislation has allowed individual carriers to increase or decrease rates annually within specified percentage ranges without regulatory authority approval. Rate changes also may be permitted automatically because of periodic changes in inflation rates or fuel price levels. Under some circumstances, rate changes can be made with only a few days' prior notice. Some major forms of traffic and commodities have been removed from rate regulation (fresh agricultural products, rail domestic coal movements, boxcar traffic, and many others of lesser importance). Also, contract rates now are used for large volumes of traffic that formerly moved largely under common-carriage rates, and released-value rates (see Chapter 8) are now more widely used.

Recent rate regulatory reforms appear to be designed to accomplish at least six major purposes. These are to (1) deregulate all traffic unless its regulation clearly is in the public interest; (2) encourage individual carrier ratemaking rather than bureau collective ratemaking; (3) emphasize the role of costs in ratemaking; (4) reduce the time lags and paperwork required for rate changes; (5) encourage negotiated rates between individual shippers and carriers; and (6) bring most ratemaking under the same anti-trust provisions applicable to businesses in general. Needless to say, these apparent goals are highly controversial.

Procedural changes in ratemaking have occurred and still are occurring so rapidly that it would be useless to attempt to list all of them here. Meantime, those concerned with rates and ratemaking must keep a keen eye on pronouncements from Washington, D.C., state capitals, traffic associations, courts, the U.S. Department of Justice, and their own trade associations and carriers. In particular, shippers, as well as carriers, must become more aware of possible antitrust violations. The Sherman Anti-trust Act and its applications and interpretations soon may become as important to transportation practitioners as the Interstate Commerce Act has been in the past.

The recent and pending changes in ratemaking and rates have created uncertainties among both carriers and shippers. Yesterday's known procedures may be obsolete or even illegal today, and today's procedures may be equally outdated tomorrow. But the new procedures have made many more alternatives or choices available to both shippers and carriers. And they have not removed the common-carrier obligations to serve and to charge reasonable and nondiscriminatory rates (see chapter 8), although it now may be more difficult to prove violations of these obligations.

Major Shifts in Ratemaking Practices

Since the late 1970s, as carriers have learned to operate in a less regulated environment, ratemaking practices have changed dramatically. Three areas typify the nature of these changes. First, *rate negotiation* has become an increasingly important part of the duties of carrier sales representatives and shipper traffic managers. The move away from collective ratemaking has intensified the level of rate competition among carriers within and across transportation modes, making a willingness to negotiate rates a major element of carrier marketing efforts. Many large shippers have been able to use this new environment to reduce overall shipping costs.

Another aspect of this change is seen in the widespread use of *discounting*. Discounting was not permitted under most previous ratemaking practices. In this new environment, it has become a way of life. Discounts are available under a wide range of circumstances, but many apply to accumulations of shipments from the same shipper to a variety of destinations over a given period of time. In many cases, the depth of the discount is tied to the total weight shipped with the carrier over a given time period. These discounts somewhat resemble the agreed rates discussed earlier in this chapter, but represent a slightly different concept. In the case of agreed rates, shipper-specific agreements are usually the case. With discounted rates, the rates are available to anyone who meets the conditions and may be claimed without a previous formal agreement, if appropriate records are kept.

Finally, *railroad contract rates*, prohibited until the Staggers Act of 1980, have come to dominate much of railroad ratemaking. Under this legislation, the railroads were given the authority to negotiate contracts for their services. By 1984, well over 13,000 contract rates had been filed by railroads. The very nature of contract ratemaking has increased railroad competitiveness and responsiveness in many markets.

SUMMARY

Anyone may wish to have anything transported from any place to any other place. The possible combinations of products, places, routes, carrier modes, and individual carriers and services are mind boggling. Beyond doubt, no other pricing system is as complex as that of transportation.

The transportation pricing system, including both its procedures and its prices, has been greatly simplified. This simplification itself, though, has required a formidable host of practices, documents, and jargon. Regulatory reform, along with computerization, is changing the details of this process, but it does not appear to be making it less complex. There is no easy way for those transportation buyers or sellers who wish to become competent in pricing. As old obstacles are removed, new ones appear. But as the following chapter shows, there is some order in the structure.

ADDITIONAL READINGS

Altrogge, Phyllis D., "Railroad Contracts and Competitive Conditions," *Transportation Journal* 21(2) (Winter 1981), 37–43.

Bagley, John W., James R. Evans, and Wallace R. Wood, "Contracting for Transportation," *Transportation Journal* 22(2) (Winter 1982), 63–73.

Blackwell, Richard B., "Pitfalls in Rail Contract Rate Escalation," *I.C.C. Practitioners' Journal* 19(5) (July-August 1982), 468–502.

Coyle, John J., Edward J. Bardi, and Joseph L. Cavinato, *Transportation*, St. Paul, Minn.: West Publishing Co., 1982.
Chapter 13, "Rate-Making in Practice," pp. 247–78.

Fair, Marvin L., and Ernest W. Williams, *Transportation and Logistics*, Rev. ed., Plano, Texas: Business Publications, 1981.
Chapter 17, "Rate Making in Practice," pp. 301–28.

Flood, Kenneth U., Oliver G. Callson, and Sylvester J. Jablonski, *Transportation Management*, 4th ed., Dubuque, Iowa: Wm. C. Brown, 1984.
Chapter 6, "Freight Tariffs and Their Interpretation," pp. 94–126.
Chapter 7, "Freight Classification," pp. 127–72.

Lieb, Robert C., *Transportation*, 3rd ed., Reston, Va.: Reston Publishing Co., 1985.
Chapter 10, "Rate-Making Procedures," pp 210–14.
Chapter 11, "Freight Classification Systems, Terminology, and Innovations," pp. 215–32.

McElhiney, Paul T., *Transportation for Marketing and Business Students*, Totowa, N.J.: Littlefield, Adams, 1975.
Chapter 10, "Freight Rates and Tariffs," pp. 163–91.

Taff, Charles A., *Management of Physical Distribution and Transportation*, 7th ed., Homewood, Ill.: Richard D. Irwin, 1984.
Chapter 14, "Commodity Classification and Its Impact on Transport Pricing," pp. 353–75.
Chapter 15, "Transport Pricing as an Element of System Costs," pp. 377–427.

Tyworth, John E., Joseph L. Cavinato, and C. John Langley, Jr., *Traffic Management*, Reading, Mass.: Addison-Wesley Publishing Co., 1987.
Chapter 3, "Transportation Pricing in Transition," pp. 57–75.
Chapter 4, "Tariff Pricing Systems," pp. 79–113.

CHAPTER 18
FREIGHT-RATE STRUCTURES

Now that much of the basic terminology of rates has been introduced, it is appropriate to consider the structure of freight rates. (*Structures*, as used here, refers to the relationship of line-haul transport charges to the distance moved and the comparative interrelationships of different kinds of rates and of rates in different geographical areas.)

In this discussion, some of the rates identified in the preceding section will be further described, and some new rate terminology will be introduced. Also, as in the preceding chapter, rail rates will form the basic reference point for discussion since an understanding of this most comprehensive rate system will lead concurrently to an understanding of the usually less complex rate structures of other modes.

At the extreme opposite ends of the rate-structure spectrum, one might imagine, on the one hand, a rate that for a given unit or weight of a particular product does not vary at all with the distance moved — a postage-stamp or fixed rate. The other extreme would be a rate that increases in direct proportion to the distance moved — a pure distance or straight mileage rate. Most freight moves under rates falling somewhere between these two extremes, under modified mileage rates, under rates that may not vary at all over considerable distances (a modified mileage or postage-stamp combination known as blanket, group, or zone rates), or even under rates that may vary inversely with distance (as fourth section rates, or movements to intermediate points under the formerly popular basing point rate structure). Each of these rate structures has its advantages and disadvantages, its supporters and opponents.

MILEAGE RATE STRUCTURES

The straight mileage rate, wherein the charge increases in direct proportion to the distance moved, is the most simple of distance-rate concepts. If the charge for moving one ton for 1 mile is 5 cents, then the charge for moving one ton for 100 miles is $5. The simplicity, orderliness, and apparent equity of such a rate structure is appealing at first glance. It is seldom used in practice, however, and for good reasons.

Terminal Cost Effects

Carrier costs are made up of both terminal and line-haul costs. A considerable portion of terminal costs are fixed regardless of the distance moved. That is, a particular shipment may cost the carrier $10 for direct handling and billing whether it moves 1 or 1,000 miles. Thus a carrier must charge at least $10 plus the direct line-haul costs incurred for the movement if it is to recover even the direct costs of providing the service. Assuming a truck shipment with direct over-the-road movement costs of $1 per mile, if the shipment moves 1 mile, the carrier must charge a total of $11 to recover all direct costs — in effect recovering the terminal costs at a rate of $10 per mile. If the shipment moves 1,000 miles, the carrier can recover the terminal costs at a rate of 1 cent per mile. The farther the shipment moves, the lower the terminal costs per weight-unit mile. Figure 16.5 in Chapter 16 illustrates this situation.

If one should assume that line-haul costs are directly proportionate to the distance moved, one might devise a cost-based rate structure that would include a flat charge, determined by the carrier's terminal expenses in connection with a given shipment, plus a straight distance line-haul rate — in other words, a terminal charge plus straight mileage rate. Terminal charges and line-haul charges are made separately in some countries, but U.S. carriers have found it to be less confusing and more convenient to quote a single rate or charge including both the terminal and line-haul elements.

There is no reason other than convenience in rate quotation and custom why line-haul and terminal charges should be amalgamated, but most carriers and shippers in this country seem to prefer it this way. Conversely, there is no strong logical argument for separating the two — supposedly, the total amount charged and paid will be the same in either case. Carriers can and do at least partially handle the terminal cost problem, particularly for very small shipments or shipments that move only short distances, by minimum charges (either absolute fixed minimums or by charging for a specified weight even though the actual weight may be less) and by higher rates per unit of weight-distance on small shipments and short hauls.

Tapering Rates

One cannot safely assume that all line-haul costs are directly proportionate to distance, however. The amount of proportionality may be debatable (and it varies between modes and even between carriers of the same mode), but most transport students and practitioners agree that line-haul-per-unit costs generally decrease as distance increases. (This can be seen easily in comparing personal automobile fuel consumption on short and longer trips.) Even if this were not so, or if the rate makers should overemphasize the amount of the decrease, the effect on rate structures would be the same. Insofar as rates are influenced by costs, it is the imagined cost rather than the actual cost (if the two are different) that is pertinent at least in the short run. (In the long run, the wrong misconception might lead to bankruptcy.)

Actually, then, distance rates, or more precisely distance-related rates, are generally influenced by the spreading of some or all of the terminal costs over the entire distance of the movement, by the rate makers' image of the behavior of line-haul costs over distance, and by the carriers' estimation of the values of the service to the shippers. Further, this latter estimation includes estimates of the strength of competition from the carriers and from producers located on the lines of other carriers as well as ideas concerning the relative sizes of fixed and variable costs, unallocable costs, and out-of-pocket costs.

The result is that in practice, distance rates are commonly tapering mileage rates; they increase with the distance moved, but not as rapidly as distance increases. For example, total charges for moving a particular shipment 100 miles might be $6, but it might move 200 miles for $10, 300 miles for $13, and 400 miles for $15. Such rates normally start with a minimum charge.

Graphic comparisons of the various types of mileage rates and the postage-stamp rate are shown in Figure 18.1. It should be understood, of course, that successive distance-rate quotations are not infinitely divisible, as indicated by the smooth lines shown for distance-rate profiles in this figure. In reality, a magnified distance-rate profile would show a series of stair steps representing rates to and between successive stations along the carrier's route. The smooth lines shown for distance rates in Figure 18.1 may be considered as intersecting midpoints of these numerous small steps.

All rate structures, with the exception of pure postage-stamp rates, discussed in this chapter, are in some way related to distance. The directness of this relationship varies greatly, however. Railroad class rates in general tend to show a more direct relationship to distance than do commodity rates, but even class rates are not straight distance rates and commodity rates do not ignore the distance factor.

Logically, insofar as rates are influenced by costs, one would expect to find rates more closely approaching the straight mileage structure among carrier modes where (1) variable costs are high relative to fixed costs, (2) allocable costs are high relative to unallocable costs, (3) line-haul costs are high relative to terminal costs, and (4) line-haul costs are most

Figure 18.1   Illustrative Rate Profiles

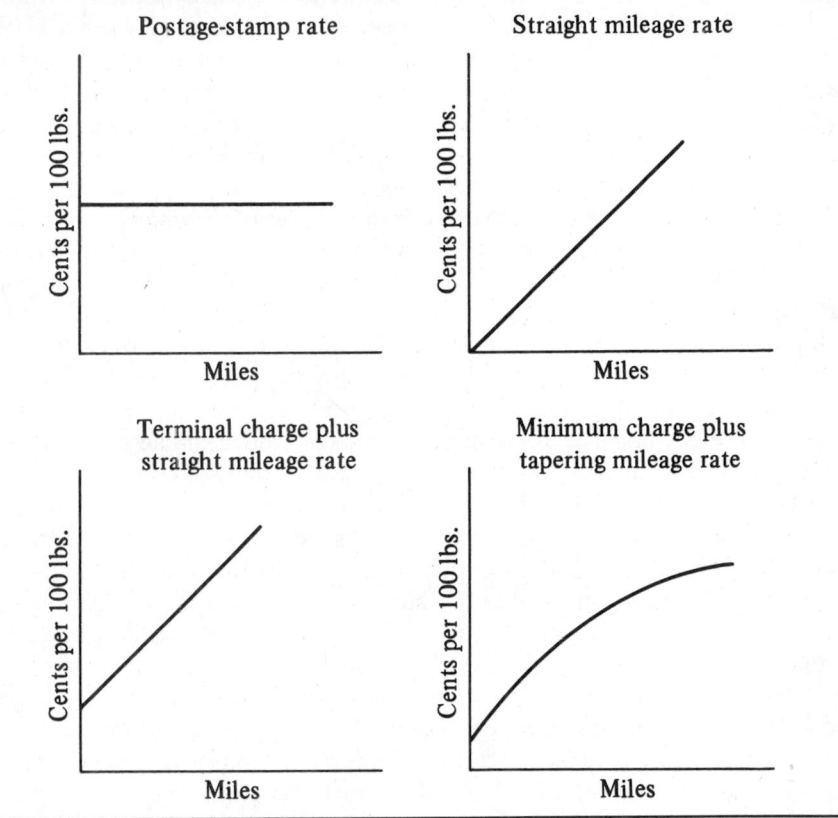

directly proportional to distance. As these conditions generally are more closely approximated in motor and air carriage than in water, rail, and pipeline transport, it should not be surprising that rates of the first two modes tend to be more closely related to distance than is true of the latter modes. Rates of secondary carriers, with the exception of the U.S. mail, naturally tend to follow the rates of the primary line-haul carriers used.

Export and Import Rates

Export and import rail rates are similar to other class commodity distance-related rates in their overall patterns. Differences between the rates on domestically originated and destined products and products going to or coming from foreign sources by ocean carriage, however, are worthy of some brief comment. These differences have persisted for more than a century. The two principal differences are that these rates may be considerably lower in some instances than applicable rates on domestic movements of similar traffic, and they may be structured in such a way as to equalize port or seacoast advantages. Note the word *may*. These permissible differences are not required or found on all products.

A vague but recognizable geographic pattern of export-import rates can be distinguished. At least five principal directional flows of traffic are involved: between the North Atlantic Coast and the Midwest, between the South Atlantic Coast and the Midwest, between the Gulf Coast and the Midwest, between Gulf and Atlantic Coast points and interior areas in the Southeast, and between the Pacific Coast and the Midwest, East, and South.

Lower export rates are designed to aid U.S. producers competing with foreign producers in foreign markets. This obviously benefits domestic producers. It also creates or stimulates business for the seaport cities and the carriers involved without disadvantaging U.S. producers. Not much controversy exists about lower export rates.

Justification for lower import rates on products that are or might be produced in this country, however, is not as clear. Their effect may be to create additional business for some carriers and port cities, while decreasing the traffic of nonport carriers and the output of domestic producers. Each such case would seem to require an analysis of its individual merits before any general conclusions are reached.

Export-import seaboard and port equalization rate schemes are more controversial. The equalized rates are not for the domestic portion of the movement, but rather for the total movement, domestic plus ocean. Owing to geographical location or other factors, ocean rates between some U.S. ports or coasts and given foreign areas are higher or lower than from other ports or coasts. In a competitive situation, if domestic export or import rates to or from two ports (or coasts) were equal, the one with the lower ocean rate would be favored. Domestic carriers serving the port or coast with the higher ocean rate would not participate in the movement.

Competition between railroads serving different Atlantic Coast ports led to several severe railroad rate wars during the 1870s. In 1877, a compromise agreement was reached which established differentials between the ports concerned. Those ports favored with lower ocean rates received higher rail rates, and vice versa. Although the specific rates and relationships have been altered over the years and some differentials have been eliminated recently, this still is the basic pattern of seaboard and port equalization.

BASING POINT RATE STRUCTURES

In order to eliminate any possible terminological confusion, it is desirable to distinguish between basing point *pricing* and basing point *rates*, particularly as both involve transportation service and both are highly controversial.

Basing Point Pricing

Perhaps the most discussed single basing pricing system is that formerly used for many years in the steel industry — the so-called Pittsburgh-plus system — in which quoted delivered prices from all mills, wherever located, included an equivalent of the freight rate from Pittsburgh. Other industries have used similar systems, and some industries have used a multiple basing point system in which instead of one nationally controlling basing point, several regional basing points were established around the country. In this latter system, the price quoted buyers includes an equivalent for the freight rate from the nearest basing point mill in their region.

Such a system of freight equalization is designed to neutralize the advantages or disadvantages of geographical location by putting all competing sellers on a par insofar as freight rates are concerned, in effect (from the sellers' and buyers' viewpoints) the equivalent of a postage-stamp or fixed rate. Defenders of such practices maintain that equalization of freight charges puts seller competition on a mill-cost-only basis, thus giving an edge to the most efficient plant, and that it gives buyers a greater choice of sellers with whom they may do business. In other words, it leads to keener competition.

Opponents, however, argue that such pricing practices are conspiracies designed to prorate business, maintain the status quo among present producers, and lessen competition. From a transportation viewpoint, the transportation equivalent paid by the buyer may have little relationship to the actual transportation costs (or rates) of the hauling carriers, and the system also may lead to a misallocation of limited resources due to extensive cross-hauling of identical or similar goods. Generally, basing point pricing systems have been severely frowned upon by regulatory authorities and courts under the provisions of the antitrust acts, although the practice of freight absorption as such is not illegal if engaged in as a part of valid competition (whatever that may mean).

It should be clearly understood that basing point pricing is a device used by sellers of products and does not involve carrier participation. The carrier is paid the authorized rate for any movement regardless of whether the buyer is charged for phantom freight or the seller absorbs freight. There is no reason for a carrier to be interested in, or even to know about, seller-buyer arrangements.

Basing Point Rates

Basing point rates, however, are a carrier invention which grew out of carrier competition or out of the desire of particular carriers, for reasons of their own, to build up particular localities as centers of distribution or other economic activity at the relative expense of other communities. Although the latter could not be easily defended as a legitimate carrier activity, basing point rates established as a method of meeting competition are perhaps as defensible as many other kinds of legitimate competition. Individuals or localities favored by a particular form of competition generally defend it staunchly, whereas those harmed by it can usually convince themselves that it is bad. Or, as someone has said, "Everyone believes competition is a good thing for the other fellow."

A basing point rate structure, of course, is a distance-related structure. Its peculiar characteristic is that the total rate is made up of a rate from origin to the specified basing point or terminal plus an arbitrary from the basing point to destination.

In classic examples such as the so-called old southern basing point system and many early westbound transcontinental and Pacific Coast north-south rail rates, the arbitrary used was relatively high in weight-mileage charges as compared to the longer haul between origin and the basing point. Often the arbitrary added from the basing point to nearby destinations was the full amount of the local or short-haul rate between the basing point and destination. Further, the arbitrary was added even to shipments destined for points between the origin and the basing point on the same line and which, therefore, were never actually transported to the basing point (an example of long-and-short-haul ratemaking formerly regulated under the Interstate Commerce Act).

Upon what competitive grounds might such a rate structure be based? Let us imagine a railroad operating from point A to B to C to D. Water carrier competition, or some other competition, exists between points A and C, but not to points B and D. Further, this competition is from a low-cost carrier who can and does quote lower rates from A to C than would normally be charged by the railroad.

In this competitive pricing situation, if the railroad wishes to participate in the traffic from A to C, it will have to meet or beat its competition by charging a lower rate than it otherwise would. For illustration, let us suppose that the low-cost water carrier charges 60 cents per 100 pounds for a particular commodity between A and C and that the railroad feels that it must charge this same rate. Note that the water carrier does not serve B or D, however, and assume that shipments destined for those points must either go all the way by rail or go by water to C and thence by rail on to D or back to B.

The railroad rate makers, then, might well reason that since the lowest alternative rate from A to either B or D is the 60-cent water rate to C plus its own short-haul rate from C to those points (which we will assume is 30 cents in both cases), an appropriate charge from A to B (a shorter haul than to C) is 90 cents, the only possible charge from A to C is 60 cents, and it is also possible to charge 90 cents from A to D, which is farther than C. This situation is diagrammed in Figure 18.2.

Citizens at B might vigorously protest such rates. They would allege discrimination, saying that shipments to C are not paying their proportionate or fair share of the rail carrier's transportation costs. Someone else then, namely the citizens of B, must make up this deficit by paying more than their fair share since the carrier must cover all its costs (including whatever profits are necessary to retain and attract its required capital) if it is to remain in business and provide the desired services.

An even more practical argument from B would be that the use of C as a basing point builds up the economy of C at the expense of B. For example, a wholesale distributor at C, buying merchandise from a manufacturer at A at the same price paid by a B wholesaler, would have a 30-cents-per-100-pounds price advantage over a competitor at B. This would mean that the distributor at C could underprice the B wholesaler at any point between C and B and could even deliver goods into B at the same price as the local B wholesaler!

The railroad would reply that rates to B and to C are based on entirely different competitive situations and that even though its rates to C are necessarily depressed, rates to B are no higher as a result of this. In fact, the railroad might point out that if its rates to C were higher, it would lose a substantial part of its traffic to that point and the effect might cause even higher rates to B. It would argue that even if the rates to C are not covering the total cost of movements to that point, they are at least covering out-of-pocket costs plus an additional amount that can be applied to overhead costs. The loss of this contribution to overhead, then, would mean that rates to B, D, and other noncompetitive points would have to be increased in order to cover the carrier's total costs!

Citizens of C would maintain that they have a natural advantage owing to their favorable geographic location which enables them to benefit from carrier competition. Artificial removal of this natural advantage, they would say, would be discriminatory against C. Citizens of D

Figure 18.2   A Basing Point Rate Situation, Showing a Long-and-Short-Haul Deviation

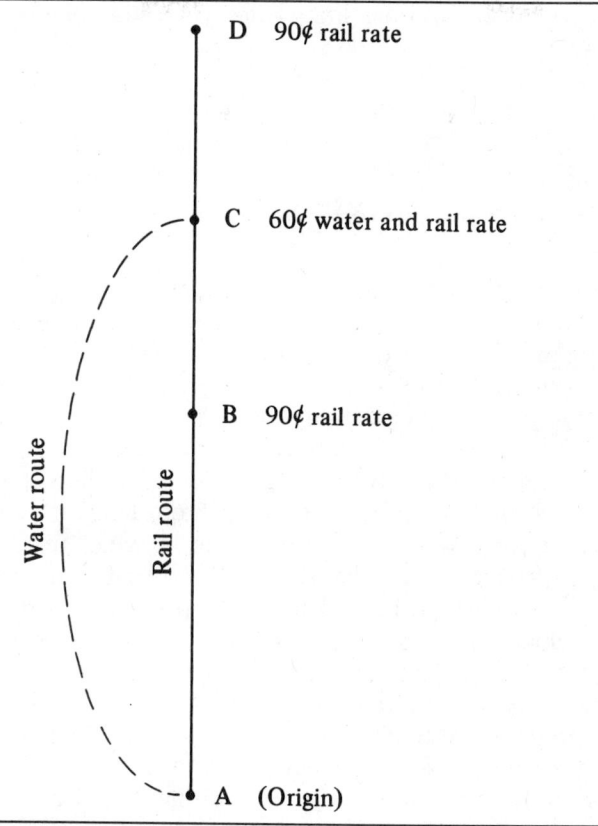

might or might not enter the controversy. If they did, they would use arguments similar to those of B.

This somewhat simplified sketch describes the essential elements and arguments for and against a classic basing point rate structure, which might have come about either by rail-versus-water or rail-versus-rail competition. The economic causes and effects of such a situation can be analyzed, but there is no general agreement on its absolute rightness or wrongness. Rather, a neutral analyst would be likely to decide for or against a basing point rate structure according to the analyst's views on cost-based versus competitive carrier pricing.

Even though the classic basing point rate structures have to a considerable extent broken down or evolved into other forms, important vestiges of them remain in existing rail rate structures. To some extent, although to a much lesser degree due to different cost characteristics, basing point influence has affected truck rates that are competitive with, and patterned after, rail structures. Some knowledge of historical causes, effects, and arguments for and against classic basing point rate structures is therefore essential in understanding important present rate patterns.

BLANKET RATE STRUCTURES

A blanket rate structure, sometimes referred to as group or zone rating, applies the same rate from a given origin (or destination if it is an originating area blanket) to all points within a specified geographical area. In effect, within the area in which this common rate prevails, it is a postage-stamp rate. Blanket rate structures, however, do make use of the distance-rate technique in that the typical product moving for a considerable distance may move through a series of blanket zones, each with a higher rate than the preceding one. Often, blanket rate zones are separated by intermediate buffer zone areas in which rates are quoted on some type of distance-rate basis. Because of rail cost characteristics and the wide area coverage by this mode, blanket rates are most widespread in rail transport. This discussion, therefore, is centered around rail blankets. Other modes, however, do make some limited use of blanket rates.

Blanket rates are quoted both in class and commodity tariffs and on short or intermediate hauls, as well as on long movements. They are most typically used and most highly developed in transcontinental or long-haul movements under rail commodity rate tariffs, however. Blankets on other types of movements usually are fewer and smaller. Either origin or destination points, or both, may be grouped together under a common rate blanket. For purposes of simplicity of exposition in the following discussion, the authors will discuss only destination blankets unless otherwise indicated. The same principles and arguments can easily be applied to origin blankets.

Blanket Forms

In respect to their size and shape, rate blankets are found in at least four distinct forms.

The form of blanket that most readily comes to mind is the very large one that may cover several states or even several different regions of the country. Extreme versions of this type of blanket were pictured and described by Stuart Daggett and John P. Carter in *The Structure of Transcontinental Railroad Rates* (Berkeley and Los Angeles: University of California Press, 1947). One of these involved rates on eastbound California wine that were blanketed for all destinations roughly east of the Rocky Mountains (more specifically, beyond the eastern boundary of Arizona and beyond Salt Lake City). Another similar blanket shown by these authors, with only a few minor differences, applied to eastbound California dried fruits and vegetables.

As noted, these two examples must be considered as unusually large blankets that apply to a postage-stamp or fixed-rate system over by far the larger portion of the country's territory and inhabitants. Fairly large blankets covering both origin and destination points, however, are not at all uncommon in both eastbound and westbound rail-commodity movements. In fact, this is the typical rate pattern of such traffic. Figures 18.3 and 18.4 show a profile and a map illustrating eastbound rail rates for one important product, lumber, originating in the Pacific Northwest. (Rates are now much higher than those shown.)

Another and much smaller form of blanket often includes the small outlying communities around a larger or key point city under a common

Figure 18.3   A Rail Blanket Rate Profile: Lumber Rates, in Cents per 100 lbs., to Various Points from Portland, Oregon, to the Gulf Coast, via the Southern Route

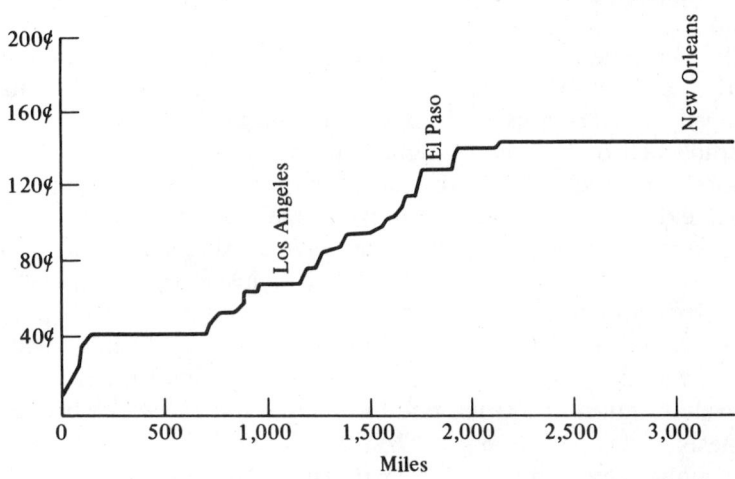

Source: Roy J. Sampson, *Railroad Shipments and Rates from the Pacific Northwest* (Eugene: University of Oregon, Bureau of Business Research, 1961).

rate blanket with the larger city. This relieves the carrier from the burden of publishing and administering many small arbitraries and places buyers or sellers in the entire given metropolitan area upon an equal competitive basis insofar as transport charges are concerned. One effect of this may be that economic activity that otherwise would occur in the central city is encouraged to develop in some of the outlying small communities.

Other blankets take the form of long and narrow strips that group together several successive points along the route of a particular railroad or along somewhat parallel routes. These blankets usually are found through areas of scant population and low traffic density. They are primarily a method of lessening the work of publishing and quoting rates and have little effect on either local economic activity or carrier revenues.

A fourth definite form of rate blanket is one that also is long and narrow, but usually not as narrow as the type just described. This form runs crosswise to the prevailing flow of traffic, which means that it is commonly found running north and south near or east of the Mississippi Valley where the great east-west rail traffic arteries are intersected by north-south rail lines or by north-south water carrier routes. Also, rivers have influenced blanket zone boundaries through the historical use of river crossings as rate break points where rates increase sharply.

These transverse blankets permit carriers connecting with transcontinental or long-haul carriers to participate in traffic movements originated or terminated by the latter carriers without any increase in rates. This benefits the transverse carriers, allows greater routing flexibility, and permits shippers and receivers a greater choice among the long-haul carriers.

Blanketing practices extend well back into the nineteenth century before the establishment of the ICC. The commission, however, has not discouraged blanketing as such, and numerous important blankets have been established during the present century.

In some instances, the coming of motor carrier competition has disturbed existing rail blanket patterns. One can imagine two adjacent blankets with a sizable rate difference between them. In such a case, a shipper desiring to send goods to a point just inside the nearer boundary of the farther and higher rated blanket might ship by rail to a point just at the farther edge of the nearer and lower rated zone. Then, conceivably, it could have the shipment transferred onto a truck and hauled to its ultimate destination at a truck rate lower than the difference between the two zones.

Such maneuvering involving the transfer of lading, however, may be both expensive and impractical. Often the rate differences between two adjacent blanket zones are not sufficient to justify it even in those instances where it might be geographically feasible. Many of the blanket

Figure 18.4   A Rail Blanket Map: Lumber Rates, in Cents per 100 lbs., from Western Oregon and Washington Origins to Various Transcontinental Destinations

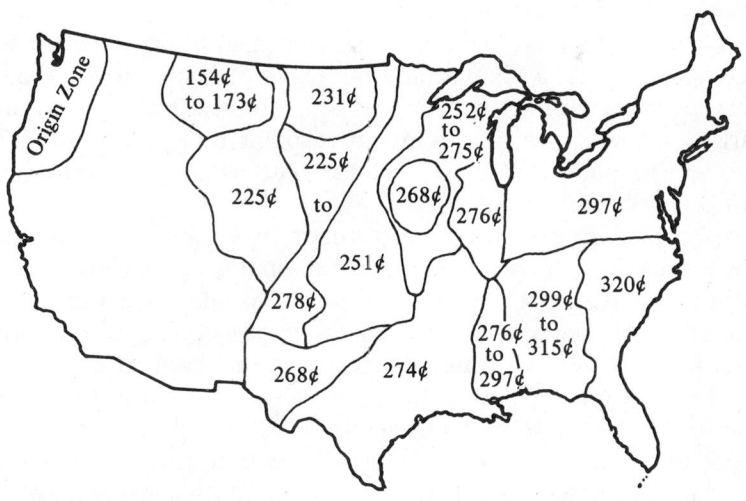

Source: Roy J. Sampson, *Railroad Shipments and Rates from the Pacific Northwest* (Eugene: University of Oregon, Bureau of Business Research, 1961). Revised to June 1978, courtesy Western Wood Products Association.

boundaries are located in areas where available truck transportation is not abundant, and many of the commodities moving under blanket rates are of the type least suited to truck transport. Finally, buffer zones with rapidly increasing distance rates may be inserted between blanket zones with large rate differences if railroads fear such behavior (see Figure 18.4). In general, truck competition between adjacent zones has disturbed blanket rate patterns much less than some earlier transport students and motor carrier enthusiasts thought probable. Recent increased emphasis on cost-based pricing, however, is rapidly breaking down the major traditional blankets.

The Rationale of Blanketing

Rate blankets have been established for various reasons. By grouping a considerable number of points together, they greatly simplify rate publication, quotation, and administration, which benefits both carriers and their customers. Particularly, they may facilitate shipper use of simplified rate maps, cards, circulars, or books based upon the applicable tariffs in lieu of continual resort to the more complex tariffs themselves. Carrier and shipper savings from this feature alone at least partially offset carrier revenue losses on longer hauls or shipper additional payments on shorter hauls within a given large blanket.

Other reasons have probably been of even greater importance, however. Blanket rates provide a compromise method by which carriers may meet their competition without resorting to long-and-short-haul rates. Instead of charging a lower rate to a competitive point than to an intermediate noncompetitive point, the carrier may choose to charge the same lower rates to both points.

For example, in the situation pictured in Figure 18.2 and already described, the carrier might choose to establish a 60-cent blanket covering shipments from A to both B and C. This still would allow the rail carrier to meet its water competition at C and prevent or control the movement of goods from A to C by water for eventual backhaul to B. The carrier no doubt would receive less revenue on a given volume of traffic from A to B, but the lower rate might generate additional traffic to B, and this intermediate point might be much less important than C as a revenue producer in any case. Even if the carrier should receive somewhat less revenue as a result of its rate blanket, this action would not be a fourth-section deviation and normally would be unquestionably legal. Community B's arguments alleging local discrimination would be considerably weakened, and the carrier might not have to incur hearing and litigation expenses in fighting B's protests.

Pressures from producers or purchasers in a given area, many of whom wish to have rate equality with other area sellers or buyers, or who may wish to have a larger geographic area in which to sell or buy without rate penalties, also have contributed to blanket rates. The arguments used by such groups, and the counterarguments used by their opponents, are similar to the arguments for and against the basing point pricing system discussed above. But whereas basing point pricing is in ill repute legally, blanket ratemaking as such does not suffer from legal handicaps.

Producers in one region who are competing in a common outside market with producers of similar items in other regions (which may be nearer the common markets) clearly have applied considerable pressures for large destination blanket rates in common marketing areas. By this device, sellers located in the first-named producing region may be able to expand their marketing territory into areas formerly dominated by their competitors. As different railroads may serve the different producing regions, railroad interest in the expansion of markets usually is similar to producer interest. If the producer customers of a particular railroad or group of railroads serving a given region increase their sales, rail traffic of the serving rail line or lines increases correspondingly.

Many sellers and buyers also like the flexible routing arrangements available within a blanket zone without additional rates. This is particularly important to shippers who make use of diversion and reconsignment in their marketing operations (see above). Cars may be freely diverted or reconsigned in a given zone without any increase in the freight rate itself, subject to any applicable tariff restrictions or additional service charges. In addition, a series of diversions or routing over known slow routes provides additional time for completing sales of moving cars. In effect, the shipper is receiving benefits similar to those which would be available under the delayed rate proposals, while the carrier's vehicle is being used as a storage place for the goods (and the carrier has a considerably greater responsibility than that of an ordinary warehouse business for loss or damage of goods). Again, carriers eager for traffic that might otherwise be lost to them because of interregional producer competition may be willing to make considerable concessions to allow producers in their own region to expand or remain in business.

Shippers and receivers almost always like to be in a position to use, or to threaten to use, alternate competing carriers. Potential loss of traffic to a rival carrier is a powerful stimulus in inducing top-quality service and favorable consideration of customer problems from an individual carrier. Blanket rates, which may allow shippers to choose from among several originating or connecting carriers, give these customers a powerful bargaining tool in dealing with individual carriers and thus may create pressures for such rates.

Pressures of intermediate or terminating carriers on originating carriers also have influenced the formation, size, and shape of blanket zones. Obviously, a geographically large blanket usually requires the participation of many railroads, each of which wants an opportunity to participate in important traffic movements. This influence is especially noticeable in the location and shape of those relatively narrow transverse blankets previously described that run crosswise to the prevailing traffic flow and begin the process of dividing the large originating eastbound traffic streams into a number of smaller streams, or the reverse. But the influence of intermediate and terminating carriers on originators is not limited to this situation.

Carriers that are originators of the products of one region also are terminators or intermediate carriers of products of other regions. This means that rate structures on long-haul traffic, as well as rate revenue divisions among the participating carriers, must be established on some mutually agreeable basis. In other words, long-haul rates are influenced to some extent by the preferences and relative bargaining positions of carriers other than the originating line or lines. These various reasons for the creation of rate blankets outline the principal advantages of, or arguments for, such structures. In summary, although rate simplification and the desire among both customers and carriers for widespread and unhampered carrier participation are important, perhaps competition is the most important cause as well as the most important advantage of blanketing practices. Although at first glance a map picturing a blanket rate structure may appear to be completely chaotic or arbitrary, study of the location of carrier routes and of the competitive conditions existing at the time of its formation usually will reveal a surprisingly logical pattern.

The competition leading to blanketing may be intermodal or intramodal carrier competition. Or it may be interregional or intraregional producer or consumer competition, involving both a desire for uniform rates in a given area and a desire for flexible routing. Often a structure brought forth to deal with a particular competitive problem tends to remain long after the peculiar competitive situation has ceased to exist. Although they do change, rate structures have an inherent stability. Typically they change only gradually. Many vested interests, shipper, consumer, and carrier, local and regional, usually are built up around any major rate structure that exists for any length of time, and such interests can be expected to fight vigorously any proposed changes adverse to their own economic welfare.

The Effects of Blanketing

It is clear that an effect of blanket rates is to give sellers a wider choice of territory and buyers in marketing their products and to give buyers correspondingly wider choices. Also, users are given a wider choice of carriers, at least of the mode quoting such rates (although other modes may be excluded). These effects no doubt increase competition, although producer delivered-price differentials may be decreased. This wider participation of buyers and sellers as well as carriers may even lead to lower consumer prices through lower seller and carrier profit margins and to better qualities and services. Many sellers and buyers, however, especially those who are economically harmed by blanket rates, and even many neutral students of transportation economics and management oppose blanketing practices.

The arguments used or the disadvantages cited by opponents of blanket rates are similar to the arguments against, and the disadvantages of, basing point pricing, postage-stamp and basing point rates, and similar freight equalization or nonmileage rate devices.

To summarize, opponents of blanket rate structures point out that to a considerable extent they ignore distance and resulting cost-of-service differences and lead to cost-increasing circuitous routing and cross-hauling. Some pay higher freight charges than would be exacted under a structure more closely related to distance and the carriers' costs of providing particular services, while others pay less.

It is said, too, that such structures offset natural locational advantages of some shippers or buyers (as a shipper of eastbound products who is located near the eastern boundary of an origin zone, or the buyer of western-produced goods who is located near the western edge of a destination group). Also, opponents say that locational advantages of producing regions located nearer consuming regions are offset by large destination blankets which allow more distant producing regions to penetrate the natural market of the nearer group.

Parenthetically, it should be noted that those who use the expressions "natural market" or "natural locational advantage" in this sense are equating these expressions primarily to distance from market. It has been counterargued that a natural locational advantage is the effect of any circumstances enabling producers or regions to obtain lower rates (and thus quote lower delivered prices) than their competitors or rates lower than they would have to pay under other circumstances. Likewise, a natural market is one in which a seller or a producing region can sell at a lower price than rival sellers or regions. Under such concepts, locational advantage or natural markets might be determined by the relative distances of competitors from the markets in question. On the other hand, nearness in distance might be offset by various other equally natural competitive advantages that result in lower rates and possibly lower prices in common markets for the more distant sellers.

Since good arguments can be made both for and against blanket rate structures, it is likely that those sellers, consumers, modes of carriage, and individual carriers who benefit from them will find grounds for their continuance. Likewise, their counterparts who feel themselves harmed will complain. As in many freight-rate and other economic controversies, there is no absolutely good or bad solution. Insofar as neutral observers or scholars are concerned (if such exist), their judgments on blanket rate structures as well as on other types of rates are likely to be based upon their personal values concerning such matters as cost of service versus value of service and the relative merits of different varieties of competition. Regardless of arguments, this type of ratemaking is well established, almost as old as the railroad industry itself, and is surrounded by strongly entrenched economic interests. Such rates are therefore likely to continue to play their significant role in our transportation economy through the foreseeable future, although large blankets are coming under increasing pressures.

THE POSTAGE-STAMP RATE STRUCTURE

The postage-stamp rate, as its name implies, is chiefly used as a government-determined price for the movement of mail (a form of freight transportation, although often not treated as such in transport textbooks). This method of rate quotation is used for the movement of small parcels, either on a nationwide basis or within defined geographic zones, with charges increasing as zones are crossed in many countries. Also, limited application of the postage-stamp concept is made in almost all actual mileage freight-rate structures as well as in blanket rates (see the following).

Postage-stamp pricing is not only confined to the movement of mail and freight. The same device is commonly used in transporting passengers by streetcar, bus, and subway within cities and often in commuter services. To some extent, too, it appears in intercity passenger transportation. But it extends even beyond these areas to marketing and pricing areas not usually thought of as being directly connected with transportation. The department store that charges the same price for a piece of merchandise whether it is carried from the premises by the buyer or delivered six blocks or six miles by the store is engaging in postage-stamp pricing. So is the large manufacturer in the Northeast that sells its toothpaste at the same price in New York as in San Francisco. Numerous other examples of the use of this pricing concept could be cited. The most notable extension of postage-stamp rates has been into the package express services generally analogous to postal service.

Proposals

It was even seriously proposed in earlier years that all U.S. railroads should base their rates mainly upon a postage-stamp system. In 1898, for example, the so-called Cowles Plan proposed U.S. Post Office Department control of railroads, with passenger fares set at a specified charge per trip regardless of the distance traveled and the only fare differences dependent upon the kind of accommodations used. Under this plan, the use of freight cars would also have been paid for at a fixed rate, varying only with type of car, regardless of distance, contents, or weight of the shipment, in effect, a combination of the postage-stamp and cube-rate concepts.

As late as 1935, the Hastings Plan calling for three railroad fares based upon short distance (up to around 50 miles), regular train service other than short distance, and express train service was submitted to the Senate Committee on Interstate Commerce. A later modification of this plan proposed that fares would be based on the number of 250-mile concentric circular zones traversed. The Hastings Plan dealt only with passenger fares, but apparently it was intended that if adopted it later would be extended to freight service. As the proposed level of fares was fairly low, the plan involved railroad subsidies by the federal government, at least during an initial transitory period. The House Committee on Interstate and Foreign Commerce voted in 1940 to postpone indefinitely an investigation of the proposal.

Effects

Advocates of postage-stamp rates maintain that such rates remove all personal and local discrimination by placing all persons and places upon an equal basis; that rate-quotation problems and tariffs are reduced to the ultimate in simplicity, thus greatly benefiting both shippers and carriers; and that tickets, or stamps, could be sold in numerous places besides ticket offices in the same ways that postage stamps now are sold. Further, both the Cowles Plan and the Hastings Plan, because of their unusually low level of proposed fares and rates, envisioned a great increase in carrier patronage based upon the assumed elasticity of demand for transport services. Proponents of these plans felt that the resulting full use of carrier capacity would eventually lower carrier per-unit traffic costs to a point where very low rates or fares could be profitably maintained.

Opponents of postage-stamp pricing, on the other hand, point out that inevitably under a non-distance-related rate structure, some users must subsidize other users or some users must pay considerably more than is justified by the carrier's cost of providing the service. If a person (or ton of freight) moves for 500 miles at the same price as another moves for 50 miles, for example, the carrier's costs must be somewhat higher on the former movement. Then if the carrier must recover all of its costs from all movements (as it must in the long run to remain in business unless it is subsidized by the general taxpayer), a portion of the charge paid for the short movement may be used to offset the higher costs involved in the long movement. Or if the price is set at a level sufficient to cover long-movement costs, the carrier will be making unduly high charges for short movements.

Under such a pricing system, one might expect that demand elasticities or inelasticities would considerably increase the patronage of those benefiting most from the prevailing established price, whereas those benefiting least or disadvantaged by the price would decrease their use of transport services or turn to alternate sources of supply. Such an effect, of course, could be construed as either personal or regional discrimination, and it would obviously have effects on established location and distribution patterns. It would probably also result in significant shifts in the balance of the carriers' utilization of their capacities and might have an adverse effect on carrier net revenues.

At first glance, it might appear that this discussion of postage-stamp rates is unduly lengthy in proportion to their importance. The concept, even if not the pure form, however, is so widespread among other existing and important rate structures that its implications must be clearly appreciated before one can understand and analyze these other structures.

Even in the age of increased reliance on cost-based rates, this pricing concept can be justified in many cases. Where actual line-haul costs are very low relative to the total costs of service, distance has a small effect on the overall cost of transportation service. For example, the cost of moving a tractor-trailer with a 20,000-pound load over the road is approximately $1.25 per mile, including driver, fuel, and depreciation. This means that a 400-mile trip will cost about $500. The allocated cost of moving a one-ounce letter in this vehicle and as part of the 20,000-pound load is approximately 0.16 cents. This is only six-tenths of one percent of the cost of mailing a letter. In a situation such as this, the related costs of movement, such as handling and pickup and delivery, are so large relative to line-haul costs, that the costs of all movements are for all practical purposes the same.

ADDITIONAL READINGS

Bigham, Truman C., and Merrill J. Roberts, *Citrus Fruit Rates*, Gainesville, Fla.: University of Florida Press, 1950.
   Chapter 3, "Development of the Rate Structure," pp. 49–83.
   Chapter 4, "Comparison of Rates," pp. 84–92.
   Chapter 5, "Appraisal of the Rate Structure," pp. 93–115.
Daggett, Stuart, and John P. Carter, *The Structure of Transcontinental Railroad Rates*, Berkeley, Calif.: University of California Press, 1947, pp. viii, 165.
Locklin, D. Philip, *Economics of Transportation*, 7th ed., Homewood, Ill.: Richard D. Irwin, 1972.
   Chapter 8, "Railroad Rate Structures," pp. 171–210.

Sampson, Roy J., *Railroad Shipments and Rates from the Pacific Northwest,* Eugene: Bureau of Business Research, University of Oregon, 1961.
   Part Three, "Southbound Rail Rates," pp. 33–60.
Troxel, Emery, *Economics of Transport,* New York: Rinehart & Company, 1955.
   Chapter 25, "Structures of Freight Rates," pp. 587–614.
Tyworth, John E., Joseph L. Cavinato, and C. John Langley, Jr., *Traffic Management,* Reading, Mass.: Addison-Wesley Publishing Co., 1987.
   Chapter 5, "Freight Rates," pp. 115–36.

CHAPTER 19

TRANSPORTATION COSTS AND LOCATION OF ECONOMIC ACTIVITIES

In the three preceding chapters, the authors have attempted to blaze a trail for the tenderfoot lost in the wilderness of proliferating freight rates. This chapter will continue by considering some of the effects of freight rates or transportation costs upon the levels and the types of economic activities carried on in particular localities, regions, or areas. (For simplicity of exposition, *freight rate* will be used in this discussion as a synonym for *shipper transportation cost*. The economic effects described below are similar whether the shipper pays a carrier or pays the costs of private transportation.) After a brief review of some further relationships between competition and rate structures, we will discuss three questions insofar as they are affected by freight rates: (1) Where does economic activity locate? (2) Once located, where is the product marketed? (3) What are the relationships between freight rates and area (local, regional, national, etc.) economic development? These questions deal with what might be called *spatial economics*.

In this connection, it is well to remember that by its very nature, no freight rate can be neutral as an influencer of economic activity, not even if the rate is set at a zero level (free transport). Any existing rate or rate structure in a competitive producing or consuming situation and any change in existing rate relationships necessarily benefit some and harm others. Thus, as transport exists in a highly competitive world, it is desirable that those involved with transportation understand something of the nature of the varieties of competition directly affecting their livelihoods.

COMPETITION, TRANSPORT COSTS, AND SPATIAL ACTIVITY

On the demand side of the demand-supply determinants of prices, there are very close and circular interrelationships between competition, freight rates, and spatial economic activity. As has been developed to some extent in the preceding chapter, the presence or the absence of competition affects both the level and the structure of freight rates. The level and structure of rates affect both the types and the volumes of economic activity carried on in particular localities. Existing rates, often competitively determined, help to determine an area's stage of economic development. The area's stage of development (or its type and level of production and consumption) further affects competition and rates. The circular interrelationship is never-ending. Thus it is not too farfetched to maintain that the whole body of the theory and practice of economic development (past, present, and future) is intimately tied to transportation costs (or freight rates).

The pertinent varieties of competition affecting freight rates, and thereby spatial economic development, include competition among carriers, producing centers, consuming centers, and commodities. Each of these is worthy of additional attention at this point.

Carrier Competition

Carrier competition may be intermodal (between modes, such as rail versus truck), intramodal (between carriers of a given mode, such as several trucklines competing for a shipper's freight, several railroads competing for traffic, or several airlines competing for passengers), or both, and it may be over parallel (approximately equidistant) or extremely circuitous routes. The preceding chapters discussed some examples of carrier rate competition.

But service levels are also important. Like other sellers, carriers engage in spirited service or quality competition such as greater speed, lesser damage, pickup and delivery, transit, and a host of others. Also, like many other sellers they may spend considerable effort in promotional competition, including direct-sales solicitation, advertising designed to convince buyers that a particular service is better or cheaper than that of competing carriers (whether it is or not), and the like.

These various forms of carrier competition bring lower rates to some points than would otherwise be forthcoming, and (perhaps as an offset to carrier revenue) losses may bring higher rates to some noncompetitive points. For example, as noted in the preceding chapters, competition is in considerable part responsible for blanket rates, discounting, and similar deviations from distance rate structures. It is well to remember that transportation rates are, in most cases, *distance related* (greater for longer distances than shorter distances) but not *distance proportional* (so much per mile). We have already noted the tapering principle in the preceding chapters, which by itself makes this statement true. Here we wish to emphasize carrier competition, which is another reason why transportation rates are not distance proportional.

Producing Center Competition

The freight-rate effects of competition between producers or groups of regional producers served by different carriers also were considered in Chapter 18. Such producing center competition is especially keen when products of the different centers are identical or reasonably close substitutes. Examples coming readily to mind are western and southern softwood lumber or California and Florida oranges marketed in the Northeast.

The more nearly identical competing products are, either physically or in the buyer's mind, the less can be the price difference between them. Prices charged consumers, of course, must include the costs of transportation (freight rates) plus all other costs of production and distribution (including profits).

Given producers or regional groups of producers may feel, at least in the short run, that their nontransport costs cannot be substantially lowered. Presumably in a highly competitive situation, these other costs would already be as low as the producers' controls could bring them. But competitively squeezed producers may be able to get lower freight rates if the carriers serving them can be convinced that the alternative is producer closure and consequent carrier loss of traffic. It may thus be considerably easier in many instances for producers to lower their transportation costs than their other costs. Such action, in addition to harming competitors in other areas and leading to protests of rate discrimination and demands for readjustments, may significantly affect the economies and the development of the regions concerned.

Producer competition may result in the primary effect just described in which freight rates to a common marketing center are lowered for one regional producing group. A secondary effect also may result, in which rates on inbound raw materials are lowered for a particular group in order that lower costs may enable it to quote a lower price on its finished product. For example, a primary effect would be the establishment of lower rates on Oregon lumber to the Northeast, thus aiding Oregon mills in competition with southern lumber mills. A secondary competitive effect might be the granting of lower freight rates on logs bound to Oregon sawmills, thus reducing Oregon costs to the point where its product can compete even without lower rates on the finished product. The end result is the same in either case, but the secondary form provides much less ammunition for attacking producers in other regions.

Consuming Center Competition

Competition between consuming centers, or directional competition, also may have considerable impact on the economic activities of given areas. A profit-minded and well-informed producer naturally wishes to sell in the market where the net return above all costs, including both transportation and other costs, is greater.

The most profitable market is determined both by the relative local prices prevailing in the alternative markets and by the producer's costs of transporting goods to those markets. Other costs of production and distribution should be about the same, regardless of where the product is sold. If market prices are the same, the producer will sell to the area with the lowest freight rate. If freight rates are the same, the producer will sell in the market with the highest price. If, as is likely, both prices and freight rates vary between the different markets, the producer will choose that combination (not necessarily either the highest price or the lowest rate) that will maximize net return.

To a pure theorist, or from an overall long-run view, the situation just described might appear to be an aberration. Under purely competitive textbook conditions, the producer's net would tend to be the same in all markets. But even though we do live in a competitive world, it is not purely competitive. Producers more often than not do have choices between more profitable and less profitable alternatives if they are well informed about ever-changing market conditions.

Freight rates may be price determined as well as price determining. It is often difficult to tell whether differences in local prices are caused by freight rates or whether differences in freight rates are responses to differences in local prices. This, however, poses no particular problem to producers with goods to sell. To them a given price and rate pattern exists at a given time, offering them an opportunity to increase profits by selling in the appropriate market. And actually, owing to various factors (market imperfections, as an economist might describe them), such a situation may exist for a considerable period of time.

We might use a simple example to illustrate some of the possible spatial economic effects of directional competition. Let us suppose that Illinois widget producers can sell either in New York or California markets which are served by different rail carriers and, further, that the market price and freight-rate combination is such that it is most profitable for them to sell in New York. But the rail carriers connecting Illinois and California, desiring to participate in hauling this lucrative traffic, decide to lower their rate on widgets to a level that makes it more profitable for producers to shift their sales from New York to California.

A probable reaction of the Illinois to New York carriers is a similar rate cut. Eventually, it is likely that rate adjustments will be reached that will permit both groups of carriers to participate in this traffic. As a result, consumers in both California and New York will be buying widgets at lower prices than previously. Then with these lower prices, the elasticity of demand will permit considerably more widgets to be sold in the two markets than were formerly sold in New York alone. To satisfy this demand, producers must increase their outputs, or new producers must enter the field, or both. Thus the Illinois widget industry grows.

It may be, however, that widgets are also produced in Texas for the New York and California markets. If so, Texas producers will correctly allege that the rate cuts have placed them at a competitive delivered-price disadvantage relative to their Illinois competitors. If this results in serious sales losses for the Texans, they will have no difficulty in convincing the different carriers operating between Texas and the California and New York markets that rate reductions will mutually benefit both these carriers and Texas producers. Such reductions, designed to restore previous competitive relationships, may further reduce prices in the consuming areas, lead to still more widget consumption, and alter the widget industry in both producing areas.

Although the illustration used is simple, further reflection on consuming center competition could lead one into many possible complex effects. In addition to directly affecting the economies of the consuming centers involved and a single producing area, the competition of directions may also bring in elements of both carrier competition and producing center competition.

Commodity Competition

Competition between commodities exists when raw materials or components of finished goods may be processed, manufactured, or assembled either at the point of origin, the point of consumption, or perhaps somewhere between. For example, mills near wheat-producing areas may grind grain into flour which is then shipped to consuming centers, or the grain itself may be shipped to consuming centers or intermediate points for manufacture. Cattle may be slaughtered in cattle-growing areas and sent to consuming areas as dressed meat or they may be shipped on the hoof to packing houses in consuming centers.

The problem of where processing or manufacture shall occur is one of the classic topics of industrial location theory which will be further considered. It is also an extremely practical problem, often a matter of

economic survival, for individual processors or manufacturers, their employees, and the communities or regions in which they are located.

The establishment, failure, or survival of this type of production in a
given locality may be largely dependent upon the comparative levels of
the freight rates applicable to the raw material and the finished product.
If rates on wheat and flour are such that it is less costly for a miller to
ship wheat in its original form than in the form of flour after taking into
account the weight losses involved in manufacturing, for example, milling
normally will occur near consuming centers. A different rate pattern,
making it less costly to ship flour than wheat, would influence the location of mills in or near wheat-growing areas. The same principle is applicable to numerous commodities at various stages of production. (Such
simplified generalizations, of course, assume that other things affecting
production costs at the different possible locations are equal or are not
unequal enough to offset freight-rate differences. This may not be true.
On the other hand, inequalities among other things may reinforce rate
differences. We are concerned here only with freight-rate effects, not with
the host of other things that might influence production costs and help
determine location.)

In addition to comparative rate levels between raw and finished products, rate structures that permit stoppage in transit for various kinds of
finishing operations may be powerful determinants of plant location. Many
communities, intermediate between raw materials producing areas and
heavy consuming areas, owe their important position in some processing,
fabricating, or assembling industry to a long-established favorable transit
privilege granted it by some railroad. It may have been the whim of a
long-dead railroad official who was influenced by stock ownership in a
local plant, by ownership of real estate in the favored community, or by
some more worthy or less tangible reason.

During the more than a century in which railroad freight rates and rate
structures have played an important role in determining "how much of
what shall be done where," many delicate balances between raw materials
rates and finished goods rates have grown up and become more or less
accepted by all concerned in numerous industries and communities (as is
also the case for many rates from rival producing centers to common
markets). Rates of other forms of carriage have sometimes modified these
production and distribution patterns, but not significantly in most instances. Other modes, rather, have tended to adapt to existing patterns
of economic activity and existing rail rates.

Sometimes rate structures or other factors have concentrated finishing
operations at the raw materials producing center, sometimes in consuming
areas, and sometimes in between. Often the balance between rates and

other factors is such that some finishing occurs both at raw materials and consuming centers as well as between the two.

In a multi-finishing-point locational pattern, output may be fairly evenly divided among the various points or it may be heavily concentrated in one area with relatively small outputs occurring elsewhere. Regardless of the proportionate shares, however, and regardless of the original causes of the existing division of output, the competitive relationships often are so delicately adjusted that even a slight change in freight-rate relationships will throw the entire mechanism out of balance. As changes in the delivered-price possibilities of the different producing areas vary, output will be shifted toward or away from raw materials areas, consuming areas, or transit points. Production and employment will increase at the favored locations, while mill and factory doors are closing and merchandising and service incomes are diminishing in those areas adversely affected by the rate change.

TRANSPORT COSTS AS LOCATION DETERMINANTS

Freight rates (or producers' transport costs) are generally considered to be only one factor, but often a very important factor, in determining where a particular plant will or should locate, or how much of what kind of economic activity will occur in particular areas.

Economic Rationality

In a competitive situation, producers naturally will prefer a location which, all cost factors taken into account, will enable them to lay down their goods in their potential market at a price lower than, or at least as low as, the prices of competitors. They must meet or beat the competition if they are to prosper. Even if competition is not keen, producers will prefer the lowest-cost location, as this will increase their profits. This lowest-cost location principle is as valid for a neighborhood grocery store as for a giant manufacturing concern with national or worldwide markets, and it underlies all location and market-area theory and rational practice.

Many businesses have located and thrived in economically irrational locations, of course, because of combinations of circumstances that may or may not be explainable. Also, many barely literate persons have become multimillionaires. These numerous exceptions do not negate the value of a choice business location or of education, however. It is possible, although not subject to proof, that many of these exceptional successes would have been even more successful with the benefits of a good location or a good education. (This assumes, of course, that other things in the personal makeup of the individuals concerned which contributed to their successes would not have been changed by preferred business locations or better educations.) As a generalization, no one would seriously dispute the proposition that those with the greatest competitive advantages, whether in location or education, are most likely to be successful, whereas those operating under the greatest competitive handicaps are most likely to fail.

In the remainder of this chapter, since this book is on transportation rather than on the whole gamut of location, marketing, and development, we will be primarily concerned with the transportation cost or freight-rate aspects of location, market areas, and regional economic development. This emphasis does not imply that other cost or even noncost factors should be ignored. Location and marketing are not always economically rational. Neither is it true that economically rational action always dictates that products locate at the point where their total transportation costs (inbound plus outbound) will be lowest, any more than it is always economically rational to sell in markets accessible by the lowest freight rates. An economically rational producer, as usually defined, tries to maximize profits. This involves minimizing total costs of production and distribution, of which transportation is only one, and selling in the markets where prices yield the largest return over costs (or if forced to sell at a loss, in markets where prices most nearly cover costs).

The following discussion, then, will assume that producers are economically rational and well informed, and that other things (nontransport factors) are equal. Starting from this base and with an understanding of the principles involved, readers or decision makers can relax these analytical assumptions as they choose to fit particular circumstances.

Because of space limitations, our discussion will also be mainly concerned with theory. In practice, almost every decision must be based on numerous factors that differ in detail. It would be difficult even to list all these factors and impossible to properly weight them to cover all potential situations. But the practitioners with a working knowledge of theory can reach workable answers in a variety of situations. It is possible to have good theory and bad practice, but it is virtually impossible to have good practice without good theory (even though practitioners may not consciously realize that they are applying good theory or any kind of theory and may not admit it even if they do realize it).

If we conceive the term *transportation cost* in a broad sense, we can convincingly argue that all regional or spatial production and distribution cost differences (except a few kinds of extractive production such as mining, fishing, and certain kinds of agriculture requiring particular localized natural resources) can be reduced to transportation cost differences. In other words, the economically rational location of all forms of refining, processing, manufacturing, fabricating, assembling, and distribution, as well as some extractive operations, is in the final analysis based upon transportation considerations alone.

INTRODUCTION TO LOCATION THEORY AND TRANSPORTATION

Traditional location theory has been concerned with two principal types of problems: (1) Where does productive economic activity (a firm or an industry) locate in order to maximize its profits, assuming that markets are fixed, or, stated another way, why do particular patterns of location develop? (2) Where is it most profitable for the firm or industry to market its product, assuming a given or existing locational pattern? This version is often called *market-area theory*. Both of these problems have been approached from a least-cost viewpoint, and transportation costs have been considered an important location factor.

Some theorists, principally geographers or historians, also have been interested in the factors determining the location of cities. And more recently, considerable theoretical and practical attention has been given to what is variously called regional economics, regional development, or even regional science. City location and regional economic development, also, as will be shown, are closely related to transportation and its costs.

The spadework of J. H. von Thünen (for agriculture) and Alfred Weber (for industrial operations) is considered classical in the fixed market approach to location. Frank A. Fetter and August Lösch have done almost equally classical work in the fixed production points area. Other theorists have elaborated upon, refined, or empirically tested much of the work of these pioneers and perhaps have even developed some new theory. Location literature is large and growing, encompassing so much that even a brief mention of all its notable contributors would exceed our space limitations.

Those interested in any aspect of transportation, therefore, might find it interesting and rewarding to delve more deeply into this literature and especially into the relationships among transport costs and location, marketing areas, and regional or community economic development. In order to acquaint readers with the bare skeletons of some of this theory and to stimulate further interest in it, the authors outline what they feel are the most pertinent portions of von Thünen's and Weber's theories and of city location in the following three sections of this chapter. The fourth section treats market-area theory in the same way. The final section of the chapter deals with the location of logistics channels.

AGRICULTURAL LOCATION:
J. H. VON THÜNEN

The theoretical work of von Thünen, one of the earliest efforts systematically relating transport costs to specific locational patterns, was based upon some forty years of his experience in managing a large nineteenth-century German agricultural estate. He was primarily interested in finding what kind of crops and methods of cultivation were most profitable under certain marketing conditions.

Although his voluminous study was empirical in that it was based mainly upon a careful study of his own records and accounts beginning in 1810 and extending until his death in 1850, von Thünen expressed the theory for which he is famous in a very formalized way. The principal criticism of his published study is not of the theory itself. His logic is virtually unassailable within the framework of its assumptions, and his empirical data were monumental. Rather, it has been his highly simplified assumptions that have been questioned by some.

In setting forth his theory, von Thünen assumed an isolated state made up of one central city located in the center of a large plain. The plain was of equal fertility, climate, and terrain throughout its extent and was used for agriculture. The city received all its agricultural products from its surrounding plain or hinterland and was the only market available to the farmers on the plain. The farmers were conscious profit-maximizers and were perfectly free to engage in whatever type of agriculture they chose. But prices for agricultural products were set by the city market and were not subject to farmer control. Finally, there was one form of transportation, equally available to all farmers on the plain and moving from all points in a direct line to the city, with freight rates set on a straight ton-mileage basis regardless of the kind of product hauled. The problem to which von Thünen addressed himself, then, was what kind of agricultural production would occur in what parts of the plain.

By his assumptions, making most of the variables equal, von Thünen kept his variables and unknowns to a manageable number even for the precomputer era. Transportation costs, the key variable, could be computed from any point simply by weight times miles times whatever rate the analyst chose. Costs associated with the two unknowns — types of crops and methods of cultivation — also could be set at any chosen level. Actually, von Thünen's extensive records provided a basis for establishing transportation, crop, and method costs, and city prices.

The problem was attacked by a model or equation as follows: profits equal market price minus production costs and transport costs. Market price was given and was the same for any product grown by any method at any point in the plain. Production costs also were given and were the same for any crop and method at any point. Transport costs varied directly with distance from the city. Now it was only necessary for von Thünen to feed his numbers into the model to determine which crops and methods were most profitable at various distances from the market.

Note that all points at an equal distance from the city paid the same transportation costs for the same product. This means that whatever crop and method are most profitable at any given point are also most profitable at all other points the same distance from the market; and if all these equal-distance points are connected, a circle is formed around the city. Thus crops and methods are grouped into a series of concentric circular zones, with only one crop and method prevailing in any one zone.

As one might guess, within the limits of early nineteenth-century transport technology and assuming a straight ton-mileage rate, von Thünen proved that perishable products and products heavy in relation to their value will be produced near the market; items that are less perishable and more valuable per unit of weight will be produced farther away.

Specifically, he found that items such as milk and vegetables would be produced in the first zone surrounding the city (remember, neither fast nor refrigerated transport was available). Zone two would grow timber for lumber and fuel (high weight, low value). Zones three, four, and five would grow grain with the intensity of cultivation decreasing as one moved from zone three to four to five. Zone six, the outermost area of the plain, would produce livestock for slaughtering and cheese. Figure 19.1 diagrams this situation.

The decreasing intensity of cultivation with increasing distance from the market was explained by von Thünen's observation that net farm prices were gross city prices minus transport costs. Thus the farther a given farm is from the city, the lower its net price for a given quantity of product. A given quantity of land near the city, yielding high net prices per unit of product, can be made much more profitable with intensive applications of labor and capital which increase its per-acre output. But land farther away with lower net prices cannot profit proportionately as

Figure 19.1   Von Thünen's Zones

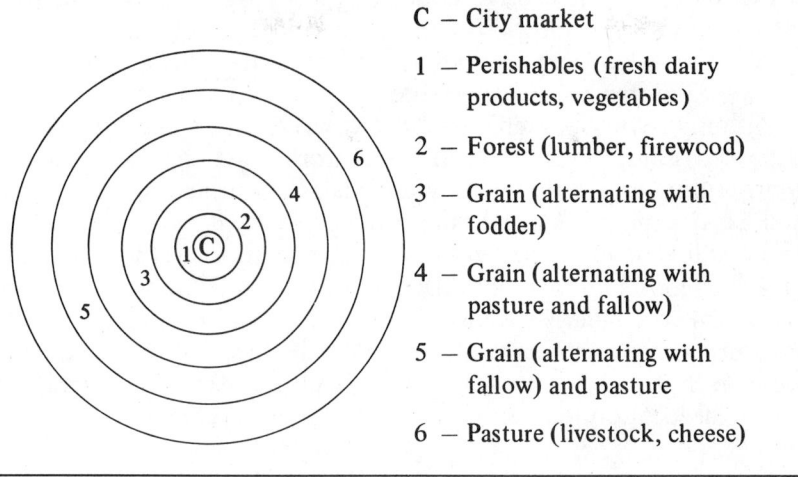

C — City market

1 — Perishables (fresh dairy products, vegetables)

2 — Forest (lumber, firewood)

3 — Grain (alternating with fodder)

4 — Grain (alternating with pasture and fallow)

5 — Grain (alternating with fallow) and pasture

6 — Pasture (livestock, cheese)

much by such intensive use of labor and capital, and consequently its owners cannot afford to spend as much for these services as can landowners nearer the market. Thus extensive agriculture, relying more on land and less on labor and capital for its inputs, becomes more profitable as distance from the market increases.

Distance and the cost of overcoming distance (transportation) thus become the important variables in what crops are produced in a given area as well as the methods of production. When the characteristics of the commodities are added (weight, value, perishability, for instance), transportation determines the location. As an aside, the transportation characteristics of various products have been mentioned in prior chapters relative to the factors considered in freight classification — which was not well developed in von Thünen's time. Indeed, it can be said that von Thünen's location theory for agricultural production laid the basis for modern freight classification.

Further, a theory of rent or of land value based on site location also was developed by von Thünen's analysis. As net farm prices per unit of output decrease with increased distance from the market, land nearer the market yields its owners greater returns per acre than more distant land. Thus, as economic values are based on economic yields, those sites nearest the market are most valuable and can command the highest sale or rental prices. Given specific price and cost data such as those used by von Thünen, the relative values of different sites can be easily calculated.

Von Thünen's theory could be proven by his agricultural records as mentioned above. But even today, one can empirically prove von

Thünen's theory by observing agricultural production and land values in the United States and other countries. What will be produced at a given site depends on transportation costs and the characteristics of the commodity — and land values will turn on the availability and cost of transportation as far as agriculture is concerned.

Although von Thünen's analysis was very formalized and his assumptions necessarily highly restrictive, his work must be classed as a notable contribution to location theory and its relationship to transportation as well as to some other areas of economic theory. It was a pioneering effort which still is much discussed more than a century later for its conclusions as well as for its methodology. By modifying von Thünen's assumptions to fit today's very different transport technology and real-world facts, today's students or analysts can obtain valuable insights into the theory of location not only as it concerns agriculture but also in the fields of industrial location, distribution, and regional development.

INDUSTRIAL LOCATION: ALFRED WEBER

Alfred Weber, also a German economist, published his *Theory of the Location of Industries* in 1909. Although much of his work was original, some of it drew upon work done by Wilhelm Launhardt, a German mathematician, during the 1880s. Also, in a different context, it built upon von Thünen. Weber was concerned with manufacturing and processing operations.

Like von Thünen, Weber's analysis was highly formalized and hemmed in by limiting assumptions. His assumptions, though, were perhaps less restrictive and somewhat more in accord with the real world than were those of von Thünen. Also, Weber dealt with several different types of locational situations.

To understand Weber's conclusions relating transportation to location, one must clearly understand his assumptions and terminology. Like von Thünen, he assumed equal transport accessibility and straight ton-mileage rates regardless of the product carried. Also, his market was fixed in a specific place. Several assumptions were made regarding the work force, its skills, and labor costs. For our purposes, however, we can assume that the necessary labor is equally available at the same costs in all locations. Some of the raw materials used in production are *ubiquities* (available everywhere at the same price). Examples would be sand, air, or water. Other raw materials are *localized* (found only in specific fixed locations). Examples would be mineral deposits such as iron ore, copper, lead, or timber or any raw material found only in a specific location. These are also assumed to have the same price wherever found. Further, some raw materials are *pure*, that is, they do not lose weight in processing or manufacturing; others are *gross* and do lose weight in processing or manufacturing. Here Weber introduced technology and process.

Although Weber used much more involved terminology and assumptions, these are sufficient for the portions of his work to be discussed here. We will consider two cases, one dealing with a single market and a single raw material, and the other dealing with a single market and two raw materials. Several different locational situations and their solutions will be presented under each of these cases, however. Once the solutions to these relatively simple situations are understood, readers will be well on their way toward understanding Weber's concept of the role of transport in location and better fitted to apply his type of analysis in solving much more complex problems.

Three different situations may be imagined under Weber's one market, one raw material case. First, the raw material may be ubiquitous (equally available everywhere). If so, production obviously will occur at the market. It would not be rational to pay freight charges on a raw material that can be obtained without transportation cost at the consuming point of the finished product. Perhaps the reader has noticed that beverage bottling plants for soft drinks tend to be located at their market. Who would ship water (unless it had some particular attribute that made it distinctive)? Second, the raw material may be a pure (non-weight-losing) material localized at a point away from the market. Then production can take place either at the raw material source or at the market. Or if we ignore extra handling costs, production could occur at any point on a direct line between the raw material source and the market. Little is lost in the process and many products are derived from crude oil refining, for example. Thus we find refineries near the oil fields, near the markets, and sometimes in between. Third, if the raw material is gross (weight-losing) and localized away from the market, production will take place at the source of the raw materials. Copper is smelted close to the mine since such a large amount of ore must be processed to get a small amount of copper. It would be uneconomical to ship all the waste a long distance. Timber is made into lumber near the forest, iron ore is "beneficiated" or concentrated near the mine (unless it is of very high quality), and phosphate rock is concentrated or transformed into fertilizer near its source. Any process which involves weight loss will tend to pull manufacturing toward raw material sources.

Turning to the second case, Weber assumed two raw material sources and a single market. Four situations can exist here. First, if both raw materials are ubiquitous, processing and manufacturing will be at the market. Second, if both raw materials are pure but localized away from the market, production will be located at the market and the cost of transporting one raw material to the other will be eliminated. The only exception to this would be where one raw material must pass directly through the source of the other raw material on its way to the market. Third, if both raw materials are pure but one is localized and the other is ubiquitous, production will occur at the market and involve transportation costs of only the localized raw material. Fourth, if both raw materials are gross (weight-losing) and both are localized away from the market, the Weberian locational triangle is involved.

This last situation is the most complex and most comparable to the majority of real-world, industrial location problems. Both raw materials lose weight, thus costs cannot be minimized by market-point production unless the market is located on a straight line directly between the two materials and unless the combination of weight-losing characteristics of the two materials or the proportionate representation of each in the finished product, or both, fall within certain percentage limits. Readers can demonstrate this for their own satisfaction by a few simple calculations using varying weight-loss and combination patterns. Likewise, ton-mileage can be kept to a minimum by moving one raw material to the other's source for production only if the two material sources are on a straight line with the market and only if the weight-losing and combination characteristics of the materials fall into limited percentage relationships (again, this can be demonstrated by a few calculations using varying assumptions).

It is in the less restricted situation of two localized gross materials located away from the market and not located such that a straight line will connect them and the market that the Weberian solution becomes less obvious but of more general practical importance. In picturing this situation, imagine three straight lines, with one connecting the two raw materials sources and with the other two connecting each source with the market — a triangle with the market at one corner and a raw materials source at each of the other two corners. Obviously production will not occur at any point outside the triangle, as this would mean more transportation than is necessary. It must occur, then, on one of the legs of the triangle (including the corners) or at some point within the area of the triangle. But where?

Simple calculations using any assumed weights and weight-losing characteristics on a scale model of such a locational triangle or even simple inspection should show that ton-mileage cannot be minimized by producing at any corner or on any leg of the figure. Production therefore occurs at some point within the triangle, that point being the one where the two raw materials can be brought together and the finished product shipped from there to the market with the least ton-mileage expenditure. A Weberian locational triangle is pictured in Figure 19.2.

Just where within a triangle a specific least-cost point will fall will be determined by a combination of the relative quantities of each of the materials used and by their relative weight-losing characteristics. If equal quantities of the two materials are required, but one loses more of its weight when combined into the finished product, for example, the production point will be located nearer the greater weight loser. Or, if absolute weight losses are equal but one material is used in greater quantities than the other, the two will be brought together for production nearer the material used in greatest quantity.

To borrow physical science terminology, the center of gravity — where total ton-mileage of raw materials and finished product is minimized — is a balance or equilibrium resulting from the relative weight pulls. Greater weights pull harder than lesser weights, and larger weight losses pull harder than smaller weight losses. The computations involved in finding the exact center of gravity can become involved for the ordinary arithmetic-and-pencil mathematician, but the principle is easy to understand and the calculations can easily be done by a slightly higher level of mathematics or a computer. Some students have demonstrated the relative strengths of the various pulls by a simple physical model consisting of a triangular frame over the corners of which run interconnecting lengths of string with weights attached.

Weber's contribution, like von Thünen's, called attention to the influence of transportation costs upon the spatial location of specific kinds of economic activity. Also, it further explained why some types of production are said to be market oriented (ubiquitous or low weight-losing materials), some raw materials oriented (high weight-losing materials), and why a great many are most profitably located at a specific determinable point in an area intermediate between raw materials sources and the market. (The so-called footloose industry — that is, one that can locate equally well in any spot or in a wide variety of locations — in terms of this chapter must be a misnomer or at least so rare as to be a great curiosity.) Not the least of Weber's contributions was the presentation of a methodology that can be expanded far beyond his basic use of it in dealing with a variety of details and more complicated situations.

Like von Thünen, Weber has been criticized for his unrealistic assumptions. His variables were few. (His work preceded the electronic computer by a half-century.) Most producers use several raw materials and sell in several markets. Blanket, tapering, and similar deviations from distance

Figure 19.2 Weber's Locational Triangle

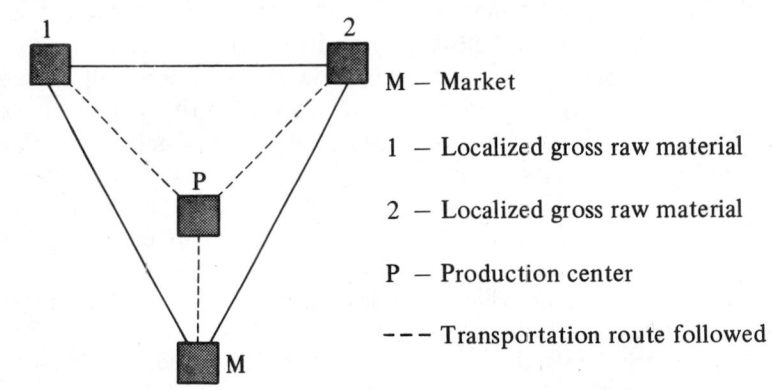

M — Market

1 — Localized gross raw material

2 — Localized gross raw material

P — Production center

- - - Transportation route followed

structures were not brought into his basic analysis, nor were transit privileges, existing carrier route patterns, and many other transport and nontransport factors that often affect, or are thought to affect, location in the real world.

Such criticisms at best are invalid as they are based on a misconception of the nature and purpose of theory. A theory is a model, perhaps based to some extent upon an abstraction from the real world (and sometimes not), making use of a limited number of variables chosen by the theorist according to his or her judgment of their relevance for a particular explanatory or predictive purpose. As such, Weber's theory was well constructed and answered his questions. It seems doubtful if his questions could have been better answered, and it is certain that his analysis would have been much more lengthy and complicated had he used a computer to grind out solutions from a great mass of complicated empirical real-world data. Those interested simply in understanding fundamental location principles as related to transport can be thankful for Weber's unrealistic assumptions.

Those interested in the practice of location, however, can and do modify and build upon the Weberian framework in many ways. Especially since the advent of high-speed computers, it is possible to expand his simple models to include almost any number of markets, numerous raw materials (in any desired quantities, ubiquitous or localized at many sources, pure or gross in any degree) as well as various freight-rate structures and levels, and even such so-called nontransport factors as differing labor costs, tax rates, land values, and raw materials and finished goods prices in different areas. As stated earlier, simple location theory has blossomed into complex practice. But the fundamentals remain unchanged. The location of production depends on the interaction of transportation costs and production costs (including technology and process).

THE LOCATION OF CITIES

Except in those resort and retirement areas where cities grow up because of such attractions as unusual scenery, climate, or similar manifestations of nature, or legalized gambling or quickie divorces, cities have been founded and exist primarily to serve the needs of commerce. This is their principal reason for being.

Cities may also make it possible for one to enjoy cultural advantages not readily brought into the hinterlands. (This could be considered a necessary fringe benefit or an offset to other conditions which encourages persons to live in cities.) Another incidental result of cities is that they concentrate many people in small areas, thus perhaps making it easier to house, feed, clothe, amuse, police, and cater to the needs and demands of large populations.

Cities serve commerce by bringing together in one place the necessary quantity and kind of labor and facilities needed to perform large-scale manufacturing, storage, and distribution functions, including concentration and dispersion of goods, breakbulk operations and trans-shipments, and their associated financing and numerous other business services. Second, they provide large markets in concentrated areas for almost every kind of product. Thus, as most cities exist to serve commerce (which depends upon transportation) and also are large consumers of the output of commerce, it is reasonable to expect that there is a relationship between transport and the location of cities.

If one looks carefully at a detailed map of the world showing major transportation routes as well as population concentrations, a striking fact is discernible. Almost all great cities, and even most of the not-so-great, are located either where transportation routes intersect or where goods change from one mode of transport to another. The principal exceptions are the resort cities mentioned and those communities based upon the exploitation of some fixed natural resource.

This situation is hardly coincidental. Since long before the dawn of written history, people met and exchanged products where trails or trade routes crossed or where navigable waters ended and land routes began.

It was only natural as time passed that some persons would take up permanent residence at the most important of these trading places to make their living by providing food, housing, and other necessities for the traders and by aiding in the performance of the labor involved in transferring goods from one mode of carriage or from one person to another. It was also natural that some of these permanent residents would see profitable opportunities in supplying storage space for traders and eventually go into the merchandising business and even into manufacturing and financing operations. The success of these residents attracted others to do likewise or to serve the needs of the now growing community. Thus the crossroads, the harbor, the fall line, or the end of the rail line developed into a trading post and eventually into a great redistribution, merchandising, manufacturing, financial, cultural, and consuming center.

It is unnecessary to go further into this aspect of history which is amply documented in our own country's development as well as elsewhere. It is clear that transportation factors have been and are major determinants in city location and development. Chambers of commerce and other civic groups are well aware of this and leave no stones unturned in their quest for more favorable freight rates and more and better carrier services and transport facilities.

Not all transport-induced city growth has come from the existence of natural or even manmade transport routes, however. Transit privileges and rates and basing point and rate structures, discussed in Chapter 18, have given advantages in manufacturing and distribution to cities otherwise without significant natural advantages. Some large communities have grown up and still are very dependent upon such artificial rate benefits.

Other cities once favored by natural or artificial transport advantages have become diversified with size and age and have managed to remain important or could remain important even with the loss of the advantages that led to their founding and earlier growth. As a city develops a broader economic base and devotes relatively more of its efforts to producing goods and services for its own inhabitants, it naturally develops more resistance to particular transportation shocks. No large city, however, is self-sufficient enough to survive for any lengthy period of time without good transport facilities and rates.

In summary, then, city location and growth are related to transport in more than one way. As servers of the commerce of wider areas, they are initially located at points where the most and best services can be supplied, and they grow and prosper as the commerce served grows and prospers. As their size and importance increases, their employment opportunities attract additional people. Additional industry is attracted because people are available as employees and consumers and because of the convenience of the available services as well as the existing transport routes. This development, in turn, leads to pressures for the development of even better transport services and often for the creation of new routes or the extension or deviation of existing routes in other areas to serve the city. Transportation and the city feed upon each other for their mutual benefit.

TRANSPORT COSTS AND NATURAL MARKETING AREAS: FETTER, LÖSCH, ET AL.

The fixed-production-points-and-variable-markets question (as contrasted with the fixed-market-and-variable-production-points approach illustrated by von Thünen and Weber) is the second major topic of traditional location theory. As several aspects of this problem have already been commented upon in this and the two preceding chapters, discussion will be brief and mainly confined to theoretical features. Frank Fetter, an American economist, and the German economist August Lösch, among others, have made notable contributions to this theory.

Unless otherwise indicated, the discussion assumes rational and informed sellers and buyers and a natural market area as a space in which a seller has a laid-down cost or price advantage over competitors if both transportation costs and all other costs of production and distribution are considered. (A seller, as the term is used here, may also be engaged in industrial, agricultural, or extractive operations rather than in distribution alone. This makes no difference in the cases we will consider.) There are many reasons why sellers might find it desirable or profitable to sell in areas in which they do not have such an advantage and even to sell in some markets at less than their total laid-down costs. Such reasons are beyond the scope of our discussion, however. To illustrate transportation cost effects, we can limit our consideration to transport costs and their changes by assuming that other factors remain constant.

For simplicity, we can imagine that our marketing operations occur in a von Thünen–type plain where transport is equally accessible on a direct line between any given selling center and all its potential buyers, and freight rates are on a straight ton-mileage basis for the particular product concerned. In addition, assume that all buyers in the plain have an equal demand (willingness and ability to pay) for the product, but as prices increase, less will be bought until at some level of prices, no sales at all will be made. The basic principles illustrated by this device can be applied in real-world problems involving a variety of freight-rate structures and levels as well as varying other production and distribution costs.

One Seller

First, assume one seller is located in the center of our plain. What will determine the extent and shape of its marketing area? Obviously the extent of its operations (the distance from the seller's base at which it will be able to sell) will be determined or limited by other given costs plus transport, costs which vary directly with distance. At some point, an equal distance in all directions from the selling point, high prices will cause sales to cease, thus defining the marketing area. As all sales stop at an equal distance from the selling point, clearly the shape of the marketing area is a perfect circle centered on the selling point (see Figure 19.3[a]).

Two Sellers

Second, assume the same conditions, except that two sellers of the same product with equal other (nontransport) costs are now located on our plain. What will determine the sizes and shapes of their respective natural marketing areas? Each seller will have an advantage at all buying points closer to it than to its competitor's base, thus no buying points except those on an imaginary line intersecting the plain at an equal distance from each seller can have the same laid-down costs or prices. It is fairly obvious, therefore, that the boundary between the two natural marketing areas would be a straight line midway between the sellers which intersects at right angles another straight line drawn directly connecting the sellers (Figure 19.3[b]). Each seller would dominate in the territory on its own side of the boundary, and the other seller would be excluded.

Third, assume these exact conditions, except that freight rates from seller X to all points are increased across the board by some specified percentage or amount, while rates from seller Y remain unchanged. What happens to the sizes and the boundary between the two marketing areas? Clearly, as seller X's costs to all points now have increased, X's natural marketing area will be reduced as seller Y's area increases. The equal-cost point on the direct line between the two will be pushed closer to seller X. But the market area dividing boundary will no longer take the form of a straight line. Instead, as insertion of hypothetical cost figures for the two sellers on a scale diagram easily shows, the boundary line will bend backward around seller X in a hyperbolic curve (not a segment of a perfect circle) whose ends will not come together even if extended to the ends of our plain (Figure 19.3[c]). The specific location of this dividing line will be determined by the amount of X's rate handicap.

Figure 19.3   Natural Market Areas under Various Transport Rates

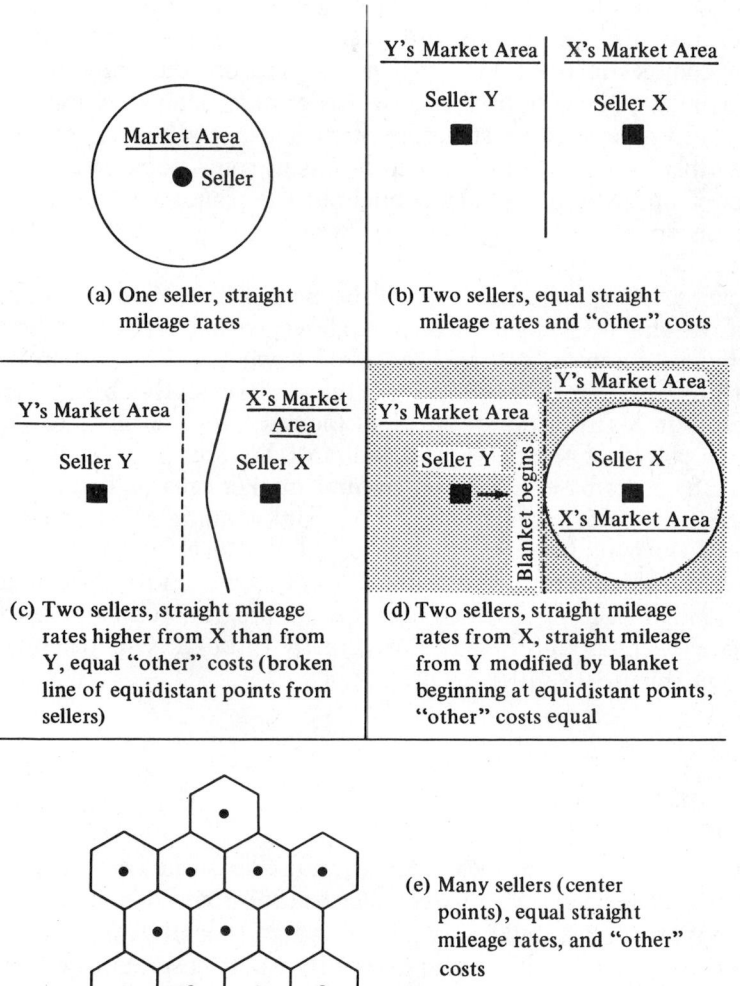

(a) One seller, straight
    mileage rates

(b) Two sellers, equal straight
    mileage rates and "other" costs

(c) Two sellers, straight mileage
    rates higher from X than from
    Y, equal "other" costs (broken
    line of equidistant points from
    sellers)

(d) Two sellers, straight mileage
    rates from X, straight mileage
    from Y modified by blanket
    beginning at equidistant points,
    "other" costs equal

(e) Many sellers (center
    points), equal straight
    mileage rates, and "other"
    costs

Incidentally, note that the same kind of market-area-boundary shift would occur if instead of an increase in X's freight rates: (1) Y's rates are decreased; (2) rates from both selling points are decreased, but with greater decreases from Y; or (3) rates from both are increased, but with greater increases from X. Also, with transportation costs remaining identical for the two sellers, the same market-area shifts would come from relative changes in their other production and distribution costs.

As a final modification of the two-seller case, let us assume that the straight ton-mileage rate structure from seller Y's base is modified by adding a blanket rate from Y which begins at some point on a direct line between Y and X and extends throughout the plain to points at this particular distance or greater distances from Y. Rates from X remain unchanged. What is the market-area effect?

Insofar as X is concerned, it will be placed in a similar condition to that of the single seller first described above; its market will be limited to those buyers whom it can reach at a laid-down price lower than its competitor's. Then, as Y's costs do not change once the blanket zone is reached, but X's transportation costs increase on a straight ton-mileage basis, all points of the outermost limits of X's area will be at an equal distance from its base. Seller X's natural market area will therefore take the form of a perfect circle with a boundary running through the points where its outbound transport costs equal the level of Y's blanket rate. Seller Y will dominate the remainder of the plain; and if its blanket rate is low enough in comparison to X's mileage rate, it can dominate the area beyond X even though it may ship directly through X to reach some of its buyers (Figure 19.3[d]).

Many Sellers

As our final case, we will consider a multiseller situation. Imagine again our von Thünen plain with its peculiar transport and demand conditions. Instead of one or two sellers, assume that a considerable number of sellers of the same product, all with equal nontransport costs (and with straight ton-mileage costs), are located at various points throughout the plain. What determines the size and shape of the natural marketing area of each seller?

Market-area size is fixed by laid-down, delivered costs, and as we have assumed other costs equal, this reduces to transport costs. The area in which each seller will have an advantage, therefore, is determined by the geographical location of the seller in relationship to immediately surrounding competing sellers and the distance from them. With given specific transport-cost figures, this can easily be computed.

It may not at first be obvious what shape the marketing areas (or the imaginary lines bounding them) of the various sellers will take. Marketing areas cannot take the form of circles as this would mean either that some parts of the plain would not fit into any seller's area or the natural marketing areas would overlap. Both these solutions are excluded by our assumptions and definitions.

To completely cover the plain without overlap, then, requires that all market areas must take the shape of some regular polygonal figure. Squares or regular triangles with a marketing point located at the center of each would satisfy our requirements that the entire plain be covered without overlap, but distances (and thus transport costs and prices) would be considerably higher from centers to buyers located in or near corners than to other buyers. As one of our basic assumptions is that higher prices result in fewer sales, it follows that sales in the plain as a whole as well as of individual sellers can be increased by reducing the price differentials applicable to these corner buyers if this can be done without offsetting transport cost and price increases elsewhere. What shape of figure can do this?

It can be demonstrated rigorously by mathematics, or perhaps to a nonmathematician's satisfaction by doodling on a sheet of regular graph paper, that a group of regular hexagons — figures with six equal sides and angles — not only completely covers the plain without overlap, but best meets the requirements of reducing transport costs and consequent price differentials to outlying buyers. This form of market area both enables each seller to maximize profits over a given geographic area by selling more at lower transport costs and allows a larger volume of total sales by all sellers in the plain as a whole. Under our assumed conditions, then, the entire plain would be divided into a honeycomb-like arrangement of natural marketing areas, each with a seller at its center. As a physical analogy, we might imagine a group of tangent circles being pressed together from without (by rational desires for maximum profits) until they assume the form of a group of hexagons. Figure 19.3[e] shows such a situation.

The above few simple examples illustrate the principal workings of transportation cost effects in market-area determination. Insofar as the real-world conditions surrounding competitive marketing differ substantially from the rigid assumptions of our models, as they do, real-world marketers necessarily must analyze their problems by appropriate modifications of the models. But, we repeat, a good grasp of fundamentals greatly aids one in dealing with problems involving numerous complex details.

LOCAL MARKETS: REILLY AND CONVERSE

The models discussed above are most often used in nonlocal or long-distance marketing-area analysis, but they might easily be modified to fit strictly local situations. In addition to these, various models have been especially designed for analyzing or predicting local trade patterns, or for measuring or predicting the interactions between areas. These latter models also might be adapted to long-distance situations.

In general, this latter group of models postulates that size of an area or city exerts a demand pull and that distance brings a supply drag. Trade or other interaction between two communities varies positively according to their sizes and negatively according to distance. In the simple size-distance formulation of such models, there is an implicit assumption that other factors are equal. On the demand side, this means similar cultural, social, and physical environments, and income levels; for supply, it means that distance, usually under a straight-distance formula, is the only pertinent cost difference to be overcome. For completeness and because overcoming distance involves transport costs, some of these so-called gravitational or gravity models will be briefly described.

One of the most celebrated of these models in retailing circles is W. J. Reilly's so-called Law of Retail Gravitation. One version of this law purports to show, strictly and directly based upon population and distance, how the volume of retail trade patronage of an intermediate city, Z, is divided between two other cities, X and Y. Reilly's conclusion, expressed in proportional terms for X and Y, is derived from the following equation:

Z's trade with X *divided by* Z's trade with Y *equals* (the population of X *divided by* the population of Y) *times* (the distance between Z and Y *divided by* the distance between Z and X) *squared*.

Paul D. Converse did a number of empirical studies using Reilly's Law of Gravitation and developed the idea of determining the "breaking point" or boundary between the retail market areas of two trading centers. The location theory here may be expressed as:

The distance of X's boundary from X *equals* the distance between X and Y *divided by* [one plus the square root of (the population of Y *divided by* the population of X)].

Another interaction theory, which has been developed to compare (among other uses) the relative transport significance of different areas, gives its results in the form of a so-called transportation index. This index or measure of the interaction between two communities, X and Y, may be computed as follows:

Transportation index *equals* (the population of X *times* the population of Y) *divided by* the distance between X and Y.

Various other similar models, some of which include sociological and other noneconomic factors, have been developed for specific purposes. If viewed simply as first-approximation explanatory devices, these models may be useful. Despite the sometimes extravagant claims of some of their builders and users who view these formulas as realistic substitutes for expensive field research, however, their success in actual prediction has not been spectacular.

It seems reasonably certain that distance, or transportation costs related to distance, exerts a considerable drag on long-distance flows, and that this retarding effect tends to become relatively greater in comparison to pull factors as distance increases. In local marketing, however, the distance factor may be such an insignificant portion of other cost and demand elements that it becomes submerged and of little effect.

In addition, no one has conclusively demonstrated that population size alone generally determines the attraction between different communities in a Newtonian sense. Gravity models, which exclude by assumption numerous physical, social, cultural, and income factors and institutional ties, are likely to exclude thereby the major forces of gravitational attraction. When these models are constructed to include some of these additional pertinent variables, they may be more useful real-world working tools. If this is not done, their usefulness in actual decision making is limited.

RETAIL LOCATION: APPLEBAUM AND GOLDSTOCKER

Turning to the problem of specific retail locations within a trade area, each decision is a separate study with a separate set of variables. While it is probable that no one set of variables applies to all retailing, it is possible to detail the most important variables in all retail location studies. Both Applebaum and Goldstocker have done pioneering work here.

Applebaum lists sixteen steps to be undertaken in choosing a specific site. Essentially three factors appear as important in all retailing locations: the economic base, population and its characteristics, and transportation availability and its configuration. Economic base refers to employment characteristics, income changes, employment stability, past growth trends, and future projections. These are always important for a retail store location. Population and its characteristics refers to total population, where people live, their socioeconomic and age characteristics, shopping habits, level of expenditures, and mobility. Transportation availability and its configuration refers to road networks, land use and zoning, projected highway and street changes, traffic patterns, and street configurations. These three variables (economic base, population, and transportation) are pivotal factors in retail location.

Goldstocker applied specific factors to specific types of retailing activity. These illustrate the pivotal three factors of economic base, population, and transportation. For example, a fast food service chain such as McDonald's gives great emphasis to "gaps in the map" — that is, after mapping out the location of competition, what remains as potential new locations? However, important factors in any fast food service outlet location study are (in order of importance): (1) good and heavily traveled arterial streets, (2) location of young families — two or more children younger than teenagers, (3) areas with two automobiles per family, (4) middle-income neighborhoods, and (5) nearness to shopping centers, as well as physical factors such as availability of land, zoning, and adequate utilities. Notice the importance of transportation — two of the five factors. Other types of retailers would emphasize other factors, but all would be derivations of the pivotal three: economic base, population, and transportation. Each decision is literally a study in itself.

LOGISTICS SYSTEMS AND LOCATION

While a great deal more will be said about logistics systems in Part VI, transportation and location decisions are important enough in designing these systems to be considered briefly at this point.

Logistics systems have two facets — physical supply, sometimes called inbound logistics, and physical distribution, often referred to as outbound logistics. The idea is to design systems to bring raw materials, parts, or subassemblies into a point of production or into a place where processing takes place by the most efficient and lowest-cost method (inbound logistics). On the other hand, outbound logistics or physical distribution concerns distributing or passing on to the next phase of production or to the ultimate market the output of the production process — again by the most efficient or lowest-cost method. Depending on the length of the production chain, these functions may occur once each or several times as goods flow from raw materials to ultimate market. In effect, transportation in logistics systems provides the links between processing or production facilities or between processing centers and the ultimate market.

It should be understood that transportation is but a part of logistics systems — we might say the most important part but still only one of many functions that take place in a logistics system. Storage and inventory control, order taking and record keeping, mixing, labeling, repackaging, marking, and sorting are some of the functions that complement transportation in a logistics system. We will discuss these interrelationships in more detail in Part VI and here concentrate mainly on the linkage or transportation function and how this impacts on location.

In location theory above, you will recall that cost minimization was a pivotal factor. So too in logistics system design. You will also recall from the preceding chapters that there is a considerable difference between unit load (truckload or carload) rates per 100 pounds and less-than-truckload or less-than-carload rates per 100 pounds. This difference in rates becomes an important factor in where to locate consolidation centers and distribution centers. The general rule is to ship as far as possible at the lowest unit load rate (carload and truckload) and minimize the use of the higher rates in less-than-truckload or less-than-carload shipments.

A few simple examples will illustrate the locational factors. Figure 19.4 shows the principle of consolidation centers. Suppose a firm owns three plants in different locations (cities X, Y, Z) but is serving a single customer some distance from any of the plants. Depending on the difference in LTL rates and unit load rates (TL or CL), it may be beneficial to establish a consolidation center in City A where the output of the three plants shipped LTL is consolidated into unit loads for the longer haul. Analysis of comparative rates and location of plants may show that consolidation somewhere in between the plants and the customer is worthwhile. Of course, service levels are also important.

Likewise, assume you are a purchasing manager receiving parts from three vendors or suppliers in varying quantities at different times. Now establishment of a consolidation center may be beneficial, and instead of having each vendor ship LTL to your plant, shipments are consolidated into unit loads at a consolidation center to take advantage of lower TL or CL rates. A bit of research into comparative rates and location of suppliers or vendors may show that a consolidation center can be cost saving. If the three suppliers are shipping different parts, various mixing rules or the existence of FAK (freight all kinds) rates will be important for the unit load portion of the movement. And again, how often and how quickly parts are needed (service levels) will be a factor.

The location of consolidation centers is really an exercise in Weberian gravity models on a smaller scale. High LTL rates compared with TL rates

Figure 19.4 Consolidation Centers

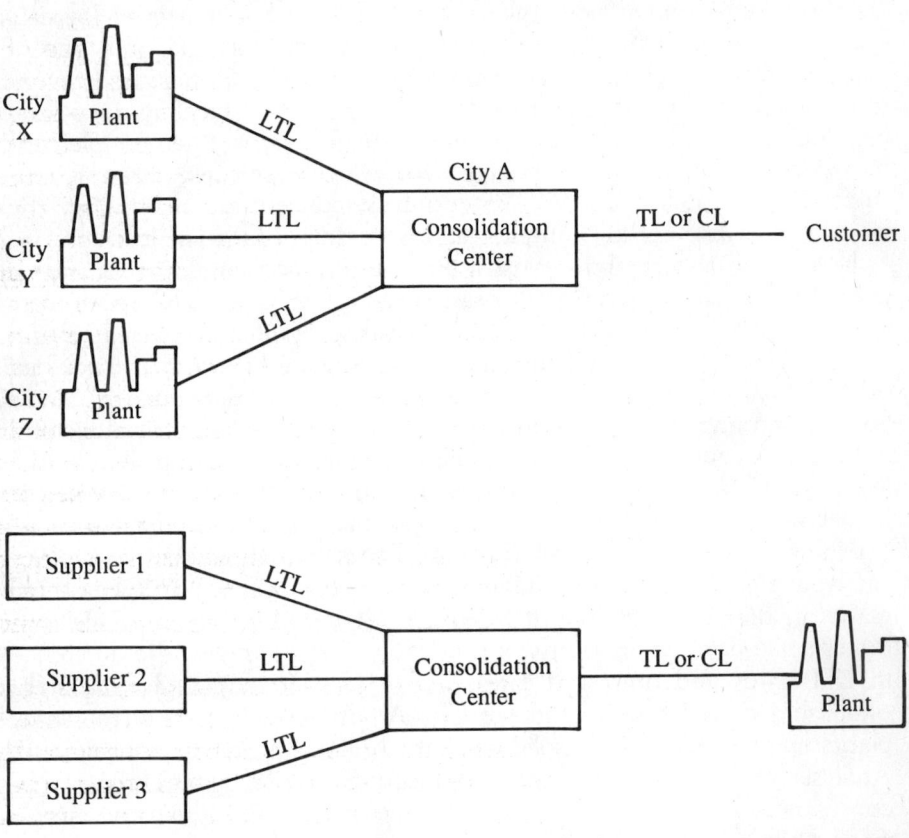

draws consolidation centers closer to suppliers or multiple plant locations and farther away from plants or customers. The exact pull will depend on the amounts shipped and the difference in the LTL rates as compared with the TL rates.

Figure 19.5 illustrates distribution centers which are generally found in the physical distribution aspect of logistics systems. Suppose you are a supplier with three separate customers (A, B, C), none of which desires a unit load (truckload or carload) in a given time period. Depending on the service level required and the difference between LTL rates and unit load rates (CL or TL), it may be beneficial to locate a distribution center somewhere between your location and your customers. Very likely this distribution center will be close to your customers and will receive

Figure 19.5 Distribution Centers

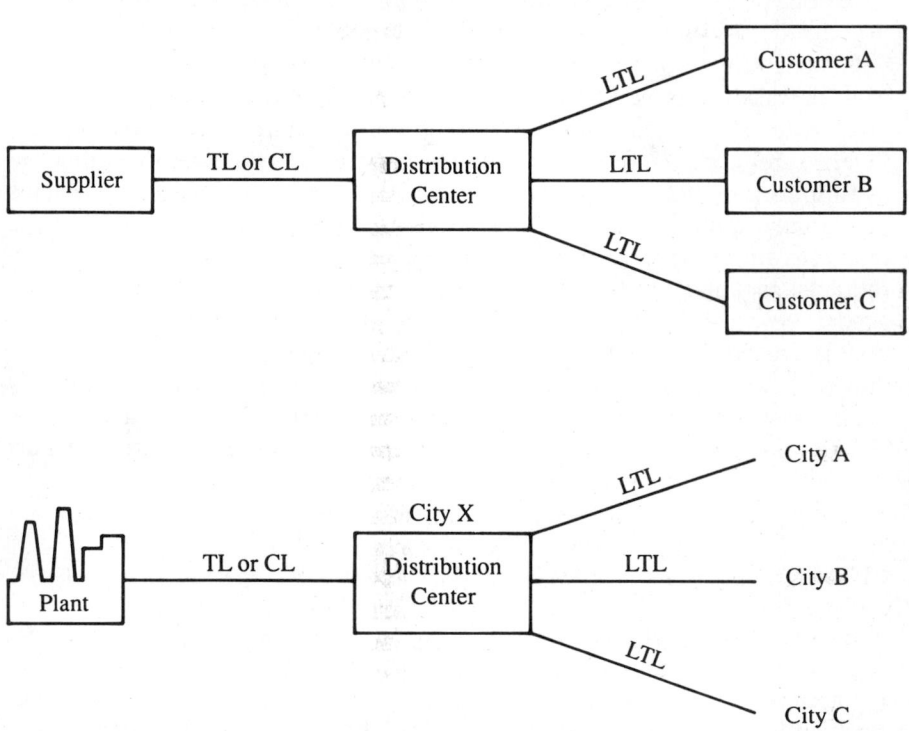

shipments in carloads or truckloads, sort and mix products to fit the customers' orders, and ship LTL for the shorter distance.

Likewise, assume your output is sold in three different markets in three different cities, none of which requires a carload or truckload in a given week. It may be beneficial to set up a distribution center in City X, ship unit loads to this distribution center, sort and mix to meet customer requirements in City A, City B, and City C. An example of this type of distribution center operation is a chain of grocery stores in three separate locations. Inbound groceries come in carload and truckload lots into the distribution center at the lowest possible rates; shipments to each store go out LTL in precisely the quantities needed by each store in each city each day or two.

Once more a type of gravity model can be used to establish the proper location of the distribution centers using comparative LTL and TL/CL rates. Higher LTL rates draw distribution centers toward customers and away from suppliers or the plants.

In both consolidation centers and distribution centers, it makes no difference whether for-hire transportation or private transportation (do-it-yourself) is used. The only complication is that as a decision maker, you must know your costs of private transportation. Also notice that in each of these examples, levels of service requirements (frequency, amounts or quantities, and reliability) become important. The analysis uses actual freight rates (or private carrier costs) — not the oversimplified ton-mileage assumptions of von Thünen and Weber. In fact, these location problems are merely applications of the location theory devised at an earlier time but with more realistic inputs from the actual marketplace. The theory remains as valid as ever — only the application is updated to reflect actual costs and circumstances. Finally, it should be obvious that a change in the relationships between less-than-truckload and unit load (TL and CL) rates via negotiations and bargaining can positively or negatively affect the location of either consolidation or distribution centers.

We shall return to both consolidation and distribution centers in Part VI.

SUMMARY

Transportation costs and location theory are inseparable. Traditional location analysis assumes either fixed markets and undetermined producing centers or fixed producing centers and undetermined marketing areas. Both industrial (or agricultural) location theory and market-area theory assume given transportation facilities, however. Analysis involving the determination of transport routes and facilities under varying production and marketing assumptions and the relationships between such routes and city location are not so well developed. Both the fixed (or given) transport and the variable (or undetermined) transport type of analysis, however, lead directly into the analysis of the types and levels of regional or spatial economic activity. In practical applications, the models provide the tools of analysis for location of markets, extent of markets, location of retail establishments, and location of consolidation centers or distribution centers in logistics systems.

Having gained some understanding of the role of transportation costs and rates in domestic transportation, the next part (two chapters) will consider carrier management.

ADDITIONAL READINGS

Applebaum, William, "Guidelines for a Store Location Strategy Study," *Journal of Marketing* (October 1966), 42–45.

Ballou, Ronald H., *Business Logistics Management: Planning and Control*, 2nd ed., Englewood Cliffs, N.J.: Prentice-Hall, Inc., 1985.
Chapter 11, "Facility Location Decisions," pp. 300–55.
———, "Potential Error in the Center of Gravity Approach to Facility Location," *Transportation Journal* (Winter 1973), 44–50.
Converse, Paul D. "New Laws of Retail Gravitation," *Journal of Marketing* (October 1949), 379–84.
Coyle, John J., Edward J. Bardi, and C. John Langley, Jr., *The Management of Business Logistics*, 4th ed., St. Paul, Minn.: West Publishing Co., 1988.
Chapter 13, "Nodal Location," pp. 456–87.
Daggett, Stuart, *Principles of Inland Transportation*, 4th ed., New York: Harper, 1955.
Chapter 19, "Varieties of Competition," pp. 365–80.
Chapter 22, "Theories of Location," pp. 426–55.
Fair, Marvin L., and Ernest T. Williams, Jr., *Economics of Transportation and Logistics.*, rev. ed., Plano, Texas: Business Publications, 1981.
Chapter 5, "Goods Movement and the Location of Economic Enterprise," pp. 66–89.
Farris, Martin T., and Stephen K. Happel, *Modern Managerial Economics*, Glenview, Ill.: Scott, Foresman and Co., 1987.
Chapter 17, "Location of Production and Markets," pp. 466–95.
Fetter, Frank, "The Economic Law of Market Areas," *Quarterly Journal of Economics*, 39 (1924), 520–29.
Goldstocker, Jac L., "A System Framework for Retail Location," in *New Dimensions in Retailing: A Decision Oriented Approach*, edited by J. K. Ryan, Jr., J. H. Donnelly, Jr., and J. M. Ivancevich, Belmont, Calif.: Wadsworth Publishing Co., 1970.
Greenhut, Melvin L., *Plant Location in Theory and Practice*, Chapel Hill, N.C.: University of North Carolina Press, 1956.
Part 1, "Review of Location Theory," pp. 3–100.
Part 4, "A General Theory of Plant Location," pp. 251–91.
Hoover, Edgar M., *The Location of Economic Activity*, New York: McGraw-Hill, 1948.
Part 1, "Locational Preferences and Patterns," pp. 15–141.
Isard, Walter, *Location and Space-Economy*, Cambridge, Mass.: M.I.T. Press, 1956.
Chapter 2, "Some General Theories of Location and Space-Economy," pp. 24–54.
Chapter 7, "Market and Supply Area Analysis and Competitive Locational Equilibrium," pp. 143–71.
Chapter 8, "Agglomeration Analysis and Agricultural Location Theory," pp. 172–99.
Johnson, James C., and Donald F. Wood, *Contemporary Physical Distribution and Logistics*, 3rd ed., New York: Macmillan Publishing Co., 1986.
Chapter 8, "Warehouse and Plant Location," pp. 293–332.
Locklin, D. Philip, *Economics of Transportation*, 7th ed., Homewood, Ill.: Richard D. Irwin, 1972.
Chapter 4, "Freight Rates and the Location of Industries and Market Centers," pp. 67–90.
Lösch, August, *The Economics of Location*, New Haven, Conn.: Yale University Press, 1954.
Chapter 6, "Site and Reasons for Town Settlement," pp. 68–84.
Part 2, "Economic Regions," pp. 101–220.
Moses, Leon F., "A General Equilibrium Model of Production, Interregional Trade, and Location of Industry," *Review of Economics and Statistics* (November 1960), 393–97.
Mossman, Frank H., and Newton Morton, *Logistics of Distribution Systems*, Boston: Allyn and Bacon, 1965.
Chapter 3, Appendix, "Summary of Plant Location Theory," pp. 105–12.
Nicholls, J. A. F., "Transportation Development and Loschian Market Areas: An Historical Perspective," *Land Economics* (February 1970), 22–31.

Reilly, William S., *Methods for Study of Retail Relationships*, Austin, Texas: University of Texas Bureau of Business Research, Research Monograph No. 4, 1929.

Richards, Hoy C., "Transportation Costs and Plant Location: A Review of Principal Theories," *Transportation Journal* (Winter 1962), 19–24.

Rose, Warren, *Logistics Management*, Dubuque, Iowa: Wm. C. Brown, 1979.
    Chapter 2, "Location of Fixed Logistics Facilities," pp. 24–42.

Smith, David M., *Industrial Location*, New York: John Wiley, 1971.
    Part 3, "Industrial Location Theory: A Synthesis," pp. 177–273.

Talley, Wayne Kenneth, *Introduction to Transportation*, Cincinnati: South-Western Publishing Co., 1983.
    Chapter 7, "Location," pp. 127–40.

von Thünen, Johann Heinrich, *Von Thünen's Isolated State*, edited by Peter Hall, translated by Carla M. Wortenberg, London: Pergamon Press, Ltd., 1966 (original work 1826).

Weber, Alfred, *Theory of the Location of Industries*, translated by Carl J. Friedrich, Chicago: University of Chicago Press, 1929 (original work 1909).

Yaseen, Leonard C., *Plant Location*, rev. ed., New York: American Research Council, 1960.
    Chapter 2, "The Transportation Factor," pp. 14–44.

PART V
CARRIER MANAGEMENT

In Part VI we will discuss shipper or distribution management — the demand side of transportation. In this part, we turn to carrier operation and management — the supply side. Many students find employment opportunities with carriers upon completion of their education, so the next two chapters will be of interest to that group. But even if students find employment with shippers in distribution or traffic departments, the problems of carriers who supply transportation will be of importance in those jobs. And if students are not employed in either carrier or shipper management, some understanding of how carriers operate will help their general understanding of transportation and its role in the economy.

This understanding is even more important in an environment where the lessening of transportation regulation has modified significantly the way in which carriers approach the management of transportation operations. In this less regulated, more competitive environment, carriers have had to develop additional information about their operations to remain successful. In this part of the book, we discuss the elements of the carrier operating environment, the nature of carrier organization and services, and how carriers have had to react to learn more about their operations.

CHAPTER 20

THE CARRIER OPERATING ENVIRONMENT

In some ways, the management of transportation carriers is similar to other business enterprises. Many of the functions are the same, and many of the tasks and goals of management are similar. However, there are several factors that make the management of transportation carriers unique and different from general management. This chapter will discuss some of the environmental factors that contribute to this difference and discuss some general aspects of carrier organization and operation.

THE ENVIRONMENT OF CARRIER MANAGEMENT

Perhaps the major unique factor in carrier management is the existence of regulation. Of course, all businesses are regulated to some degree, and society specifies rules of business conduct in general in the antitrust statutes, and laws about fraud and misrepresentation, weights and measures, and so forth. However, transportation takes place in an environment regulated to a higher degree than almost any other business. This is true even though we live in the so-called era of deregulation of transportation. But before we analyze that interesting change, we should be aware that transportation continues to be regulated. It is principally the *degree* and *type* of regulation that has changed.

The regulation of transportation takes three forms: regulation of the physical factors in carrier transportation, regulation of the economic dimensions of carrier transportation, and social regulation via policies that both benefit and hinder carrier operations. Each of these forms of regulation has a different character and concerns different aspects of transportation, but all have the same goals: protection of the public and promotion of the best possible system of transportation.

The regulation of the physical aspects of transportation illustrates these goals. The safety of the user and co-user of highways, airways, streets, railways, and ocean shipping lanes is involved. Society acts to protect itself and its parts from physical danger and disorder. At the same time, physical regulation may involve the concept of reliability. It is in the interest of society that safe transportation be readily available and that once a journey of a passenger or a shipment has begun, it will be completed in a fast, efficient, and reliable manner. To these ends, regulations concern three physical areas of transportation: the conditions of equipment, the qualification of operators, and operating procedures.

Many examples of physical regulation of equipment conditions are possible. In the case of private automobiles, some states require safety checks of lights, brakes, steering mechanisms, windshields, and so forth. Commercial highway vehicles are regulated by states as to weight, length, width, and height to protect both the highway itself and the co-user of the highway. In air transportation, the Federal Aviation Administration passes upon air worthiness and levels of maintenance. The U.S. Coast Guard regulates the equipment and physical condition of boats and ships. The Federal Railroad Administration sets standards for railroad beds, alignment, surface structure, and so forth.

Qualifications of transportation operators are known to all through driver's license requirements in each state. Commercial drivers must pass an even higher driver's license standard. Truck drivers are regulated as to permissible hours of continuous service, as are air pilots. Physical qualifications of operators are also important in air transportation. In water transportation, pilots must meet regulatory levels to be licensed.

There are many regulations and rules concerning operating procedures. Perhaps the best known is the speed limit for automobiles and trucks. Buses must stop at all railroad crossings, planes must fly at specified altitudes and approach a landing field in a specific manner, ships must pass one another in a designated fashion, the physical distances between vehicles is usually regulated in air and water, and stoplights regulate traffic flow. Perhaps no other business produces its services under as many rules and regulations as transportation.

The economic regulation of transportation is discussed in detail in Part III. Suffice it to say at this point that three aspects are involved in economic regulation: entry and exit, rates and earnings, and service. Often, for-hire carriers must have certificates of public convenience and necessity and prove that their service is needed. In spite of deregulation, the rates and earnings of motor, rail, and water carriers continue to be regulated. The degree of rate regulation is less than it once was but there are still limitations. This is true also of frequency and types of service.

Social regulation by policy decisions refers to the interesting problem of public support for transportation and various repayment devices, such as fuel taxes, tolls, fees, and charges. Likewise, society regulates ownership patterns, such as mergers and consolidations, and the structure of competition. Environmental restraints concerning vehicle emissions, noise, ocean pollution, and highway and airway congestion are also social regulations. We shall explore some of these social policy regulations later in this book, but the important point here is that society regulates transportation far more than it regulates almost any other business. And since carriers supply transportation, it seems fair to say that carrier management takes place within an environment made up of multiple rules and regulations.

LEGAL OBLIGATIONS IN COMMON CARRIAGE

One major factor that differentiates many carriers from other businesses is their designation as common carriers. Indeed, it is this aspect of carriage that forms the basis for much of the economic regulation of carriers discussed above. Common carrier designation is a special type of business undertaking found in transportation and a few other areas of business in our economy. Special legal obligations have been placed upon these businesses by society because of society's extraordinary dependence on and need for their services. Basically, a common carrier must fulfill four duties: the duty to serve, the duty to deliver, the duty to charge reasonable rates, and the duty to avoid discrimination.

To ensure that these obligations are met, society may impose regulations or restrictions on those undertaking this necessary service. Society also imposes duties or obligations on the users of the service, in this case, the shippers. Hence, the duty to pay for the movement in a prompt and complete fashion is imposed upon the shipper. (Shippers may be relieved of their basic obligation to pay if (1) they sign the "without recourse" clause of a bill of lading or (2) carriers deliver without collecting charges due or contrary to the shipper's order.)

Likewise, society in its regulation of these special types of businesses imposes a duty upon itself to ensure that the common carrier is not legally prevented from earning enough revenue to carry on its business. This is the basis of the very knotty problem of rate-level regulation and the definition of a reasonable rate of return. This problem of social regulation of earnings is discussed in some detail in Parts III and IV. Here we are concerned principally with the duties imposed upon the common carrier.

The Duty of Service

One of the oldest of the common-carrier obligations is the duty to serve all comers. It is on the basis of this obligation that the carrier is common or public. One making a general offer to the public as being willing to perform certain kinds of carrier services must actually perform these services upon reasonable demand.

Qualifications of the Duty to Serve

Ordinarily a carrier desires to serve all customers, since it is in the business of transportation. However, extraordinary circumstances may arise when its duty to serve must be qualified. It does have the right, within limits, to refuse service.

A carrier, for example, is obligated to serve only its own public. This qualification extends to kinds of goods and kinds of persons. A motor common carrier of sand cannot be forced to haul petroleum. A court has held that a railroad may refuse to take dogs as baggage. In another case, a court held that a railroad need not install scales that would serve the public in weighing goods but that are not essential to the railroad business. Likewise, a carrier of passengers holds itself out to serve only the traveling public and cannot be forced to carry newspaper sellers or similar vendors on its trains. In the absence of published tariffs including a particular commodity, a carrier cannot be made to install special equipment to handle a specific type of goods. Also, a carrier of freight does not have to carry passengers.

The offer of the shipper must be reasonable as to time and condition. Shipments may be picked up only during ordinary business hours. The duty to serve does not force carriers to accept shipments at all hours. Likewise, a shipper must present goods at the proper place and cannot expect the carrier to extend a published pickup and delivery area to unusual distances or for unusual weights. Of course, if the carrier's pickup and delivery tariff provides for special areas or weights, the carrier has included this in its public offering and must serve accordingly. Also, a carrier may not be forced to accept a shipment it cannot deliver either because of unusual conditions or because it does not or cannot serve the delivery point. The public of a motor carrier cannot extend, for example, to points the carrier is not certificated to serve, and a carrier is allowed to require reasonable notice of intended shipment.

Finally, the obligation to serve is qualified by certain circumstances. A carrier may refuse to haul dangerous commodities or objectionable persons. Poorly packed dynamite need not be carried, nor deceased persons if the carrier wishes to refuse. Indeed, a carrier may always refuse to service poorly packed shipments, since it is liable for loss or damage of freight during shipment. Offensive or objectionable persons may be refused, as may goods that might impregnate or contaminate other goods. Nor can a carrier be forced to carry items of extreme value such as diamonds, money, or valuable papers, which expose it to unusually large liabilities for loss.

Adequacy of Service

In addition to the duty to serve all comers within its ability, a common carrier must supply adequate facilities and services. Adequacy has been interpreted to mean that facilities must be available for normal or usual demands, facilities must be in reasonably good condition for the type of traffic, and the service must be performed with reasonable dispatch.

As to normal demands, a carrier cannot be forced to provide for infrequent peak shipments. Wherever such conditions prevail, as in seasonable shipments of some agricultural goods, the carrier must distribute its facilities fairly among its customers. Reasonably good condition means that vehicles, ways, and equipment must be adequate for the type of service offered. For instance, vehicles used to haul livestock are not adequate to haul food in the absence of thorough cleaning or modification. Cars to haul grain are not adequate if their state of repair is such that they leak. The matter of reasonable dispatch will be considered below under the duty to deliver.

A carrier may be forced to do whatever is necessary to fulfill the need for adequate service, yet it cannot be forced into a new line of business or into a new geographic area not previously served. The carrier's duties are limited by its established routes and its certificate to serve. However, once the carrier has entered into an area or line of business voluntarily, it may not abandon or withdraw its service without permission from the appropriate regulatory authorities.

Withdrawal of Service

Common law holds that a rail carrier has accepted a franchise or charter from the sovereign and enjoys the privileges thereof. Hence withdrawal of services can come only on permission of the sovereign or a representative. Statutory law has placed control over interstate rail abandonments or withdrawal of service generally in the hands of the ICC. In the case of motor carriers, however, federal regulatory authorities have no control over abandonment or withdrawal of service.

A rail carrier cannot withdraw from a segment or part of its service solely because it is unprofitable to serve that segment. If profit is made on a part or on the service as a whole even though a portion is unprofitable, the unprofitable portion may not be abandoned. Regulatory authorities may impose various conditions during a trial period and force the carrier to prove not only that the service is unprofitable but that it has no chance of ever being profitable.

The carrier may, of course, withdraw all its service if the total is unprofitable. It cannot be made to serve indefinitely at a loss due to the Fifth and Fourteenth Amendments of the U.S. Constitution. But even here regulatory authorities will require it to be clearly established that the whole service is unprofitable, and the permission of the representative of the sovereign is required. Reference to the statistics on the total rail network in Chapter 2 shows that withdrawal and abandonment have been permitted.

These limitations on abandonment or withdrawal have been highly important in recent times in the rail passenger transportation business. Until the Transportation Act of 1958, many abandonments were controlled by state regulatory authorities who tended to be very reluctant to permit withdrawals. Subsequent to allowing ICC control under specified conditions in the 1958 act, abandonments of rail passenger service greatly accelerated. The Regional Rail Reorganization Act of 1973 established separate criteria for the abandonment of excess rail mileage in the northeastern United States.

The Duty of Delivery

It is the duty of a common carrier to deliver the goods entrusted to its care. This duty is a common-law obligation, although it also appears in various forms in statute law. It is commonly referred to as *carrier liability* and is perhaps the oldest of all carrier obligations.

Because of the shipper's absolute dependence upon the carrier to protect its goods, plus the ease with which carriers could consort with robbers or pirates, the common law of carrier liability was very strict. In 1703, Lord Holt, in the famous English case of *Coggs* v. *Bernard* (2 Ld. Raymond 919), stated the common-law liability of carriers as: "he is bound to answer for the goods in all events." The justice further stated:

> The law charges this person thus intrusted to carry goods, against all events, but Acts of God, and of the enemies of the King. For though

the force be ever so great, as if an irresistible multitude of people should rob him, nevertheless he is chargeable. And this is a politic establishment, contrived by the policy of the law, for the safety of all persons, the necessity of whose affairs oblige them to trust these sorts of persons, that they may be safe in their ways of dealing; for else these carriers might have an opportunity of undoing all persons that had any dealings with them, by combining with thieves, etc., and yet doing it in such clandestine manner as would not be possible to be discovered. And this is the reason the law is founded upon in that point.

The general obligation of the land common carrier, then, is to deliver goods in the same condition as they were received, with reasonable dispatch, and to the right party. Different liabilities apply to ocean carriers, which are excluded from the scope of this discussion. Air carrier liability still is evolving, with some similarities to and some differences from that of land carriers.

Limitations of Liability

As noted above, the common law originally held the carrier absolutely responsible except in the case of acts of God or acts of the enemies of the king. Statutory law over time has added four other limitations, namely, acts of public authority, acts of the shipper, inherent nature or vice of the goods, and a highly qualified acts of riots or strikes.

Acts of God refer to some extraordinary and unavoidable events such as flooding, lightning, tornado, or extreme ice and snow. Bad weather that might reasonably be expected to occur from time to time is not an act of God. Acts of the king's enemy (or the public enemy) refers to organized foreign or public enemies and is important principally in wartime. Acts of public authority concern seizure of goods by legal process or by quarantines laid by public officials. The carrier's liability is limited by acts of the shipper when goods are not properly marked or are not packed or loaded according to accepted regulations or standards. Shipper acts that mislead the carrier, such as failure to declare extraordinary values of the goods, cannot be used to make a carrier liable.

Inherent nature or vice of the goods refers to such things as livestock injuring one another, molasses fermenting while in transit, or goods that damage other goods, assuming the carrier is not negligent. The uniform bill of lading exempts the carrier from liability for loss, damage, or delay due to riots or strikes unless the carrier is negligent. The meaning of negligence, particularly when labor disputes are involved, is hard to define. It should be obvious that the exact definition and application of all these legal terms are a study in themselves and far beyond the scope of an introductory textbook. Everyone concerned with transportation, though, should have some familiarity with these matters.

None of the above limitations of liability applies if the carrier is guilty of contributory negligence or lack of due diligence. The burden of proof is on the carrier. It must show that it was not negligent and that due diligence was exercised. The carrier cannot contract out of negligence.

A carrier is expected to deliver with reasonable promptness. What is reasonably prompt varies with circumstances, but a carrier cannot be charged with loss due to delay unless the delay is unusually long and unreasonable. Carriers may voluntarily bind themselves to meet a time limit and pay special damages in case of default on that part of their contract. This is done for a consideration, of course, but some shippers feel that delivery under a time limit is worth the extra charges, particularly where highly perishable goods are involved.

A carrier may, on occasion, attempt to overcome some of the statutory limitations of liability by special contract and considerations. Thus a released-value agreement and rate may be in effect. Here the carrier agrees to carry the goods at a lower rate if the shipper agrees to release it from liability above a stated value. Such rates are in effect generally on household goods and baggage. The shipper may, of course, pay the regular rate and force the carrier to assume full liability. However, it is often worthwhile for the shipper to use the released-value rate and buy insurance to cover losses for which the carrier is not responsible.

Generally, the amount a shipper can recover in case of loss or damage is the value of the goods to the owner at destination at the time the shipment should have arrived. There are many variations of this and many ways of determining this value. Again this indicates the specialized legal nature of the subject of liability.

Duration of Carrier Liability

The carrier's liability commences upon delivery of the goods to it — when the shipper has nothing more to do with the shipment. Many problems arise concerning when the carrier becomes liable and assumes the obligation to deliver. In carload and truckload shipments, this generally is when the motive power is attached. In smaller shipments, liability is assumed when the shipment is loaded on the vehicle. The presence or lack of presence of an agent of the carrier may be of importance here.

Carrier liability ends upon delivery to the correct consignee. However, there are various rules or regulations on this. Generally, the liability to deliver as a common carrier ceases when reasonable notice has been given to the consignee of the arrival of the shipment. (Reasonable notice usually is interpreted to mean forty-eight hours in rail transportation and seven days in motor transportation.) After these times, the carrier's liability as a common carrier ceases and the liability becomes that of a warehouse business only. Liability as a warehouse business is limited to acts of negligence, which means the responsibility for ordinary care only.

It should be stressed that the duty to deliver is not a matter of commission regulation; it is a matter of common and statutory law, and statutes may vary somewhat between states. Liability matters are settled according to court decisions and not before regulatory bodies.

The Duty of Reasonable Rates

A common carrier must charge reasonable rates. Originally this duty or obligation arose because the carrier was in the position to exploit the use of its service. Common callings, under English common law, included various types of persons and business undertakings such as wharfingers, ferrymen, innkeepers and victualers, millers, blacksmiths, tailors, bakers, brewers, draymen, teamsters, and common carriers. Because entry into these undertakings was limited and controlled either by guilds or by the government, customers often had very limited choice, and the possibility of exploitation existed. Therefore the sovereign and the courts imposed the duty of charging only reasonable prices for these services. In effect, this meant maximum rate control, although the definition of what was reasonable probably was as difficult then as it is now.

Recently the idea of reasonable rates has taken on a new connotation. The idea has developed that rates or charges can be too low; thus the problem becomes one of controlling minimum as well as maximum rates and charges. A rate or a price that is unreasonably low basically is one that does not permit the carrier to earn enough revenue to fulfill its obligations to serve. Recognition of this point is included in the shipper's obligation or duty to pay. But the matter is not that simple. A rate on one particular commodity may be unreasonably low if it causes unduly high rates to be charged on another commodity. Here a matter of comparative rates and discrimination is involved. Again, a rate may be unreasonably low if it is designed to drive competing carriers of the same or different modes out of business. This involves intramodal and intermodal competition.

Federal and state regulatory commissions have been given the authority to determine reasonableness, subject to court review. The evolution and application of this concept and some of its problems are discussed in greater detail in Parts III and IV.

The Duty of Nondiscrimination

Another common-law duty of common carriers is the obligation to avoid discrimination. This duty is related to the other three, but it has become more refined and defined in statutory law than have the other duties.

Our society opposed discrimination on at least two grounds: the philosophical-political and the economic. Our philosophy of democracy is based on the ideal of fair play and equal treatment for all. Discrimination implies unequal treatment and hence is objectionable from a philosophical viewpoint.

Economically our society is based on the idea of competition and relative price stability. Discrimination may involve capricious pricing and perhaps even changing prices from day to day, as the firm practicing discrimination may prefer a favored few while prejudicing other customers. This is a move away from stable price relationships necessary for competitive economic growth and development as well as away from our ideal of equal opportunity for all.

Discrimination implies a degree of monopoly power. If all firms were perfectly competitive, none could discriminate. Hence, as our society generally disapproves of monopoly, it naturally disapproves of this manifestation of its power.

Definition of Discrimination

Discrimination, defined in simplest terms, is different treatment under similar circumstances or similar treatment under different circumstances. In transportation, discrimination usually takes two forms, service discrimination or rate (price) discrimination. Thus our preliminary definition could be amended to read: "Discrimination is different service or rates under similar circumstances, or similar service or rates under different circumstances."

The common-law definition of discrimination is quite vague and is stated in general terms only. It is necessary, then, as a practical matter, to look to statutory law for an explicit prohibition against various types of discrimination. In these prohibitions, discrimination in transportation is well defined. For example, Section 2 of the 1887 Act to Regulate Commerce (Interstate Commerce Act) stated in part:

> If any common carrier . . . shall, directly or indirectly, by any special rate, rebate, or drawback, or other device, charge, demand, collect or receive from any person or persons a greater or less compensation for

any service rendered . . . in the transportation of persons or property . . . than it charges, demands, collects or receives from any other person or persons for doing for him or them a like and contemporaneous service in the transportation of a like kind of traffic under substantially similar circumstances and conditions, such common carrier shall be deemed guilty of unjust discrimination, which is hereby prohibited and declared to be unlawful.

Section 3 of the same act noted various types of discrimination by stating:

It shall be unlawful for any common carrier . . . to make or give any undue or unreasonable preference or advantage to any particular person, company, firm, corporation, association, locality, port, port district, gateway, transit point, region, district, territory, or any particular description of traffic, in any respect whatsoever, or subject any particular persons . . . [list again repeated] to any undue prejudice or disadvantage in any respect whatsoever.

Types of Discrimination

It is obvious from the above that there are at least four types of discrimination and many subtypes or applications. These are discrimination of persons, organizations, places, and types of traffic. Both service and rate (price) discrimination could exist either in favor of or to the detriment of each.

Persons with similar transportation circumstances and conditions must be treated alike. A carrier cannot provide more service to a particular shipper than it provides to a substantially similar shipper, or vice versa. Organizations, whether corporations, associations, or firms, must receive equal service and rates if the transportation situation is similar. One town, district, region, or locality cannot be treated differently from a service or rate viewpoint than a similar locality. And all types of traffic and commodities that are similar from a transportation viewpoint must be given similar treatment as to service and price.

It is simple to state the principles involved, but it is most difficult to define similar circumstances and conditions or to give meaning to the terms *advantage, disadvantage, preference,* and *prejudice.* The difficult task of defining these terms and giving meaning to these statutory prohibitions is a never-ending problem of transportation regulatory commissions and the courts. Some of the implications of commission and court interpretations are considered in the portions of this book dealing with rates and regulations.

Permissible Forms of Discrimination

Discrimination is common in our economy, particularly price discrimination. For an equal service, doctors charge unequal prices; magazine subscriptions are persistently advertised at special rates for new subscribers; price discounts for quantity purchases, whether it is the large economy size or large industrial purchases, are common; electric utilities lower the price per unit of use as more units are used; theater tickets for the same performance typically vary as to location or time; in short, different prices for substantially the same thing is a common phenomenon in our society, and in most cases this discrimination is widely accepted.

It is apparent, then, that there are two categories of discrimination: that which is legal and acceptable and that which is not. This is particularly true for price discrimination. What is objectionable and illegal is not price discrimination as such, but undue price discrimination. But this raises another problem. Just what is undue price discrimination?

In a competitive economy, prices are based substantially on cost. Economists, recognizing this fact, long ago defined undue price discrimination to mean differences in prices not reflecting differences in costs. Hence, if savings can be made and costs reduced by packaging items in the large economy size, the price should be less per unit; if large users of electric power allow the producing company to gain economies of scale and lower its costs, the large user should gain part of these economies in lowered prices, and so forth.

Under this cost-oriented definition, price discrimination takes on a different dimension. Now the matter becomes one of the cost of producing the service. Differential pricing, or charging customers different prices, is not objectionable if the different prices actually reflect differences in costs. A major problem in transportation discrimination, then, is one of tracing or ascertaining the cost of producing the service in question. It should be noted, though, that the determination of exact per-unit costs in transportation is very difficult and is thought by some to be impossible. Thus, following the economist's definition, a great deal of price discrimination exists in transportation because costs are unknown and much of this discrimination is not definable.

It should also be clearly understood that the duty to avoid discrimination does not necessarily prohibit charging different prices or rates for different types of traffic. A ton of gravel is not transported at the same rate as a ton of automobiles. Some consideration is given to the value of the service involved. Transporting the ton of automobiles usually creates more place utility than transporting the ton of gravel, hence the rate on automobiles can be and is higher without violating the statutes.

The problem of similar items or circumstances also is quite complex. Various types of freight have different transportation characteristics and no two types are completely alike. The same may be said for localities, persons, and organizations. This was recognized in regulatory law by making *undue* preference and prejudice unlawful. Thus it becomes a matter of the degree of discrimination or what is undue. Again, the final responsibility of deciding what is permissible and what is undue has been placed in the hands of the regulatory commissions and the courts.

Finally, it should be noted that some discrimination in transportation is permitted on the grounds of public policy. For example, persons employed by religious or charitable organizations may be allowed to travel at special low rates; federal government traffic was given special low rates on railroads until the 1940s and still qualifies for special rates under provisions of the Interstate Commerce Act. The Hoch-Smith Resolution of 1925 provided for special rates on certain classes of agricultural goods as a matter of public policy. Proponents of these and similar forms of discrimination feel that their advantages outweigh their disadvantages.

In addition, the obligation to avoid discrimination does not mean that certain types of quantity discounts are not allowed. Rates based on truckload quantities are substantially lower than LTL rates. Presumably there is a cost differential between the two types of traffic, but there may be some question whether the degree of price differential reflects the actual amount of cost differential. There are some examples of trainload rates which are lower than carload rates. However, these quantity discounts generally are noncumulative. Cumulative discount-type rates generally have been considered to be discriminatory in this country on the grounds that they tend to favor large shippers over small shippers, although such rates are widely used in several other countries. (It should be noted that current discount practices in the motor carrier industry, as described in Chapter 17, are often tied to cumulative traffic movements.) It should be further noted that some practices that are illegal domestically are permissible in international ocean transportation. In this area, price discrimination and price differentials are widespread.

In summarizing the duty to avoid discrimination, it can be said that the common carrier is under the obligation of avoiding undue discrimination. However, discrimination is sometimes difficult to define, and the application of this obligation by way of commission regulation is one of the most challenging and most complicated areas of domestic transportation.

LEGAL OBLIGATIONS
IN CONTRACT CARRIAGE

Most of the common-carrier obligations discussed above are covered in the individual contracts between contract carriers and their shippers. There are no common-law obligations of the contract carrier as such outside of the contract for its services. However, when the individual contract does not cover an obligation such as liability, the laws of the state of jurisdiction will apply. Since a contract carrier provides a highly specialized and limited type of service, it does not offer to serve the general public in the same manner as a common carrier. Its public is very limited. Indeed, if it does offer to serve all comers and enter into a substantial number of contracts, it risks being declared a common carrier and being brought under the duties and obligations of a common carrier or of incurring the penalties of engaging in unauthorized common carriage.

It should be noted that recent statutory laws and regulatory policies have encouraged many carriers to offer both common and contract carriage services. Prior to the late 1970s, a carrier generally could offer only common *or* contract services, not both.

INDUSTRY STRUCTURE
AND OWNERSHIP PATTERNS

To a considerable extent, the ownership pattern and industry structure of each mode of transportation reflect the economic, regulatory, and historical environments in which that particular mode grew. These differences mean that each carrier possesses a distinctive ownership pattern that in turn affects the nature of carrier management decisions.

For example, all railroads are corporations, many of them very large. The structure of the railroad industry is oligopolistic, consisting of a relatively few carriers, each with a considerable degree of monopoly within its service territory. This industry structure reflects the need for massive amounts of capital during the period of railroad construction and development from 1830 to roughly 1910. The physical components of a railway were expensive, requiring large amounts of corporate debt to fund them. Additionally, equipment was and is costly and each carrier owns huge numbers of cars, locomotives, shops, and terminals. Since the railway is privately owned, two major railroad problems are maintenance of the way and equipment and management of finances in order to raise money for their replacement as well as to refinance older debt incurred during the development period. As we shall discuss in detail in Chapter 28, many railroads received grants of land from governmental agencies. Some of this land contains valuable natural resources such as timber, coal, oil, uranium, and so forth. Additionally, a portion of the land purchased by or given to railroads is today valuable city real estate. Hence, current railroad management often involves massive real estate and land development problems. Although other carriers own real estate for their terminals and offices, this aspect is a much less important management problem for them. Likewise, since all other modes with the exception of pipelines use publicly provided ways, both maintenance problems and the fixed-cost nature of the ways are not as important to them.

The airlines are also oligopolistic and are usually large businesses. Competition in any given market frequently involves relatively few carriers. Equipment is especially costly in air transportation, as is equipment maintenance. The airway is furnished and operated by the federal government with terminals provided by local governments. Airlines pay for the use of terminal facilities through landing fees or space rentals. No direct charge is made by the federal government for using the airway. Hence, the airlines' terminal and airway costs are variable, not fixed costs like those of railroads and pipelines. But airplanes themselves are expensive, and airlines must borrow capital from many sources, including governments in the case of foreign firms. Aircraft leasing is also important. Therefore, airlines also have a financial management problem related to their fixed costs for equipment and maintenance.

The motor carrier industry involves almost every type of industry structure from large corporations such as the nationwide LTL carriers to individual proprietorships in the case of local pickup and delivery carriers and owner-operator commodity truckers. Some carriers are highly specialized, hauling one or a few commodities sometimes with specialized equipment, whereas others are general commodities carriers, which haul everything. Additionally, many carriers serve a limited geographical territory, and others are nationwide in scope. It can indeed be said that there is no one industry called trucking, but rather a variety of different industries. The overall industry structure approaches imperfect competition; most markets are served by a fairly large number of carriers, although this varies in that some specialized carriers are nearly oligopolistic. Costs tend to be highly variable and profit margins small. Equipment leasing is widespread, and terminal needs vary by type of operation. Typically, large numbers of vehicles are involved, and management problems revolve around operations, sales, and personnel problems.

Pipelines tend to be large and almost monopolistic. Fixed costs are immense, but capital generally comes from petroleum companies which jointly own the carriers. Inland water transportation costs are highly variable and there are many companies involved. Here there is a degree of specialization by service territory, and the operation of inland water carriers resembles that of motor carriers in industry structure.

Ownership of carriers is usually private, although the special public corporations involved with Amtrak and Conrail prior to its privatization in 1987 are exceptions. Mergers are controlled in most modes, especially when common carriers are involved — the exception being in air transportation. This regulation varies by mode and has recently been modified by deregulation. (We shall devote Chapter 26 to the problem of carrier merger and consolidation.)

The reason for surveying the industry structure and ownership patterns is that carrier management faces different problems and challenges in each mode of transportation. Generalizations are difficult, but managerial problems are definitely colored by the structure of the particular type of transportation involved.

CARRIER COMPETITION

All carriers do not compete with all other carriers and all other modes for all possible freight and passengers. To be sure, there are wide areas of carrier competition and the markets do overlap. Nevertheless, carriers operate within *ranges* of competition.

Carrier competition essentially is both intramodal and intermodal. In intermodal carrier competition, each mode tends to have an inherent advantage and is able to specialize in some types of service without danger of competition from other modes. For example, railroads and water carriers compete for the movement of heavy, low-value goods, but very little of this traffic is carried by airlines. Airlines and trucks compete to move high-value goods requiring quick delivery and an emphasis on service, but water carriers generally do not compete in this market. Pipelines and water carriers compete in carrying liquids with little competition from airlines. Trucks generally compete in most markets and provide at least a portion of the movement of most goods — typically the pickup and delivery portion, although they also compete with railroads in the long haul of some goods. Railroads are the other most generalized competitor for freight, but increasingly they are limiting themselves to competition for unit loads moving relatively long distances. Each mode tends to have an inherent advantage within certain limits of price and service.

Intramodal competition refers to carriers of the same mode competing with one another. Truck lines compete with other truck lines, airlines with other airlines, and so forth. In intramodal competition, both price (rates) and service are the basis for competition. Since deregulation, a great deal of emphasis has been put on price competition, and it is common for carriers to underprice one another, within limits, to obtain freight and passengers. However, service competition remains a very real factor, and many of the carriers' customers may be willing to pay a somewhat higher rate or fare in return for better service. In freight transportation, on-time delivery, minimum damaged and lost goods, delivery and pickup at odd hours, promptness, direct routing, reliability, and special factors may be important service competition considerations. In passenger transportation, these considerations may be comfort, food and drink, entertainment, speed, convenience of purchase and boarding, and destination facilities. A glance at carrier advertisements in newspapers, industry journals, and other media reveals that many carriers stress both their rates and their service.

One of the principal tasks of carrier management is to identify what transportation markets it wants to enter. Carrier management must decide, "what business are we in?" The key here is the concept of inherent advantage — what sort of business or competition can the carrier do best? Once this decision is made, carrier management has the task of organizing, operating, and marketing in that segment of the market in such a way as to be profitable and successful, which will usually turn on how well the carrier fulfills shipper or passenger needs.

The market segment chosen can sometimes be too small, in other cases too large. Yet carrier management must realize that it can't be everything to everybody. Hence, carrier competition will vary with each market and within each industry, too. Some shippers will find many carriers competing for their business, whereas others may feel limited to a given carrier or a few carriers depending on product characteristics, length of journey, freight rates, service requirements, and the like. However, the key to carrier success is innovative marketing — finding a market sector where it has an inherent advantage and then tailoring its service to shippers' needs.

Since markets vary, it is difficult to generalize about carrier competition except to say that each carrier tries to identify the area it serves best and in which it has an inherent advantage; that the degree of carrier competition varies from one geographic market to another and from one mode to another; and that carrier competition is based on both price and service. From a carrier management viewpoint, however, it is important to know what intermodal and intramodal competition carriers face and to attempt to discover where a carrier can best carve out a market niche.

CARRIER COOPERATION AND COORDINATION

At the same time that carriers compete with one another, they also enter into various cooperative and coordinating arrangements. Cooperation and coordination are not the same, even though the terms are sometimes used synonymously. The distinction between them is in terms of the mode of transportation. *Cooperation* means firms of the same mode of transportation working together in some beneficial way. Interchange of railroad equipment is a good example of cooperation. *Coordination,* on the other hand, refers to two firms in different modes of transportation working together. TOFC (or piggyback) service is a good example of coordination.

Carrier Cooperation

Cooperation by firms of the same mode has taken place for many years. Originally railroads cooperated in what were known as pools. These cooperative agreements divided up either tonnage or revenues or both and were determined to be noncompetitive and illegal by the Act to Regulate Commerce in 1887 and by application of the Sherman Antitrust Act of 1890. Modern-day cooperation between carriers is not aimed at lessening competition and thus is usually legal. The two aims of cooperation are to facilitate physical interline operations and to facilitate legal joint carrier actions.

Cooperation aimed at facilitating physical interline operations takes place through equipment interchange and standardization, and joint use of terminals and other facilities, as well as through routes and rates, interline agreements, and advisory board activities. Equipment interchange, most highly developed in railroads, has existed for many years. Freight cars freely circulate from one railroad to another without regard to ownership. These cars may be owned by one of a number of railroads, private car companies, or shippers themselves. Equipment interchange is less highly developed in the motor and air modes but does exist.

This beneficial interchange of equipment depends on physical standardization and a method of payment. Rail equipment standardization concerns height, width, length, couplings, braking systems, type of wheel, and of course, track gauge; standardization of the latter has existed in the

United States, Canada, and Mexico for many years. State highway laws are responsible for a similar equipment standardization of trailers. In rail transportation, even maintenance and repair rules are standardized under the Master Car Builder Rules of the Association of American Railroads (AAR). These rules define conditions under which a railroad may refuse to receive a car in interchange, assign responsibility for various types of repairs between owning and using railroads, and contain a detailed list of prices to be charged for repair of cars. Similar rules for truck trailer exchange do not exist.

The distribution, accounting, and payment for use of rail cars is also standardized. The AAR has a Code of Car Service Rules, which prescribes when and in what manner cars will be sent to their home owners. The Code of Per Diem Rules specifies the charges that must be paid for cars by the using line to the owning railroad. The amount of per diem payment comes under the jurisdiction of the Interstate Commerce Commission and from time to time has been somewhat controversial. No similar set of rules exists for truck trailers, and physical interchange of that equipment is basically a matter of bilateral agreement between motor carriers.

Joint use of terminals, interline switching, interline drayage, and other means of ancillary physical cooperation also exist. In rail transportation, the switching of rail cars in large terminal points such as Chicago is so important that separate switching railroads and so-called belt-line railroads have developed. In motor transportation, interline drayage is an important factor, and in some cities some carriers, sometimes called local cartage carriers, specialize in pickup and delivery.

Through rates and routes have been highly developed over the years and facilitate interline transportation. A *through route* has been defined by the U.S. Supreme Court as "an arrangement, expressed or implied, between connecting railroads for the continuous carriage of goods from the originating point on the line of one carrier to destination on the line of another" (*St. Louis-Southwestern Ry. Co. v. U.S.*, 245 U.S. 136, 1917). As noted in Chapter 17, through routes carry through rates, which are usually lower than the combination of local rates. Through rates may be joint rates (involving two carriers) or local rates (involving one carrier but less than the combination rates on through routes). Carrier personnel commonly refer to through routes and joint rates in the same breath, although through routes and local rates do exist (rate terminology and distinctions are discussed in Chapter 17). It should be noted that the ICC has the power to prescribe through routes among carriers in both rail and motor transportation. This power has existed since the passing of the Transportation Act of 1920 (for railroads) and the Motor Carrier Act of 1980 (for highway transportation).

Interline agreements using through routes and joint rates, interline switching, interline drayage, and joint use of terminals also exist. In motor transportation, these agreements most often are between noncompeting carriers that meet end to end, or between pickup and delivery carriers and line-haul carriers. Airlines sometimes have similar agreements between overseas carriers and national carriers concerning joint use of terminals, through routes and joint rates, and so forth. In pipeline transportation, through billing, connections, and switching of crude petroleum and petroleum products allow freight to move almost nationwide through interline agreements. These agreements facilitate the flow of commerce and are considered highly beneficial to the shipper and the passenger.

Shipper advisory boards are another cooperative undertaking, primarily in the rail field, where groups of carriers and shippers meet periodically to exchange information and discuss mutual problems. This activity, organized by the AAR in 1923, often deals with freight car distribution, projection of seasonal needs for equipment, and other matters of common interest. Similar types of organizations are found in some areas where motor carriers and shippers meet; an example is the Southern Shipper-Motor Carrier Conference.

Other carrier cooperative ventures that facilitate joint action are cooperative ratemaking, joint or collective ownership, and interfirm public relations. The matter of cooperative ratemaking has been regulated in recent times. Originally, each carrier established its own rates, but later cooperative ratemaking through rate bureaus was undertaken. In the rail field, this activity was important relative to uniformity in classification as discussed in Chapter 17. With the passage of the Reed-Bulwinkle Amendment to Section 5 of the Interstate Commerce Act in 1948, rate bureaus and cooperative ratemaking were exempted from the antitrust laws. However, in 1980, both the Motor Carrier Act and the Staggers Act placed restrictions on this antitrust exemption, as discussed in Chapter 13. Essentially, the recent restrictions allow antitrust immunity to rate bureau action only where through routes and joint rates are concerned.

An unusual type of cooperative undertaking is the joint and collective ownership found in pipeline transportation. This sort of ownership of pipelines is very common and has come about because of the large capital requirements of pipelines plus the close connection of pipelines to the parent petroleum industry firms. Pipelines are often "undivided-interest" undertakings with various petroleum companies or other pipelines financing and owning a share of the whole but none owning a specific physical portion of the pipeline. Thus, a new pipeline might be owned collectively by any number of existing pipelines or petroleum companies, but will be operated as a separate and independent entity.

Interfirm public relations is the final form of cooperative carrier under-takings. This involves the familiar trade associations that exist in almost all areas of transportation. Their main tasks are to improve public rela-tions of their branch of transportation, lobby and protect members' inter-ests in various ways, and carry on research and development. Some, like the Association of American Railroads, are also active in standardization and rulemaking to facilitate interline movement. Besides the AAR, major groups include the American Trucking Associations, the American Water-ways Operators Association, the Air Transport Association of America, the Association of Petroleum Pipelines, and the Private Truck Council of America. In highway transportation, there will generally be a trucking association at the state level as well. Additionally, some regional associa-tions of carriers exist.

As a general rule, most of these carrier cooperative ventures are vol-untary. When they promote more efficient and better transportation for the shipper and the public, these activities have usually been held to be legal. Cooperative activity of this sort has much to recommend it.

Carrier Coordination

Carrier coordination means that firms in different modes of transportation coordinate their services and work together in some way. Separate ownership is involved — otherwise, it would be integration wherein one firm owns carriers in several different modes. The distinction is important since integration is somewhat controversial, whereas coordination is not. Many groups, including regulatory authorities, are concerned when a railroad attempts to buy and integrate a truck line into its operation, but these same groups are not alarmed if a railroad and an independently owned truck line enter into an agreement to coordinate their services. Prior to the deregulation movement discussed in Chapter 13, regulatory authorities usually restricted this type of ownership pattern. But coor-dination between independently owned carriers in different modes was encouraged.

Legally, two types of coordination may be required by the ICC. In 1912, the ICC was given the power to require physical interconnection between rail carriers and water carriers. Later, rail carriers were forced into publishing through routes and joint rates with water carriers on the Mississippi River. In the Motor Carrier Act of 1980, the power of the ICC to require coordination with inland water carriers was extended to motor carriers. Under rail-water coordination, the large-volume iron ore move-ment went by rail to the head of the lakes, by water carriers to points in

Ohio, Illinois, and Michigan, and by rail inland to steel plants. This is a good example of a beneficial aspect of carrier coordination.

If one considers maritime transportation along with the five domestic modes, there are fifteen potential types of coordinated service as noted in Table 20.1. The first eight (rail-truck, truck-air, rail-inland water, truck-pipeline, maritime-rail, maritime-truck, maritime-pipeline, and truck inland water) are found in varying degrees in the United States. The remaining seven, although possible, rarely are undertaken. It is to be emphasized that coordinated carrier service calls for separate ownership of the respective carriers where a through and joint rate and route exist. There are many examples of integrated carrier service (with one ownership), such as LASH and Seabee vessels; truck pickup and delivery around rail, inland water, pipeline, air, and maritime terminals in carrier-owned trucks; and TOFC Plan II, but these do not have a separate-ownership pattern.

The flexibility of the motor truck causes it to be combined most readily with other modes. In many cases, after the versatile truck has picked up the freight at the door of the shipper and hauled it to the terminal, the trailer itself moves by some other mode to a distant terminal where again the flexibility of the truck and streets and highways allows delivery to the receiver's door. The most common truck-other combination is the familiar piggyback, or TOFC, service. Here the economy and efficiency of long-haul rail service is combined with the convenience of the flexible truck. This service started many years ago on an experimental basis and grew rapidly since the 1950s. Piggybacking has now firmly established itself as an integral part of domestic transportation.

It should be noted that a good deal of TOFC service involves railroads hauling the trailers of their truck subsidiaries or their own pickup and delivery vehicles. Although this type of service, called Plan II service, is both piggyback and intermodal, it is not considered coordination as we use the term here to mean joint service of separately owned modes of transportation. Since this service was effectively deregulated under the ICC interpretation of the Staggers Act of 1980, there has been considerable interest and growth of Plan II-type piggybacking by the railroads.

Another widely used coordinated service is COFC, or container-on-flatcar. Containers are very flexible and COFC service is but one application. After all, a truck is really only a container on wheels. Service whereby specifically designed truck trailers or vans are detached from their wheels and loaded on specially built rail cars is common. Sometimes these vans are further loaded on ships and sometimes airplanes for overseas points, making another type of coordinated service. Special maritime vessels called containerships have become prevalent in the last twenty years, so that containerized international transportation has grown greatly.

Table 20.1 Coordinated Transportation Service

Modes	Application
Rail-truck	TOFC or piggyback
Truck-air	Pickup and delivery around airports
Rail-inland water	Iron ore and grain shipments
Truck-pipeline	Pickup and delivery around pipeline terminals
Maritime-rail	COFC or container on flatcar (land bridge)
Maritime-truck	RO/RO or roll-on, roll-off service
Maritime-pipeline	LOOP
Truck-inland water	Pickup and delivery around inland water ports
Inland water-pipeline	
Maritime-air	
Rail-air	
Rail-pipeline	
Inland water-air	
Maritime-inland water	
Pipeline-air	

Actually, there is little to prevent these flexible containers from using several modes of transportation.

The field of containerization affects transportation and may be considered an integral part of the subject. In reality, any shipment packed in a box is containerized; thus, containerization is really a matter of degree. The point of containerization is to minimize expensive handling of freight as well as loss and damage. Great strides have been made in the use of large containers, usually measuring 8 by 8 by 20 feet, and standardization is slowly coming in size and handling in rail, highway, and maritime transportation. Smaller containers are widely used in air freight.

Two newer types of coordinated service involve RO/RO ships and LOOP. RO/RO stands for roll-on, roll-off service whereby truck trailers are shipped in specially designed vessels to points lacking sophisticated port facilities needed for container handling. These services are similar to TOFC with maritime vessels substituting for rail cars. RO/RO service is very important to less developed countries or newly emerging nations where port facilities are crude, but interior roads exist for the delivery portion of the shipment. LOOP stands for Louisiana Offshore Oil Port and is a relatively new project off the Gulf Coast of Louisiana where very large crude oil tankers discharge their cargo in deep water into a pipeline connected to inland storage facilities. The LOOP system, owned jointly by groups of pipelines, services all tankers and is interconnected to the domestic pipeline network.

The rationale of these various combinations of line-hauls, as well as other coordinating devices, is that the results are highly beneficial to all concerned — carrier, shipper, and the public. This is the major reason these services are permitted and encouraged. Carriers share traffic they might not otherwise handle. Less labor is involved as transloading is easier. Generally, equipment utilization is better and costs are often lower and efficiency higher. Shippers benefit from better service — through routes, door-to-door service, through billing by one mode, and fewer arrangements to negotiate. Less loss and damage to lading is also a usual result of coordination. The public benefits from better utilization of the transportation system and better resource allocation.

If coordination is both beneficial and noncontroversial, why is it not more common in domestic transportation and why has it been so long in coming? The answer is twofold: (1) the natural tendency in a competitively structured system of transportation for each carrier to want the greatest possible total tonnage, and (2) the lack of promotion of intermodalism. Although some regulatory obstacles existed for a time, these have mostly been removed by recent legislation. As noted above, in the past, it proved necessary to give the ICC power to enforce rail-water coordination and, recently, motor-water coordination. Obviously, these carriers were hesitant to share tonnage with one another, or such regulation would have been unnecessary. Carrier attitude is perhaps the greatest obstacle to more carrier coordination.

CARRIER ORGANIZATIONAL PATTERNS

Given the fact that carriers are basically selling a service, the two major organizational functions are operations and sales. Traditionally, carriers have been oriented mainly toward operations. Indeed, many critics of carrier management contend that far too little attention has been paid to the marketing side of the carrier business.

To a considerable degree, the organizational patterns of carriers reflect the two influences of geography and routes. Most carriers operate over a wide geographic area — some are transcontinental and international in scope. Wide geographic dispersion of operating units makes for a much more complicated managerial problem than if all functions are concentrated in one or a few plants, such as occurs in most manufacturing. Control and accountability are difficult when geographic distance intervenes, and several organizational patterns can be found among carriers.

Routes are the other factor influencing carrier organizational structure. Being operationally oriented, management structure tends to reflect the routes over which a carrier operates.

The organization of the railroads is a good example of these influences of geography and routes. Railroads are basically linear, running between major points. Historically, the railroads were the first big business in America, and a great deal of early management structure developed here first. The division tends to be the autonomous management unit. Many rail divisions are 200 or so miles in length along a linear route, for traditionally a freight train would cover 100 to 120 miles per operating shift and labor regulations led to crew changes every 100 miles. Hence, a division point or headquarters would control trains 100 miles in either direction with the next division point picking up responsibility when a new crew took over operation of the train. Each division has a high degree of autonomy, with a division superintendent, its own repair and maintenance operations, trainmasters, clerks, signaling department, wrecker crews, track gangs, local operating crews, and through train crews — each division is literally a small railroad in itself. The train proceeds from autonomous division to division on its journey to its ultimate destination, dropping off and picking up cars at each division point. Local trains operate to intermediate points within a division, dropping off or picking up cars 100 miles or so on either side of the division point. Major classification yards near end terminal points make up trains of cars, usually sequentially, for specific end terminal destinations. Sales and marketing tend to be centralized in railroading with sales or traffic offices in major cities along the route.

Motor carriers tend to be organized on a regional basis, with the terminal the center of the organizational structure, terminal managers controlling the entire operation, and each terminal functioning as a separate motor carrier. Over-the-road trucks (line-haul vehicles) operate between terminals with unit loads, and freight is picked up and delivered to and from terminals in smaller vehicles. Sales tends to be decentralized with each terminal having its own sales staff, given the multiplicity of customers and goods handled. Most terminals also have rate and tariff departments, loss and claims personnel, billing and collection, dispatchers, equipment maintenance facilities, dock supervisors and workers to load and unload vehicles, and so forth. Sometimes terminals are grouped into geographic districts or divisions, but usually each terminal has a high degree of autonomy and is geographically separated from the carrier headquarters.

Airlines, pipelines, and water transportation tend to have much more centralized management structures. Given automation, pipelines have much smaller terminal staffs than either railroads or motor carriers. Operations are usually centralized and use electronic devices to control flow.

Since the number of customers is small, sales and marketing can be easily centralized. In airlines, centralization is also common, but sales personnel are stationed at each major point to deal with customers or, more important, travel agents. Operational personnel and ticket agents are, of course, located in the terminal served by the air carrier. All but minor maintenance is usually found at large centralized maintenance bases. Where the hub-and-spoke route configuration is used, hub terminals will have more autonomy and will manage a large number of crews, ticket personnel, and maintenance and ramp crews. In water transportation, major decentralization takes place at port terminals with the boats or ships being pretty much self-contained and self-sufficient. The sales department tends also to be centralized to major shipping ports. Once again, routes served tend to establish where management takes place.

Since many carriers interconnect or interline, it is not unusual to find sales and marketing personnel in cities not directly served by a specific carrier. In railroading, off-line agents in most large cities are common, since the shipper has the legal right to specify the route used. Some major truck lines also maintain sales offices in cities they do not serve. Airlines will employ sales personnel to call on travel agents in cities not on their routes. Steamship and inland water carriers also have traveling sales representatives assigned to large territories away from their ports. And it is common for transportation carriers to be listed and advertise in the yellow pages of cities not directly on the carrier routes.

ADDITIONAL READINGS

Bowersox, Donald J., Pat J. Calabro, and George D. Wagenheim, *Introduction to Transportation*, New York: Macmillan Publishing Co., 1981.
  Chapter 17, "Transportation Careers and Organizations," pp. 341–55.
Daggett, Stuart, *Principles of Inland Transportation*, 4th ed., New York: Harper and Brothers, 1955.
  Chapter 12, "The Duty of Service," pp. 229–43.
  Chapter 13, "Common Carrier Liability," pp. 244–62.
Fair, Marvin L., and Ernest W. Williams, *Transportation and Logistics*, Rev. ed., Plano, Texas: Business Publications, 1981.
  Chapter 11, "Service Obligations and Liabilities of Public Carriers and Warehousemen," pp. 182–96.
Farris, Martin T., "The Role of the Common Carrier," *Transportation Journal* 10(4) (Summer 1967), 28–34.
Flood, Kenneth U., Oliver G. Callson, and Sylvester J. Jablonski, *Traffic Management*, 4th ed., Dubuque, Iowa: Wm. C. Brown, 1984.
  Chapter 19, "Carrier Liability," pp. 509–44.
Locklin, D. Philip, *Economics of Transportation*, 7th ed., Homewood, Ill.: Richard D. Irwin, 1972.

Chapter 22, "Discrimination between Places and Commodities," pp. 511–38.
Chapter 25, "Railroad Service and Service Regulation," pp. 580–606.
Miller, John M., and Fritz R. Kahn, *Law of Freight Loss and Damage Claims*, 2nd ed., Dubuque, Iowa: Wm. C. Brown, 1961.
Chapter 1, "Source of Carrier Liability for Loss and Damage," pp. 1–11.
Chapter 2, "The Transportation Contract," pp. 12–85.
Chapter 3, "Common Carrier Liability Generally," pp. 86–114.
Chapter 4, "Specific Phases of Carrier Liability," pp. 115–521.
Wycoff, D. Daryl, and David H. Maister, *The Domestic Airline Industry*, Lexington, Mass.: Lexington Books, 1977.
_____ , *The Motor Carrier Industry*, Lexington, Mass.: Lexington Books, 1977.

CHAPTER 21

CARRIER MANAGEMENT

In the previous chapter we discussed the nature of the carrier operating environment. In this chapter we discuss the nature of carrier management and how management practice has been forced to change in a less regulated environment. In addition, we will address some terminal and special line-haul services offered by carriers as part of their overall transportation service package.

CARRIER MANAGEMENT ACTIVITIES

Carrier management activities can be divided into four main categories: operations-maintenance, sales-marketing, pricing-ratemaking, and administration-coordination. The latter category includes a whole group of activities, such as finance, accounting, billing and collecting, purchasing, insurance, personnel training, safety and security, real estate development, taxes, permits and licenses, legal affairs, public relations, equipment selection, claims, and planning.

Operations-Maintenance

Carriers have traditionally been operations oriented. Most people think of transportation in terms of its equipment operations — trains, trucks, planes, buses, barges and towboats, ships, cars, pipelines — all providing service to its customers. Operations is obviously the most visible activity of transportation carriers. It includes operating equipment, dispatching crews, loading and unloading freight and passengers, ticketing and rating freight bills, scheduling and accounting for equipment — literally providing the service.

A somewhat less visible aspect of operations is maintenance. Considerable sums of money and numbers of employees are dedicated to keeping equipment and the way (in the case of railroads in particular) in good operating order. Certain minimum levels of maintenance are often specified by public authorities and regulation. Additionally, preventive maintenance is often practiced, whereby parts of vehicles are replaced and inspections made on a scheduled basis.

In managing operations, many criteria of efficiency are possible. For example, shipments should be routed to move in a straight line wherever possible to minimize distance. Equipment should be used to its greatest capacity — either weight-carrying capacity or space capacity, called cube in freight transportation or seats occupied in passenger transportation. Here the load factor becomes important. This is a measurement of the degree of capacity utilized. For example, if an airplane has 150 seats and 75 are occupied, the flight is said to have a 50 percent load factor.

Dispatching should be accomplished in such a manner as to minimize empty backhauls of equipment or deadheading of crews. In recent years, minimizing fuel consumption has taken on more importance as an operations and maintenance criterion. Excessive speeds may be very costly in fuel consumption. Also, increasing labor productivity is an important consideration since labor costs are usually the largest single cost of operation.

The economics of these operating criteria are quite simple. Many of the costs of operation become fixed costs once the service is undertaken. Once equipment is purchased, its repayment is a fixed cost. Once crews are hired, trained, and scheduled, their cost becomes fixed, at least for a time. Labor agreements reinforce the fixed nature of crew costs. Considerable fuel is necessary to move an empty vehicle (train, plane, truck, bus, or ship), and as the vehicle is loaded with freight or passengers, fuel use does not increase proportionately with the increased load. Minimum maintenance and preventive maintenance are also fixed costs of operations. Under all these circumstances, operations at or near capacity fully utilizing crew time and equipment and avoiding circuity are more efficient and profitable for the carrier.

A continuing management problem in transportation operations and maintenance is that of balancing the efficiency criteria noted above with service criteria of frequency, reliability, and safety. For example, airplanes and buses should be filled to capacity for efficiency, but the carrier must also keep a schedule and equipment may have to be dispatched with less than a full load. And for-hire motor carriers, railroads, towboats, ships, and pipelines all operate on a predetermined schedule. Only contract carriers, independent carriers, tramp steamers, and private carriers do not have the obligation of maintaining specific schedules. Reliability, frequency, and safety of service are the most important attributes of the for-hire common carriers. Hence, trade-offs are inevitable between reliability-frequency-safety and operating at capacity, minimizing backhauls and deadheading, distance, fuel use, and crew costs. Operations can be a real management challenge.

Sales-Marketing

Transportation is, after all, a service — and as we have seen above, considerable ranges of competition exist. Hence, sales and marketing are a very important carrier management activity. Each carrier must engage in sales and marketing activity and should have a marketing strategy and goals.

Sales efforts by carriers vary. For many years, observers have been critical of carrier sales and marketing efforts — particularly in some modes such as railroad and maritime transportation. To some degree, these criticisms were accurate, especially with a regulated environment and with limited choice on the part of shippers and passengers. Moreover, selling service is somewhat different from selling products and in some ways presents a greater challenge to the sales and marketing personnel. However, given less government regulation and more competition among carriers — both intermodal and intramodal — sales and marketing of carrier service have become more important.

Essentially, the sales and marketing activity presents the carrier services to the potential shipper and passenger. In freight transportation, salespersons have traditionally been called solicitors, for they literally ask for shippers' business. But the sales and marketing effort must be more than solicitation. It should emphasize the strengths of the service, attempt to balance movement in both directions, zero in on profitable freight and passengers, balance backhauls, and create freight and passenger volume.

But volume alone is not enough for modern, alert carrier management. Profitability is a more important criterion. The marketing effort should attempt to ascertain what movement of freight and passengers is most profitable and make an extra effort in that area. Many carriers faced with increased competition and deregulation are finding that an emphasis on the volume criterion can be deceptive.

Part of the marketing effort will include advertising and promotion. Some modes of transportation, particularly in freight, have traditionally done very little advertising; others such as airlines have always used advertising. However, modern and innovative carrier management in today's business environment realizes that advertising is an integral part of the marketing effort.

Finally, attitude is probably the most important attribute of carrier marketing. The salesperson should be trained to ask: what can we do to help the shipper or the passenger? The successful carrier sales effort today is centered around the so-called marketing concept — assisting the customer in all possible ways. Some carriers devote substantial time and effort to determining specific customer needs, analyzing their shippers' operations with a view to offering improved service, and assuming the role of partner in solving customers' problems. The carrier that attempts to discover the customer's needs and tailors its operation to those needs gets the business.

Pricing-Ratemaking

Although pricing-ratemaking may be thought of as part of marketing, it is really more than that. The price or rate is only one aspect of marketing, and in the creation of freight and passenger demand, service, reliability, and selling are also important. On the other hand, rates and prices generate revenue and therefore must be established with some reference to costs. Hence, the purpose of pricing and ratemaking activities is twofold: pricing as a marketing tool to generate freight and passenger demand in competition with other carriers and modes, and pricing to generate enough revenue to cover costs of the service and show a profit.

Carrier pricing and ratemaking is complicated by two factors: utilization levels and the high degree of common and joint costs in most carriers. Theoretically, each rate or fare should cover the cost of that service and contribute to profit. But this implies some level of utilization — an average-sized shipment or average number of seats filled or assumed load factor. As noted above, many operational costs are fixed or almost fixed. Therefore, specific shipment costs or passenger costs are a function of the utilization of available capacity, and per-passenger costs or per-ton costs will vary with how well capacity is used.

Further, most carriers have a considerable degree of overhead or common and joint costs. Many expenditures covering the entire operation can be allocated only arbitrarily to specific passengers or shipments. For example, how does one assign marketing expenses to specific shipments or passengers? Major effort may be expended on only a few shippers or a few passengers at any one time, but marketing costs must be covered by total revenues. These costs are common to the entire operation, as are most administrative costs, capital costs, taxes, and so forth. These common costs cannot be separately assigned to a given shipment or passenger. If per-unit costs cannot be assigned, how can price be intelligently established to cover costs and generate a profit?

In view of these problems, many carriers use the so-called contribution theory in their pricing or ratemaking. They identify as many separable costs as possible, such as fuel and crew costs. These costs establish a minimum below which rates cannot go. Next, rates are established over and above separable costs on the basis of managerial estimates of the elasticity of demand for a particular shipment or passenger class. The object is to establish a rate or fare that covers separable costs and makes the greatest total contribution to fixed and common costs, considering demand characteristics.

Under this system, some rates and fares will be higher than others, and some will be lower than others. Indeed, the system of freight classification discussed in Chapter 17 is based on this theory. The concept is also widely used in excursion and promotional air fares. Separate rates or fares are set for each commodity or passenger class with the goal of maximizing revenue and making the greatest possible contribution to fixed and common costs over and above separable costs.

It should be noted that the contribution theory assumes three things: excess capacity, elasticity of demand, and ability to separate customers. If a carrier is operating at full capacity, it would be foolish to lower rates or fares on a given commodity or passenger class to promote traffic. But if excess capacity is available , the carrier can spread the common and fixed costs of operation over more freight or passengers and gain more profit from the added traffic. Of course, this assumes that freight or passengers will be attracted by a lower rate (demand is elastic). If a lower price will fill excess capacity, it is better to earn something than nothing. This theory also assumes that freight or passengers can be separated and identified so that special low rates or fares can be made just for them. In the long run, all revenue must cover all costs plus a profit, but in the short run, added traffic priced anywhere above separable costs is better than having excess capacity.

Obviously, then, the keys to successful pricing in transportation are knowledge of carrier costs and knowledge of the demand characteristics of commodities and passengers. Innovative and alert carrier management will give its major emphasis to pricing and ratemaking.

Administration-Coordination

Many activities fall into this group. Some of them are finance, accounting, billing and collecting, insurance, purchasing, taxes and licenses, security, legal activities, claims settlement and prevention, personnel and training, equipment selection, public relations, and planning. In some cases, one or more of these activities could stand alone, depending on its importance to the particular carrier. For example, many railroads are large landowners, and hence their real estate and development activities will often be organized under a separate vice president. Finance is another activity that is often administered by a separate vice president, given the necessity of many carriers to raise capital for equipment replacement, terminal expansion, and upgrading of the way (as in railroading). Another function that is often organized separately is that of personnel and training, since rail, motor, and air carriers find that over 50 percent of their costs involve labor. The degree of importance of each activity will vary according to the carrier's characteristics.

Internal coordination is a major administrative activity for all carriers, however. Operations and maintenance must be coordinated with sales and marketing. Pricing and ratemaking decisions cannot be made without consultation and coordination with both sales and operations. Equipment selection will be influenced by the needs of operations. Personnel and training must be closely coordinated with operations. Public relations and advertising must be coordinated with sales. And so it goes through all parts of carrier management — the need for internal coordination, interchange of ideas, communication, and teamwork is mandatory. Coordination is a prime task of carrier management at all levels.

TERMINAL AND SPECIAL LINE-HAUL SERVICES

No look at carrier operations and management would be complete without a view of terminal and special line services offered by carriers. These services are important to the provision of full transportation service and are a significant contributor to the nature of the shipper-carrier relationships discussed in Part VI.

Terminal Services

Terminals are of major importance in domestic transportation. A terminal is more than a place where the line-haul for freight and passengers stops and starts. It is a place where various necessary carrier operations take place, where changes in the shipment occur, and where various special services are performed for shippers, sometimes as a part of the line-haul charge and sometimes at extra charges. Finally, a terminal is a place where carrier cooperation and coordination take place, as discussed in Chapter 20.

Terminals vary in physical size from relatively small installations used by buses or trucks to the very large airports in metropolitan areas or rail marshaling yards in or adjacent to key shipping points. Many acres of land are necessary for rail terminals, airports, and seaports, whereas only small amounts of land are necessary for motor operations. Of course, the flexible motor vehicle depends upon the many miles of public streets and highways for part of the same terminal function the railroad uses its yards to perform.

Because of the need for space for terminal operations, there is a definite relationship between transportation terminals and the problems of urbanization. In the case of the motor carrier, it is often traffic congestion on the public streets; in the case of the rail carrier, the problem is sometimes urban blight and deterioration near its yards and shops, and in the case of the air carrier, noise and safety factors cause urban problems. Since terminals are a focal point of movement, they markedly affect the flow of traffic and people in an urban system. Hence, terminals are a very important factor in urban systems' analysis and planning as well as an integral and essential part of intercity domestic transportation. Our concern here is primarily with the transportation role of terminals.

Functions of Terminals

Terminals have five basic functions: concentration, dispersion, shipment service, vehicle service, and interchange.

A terminal provides a point of consolidation. This function is performed for the transportation of both freight and people. People are consolidated or concentrated into groups in the terminal according to the size of the transportation vehicle. People load themselves into planes, trains, and buses, thereby simplifying the problem of getting the concentration to be shipped onto the vehicle.

With goods, the concentration is similar. Freight moves to a terminal point, either by carrier-provided pickup vehicles or by the shipper's own actions, and is consolidated or concentrated into vehicle lots. The terminal provides the point for this concentration. Once the concentration is complete, the shipment can start on its journey. But in order to gain economies of lower costs and use of vehicles, each shipment is concentrated to some degree and does not move separately. This is true whether the function of concentration is applied to packages or carloads. With packages and individual items, the concentration into larger units to fit the vehicles is obvious. But the same function is involved when rail cars are made into trains in terminals or barges are assembled into tows.

To facilitate the function of concentration, goods are handled in terminals. This may involve the physical movement of many items in small packages, or it may involve the handling of vehicles such as making up railroad trains. This handling is expensive and makes up a major part of the terminal costs. It also subjects the shipment to the possibility of loss or damage. The expense and hazards of this concentration are two of the great problems of domestic transportation.

Allied to concentration are the tasks of dispatching vehicles and crews. The terminal furnishes a point where this function is carried on.

The function of dispersion is the opposite of concentration. This is also an important function of terminals, performed for both people and goods. In intercity transportation, the terminal is the point of destination. From the terminal people disperse to their homes, offices, jobs, and so forth; goods disperse to their ultimate destination. The fact that people unload themselves and generally provide their own dispersion makes this function fairly simple in passenger transportation. However, in the movement of freight, the delivery aspect of the dispersion function is expensive and time consuming. The function remains the same whether the goods are in small parcels or in vehicle or carload lots. Freight cars have to be dispersed upon arrival at a terminal; full-load trucks have to be delivered or dispatched locally. And the task of dispatching vehicles and crews in delivery is carried on at the terminal.

The two functions of concentration and dispersion are often carried on simultaneously. When freight cars are picked up for concentration into trains, other cars may at the same time be dispersed. When LTL shipments are picked up for concentration into over-the-road units, other shipments may be delivered. Both functions can often be performed by the same vehicle or crew.

Terminals provide a place where shipments are serviced in various ways. In passenger transportation, the provision of waiting rooms and ticketing are the prime shipment-service functions of terminals. In the transportation of goods, the same functions take place but in a somewhat more complicated manner. Thus terminals provide storage and elevation for goods being shipped and protection for goods against the elements, theft, and damage. This is essentially the same service a passenger waiting room provides. Terminals likewise provide a point at which routing and billing of shipments take place. This is the same documentation service as the ticketing of passengers. These shipment-service functions of storage and documentation are provided for shippers or passengers as part of the line-haul charge.

Carriers, too, use terminals for their own function of vehicle service. The terminal is a place to store vehicles until they are needed in the concentration or the dispersion function. It also provides a space to maneuver vehicles where needed. Cleaning, repairing, and servicing vehicles are generally undertaken at terminals. Repair shops often are maintained, and vehicles are made ready for departure.

Sometimes the terminal provides the carrier with its principal place of doing business. While this is not a vehicle service aspect, it is a related terminal function. The terminal may be the site of carrier executive offices, sales offices, and administrative offices, although some of these carrier functions may be carried on at locations other than terminals.

Finally, terminals provide the place for interchange of passengers and freight. This interchange may involve moving people from plane to plane, rail car to rail car, or bus to bus. Goods, too, are interchanged. Interchange may be between vehicles of the same line or between different lines (cooperation). It may even involve interchange of shipments between different modes of transportation (coordination).

These five terminal functions of concentration, dispersion, shipment service, vehicle service, and interchange are essential to the movement of all goods and people in intercity transportation. They are generally included in the line-haul charge of carriers and must be provided in a nondiscriminatory and adequate manner. There are, however, other terminal services that are accessorial or optional in some cases.

Accessorial Terminal Services

The terminal functions already discussed are essential to shipment of all goods and passengers. Accessorial terminal services are not essential to all shipments but are offered by carriers, in many cases voluntarily, but often at an extra charge. These include the following five services: pickup and delivery, loading and unloading, weighing and reweighing, industrial switching, and storage and elevation.

Although motor carriers generally have provided pickup and delivery as part of their regular line-haul freight service, it is incorrect to say that free pickup and delivery is universal. Prior to the 1930s, this service was not provided as part of the line-haul freight service by railroads. There often is a pickup and delivery charge on air cargo and air freight. Passengers are rarely picked up or delivered; carriers usually rely on public transportation or special limousine companies to provide this service at an extra charge. Additionally, there are size, weight, and geographic limits to free pickup and delivery even when it is part of the line-haul service.

If a shipper performs this service in its own vehicles, an allowance may be offered by carriers. In some cases, the shipper must specifically request pickup and delivery, otherwise it will not be offered. Naturally, when pickup and delivery are at a point quite distant from the terminal, additional charges are to be expected. The same may be said for unusually bulky or heavy goods. The rules establishing the boundaries of free pickup and delivery districts are found in pickup and delivery tariffs. The weight and size limitations before extra charges are assessed, along with the various pickup and delivery charges, are also found in pickup and delivery tariffs. (Tariffs are discussed in Chapter 17.)

In carload and truckload shipment, it is the obligation of the shipper or the consignee to load or unload the shipment. Generally the shipper does this, but upon request the railroad may load and unload cars for a shipper or consignee at a charge. This service also provides for checking, sorting, coopering, and other tasks allied to the loading and unloading function. In motor transportation, loading and unloading is usually provided as part of the line-haul service as long as it can be done by one person and does not involve unusual tasks. There are various exceptions to this general rule, of course.

Since freight charges are based on weight, the weighing of shipments is part of the line-haul service. The weight of a shipment must be accurately determined in order to protect both the shipper and the carrier and to avoid discrimination. Most of the weighing is done on the carrier's scales or by carrier-supported independent weighing and inspection bureaus. There are five rail and sixteen motor weighing and inspection bureaus that carry on this function.

Reweighing is also done by these bureaus. If the shipper questions the weight assigned by the carrier, the shipment will be reweighed. The charge for this service is assumed by the carrier if reweighing determines that the initial weight and charge were in error by more than a recognized tolerance. Otherwise, the shipper pays for this reweighing service.

In order to avoid repeated weighings on standardized shipments, an average weight agreement is often arranged between shippers and carriers. This device helps both parties by cutting the carrier's cost and by expediting the shipment. When shipments are of standard size such as cartons of canned goods, citrus cartons, fruit boxes, barrels of liquid, and so forth, a test over time can determine the average weight of such containers, and the weight of a shipment can be readily ascertained without physically weighing each shipment each time. Weighing and inspection bureaus administer weight agreements and supervise transit-privilege administration and various other functions.

The movement of rail cars within a terminal, as distinguished from movement between terminals or stations of a carrier, is called *switching*. There are several types of switching services, some of which are performed as part of the line-haul charges and some of which are performed at extra charges. If an industry owns rail sidings or tracks within a plant, industrial switching is involved at an additional charge.

Just as motor carriers use pickup and delivery as a competitive device, railroads sometimes use switching in the same manner. Line-haul charges usually include the switching and spotting of cars on industrial tracks; but in large terminal areas, a shipper may not be located on the tracks of all carriers. Here it may have to pay an extra charge (unless it is absorbed by the carrier) to send or receive cars on a certain rail carrier. Sometimes the carriers have a reciprocal switching agreement whereby the parties to the agreement reciprocate and do not charge for switching cars among themselves. In large terminal areas, special belt-line or switching railroads may exist that do nothing but switch cars from carrier to carrier or shipper to shipper. These belt-line companies may be owned by all the carriers jointly as a union or terminal railroad, or they may be separately owned. These companies' charges for their services may or may not be absorbed by the carriers.

Switching often is carried on over a wide area. The municipal boundaries of a city are not necessarily the switching district or switching limit. The Chicago switching district, for instance, covers 400 square miles and is 40 miles in length from north to south and 7 to 15 miles wide from east to west, with 5,000 miles of track. This district is served by many railroads, several of which are line-haul carriers.

Flotage and lighterage services in harbors are another form of switching, using barges instead of tracks. These special services, which are particularly important in port areas, may or may not be offered at an extra charge.

Storage of freight on the premises of the carrier and elevation service for grain at terminals and ports are other optional services. Sometimes storage will be provided free of charge at the owner's risk, but more often a warehousing or storage charge is made. Elevation for weighing, inspection, or transfer from car to car is part of the line-haul service, but elevation for storage is an accessorial service provided by many carriers at an extra charge.

Accessorial Line-Haul Services

In addition to line-haul terminal services and the various optional or accessorial terminal services, carriers also voluntarily offer a group of services that are accessorial to the line-haul. There may or may not be an extra charge for these supplemental or accessorial services. Six of these services are discussed here: reconsignment and diversion service, stopping-in-transit service, pool-car service, protective services, tracing and expedition, and transit privileges.

Reconsignment and Diversion Service

Although the terms *reconsignment* and *diversion* are often used interchangeably, there is a technical difference between the two services. *Diversion* means to change the destination of a shipment while it is en route, whereas *reconsignment* means to change the consignee of a shipment after it has arrived at its initial destination, but before delivery. These services are found most frequently in rail transportation, although some motor carriers also offer reconsignment and diversion.

A shipper or owner may wish to change the destination of a shipment or change the consignee on a shipment for several reasons. In at least eight conditions, this privilege proves valuable to the shipper.

1. The shipper may wish to start the shipment on its way prior to sale in order to avoid spoilage. If goods are perishable, they must move to market in as short a time as possible. The shipper consigns the car to itself; and after it has sold its contents, it reconsigns the shipment to the buyer.
2. The shipper may wish to avoid demurrage or detention charges. Only a limited number of hours or days are allowed for loading. Thus, in order to avoid penalty, the shipment may leave only to be reconsigned or diverted after it is sold.
3. The shipper may wish to send the shipment on its way to facilitate the flow of work in its plant. Limited loading facilities exist at most production points. Rail cars or trucks must be started away from the plant in order to accommodate more vehicles even though sale has not been made.
4. The shipper may wish to reconsign or divert a shipment on its way to market for price or service reasons. With a constantly changing price for goods, diversion allows the owner to change the destination of the shipment en route in order to get the highest price. Competition often calls for quick delivery, and many sales are made on the service aspect of ability to deliver in the shortest possible time. When a producer is some distance from the market, the shipment may be billed to the shipper itself and sent on its way. By diverting or reconsigning after it is sold, the distant producer often can offer as quick a delivery as the producer closer to the market.
5. The reconsignment and diversion privilege may be used to slow down a shipment until it is sold or until it is needed. In this manner, the

service provides a means of delay which may be as valuable as speed in some circumstances.

6. The buyer of the goods may resell the shipment to another buyer and use the reconsignment and diversion privilege. Some shipments may be sold several times while they are en route.

7. The buyer may cancel its order after the shipment has left the production point. By reconsignment and diversion, the seller may be able to dispose of the goods without loss due to cancelation.

8. The shipper may wish to avoid financial loss due to bankruptcy of the buyer.

Although there are no doubt other conditions under which this service is used, it is apparent that this valuable privilege is one of the important services of a carrier. This privilege is granted under certain uniform rules and charges, and shippers should know the circumstances under which it may be used.

From the conditions stated, it is obvious that the reconsignment and diversion privilege is more important for some commodities than for others. If goods are perishable, if the market price fluctuates daily, and if delivery time is a prime factor in selling goods in competition with producers closer to the market, the reconsignment and diversion service is highly valuable. If these conditions do not exist, the service is not so important. The service is therefore offered and used most frequently in the shipment of lumber, citrus, fresh fruits and vegetables, and dairy products. In these shipments, the rail carriers are particularly liberal in granting such privileges, often allowing some free reconsignment or diversion before a charge is made for the service, and only nominal charges thereafter. It is estimated that over half the rail traffic out of California and Florida is reconsigned at least once.

Reconsignment and diversion is important to the general public as well as to the individual shipper. It allows more producers to compete in a market and extends the economic supply to a wider area. Additionally, the effect of reconsignment and diversion of shipments on price can be considerable. Any marked variation in price in a given market can soon be brought into line by having shipments diverted to it.

Stopping in Transit

Another important accessorial line-haul service offered by the carriers is the right to stop shipments in transit for loading or unloading. This benefits the shipper or the consignee because it can apply the cheaper minimum carload rate even though a part of the journey is made with only a part of the vehicle filled. If the shipment had to proceed on less-than-minimum rates for both parts of the journey, the overall rate might be much higher.

Under this service, a producer may sell goods at two or more points or to several customers, ship the goods in a single car at the lower carload rates, and stop the car to partially unload at the point of each sale. Of course, the carload rate to the most distant point is charged. Also, a manufacturer may have two or more plants and use the privilege of stopping in transit to complete loading to ship at lower carload rates from both points without having a full carload at either point. For commission merchants and persons who buy and sell, the advantage is obvious.

This service was developed by railroads as a competitive device. However, many motor carriers also offer similar services. Stopping in transit to complete loading or unloading should not be confused with transloading. In transloading, the carrier may combine several loads of different shipments in a single vehicle for convenience.

Pool-Car Service

Another accessorial line-haul service offered by carriers, both rail and truck, is the pool car. This is a type of shipper operation much like the concentration function carried on by the carriers themselves. The carrier allows several shippers from one point of origin with the same type of commodity or a single shipper with several small shipments to pool shipments for the same destination. In this manner, shipments are moved at lower carload or truckload rates and at more frequent intervals than would be possible for smaller movements. Distribution or concentration of pool-car shipments is typically not handled by the carrier. Warehouses or local cartage firms often offer this service at a small charge.

The advantage of pool-car service is not only that the smaller shipper can get lower rates but also that inventories can be kept under more careful control, thus reducing costs.

Protective Services

In the shipment of perishable goods, protection of the shipment can be of vital importance. Protection here refers to protection against the elements, not protection against theft or pilferage.

A charge is made by the carrier for icing, refrigeration, ventilating, or heating cars. These services are made available to assist the shipper to bring goods to market in good condition. The feeding and watering of livestock is another type of protective service offered by the carriers at an additional charge.

Tracing and Expediting

The shipper often needs to know the progress of its shipments. Many carriers provide a tracing service for carload or truckload movements. No charge is made for this service even though rather elaborate means are often employed to keep track of shipments. In fact, some carriers use their complex tracing service as a competitive aid in selling their transportation service.

Expediting or speeding up a shipment uses tracing procedures. When assembly lines are threatened with shutdown or repair parts are necessary for production to resume, the shipper and the consignee both want to know not only how the shipment has progressed but also if the shipment can be speeded to destination. In some firms, one particular person in the traffic department is assigned to this task. These functions will be further discussed in Chapter 23.

During military emergencies, expediting is used extensively to speed shipments of high priority. Various techniques have been developed, and carriers cooperate in this service in order to retain the good will of important shippers.

Transit Privilege

The final accessorial line-haul service discussed here is the transit privilege. This privilege or service has a long history in rail transportation and is found in modern motor transportation as well.

With transit privileges, a shipment may be stopped while in transit from origin to destination and physically changed in form before proceeding to destination. The advantage is that the carrier considers the whole movement, even with a stop to change form, as a single movement and charges the long-haul rate rather than two short-haul rates. Thus the economies of long-haul rates are made available to the goods.

There are many types of transit privileges. The most common are milling in transit on grain, storing in transit, fabrication in transit, refining in transit, and treating or processing lumber in transit. In the common milling-in-transit privilege, grains move to the point of milling, are unloaded and milled into flour, and proceed to market as flour all under the long-haul or through rate. This allows more milling points to compete in a given market, thus neutralizing the location advantages of nearness to the market. Transit privileges are administered by weighing and inspection bureaus. A more detailed discussion of various transit rates and their effect on marketing and the location of industry is included in Part IV.

MANAGEMENT IN A LESS REGULATED ENVIRONMENT

In a highly regulated environment, carriers could operate successfully if they were reasonably efficient and fortunate enough to have a favorable traffic mix. In such an environment, with entry control and collective ratemaking, the competitive situation faced by the carrier changed slowly from year to year. An individual carrier did not have to know a great deal about the cost of providing service in many cases. This was especially true for a railroad or motor carrier because collective ratemaking and the cost-finding efforts of others would determine the level of rates used and their adequacy. Without rapid changes in the number and makeup of competitors, carrier selection often was based on the level of service given — measured in terms of such factors as transit time, on-time delivery, and loss and damage rates. In such an environment, inefficient carriers would go out of business, but much less quickly than is the case today.

Example of Motor Carrier Operation

In the new carrier environment, it is much more difficult to assure successful operation. In this era of intense rate and service competition, coupled with greater operating freedom, the management of an individual carrier must know much more about its operations to succeed. This need is a result of the complexity of carrier operations and the fact that virtually no two traffic movements are identical. An example of the nature of this complexity can be seen in the alternative ways that a shipment may move through a general commodity motor carrier system. In the somewhat simplified model shown in Figure 21.1, the carrier receives freight from two basic sources — another carrier that delivers what is known as interline received freight to the carrier's dock or from a shipper initiating freight for the carrier's system. In the latter case, the carrier must pick up the freight from the shipper and bring it to the terminal in preparation for line-haul movement.

Since pickup and delivery operations, to be efficient, are generally assigned to regions within a community, freight on any given vehicle will have a large range of ultimate destinations. Therefore, dock or terminal

Figure 21.1 Example of Carrier Operation

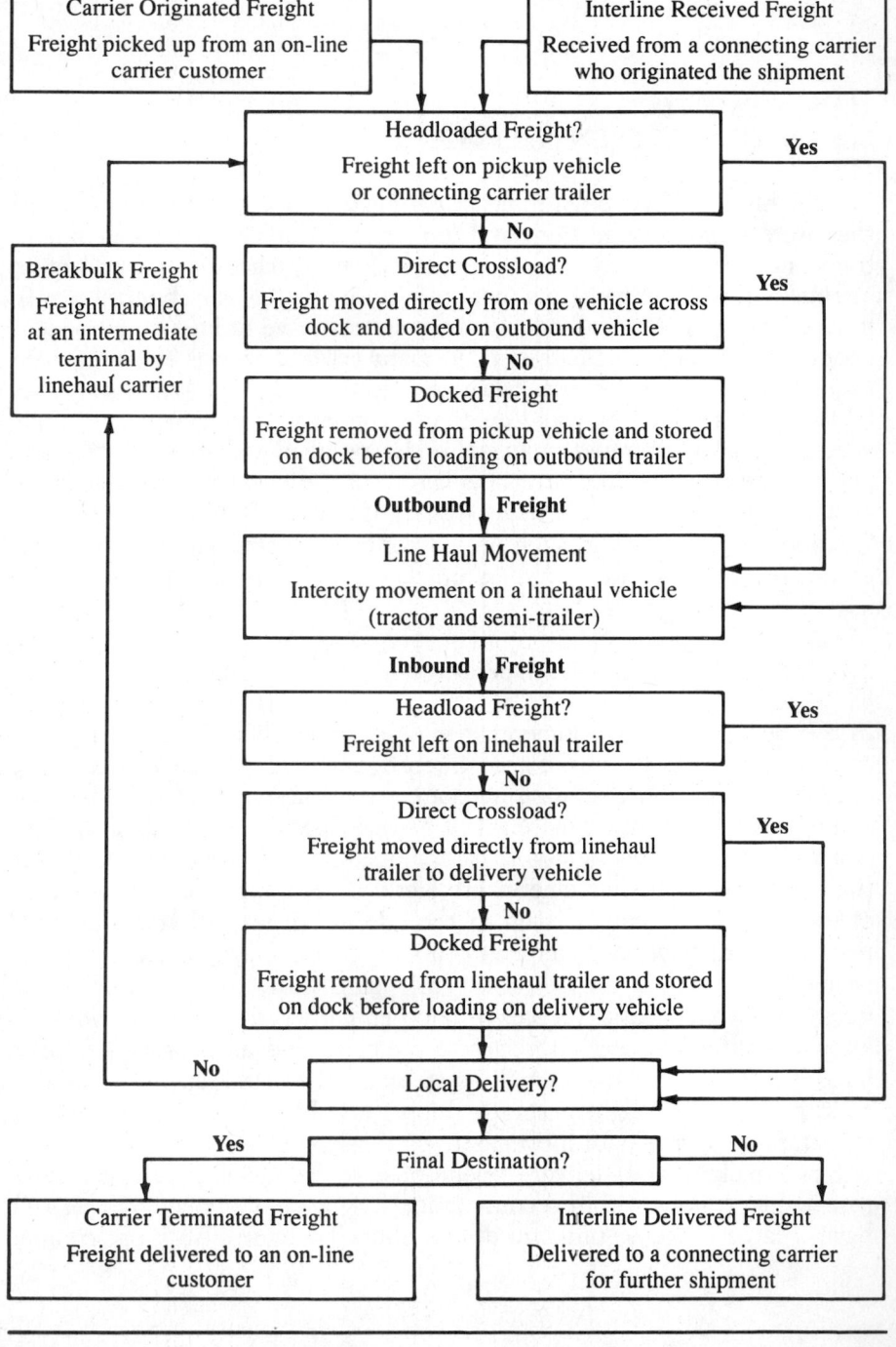

operations will be used to concentrate freight for efficient line-haul movement. In addition, the freight will be placed on trailers more suited for line-haul movement. (Since pickup and delivery service usually requires handling of freight at shipper and consignee locations, and because of the amount of time spent traveling between customer locations, equipment used in this service is often smaller than that used for line-haul movement. In effect, it is not possible to fully utilize the capacity of a 45-foot trailer in the time allowed during a pickup and delivery driver's shift.)

Freight reaches line-haul trailers in one of three ways. First, if the shipment is of sufficient size, a line-haul trailer may have been used to collect the freight. In this case, the freight is left on the trailer and is referred to as headloaded freight. Additional freight for the same destination may be placed on the trailer also. Second, the freight may be directly crossloaded from the pickup vehicle to the line-haul trailer. Third, the freight may be downloaded from the pickup vehicle, placed on the dock, and later moved to the line-haul trailer (intermediate docking). The handling costs, and therefore overall costs, of freight handled in each manner will be different. Even if handled in the same fashion, the different physical characteristics of individual shipments will dictate different handling times and, therefore, different costs.

Once the freight has been placed on the line-haul trailer, it will be moved to the next terminal on the way to its destination. At the destination terminal, the freight again either remains on the trailer until delivery or is directly crossloaded to a delivery vehicle or held on the dock for later loading into a delivery vehicle (intermediate docking). The delivery vehicle will then move the freight to a consignee's dock or to a connecting carrier for further movement.

In a larger carrier system, the freight may also be *breakbulked* at intermediate points. The principle of breakbulking is based on trade-offs between line-haul efficiency and effectiveness and additional freight handling costs. Figure 21.2 illustrates a breakbulk operation. In this example, a carrier has terminals in Memphis and Chicago that generate freight to Seattle and San Francisco. On the average, the carrier generates one-half trailerload of freight from each origination terminal to each destination terminal per day. To meet a delivery schedule requiring that the freight tendered be shipped the same day, it would require four tractors and trailers departing from the two origination terminals each day. If a breakbulk terminal is established in Denver, the carrier can send two tractors and trailers per day to Denver, where the Chicago-San Francisco freight and Memphis-Seattle freight are crossloaded. Then all San Francisco freight is on one trailer and all Seattle freight on the other. The carrier can provide almost the same service as if direct moves were made, as well

Figure 21.2 Example of Breakbulk Operation

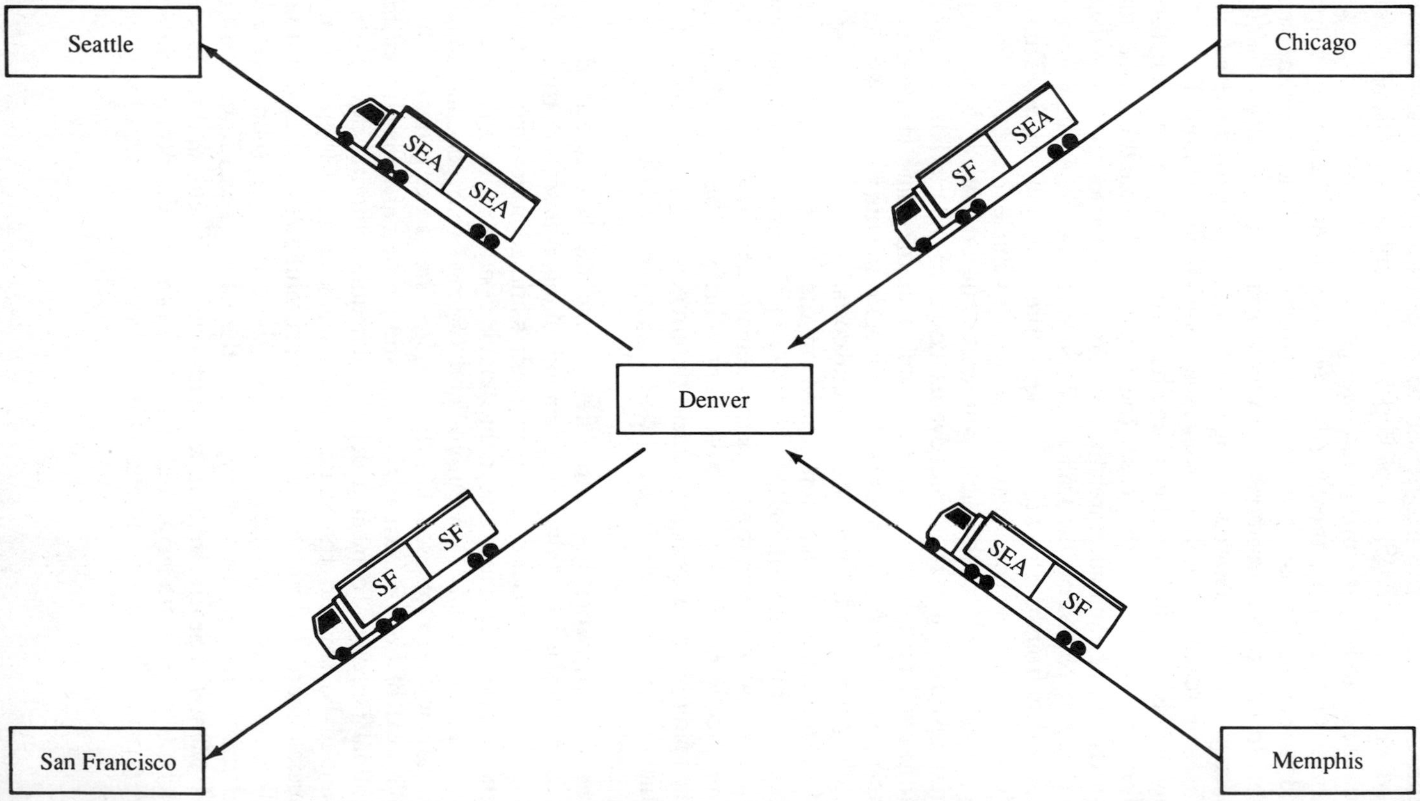

as reduce overall costs, if the added dock labor at Denver is less than the equipment, fuel, driver, and other costs related to the eliminated direct moves.

The Nature of Transportation Costs

The example shown above demonstrates in a small way the complexities of carrier operation. While the use of averages can reduce the need for carrier information concerning the specifics of operations, there are limits to this. The following simple example demonstrates the problem. If you were to enter the limousine business, you might determine that you would incur the following daily expenses: driver time at $100 per day, automobile depreciation at $40 per day, and average fuel costs of 5 cents per mile. If you drove the vehicle an average of 1,000 miles per week, you could conclude that the average cost per vehicle-mile is 75 cents.

If you now chose to use this estimate as a basis for charging for your services, you would charge each customer 75 cents per vehicle-mile. Therefore, if you had a customer who used your services in the city for an entire day, but required only 50 vehicle-miles, you would collect $37.50 for the day. Similarly, a customer who went between cities would travel perhaps 300 miles and pay you $225 for your services. In effect, in providing service to the first customer, you would incur expenses of $100 for your time, $40 in depreciation, and probably something over $2.50 in fuel, since city driving fuel usage is usually much poorer than road usage — a total of perhaps $145. The second day you would incur the same driver and depreciation expenses, but fuel costs of perhaps $10 — or a total of perhaps $150. On the first day your average cost was $2.90 per mile, while on the second day it was 50 cents per mile. Given your costing and pricing practices, you would probably soon go bankrupt, being uncompetitive for profitable "long-haul" traffic and too competitive for the unprofitable "short-haul" traffic.

The importance of this example is that it demonstrates that a carrier must know its costs to price effectively. In a collective ratemaking environment, it is assumed that enough competitors will understand their costs to develop meaningful prices for most carriers participating in the appropriate tariffs. From an individual perspective, success then again becomes a matter of being reasonably efficient and having the right traffic mix. For this example, as long as everyone competing in the limousine business generated about 1,000 vehicle-miles per week, all carriers would be "profitable."

Carrier Information Systems

In the operating environment of the 1980s and 1990s, individual carrier managements must capture the data needed to develop a great deal of information about their operations and to use this information to improve management practice. In an era of more nearly cost-based pricing, a lack of information will result in poor pricing practices, as is illustrated above. If a carrier's management finds that costs exceed market prices for its services, it must be able to evaluate how efficiently it is using resources to produce services. If management is told that a carrier's service is poor, it must be able to document and quantify performance, in terms of such things as on-time delivery and loss and damage claim rates. Such analyses are required if a carrier is to become as competitive as possible, reaching the level of "achievable excellence."

In the course of their day-to-day operations, carriers generate a vast amount of data. Even a relatively small carrier with gross revenues of $12 to $15 million dollars per year will generate perhaps 10 million pieces of data concerning such things as revenues, shipment characteristics, shipment movement patterns, labor use, fuel use, equipment maintenance, and myriad other things in the normal course of operation. Most of this data is used to facilitate the movement of freight through the carrier's operating system and to charge for the carrier's services. The problem lies in determining how much of this data is necessary for decision-making purposes and therefore should be captured in a way that facilitates easy later use.

In developing a meaningful picture of carrier operation, the carrier must not only collect data related to traffic, the operating system, and revenues and expenses, it must also evaluate how these are connected. The diagram shown in Figure 21.3 illustrates this concept. The carrier will normally generate the traffic characteristic, operating, and financial data, but fail to tie it together or keep it in an organized manner (embodying modern data base management practices). The key for management is the development of the "connectors" shown in the diagram — the relationships between a shipment's physical characteristics and dock handling labor requirements or line-haul fuel efficiencies and specific line-haul routes, for example. How these are developed is beyond the scope of this book. Suffice it to say that it requires bringing the tools of the cost accountant and the industrial engineer together in a carrier operating environment. It also means widespread use of computer technology to aid in data analysis and management of day-to-day operations.

There are many computer applications coming into ever-broader use in transportation today. The airlines have long used computers to aid in efficiently scheduling aircraft use, and railroads and larger motor carriers

Figure 21.3 The Carrier Information Environment

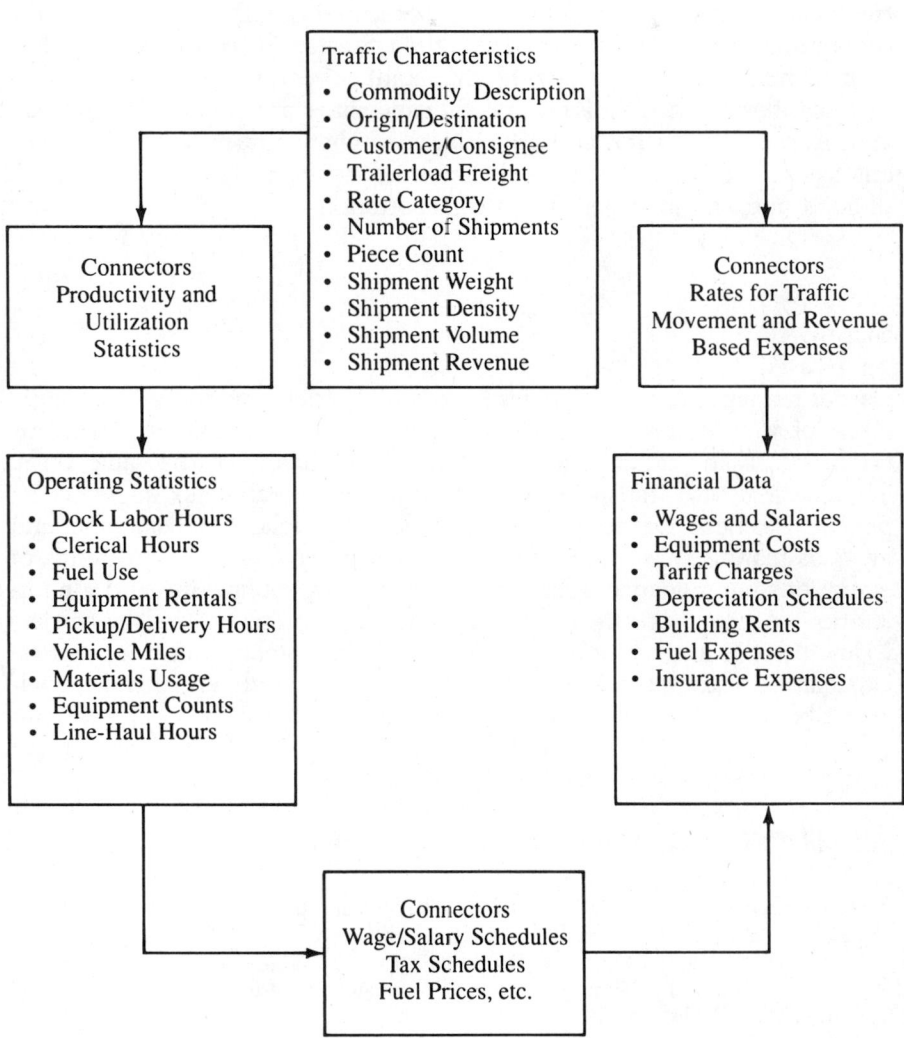

Traffic Characteristics
- Commodity Description
- Origin/Destination
- Customer/Consignee
- Trailerload Freight
- Rate Category
- Number of Shipments
- Piece Count
- Shipment Weight
- Shipment Density
- Shipment Volume
- Shipment Revenue

Connectors
Productivity and
Utilization
Statistics

Connectors
Rates for Traffic
Movement and Revenue
Based Expenses

Operating Statistics
- Dock Labor Hours
- Clerical Hours
- Fuel Use
- Equipment Rentals
- Pickup/Delivery Hours
- Vehicle Miles
- Materials Usage
- Equipment Counts
- Line-Haul Hours

Financial Data
- Wages and Salaries
- Equipment Costs
- Tariff Charges
- Depreciation Schedules
- Building Rents
- Fuel Expenses
- Insurance Expenses

Connectors
Wage/Salary Schedules
Tax Schedules
Fuel Prices, etc.

have used computer-aided systems for shipment tracing, billing, and dispatching. Similarly, applications for personal computers are now becoming available to a wider range of even very small carriers. These applications range from costing systems tying operations to pricing systems, to electronic data interchange between carriers and their customers, to satellite tracking systems capable of locating vehicles instantly to within a 90-square-mile area anywhere in the United States. All of this means that carrier management is reaching the point where the tools needed to significantly enhance decision-making capabilities are readily available. Of course, as is always the case, the ability to change does not ensure that change will occur. In addition, as in all industries, there will be instances of good and bad management in transportation.

SUMMARY

Carrier management is an interesting and challenging profession. Management of a transportation carrier involves the same basic management functions as any other enterprise and requires many of the same skills. The problem with transportation is that it is a very complex, highly competitive business. Carrier management activities follow the same general areas as management in any industry and may be thought of in terms of operations-maintenance, selling-marketing, pricing-ratemaking, and administration-coordination. In the less regulated environment faced by carriers today, there is a need for improved management practice, drawing on the capabilities of the computer and reflecting significantly enhanced knowledge about the operations of individual carriers.

ADDITIONAL READINGS

Bowersox, Donald J., Pat J. Calabro, and George D. Wagenheim, *Introduction to Transportation*, New York: Macmillan Publishing Co., 1981.
   Chapter 16, "Transportation Carrier Management," pp. 317–38.
Coyle, John J., Edward J. Bardi, and Joseph L. Cavinato, *Transportation*, 2nd ed., St. Paul, Minn.: West Publishing Co., 1986.
   Chapter 20, "Carrier Management I," pp. 413–30.
   Chapter 21, "Carrier Management II," pp. 431–50.
Davis, Grant M., Martin T. Farris, and Jack J. Holder, Jr., *Management of Transportation Carriers*, New York: Praeger Publishers, 1975.
   Chapter 2, "The Regulatory System," pp. 21–48.
   Chapter 3, "Transportation Competition," pp. 49–62.
   Chapter 4, "Route Structure," pp. 63–75.

Chapter 5, "Ownership Patterns," pp. 76–89.

Chapter 6, "Pricing and Rate Making," pp. 90–144.

Fair, Marvin L., and Ernest W. Williams, *Transportation and Logistics*, Rev. ed., Plano, Texas: Business Publications, 1981.

Chapter 15, "Management, Labor, and the Efficiency of Carrier Operations," pp. 253–76.

Harper, Donald F., *Transportation in America: Users, Carriers, Government*, 2nd ed., Englewood Cliffs, N.J.: Prentice-Hall, 1982.

Chapter 15, "Decision Making in Transportation Companies," by Frederick J. Beier, pp. 338–67.

Koot, Ronald S., and John E. Tyworth, "The Determinants of Railroad Track Maintenance Expenditures: A Statistical Analysis," *Transportation Journal* 21(1) (Fall 1981), 24–43.

Shrock, David L., and Mary Ann Stutts, "A Comparative Analysis of Carrier Print Advertising," *Transportation Journal* 21(1) (Fall 1981), 67–76.

Taneja, Nawal K., *The Commercial Airline Industry: Management, Practices and Policies*, Lexington, Mass.: Lexington Books, 1976.

Wood, Donald F., and James C. Johnson, *Contemporary Transportation*, 3rd ed., New York, NY: Macmillan Publishing Co., 1989.

Chapter 15, "Managing Carriers in Private Sector," p. 385–416.

Wyckoff, D. Daryl, *Railroad Management*, Lexington, Mass.: Lexington Books, 1976.

PART VI

PHYSICAL DISTRIBUTION MANAGEMENT

In other parts of this book, we have considered various aspects of our domestic transportation system — its history and economic significance, its economic characteristics and performance, its services, costs, and rates, its regulation, and our public goals in its operations. In all this, our concern has been with the effective use of the system for individual shippers and for the overall public welfare of our profits-oriented, free-enterprise economy.

Even the best physical transportation plant cannot adequately serve our individual and social needs unless it is properly used in physically distributing products. This requires a high level of technical and managerial ability on the part of both providers and users of transportation. For the user, the transportation activities of individual firms must be properly supervised and coordinated with other operations of the firm. Choices must be made among transportation alternatives. New ways of improving transportation efficiency for the firm and for the entire economy must be sought constantly. For the provider of transportation services, new and improved ways of meeting shipper needs must be developed.

The complexities of our transportation system have led to the development of a specialized area of management, which we call *traffic management*, at the individual-firm level. As transportation conditions and competitive pressures have changed, so has the traffic management function. To efficiently fulfill this function, today's traffic managers must have a broad understanding of the external and internal environment of their businesses plus general management talent and special knowledge of transportation.

In this part, we will view the general nature and scope of the administration of the physical distribution function at the level of the individual firm, with particular emphasis on the role of traffic management in this process. This introduction, together with the earlier portions of this book, is designed to be a taking-off point for those interested in more advanced and technical studies in traffic management or any other phase of physical distribution management. For those interested only in an intelligent layperson's or informed businessperson's knowledge of the field, on the other hand, this part should lead to a better understanding of the importance of the proper use of transportation in our dynamic economy.

CHAPTER 22

EVOLUTION AND STRUCTURE OF SHIPPER RESPONSIBILITY

PHYSICAL DISTRIBUTION AND INDUSTRIAL TRAFFIC MANAGEMENT

Physical distribution is that aspect of production concerned with the movement of goods through space (transportation) and time (storage and warehousing). These movements add to the utility and thus to the value of goods, as well as to their cost. A firm's objective in physical distribution is to add as much value as possible with the least increase in cost or to strike a satisfactory or acceptable balance between value-added and cost-added.

The term *physical distribution* often is used to refer in a narrow sense only to outbound movements, with its counterpart — *physical supply* — being used in reference to inbound shipments. As employed in this book, however, unless otherwise specified, a firm's physical distribution process encompasses both inbound and outbound movements and related activities.

Transportation is a necessary component of physical distribution and usually is the most costly part of the process. In fact, until quite recently most firms and individuals acted as if transportation were the only significant element in this process, and they viewed transport services only as cost-additive and not as a means of adding value or of reducing nontransport costs. Today, however, it is being recognized more and more that the effective management of a firm's transportation involves interrelationships with other functions such as purchasing, inventory control, production scheduling, warehousing, internal materials handling, package engineering, advertising and sales, plant location, and even broad marketing, product, and customer-relations policies. All these interrelated activities, then, and perhaps others, may properly be included within what we call the physical distribution process.

EVOLUTION OF THE TRAFFIC MANAGER

As transportation has always been a necessary element in trade, it follows that we have had transportation managers for as long as we have had commerce of any kind; in fact, this management must predate even our earliest and simplest forms of organized commerce. But it was not until the development of efficient modern transportation technology, which allowed mass production and mass distribution over large geographic areas, that full-time specialists in transportation, so-called traffic managers, became important in industrial and commercial firms using far-flung transportation services. Industrial or commercial traffic management became recognized as a separate occupation only after railroads became an important or dominant form of land transport and steamships began to replace sailing vessels during the nineteenth century.

In most firms the traffic manager has not been highly placed in the management hierarchy. By generally accepted definitions, a manager's functions include the planning, organizing, directing, coordinating, and controlling of some activity or activities. This involves whatever cooperation may be appropriate with other managers plus the follow-up necessary to determine whether a job is being satisfactorily performed and the authority to take remedial action if it is not. By all definitions a manager is a decision maker. Judged by these criteria, the limited scope of the functions of the so-called traffic manager of the past, and even a large number today, has dictated their classification as low-level managers.

The Early Railroad Era

Traffic management as a distinct occupation came during the preregulation railroad era. In those free-wheeling days of the mid-nineteenth century and following, railroads had a relatively free hand in setting their rates and services. Discrimination between localities and even between individual customers in a given locality was widespread. Rate advantages or services advantages such as transit privileges not available to competitors were eagerly sought by rival industrial or commercial firms and were just as eagerly granted by fiercely competing railroads.

It is well known that the squeaky wheel gets the grease. Aggressive firms whose transport costs were a large proportion of their total costs or who stood to benefit by service concessions were prone to squeak loudly. They hired traffic managers, often former railroad personnel with railroad connections, as their representatives. A major function of these first traffic managers was to obtain favorable rail treatment for their firms either by persuasion or by the potential threat of diverting substantial traffic to other rail lines. Such persons clearly were not managers in the accepted definition of that term. Rather, they were more akin to salespersons or lobbyists.

The Regulated Rail Monopoly Era

This situation changed with the coming of effective railroad regulation. Discrimination was outlawed. Rates and services, published in tariffs, were public knowledge and were equally available to all users under substantially similar circumstances. The traffic manager no longer could secure extraordinarily favorable concessions for his firm, at least not legally. Rational economic grounds for choosing among different carriers were limited. For practical purposes, only rail transport was available for large or lengthy movements except in coastal areas and on a few interior routes where water transport managed to survive. And even if alternate rail carriers or routes were available, rates and services generally were identical, or almost so.

In this new environment, the traffic manager became a specialist on rates and routes whose principal stock in trade was the ability to read the increasingly complex and numerous rail freight tariffs. This skill usually was acquired by several years' experience as a rate clerk in a railroad traffic department or by a long apprenticeship in an industrial traffic office or shipping department, perhaps supplemented by correspondence or night-school courses.

Higher echelons of management generally had little knowledge or understanding of the work of the individuals in their small offices surrounded by volumes or incomprehensible rate books. They were looked upon, usually rightly so, as rather narrow specialists or technicians. Their services were recognized as necessary, but were regarded as ranking but little higher than that of shipping clerks. In fact, shipping clerks often were responsible for such traffic management as existed in smaller firms or in organizations with relatively low transport costs; and in other cases, the promotional route to traffic manager was up through shipping department ranks.

The major tangible criterion by which higher management usually evaluated the efficiency of the traffic manager was the level of transport costs paid by the firm. If freight charges per unit of product declined, the traffic manager was efficient; if these costs increased without some clearly understandable reason, such as a freight-rate increase or market extension into more distant areas, he might be replaced. It is not surprising, therefore, that the traffic manager's goal generally was to minimize the firm's direct transportation outlays. This clearly was what top management desired. It was probably unusual for a traffic manager to see that the lowest possible transport costs did not always necessarily mean the lowest possible total production costs, and it certainly was exceptional when such an astute traffic manager had the aggressiveness and persuasiveness to convince higher management of this.

The rates-and-routes technicians were not completely passive, of course. Often they did represent their firms as specialists and as special pleaders before carriers, carrier associations, and regulatory agencies. These activities frequently did benefit the firm, the industry, or the economy generally by influencing the level of rates and the quantity and quality of services. However, these advocate functions did nothing to enhance the traffic manager's status as a manager; rather, they confirmed the traffic manager's status as a specialist and a technician.

In their capacity as specialists, the more effective traffic managers sometimes were called upon for advice on transportation matters by top management or by various functional departments or divisions of their firms; they performed staff duties in addition to handling technical details. Usually, however, the traffic manager's advice, if sought at all in connection with locational, marketing, and production matters, was considered along with advice from several other sources in reaching a decision.

Seldom, if ever, did the traffic manager act as a major decision maker on matters of great importance to the business. Most decisions related to requests for carrier transportation equipment for loading, routing, and documentation of shipments, routine handling of loss and damage claims, freight-bill audits, and the supervision of the small staff of clerks and assistants, if any. Sometimes responsibilities were extended to include some phases of packing, marking, and the actual loading of merchandise aboard rail cars. But at most, the traffic manager's operational decisions were on a par with those of office managers and shipping department foremen.

The Rise of Transport Competition

The emergence of effective intermodal transportation competition, which has developed rapidly since the 1920s, again called for a different type of traffic manager. Many shippers were freed from exclusive dependence upon the rails. The traffic manager in many cases was given a choice between different modes of transport, between common and contract carriers, or even between for-hire and private transport. These alternative services varied considerably in quality and cost. By making the proper choice, a traffic manager might considerably reduce the firm's transport costs, improve customer services, and consequently create good will and retain or generate business for the company, or even influence production schedules and inventory and marketing policies. Traffic management decisions, in other words, could significantly affect the prosperity of the firm.

Under such conditions, the rail rates-and-routes expert alone was not qualified for the traffic manager's role. The old expertise still was necessary, but no longer sufficient. The new role required comprehensive knowledge of the rates and service characteristics of all forms of transportation as well as some knowledge of the effects of various kinds of alternative transport services upon the company's overall operations. The effective traffic manager, in addition to being a technician and a staff specialist, became also something of a generalist and a real decision-making manager. Industrial traffic personnel increasingly came from sources other than railroad rate departments and industrial shipping departments. Even some college graduates (rank heresy to old-line, rail-spawned traffic practitioners) began to infiltrate the mysterious realm of traffic management.

This transformation did not occur overnight. In fact it is still in process. Many of the older generation of traffic managers could not or would not adjust wholeheartedly to the new environment. Even more important, higher management often failed to recognize that a changed technological environment had expanded the horizons of physical distribution and called for a new breed of traffic manager. Consequently, the traffic management function all too often was still regarded as a necessary evil requiring only the services of a narrow specialist whose performance was judged by how effectively direct transport costs were minimized. Thus, without adequate recognition in status and pay, many traffic managers continued to follow the path of least resistance by doing what had been expected of them historically. This situation still exists in numerous firms.

In the better managed and more progressive companies, however, especially those in which transport costs were a large portion of distribution or total costs, opportunities did increase for the traffic manager. By doing a better job for the firm, the traffic manager received greater financial rewards and became recognized as a legitimate member of the management team — a low-ranking member, perhaps, but nonetheless a member. As the traffic manager's influence on the profitability of the firm was recognized, decision-making authority was broadened, and advice was sought more often by top management and by other management officials. In the current era of lessened transportation regulation, many firms have continued to expand the traffic manager's role in efforts to take advantage of opportunities being provided by added carrier rate and service competition and the greater freedom to negotiate rate and service packages with individual carriers.

In summary, the traffic manager as such is generally regarded as a technician and staff specialist. In many firms, the traffic manager is viewed only in this light and typically performs in the manner expected of a technician. However, in a growing number of firms, the importance of traffic management is fully recognized and the traffic manager performs and is seen as an important part of the management group.

The Total-Cost Concept of
Physical Distribution Management

Since the late 1950s, the advent and growing use of electronic computers, coupled with increasing competitive pressures to produce and distribute goods as efficiently as possible, has focused interest on a new concept of total-cost physical distribution management. Widespread interest has developed in the interrelationships between the type of transport used and other production and distribution costs. This development, or the application of it, has been variously labeled as physical distribution management, business logistics, rhochrematics (a word that is a combination of Greek words meaning roughly "the science of materials flow"), and similar terms. In some instances, new managerial titles and departments corresponding to these terms have been created.

Perhaps the only really new portion of this concept, at least for those businesses that have long been blessed by good and well-recognized traffic departments, are the new terms themselves. Certainly the best traffic managers and higher management officials in the best-managed businesses have long been aware that minimizing transport costs does not in all circumstances maximize profits. For example, sometimes the use of a higher-priced mode such as air carriage, rather than a lower-priced mode, will decrease some other cost or costs considerably more than it increases transport costs; or perhaps the provision of better customer service through premium transportation will pay off manyfold in good will and increased business volume.

The importance of this so-called new total-cost concept should not be minimized, however. Management officials generally, academicians who have shown little interest in transportation for many years, and even some of the traditional type of traffic managers have been intrigued by it. New and much needed attention and thought have been devoted to the role of transportation in physical distribution. The popular concept of the humdrum activities of the traffic manager has been glamorized. The title of physical distribution manager or vice president, logistics, is likely to carry more popular and corporate prestige than the title of traffic manager. Even more important, the new title and the top-management thinking back of it are likely to result in increased responsibility and authority for its recipient and to attract or develop better managers.

A new managerial title or a renamed corporate department alone, of course, does not improve the efficiency of a business. If retitled individuals continue doing only the same things in the same ways, nothing is bene-fited except their ego. Physical distribution management includes traffic management, but it is more.

The traffic manager in reality is a purchasing agent and heads a de-partment devoted to the efficient buying of those transportation services needed by the firm. If the traffic manager takes into full account the total operational and distribution costs and profits effects of purchases of trans-portation services and has the corporate influence or authority to obtain cooperation from other departments or divisions in tailoring transport and other activities to an optimum blend, the person is practicing physical distribution management (or business logistics, rhochrematics, etc.) re-gardless of the title used or of the corporate organizational structure. Con-trarily, if the cooperation of other managers (those in charge of such activities as production scheduling, inventory control, purchasing, market-ing, and related functions) and of top management itself is not or cannot be obtained, the person can never be more than a traffic manager.

An increasing number of firms are creating departments and managers of physical distribution. Some of these, unfortunately, are little more than changed labels. But many are managing physical distribution in the best sense by coordinating the activities of the traffic department with the activities of other departments. This calls for a physical distribution posi-tion in the management structure higher than the position of the traffic manager and the various other departmental managers concerned. Usually, to be effective, this means that the manager of physical distribu-tion must have vice-presidential authority (even if not that title) and the ear of top management. Usually no lesser position can bring about the necessary cooperation between departments and managers with traditional suboptimizing goals.

Figure 22.1 shows a portion of a simplified organization chart of a manufacturing firm illustrating the control of physical distribution. This chart, while perhaps reasonably representative, does not purport to be ideal. What is best for one firm is not necessarily best for another. There are almost as many organizational forms, formal and informal, as there are individual firms. Specific interrelationships among the traffic department and other departments will be elaborated upon in Chapters 23, 24, and 25.

Many traffic managers have aspired to, and some have achieved, the position and title of vice president in charge of physical distribution, or some such. The typical well-informed traffic manager's qualifications for such a position certainly are as good as those of the typical manager of marketing or related functional areas, but probably no better. It is essen-tial that a physical distribution manager be well versed in transportation, but it is equally essential that such a manager be well versed in many

Figure 22.1 Segment of Organization Chart for Coordinating Physical Distribution Management

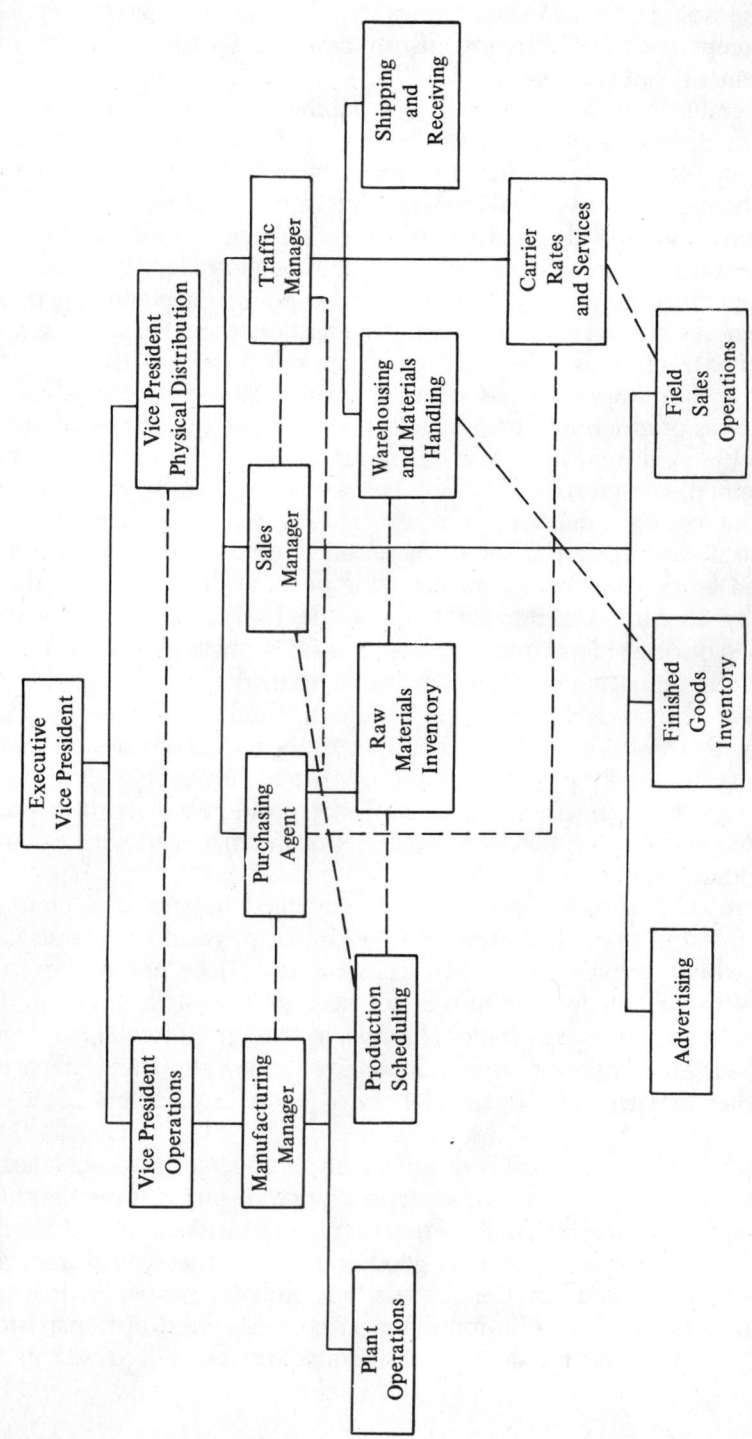

Solid lines indicate line authority and responsibility. Broken lines show principal channels of interdivisional and interdepartmental information and coordination.

other phases of the company's activities and of the industry concerned. The physical distribution manager must be a specialist in general management rather than in a functional area. Subordinate managers will be functional specialists. It is just as likely that a competent manager from a nontransportation area can acquire the transportation understanding necessary for overall physical distribution management as it is that a traffic manager can acquire the necessary grasp of nontransport functions.

In selecting a physical distribution manager, top management in a particular firm will consider many things. These will include the nature of the firm's and the industry's distribution problems, the share of distribution and total costs attributable to transportation, the present corporate organization structure, qualifications of potential candidates for the position (both inside and outside the firm), and perhaps individual personalities, historical intrafirm relationships, and what similar or competing firms have done.

Although information is sketchy and the situation is changing, it appears that at least a majority of those individuals now bearing the title of physical distribution manager (or similar titles) have been chosen from the ranks of general line managers, that is, from operations positions rather than from direct distribution positions. Traffic managers and sales managers seem to have contributed about equally to most of the remainder of these positions, with a small number coming from several other functional areas.

In companies without a specifically designated physical distribution manager, such interdepartmental coordination of physical distribution as exists apparently is directed by general management officials in a majority of firms, with traffic departments, sales departments, and purchasing departments (in that order) being next in importance. In many such firms, standing interdepartmental committees or other less formal means of coordination may perform just as effectively as would a formalized organization structure and a titled physical distribution manager. Organization charts and titles do not always guarantee, and are not always necessary for, an effective level of performance.

To summarize briefly, the total-cost management concept of physical distribution represents the latest stage in the evolution of the functions of the traffic manager. Although traffic management has existed in some form as long as traffic itself, the traffic manager's separate position in business organization arose out of the peculiar needs of the early railroad era. As these needs changed with changing institutional and technological environments (regulated rail monopoly, followed by extensive intermodal competition), the traffic manager likewise changed. Finally, the business cost squeeze of the 1950s, attributable in part at least to considerable saturation of the pent-up demands of the war years, higher labor costs, and an international increase in productive capacity, efficiency, and competition forced many firms and industries to search for new methods of cutting cost.

To their surprise, many managements found that greater opportunities for efficiencies existed in proper utilization of transportation than in any other area. Costs of labor, raw materials, and capital in many cases are only slightly under management control, and a great deal of attention has been given to the improvement of production methods and techniques for many years. But the management of transportation from the overall view of profit maximization offered an unexploited new frontier, hence the interest in the total-cost management concept of physical distribution and the increasing recognition given to the function of traffic management in this process.

DUTIES AND ORGANIZATION OF THE INDUSTRIAL TRAFFIC DEPARTMENT

Now that we have considered the overall role of the industrial traffic manager in a firm, we can appropriately turn to a more specific examination of how a traffic department may be organized and the nature of its responsibilities. In the following discussion, it is not necessary to assume that the traffic department is or is not a part of a formal structure headed by a physical distribution manager unless the authors so indicate. There is no inherent reason why a traffic manager reporting directly to a vice president of physical distribution or logistics should have significantly different responsibilities or a significantly different internal organization in a department than one reporting to some other higher management official.

Traffic Responsibilities

As pointed out above, the traffic manager is a combination of technical expert, staff adviser, and line manager. Almost all line managers have some staff advisory responsibilities, of course, and many staff officials in addition to their research, planning, and recommendation functions also exercise some line authority within their own fields of specialization. Most management officials fall clearly either into the line or the staff division, however, with the other function being relatively minor. This is not generally true of traffic managers. Instead, they are unique in that they cannot clearly be classified primarily either as line managers or staff experts.

Line Duties

Like most managers, line or staff, traffic managers exercise line control over subordinates in their own departments. Their major line responsibility, however, is in acquiring transportation services for the company.

Buying appropriate transportation often is a complex activity requiring decisions among many alternatives. The traffic manager must consider all available services and rates of all modes of carriage and even of individual carriers among these various modes from the viewpoint of what best fits the company's need for a specific shipment. As you know, services and rates vary considerably among modes and carriers both at any given time and over periods of time. Likewise, each shipment made by a company may have individual characteristics and needs of its own. Buying the right transportation for a particular movement, therefore, calls for the traffic manager's expertise in transport matters plus an intimate understanding of the general characteristics of the firm and industry, and a detailed knowledge of any peculiarities (physical or otherwise) of a particular shipment.

Purchasing transportation is very different from purchasing groceries in a supermarket. It is true that the grocery shopper may have a bewildering variety of prices, sizes, and labels (supposedly denoting quality) to choose from as does the traffic manager. But here the comparison ceases. The food shopper chooses from among what is available, carts it away, and the transaction is finished. The traffic manager, however, typically spends a great deal of time attempting to get something that is not currently on the shelf. By negotiating with individual carriers, carrier associations, or regulatory agencies, individually or through one or more shipper associations, the traffic manager actively and often successfully attempts to change prices, quantities, and qualities of transportation.

Further, the traffic manager usually must choose a bundle of transportation services with an eye to what the consignee of a shipment desires; a customer may have peculiar requirements for line-haul or terminal services, or even biases which must be considered. Sometimes sacrifices in terms of immediate convenience and costs to the traffic manager's own firm must be made for the sake of long-run customer good will and repeat orders. Often the traffic department's work is made more difficult (as well as considerably more costly) by promises made by product salespersons who have little if any knowledge of transportation matters pertinent to the product.

In addition to choosing from among the various alternative modes and carriers, the traffic manager must choose a specific route over which the shipment will move, contact the carrier for equipment, and perform the necessary paperwork. The manager must follow up to see that the ordered equipment actually is received when promised, perhaps supervise loading of the cargo, and see that it is dispatched on schedule. Additional follow-up may be required to ensure that the cargo arrives on time and in good order and corrective action must be taken if it does not. Finally, the carrier's billing must be checked to ensure that the company has not been overcharged.

From the foregoing, which is only the briefest thumbnail sketch of the major traffic management line function, it can be seen that the life of the traffic manager cannot be a dull one. Instead, the manager is faced with a continuous stream of problems and crises, all important to the company, which require immediate decisions based upon expert knowledge and good judgment. Also, the manager is responsible for modifying the transportation bundle to more closely fit the company's needs, for actions designed to prevent small transportation problems from growing into large ones, and for taking corrective actions when disaster does strike.

Staff Duties

In addition to line functions, most traffic managers perform a variety of staff or advisory duties. Some of these are routine in nature, perhaps only calling upon the traffic manager's fund of existing technical knowledge for advice on minor operating problems or decisions in other departments or divisions. Some, on the other hand, require extensive special study, research, or experimentation.

For example, if a firm is considering a major capital expenditure for a branch factory or warehouse, the traffic manager may be called upon to make detailed studies of comparative transportation costs of several possible alternate locations. If the firm is considering a move into private carriage as a substitute for or supplement to for-hire services or if it is considering containerization or a major new product line, both technological and comparative cost studies might be required from the viewpoint of transportation. As a staff adviser, of course, the traffic manager would not make final decisions on such matters. However, this specially developed evidence and advice would be considered along with that of other staff and line officials, with the decision being made by top management or perhaps by a committee made up of the managers most directly involved under delegated authority from top management.

On more routine operational matters not requiring major capital expenditures, the traffic manager's role may vary from providing factual information to the legal department to giving information advice on relative lot sizes to the purchasing agent to making special transportation-cost studies for the sales manager. Responsibility for using or not using this material rests with the one requesting it.

In other cases, the traffic manager and some other department head or heads may make joint decisions on operational matters involving their respective areas. This is particularly likely when all the departments concerned are directly responsible to one official such as a physical distribution manager.

Supervision of the Traffic Manager

Traffic management in most firms is ranked as a middle-management position. As such, the traffic manager is responsible either to top management or to some intermediate higher manager. There is no dominant pattern in this chain-of-command structure, however. The traffic department may be autonomous in that it is directly responsible only to the president or senior vice president who may or may not effectively supervise its operations. It may, on the other hand, report to the head of the marketing, purchasing, or production operations, or even in rare cases to some other official. If the firm has a physical distribution manager or some similar official, the traffic manager normally is under that person's jurisdiction (see Figure 22.1).

Logically one might expect that the nature of a firm's product and the relative importance of inbound and outbound transportation costs as a proportion of total costs would determine that organizational position and status of its traffic department. That is, a firm with unusually high transport costs in relation to total costs might have its traffic department directly under top management. A firm with substantial outbound transport costs might place its traffic department within the marketing framework, and one with substantial inbound charges might make the traffic manager subordinate to the purchasing agent or even the production manager.

Reality, however, often confuses logic. In many instances (perhaps too many for efficiency), the organizational position of the traffic department has been determined by historical accident, by the personal capabilities of the traffic manager, by personal preferences or prejudices of top management, by whether or not particular individuals work well or poorly together, or for similar nonrational reasons. One of the notable accomplishments of the new interest in total-cost physical distribution management, perhaps, is the introduction of rationality in organization patterns for this function.

Internal Organization of the Traffic Department

A firm's overall philosophy of organization and the nature of its activities set the broad framework within which its traffic department is organized. Within this general framework, then, the specific internal organization geographically and functionally is based upon the peculiar specialized duties of the department.

Geographic Organization

Firms doing business at only one location do not have any problem of geographic decentralization of the traffic function. Multilocation firms, however, have to choose between centralized or decentralized administration of the traffic function or, more correctly, among the various degrees of possible decentralization. This choice sometimes is exercised by the traffic manager, but usually it is based upon overall company policy. A company tending toward centralization or decentralization is likely to apply its general policy to its traffic department, but not always. If there is any substantial deviation of the traffic control function from the general pattern, it appears to tend toward centralization.

In a highly decentralized traffic management operation, the central office staff, perhaps headed by a general traffic manager, usually provides technical information, advice, and assistance to branch or plant traffic managers. In addition, it may promulgate general broad policies, represent the company in rate hearings affecting more than one plant location in differing ways, and perhaps aid in training local traffic personnel. The headquarters office essentially provides staff services for local traffic managers who make most of their own decisions under the general supervision of local plant operating officials.

In slightly more centralized situations, the head office may recruit, assign, or replace local traffic managers subject usually to the concurrence of the pertinent local operating management. Some local traffic managers thus feel that they have two bosses. In a highly centralized operation, however, the headquarters office may make most of the important decisions such as designating specific carriers and routes or taking action on all but the smallest loss and damage claims, thus basically leaving the local traffic manager with the functions of shipping clerk and office manager.

Some large multilocation firms follow an intermediate policy between centralization and decentralization. Some local traffic managers may have a great deal of discretion and authority in making decisions, whereas others have very little. In some cases, another level of management, perhaps called a regional or a district traffic manager, may be interposed between the general traffic manager and branch traffic managers in several areas of a firm's operations.

During recent years, it appears that large multilocation firms have been tending toward more decentralization. This tendency is evident in traffic management, but it does not appear to be advancing as rapidly in this function as in some others.

A discussion of the intrinsic merits of centralization versus decentralization in general is beyond the scope of this book. There are advantages and disadvantages to each, and the merits of each are to some extent dependent upon the overall nature of the particular industry and firm. Also, in a particular situation, a decision in favor of centralization or decentralization may be considerably influenced by the supposed capabilities of the persons available to do a desired job.

Some general traffic managers or top-management officials feel that they are able to negotiate much more effectively with carriers through centralized control of carrier choice and traffic routing than would be possible if these decisions were made on an uncoordinated basis at many scattered locations. In fact, a number of very large corporations have moved toward greater centralization of certain aspects of the traffic function as the degree of carrier economic regulation has decreased. These corporations feel that the increased bargaining power gained through corporate negotiation with carriers exceeds the various disadvantages associated with a loss of local flexibility in dealing with individual carriers and local transport conditions. In addition, in the case of firms that sell sizable quantities of their product to carriers, reciprocity may be of considerable importance.

Functional Organization

Traffic departments, like other departments, are organized according to the functions they are expected to perform. Although these functions do vary to some extent between firms and over time in the same firm, there certainly is much more uniformity in functional than in geographic organization.

The major functions of traffic management have been briefly summarized above and will be discussed in considerably more detail in Chapters 23, 24, and 25. At this point, therefore, we will only refer to Figure 22.2,

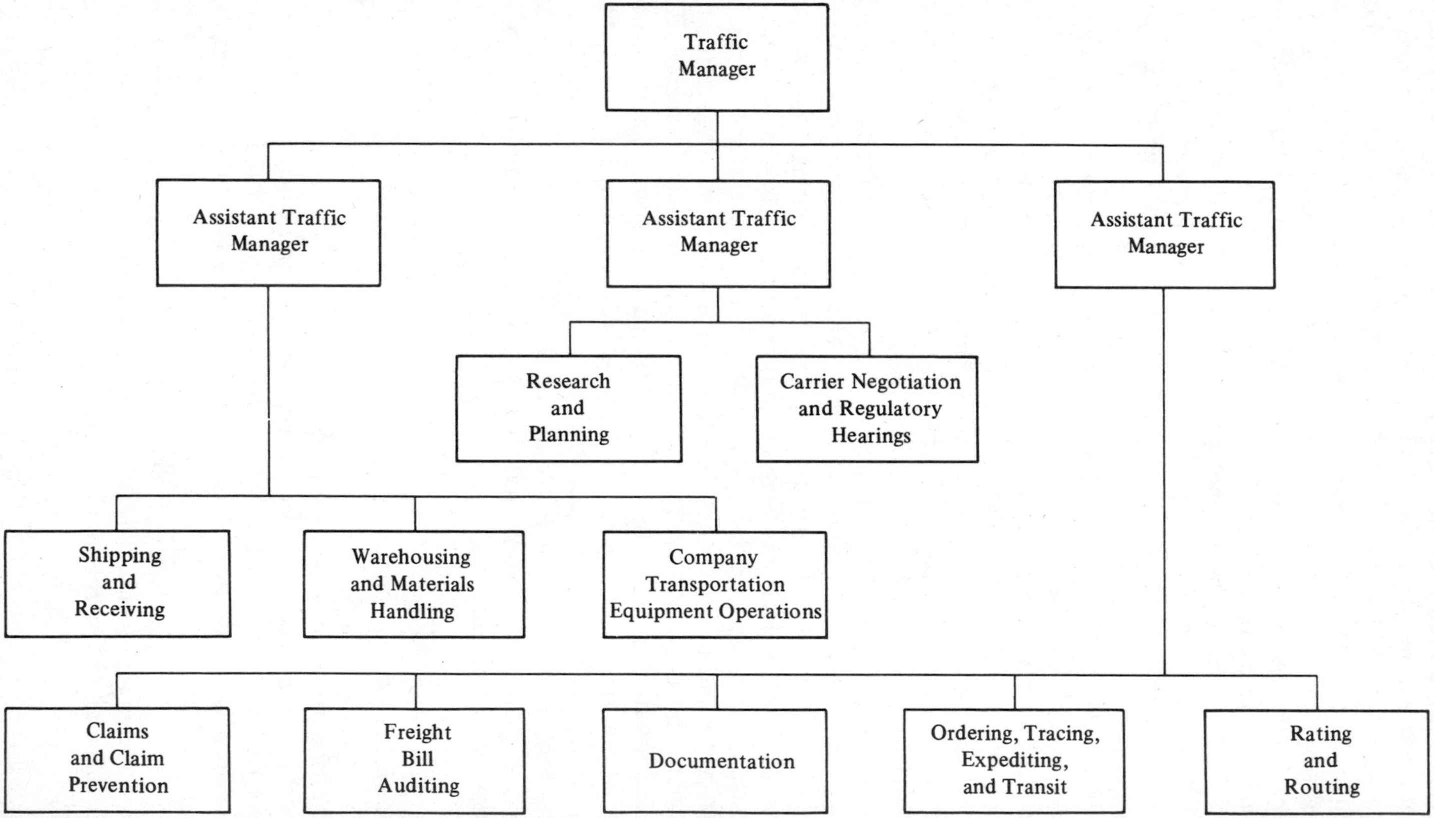

Figure 22.2 Functional Organization of an Industrial Traffic Department

which pictures a simplified representative functional organization chart for a medium-sized or large firm's traffic department. This figure may be utilized by readers in furthering their understanding of the material in the following chapters. It is not presented as the best or most used form of organization, but merely as a form that is representative of the functions typically performed and of many actual organizations. Depending upon the size of the operation, of course, each of the functions shown might be further subdivided or consolidated.

CARRIER TRAFFIC DEPARTMENTS

This book is not primarily concerned with carrier traffic management as such. It is essential that those engaged in industrial traffic work be acquainted with the organization and functions of their carrier counterparts, however. Most of the day-to-day contact of the shipper with the carrier is through the latter's traffic personnel.

Carriers are in the business of selling transportation services. They necessarily must give customers the services they want at prices they are willing to pay. Further, as the for-hire carriage business is an extremely competitive one, carriers must remain in close touch with shippers both to display their wares and to anticipate and provide required shipper services at competitive prices. These are the functions of the carrier traffic department.

Two clear-cut although necessarily closely related functional divisions exist typically among carrier traffic personnel. One group is concerned primarily with the making and publication of rates. The others essentially are salespersons of the carriers' services (traffic solicitors). Obviously, rates must be tailored to the needs of users. Thus a close two-way flow of information between solicitors (who are in continuous contact with customers) and rate personnel (who establish the prices at which solicitors must sell the carriers' services) is essential. Lack of close cooperation between these two groups can be disastrous in terms of lost customer good will and business.

There are a host of associated traffic duties related to the primary functions of carrier pricing and selling. These involve such matters as special line-haul and terminal services, public relations, promotional activities, research, relationships with other carriers and with regulatory agencies, loss and damage prevention and claims settlement, and a variety of similar activities that help make the transportation bundle complete.

Also, the carrier's traffic department and its operations department (which actually delivers the bundle of services priced and sold by traffic personnel) must cooperate closely. Promised schedules and delivery times must be met, merchandise losses and damage must be minimized, and the right kind of equipment must be made available when and where needed. Favorable rates and excellent traffic salespersons are worthless if the carrier's operating department cannot or will not perform as promised.

Any successful industrial traffic manager, in addition to understanding the general form of carrier traffic organization, must have a detailed knowledge of the organizations of those individual carriers with which the firm does business and a close working acquaintanceship with the key carrier personnel involved. A substantial amount of time is spent in negotiating with carrier traffic personnel on an individual day-to-day basis as well as with carrier organizations (rate bureaus, for example) individually or through trade or professional associations. A detailed discussion of the carrier management function is provided in Part V.

THE CHANGING ROLE OF
THE TRAFFIC MANAGER

It is becoming increasingly apparent that the traffic manager's importance to a firm's profitability will continue to grow in the future, even in firms in which the traffic management function has been very narrowly defined. The expansion of the traffic manager's role, in the short term, will be in two areas. This role expansion will involve increased interaction with the carriers that serve the firm and closer coordination with the firm's purchasing and sales functions.

Changing the Rates or Services Environment

As indicated previously, a purchaser of transportation services may directly influence the price and quality of the services purchased. Various kinds of optional carrier services are described in Chapter 21 of this book, and the procedures for establishing a new rate or changing an existing rate are discussed in Chapter 17.

The traffic manager is the firm's technical expert and direct representative and negotiator in these matters. It is this person's duty to determine, perhaps in consultation with other departments or divisions, what services or rate changes will be beneficial to the company and whether there is a likelihood that these changes can be achieved. Then the traffic manager has the primary responsibility for preparing and presenting the firm's case to individual carriers, rate bureaus, regulatory agencies, and sometimes even in the courts or before legislative bodies. This may require enlisting the aid of various other components of the firm (sales, purchasing, accounting, legal, etc.) or working through shipper organizations such as shippers' advisory boards, the National Industrial Transportation League, or industry trade associations.

Some of the desired environmental changes may be nationwide or industry-wide in scope, such as general rate decreases, demurrage charges, or attempts to curb loss and damage or to influence the building or distribution of transportation rolling stock. Changes in transportation legislation and regulatory procedures or the construction of new highways may be sought. Improvements in carrier technological development or managerial practices may be urged.

Other changes may primarily benefit the traffic manager's own company. These include such things as particular rate decreases, better local supplies and scheduling of rolling stock, the negotiation of transit privileges or average-weight agreements, the building of spur tracks, or improved methods of freight handling by individual carriers. The traffic manager may also be called upon to oppose proposed rate changes that might give the firm's rivals a competitive transportation advantage.

Negotiation in a Less Regulated Environment

Since the passage of the Motor Carrier Act of 1980, the Staggers Rail Act of 1980, and air freight deregulation, shipper/carrier relationships have become much more flexible. Although it has always been possible to negotiate changes in rate and service packages, this was often technically difficult and time consuming. In large firms particularly, the general traffic manager and perhaps several assistants could spend a substantial portion of their time attending meetings and hearings concerned with achieving changes in rate levels and the general transportation environment. In an era of reliance on the collective ratemaking process, this often involved complex sets of negotiations with groups of carriers and careful consideration of the needs of other shippers. Today, with less reliance on collective ratemaking, rate and service package negotiations with individual carriers have become commonplace — so commonplace and frequent that many carrier managers refer to this as the age of "calculator pricing."

This has meant that the traffic manager has had to become more aggressive in dealing with carriers and more knowledgeable about the operations of the specific carriers dealt with. In many instances, shippers dealing with carriers on a one-to-one basis have been able to achieve major price and service concessions. In addition, most major companies are now dealing with fewer carriers, in some instances going from several hundred carriers to fewer than twenty. This reduction in the number of carriers dealt with has significantly simplified the rate determination process and increased the shipper's negotiating power as its business is spread over fewer and fewer carriers. It has also meant that traffic managers have had to become more adept at the process of negotiation, with a resultant change in their role in the firm. Although traffic managers have remained technical specialists, their role has somewhat reverted to that of early traffic managers in the era before railroad regulation.

Contract Rates

For many traffic managers, this era of increased rate negotiation is merely an extension of efforts performed in dealing with contract carriers and contract negotiation. When contract carriage is an appropriate alternative for freight movement — most often when high volumes and regular traffic patterns are involved — individual contracts defining rate and service specifications, such as liability levels or service frequency, must be negotiated. This form of carriage has long been a valuable tool for the astute traffic manager, as it has usually provided the firm with lower rates and better service than that provided through common carriage. The advantages of contract carriage may become even more pronounced in the future as common carriers increase shipper-specific rate negotiations and establish contract carrier affiliates.

Purchasing and Sales Policies

As inbound and outbound freight costs often are sizable portions of a firm's expenditures, the interrelationships between traffic and purchasing and sales departments are fairly obvious. The traffic department sometimes is supervised by the sales manager or the purchasing agent. Ramifications of the traffic function, however, may extend further into buying and selling policies than is observable at first glance.

Where, How Much, and When to Buy or Sell

In the past and even to some extent today, those responsible for buying and selling have tended to ignore the traffic management function. Purchasing and sales personnel have suboptimized their own functions by buying or selling wherever, whenever, and whatever quantities seemed most desirable from their individual or departmental viewpoints, or in view of production schedules or inventory limits. The traffic department has been presented with an accomplished agreement and has been expected only to move the goods involved. This is completely contrary to the more recent concept of physical distribution management. In an era of increased rate negotiation, it is an even less acceptable practice.

Delivered or laid-down prices, whether for a firm's inbound or outbound goods and regardless of the method of price quotation used, are made up of origin prices plus transportation costs. Even the most suboptimizing of purchase agents could readily see that a purchase involving an f.o.b. origin price of $10 per unit plus an inbound freight rate of $2 per unit would be preferable to an f.o.b. origin price of $8 and a $5 transportation cost. Likewise, given the pertinent transportation cost information, a salesperson might recognize that goods sold in one territory are less profitable than those sold in another, but operating within a given territory on a commission basis or being judged by sales volume, the person would probably attempt to sell as much as possible anyway.

One of the most obvious and common interrelationships between traffic and purchasing and sales departments, therefore, is the furnishing by the traffic department of freight rate and other pertinent transportation costs from and to various origins. This enables the purchasing department to choose its supply sources and the sales manager to deploy the sales force and concentrate sales efforts in those geographic areas most profitable to the firm.

It is a little more difficult to show purchasing and sales personnel that the quantities bought and sold in any given transaction may significantly affect the transportation cost and thus the firm's profit position. Buyers want to reorder in some predetermined quantity when inventories decline to a certain level or to buy in quantities designed to meet some predetermined production schedule. Sales representatives prefer to sell large orders, but will sell in small quantities if large orders cannot be obtained. Any exotic traffic gibberish about carload minimums, LTL versus TL, consolidated shipments, incentive rates, and the like, even if understood, is likely to be disregarded unless there is considerable respect for and a close working relationship with the traffic department.

The quantities bought and sold or the frequency of transactions, of course, do affect inventory levels, warehousing needs, and sometimes production scheduling. These things in turn may directly affect the financial requirements of the company for carrying inventory and the company's customary relationships with its customers and suppliers. No traffic manager would argue that the per-unit volumes and the calendar frequencies of the company's purchases and sales should be adjusted exclusively to the needs of the traffic department. Most would agree, however, that transportation factors ought to be considered along with other pertinent needs of the firm and that often significant transportation economies can be achieved by minor adjustments in buying and selling policies without any adverse effects, or with relatively insignificant effects, upon other company operations.

Even if the traffic manager cannot eliminate the expensive small-lot problem, it may be possible to work with purchasing and sales personnel to reduce cost. Instead of shipping each lot individually, the company may use the services of freight forwarders or even consolidate small shipments into volume shipments itself. It may cooperate with other small-lot shippers in the use of a pool car or in forming a cooperative shipping association. Small shipments from or to several different origins or destinations may be arranged through stoppage in transit for partial loading or unloading. An ingenious traffic manager, given a modicum of cooperation, can find many ways to skin a cat. Given the increased ability of the traffic managers of many firms to positively affect rate and service levels being provided to their firms in the current regulatory environment, coordination between traffic and sales and purchasing departments becomes even more important. In fact, if the greatest potential benefits are to be achieved for the firm as a whole, the interactions among these three functional areas must take place at the corporate level in most cases.

Reciprocity

Many companies follow reciprocal buying and selling policies. As pointed out earlier, this may even extend to the purchase of transportation services. In such cases, the traffic department usually is the affected rather than the initiating department; that is, transportation is bought from those who buy the company's products. By working together on such policies, sales and traffic departments may be able to benefit their firm considerably.

Reciprocity policies may be worked out at the departmental level or the decision may be made by top management. In either case, the traffic manager's advice on such reciprocity policies as affect the choice of a carrier obviously should be sought; and once the decision is made, the traffic manager should cooperate with it insofar as possible as long as the policy is in effect.

Traffic Coordination

It is also possible for many companies to coordinate inbound and outbound freight movements associated with a particular facility or group of facilities to develop a traffic balance more favorable to the carrier providing service or to private carriage. Not all inbound and outbound traffic flows lend themselves to the creation of traffic balance. For example, both the flow of parts into an automobile assembly plant and the outbound flow of finished automobiles may be accomplished by rail, but the inbound flow may be accomplished using general-service freight cars, whereas the outbound flow will require the use of specialized auto-hauling equipment. However, where similar equipment can be used for both inbound and outbound traffic, successful coordination of those movements requires that the traffic manager serve the entire firm, not just a part of it, such as sales or purchasing. In addition, it means that a company must be willing and able to carefully evaluate all its transportation needs as a set before the traffic manager begins negotiations for services to meet those needs.

SUMMARY

The role of the traffic manager has evolved, as the nature of transportation competition has become more complex, into that of a highly trained specialist. In this role, the traffic manager acts as the interface between a firm and the carriers that provide it with transportation services. In spite of the importance of this function and the development of the physical distribution management concept, the traffic manager has continued to be viewed as a low-level manager by most companies. However, an environment of lessened transportation regulation has led to increased opportunities for the negotiation of improved rate and service packages by individual companies. In such an environment, even companies still narrowly defining the role of the traffic manager are viewing this specialist with renewed respect.

ADDITIONAL READINGS

Ballou, Ronald H., *Basic Business Logistics*, 2nd ed., Englewood Cliffs, N.J.: Prentice-Hall, 1987.
Chapter 1, "Logistics — An Essential Subject," pp. 2–22.
Bowersox, Donald J., David J. Closs, and Omar K. Helferich, *Logistical Management*, New York: Macmillan Publishing Co., 1986.
Chapter 1, "Logistical Management," pp. 3–33.
Coyle, John J., Edward J. Bardi, and C. John Langley, Jr., *The Management of Business Logistics*, 2nd ed., New York: West Publishing Co., 1980.
Chapter 1, "Logistics Management: An Overview," pp. 3–30.

Chapter 2, "Logistics Environments," pp. 35–62.

Harper, Donald V., *Basic Planning and the Transportation Function in Small Manufacturing Firms*, Minneapolis: University of Minnesota, 1961.

Johnson, James C., and Donald F. Wood, *Contemporary Physical Distribution and Logistics*, 3rd ed., New York, NY: Macmillan, 1986.

Chapter 1, "The Physical Distribution and Logistics System: Its Concept and Growth," pp. 3–32.

Lambert, Douglas M., and James R. Stock, *Strategic Physical Distribution Management*, Homewood, Ill.: Richard D. Irwin, 1982.

Chapter 1, "Distribution's Role in the Economy and the Firm," pp. 2–27.

Mossman, Frank H., and Newton Morton, *Logistics of Distribution Systems*, Boston: Allyn and Bacon, 1965.

Appendix B, "Constructive and Routine Duties of the Traffic Department," pp. 367–76.

Taff, Charles A., *Management of Physical Distribution and Transportation*, 6th ed., Homewood, Ill.: Richard D. Irwin, 1978.

Chapter 1, "Conceptual Framework," pp. 3–23.

CHAPTER 23

TRAFFIC MANAGEMENT FUNCTIONS

The preceding chapter reviewed the evolution of traffic management and briefly surveyed its overall role in the managerial and distribution process. This chapter will consider in more detail some (but by no means all) of the more routine activities performed by the industrial traffic manager relating to traffic management and traffic control decisions. We cannot go into these operations in great detail, but we can describe some of the more important types of activities and the reasons behind them. These activities vary in detail and degree from firm to firm, but in total they account for a good portion of the typical traffic manager's normal functions.

DIRECT DAY-TO-DAY RELATIONSHIPS WITH CARRIERS

A traffic manager is faced with the problem of moving something from its present position to another location and doing this in a manner and at a cost that will make the greatest contribution to the firm's continued success. This involves a basic decision as to choice of carrier. While the traffic manager may be faced with the choice of private or for-hire carriage on a routine basis, this is not usually the case. Most often the choice is among alternate for-hire carriers. (Chapter 24 will discuss the private versus for-hire alternatives.)

Selecting a Carrier

In selecting a mode of carriage and an individual carrier from that mode, several factors must be considered. Which mode and which individual carrier, assuming that alternatives are available, will best perform the service from the selling firm's viewpoint? From the buying customer's viewpoint? Does the customer have any special needs or preferences, or does the selling firm have a policy regarding how its traffic is allocated

552 PHYSICAL DISTRIBUTION MANAGEMENT

among competing carriers? What are the comparative freight rates and associated transport costs of the available carriers? What is the likelihood of loss, damage, or delays en route by the various alternatives? All these and a host of similar questions must be answered.

This does not imply that conscious and time-consuming decisions are made on all these matters for every shipment. Generally, the same types of goods are shipped via the same carriers to the same destination areas or consignees. But explicitly or implicitly, choices among carriers do have to be made, and the relative advantages and disadvantages of the various modes and individual carriers must constantly be reviewed as conditions change or as exceptional situations arise.

Equipment Control

After selecting the carrier, the traffic department must see that the proper carrier equipment is made available. A particular piece of equipment — railroad car, truck or trailer, barge — with a certain capacity and a specified design must be spotted for loading at a given place and time. The traffic manager must inform the carrier of the firm's specific day-to-day needs and follow up to ensure that equipment orders are met. The traffic manager must know when and with whom equipment orders must be placed and what kind of equipment is acceptable if first-choice equipment is not readily available. This means that the traffic manager must remain alert to conditions of equipment supply and demand in the firm's industry and geographic area and be familiar with existing and changing equipment technology.

When ordered carrier equipment has been received, it must be promptly and properly loaded and the carrier notified of its availability for movement. Packaging, marking, loading, stowing, and bracing of shipments must conform to minimum carrier standards and rules and must be sufficient to minimize the chances of damage en route. Actual supervision of these activities may or may not be under the jurisdiction of the traffic department, but they clearly are traffic control functions. Even a traffic manager who is not directly responsible for their satisfactory performance must at least remain well informed in this area in order that those responsible can be advised of weaknesses in present procedures and of potential or actual new developments in techniques.

If carrier equipment is not promptly loaded and started on its way, carrier costs are unnecessarily increased or their revenues lowered. This does not contribute to happy carrier-shipper relationships. Also, it contributes to equipment shortages, which at times may severely inconvenience other shippers and even adversely affect the nation's distribution and production activities. For these reasons, additional charges are levied against a shipper who holds carrier equipment for an undue length of time. These are called *demurrage* charges by railroads and *detention* charges in the trucking industry. Traffic managers must know the rules relating to these penalty charges and must schedule equipment ordering and release to minimize them.

Demurrage

Railroad demurrage rules and charges are published in tariffs like other charges. Demurrage charges begin after expiration of the free time allowed the shipper or receiver. Normally this is forty-eight hours from the first 7 A.M. after the equipment has been made available for loading or unloading, excluding Sundays and holidays. (Once demurrage has started, Sundays and holidays may be chargeable.)

Demurrage charges are a flat daily charge for the time held beyond the free time, but these charges are progressive — the daily rate becomes higher up to a maximum level as the length of time held increases. Charges may be waived, however, if a shipper or receiver can show that the delay is caused by severe weather conditions which prevent loading or unloading or by strikes. Also, shippers or receivers are not responsible for demurrage if the carrier bunches the arrival of cars in such a manner that normal loading and unloading procedures cannot provide an adequate release of equipment. The user cannot be penalized for the carrier's own shortcomings in performance.

There are two methods of accounting for and paying for demurrage. Under the *straight* method, each car is treated as a unit and stands on its own separate record. Under the *average* plan, users receive credits for early release of cars — that is, release before the free time has expired — and debits for holding equipment beyond the free time. Then at the end of the month, credits are used to offset debits, and payment is made for the excess debits.

Different demurrage rules, usually allowing considerably more free time, apply to rail shipments held in seaports when the rail movement is merely a part of a longer export or import movement using ocean carriage for a portion of the haul. Also, although water and truck carriers make use of penalty charges for undue holding of equipment, their rules and payments are adapted to their own peculiar circumstances. Truck free time, for example, is considerably shorter than rail free time, being measured in hours instead of days, and truck detention charges are usually considerably higher than rail demurrage charges.

Routing

In addition to ordering the right equipment from the selected carrier, the shipper may wish to instruct the carrier as to the route that the shipment is to follow between origin and destination. This is particularly true in the case of rail shipments, where an extremely large number of alternative routes may be available for use on long hauls. In this instance, someone must designate the specific route to be used. Usually this designation is a function of the traffic department — and is often a very important function.

Many firms, particularly smaller ones or those shipping only one or a few products, may ship over the same route or routes to the same customers over and over again. In large organizations shipping a variety of products to a far-flung group of customers, however, the technical aspects of routing (like rate determination) may require careful study and involve the application of elaborate carrier routing-guide publications or painstaking scrutiny of applicable tariffs. Central traffic offices of large firms often prepare route cards or route sheets for use of traffic personnel in decentralized local or regional offices.

We cannot go into the technical complexities of routing here. We will consider (1) why shippers may prefer to designate routes themselves rather than leave this to carriers and (2) shippers' legal rights to control their routings.

Why Shippers May Want to Route

By traditional custom and law, rail shippers have the right to route their shipments. Traffic managers are no more eager to surrender their legal and traditional rights than are any other groups. This right provides traffic solicitors (salespersons) with a motive to call upon traffic managers and treat them kindly in an effort to influence their allocation of traffic between competing carriers over various routes. This, in itself, may be justification enough of the right to route for some traffic managers. But there are even better reasons.

Sellers like to please buyers. If a firm prefers that its goods be handled by a particular carrier or a specified group of connecting carriers, the shipper obviously will make every effort to follow the consignee's routing preferences. Also, some routes have lower applicable freight rates between origin and destination than do other possible routes. (Usually, however, if no specific routing is made by the shipper, the carrier is required to use the lowest rated available route for the movement.)

Service and reliability features are of considerable importance in choosing a route. Even though most carrier services may be performed by the originating and the terminating carriers on a multiline or joint movement, shippers or receivers may have justifiable reasons for preferring some intermediate carriers (and their particular routes) over others. Experience may indicate greater loss and damage to cargoes or less reliability in meeting scheduled delivery dates over some lines and routes than over others. Climatic conditions or anticipated weather changes may also be quite important in influencing the choice of a route for certain types of products.

Some routes permit more rapid delivery to destination than others. A shipper may want goods to arrive as quickly as possible or at a specific time designated by the customer. On the other hand, the shipper may want goods to proceed toward their destination slowly either for the convenience of the consignee or to give the shipper sufficient time to complete the selling of goods that may have left the origin still unsold. Also, such useful privileges as diversion, reconsignment, stoppage in transit for further processing, or stoppage for partial unloading or further loading are available only at certain designated points and over particular designated routes. It is the traffic manager's responsibility to route according to these various needs of the company.

It may be, too, that a large shipper will follow the practice of reciprocity; it will give a substantial portion of its carriage business to those carriers who also are good customers for its own product. For example, a steel company given a choice between otherwise equal rail routes might tend to route its shipments over the lines of those carriers who buy most of their steel from it rather than using the facilities of railroads buying from its competitors. The practice of reciprocity is common in all types of businesses, and it is perfectly legal as long as it does not result in undue discriminations or preference.

Sometimes a large shipper is able to use its routing rights as a bargaining tool in obtaining more favorable services or rates from carriers. A carrier who knows that a substantial volume of business can be diverted from its own lines to a rival carrier is likely to listen to the shipper's views or grievances with considerable respect. Again, such shipper influence is perfectly legal if not improperly used to the disadvantage of competitors. The desire to control all routing for bargaining purposes is one major reason this function is often retained in the central traffic office even though many other traffic functions may be decentralized to regional or local offices.

In summary, then, exercising the right to route rail shipments, although resulting in much tedious and time-consuming technical work for the traffic department, may be of considerable economic benefit to a shipper.

Legal Aspects of Routing

Shippers by rail and water are given the legal right to route shipments under the Interstate Commerce Act. This right is not given for other modes, but conditions in other forms of transportation do not create such involved problems of routing.

Water and air carriers normally do not engage in a great deal of inter-line traffic exchange. Shipments by these modes generally move from origin to destination over one route and by one carrier. Interline exchanges are increasing in the trucking industry, but even here such exchanges are relatively unimportant as contrasted with rail interlining. But even when a trucking company accepts a shipper's routing on a bill of lading (a transportation contract), it may be held liable for any damages suffered by the shipper as a result of violation of the contract. This comes under the area of contract law, however, rather than under transportation law.

As indicated above, a rail shipper has the legal right to route its shipment. If it does not exercise this right, the carrier must move the shipment over the lowest priced, or some one of the lowest priced, available routes. There is an exception, however, in that a carrier cannot be forced to short-haul itself substantially unless to avoid short-haulage would require using an unreasonably long route. For example, a given rail carrier accepting a shipment destined to a consignee 1,000 miles distant might have interline connections for that destination at points 100 miles and 500 miles from the origin. In such a case, the originating carrier would normally be entitled to the 500-mile haul. But if the longer route results in the goods having to be moved 2,000 miles rather than 1,000 miles to reach the destination, the carrier probably could be forced to short-haul itself.

Shipper traffic departments often physically prepare the principal shipping document (bill of lading) and insert the desired route and the applicable freight rate. If the shipper inserts the route but does not include the rate, the carrier must follow the designated routing even though it requires a higher rate than some other route. If the shipper specifies the applicable rate but does not include a route, the carrier must move the shipment over the route for which the named rate applies. If there is more than one such route, the carrier may choose the routing. If the shipper's designated route and rate conflict or if the rate shown by the shipper does not apply over any route, the carrier is expected to contact the shipper for clarification. It is not clear what the carrier must do in case of such a conflict if the shipper cannot be contacted, but it seems likely that the carrier would be required to use the lowest rated route possible without substantially short-hauling itself.

Tracing and Expediting

Because of their necessity for tightly planned production or merchandising schedules, consignees often are quite concerned about the location of en route goods and when these goods will be received. Traffic departments, therefore, often are asked to obtain carrier cooperation in speeding up certain shipments or in determining where shipments presently are in order that their arrival time can be more accurately predicted. This is especially true for railroad carload shipments.

Carriers usually cooperate as much as possible in tracing and expediting, especially if the process is not abused by individual shippers. Some large carriers maintain sizable departments devoted exclusively to these activities. For example, many railroads maintain communications systems that enable them to answer an inquiry concerning the present location of a particular car within minutes or even seconds. And often it is possible to speed up an urgently needed shipment by cutting a car out of a slow train and putting it on a faster one or by using some similar maneuver. For many shippers and consignees, this is a valuable part of the bundle of transportation services.

Documentation

The Bill of Lading

The bill of lading, normally prepared in the shipper's traffic department although legally issued by the carrier (acceptance and signature constituting issuance), is the most important traffic document for both the shipper and the carrier. This key document has been called the oldest, most widely used, and least read of commercial documents!

The bill of lading acknowledges receipt of the goods by the carrier and provides evidence of title to the goods. Even more important, it is the basic contract of carriage between shipper and carrier, setting forth the rights and responsibilities of each. Like other contracts, its execution requires parties competent to contract, for legal purposes, a consideration, and a meeting of the minds of the contracting parties.

Historically, the bill of lading can be traced back into antiquity when it was used as a customary practice by the earliest Mediterranean merchants and sea traders. It evolved as an important part of the so-called Law Merchant of the medieval and early modern periods, and thus on into contemporary times. Until the present century, however, there was no necessary uniformity in the contractual terms of the document. Each carrier issued its own bill of lading containing such contractual terms as it preferred. Carriers might even by terms of the contract escape from their common-law liability for delivery or drastically limit the amount recoverable by a shipper whose products were lost or damaged by the carrier.

Carriers were prohibited from using bill of lading provisions to contract out of their duty of delivery by the Carmack Amendment in 1906. It later developed, however, that carriers still could contract to limit the amount of the shipper's recovery. The first Cummins Amendment in 1915, therefore, prohibited any limitation of liability. This was relaxed somewhat by the second Cummins Amendment, 1916, which does allow some limitation of liability, although not a release for liability as such, in return for a lower freight rate (except on ordinary livestock). This makes possible the use of the so-called released-value rate (see Chapter 17). This released-value option has been greatly enhanced by recent changes in transportation regulation.

Although the above-named amendments specified what carriers could and could not do contractually in terms of loss and damage liability, they did not require a uniform bill of lading. Actually, some railroad and shipper groups attempted to established a uniform bill during the 1890s, but their success was limited. In 1908 in response to shipper petitions, the ICC recommended such action, but it had no power to require it. Congress in 1910 gave the ICC authority to prescribe a uniform bill of lading for railroads after appropriate hearings. The hearings started in 1912, but World War I intervened and the ICC did not prescribe the uniform bill until 1922. This 1922 bill of lading, although modified to some extent by later ICC action, is essentially the same document now used for all railroad shipments.

Part II of the Interstate Commerce Act gave the ICC about the same regulatory controls of the form of motor carrier bills of lading as it has over railroad bills. The commission has not seen fit to require that motor carrier bills be standardized, however. But, as the basic laws are similar, the actual contractual contents of rail and truck bills must also be similar, even though they may differ in physical size, shape, and some wording.

Kinds of Bills of Lading

Bills of lading may be classified as government, livestock, and commercial. These terms are self-explanatory. The government bill is used for governmental shipments, the livestock bill for shipping livestock, and the commercial bill for the great mass of ordinary business or personal shipments.

The commercial bill of lading may be either a domestic or an export or ocean document. Although we are not primarily concerned with foreign ocean transportation in this book, we will point out that the ocean variety is quite different from the domestic bill. The latter, of course, is most important to most shippers.

The domestic commercial bill of lading (and the ocean variety too, incidentally) may be either a straight or an order bill. The latter is a negotiable instrument, it may be endorsed to other parties, and the purchaser of the properly endorsed document acquires title to the goods covered by the document. The straight bill, on the other hand, is not negotiable. The difference between the two forms might be thought of as being equivalent to the difference between a personal check payable to John Doe and one payable to the order of John Doe. Carriers must be very careful in delivering goods consigned under an order bill, since they may be held liable for misdelivery if they deliver without requiring the presentation of a properly endorsed bill.

The face or front side of a uniform bill of lading filled out by the shipper or the carrier is fairly self-explanatory. It contains routine operational information such as the names and addresses of the consignor and consignee, routing instructions, the rate, a description of the kinds and quantities of the things shipped, payment method, and similar items. The fine print on the back of the bill spells out the contract terms, especially matters of the carrier's liability (or the lack thereof) under various circumstances. An example of a motor carrier bill of lading is presented in Figure 23.1.

As already mentioned, railroad bills of lading are standardized, and truck bills in general are similar in nature although varying in detail and not standardized. Freight forwarders often use the bills of the mode of carriage performing the line-haul movement. Airbills are used for airfreight movements. These are not all uniform, although many are through voluntary actions of the airlines. Pipelines, operating under conditions different from other for-hire carriers, use a tender of shipment form in lieu of a bill of lading. The ocean bill, as previously indicated, is quite different from the domestic variety. Finally, contract carriage is governed by the terms of the individual carrier contract existing between shipper and carrier.

Although space precludes any further detailed discussion of the bill of lading, the authors feel that this vital shipping document should be thoroughly understood by everyone — shipper or carrier — who is concerned with it in any way. We highly recommend that such persons obtain copies of each type of bill of lading and study them carefully front and back. They are transportation textbooks in miniature.

Figure 23.1 Motor Carrier Bill of Lading

Hurley Trucking Company, Inc. 1001 South Fourth Street
Phoenix, Arizona 85004

STRAIGHT BILL OF LADING
—Original—Not Negotiable—Domestic

ROUTE: Hurley Trucking Co., Inc.		SHIPPER'S NUMBER	
TO: CONSIGNEE		FROM: SHIPPER	
STREET		STREET	
DESTINATION	ZIP	ORIGIN	ZIP
C.O.D. AMOUNT $		REMIT C.O.D. TO:	

NO. PKGS.	DESCRIPTION OF ARTICLES, SPECIAL MARKS AND EXCEPTIONS	HM	*WEIGHT (SUB. TO COR.)	CLASS OR RATE	CK. COL.	

Subject to Section 7 of conditions, if this shipment is to be delivered to the consignee without recourse on the consignor, the consignor shall sign the following statement.

The carrier shall not make delivery of this shipment without payment of freight and all other lawful charges.

(Signature of Consignor)

☐ PREPAID
☐ COLLECT

Received $_____ to apply in prepayment of the charges on the property described hereon.

Agent or Cashier

PER _____
(The signature here acknowledges only the amount prepaid.)

This is to certify that the above named materials are properly classified, described, packaged, marked and labeled, and are in proper condition for transportation, according to the applicable regulations of the Department of Transportation.

X _____

Charges Advanced $

SHIPPER	Hurley Trucking Co., Inc.
PER	PER DATE:

HTC-F-01-02-02   5/83

Source: Hurley Trucking Company, Inc., Phoenix, Arizona. Used by permission.

Other Traffic Documents

Shipments move on "ways" of paper as well as upon ways of steel, concrete, water, or air. In addition to the often voluminous records needed for strictly internal use, the traffic department is routinely concerned with many other shipping documents such as arrival notices, delivery receipts, freight bills, inspection reports, claims reports, and the like. Carriers also struggle with mountains of paper. A key carrier document is the waybill, made for every shipment, which contains information similar to that on the face of the bill of lading and which accompanies the shipment from origin to destination.

One is justified in wondering how transportation was accomplished in earlier and less complex eras when paper was less plentiful and more expensive! The paperwork problem of both shippers and carriers has become so complicated and expensive that various methods are being sought to bring it under control. These methods run the gamut from electronic computers and IBM cards to snap-out carbon insert forms. There is agitation for fewer and simpler forms, but the problem is far from solved.

Traffic Claims

The preparation and collection of claims against carriers and claims prevention are an important traffic management function. Depending upon circumstances, this may be handled almost entirely by the traffic department, or it may be a cooperative effort of traffic and other areas of management. Claims can be divided into two types, namely, those for loss and damage to goods shipped, and reparations and overcharges.

Loss and Damage Claims and Prevention

The liabilities of common carriers for lost or damaged shipments are part of the so-called common-carrier obligation. Payments are not made automatically, however. Before an L & D claim is paid, the shipper or receiver (whoever has title to the goods in question) must file and substantiate a claim. The amounts involved often are substantial, perhaps amounting to as much as $2 billion annually in the economy as a whole.

The filing of claims is governed by statutory law and the transportation contract (bill of lading). For example, damage claims generally must be filed with carriers within nine months (six months for express) after delivery of the shipment, and claims for lost shipments must be made within nine months of the reasonable delivery date of the goods. If the carrier refuses to pay the claim, suit must be brought in a court of law within two years of the date of refusal.

Further, a loss and damage claim must be supported by evidence acceptable in court. Although nothing is specifically prescribed by law as to what is acceptable, supporting evidence customarily includes some kind of standard form plus the bill of lading, invoice, and freight bill (preferably original copies) covering the shipment. Other evidence might include inspection reports, appraisal and salvage reports, and photographs.

Clearly, inadequate knowledge of the pertinent rules or laxness in procedures by the traffic manager may be harmful to a firm's efforts to recover for lost or damaged shipments. But recovery of past damages is only part of the story. Efforts to prevent loss and damage from occurring may be of even greater importance.

Lost and damaged shipments are a sheer waste to the nation's economy, resulting both in lost production and in higher freight rates and higher consumer prices. L & D claims are costly to process for both the shipper and the carrier. Even if the claim is paid in full, many hours and a considerable amount of paper have been consumed. Very small claims may never be filed, and larger claims may be compromised by underpayment or overpayment to reduce the processing load. Further, damaged or lost merchandise may severely inconvenience consignees, disrupt production or sales schedules, and create problems of lost good will between shippers and receivers, and between both these groups and carriers. It has been estimated that the indirect costs related to shipment loss and damage may be as much as seven times as great as the direct costs.

Loss and damage prevention involves a combination of research, education, and supervision on the part both of shippers and of carriers. The cause first has to be discovered. Published statistics indicate that at least two-thirds of the loss and damage to shipper goods may be controllable. About one-third may be attributable to rough handling by carriers either at terminals or en route, and another one-third may be due to improper packaging, marking, or loading by the shipper. The remainder is the result of unknown or uncontrollable factors.

Once the cause is known, devices or procedures must be developed to eliminate or reduce the loss. These techniques then must be thoroughly taught to the actual shipper or carrier personnel engaged in the physical handling and movement process. And continual supervision is required to ensure that the techniques are applied. This sounds very elementary. But a large amount of time is spent by carriers and shippers individually and through various associations in trying to solve the L & D problem. And losses continue to climb!

Overcharges and Reparations

Overcharge claims are made when a shipper feels that payment of more than the lowest applicable published rate for shipment can be demonstrated. This may be a simple arithmetic mistake, or it may be the result of a rate clerk's error in using tariffs. In principle, this is not a complex process. As you know, a shipper is entitled to pay the lowest published rate. If the shipper pays more and can uncover this and prove it to the carrier, the carrier is legally obligated to make the appropriate refund. Auditing of freight bills, then, is designed to discover overpayments. This function may be performed within the shipping firm, or it may be farmed out to independent freight auditors who operate on a percentage-of-recovery commission basis.

Reparations claims are made for a different type of refund. Common carriers are required by law to charge reasonable rates, those not so high as to be exploitative of the shipper nor so low as to be noncompensatory for the carrier. A reasonable rate is called a *lawful* rate. Shippers must pay the published tariff rate, the *legal* rate, related to the movement of their goods, whether or not this rate is reasonable. In other words, it is possible for a rate that was reasonable and lawful at one time to become unreasonable with the passage of time, as carrier costs or competitive conditions change.

If a shipper can demonstrate to the satisfaction of the ICC or the courts that it has been paying an unreasonably high rate, it is entitled to recover from the carrier the difference between a reasonable rate and the rate actually paid for past shipments. These reparations payments cannot be made even if the carrier is willing to pay, however, without a specific order from the ICC or from the courts. Further, reparations awards are governed by a statute of limitations, which prevents refunds for back shipments beyond a period of two years for private shippers or three years for government shipments.

A reparations claim must be made according to a prescribed form and procedure, and the shipper must be able to document the amount claimed. Due to court decisions holding that the original Parts II and IV of the Interstate Commerce Act did not provide specifically for reparations, interstate motor carriers and freight forwarders were not liable for reparations until these statutes were changed by Congress in September 1965.

Shipment Consolidation

As was indicated earlier, one of the major problems of many shippers relates to the movement of small shipments, often requiring the use of high-cost transportation to facilitate service. One tool at the disposal of the traffic manager is to address the small-shipment problem as one of shipment consolidation. Shipment consolidation involves combining shipments destined for the same consignee, where possible, or to the same general area, taking advantage of lower line-haul rates for larger shipments as well as receiving the better service given to shipments requiring less frequent terminal handling by the carrier. In some cases, the line-haul cost savings may more than offset the carrier's added charges for delivery to multiple consignees at the destination point. This type of trade-off is a good example of how a traffic manager can positively affect a company's profitability. Although it is not possible for all shippers to effectively use shipment consolidation as a cost reduction tool, many companies can do so with careful planning as they schedule shipments to their customers or are able to coordinate movements from several plant locations or for various divisions of a larger corporation. Fortunately, both the motor carrier industry and the railroads have been particularly cooperative in facilitating shipment consolidation by shippers.

Movements Through Shipper Cooperatives

A second way that the traffic manager is able to combat the high cost of small-shipment movement is through participation in shipper cooperatives, particularly in the movement of inbound shipments. These cooperatives, as described in Chapter 5, are private, nonprofit organizations performing services for their members similar to those of freight forwarders. Such organizations act as consolidators for their members, allowing various individual shippers to take advantage of the lower line-haul rates (per hundredweight) afforded to large shipments. Such organizations, as their names imply, require the close cooperation of their shipper members and are usually made up of similar types of shippers, as seen in the case of grocery store cooperatives. Again, the carriers have been very helpful in facilitating movements tendered by shipper cooperatives.

INTERNAL OPERATING RELATIONSHIPS

Traffic management, however broadly or narrowly it may be defined, is directly related to many of a firm's other operational and staff functions. An individual business is a system or an organism. Actions taken in one portion of the firm affect other portions. Things done in the sales department of a business affect the traffic department, and vice versa.

It follows that if a business is to give its best performance, its activities must be effectively coordinated at all levels. Ultimately this is a responsibility of top management, but in practice much of it is done on the initiative of lower-level managers. If these lower-level managers do not understand the need for joint action or are not willing to cooperate with one another, top management may be faced with a serious educational or replacement problem, or the firm may operate at a low level of performance if it survives at all.

We are concerned here only with coordination between the traffic function and other areas of a business that takes place on a routine basis. The role of the traffic manager may be only advisory in this coordination, or it may involve joint decision making by traffic and other managers. Whether the traffic manager's role is advisory or decisional will vary depending on the nature of the problem and the traffic manager's status in the organizational hierarchy.

LEGAL PROBLEMS

Some firms maintain their own legal department, others have attorneys on retainer, and still others seek attorneys only when specific legal problems arise. Some businesses use a combination of these methods. Whatever organizational arrangement is used, however, relationships between a firm's attorneys and its traffic department should be about the same.

Much of the traffic manager's work can be described as quasi-legal in nature. For example, the traffic manager enters into transportation contracts, files various kinds of claims, and appears before regulatory agencies in rates and services cases for the company. This requires a good working knowledge of the applicable laws and legal procedures. But unless the traffic manager is an attorney, that person cannot represent the company in a court action. This means that when something goes wrong — a lawsuit arises over a contract, a carrier is sued for nonpayment of a claim, or a court appeal of a regulatory decision is made — the attorneys must take over.

Most attorneys are not transportation experts, however, and even those who are usually have not been involved in the earlier stages of the actions that ultimately are taken to the courts for decision. The traffic department, therefore, assists the attorney in preparing the case by indicating what has transpired earlier, collecting and assembling pertinent data, and advising upon the peculiar transportation technicalities of the case. In other words, even though the attorney must present the case in court, actually the attorney and the traffic manager act as a team with both contributing their own special knowledge and capabilities to the combined effort.

Wise traffic managers realize that almost any of their quasi-legal actions conceivably could lead to a court case and that they must conduct themselves accordingly. Careful records must be kept, correct procedures followed, and legal advice sought on any questionable point. Much litigation is prevented by knowing when to seek legal advice and much is won by building up a record for the potential use of attorneys if the need arises.

TRANSPORTATION INSURANCE

Insurance is just as real a transportation cost as any other cost. Typically, however, in firms involved in domestic shipping (as contrasted with ocean shipping), transportation insurance falls into an organizational no-man's-land, not clearly understood and often neglected by both the traffic department and whoever is responsible for handling the firm's major insurance coverage.

Basically there are two kinds of transportation insurance. *Liability* insurance protects the insured from damages caused to others as a result of the insured person's actions. *Indemnity* insurance provides protection against losses suffered by the insured. Both these kinds of insurance are available and may be quite important to both shippers and carriers. Our present interest is only in shippers' insurance, however.

Transportation Liability Insurance

Liability insurance is primarily of importance to those shippers who use private transportation. This is the personal liability and property damage (PL & PD) type of insurance familiar to every automobile owner. If a firm operates a fleet of trucks or other private transportation equipment, this coverage must be provided to protect the company against claims for personal injuries or damages brought by outsiders. It does not cover damages to the firm's own equipment and goods.

Virtually all companies engaged in private transportation have this kind of insurance, although not always in an adequate amount. Its purchase may be handled by the traffic department or it may be handled by some other department or official in the company. In any case, it is closely related to the traffic management function.

Transport Indemnity Insurance

Shippers using private transportation need indemnity protection against loss and damage both to their transportation equipment and to the goods hauled in this equipment. The indemnity need of one using contract carriage will vary depending upon the nature of the carrier's liability under the contract. Those using common carriage may need some form of indemnity protection for goods in the hands of carriers.

As land common carriers have a high degree of liability for goods entrusted to their care, one might wonder why such goods need to be further insured. (The situation is quite different with water carriage where carrier liability is very limited, but marine insurance is beyond the scope of this book.) Actually, many shippers do not carry indemnity protection (transit insurance) on goods shipped by common carrier. Instead, they rely upon the carriers' liabilities for loss and damage (duty of delivery) and assume the risk of any nonrecoverable loss themselves.

But there are several reasons why it is sometimes desirable for a shipper to obtain transit insurance even on goods shipped by land common carriers.

1. The carrier is not liable for an act of God or an act of the public enemy, and may be exempt from liability on various statutory grounds.
2. Even though legally liable, the carrier might not be financially able to pay a large claim, or payment might be delayed for months or years pending a court decision.
3. Shipments may be made under released value rates which limit the amount necessary to be paid by the carrier. It often is less expensive to ship under a released value rate and buy full insurance coverage than to ship under a higher rate with more complete recovery available from the shipper.

In summary, then, transit insurance to indemnify the shipper may be desirable because of the greater likelihood of prompt payment of claims and because it provides more protection. Whether or not this is worthwhile will depend to a considerable extent upon the nature and value of the goods being shipped. Even though there is a likelihood of many small and regular unrecoverable losses, the shipper may be willing and able to absorb these (self-insure). Such losses can be taken into account in pricing the merchandise. On the other hand, the likelihood of loss on a given shipment might be very small, but the value of the shipment might be such that its unrecoverable loss would seriously affect the firm. In such a case, it would be prudent to insure.

Shippers' transit insurance is available in various forms. It may be purchased for a specifically named item or group of items for a single trip, or it may be obtained for any items fitting into a broad general classification for a series of trips. The value of the merchandise shipped may be specifically stated, or the insurance contract may provide that values will be determined upon invoice or market prices (usually with some stated upper limits). This insurance may be obtained for either private or for-hire movements.

The Traffic Manager's Insurance Role

Insurance, like transportation, is a complicated technical field. Normally one would not expect a traffic manager to be an insurance expert any more than one would expect an insurance expert to be highly knowledgeable in transportation matters.

Transportation insurance, however, is only one phase of insurance, and it is equally a phase of transportation. Competent traffic managers should at least know what kinds of transportation insurance are available and what kinds and how much companies need for protection. They are, or should be, in a better position than anyone else in a firm to assess the risks inherent in particular shipments, modes, and routes. If the company is not adequately protected in general or on a particular transaction, the traffic manager should take whatever steps are necessary.

In firms with an insurance department or with some specific official designated to handle all insurance matters, the traffic manager should be responsible for providing the necessary transportation advice or in aiding in the making of insurance decisions. Under other conditions, the traffic manager may be responsible for obtaining some or all portions of the necessary transportation insurance.

Where neither the traffic manager nor anyone else has a clear-cut organizational responsibility for transportation insurance and if there is a need for such insurance either on a specific shipment or on a continuous basis, a good traffic manager will apprise top management of the situation. In insurance matters, transportation as well as other kinds, it is not safe to assume that someone else is taking care of things. In order to do the job well either as an adviser or as an individual or joint decision maker, the traffic manager must have a working knowledge of transportation insurance.

INTERNAL WAREHOUSING
AND MATERIALS HANDLING

Intraplant movement and storage of raw materials and finished-goods inventories often fall under the supervision of the traffic manager. This logically is a part of the transportation function since plant inventories are merely temporarily at rest in their movement from origin to final destination. Storage and processing can be viewed only as an intermediate step in the transportation process. Further, as the traffic department has responsibilities in getting goods into the plant and in getting them aboard outbound transportation equipment in proper order and on to their destination, it is not at all illogical that this department should handle goods (except for the actual processing or manufacturing operations) while they are within the plant.

We will not discuss the many techniques and mechanical devices used in the internal movement and storage of goods. This is a comprehensive field in itself and one in which many new developments have brought increased efficiency and promise much more. Each system of intraplant storage and movement must be developed for a particular situation. Thus there are almost as many systems or variations of systems as there are firms and plants. The traffic manager who does have supervisory responsibilities in this area will find no shortage of current literature dealing with it.

PACKING, MARKING, AND LOADING

Whether or not the traffic department is responsible for the internal handling of goods, it certainly has a significant responsibility in seeing that outbound shipments are properly packed or packaged, marked, and loaded. Again, these physical operations may or may not be directly under traffic supervision. But if not, close cooperation should be maintained between those who are responsible and the traffic department. As indicated earlier, perhaps one-third of all loss and damage to shipments en route can be traced to improper packing, marking, or loading.

Two things should be kept in mind when packing or packaging goods for shipment. First, the shipment must be protected from the hazards of the voyage. These include such things as climate, rough handling by carriers, and pilferage. Second, packaging adds to costs. The materials used for packaging cost something, as does the labor for doing the packing. Further, packaging increases the weight of the shipment and thus adds to the freight bill. The ideal packaging is enough to protect the shipment adequately, but not more.

Classifications, tariffs, and other carrier publications specify minimum packaging requirements for many types of commodities under various conditions. Also, professional package engineers or consultants, trade associations, manufacturers of various kinds of packaging materials, and many current journals and periodicals are useful in solving packaging problems. During recent years, much research has gone into developing various kinds of containers, pallets, strapping methods, unitized load devices, and lightweight packaging materials designed to increase protection and reduce costs of shipment. Information on these matters is a part of the traffic manager's expert knowledge which should be available to, and widely used by, whoever actually does the physical packing job.

Very little needs to be said about the marking of shipments except that markings should be correct, clear, and consistent with the information shown on the bill of lading. Poorly marked shipments go astray more frequently than well-marked ones; and once shipments have strayed, inadequate markings make it more difficult to locate the shipper or consignee.

Finally, proper loading onto outbound transportation equipment is a traffic function whether or not loading actually is under the supervision of the traffic manager. The loading methods used will depend upon the nature of the goods, the type of packaging, the kind of outbound transportation used, the physical layout of the plant itself, and the kind of materials-handling equipment available.

Proper loading is concerned with protection of the goods shipped, with facilitating their unloading at destination (or partial unloading en route), and with minimizing loading costs (labor and protective dunnage). Shipments must be stowed in the vehicle and braced in a manner to accomplish these objectives.

Loading is another of the traffic manager's areas of expertise and one in which there have been many recent developments. Much of the old expensive hand loading has been outmoded by mechanical loading using conveyors, chutes, fork-lift equipment, and specially designed carrier vehicles. Also, new protective devices such as inflatable rubber dunnage, strapping materials, and even shock-resistant rolling stock are coming into use. Progress in loading efficiency is keeping pace with developments in packaging technology and promises equally great savings in the future. Traffic managers themselves (or through cooperative action with or advice to other managers) are responsible for seeing that their firms benefit from these innovations.

OTHER ROUTINE ACTIVITIES

Other normal duties of a traffic department include the supervision of the firm's private transportation operations, if any, making arrangements for the personal transportation of company officials traveling on company business, and sometimes handling the details of household goods movements for transferred company personnel. Also, like other managers, traffic managers must be concerned with the recruitment, supervision, training and development, and promotion of personnel in their departments.

SUMMARY

Although not all the day-to-day traffic control decisions and activities of a typical traffic department have been elaborated upon or even mentioned, the importance of these functions should be clear from the foregoing. If they are done well, the individual firm benefits by lower costs and the efficiency of the nation's production and distribution is improved. If they are done poorly, the firm's costs are unnecessarily high, which may lead to individual disaster and harm to the overall national economy.

It should be clear, too, that the routine of traffic control is not a cut-and-dried process. An infinite variety of problems requiring decisions and implementing action are continually arising. The handling of these problems requires a technically skilled but broadly based individual. In addition to a knowledge of "rates and routes," the effective traffic manager must have a better-than-passing knowledge of economics, psychology, law, and some phases of engineering plus an extensive understanding of the firm, its industry, customers, and competitive environment, and transportation institutions and technology. And among other characteristics, the traffic manager must be imaginative, flexible, courageous, and durable.

Although the traffic manager is a specialist and thus primarily responsible for the firm's traffic-control procedures, the fact that traffic management decisions may significantly affect the jobs of others should not be forgotten. Coordination is not a one-way street. On some matters, the traffic manager should make decisions with due regard for the advice of other members of management. Some matters may require joint decision making, whereas in others the traffic manager's role is purely an advisory one.

Traffic control offers both challenges and opportunities. It is an area of business in which much improvement can be made and in which new developments and techniques promise to continue replacing older methods within the foreseeable future. Although its practitioners often go unpraised, its effective performance is vital to the welfare of individual business firms and to the nation's economy.

ADDITIONAL READINGS

Bagley, John W., James R. Evans, and Wallace R. Wood, "Contracting for Transportation," *Transportation Journal* (Winter 1982), 63–73.

Brown, Terrance A., "Shippers' Associations: Operations, Trends, and Comparative Prices," *Transportation Journal* (Fall 1981), 54–66.

Coyle, John J., Edward J. Bardi, and C. John Langley, Jr., *The Management of Business Logistics*, 4th ed., New York: West Publishing Co., 1988.
   Chapter 10, "Traffic Management," pp. 355–90.

Flood, Kenneth U., Oliver G. Callson, and Sylvester J. Jablonski, *Transportation Management*, Dubuque, Iowa: William C. Brown, 1984.
   Chapter 1, "The Changing Environment of Purchasing and Selling of Transportaion Services," pp. 1–26.
   Chapter 18, "Shipping Documents," pp. 463–508.

Johnson, James C., and Donald F. Wood, *Contemporary Physical Distribution and Logistics*, 3rd ed., New York, NY: Macmillan Publishing Co., 1986.
   Chapter 6, "The Traffic Management Function," pp. 201–47.

Lambert, Douglas M., and James R. Stock, *Strategic Physical Distribution Management*, Homewood, Ill.: Richard D. Irwin, 1982.
   Chapter 5, "Decision Strategies in Transportation," pp. 144–79.

Taff, Charles A., *Management of Physical Distribution and Transportation*, 6th ed., Homewood, Ill.: Richard D. Irwin, 1978.
   Chapter 17, "Evaluative Factors in Routing," pp. 452–82.

Tyworth, John E., Joseph Cavinato, and C. John Langley, Jr., *Traffic Management*, Reading, MA.: Addison-Wesley Pub. Co., 1987.
   Chapter 2, "Transportation Services and Selection," pp. 25–52.

CHAPTER 24

THE LOGISTICS FUNCTION

The previous two chapters dealt with the evolution of the traffic management function and the role of the traffic manager in providing the company's interface with the transportation industry. In addition, they also mentioned several areas where the traffic manager plays an important advisory role in formulating routine operating policy for the firm. This chapter emphasizes the evolution of the logistics function from physical distribution management to the integrated, total firm approach that will dominate in the 1990s.

PHYSICAL DISTRIBUTION MANAGEMENT CONCEPTS

The physical distribution management concept is principally a post–World War II phenomenon, as Chapter 22 discussed. As companies have added product lines and sought to serve a more diverse set of customer locations, their distribution systems have become more and more complex. This complexity is reflected in the sensitivity of the interrelationships among the various parts of the distribution system. To keep costs under control while maintaining acceptable service levels, companies began to apply a systems approach to the analysis of their distribution operations. Indeed, the objective of adopting the physical distribution concept is generally defined as achieving distribution cost minimization subject to a given level of service and, concurrently, avoiding suboptimization within the system that would increase overall distribution costs. This section addesses the basic elements of the physical distribution system, the application of the systems concept to integration of these elements, and the role of customer service in distribution decisions.

Elements of the Physical Distribution System

The physical distribution systems of most companies will be made up of five elements necessary to facilitate goods distribution. These elements include inventory and inventory control, warehousing and storage, materials handling, packing and packaging, and transportation. Each of these elements plays a key role in the physical distribution process, as shown in Figure 24.1, and decisions affecting the attributes of any one of the five will affect the required attributes of the remaining four.

Inventory and Inventory Control

The basic function of inventory is to act as a buffer between supply and demand. It may be used to build raw material stores that are available from their source on a seasonal basis but are required for production on a year-round basis. The accumulation of grain at flour mills is an example of this use of inventory. Another use of inventory is the formation of safety stock, that inventory held to meet fluctuations in demand or delivery times that might be faced during stock replenishment periods.

Inventory control is the process of managing physical inventories throughout the supply-distribution chain. This process is concerned with determining appropriate inventory levels at the various storage points within the physical distribution system, as well as with determining where specific items should be stocked. A recent trend in inventory control is more selective stocking policies rather than maintaining stocks of all parts or products at each storage point in the system. As transportation systems have improved, particularly with the growth of air package express services, many manufacturers have found that it is possible to store critical replacement parts at a limited number of service locations without appreciably limiting their ability to provide rapid response to virtually any point in the country or even the world.

Inventory stocking decisions relating to inventory level and location and ordering decisions relating to order size and frequency may significantly affect a company's warehousing and transportation requirements and costs. Indeed, the relationships among these functions are so interwoven as to make adaptation of the systems concept within the physical distribution management function essential to the success of most companies.

Warehousing and Storage

The basic function of warehousing and storage facilities is to accommodate goods accumulation and distribution. Aside from warehouses used to facilitate long-term storage of raw materials or products, as in the case of warehouses used to store whiskey during the aging process, warehouses

Figure 24.1 The Process of Physical Distribution

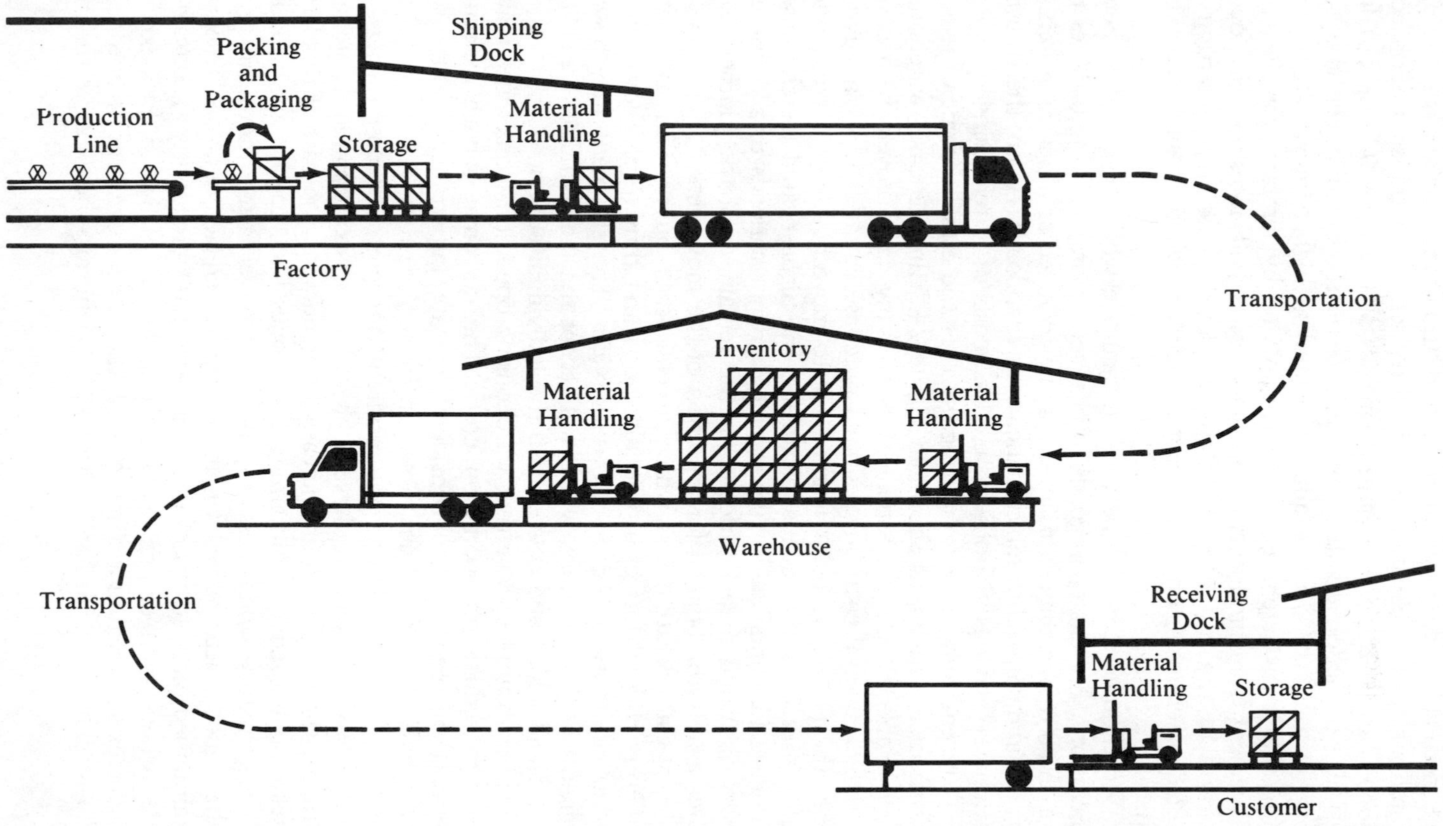

are normally used to facilitate the distribution process. For example, warehousing may be used to achieve reductions in transportation costs. Goods can be shipped in large quantities at low rates (CL or TL) from distant production points to warehouses near consuming centers. Then local distribution in small quantities (and at higher rates) can be made from the local warehouse. Instead of paying higher rates for the entire movement from producer to consumer, lower bulk rates are used over a portion of the distance, the transportation cost savings offsetting the added warehousing costs. This is an example of what is called a breakbulk operation.

Warehouses may also be used to facilitate what are called makebulk operations. For example, goods from several manufacturing facilities that are to go to the same consignee may be collected at a nearby warehouse facility and shipped in mixed carloads or truckloads. Again, the transportation cost savings will offset the added costs of warehousing.

A recent trend in warehousing involves the establishment of regional distribution centers, as shown in Figure 24.2. In this case, warehousing may enable a seller to supply each of many small buyers with several products. Even if each buyer should purchase in carload lots, a shipment from the producing plant might have to move at higher mixed carload rates, that is, at the rates applicable to the highest-rated merchandise in the carload shipment. But by shipping straight carloads to a distributing warehouse and mixed carloads for the remainder of the journey, lower rates again are obtained for a portion of the movement.

Pool-car operations, in which several small buyers join together in ordering carload lots of a particular good and thus receive lower freight rates, often use public warehouse services. The shipment may be consigned to the warehouse, which will accept the merchandise, break it up into smaller lots, and deliver it to the individual buyers.

These examples show that warehousing operations sometimes may be used to reduce transportation costs. The customer service aspects of warehousing usually are of considerably greater importance than transportation cost-savings features, however. In fact, the total costs of warehousing are much greater than any resultant transportation cost savings.

As speed and reliability have improved in transportation and communications, there has been an increasing tendency on the part of retailers to push the burden of maintaining inventories back toward the producer. During the age when messages could not travel faster than a horse and when goods were moved by animal-drawn vehicles, retailers necessarily maintained large stocks of goods and ordered infrequently. Today, however, when orders can be placed on one day and delivered the next from distances several hundred miles away, the retailer can gear inventories to almost immediate demands. The seller performs the storage function.

Figure 24.2 The Regional Distribution Center Concept

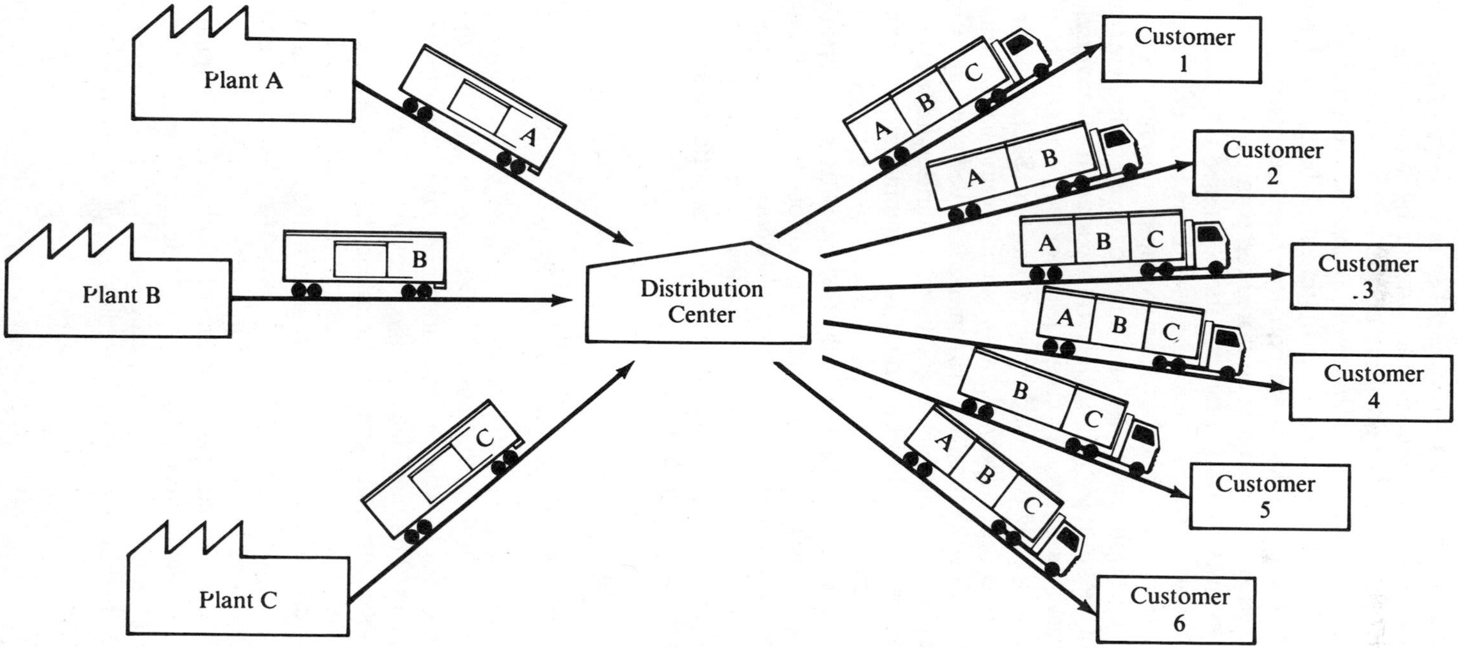

Thus, in a competitive situation, the seller must be prepared either by strategically located distribution warehouses or by fast transportation, or both, to make quick delivery on short notice.

Warehouse space also is necessary at points where commodities are stopped for processing or fabrication in transit. Inbound and outbound daily flows of materials seldom are equal at such points. Raw materials and processed goods usually must be stored temporarily, and transit points may be used as distribution centers for the processed commodity.

Similar temporary storage needs exist where one form of transportation makes connections with another. For example, warehouses in seaport cities act as collection points for small rail or truck shipments awaiting the arrival of steamships for further transportation. Conversely, such warehouses serve as temporary receptacles for large quantities of goods brought in and speedily unloaded by water carriers. Such goods are more gradually dispersed (in smaller volumes) by connecting land carriers. Early railheads connecting rail lines and wagon roads served the same functions. Similar situations still exist where goods must transfer from one mode of domestic carriage to another or where bulk shipments are dispersed or small shipments concentrated.

In summary, warehousing is closely tied in with transportation and plays an important role in the dynamic distribution process. Warehousing facilities necessarily come into being at distribution centers and transit centers, as well as where modes of transportation change and where seasonal production occurs. These facilities serve the needs of buyers, sellers, and transportation firms.

Materials Handling

The materials handling function is often defined as the internal movement of goods within a production or warehouse facility. It also involves the transfer of goods between storage and production facilities and transportation vehicles. The materials handling methods selected to accommodate goods movement can significantly affect the other elements of the distribution system. For example, the use of automated handling equipment, such as draglines, continuous chain systems imbedded in receiving dock floors or suspended overhead and used to pull carts of goods from dock to storage areas, will affect required aisle widths and overall facility design and cost. In addition, the use of mechanical equipment, such as forklift trucks, will affect not only dock design but also the type of packaging that may be appropriate, since mechanical handling is often rougher than manual handling. Materials handling methods may also affect the suitability of certain types of transportation equipment for goods movements.

Packing and Packaging

Packaging refers to the box or container into which a product is placed after production. This container often has two purposes, to provide advertising or information related to the contents and to protect the contents during transit. Packing refers to the package internal or external efforts taken to add to product protection. Two of the newer materials used for packing are so-called bubble wrap and styrofoam beads. In most instances, these materials serve to cushion the severe shocks received by package contents while being handled at docks and warehouses or while in transit. In addition, the container itself provides additional protection for the shipment.

To facilitate the efficient handling and transportation of many products, efforts have been made to develop packaging systems that are suited to mechanical materials handling methods. This has involved palletization of shipments wherever possible, often with groups of cartons placed on individual pallets banded with metal straps or encased in shrink-wrapped plastic for protection against damage and loss. These attempts to facilitate mechanical handling of shipments have enhanced the use of forklift trucks, among other types of equipment, in distribution. An idea of the potential magnitude of the savings possible from such changes in packaging methods can be seen in the following example. It may take as much as two and one half hours of manual labor to download and store 1,500 pounds of styrofoam cups from a delivery truck if they are handled in individual boxes weighing 10 pounds each. If this load is palletized, it might be downloaded and stored in less than twenty minutes.

The ultimate package is often said to be the shipping container. The basic idea of containerization is to place several or many small units inside a protective covering which can be handled and shipped as a unit. Actually, a boxcar or a truck van is a container, but the great present interest is in developing containers that can be hauled aboard a rail car, a truck, an airplane, or a barge or steamship and preferably interchanged among these various modes.

There are many advantages to containerization. Goods are better protected from handling and shipment damage, pilferage, and loss. Packaging expense can be cut, and handling labor can be expedited at lower cost. Some firms have substantially reduced costs and virtually eliminated en route loss and damage by containerization. Carriers, who also benefit from the more rapid turnaround of equipment and fewer L & D claims, have been very cooperative with shippers in solving container problems and in pushing the movement. A piggyback van is one form of carrier-promoted interchangeable equipment.

Numerous problems arise with containers, however. They are costly and may increase the weight shipped. The shipper and the receiver as well as the carrier may have to change their handling techniques. Shipper-owned containers must be returned to their owners, and an empty container occupies as much space and may be almost as costly to handle and transport as a full one. This means that maximum container efficiency requires two-way use, a situation that does not fit the operational pattern of many shippers. (Many carriers own containers, thus solving the empty-return problem at least for shippers.)

Several groups are working on the problem of standardizing containers. The ideal type sought is a container that can be hauled in multiple units by any mode of carriage. That is, several units might be taken by truck to a railway station and added to several other units to load a flatcar. Then several flatcars might in turn discharge their containers onto a water carrier. At the end of the water movement, the process might be reversed. Such coordination, of course, requires that some standard or uniform size or sizes be adopted to facilitate interchange.

Although containerization is not the answer to all loss and damage and handling problems, it does offer substantial savings under the right conditions. Many shippers cannot containerize and probably never will be able to do so. As the state of technology improves, however, and appropriate institutional and rate adjustments are made, many more shipments will surely move in containers. All traffic managers should keep up with developments in this rapidly changing field, or at least with those developments that are of potential use to their firms, and be prepared to give advice and make recommendations to top management regarding expenditures for this type of equipment.

As indicated above, a switch to containers may involve changing handling methods and obtaining new materials handling equipment. Also, the traffic department itself in many firms is responsible for internal materials handling. In either case, the traffic manager has the responsibility for remaining current on the various types of handling equipment available (both its costs and what it can do to improve the firm's efficiency) and advising top management appropriately.

Transportation

Transportation is the element that ties the distribution system together, literally. Since raw materials sources, parts vendors, production facilities, warehouses and storage points, and customers are often located at widely dispersed points, good transportation must be available if the flow of materials is to be achieved efficiently and effectively. The economic significance of transportation was discussed in Chapter 1. Its importance to the success of an individual company and its effect on the remaining elements of a company's distribution system are as important, albeit on a smaller scale, as transportation is to the general economy.

The mode of transportation selected, as well as the specific carrier within that mode, will affect required inventory levels, packing and packaging requirements, the type of materials handling equipment needed, the type, number, and location of warehouses and distribution centers required, and many other aspects of a company's distribution system. The traffic manager must be aware of these impacts at a highly detailed level and advise top management of their effect to enable them to make intelligent decisions relating to the structure of the overall physical distribution system.

Cost Trade-offs Within the Physical Distribution System

As stated earlier, the physical distribution management concept is often referred to as a prime example of the application of the systems concept. Specifically, as physical distribution managers attempt to minimize the overall cost of distribution, subject to customer service constraints, they must carefully consider a wide variety of cost trade-offs among the elements of the system. Many of these types of cost trade-offs were suggested in the preceding section. This section provides two examples of how these trade-offs might be analyzed in attempting to achieve cost minimization.

The Basic EOQ Model

The classic example of application of the systems approach to physical distribution management is that of determination of an economic order quantity (EOQ). In determining an EOQ, the manager seeks to define the optimal order size related to a particular product with a known annual demand that will in turn minimize total inventory cost. In effect, the manager tries to balance the costs related to product ordering, which will increase as more orders are placed and smaller quantities are ordered each time, and those related to carrying inventory, which will increase as the number of orders decreases and the average amount on hand increases.

Ordering costs include such things as the cost of clerical effort required to place an order and to handle the goods upon their receipt. Order carrying costs include costs related to warehouse maintenance and the cost of money invested in inventory, among other things. The trade-offs between these two types of costs are shown graphically in Figure 24.3, which plots ordering costs, carrying costs, and total inventory costs against order size. Emphasis on either of the factors that make up the total cost curve in isolation will result in a suboptimal total cost for the system. At one extreme, a single order per year will minimize ordering costs while maximizing inventory carrying costs. Similarly, not ordering until a sale has been made would minimize inventory carrying costs while maximizing ordering costs. As is apparent from the example presented in Figure 24.3, neither result is likely to be optimal from a systems perspective.

Figure 24.3 Graphical Presentation of Economic Order Quantity (EOQ) Cost Trade-offs

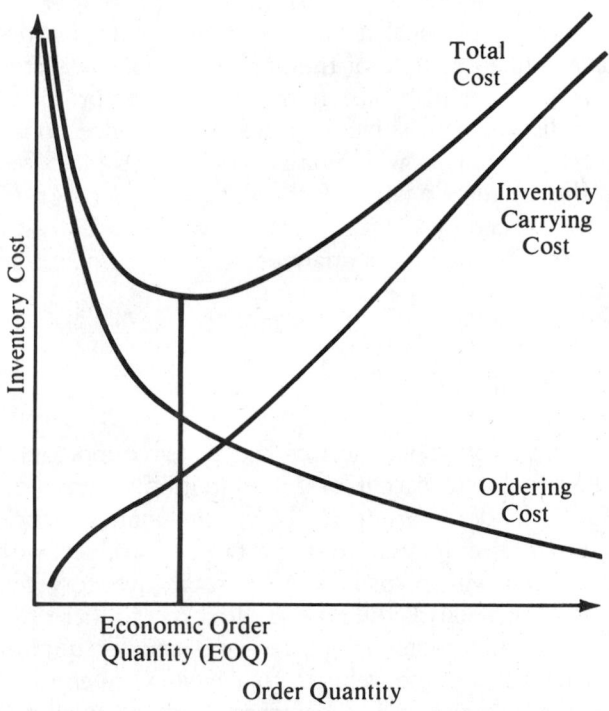

The Modal Choice Decision

Another example, broader in scope, demonstrates how transportation mode selection can affect the relative cost of each element of the distribution system. In this instance, it is assumed that the physical distribution manager, with advice from the traffic manager, is considering selection of either rail or motor carrier transportation to support the continuing movement of a specific product. If this decision were to be made on the basis of transportation cost alone, as shown in Figure 24.4, the rail carrier should be selected.

However, if the systems approach is used and the different operating characteristics of rail and motor carriage and their respective effects on the other four elements of the distribution package are considered, another decision might be reached. Since railroad transportation is often slower and less reliable than truck transportation, the levels of safety stock associated with rail movement may be larger. In addition, since railroads are most suited to volume movements, the quantities shipped at one time may be larger, necessitating higher average inventory levels. Larger inventories will have an impact on the company's warehousing needs, increasing space requirements and costs associated with the particular product. Since rail movement is generally rougher than motor carrier movement, packaging costs may also increase as improvements required to protect the product during shipment are made. In addition, since the company may need to install a rail siding to facilitate rail shipments, the cost of materials handling may go up. In effect, every cost associated with the movement of this particular product, except direct transportation cost, will be higher if the product is shipped by rail. Indeed, as shown in Figure 24.4, a decision to use rail movement that seems appropriate to the traffic manager may prove to be inappropriate when viewed in a systems context.

Additional Applications

As applied in a physical distribution management setting, the systems concept involves careful analysis of the interrelationships among the five basic distribution elements. This analysis will usually involve the definition of cost trade-offs between the parts of the distribution system, as described in the examples presented above. Additional application areas are described here. First, in a decision to automate a warehouse facility, a company must weigh the added fixed costs related to materials handling operations through the use of mechanical equipment with high initial cost versus reductions in the labor costs associated with manual materials

Figure 24.4 Example of Use of the Systems Approach to the Modal Choice Decision

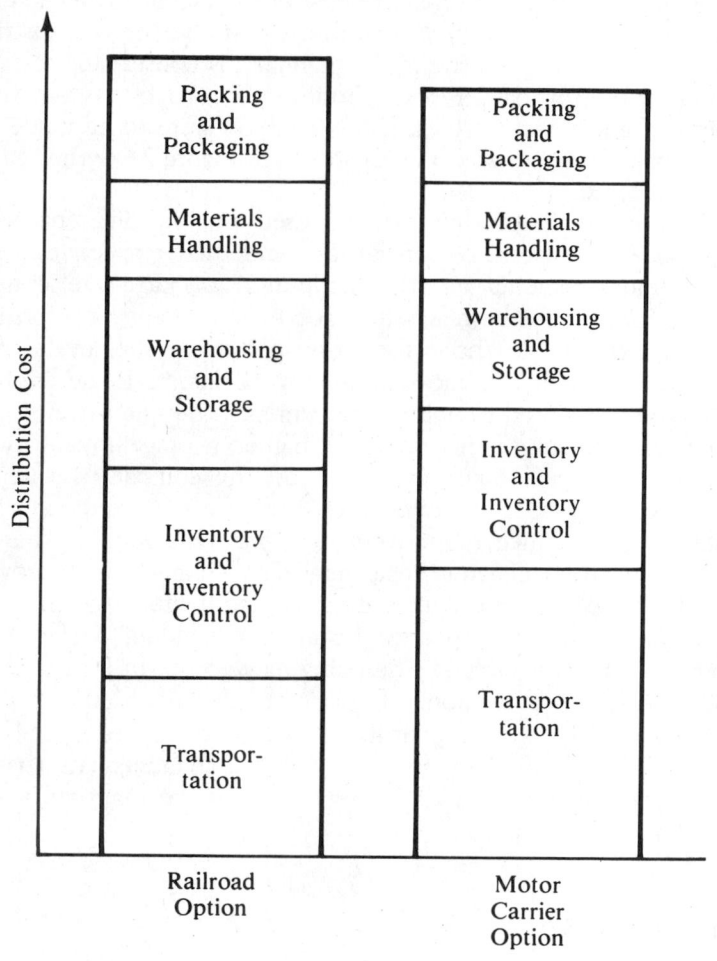

handling. Associated with these costs would be the need for increased product protection to withstand the added shocks inherent in mechanical handling. Similarly, a decision to establish a regional distribution center would increase overall product handling costs as added handlings are added between factory and consumer, but decrease line-haul transportation costs through shipment consolidation. In each case, the net cost of distribution must be reduced if the change in procedure or system structure is to be adopted.

Trade-offs are also involved in determining the level of service provided by a distribution system and the costs associated with provision of that service. This often entails consideration of a number of imponderables, since the relative value of any given level of service is often difficult (if not impossible) to determine quantitatively.

CUSTOMER SERVICE

The five distribution elements discussed so far in this chapter are most closely related to the physical movement and storage of products within the physical distribution system. The degree to which these elements satisfy the needs of a company's customers may be broadly defined as customer service. In this section, we will discuss the various attributes of customer service and how the traffic manager and transportation can influence a company's customer service level.

Elements of Customer Service

Customer service is made up of a number of attributes that relate the performance of a company's distribution system to customer satisfaction. Some of these attributes include the accuracy of orders received (were they filled properly?), the portion of an order filled from inventory (and therefore not backordered or just omitted from an order shipment), the proportion of goods that arrive in a damaged condition, the length of the order cycle (the time from customer placement of an order until the order is received by the customer), and the variability of order cycle time, among other things. Considering the scope of customer service attributes and their diverse nature, it is obvious that a single measure of overall customer service performance is not possible. The relative importance of each of the customer service attributes will vary with the level of competition a company faces, the nature of its products, and the value, to the customer, of individual shipments.

Transportation is one of the most important determinants of customer service. The loss and damage rate suffered during transit will be directly affected by the traffic manager's carrier selection decision and the quality of the advice the manager gives during the package design process. Order cycle time and variability will also be directly affected by mode and carrier selection.

The Order Cycle

The role of the traffic manager and transportation in determining customer service can be further highlighted by looking at the order cycle in greater depth. As Figure 24.5 shows, the order cycle is made up of four distinct phases. The first is order transmission, the process of getting an order from the customer into a company's distribution system. This may be accomplished through sales visits, telephone conversations, electronic data transmissions, or the postal service. Order processing, the second phase, includes such activities as order registration, product availability checks, pricing, invoice preparation, and customer credit checks. The third phase, the order filling process, consists of the warehousing or distribution center operations and involves picking the required products from stock, preparing the order for line-haul shipment, and preparing required shipping documents, such as bills of lading. The last phase involves the actual shipment of the order to the customer.

Figure 24.5 Elements of the Order Cycle

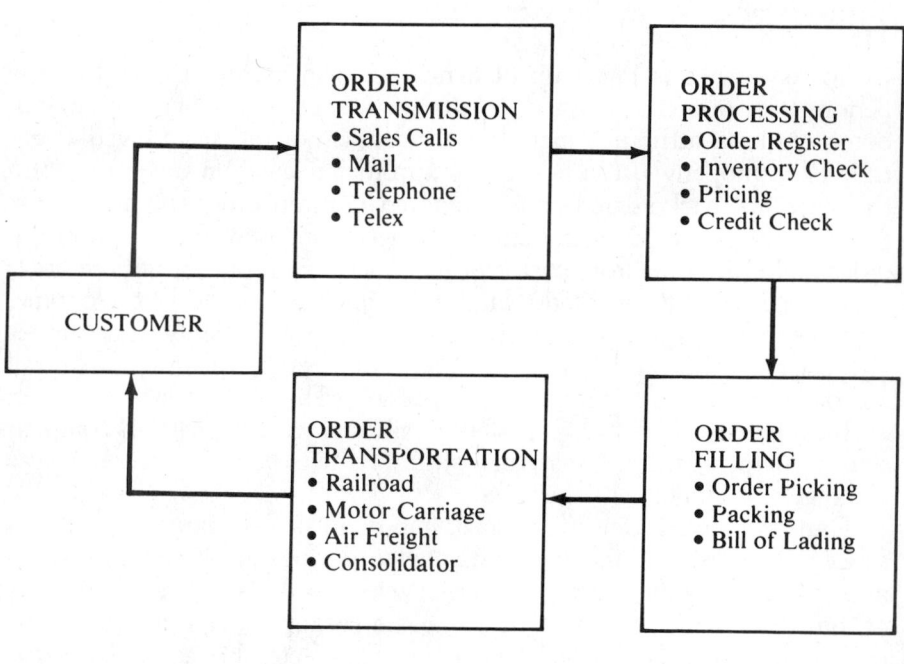

As stated earlier, the transportation decision will directly influence overall order cycle time and variability. In addition, the transportation decision will affect the design of the remaining order cycle elements. For example, similar overall order cycles could be accomplished through automated order transmission and processing and the use of rail transportation, or through the use of motor carrier transportation and slower order transmission systems, such as mail order or manual internal order processing.

THE NEW LOGISTICS ENVIRONMENT

As the operations of many companies have become more complex, with international operations and greater expansion of product lines to meet the needs of specialty markets, the traditional environment of physical distribution or logistics management has been expanded. This expansion is seen in the adoption of a total firm approach to logistics and is sometimes referred to as neo-logistics. In effect, this approach fully embraces the systems concept underlying the basic logistics function and applies it to all aspects of goods and materials flow from raw materials source through processing to delivery to the ultimate consumer. This expands the depiction of the physical distribution process shown in Figure 24.1 to the broader concept depicted in Figure 24.6. In this expanded view, the logistics manager is also interested in many aspects of purchasing and materials management and production and operations management.

We need to review the nature of many businesses in the 1990s to see why these changes have occurred. Firms have become larger. Their product lines proliferate. They operate in international markets. In effect, they have become more complicated, and these complications have made logistics practice more difficult. For example, many domestic firms have developed truly international operating environments through the incorporation of offshore manufacturing operations. This complicates the movement of goods and materials because basic parts, such as computer chips, may be produced in the United States, shipped to be joined with other parts and converted to subassemblies in one country, further processed in a second, and returned to the United States for final assembly. Finally, the finished goods may be shipped to international markets for sale. That this is economically feasible is a tribute to the quality and efficiency of the international transportation system. The trade-offs involved in such operations are a prime example of the role of transportation in facilitating geographic division of labor and specialization, as discussed in Chapter 9.

Figure 24.6 The Total Firm Approach to Logistics

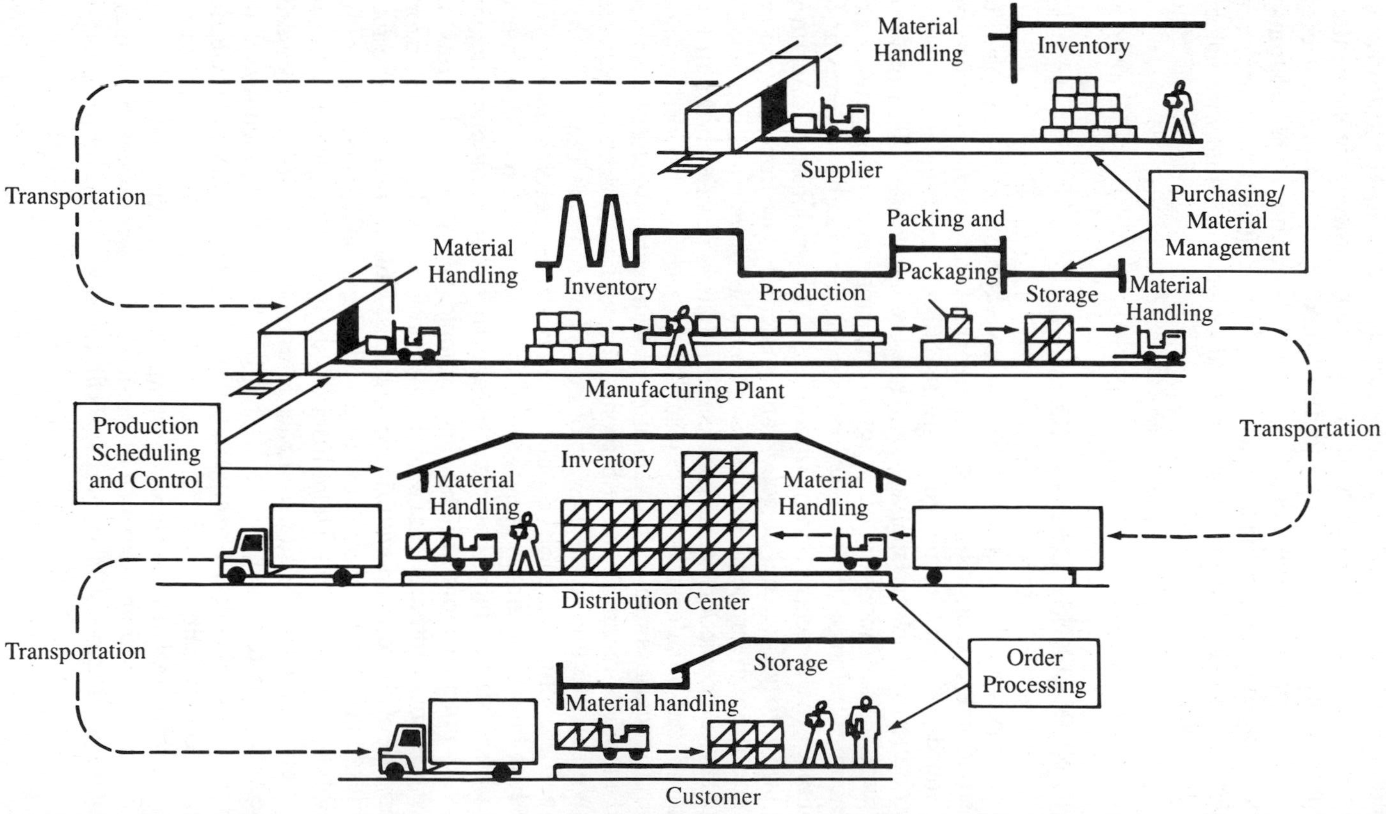

In the evolution of this new, total firm approach to managing the flow of goods, we have seen the role of the traffic manager evolve from responsibility solely for managing the shipper-carrier interface to the physical distribution manager's responsibility for a wide range of activities related to the movement of goods from production facility to the consumer. At the same time changes were taking place on the supply side, the movement of goods from material source to the manufacturing facility. In this instance, the traffic manager's counterpart, the purchasing manager, was also evolving from technician to manager. The new type of manager, often referred to as a materials manager, has influence over decisions involving many of the same elements as addressed by the physical distribution manager, including inventory and inventory control, warehousing and storage, packing and packaging, materials handling, and transportation. The materials manager uses many of the same tools as the physical distribution manager but views the flow of goods from a different perspective.

The similarities in techniques used for analysis and the ability to tie inbound and outbound traffic flow together have resulted in significant savings in some cases where vehicle movements have been coordinated, reducing empty backhauls for both private fleets and commercial carriers. (It should be noted that this will not reduce empty backhauls to zero. In many cases, different types of equipments are required for moving raw materials and subassemblies than for moving finished products. Also, even if similar vehicles are used, finished products often require more cubic capacity than the inbound materials. An example would be inbound movement of flat steel sheets that are later formed into washing machine shells.) One major change has involved increased interest in the transportation costs associated with inbound traffic movement. Firms are finding that major cost savings are available if they control inbound transportation rather than allow suppliers to control this function, as when a firm purchases goods f.o.b. delivered.

The common thread to all parts of the logistics process is inventory and inventory control. The most current trends have involved emulation of the Japanese in adoption of so-called just-in-time manufacturing techniques. The goal of these techniques is to significantly reduce the amount of inventory throughout the supply and manufacturing system. For just-in-time techniques to be successfully implemented, the firm must have reliable sources of supply and in turn be supported by reliable transportation carriers. While sizable cost savings are available from the inventory reductions usually associated with just-in-time techniques, there are risks involved. In many cases a systems breakdown will involve costs related to emergency shipments or production runs and payment for idle workers when parts are not available. An in-depth discussion of just-in-time techniques and their advantages and disadvantages is beyond the scope of this book. It is important, however, that the transportation student realize what this has done to the way logistics practitioners view their environment.

The horizons of the productions and operations manager have similarly been expanded by changes in the nature of the operating environment. For our purposes, these changes are important only as they relate to logistics. Much like the materials manager, the production manager is interested in inventories. In the physical flow chain, production is the source for the physical distribution manager and the ultimate customer for the materials manager. Therefore, production scheduling affects both the availability of goods for distribution and requirements for materials from the supply chain. To reduce inventories throughout the system requires careful coordination of activities across all logistics-related areas. In addition, plant location decisions require input from traffic and purchasing managers on customer and supply source locations and the transportation costs related to materials and finished goods movement.

SUMMARY

In this chapter we have seen how the concerns of the traffic manager have been expanded to encompass more than just transportation. In adapting the systems concept to distribution, the traffic manager became the physical distribution manager, dealing with trade-offs between the cost of transportation, inventory and inventory control, warehousing and storage, packing and packaging, and materials handling. In addition, the physical distribution manager must consider the customer service aspects of distribution, providing service that will enhance the image of the firm while at the same time controlling distribution costs. Firms are now looking at an expansion of this concept to reflect all aspects of the physical flow of goods through the firm, embodying a total firm approach to logistics.

ADDITIONAL READINGS

Ballou, Ronald H., *Business Logistics Management: Planning and Control*, 2nd ed., Englewood Cliffs, N.J.: Prentice-Hall, Inc., 1985.
Chapter 1, "Business Logistics — A Vital Subject," pp. 1–24.
Chapter 2, "Logistics Decision Making — An Overview," pp. 25–51.

Bowersox, Donald J., David J. Closs, and Omar K. Helferich, *Logistical Management,* New York: Macmillan Publishing Co., 1986.
  Chapter 2, "Logistical Strategy and Decision Processes," pp. 34–69.
  Chapter 9, "Foundations of Logistical Policy," pp. 267–302.
Hutchinson, Norman E., *An Integral Approach to Logistics,* Englewood Cliffs, N.J.: Prentice-Hall, Inc., 1987.
  Chapter 1, "Logistics and Management," pp. 1–13.
  Chapter 2, "The Elements of Logistics," pp. 14–27.
  Chapter 3, "An Integration of Logistics," pp. 28–45.
Johnson, James C., and Donald F. Wood, *Contemporary Physical Distribution and Logistics,* 3rd ed., New York: Macmillan Publishing Co., 1986.
  Chapter 2, "Physical Distribution and Logistics: Interfaces within the Firm," pp. 35–64.
  Chapter 3, "Customer Service and the Order Cycle," pp. 67–99.
Mentzer, John T., and Allan D. Schuster, "Computer Modelling in Logistics: Existing Models and Future Outlook," *Journal of Business Logistics,* 3, No. 1 (1982), Special Supplement, 1–55.
Poist, Richard F., "Evolution of Conceptual Approaches to Designing Business Logistics Systems," *Transportation Journal,* 26, No. 1 (Fall 1986), 55–64.
Poist, Richard F., "Evolution of Conceptual Approaches to the Design of Logistics Systems: A Sequel," *Transportation Journal,* 28, No. 1 (Spring 1989), pp. 35–39.
Stock, James R., and Douglas M. Lambert, *Strategic Physical Distribution Management,* 2nd ed., Homewood, Ill.: Richard D. Irwin, 1982.
  Chapter 2, "The Integrated Logistics Management Concept," pp. 38–69.
  Chapter 4, "Customer Service," pp. 112–69.
Taff, Charles A., *Management of Physical Distribution and Transportation,* 7th ed., Homewood, Ill.: Richard D. Irwin, 1984.
  Chapter 6, "Inventory Control" pp. 143–73.
  Chapter 7, "Warehousing Management," pp. 175–97.
  Chapter 10, "Industrial Packaging," pp. 261–76.
  Chapter 11, "Material Handling," pp. 277–92.

CHAPTER 25

LOGISTICS INTERFACES

In the last chapter we dealt with the coming of age of logistics management. Even in this new environment, the traffic manager remains an important player in logistics operations. In addition to an operational role as the contract point between the shipper and carrier, the traffic manager provides critical input for many nonroutine company decisions. In this chapter we examine the advisory role of the traffic manager in making nonroutine decisions requiring capital expenditures and in managing international transportation. We also examine the concept of third-party logistics and the management tools required for success in logistics.

TRAFFIC MANAGER ADVICE ON
CAPITAL EXPENDITURE DECISIONS

In continuing to define the traffic manager's advisory function, those nonroutine decisions that call for major capital expenditures should be emphasized. Such decisions are usually made by top management, who should call upon the traffic manager for advice in those matters involving transportation. Lack of consideration of the transportation implications of proposed actions can result in costly mistakes that the firm, because of the extended life of most major capital expenditure projects, may have to live with over a long period of time.

One type of investment or capital expenditure decision in which the traffic manager's advice would be pertinent is the choice between private and for-hire transportation services. Another might be containerization and, often related to this, the type of intraplant materials handling equipment used. The transportation advantages or disadvantages of proposed or existing warehouses or branch plants would be still another area involving transportation, as would some types of product innovations. Other situations might be added to this list, but these are important and fairly typical top-management problems closely related to the traffic management function.

Decisions on Transportation
Equipment Expenditures

Sometimes a shipper's choice of a carrier will be largely determined by its peculiar problems such as service needs and location. Often, however, situations may exist in which choices must be made among common, contract, or private carriage, or even some combination of these legal forms, as well as among for-hire carriers.

Contract carriage may offer an acceptable alternative to common carriage both in costs and services in some situations. Contract-carrier rates often (although not always, by any means) are lower than common-carrier rates for comparable shipments. Further, by its very nature, contract carriage is a specialized service geared to the individual needs of its particular customer or a few customers. But contract carriers must be assured of a sufficient volume of traffic to make it profitable for them to operate and often must have a backhaul from some source. It usually is not profitable to operate a transportation business that moves goods in only one direction (except oil pipelines, of course).

The alternative to contract carriage for those who are not satisfied with common-carrier services or rates is to go into private carriage. Many firms have done this, especially in motor carriage.

Private Truck Carriage

It is estimated that around 15 percent of all intercity freight in this country and around two-thirds of truck ton-mileage move by private transportation. More than 90 percent of the nation's truck fleet is owned by private shippers. The trend toward private truck transportation has been upward since World War II, but appears to have accelerated during recent years. Various factors, all basically growing out of dissatisfaction with existing for-hire carrier services or prices, account for this trend.

Transportation costs certainly are an important factor in the switch to private carriage. Private trucking costs, particularly on shorter and intermediate-length hauls, often are demonstrably lower than common or contract truck carriage or even rail-carrier rates. In addition, as shipments are handled and transported only by the shipper's own employees, loss and damage (and sometimes packaging expenses) may be less than in for-hire carriage.

Private truck operators have some distinct cost advantages over for-hire operators. They are not obliged to maintain excess capacity. Instead, they may maintain only enough equipment for their normal traffic needs and turn to common carriers for the transport of unusually heavy or peak volumes. Also, they may use their own equipment for hauling merchandise subject to high freight rates, leaving the lower rated, less profitable traffic for common carriers. Further, they usually do not incur the economic regulatory expense incident to for-hire carriage and may be able to make more efficient use of their labor and operate with lower wage scales than can for-hire carriers. And of course they obtain the transportation profits (if any) that otherwise would go to for-hire operators.

A principal cost disadvantage of private truck carriage is the backhaul problem mentioned in connection with contract carriage. Some shippers are able to route and schedule their outgoing trucks in such a manner that inbound supplies and materials can be brought in on the return trip. Others have resorted to legally questionable gray areas, if not outright illegal devices, such as buying and selling merchandise not related to their primary business in order to avoid "dead-heading." Without some such arrangement, it is often difficult to justify private truck carriage on a strict cost basis. However, since the *Toto* decision in 1978, it has been possible for private carriers to obtain common-carrier backhaul authority. In addition, the opportunities for intercorporate hauling, where one corporate subsidiary hauls goods for another for a fee, have been enhanced by provisions of the Motor Carrier Act of 1980. Both of these changes have helped some private carriers relieve their empty backhaul problems.

It is also possible that a firm whose principal business is manufacturing, processing, or merchandising may not be able to operate transportation equipment as efficiently as a for-hire carrier, even under physically similar conditions. One gains expertise or know-how by specialization. More important, the manufacturer, considering transportation a sideline to the firm's major interest, may thus run a loose operation. A for-hire carrier, on the other hand, relying only on transportation profits, would be highly motivated to watch costs and improve operating efficiency.

It is probable that service factors are more important than potential cost savings in most shippers' decisions to go private. Common carriers are geared to the needs of a wide and diversified shipping public rather than to the special needs of an individual shipper. Customers often want faster delivery, fewer delays, and different delivery schedules than are available by common carrier between a particular shipper and customer. Thus, in order to remain competitive with other shippers who can and will better please customers, a firm may be forced to abandon common carriage even at the expense of some additional transport cost.

The traffic manager will seldom be in a position to make the final decision on changing from for-hire to private carriage. This involves capital expenditures as well as changes in the firm's operating patterns and costs. Such decisions properly are made at higher levels. Suggestions or recommendations for changes sometimes come from the traffic department, but probably most often originate from sales personnel.

In presenting top management with comparative estimates of costs and services of for-hire versus private transport, the traffic manager obviously is the company's expert, but may have to conduct detailed cost studies. In addition to line-haul operating costs and labor costs, fixed terminal expenses, additional administrative expenses, and depreciation on equipment must be calculated. It is easy to make overly optimistic estimates of the costs of private carriage as many firms have discovered too late.

Although many average cost figures are published, it is preferable to make cost studies in the context of a particular firm's operating environment and peculiarities. Trucking costs vary widely in different sections of the country because of differing labor, fuel, and taxation costs and different operating conditions. They also vary even within the same locality depending upon the type of equipment used, the commodity hauled, and the length of haul.

When the best possible cost estimates have been developed, these can be weighed against the estimated service advantages of private transport. Even then, however, a firm may have alternatives other than private transport. The mere threat of private carriage may be enough to cause for-hire carriers to change their rates and services in ways beneficial to the firm in question. This alternative should always be explored and called to top management's attention.

Finally, some attention should be given to the broader implications of private versus common carriage. The distribution system upon which much of our economy depends is serviced mainly by common carriers. A large number of shippers cannot possibly rely entirely or even in considerable part on private transportation. It is essential for these shippers and for the general public that our strong common-carrier system be maintained.

Insofar as an overextension of private transportation does tend to erode the overall strength of our established distribution system, it cannot be considered to be completely in the public interest. One cannot and should not expect a firm in a profit-oriented society to neglect its own interest in favor of some ill-defined public interest concept. One should expect responsible management to consider this along with other pertinent factors; and such consideration need not be completely altruistic. If its own industry or the economy as a whole suffers, an individual firm is not likely to prosper.

Interestingly, one of the outcomes of the trend toward transportation deregulation may be a move away from private carriage in some sectors. This movement would be the result of increased competition among for-hire carriers that could bring price and service packages in line with the perceived benefits of private carriage in many cases. This could be the case especially as more nonunion carriers compete for the type of steady, high-volume business usually associated with private intercity carriage.

Other Private Transportation Equipment

Many large private shippers, as well as the armed forces, own railroad cars or lease cars from independent car-owning companies. These cars usually are of specialized design to handle some particular type of commodity (as petroleum products, chemicals, fresh or frozen fruits and vegetables, meat, etc.). They usually are assigned to the use of the owning or leasing shipper, who pays regular rail freight rates. The car owner, however, receives a mileage allowance (as specified in the applicable tariffs) from the railroads over whose lines the cars move.

Shippers by water often own all or a large part of their required transportation equipment. Many oil companies also, in effect, rely upon private pipeline transport although legally their pipeline operations may be classed as common carriage. There is as yet very little private transportation of freight by air.

The advantages and disadvantages of private transportation or private equipment ownership in these other modes are similar in nature to the advantages and disadvantages of private truck ownership: the shipper may benefit from having the type of equipment most suited for its needs available when it wants it and may possibly (but not always) obtain better service or ship at lower costs. Likewise, the traffic manager's advisory role is to point out to top management the comparative cost and service features of the various alternatives.

Warehousing and Warehouse Location

Many persons still think of warehouses as being primarily places of static storage such as basement corners, garages, and attics. Except for such facilities as grain elevators, tank farms, or dockside warehouses, that are located adjacent to line-haul transportation facilities, the layperson seldom views warehousing as a vital part of our distribution system designed both to improve customer services and reduce transportation costs. Shippers may engage in private warehousing operations by owning or leasing space. Or they may rely upon for-hire public warehouses whose business is storage and related services.

Kinds of Warehouses

Public warehouses have a legal status similar to that of privately owned public utilities and are actually regulated as public utilities by some state regulatory commissions. In addition to storage and protective services, they may provide a variety of services associated with distribution. They are open to everyone at established tariff charges or negotiated charges.

All public warehouses are subject to the Uniform Warehouse Receipts Act. Two kinds of warehouse receipts, negotiable and nonnegotiable, may be issued for goods stored in public warehouses. These receipts might be compared to order and straight bills of lading; that is, the nonnegotiable receipt permits delivery only to a specified person or firm, whereas the negotiable receipt permits delivery to the bearer or to the holder of the properly endorsed document. Negotiable warehouse receipts are used both in selling stored goods and in obtaining loans on them. The buyer or lender is protected in that the receipt issued by the warehouse guarantees that the goods are in its custody and will be surrendered to (and only to) the person holding the receipt.

Field or custodian warehousing is a hybrid between the private and public varieties. It permits the issuance of negotiable warehouse receipts covering goods stored on private premises. These goods, even though stored in the owner's building, must actually be in the custody of a public warehouse. In effect, it is public warehousing brought to the owner's place of business. An owner who wishes to borrow against stored goods may use this device rather than incurring the expenses of physically moving the goods into a public warehouse.

Warehousing Costs

Warehousing costs, either private or public, may be quite high. They include capital and operating costs for the facilities as well as administrative and clerical costs. In addition, there are substantial costs involved in holding inventories. Working capital is tied up in stored merchandise; and in addition to physical handling costs, the merchandise may be subject to taxation, spoilage, breakage, theft, and obsolescence. Insurance protection must be provided. It is generally believed that the average annual costs of holding inventories may be as much as 20 to 25 percent of the value of the goods held.

Faced with such costs and with the trend toward lower inventories on the part of retailers, it is not surprising that producers and intermediate distributors actively seek lower cost alternatives. One such alternative is the substitution of faster and higher priced transportation; warehousing and inventory costs are traded off against transportation costs until some optimum balance minimizes total physical distribution costs. This optimum must take into account the quality of customer service.

Many firms during recent years have made substantial cost reductions by eliminating or reducing the number of their regional distribution warehouses, and thus reducing their inventories. To maintain prompt and reliable customer services, premium transportation such as air carriage is provided from a central warehouse or from only a few locations. The great reductions in inventory holding and warehousing costs much more than offset the consequent increases in transport costs.

Various large firms have reported spectacular savings with no deterioration in customer services, or even improved services, by such actions. Others have found that cost savings were not as great as anticipated, or that customer services and relationships suffered, or both, under centralized distribution. Every firm is an individual. Methods that work well for one may be very unsatisfactory for another. Careful studies of costs and service factors and consideration of the implications of changed methods for other functional areas of the firm should precede any decision to shift from decentralized to centralized distribution or vice versa.

The Traffic Manager's Role in Warehouse Location

Three basic types of questions arise in connection with the location of warehousing facilities. First, are existing services necessary and adequate? Should they be expanded, reduced, or maintained at approximately the present levels? Second, are new warehouses needed? And third, if new warehouses are needed, where should they be located? A related subsidiary question is whether the facilities should be private, public, or field warehousing.

Decisions to change existing warehousing methods may significantly affect all phases of a firm's activities. In addition to customer relations, marketing, transportation, and production operations are involved. The firm's capital structure may be changed, thus calling for different financing methods. Different administrative, inventory handling and control, clerical, accounting, personnel, and labor relations problems may arise. Quite clearly those officials responsible for all these and any other affected activities should be consulted by top management before a decision is reached.

The traffic manager's responsibility is to determine and report the transportation costs and available or obtainable transportation services associated with all the various alternative methods and locations under consideration. Top management, then, must consider these transportation factors alongside other advantages and disadvantages of the proposed action. Transportation sometimes is an important determinant in the final decision, sometimes not. It does establish limits or boundaries within which the decision must be made.

In the precomputer era, calculating the comparative transportation advantages and disadvantages of even a few alternative locations was a difficult or impossible task. The number of variables that can be handled by mechanical calculation is fairly limited. Today, however, masses of information can be fed into computers and answers received in short order. In fact, not only transportation data but all kinds of pertinent information may be computerized, thus making it possible to pinpoint the preferable locations with an accuracy undreamed of a few years ago.

The computer does not make traffic experts or any other functional experts obsolete, however. Instead, it increases their usefulness. If incomplete or incorrect information is fed in, computer-based decisions can lead to horrendous mistakes. The computer clan has a favorite expression, *gigo*, meaning "garbage in, garbage out." In developing information for locational or any other types of decisions, the traffic manager must attempt to include all pertinent transportation data in a correct form. The computer must be asked the right questions and given the right information before it can give the right answers.

Traffic Management and Plant Location

Whether or not additional plants should be established and where they should be built are other top management decisions requiring transportation advice. Location theory and some aspects of location practice as related to transportation have been discussed in Chapters 13 and 14. Most of the discussion of warehouse location in the preceding section is equally applicable to plant or branch plant location.

It is not necessary to repeat the foregoing discussions here. Instead, we mention plant location specifically to re-emphasize the importance of traffic management's advisory role in such decisions and to point out that its role and the procedures used are similar whether the locational problem concerns plant or warehouse facilities.

Traffic and Major Product Innovations

Making major product innovations without adequate consideration of transportation factors is as rash as ignoring transportation advice in reaching locational decisions or in deciding to expand marketing activities into new geographical areas. Top management, when considering a new product line, should never forget that transportation costs are a part of the buyer's price. Thus whether or not a given product can be sold in a particular area and how profitable its sale will be depend to some extent upon transportation costs.

Marketing research personnel who determine whether or not a demand exists or can be developed for a new product and engineering personnel who design the product cannot be expected to be knowledgeable on transportation matters. If left to follow their own inclinations, the new product's delivered costs may be unduly high. Traffic personnel, therefore, should be asked several questions about the proposed new item. For example, what mode of transportation is most suitable? Are adequate transportation facilities available into the proposed marketing areas, or if not, can they be obtained? What will be the level of the applicable freight rates, and can more favorable rates be negotiated? What are applicable freight rates on potentially competitive products? What are the proposed product's loss and damage characteristics and packaging requirements? Are special carrier services needed, and if so, can they be obtained? And at what costs?

The above transportation questions that should be asked about a product innovation are merely suggestive rather than complete. A responsible traffic manager will not be content to answer only the questions that are asked by top management or by others concerned with the decision. Others may not know which questions to ask. It is the traffic manager's duty to raise all the relevant questions and to provide their answers.

Many instances could be cited in which minor design or packaging changes suggested by traffic managers have greatly reduced transportation costs or in which traffic management's knowledge of service limitations have prevented serious mistakes. For example, the removal of clothes dryer handles during shipment can reduce potential damage at this time that, while minor, could cause customer dissatisfaction after purchase. In addition, the traffic manager may be able to suggest changes that make the product easier to ship. If a large product can be designed in such a way as to facilitate its shipment in modules, the difficulty and expense associated with the movement of oversized shipments may be avoided. One could cite an equally large number of examples of firms that have experienced difficulties through failures to seek proper traffic advice.

Electronic Data Processing

Electronic data processing is becoming more and more essential in developing information for management control. This is as true in traffic management as in other functional areas. In traffic control, electronic data processing has proven to be particularly useful in the preparation and updating of rate and route sheets, in analyzing the comparative costs of movements by different modes, routes, and carriers, and in determining the best locations (from a transportation viewpoint) of branch plants and warehouses. In addition, electronic data processing can be used to increase the speed and accuracy of various routine clerical functions such as freight-bill auditing. Some attempts are being made to reduce complex tariffs to computerized form, thus eliminating traditional rate clerk functions and making rate quotation more reliable and rapid.

Electronic data processing is here to stay. As technology advances and more traffic-oriented software becomes available, reduced prices for tremendous computer capability and competition in general are making it essential that electronic data processing techniques be routinely used in traffic control. This is not to say that traffic managers must become experts in computer programming and operation. This is a technical field in itself. Rather, every traffic manager worthy of the name should be familiar with what a computer can do (and equally important, what it cannot do) in order to improve the firm's traffic control performance and to be able to advise top management both on the results of computer studies and on the traffic department's needs for electronic data processing facilities and support.

Another aspect of enhanced electronic data processing is the capability for direct data input and electronic data interchange. Direct computer input of data required to generate shipping documents provides the opportunity for significant cost savings and enhanced data capture for evaluation of traffic operations. Direct entry means that data could be transmitted directly to customers, suppliers, or carriers, reducing transaction times significantly and potentially reducing clerical costs for all concerned. In addition, such tools can be used to greatly improve inventory control. We all can see this at merchandising operations where scanners are used at checkout counters. These devices not only provide for accurate pricing at the point of sale but also can be used to automatically track sales and, therefore, inventory levels.

MANAGING INTERNATIONAL TRANSPORTATION

This book is primarily concerned with domestic transportation. More and more American firms, however, are becoming involved in international distribution as exporters, importers, or both. Frequently, traffic departments in such firms are called upon to handle transportation and related matters for international freight movements. And just as frequently, traffic department personnel find that international transportation occurs in a very different institutional environment than domestic transportation (see Chapter 6). The domestic traffic manager's expertise is not useless, but it must be supplemented considerably for international distribution management.

The principal differences between domestic and international distribution, insofar as traffic department responsibilities are concerned, occur in the areas of documentation, rates, and carriers' liabilities for lost or damaged merchandise. We cannot go deeply into these differences; this would require a separate and lengthy treatise. But we can at least mention the general natures of the problems involved.

Documentation

The numbers and complexities of documents required in international trade and transportation are much greater than for domestic purposes. In addition to the documents required by buyers, sellers, and domestic carriers, additional documents are necessary for the governments of the origin and destination countries, for port authorities, for international carriers, and for financial organizations (for payment purposes) in both countries. Often as many as forty separate documents, many with multiple copies, are necessary for a single international shipment.

Freight Rates

Through freight rates from an interior point in one country to an interior point in another country still are hard to find. Normally, a foreign buyer takes delivery at the entry point in its own country and arranges for whatever further domestic transport is necessary. Thus the seller arranges domestic transportation to its own country's point of exit and from there to the foreign entry point.

In the United States (and some other countries), though, freight rates for goods destined for export, or received from abroad, sometimes are lower than the applicable rates for similar goods moving over the same routes in domestic trade. Demurrage conditions also may be different.

Steamships usually quote rates on a weight or space basis, at the carrier's option. Most steamships moving breakbulk goods are members of conferences which establish uniform rates for various trades. Shippers who sign agreements with these conferences can obtain rates lower than those available to nonconference shippers. It should be noted that quoted steamship tariff rates may not include various kinds of terminal charges and transportation surcharges, which must be determined separately.

Bulk shippers may resort to the international ship charter market and charter a steamship for a particular voyage or for a specified period of time. Many kinds of charter contracts are used. Charter rates are not set by conferences but by the prevailing conditions of international supply and demand. Sometimes they fluctuate greatly.

Carrier Liability

Export goods usually require considerably different packaging, packing, and marking than do domestic shipments. This is to facilitate handling and distribution in foreign lands as well as for protective purposes. But despite better protective packaging, loss and damage in international shipments often are quite high.

Unlike domestic carriers, international carriers are not held to a high degree of liability for losses and damage. In addition to the usual common-carrier exemptions from liability, for example, steamships are not liable for losses caused by fires, storms, shipwrecks, piracy, or errors of navigation and management. In fact, if a seaworthy vessel is provided, they have very little liability — and if they are legally liable, the maximum recoverable amount usually is quite small. International air carriers are subject to more liability than ocean carriers, but less than domestic carriers.

This means that goods moving in international trade, either by water or by air, must be insured by the seller. Customarily, at least in ocean transportation, sellers receive their payment from local financial institutions once goods are aboard a vessel in good order and have started their journey. But such advance payments will be made only if an insurance contract is part of the surrendered documentation (along with an invoice, an "on-board" bill of lading, and whatever other special documents are required for the movement).

Assistance for International Movements

Every major seaport has a complex of organizations — international departments of banks, customhouse brokers, export merchants and commission houses, export managers and agents, ship chartering brokers, marine insurance offices, international freight forwarders, and the like — who are prepared to assist export sellers in any or all aspects of foreign trade and transportation for a fee. Many beginning exporters, at least until they become familiar with the procedures involved, rely wholly upon international freight forwarders to handle all aspects of their transactions. About 1,000 of these forwarders are registered with the Federal Maritime Commission.

Assistance and helpful advice also are available from United States government sources, particularly from the Department of Commerce and the Department of Transportation.

THIRD-PARTY LOGISTICS

An interesting current trend in logistics is the use of third-party agencies to perform many traditional in-house logistics functions. These agencies, in many cases consulting arms or separate operating divisions of carrier-oriented firms, provide the expertise and facilities required to fill a wide range of logistics needs for their customers. In many cases this contract service permits the customer to reduce its logistics infrastructure significantly, freeing needed funds for other purposes.

This is not a totally new concept; public warehousing has long been used to augment storage space in distribution operations. However, this new trend goes far beyond the type of relationship normally associated with public warehousing. The contract agency, in many cases, provides virtually all required logistics services, from storage to inventory control to carrier selection. The contract agency may have greater expertise in an area still viewed by many companies as a secondary or tertiary activity, and therefore may be able to provide better, more efficient service. This is especially true for many smaller companies that are highly operations oriented and may not have the resources required to put together the critical mass of staff expertise, traffic volume, and efficient facilities required to be cost effective.

While there are significant benefits to be gained from contracting for logistics services, the firm must take the same care in making this decision as in making any other logistics decision — determining that the benefits accrued, including cost savings, exceed the cost of the service (as opposed to just removing an operations element requiring an already overworked management's attention). In addition, the contract agency must be willing to absorb a portion of the risks involved. In effect, the costs related to the provision of the service should be tied to the amount of traffic handled and not based on a totally fixed fee.

The trend is toward longer-term contractual arrangements in third-party logistics agreements. These arrangements, perhaps up to five years in length, permit the development of well-defined relationships between the service provider and the customer. Such commitments often are required to fully understand the customer needs and to put in place an infrastructure that will best meet the needs of those customers. From the perspective of the purchaser of such services, the key element is the degree of management expertise the contractor can bring to the customer's logistics operations.

THE LOGISTICS CHALLENGE

Over the last four chapters we have examined the evolution of the shipper-carrier relationship, from the highly focused traffic management function of the early railroad era to the total enterprise approach at the leading edge of management today. Over this time, the skills needed by logistics practitioners to successfully meet the challenges of their environments have changed significantly. For example, the modern descendant of the traffic manager must have a deep understanding of all elements of the logistics function, in the broadest sense — how these elements are interrelated in a modern logistics environment, and how they relate to the enterprise as a whole. This requires stepping out from the compartmentalized approach of the original traffic manager to embrace all elements relating to the physical flow of goods and materials through the firm. This in turn requires an understanding of the purchasing and materials management and production and operations management functions as well as the traditional elements of transportation and physical distribution management.

In this environment, the logistics manager must develop a package of informational and analytical tools that can be applied to complex problems. These information tools include many aspects of modern information systems management, from data base development to use of the latest in communications equipment. Timely, accurate information is a major contributor to good decision making, especially in a volatile, highly competitive environment. Equally important is the ability to evaluate the data collected. As very high powered computers with virtually unlimited computational capacity become increasingly accessible, the ability to tackle what were impossible problems yesterday becomes more commonplace. The modern logistics manager knows what analytical tools are available and how they can be used to aid in decision making. These tools include such things as advanced statistical analysis techniques, management science or operations research methodologies, and sophisticated simulation techniques. While the individual manager does not need to be proficient in the use of these techniques, which are better left to the specialist, the manager does need to understand where they should be applied and what their limitations are.

Overriding all of this is a need to be able to think critically. This ability has become an educational and business "buzzword" in recent times, but that does not diminish the need for creative thinking. In effect, critical thinking means the ability to step back from a problem or situation and evaluate it without anticipating answers based on a past set of conventional practices. This is especially necessary in a complex, constantly changing environment. Much as the traffic manager has been forced to become a generalist as transportation has moved away from collective ratemaking and tight entry control, the logistics manager also has been forced to become a generalist. This has made logistics an even more challenging and rewarding career path for many students.

ADDITIONAL READINGS

Johnson, James C., and Donald F. Wood, *Contemporary Physical Distribution and Logistics*, 3rd ed., New York: Macmillan Publishing Co., 1986.
Chapter 11, "International Logistics," pp. 415–67.
Chapter 12, "Physical Distribution and Logistics System Analysis and Design," pp. 471–506.
Mentzer, John T., and Allan D. Schuster, "Computer Modelling in Logistics: Existing Models and Future Outlook," *Journal of Business Logistics*, 3, No. 1 (1982), Special Supplement, pp. 1–55.
Stock, James R., and Douglas M. Lambert, *Strategic Physical Distribution Management*, 2nd ed., Homewood, Ill.: Richard D. Irwin, 1987.
Chapter 16, "International Logistics," pp. 640–87.
Taff, Charles A., *Management of Physical Distribution and Transportation*, 7th ed., Homewood, Ill.: Richard D. Irwin, 1984.
Chapter 12, "Location Analysis," pp. 293–314.

PART VII

TRANSPORTATION PROBLEMS AND TRANSPORTATION POLICY

To this point in the text we have considered the role of domestic transportation in our economy, the economic characteristics and performance of the transportation system, the development of regulation/deregulation in transportation, the role of costs and rates, carrier management, and shipper management. Only two matters remain to be considered: transportation problems and policy, and the future of transportation as we see it. In the next four chapters we will note a few of the problems of transportation and the attempts to deal with these problems by way of transportation policy. All transportation problems cannot be discussed or even listed due to limited space. Some problems are local or regional in nature. Also, transportation problems tend to arise, cause some type of policy action, and be solved or at least diminished in importance over time if transportation policy is well thought out and implemented. We shall concentrate here on only three broad areas as illustrations of where transportation policy has developed. *Policy*, as we use the term here, means the policy established by Congress, interpreted by the courts, often proposed by the executive, and administered by commissions, boards, or agencies.

Even though we will be discussing primarily public policy and goals, it should be clear that there are many groups in our transportation economy with many different goals. Sometimes these goals conflict and sometimes not. When there is conflict between the goals of various groups, problems of policy arise. Congress, like any elective body, is responsive to these conflicts of goals.

It is possible to generalize about conflicting goals by looking at the groups that originate goals. For our purposes, we can delineate four groups whose goals affect transportation policy in varying degrees and are sometimes in conflict. These are carriers who supply the transportation; transportation labor, which is the largest component in the cost of that supply; shippers who demand and use transportation; and the general public. When we note in a general way the goals of each of these four groups, conflicts in policy become much clearer.

The maximization of profit is the general goal of carriers. Methods of increasing profit include the elimination of excess capacity and the best possible use of capital, the elimination of excess labor and the best possible use of personnel, and the elimination of any element of service not absolutely necessary to satisfy customers. Carriers wish to accomplish these cost-saving goals without reducing rates or decreasing revenues. Indeed, a complementary goal is to charge the highest possible price (rate) that regulation, competition, and the shippers will allow.

The goals of labor, on the other hand, are higher wages for the same or less work, a steady income, and better working conditions. Job security has become a very important goal of labor in recent times. Obviously, these goals conflict in varying degrees with carrier goals.

The shippers' goals are more service at less cost to themselves, and they desire more choice among firms and modes. For the shipper, dependable, reliable, on-time, and damage-free transportation service at the lowest possible cost is of importance. Again conflicts are evident.

The general public may or may not have the same goals as carriers, transportation labor, or shippers. Public goals are more general and sometimes are not easy to define. In general, the public is interested in a sound transportation system that is available as needed and is able to take care of all ordinary and most extraordinary demands (such as defense) placed upon it. Since performance of the transportation system is the test used by the general public, it desires the best possible service at the least possible price and with a high degree of protection for itself. Finally, within the general framework or structure of our economy, the general public is concerned with the structure of the transportation industry and apparently wishes to avoid monopoly exploitation and stimulate competition for its own sake.

The next four chapters will consider these various conflicts and goals and their implementation in some detail.

CHAPTER 26

TRANSPORTATION MARKET STRUCTURE

The structure of the transportation market is of some importance, since it directly affects the performance of the transportation system. In the discussion of economic characteristics and performance (Part II), the market structure of the railroads, airlines, trucklines, pipelines, inland water carriers, maritime carriers, and both public and private passenger carriers was noted. In Chapter 14, the consequences of deregulation for the market structure of the various modes was noted. Here we shall consider how market structure is affected by carrier unification and merger, carrier integration, and carrier diversification. Unification and integration have been going on since transportation firms were first created. Indeed, there is hardly a transportation firm or transportation system in existence today that did not come about by way of unification or integration. The previous discussion of regulation has shown that the public has long been concerned about the effects of unification and integration. Various regulations have been used from time to time to attempt to control or mitigate the effects of these actions. We will consider some of the public policy questions posed by unification and integration in the latter part of this chapter. For now it is sufficient to say that public policy has changed over time just as the whole structure of transportation regulation and the transportation market has changed.

DEFINITION OF TERMS

Before discussing unification and integration in detail, it may be desirable to review the meaning of these terms. Sometimes carrier unification and carrier integration are confused with carrier coordination and cooperation (which were discussed in Part V). The distinctions among these four terms rest on two factors — ownership and mode. The various combinations with an example of each are shown in Table 26.1.

    Carrier unification involves a common ownership on an intramodal basis. *Carrier integration*, on the other hand, involves common ownership of several modes of transportation by a single carrier firm. *Carrier coopera-tion* involves several separately owned carriers of the same mode cooper-ating by way of equipment interchange, public relations, and so forth. *Carrier coordination* involves two or more separately owned carriers in separate modes physically coordinating their services such as in piggyback service, container-on-flatcar service, and so forth. Carrier coordination and cooperation were discussed in Chapter 20 as part of carrier management. Here we are concerned solely with the matter of carrier ownership patterns.

Table 26.1 Carrier Unification, Integration, Coordination, and Cooperation

Term	Ownership	Mode	Example
Carrier unification	one	one	Carrier mergers
Carrier integration	one	many	Transportation company
Carrier coordination	separate	many	Piggyback service
Carrier cooperation	separate	one	Equipment interchange

A transportation company is an example of integration. This would be a single firm owning operating entities in all modes of transportation — rail, motor, water, air, and pipeline. Such a firm theoretically would allocate its traffic to the particular mode that could do the job in the cheapest or most profitable manner. If the movement produced the most profit when carried by truck, trucks would be used. If rail movement were more profitable, rails would get the traffic. Profitability to the firm would be the sole criterion for allocation. Some persons see this as an effective free-market answer to the problems of intermodal competition and the regulatory problems that arise from a competitive transportation market.

A partially integrated transportation firm would be one owning operat-ing entities in two or more (but not all) modes of transportation. Currently, many railroads have motor carrier subsidiaries, and a few railroads own pipelines, air freight forwarders, and surface freight forward-ers. One railroad owns an inland barge carrier and a maritime carrier. Several motor carriers own international air freight forwarders and surface freight forwarders. Several airlines own regional or local motor carriers. However, there are no fully integrated transport firms in this country.

Unification occurs when two firms of the same mode merge or consolidate. Railroad, truck line, and airline mergers or consolidations are current examples of transportation unification. (Legally there is a difference between merger and consolidation, but the economic effects are similar.)

The carrier's purpose in both unification and integration is to increase profits.

CARRIER GOALS LEADING TO CONFLICT

Since transportation is of such great importance to the whole economy, any change in the structure of the transportation industry has a wide impact. Conflict in goals is almost inevitable under such circumstances. As carriers attempt to adjust the transportation plant by unification or integration, conflicts arise with the goals of transportation labor, shippers, and the general public.

A main goal of carriers is to maximize profit. They are no different in this regard from any other business firm. Three avenues of approach are available for a firm wishing to maximize its profits. First, it may raise its prices (rates), depending on demand conditions, competition, and regulatory action. Second, it may reduce its costs in some way. Third, it may increase its demand and quantity of service sold.

Increasing rates will turn on the degree of competition that exists — both intermodal competition and intramodal competition. Ease of entry or lack thereof will also be a factor in the market structure. Shipper resistance and alternatives (such as private transportation — sometimes called "do-it-yourself" transportation) provide conflict with this approach.

Increased volume and cost reduction are not exclusive approaches to profit maximization. Both may be used simultaneously. A well-managed firm always wishes to control its costs. It can do this by carefully allocating the amount of labor and supplies used in its services and by economizing on its use of capital. However, if two firms combine in some way, additional economies may be possible. When two equal-sized firms merge and the new firm does twice the business of either of the previous firms, it does not follow that twice the labor, capital equipment, or supplies will be required. Economies and cost savings may be readily effected.

When transportation firms attempt unification or integration to gain the various economies, conflicts in goals may be sharp. Unification often means that some labor will no longer be needed. This conflicts with the goals of transportation labor. Unification often means that duplicating services are eliminated. Shippers have less choice and communities get less service, again creating conflicts. If excess labor is not utilized elsewhere in the economy, the public goal of full employment may be affected. Antitrust goals may also come into conflict with unification and integration of transportation firms. All these conflicts and others are triggered by carriers rationally seeking goals of profit maximization.

Unification and integration of carrier firms may also lead to gains. Gains to the carrier are obvious. There may also be gains to shippers, to transportation labor, and to the general public. This will depend to a great extent upon the methods and the effects of unification and integration.

METHODS AND PURPOSES OF UNIFICATION AND INTEGRATION

The carrier's purpose in unification or integration is to increase profit, as previously noted. These actions may affect profits in a number of specific ways, but these can be summarized under the categories of price increases (rate or fare), cost savings, or increased volume.

Rate or Fare Increases

Transportation carriers have always set their own prices (rates or fares). As noted in Part III (particularly Chapters 13 and 14 on the "pillars of regulation"), the regulatory authorities had the power to find a rate unreasonable or unduly discriminatory (preferential or prejudicial). In those cases, the ICC or CAB could specify what rate or fare was reasonable or what rate or fare was not discriminatory. In spite of the erroneous statements in the public press that "the ICC sets rates" or "the CAB determines fares," the carriers have always had broad powers to set their own rates or fares. Indeed, studies during the height of the regulatory era showed that only about 10 percent of rates were "set" by the ICC. Essentially, the carriers had the power to set their own prices and the board or commission had the power to review.

Since deregulation in air transportation, even this review process no longer exists and in freight transportation the deregulation acts allow wide latitude for the carrier to determine rates without regulatory review within the various zones of rate freedom (discussed in Chapters 13 and 14). Also as noted in Chapter 14, under administrative deregulation the ICC has failed to exercise jurisdiction over rate review when rate discounting exceeds the limits of the zone of rate freedom in the statutes. The only exception to this is in rail transportation where rates might not be high enough to cover variable costs or might be in the "market dominance" category.

What then controls rates and fares charged by the carriers? The answer is similar to any price in our economy: supply and demand sets prices. But once that is said, can we go farther to analyze rate and fare increases? At any one time, the supply of transportation offered will turn on two things: the degree of competition and the cost of producing the service. The demand for transportation will be determined, to a considerable degree, by the value of the service to the user (shipper or passenger) and the alternatives existing for the shipper or passenger. We have already discussed these concepts in detail in Chapter 16 so we need only relate this to unification and integration here.

Degree of Competition

If by the actions of mergers (unification) or integration (one corporation owning carriers in various modes of transportation) the degree of competition in the transport market or the alternatives existing for the shipper have been changed, the structure of the market has been changed. As noted above, transportation competition can be either intramodal (between carriers of the same mode) or intermodal (among carriers of competing modes) or both. Mergers between carriers or integration across modes may decrease shipper or passenger options and allow carriers to increase rates or fares. The degree of success in raising rates or fares will turn on how much market power is gained by mergers or integration. If a rail shipper is served by two railroads and these two merge, the opportunity for a rate increase is present; if a city is served by two airlines and these two merge, the opportunity for a fare increase is present; and if a shipper is served by two truck lines and these two merge, the opportunity for a rate increase is present. But suppose more than two carriers are involved. Then it becomes a matter of the degree of competition among the carriers in a given market. The point is, unification and integration can and do affect the degree of competition — one of the purposes of unification and integration may be to decrease transportation competition and raise rates or fares.

Entry Considerations

As noted in Chapter 14, entry has been made much easier under all the deregulation acts except the Staggers Rail Act of 1980. Theoretically, if rate or fare increases take place due to unification (merger) or integration, other transportation firms attracted by higher rates or fares should be able to enter the market and restore the degree of competition. In fact, under the theory of contestable markets (much mentioned in the deregulation movement) just the ability of competitive firms to enter a market should deter a merged transportation firm from raising rates or fares. Actual entry would not be necessary under this concept — the potential of competition itself would be sufficient to keep rates and fares from being raised after a decrease in the degree of competition.

However, as we have noted in Chapter 14 on the consequences of deregulation, this theoretical concept does not always hold, and indeed airfares seem to have risen in some markets where airline mergers have taken place.

The problem is that the theory of contestable markets assumes that no substantial barriers to entry or exit exist, no operating economies of scale favoring existing carriers exist, users would be willing and able to switch quickly among carriers, and existing carriers would not react quickly to new entrants' lower rates or fares. While the idea of "contestability" is itself quite appealing, in the real world barriers to entry exist. Chapter 14 has already mentioned the limited capacity at various airports and the difficulties of obtaining "slots" or gates. Also, the matter of substantial fixed costs in the LTL trucking area has been mentioned as a barrier to potential entrants. Further, operating economies of existing firms do exist, users are sometimes bound to a given carrier by various marketing devices (frequent flyer programs were discussed in Chapter 14, for example), and the existing firms are often quick to meet lower rates of new entrants.

Can two carriers that are merged raise rates or fares? It depends greatly on how easily new entrants can come into a market and survive the competitive struggle which could follow a merger and a rate or fare increase. Chapter 14 has already discussed the number of new entrants in air and LTL trucking and how many have survived. In air transportation, there were 121 new entrants in the first ten years after deregulation but only 49 of these survived and these were mostly commuters. Indeed, exclusive of commuter airlines, there were 64 new entrants in the scheduled airlines in the first ten years after deregulation but 45 of these went bankrupt or were merged into existing carriers during this period. In motor transportation, a tremendous number of new entries took place between 1978 and 1987 but a tremendous number of bankruptcies and mergers took place too. The failure rate was 190 firms out of every 10,000 in trucking in 1985, well above the national average of 120 per 10,000 firms for all businesses that year. Chapter 14 also noted the increasing degree of concentration in the LTL sector of trucking. Entry considerations are important, but so are survival rates!

Shipper Alternatives

Finally, whether a change in market structure by way of unification or integration is successful in raising rates or fares will depend also on what alternatives exist for users (shippers and passengers). Mention has been made of private transportation — particularly in trucking but also in inland water and maritime transportation. If truck rates are increased too much, the shipper can set up its own private truck line to haul its own freight. This will be an economical alternative if the volume shipped is considerable (it will be quite difficult for a small shipper to justify use of its own vehicles) and if a backhaul can be secured to help absorb a portion of the cost of private transportation. We have already noted in Chapter 14 (Consequences of Deregulation) that under deregulation private transportation by truck has become easier and that backhaul authority (*Toto* decision) is readily attainable as well as the use of a growing commodity truck broker segment of the industry.

In addition to the alternative of private transportation, the degree of alternatives available intermodally will affect increases in rates due to mergers. Rail and truck service compete in many areas, for example. If a rail merger led to a marked increase in rail rates, the shipper might switch to trucks. As we have noted in Chapter 14, competition is intense and entry is easy in the truckload segment of motor transportation, and this segment competes not only intramodally but also for rail carload shipments. Further, the shipper may also have a number of other alternatives which could tend to hold down increases in rates because unification or integration changes the market structure. Sometimes products can be redesigned to lower transportation costs should transportation costs increase too much. Even changes in location of points of production or consolidation or distribution centers are possible should rates increase too greatly. Indeed, depending on the circumstances, many shippers could take various actions to free themselves from complete dependence on a merged transportation firm that gains substantial market power in transportation.

In summary, while unification and integration can lead to increased rates or fares and therefore maximize revenues for the merged or integrated firm, the degree of competition (intramodally and intermodally), entry considerations, and shipper (user) alternatives provide a limit to rate or fare increases.

Cost Savings

At a given level of rates (prices), any lowering of costs will obviously result in greater profits to the firm. Two approaches to cost savings are possible. These are adjusting to gain economies of utilization and adjusting the scale of operations itself.

Economies of Utilization

Given the scale of operations or plant of a particular firm, economies are possible by better use of the inputs into the productive process. Hence attempts to gain the best or optimum use of labor and supplies without varying the scale of operations is always a challenge to management. Firms vary considerably in their ability to meet this challenge.

In transportation, as noted earlier, there are many fixed and common costs. Many of these are associated with plant size. Once a railroad is constructed, for example, it is difficult to change its scale of operations. About all that can be done is to adjust labor and material inputs in such a way as to gain the best efficiency. The same is true of other large pieces of equipment or terminal facilities. In air transportation, once a fleet of planes is purchased, the main job of management is to adjust labor, materials, and service facilities so as to best utilize the plant. One cannot fly half a plane or operate with half an air crew merely because only half the seats are filled.

Additionally, operation of a transportation plant requires many specialists and persons with a high degree of training. Rate specialists, equipment specialists, and administrative specialists are examples. These positions are necessary, but sometimes the scale of operations does not justify having large groups of these specialists. In such cases, a firm may decide to use a particular specialist on two or more unrelated jobs and hope the person can continue to do an effective job. Or instead of employing a large number of specialists, the transportation system may have but a few and either try to move the specialist about as needed or send the work to a centralized location. The traveling mechanic of bygone railroad days is an example of moving the specialist to the job, and the central repair shop and the airline maintenance base are examples of moving the work to the specialist. In both cases, however, some losses are incurred in the movement of either the specialist or the work and in scheduling of work.

When firms consolidate or merge, the combined or surviving firm is often large enough to make more effective use of specialists. Centralization of work or the full-time application of specialties is feasible. Better use of capital equipment may also be possible. When airlines merge, better scheduling of all equipment may result. Small planes can serve light traffic-density routes and larger planes heavy traffic-density routes. The previous firms may not have been able to afford equipment to efficiently serve various traffic-density routes, but the combined firm now has enough planes to do so. Here service is probably improved while cost savings are made.

The same result is possible in administrative expenses. When two motor carriers merge, better use of existing office personnel may result. Each person can now specialize and be more efficient. An example is traffic solicitation. When the firm is small, salespersons must call on all kinds and types of customers, giving little attention to each. If consolidation makes a larger firm, sales tasks can be divided and better solicitation may result from specialization.

To some degree, the same statements may be made about integration. Again using sales effort as an example, a partially integrated firm can sometimes offer a service that a nonintegrated firm cannot. Also, sales representatives may easily shift from mode to mode. Hence, specialization of solicitation and promotion is possible where previously it was not. The area of maintenance provides another example of the economies possible under integration. Railroad repair shops can do some of the tasks truck repair shops do. Both use some labor in common.

In summary, both unification and integration can lead to economies in the use of administrative personnel, maintenance personnel, labor of all kinds, equipment, and capital facilities. Many of these lead to better service through specialization of labor or capital and, at the same time, lead to greater profit for the firm.

Adjusting the Scale of Operations

Perhaps better known and somewhat more obvious are the cost savings that arise from adjusting the scale of operations. Every firm is interested in adjusting its scale of operations to most efficiently fit its demand. Here capital costs are probably the most important factor. If size can be increased, specialized pieces of capital equipment that do the job more efficiently can sometimes be employed. Firms that grow to a larger scale of operation can often do tasks they previously had to have others do for them. Specialists can be hired that were not previously used. More efficient types of management and organization may likewise be possible. Unification often allows for such cost savings.

However, in this day of increased automation, efficiency, and shifting market shares, it is most often the costs saved by reducing excess capacity that are the most important. As we saw in Chapter 2, railroads in our domestic transportation system are still reducing their trackage. Physical duplication of plant and personnel is common in railroad transportation.

Many rail merger proposals stress the existing duplication of tracks, stations, terminals and yards, administrative facilities, and specialized employees, and the savings that will be accomplished by reducing duplication. This is especially so where the proposed merger is the side-by-side variety in which two firms are duplicating services in the same territory or area.

Air mergers likewise propose savings by the reduction of duplication. When route patterns can be consolidated or merged, better use of equipment is often possible. Excess capacity in administrative personnel, in ticketing, or in repair facilities is avoided. Sometimes these savings can be accomplished at little or no reduction in service, although this is not always so.

Mergers and consolidations almost always mean savings in the use of labor. Rarely are all the clerks, sales representatives, supervisors, or administrators of two firms necessary in a merged firm. Excess capacity in operating and maintenance crews can often be reduced as well. With better scheduling of vehicles possible because more are available, wasted time and inefficiencies are reduced.

Almost any side-by-side merger, regardless of mode, can make savings of this type. The amount of savings may depend upon the degree of divisibility of the units of input. Motor carriers often have small savings from side-by-side mergers because a truck is a small and readily divisible unit of input. Terminal and overhead savings in truck mergers are possible, of course. Rail and air carriers potentially can have greater savings in side-by-side mergers because they use less divisible units of input and consequently the reduction of excess equipment capacity is far greater.

Increased Volume

The second method of increasing profit by unification and integration is to increase the volume of movement. If traffic can be increased, better use of capital is often possible and service can be increased (which may in turn lead to more traffic and more profit). Many of the economies of specialization and scale noted above are equally possible when volume of movement increases.

Increased volume arising from unification may come from end-to-end mergers of rail, truck, air, or water transportation lines. Here two routes are connected to make a bigger and longer system. While end-to-end mergers may result in some savings by eliminating some duplication of terminal facilities, these mergers are usually rationalized on the basis of better service. The merged system usually gives through service to shippers, should mean fewer claims and damages because of less handling, and often makes a faster service. Traffic may well increase as through service is offered, and sometimes latent demand may be stimulated by bringing new industries or undertakings into the transportation system with fast, economical through service not previously possible.

In passenger transportation, end-to-end consolidations definitely are an advantage to the public. The need for transferring passengers from car to car or plane to plane is decreased. While the interchange of rail passenger cars has become highly developed, interchange of air equipment between firms is still rare.

Motor carriers, too, have used end-to-end unifications to improve demand and profits. The tacking of operating rights into a system with broader geographical coverage is a common way of growth in motor transportation. Here again profits can be increased by allowing the firm to participate in more long-haul traffic and by the substantial economies available when a reduction in the handling or transfer of lading is possible. Sometimes, too, rolling equipment can be more efficiently scheduled and used when two firms merge or consolidate on an end-to-end basis, and very often overhead and administrative expenses can be reduced or labor can be better utilized.

Increased volume may arise from integration because a more complete service can be offered by the integrated firm than by its competitors. An integrated firm can combine the best of several modes and perhaps lower its rates while improving services and increasing its profits.

If these various devices merely result in a shifting of traffic from one firm to another, society may be no better off than before. But if the integrated firm or the firm gaining economies through unification is able to provide service at a lower rate than before the traffic shift, the public may gain. Although the purpose of these devices is to increase carrier profits, their effects remain to be considered.

EFFECTS OF UNIFICATION AND INTEGRATION

The effects of unification and integration may vary, depending upon the time period used in analyzing effects and the type or method used for unification and integration. We have already differentiated between methods used. Now we will consider time periods in terms of immediate effects and long-run effects.

Immediate Effects

An immediate effect of unification and integration is conflict. As noted previously, the goals of the various groups concerned differ. The degree of conflict varies somewhat according to the method used. Unification proposals based on increased volume and better service (such as end-to-end mergers) cause conflict only where cost reductions are involved. Proposals of the cost-savings type, however, often bring definite conflicts among carriers and transportation labor, shippers, and the general public. This is particularly true where adjustments in the scale of operations or economies of scale are sought by decreasing labor usage or decreasing services.

Labor Decreases

Decreases in the use of all types of labor are common immediate effects of unifications. These decreases involve not only operating personnel, but also administrative staff and clerical help, and are especially found in the side-by-side mergers where duplication exists. If integration involves savings in labor costs, the effect is the same, of course. Although such decreases in labor costs may make the carrier more profitable, they often adversely involve individual workers, the community, and the general public.

The immediate effect on the worker is loss of employment, income, and job security. Much of the labor strife in transportation in recent times has centered around carrier-labor conflicts over job security. Organized worker groups generally have opposed mergers and consolidations. Congress has become enough concerned about these immediate effects on transportation labor to enact various labor-protective provisions in our public policy on transportation, as we shall note in the next chapter.

The community served by the firms involved in unification and integration may likewise be adversely affected by labor decreases. Loss of payrolls is often a very serious community problem, particularly in small towns where carriers are a large factor in the economic existence of the community. Smaller payrolls mean less business, more unemployment, and the social costs that accompany idleness. Communities have been known to oppose carrier unification quite vehemently, particularly where railroads and large payrolls are involved.

The general public may be adversely affected in the immediate period by labor decreases insofar as the general goal of full employment is undermined. Assuming no immediate shifting of labor made excess by mergers or consolidation, the attainment of full employment is postponed.

This immediate effect, as well as some of the effects on individuals and communities, may be entirely different after a period of readjustment has taken place. But these immediate effects do help explain some of the opposition to unification and integration proposals.

Service Decreases

Another immediate effect of many unifications is a decrease in service to someone. This is particularly true of cost-saving types of unifications such as side-by-side mergers that eliminate duplication. To some degree, service decreases are also involved in integration as well. In end-to-end mergers designed to increase volume, some local service decreases may be involved, but they are often offset by increasing through service. Again, service decreases may make the carrier more profitable and better adjust its plant to demand, but they cause conflicts with the same three groups: individuals, the community, and the general public. These conflicts are of a somewhat different nature, however, than those considered before.

The immediate effect of service decreases is upon the shipper and passenger. When side-by-side mergers take place or when integration limits the number of competitors, shipper choice is restricted. This is true for passenger service as well. Shippers and passengers desire a wide choice and therefore look upon service decreases as adversely affecting them.

No community wants less service from the carriers serving it. No city wants to have second-class status on any rail, motor, or air system. Every town desires main-line service of the highest and best type, if only to placate its civic pride. Unifications designed to end duplication obviously mean that all cities cannot be served as they were before. The immediate effect is conflict.

The general public as conceptualized by public policy may find a conflict in service decreases. In a general way, the economy supports competition between many firms as a laudable economic goal. Service decreases eliminate competition and the duplication caused by competition. Many times the Antitrust Division of the Department of Justice has been at odds with the actions of the ICC over mergers and consolidations. The desire for competition among many firms and the goal of a more efficient transportation system are not always in harmony.

Besides the conflict over antitrust goals and the elimination of carrier duplication, a national defense conflict sometimes arises. Transportation is absolutely necessary for defense, thus any decrease in service or reduction in plant and equipment may have the immediate effect of decreasing the nation's defense potential. Many have noted the need for excess capacity in domestic transportation to provide for rapid traffic expansion in case of emergency. Some have even suggested that defense needs justify public expenditures to maintain duplication of transportation facilities. One program of action carried on for several years involved the buying and stockpiling of excess rail passenger equipment near military bases.

End-to-end mergers and unifications designed to attain greater volume or to give through service do not involve the degree of conflict with shippers and communities that cost-saving mergers involve. Although these types may have great conflict with antitrust policy, they are not generally in conflict with defense needs.

Long-Run Effects

The long-run effects of unification and integration are rarely the same as the immediate effects. Conflicts may or may not continue after adjustment. Some of the effects undoubtedly are beneficial in the long run from several points of view, but again the effects will vary somewhat according to the type or method used.

Given time, unification or integration that increases volume seems to be beneficial to all. End-to-end mergers or consolidations that broaden service areas, allow more through traffic, and make for more financially healthy carriers are especially beneficial. The chance for stimulating new demand seems greater here than in the cost-saving type as service decreases are smaller and better services often result. Of course, the end-to-end merger may prosper because it causes a traffic shift from one carrier or one mode to another. Under such circumstances, long-run benefits will accrue only if the shift is to a less costly and more efficient carrier. Some cost savings are usually involved in end-to-end mergers, however, although to a smaller degree than in the side-by-side type. After adjustments, the long-run effect of unification or integration leading to increased volume and better service leaves only the antitrust problem unsolved.

The long-run effect of cost-savings unification and integration proposals are basically two: increased carrier earnings and more efficient resource allocation. These long-run effects may eventually overcome some of the immediate conflicts noted above, or they may not.

Increased Carrier Earnings

If cost-savings unification or integration has been properly planned, it should result in greater long-run carrier earnings. This can be beneficial to almost all parties concerned if increased earnings lead to lower rates, if they lead to better service at the same rate, or if they lead to financially adequate carriers.

Lower rates for the same level of service benefit the shipper and reduce costs. Depending upon the conditions of competition and demand in the various products shipped, this may be translated into either lower prices to the consumer or a postponement of price increases. Too many assumptions concerning competition, the pattern of growth of firms, general economic conditions of inflation or deflation, and the elasticities of demand of thousands of individual products in numerous markets are involved for any detailed analysis of the effects of lower rates. However, it is proper to generalize that lower transportation rates are a stimulus to economic growth and development and are considered beneficial to the whole economy.

Better service at the same rate has the same economic effect. Carriers and commissions may prefer to translate greater earnings not into lower rates but into increased service levels. Here again the higher level of service is beneficial to shippers and ultimately to the general public. Better service levels may even be beneficial to transportation labor by providing more jobs. Again, the long-run effect on any one individual or industry is hard to ascertain without multiple assumptions about economic conditions and particular markets. However, better service is generally considered beneficial to economic growth and development.

Finally, greater earnings may lead to a more financially adequate transportation system. Remember that Congress assumed adequacy of transportation as a prime public policy goal from 1920 to 1980. Even the recent deregulation acts continue to list financial adequacy as a goal along with increased competition. If the financial woes of carriers are such that questions exist about their ability to continue to fulfill their role in the future, increased earnings from unification or integration could be most important. Long-run cost savings may be the only hope for some carriers. In such instances, the long-run effect may be a continuation of shipper choice, service, employment, and a degree of competition, none of which might be possible without mergers and consolidations to rescue financially weak carriers.

Allocation of Resources

A second long-run effect brought about by unification or integration of the cost-saving type is a change in resource allocation. In the previous discussion of financial adequacy, a tacit assumption is made that we need various types of carriers. This may not be the case. Every industry is constantly changing; all parts of the economy are constantly in a state of shift. We fail to recognize this merely because the degree of change or shift may be small or take long periods to complete. Yet the proper balance of resources to needs is perhaps the greatest problem affecting the entire economy.

Unification and integration of the cost-saving type may act as a vehicle by which the economy attains a better balance in its use of resources. Perhaps service decreases and labor decreases (immediate effects) are needed because of basic permanent changes in technology or shifts of traffic shares. Perhaps excess capacity needs to be removed and the capital and materials employed elsewhere in the economy. With decreases in some modes and increases in others, society may attain a better balance in resource use. If a shift of resources, including capital and labor, means more productive employment outside transportation, perhaps all parties are better off. In the long run, all will benefit — labor, shipper, communities, and general public — from an economy that uses its resources in such a way that only the amount actually needed is allocated to transportation. Insofar as unification and integration act to assist in attaining a proper balance of resources, society will benefit in the long run.

The antitrust problem remains even here, for there is no guarantee that an optimum resource allocation will necessarily be consistent with antitrust goals. Likewise, if no shifting takes place and the resources remain unemployed, a major problem presents itself.

OBSTACLES TO UNIFICATION AND INTEGRATION

Enough of the kinds of conflicts have been noted to make it obvious that many obstacles stand in the way of unification and integration in domestic transportation. Unification and integration do not automatically take place. Sometimes obstacles are insurmountable; at other times they merely delay the ultimate adjustment process. For our purposes, we can note three types of obstacles: regulatory obstacles, obstacles inherent in unification itself, and environmental obstacles.

Regulatory Obstacles

Unification and integration in railroads and motor carriers cannot take place without permission from the ICC, and as previously noted, conflicts arise from various groups when it is proposed. Regulatory procedure allows all interested parties to be heard and takes into consideration their various positions. This in itself slows the process.

In air transportation, the FAA assumed jurisdiction over airline mergers after the CAB was "sunsetted" in 1985 and allowed mergers and buyouts quite freely, as noted in Chapter 14. Since 1989 the general antitrust laws have been involved in airline mergers. While the Department of Justice took only an advisory role up to 1989, it is expected that its position will not be as lenient as the FAA's in the future.

Because of the monopolistic aspects of railroad transportation and because the "rail monopoly problem" predated the antitrust law of 1890 (Sherman Act), unification in transportation has generally not fallen under the antitrust laws. The Department of Justice may enter a merger case in transportation (with the exception of air transportation since 1989) on an advisory capacity. That is, it assumes the same role as any shipper or city or protesting carrier or individual. Early attempts to use the antitrust laws against railroads were rebuffed by the U.S. Supreme Court since the earlier (1887) Act to Regulate Commerce gave the ICC jurisdiction in the area of transportation mergers. That jurisdiction continued up to the present and was applied to the other modes of transportation as they were regulated over time.

Therefore, public policy on transportation unification and integration has been specifically established by Congress. Much of this public policy is frankly protective, designed to protect groups such as transportation labor as well as the general public. Even so, some of this public policy is but partially in harmony with other general goals such as the maintenance of competition and antitrust policy. It is also hard to define what action protects the general public. Policy is not altogether clear on such matters. These goal conflicts, protective provisions, and uncertain criteria are obstacles to unification and integration.

Inherent Obstacles

Unification or integration involves a degree of voluntary action on the part of the participants. Agreement among merging or integrating firms is not always easy. Since many are corporations, many investors with diverse goals and objectives must be satisfied. This involves both debt and equity owners. Management itself may disagree. It is not easy to merge oneself out of a job, and a merged firm can have but one president and set of administrative officers. As we have seen, adjustments in the immediate period are almost inevitable when unification or integration takes place. Adjustment means change and uncertainty. The tendency to avoid adjustment and change is great in all businesses, and in some of the older transportation firms this inertia itself is a major obstacle. Therefore there are obstacles inherent in the very idea of unification or integration.

Political and Economic Environmental Obstacles

Transportation does not operate in a vacuum. Unification and integration take place in a political and economic environment. The economic environment of the nation is oriented toward individual firms and competition. Unification and integration involve group action on the part of firms and often a decrease in competition. This may present an obstacle.

From another point of view, the political climate may be a very real environmental obstacle. Transportation systems serve many towns, counties, and states. Each is a political unit with its representatives elected to promote the welfare of each particular governmental unit. Laws are passed and pressures arise from the conflicts previously noted. Some politicians may even exploit these conflicts for personal political gain and oppose unification not because it is economically unsound, but because it is politically expedient to do so. The political climate, then, may pose an obstacle to unification and integration.

In summary, because of regulatory provisions and conflicts, inertia and inherent difficulties, or the economic and political environment, unification and integration may be delayed or prevented in spite of economic and business goals.

PUBLIC POLICY ON UNIFICATION AND INTEGRATION

Public policy on unification and integration is a part of our general transportation policy. Just as our general public policy on transportation has evolved, developed, and changed over time, so has policy in this area. Basically, the policy has been restrictive — unification and integration have been controlled. The degree of control varies both over time and by mode. Additionally, public policy is not the same for unification as it is for integration.

Control of Integration

Regulatory controls have prevented the formation of fully integrated transportation firms in this country. Although the transportation company idea has been much discussed, it is necessary to look to our neighbor to the north for the best example of such an operation. The Canadian Pacific Railway Company owns railroads, truck lines, an airline, maritime water carriers, and numerous other subsidiaries. No such example can be found in this country.

Regulations affecting integration apply principally to the railroads. A number of partially integrated rail systems do exist in the United States. Many railroads own truck subsidiaries and a few own pipelines and air-freight forwarders. The reverse, however, is not true. Few truck lines or pipelines own railroads, although there is no prohibition against such ownership. (You will recall, however, that freight forwarders are not allowed to own line-haul carriers.)

The reason for this difference in regulatory treatment relative to integration is fairly obvious. It revolves around historical and economic conditions. Historically, railroads grew into large corporate giants before truck lines, pipelines, and airlines did. The dominant position of the railroads caused various controls to be placed on their ownership of the other emerging modes. No such problem was envisioned with the newer modes.

Economically, there are also several reasons for this difference in regulatory treatment. Most of the newer competitive transportation firms did not possess the financial resources to be able to consider ownership of other modes. Also, because of the economic structure of the newer and competitive modes of transportation, there was less chance of economies of scale through ownership of several modes. Railroads have large fixed expenses and common costs. Some of these could be spread to the other modes and economies easily gained in the use of people and capital. While the opportunity to offer more complete service might be appealing to motor carriers or air carriers, for example, there was less direct economic justification for such integration in the newer modes than in rail.

Our general economic philosophy in this country has been to idealize competition. Railroads already were monopolistic, and public policy was designed to prevent them from spreading their monopolistic powers to other modes of transportation. The new firms were generally competitive with railroads and with themselves. Hence, there was less concern about the spread of monopoly and the upholding of competition among the newer modes. Naturally, regulation of the possible acquisition of other modes did not come about when competitive conditions prevailed.

Regulation is concerned mainly with rail ownership of motor carriers. Many railroads own truck subsidiaries (many acquired prior to the regulation of motor carriers in 1935), but in all cases the operating rights of rail-owned truck lines were restricted. The railroad-owned motor carrier was not allowed to compete with its parent, and various restrictions were placed on the type of service that could be offered in competition with the regular truck lines. Basically, these restrictions were designed to ensure that railroad-owned motor carriers operated in an ancillary, auxiliary, or supplementary capacity to their rail parents.

In 1983, the ICC voted to lift many of the previous restrictions that it had historically placed on railroad-owned motor carriers. No longer are these rail-owned truck lines limited to pickup and delivery of freight for their railroad.

In recent times, public policy has attempted to foster intermodalism. The Declaration of National Transportation Policy, as amended by the Motor Carrier Act of 1980, explicitly lists as a goal the promotion of intermodal transportation. In furtherance of this goal, the ICC exempted piggyback service from control in 1980. Much TOFC or piggyback service is the carriage of trailers of railroad-owned trucklines, and this change in policy points to more integration in the future.

Also under the 1980 deregulation acts, the ICC has been more willing to approve railroad ownership of carriers in other modes. Thus, in 1984 CSX (formerly Chessie System) was allowed to purchase American Commercial Barge Lines, in 1985 the Norfolk and Southern was permitted to purchase North American Van Lines, in 1986 CSX was allowed to purchase Sealand (a maritime carrier), and in 1987 the Union Pacific was permitted to acquire Overnite Transportation, a large motor carrier east of the Mississippi. Since deregulation, integration in transportation has proceeded considerably.

Under the changed regulatory environment, the old concept of a total transportation company, sometimes called "megacarriers" or "full-service carriers," seems possible. The idea here is that one firm, the transportation company, owns operating divisions in all modes of transportation. Under this concept, the freight is allocated to whichever mode can carry it most efficiently and profitably. The concept of the total transportation company or totally integrated carrier was not possible until the recent regulatory changes.

Control of Unification

The matter of public regulation of unification is more complicated than the control of integration. Controls vary considerably by mode, and it is appropriate to survey this topic on a modal basis.

Railroads

The history of unification in railroads is most interesting. Practically all modern railroads evolved in this manner. The history of public policy on railroad merger and consolidation is likewise interesting. Merely the sketchiest account will be given here. (Some of the background of this problem was previously considered in Chapters 10 and 11.)

General fear of railroad consolidation and attempts at public control predate federal regulation. It will be recalled that an integral part of the early granger laws prohibited consolidation and merger of railroads. Being primarily intrastate in nature, these prohibitions had little effect and were generally not in existence for long.

The initial Act to Regulate Commerce prohibited pooling and other concerted action by rail carriers. It did not deal with consolidations and mergers as such. However, in a series of legal actions just after the turn of the century, the antitrust laws were applied to railroad consolidations. These actions were found to violate the Sherman Act in the famous *Northern Securities* case (193 U.S. 197, 1904). Rail consolidation and merger, which had previously been widespread, ceased almost entirely.

In the Transportation Act of 1920, Congress took a more permissive attitude toward rail mergers and consolidations. The ICC was given control over unification and had to apply certain criteria to each proposal before allowing railroads to merge or consolidate. The ICC was also directed to draw up a nationwide plan of a limited number of railroads. Such a plan, based largely upon a study and recommendation made by Professor William Z. Ripley of Harvard University, was eventually adopted. All mergers had to fit into this preconceived plan. Little merger activity took place under this scheme, although stock ownership and the holding company device were used to achieve some of the financial benefits of mergers.

By 1940, it was apparent that the nationwide plan had failed. Hence, the plan was abandoned and new criteria were drawn up. The Transportation Act of 1940 provided that the ICC must find a rail merger proposal "to be in the public interest," labor protective provisions were added so that workers could not be placed in a worse position because of a merger or consolidation for a period of four years, the ICC had to consider the effect of a merger proposal on other railroads in the territory, and the total fixed charges coming out of a merger proposal could not be burdensome.

No basic change has been made in public policy toward rail mergers and consolidations since 1940. For a period of time few mergers were attempted. However, starting in the late 1950s, a whole series of merger proposals for railroads erupted. Much time must elapse for hearings and for all interested parties to be heard in these proposals. However, during the 1960s and early 1970s, the ICC slowly processed more merger applications and generally looked with favor on rail mergers. A number of lines were merged or consolidated. Considerable reappraisal of the advantages of mergers came with the 1970 Penn Central bankruptcy, but interest in mergers eventually revived.

One difficulty with railroad mergers was the long time lapse necessary to gain approval. One merger proposal took over ten years in hearings. In an attempt to remedy this procedural problem, Congress in the 1976 4-R Act required the ICC to act on rail merger proposals within thirty-one months. In the Staggers Rail Act of 1980, Congress provided that the ICC must consider whether a proposed rail merger would have adverse effects on competition among rail carriers in the region, and control over mergers of smaller railroads was considerably reduced.

During the late 1970s and in the 1980s, several rather large rail mergers have been completed: Burlington Northern and Frisco Lines, the Chessie System and the Seaboard-Family Lines, Norfolk-Western and Southern, and the Union Pacific-Missouri Pacific-Western Pacific. In an exception to this policy of freely approving railroad mergers, the ICC denied the merger of the Santa Fe and Southern Pacific in 1987 on competitive grounds. However, the subsequent Southern Pacific–Rio Grande merger proposal was approved in 1988. Refer again to Chapter 14 (Table 14.6) for details of railroad mergers since 1980.

Abandonment of trackage is also related to railroad unification. The 1976 4-R Act recognized the need for speedier abandonment of excess trackage and railroad system planning as noted in Chapter 21. The Staggers Rail Act of 1980 provided for shortened procedure in abandonment proposals with unprotested abandonment allowable in 75 days and various deadlines for decisions where protests and investigations are involved. The new maximum time limit for ICC decisions in all abandonment applications is 330 days.

Motor Carriers

Because there are more motor carrier firms, unification proposals do not attract as much attention as they do in rail and air transportation. Nevertheless, a large number of mergers and consolidations have taken place. Motor carriers have created large transportation systems by these devices, and public policy questions arise from time to time. Periodically the ICC issues reports on motor carrier concentration, and some members of Congress have evidenced concern over the antitrust aspects of truck mergers.

Mergers and consolidations of small truck lines have never been controlled. In the original 1935 act, mergers involving twenty or fewer vehicles were exempt from control. Later all mergers involving two firms with combined operating revenues of $300,000 or less were exempt. The

Motor Carrier Act of 1980 extended this exemption so that mergers were exempt if the combined firm had total operating revenues of $2 million or less.

Where mergers and consolidations are controlled, the ICC must consider the effect of the proposed merger on adequate transportation service to the public, the total fixed charges resulting from the merger, and the interests of employees. All interested parties must be heard.

As with rail mergers, there has been concern over the lengthy procedure of merger hearings. Hence, in the 1980 Motor Carrier Act, Congress specified time limits within which the ICC must act in merger cases. Hearings of evidence in a merger proposal must be completed in 240 days, and the commission must render a final decision not less than 180 days thereafter.

Merger control and entry control are closely connected. Prior to the deregulation movement, entry was closely regulated and therefore mergers were also regulated. Since entry is considerably easier under the 1980 Motor Carrier Act, trucking mergers and consolidations are not as important a regulatory issue as they once were.

Air Carriers

Since there are only a small number of firms involved in air transportation, any unification proposal creates much public interest. Many of the existing airlines have grown by merger and consolidation, although such actions have been relatively infrequent. Prior to deregulation in 1978, public policy in this area was similar to that of the other modes in that all mergers had to be approved by the Civil Aeronautics Board and found to be in the public interest. Between 1938 and 1978, the CAB followed a very strict policy on airline mergers and allowed relatively few mergers — usually allowing them only where one of the merger partners was in danger of bankruptcy (the "failing carrier doctrine"). As with motor carriers, merger control and entry control were closely linked and since entry was very difficult, it was logical to make mergers difficult, too.

Since 1978, entry into the airlines has been much easier. Hence, control of mergers has been less of a regulatory issue than previously. However, the CAB retained the power to approve airline mergers from 1978 to 1985. When the CAB passed out of existence in 1985, jurisdiction over airline mergers passed to the FAA for a period of time. Generally, both the FAA and CAB allowed most unification and merger proposals since 1978. Chapter 14 (Table 14.2) details the mergers in airlines since 1978. In 1989, the Department of Justice took jurisdiction over airline mergers under the general antitrust laws as noted above.

carrier portion of its operation while still retaining the original transportation name. In another instance, a railroad company provided the initial basis for the formation of a conglomerate which later sold the railroad itself but retained a portion of its name.

Control of Diversification and Conglomerates

Use of the holding company device avoids the necessity of getting regulatory commission permission for such diversification. The transportation firm does not have to make the investment; instead, its nonregulated parent holding company invests. If the owners of a transportation firm choose to exchange their stocks for part ownership of another larger conglomerate company, this is beyond the scope of authority of the transportation regulatory agencies. Basically, only the antitrust laws apply to the nonregulated sectors of the economy and provide the only present basis for control of these activities. Even here, it is not clear what our national policy on conglomerates is and to what degree the antitrust laws really apply.

At this point, it is not clear whether the industries approach and the conglomerate movement are detrimental or favorable to transportation services. Some observers attribute the Penn Central's bankruptcy to excesses allowed by this approach. Some deplore the use of transportation revenues for nontransportation activities, whereas others argue that being a part of a diversified firm may actually strengthen transportation undertakings during times of economic stress. Some point to the use of transportation assets as providing greater borrowing power to finance nontransportation activities, whereas others note that these financial developments can take place only if the owners are convinced that it is in their own economic self-interest to exchange their stocks. Finally, some see the danger that a carrier that becomes an operating subsidiary may discriminate in favor of its parent company, whereas others maintain that the laws regulating discrimination in transportation are clear and make no ownership distinction.

In 1977, the ICC filed a report with Congress asking for regulatory control over this type of ownership. The report noted that more than one-half of the railroad industry (as measured by assets and revenues) was in the hands of conglomerate or industry ownership and expressed concern that transportation assets or revenues were being shifted to nontransportation uses. Congress did not act on this request.

In any case, diversification and the conglomerate movement in transportation have given rise to a great deal of concern and interest, and these developments will be debated extensively during the next several years. If these events do adversely affect transport services, new regulatory legislation no doubt will be forthcoming.

SUMMARY

The market structure of transportation and its changes and control provide one illustration of transportation problems and policy. Unification (mergers) and integration illustrate the conflicting goals that affect public policy in domestic transportation. These conflicts are triggered by carrier goals of maximizing profit. Two approaches to maximizing have concerned us here — unification (intramodal) and integration (intermodal). The purpose of unification and integration is to raise rates or fares, effect cost savings through greater economies of utilization or scale, by adjusting the scale of operations itself or by increasing volume or demand. The effect of these methods varies considerably. The immediate effect is conflict when cost-savings or rate/fare increase methods are used. Increased volume methods evoke less conflict. The long-run effect is more difficult to ascertain, but it seems to resolve many of the conflicts over immediate effects. Nevertheless, these conflicts lead to definite obstacles to unification and integration, many of which prevent or limit use of these techniques. Finally, because of these conflicts, public policy has evolved in an attempt to control unification and integration. That policy has changed over time, has treated the various modes in different ways, and has treated integration differently than unification. Until recently, public policy has been restrictive and protective. Although almost all proposals for unification and integration must be approved by the ICC, recent decisions in the unification area have been quite permissive. As deregulation has eased entry controls in motor and air transportation, merger controls have likewise eased.

Recent movements toward diversification through holding companies and conglomerate enterprises owning transportation firms have caused interest in an area allied to traditional unification and integration. The potential effects of these developments are not entirely clear at the present time, and public policy concerning them is still evolving.

ADDITIONAL READINGS

Barrett, Colin, "Diversification of Scatteration," *I.C.C. Practitioners' Journal* (January–February 1970), 198–208.

636 TRANSPORTATION PROBLEMS AND TRANSPORTATION POLICY

Boisjuly, Russel P., and Thomas M. Corsi, "The Aftermath of the Motor Carrier Act of 1980: Entry, Exit, and Merger," *Proceedings, 23rd Annual Meeting Transportation Research Forum* (1982), 258–64.

Conant, Michael, *Railroad Mergers and Abandonments*, Berkeley: University of California Press, 1964.
Chapter 2, "The Myth of Interrailroad Competition," pp. 25–41.
Chapter 5, "Functional Mergers: Pooling and Trackage Agreements," pp. 91–112.
Chapter 8, "Administrative Regulation of Resource Allocations," pp. 166–86.

Corsi, Thomas M., "The Policy of the ICC in Trucking Mergers, Control and Acquisition of Certificate Cases 1965–1973," *I.C.C. Practitioners' Journal* (November–December 1975), 24–38.

Crum, Michael R., and Benjamin J. Allen, "U.S. Transportation Merger Policy: Evolution, Current Status, and Antitrust Considerations," *International Journal of Transport Economics*, 3, No. 1 (February 1986), 41–75.

Daley, James M., "Holding Companies, Common Carriers, and Public Policy," *Transportation Journal* (Winter 1979), 67–73.

Dempsey, Paul Stephen, "Antitrust Law and Policy in Transportation: Monopoly I$ the Name of the Game," *Georgia Law Review*, 21, No. 5 (Winter 1987), 505–99.

Due, John F., "Factors Affecting the Abandonment and Survival of Class II Railroads," *Transportation Journal* (Spring 1977), 19–36

Ellsworth, T. P., "The Merger Merry-Go-Round: Rail Consolidations Under the 4R Act," *I.C.C. Practitioners' Journal* (May–June 1977), 446–76.

Fair, Marvin L., and Ernest W. Williams, Jr., *Transportation and Logistics*, rev. ed., Plano, Texas: Business Publications, 1981.
Chapter 20, "The Control of Carrier Structure and Services," pp. 386–406.

Farris, Martin T., and Paul T. McElhiney, eds., *Modern Transportation: Selected Readings*, 2nd ed. Boston: Houghton Mifflin Co., 1973.
Suelflow, James E., and Stanley J. Hiller, "The Transportation Company: An Economic Argument for Intermodal Ownership," pp. 401–15.

Graham, Kenneth R., "Rail-Based Holding Companies: A View of Some Indicators of Strategy, Management Change, and Financial Performance," *Transportation Journal* (Summer 1980), 73–77.

Grimm, Curtis M., "An Evaluation of Economic Issues on the UP-MP-WP Railroad Merger," *The Logistics and Transportation Review*, 20, No. 3 (September 1984), 239–60.

Heaver, Treavor D., "Multi-Modal Ownership — The Canadian Experience," *Transportation Journal* (Fall 1971), 14–28.

Johnson, James C., "Seven Transportation Megatrends for the Late 1980's," *Transportation Practitioners' Journal*, 53, No. 2 (Winter 1986), 164–80.

———, *Trucking Mergers: A Regulatory Viewpoint*, Lexington, Mass.: D. C. Heath & Co., 1973.
Chapter 4, "Introduction to Trucking Unification," pp. 55–64.
Chapter 5, "The Reasons for ICC Approval of Trucking Mergers and Consolidations," pp. 65–80.

———, and Terry Whiteside, "Professor Ripley Revisited: A Current Analysis of Railroad Mergers," *I.C.C. Practitioners' Journal* (May–June 1975), 419–452.

Jordan, William A., "Problems Stemming from Airline Mergers and Acquisitions," *Transportation Journal*, 27, No. 4 (Summer 1988), 9–30.

Lackman, Conway L., "Implications of Conglomerates for Transportation in the 1970's," *Transportation Journal* (Fall 1974), 30–45.

Lee, Tenpao, C. Phillip Baumel, and Patricia Harris, "Market Structure, Conduct and Performance of the Class I Railroad Industry 1971–1984," *Transportation Journal*, 26, No. 4 (Summer 1987), 54–66.

Lieb, Robert C., "A Revised Intermodal Ownership Policy," *Transportation Journal* (Summer 1971), 48–53.

_____ , *Freight Transportation: A Study of Federal Intermodal Ownership Policy*, New York: Praeger Publishers, 1972.

_____ , *Transportation*, 3rd ed., Reston, Va: Reston Publishing Co., 1985.
Chapter 18, "Consolidations, Intermodal Ownership, and Conglomerate Combinations," pp. 383–405.

Morash, Edward A., and Charles Elis, "Motor Carrier Mergers, Mobility Barriers, and Regulatory Reform," *Transportation Journal*, 25, No. 1 (Fall 1985), 38–50.

Pegrum, Dudley F., *Transportation: Economies and Public Policy*, 3rd ed., Homewood, Ill.: Richard D. Irwin, 1973.
Chapter 18, "Consolidation and Integration," pp. 420–40.

Sampson, Roy J., *Obstacles to Railroad Unification*, Eugene: Bureau of Business Research, University of Oregon, 1960.

Sattler, Edward L., "Diversified Holding Companies and Their Impact on the Railroad Industry," *Transportation Journal* (Fall 1980), 65–74.

Schary, Philip B., "Measuring Concentration and Competition in the Regulated Motor Carrier Industry," *Transportation Journal* (Summer 1973), 49–53.

Smith, Jay A., Jr., "Concentration in the Common and Contract Motor Carrier Industry: A Regulatory Dilemma," *Transportation Journal* (Summer 1973), 30–48.

Spraggins, H. Barry, "Rationalization of Rail Line Abandonment Policy in the Midwest under the 4-R Act of 1976," *Transportation Journal* (Fall 1978), 5–18.

CHAPTER 27

TRANSPORTATION LABOR-MANAGEMENT RELATIONS

The preceding chapter considered conflicting goals relative to the structure of carrier organizations. This chapter is concerned with another area of goal conflict. Again several groups are involved, each with conflicting or partially conflicting goals. To some degree, the conflicts here are triggered by transportation labor, whereas the conflicts described in the previous chapter are carrier-triggered. Regardless of which group sets off the problem, however, it is the types of goal conflict and the attempts to resolve them that concern us here.

CONFLICTING GOALS: CARRIER, EMPLOYEE, AND PUBLIC

As noted previously, the goal of the carrier is profit maximization. This may be attempted through unification and integration. More commonly, however, the carrier will achieve this goal by adjusting the inputs of labor, capital, and materials into its productive plant. Labor, one of the major inputs, is always susceptible to adjustment. This is particularly true where capital can be substituted for labor.

Transportation labor, on the other hand, has an entirely different set of goals. Labor is interested in wages or compensation, conditions under which work takes place, and job security or job continuity. The intensity of transportation labor's goals is equally as great as the intensity of the carrier's goals. Workers depend primarily upon their jobs for their economic existence. Their jobs are their lives, just as profit is the lifeblood of carrier existence. Transportation labor wants the best labor bargain possible and looks with little sympathy on the carrier problem of minimizing costs at labor's expense in order to be competitive and to maximize profit.

Job security is especially important to transportation labor. Wages traditionally have not been low in transportation. The conditions of employment are shaped to a great degree by the type of operation involved. Hence continuity of employment and job rights have particular importance to transportation labor. Any downward adjustment of the amount of labor affects these goals.

The general public (including shippers) has varying interests in labor-management relations. In the short-run or immediate period, the primary and overwhelming goal of the general public is *continued service*. It is literally true that in the immediate period of a potential transportation shutdown, the public is indifferent to who wins the labor-management struggle as long as service continues.

In the long run, however, the general public has conflicting or split goals. On one hand, it wants the best, most efficient transportation possible at the lowest possible cost. This may mean the use of less labor and more capital. The problem of resource allocation is again involved. On the other hand, the public is also interested in full employment of people as well as other resources. National policy favors full employment, and much concern is evidenced over rates of employment and unemployment and their effect on the economy. Society also has become very interested in the social problems brought about by labor adjustment. The human and social costs of unemployment have become a real concern as the multitude of social legislation in this area testifies. Internal conflict between society's desire for the cheapest, most efficient transportation and full employment and minimum social costs of adjustment is self-evident.

One might properly ask if this conflict of goals is not a general problem of all business enterprises in a highly industrialized economy. To some degree this is true. However, because of some of the special conditions in transportation, these goal conflicts are considerably sharpened and brought into public focus.

Service Continuity

The overwhelming special nature of the problem in transportation is the absolute necessity for service to continue. In most other industries, production can cease at least temporarily without great general loss when labor-management strife erupts. But because of the essentiality of transportation services to the economy, society cannot allow these services to cease even on a temporary basis. It is well to reiterate that without transportation, stagnation of the whole agricultural and industrial economy is quick and certain. Interdependency exists in practically all present-day economic activity. When transportation stops, production stops. *Continuous service is a must.*

There are other reasons why the general conflict of goals comes into sharper focus in transportation than in other areas. These may be classified as historical reasons and as economic and technological reasons. Each category is worth exploring.

Historical Nature of the Problem

The union movement among workers in the transportation industries is one of the oldest in the country. Early railroad unions facing a strong management in a monopolistic industry attained strength much earlier than most labor organizations. The so-called Big Five — the railroad operating brotherhoods — were formed long before most unions were effective. The Engineers Brotherhood was founded in 1863, the Conductors in 1868, the Firemen in 1873, the Trainmen in 1883, and the Switchmen in 1894. All but the last of these brotherhoods predate federal regulation of transportation, and two were started even before the early state granger regulations.

The operating labor of railroads, then, was almost completely unionized at an early date. Railroad labor strife provided some of the bloodiest and hardest fought struggles in the latter half of the nineteenth century. It involved not only the brotherhoods but also the general labor unions of the time (such as the Knights of Labor). These strong transportation unions facing equally strong transportation management gave our country its first real taste of labor-management strife.

The Teamsters Union has a long history of strength and sharp bargaining in the trucking industry. The Maritime Unions and Longshoremen are well known as strong labor organizations. Although not organized until the 1930s, the unions in air transportation are well known. In the railroads, only the Brotherhood of Railway Engineers remains as a separate craft union — the other Big Five brotherhoods mentioned above have joined the United Transportation Union, an industrial union of considerable strength. However, one of the consequences of the deregulation movement has been a decrease in union strength — particularly in trucking and air transportation — as we noted in Chapter 14. Even so, labor unions remain a major factor in transportation and the vast majority of workers in transportation are unionized. Indeed, transportation has a higher degree of unionized workers than any other industry.

There also has been a tendency to pioneer public policy in the transportation field. Some of our society's first attempts at social legislation originated in transportation. The right to bargain collectively, the eight-hour day, social security, outlawing of the "yellow-dog" contract, the cooling-off period, and other now generally accepted labor rights and policies were first introduced in the rail transportation area. It is almost as if new ideas of society's role in labor-management relations were tried and tested on the railroads before being applied to the whole economy. This historic tendency to try things out in the transportation labor-management arena is in itself a major reason why goal conflicts are brought into sharper focus in this area.

Economic and Technological Nature of the Problem

The special nature of the problem of our transportation labor-management relations is further illustrated by four economic and technological conditions: employment characteristics, carrier costs, process characteristics, and substitutability.

Employment Characteristics

The employment characteristics of transportation labor are typically the requirement of a relatively high level of skill, considerable responsibility by the worker, a minimum of supervision, and higher-than-average pay levels. Equipment operators in all modes of transportation are highly skilled. They must exercise considerable judgment while operating without an immediate supervisor close at hand. Airline pilots are perhaps the outstanding example of this need for skill and judgment, the carrying of great responsibility, the lack of direct supervision, and high pay levels. Most other types of workers in transportation are similarly situated at least to some degree. Rate clerks must make careful judgments that affect the costs of the firm. Maintenance personnel must be especially responsible to protect life and property. Freight handlers must be particularly careful and, above all, trustworthy in their work. All transportation workers are part of an undertaking of public trust. The economic good and the personal well-being of the public are entrusted to their skill, care, and responsibility.

The average level of compensation for transportation workers in 1986 is shown in Table 27.1. Note that these data are in two forms: direct annual earnings and total compensation including supplemental benefits. Railroad workers are the highest paid, followed by pipeline labor and air transportation workers. Of course, each group contains many categories of workers and some groups such as airline pilots and over-the-road truck drivers far exceed the average figures here.

Also note that Table 27.1 gives an average for all transportation ($31,498 in 1986 including fringe benefits) and this can be compared to manufacturing and other industries as well as to all industry. Generally

Table 27.1   Average Annual Earnings and Total Compensation Per Full-Time Employee, 1986 (in Dollars)

	a	b
All Transportation	25,638	31,498
Railroads	36,463	48,379
Local and Intercity Bus[1]	16,203	18,725
Trucking and Warehousing[2]	22,623	27,577
Water	28,970	33,822
Air (common carrier)	32,249	40,418
Oil Pipeline	38,667	44,000
Allied Services	20,830	25,096
Manufacturing	25,462	31,219
Communications	32,806	41,974
Electric/Gas/Sanitary	33,300	41,613
Finance/Insurance/Real Estate	25,746	30,338
All Industry Total	21,935	26,301

a = Average Earnings
b = Average Total Annual Compensation Value of Supplemental Benefits
[1]Class I intercity Bus = $21,958 average annual earnings.
[2]Class I and II ICC regulated truck = $28,130 average annual earnings and $35,715 total compensation 1986.
Source: Transportation Policy Associates, *Transportation in America*, 6th ed., Washington, D.C. (March 1988), p. 17.

transportation workers are paid more than the average worker and this reflects worker responsibility and skill. In general, society has a justifiable interest in safe, reliable, and trustworthy service as well as continuity of service. Certainly this gives a special nature to labor-management relations in transportation.

Carrier Costs

As pointed out in Chapters 4, 5, 6, and 7, labor costs make up a major portion of the costs of providing service in several modes of transportation. Although it is not true for pipelines and water carriers, labor is the largest single cost item for rail, air, and motor carrier service. Labor costs are therefore of extreme importance to carrier management and a small change in labor costs or fringe benefits is reflected in the profitability of the carrier. Any effort which lowers the labor costs or increases worker productivity will be of great interest to transportation management. Hence, the intensity of the labor-management bargain is heightened.

Process Characteristics

The transportation process is a continuous one. Transportation does not start at 8:00 A.M. and end at 5:00 P.M. The forty-hour week is a pay week only, not an operating period. Trains, trucks, planes, boats, and pipelines do not stop running between Friday afternoon and Monday morning. Because of this continuous process, the labor-management bargain has many more dimensions than the 8:00 to 5:00, forty-hour-a-week factory work bargain. The technological setting is such that both the economics of compensation and the conditions of labor are infinitely more complex in transportation than in the economy as a whole.

Union contracts in transportation often specify miles worked rather than hours worked. For example, in railroad transportation a day's work for operating personnel is 110 miles, not eight hours. Pilots can fly up to 100 hours a month according to the FAA rules but most are allowed to operate but 80 hours a month for a month's pay by contract. In over-the-road trucking, pay according to mileage is common — not hours worked. Also, drivers can drive but 60 hours a week and must have eight hours' rest between driving shifts. Provisions in contracts involve cost of meals while working, allowances for rest periods, arrangements for "deadheading" (returning to originations), allowances for layovers, and so forth. While many of these provisions are dictated by safety regulations, they become part of the labor contract and illustrate the complexity in transportation relations due to the process characteristics.

Substitutability

Finally, in recent times it has been increasingly possible to substitute capital for labor in transportation. The use of capital in place of labor varies by mode, of course, but has been extremely widespread in pipelines, railroads, maritime, and aviation. With automatic pumping-station devices, remote controls, and electric pumps, pipelines have successively decreased their use of labor while rapidly increasing their throughput. In railroads, employment has declined due to dieselization, centralized traffic control, and automation as capital innovations have increased. Operating crews are generally smaller and such things as the traditional caboose have been replaced by capital innovations. In maritime transportation, the use of the container as well as automation aboard ships and at dockside is another example of the use of capital for labor. Finally, in aviation, the use of larger planes carrying many more passengers but with the same or nearly the same number of operating personnel such as pilots provides a further example of the substitution of capital for labor. This substitution effect, which has been especially strong in transportation, serves to intensify the labor-management bargain.

It is understandable, then, why the social necessity for continued service, the historical fact of early unionization and social innovation, and the economic-technological factors of employment characteristics, carrier costs, process characteristics, and substitutability all combine to make labor-management relations in transportation a unique problem.

CHANGES IN EMPLOYMENT

The total number of workers in transportation has decreased slightly in the twenty years since 1947. Table 27.2 shows the total number of workers in transportation and changes in employment in the various modes in the post–World War II period. While total intercity ton-miles produced increased from 1,063 billion in 1950 to 2,501 billion in 1986 (an increase of almost 2.5 times) and total for-hire passenger-miles increased from 11.6 billion in 1950 to 19.4 billion in 1986 (almost doubled), total transportation employment decreased from 2,625,000 in 1950 to 2,566,000 in 1986.

Note particularly the decline in railroad, oil pipeline, and water transportation employment — all of which increased ton-miles produced in this period, as noted in Chapters 4, 5, and 6. Much of this was due to the substitution effect of capital for labor noted above and the resultant increase in productivity per labor unit. The number of employees increased in only two modes during the post–World War II period: air transport and trucking and terminals — both of which increased production of ton-miles and passenger-miles by very large percentages during this period.

These decreases in the number of employees in the face of increases in the quantity of output becomes a very real factor in the labor-management bargain even though a substantial portion of this decrease came from attrition. We shall discuss such matters as job protection directly; however, these decreases in total employment illustrate again the conflicting goals of the various groups involved in transportation labor-management relations.

Table 27.2 Employment of Operating Personnel in Transportation, Selected Years (in Thousands)

	1947	1950	1960	1970	1980	1986
Air Transport	85	86	191	351	453	560
Bus Intercity	54	47	41	43	38	36
Local Transport	199	157	101	77	79	96
Railroads	1,557	1,391	885	627	532	325
Oil Pipelines	30	29	23	18	21	18
Taxi	125	121	121	107	53	37
Trucking & Terminals	496	557	770	998	1,189	1,311
Water	284	237	232	215	213	183
Total	2,830	2,625	2,364	2,436	2,578	2,566

Source: Frank A. Smith, *Transportation in America: Historical Compendium 1939–1985,* Westport, Conn: Eno Foundation for Transportation, 1989, pp. 30 & 31 for 1947 through 1980, and Transportation Policy Associates, *Transportation in America,* 6th ed., Washington, D.C. (March 1988), p. 19 for 1986.

INSTITUTIONAL ENVIRONMENT

Because it is a unique problem, the labor-management bargain in transportation occurs in an institutional environment of its own. This environment differs from other labor-management relations from both the economic and the legal viewpoints.

Economic Environment

The two economic factors tending to make a different institutional environment in transportation are industry-wide bargaining and the necessity for service continuity.

In general, the labor-management bargain is negotiated on an industry-wide basis within a particular mode. The only significant exception to this has been the Teamsters' contract which until recently was negotiated on a regionwide intramodal basis. In 1964, the Teamsters' contract also became industry-wide. In this type of negotiation, one bargain generally covers all firms and workers in the particular union either over the entire country or in a given region.

Under regionwide bargaining there are few differentials, and under industry-wide bargaining there are none, since a given type of labor is paid the same amount and works under the same conditions all over the country (or region). Carrier costs tend to be equalized and low-cost labor areas are prevented.

Unions have often upheld industry-wide bargaining as an ideal. They have felt that each type of labor should be paid the same regardless of where it is performed. In general, unions have looked upon industry-wide bargaining as an opportunity for their best negotiators to get the best bargain and thereby erase any effect of weak local unions. Industry-wide bargaining has been a sign of labor solidarity, a united front, and equality for all across the country. Finally, it has been an ideal because the maximum sanction of complete work stoppage can be applied if a strike becomes necessary.

But when the ideal of industry-wide bargaining has been attained, the second economic institutional factor — the necessity for service — intervenes. The goal of solidarity, no differentials, maximum sanctions, and equalization conflicts with society's goal of continued service. If negotiations break down, the ultimate weapon is the strike. But a strike means discontinuance of an essential service. Society cannot tolerate this. Therefore, once the long-sought economic institutional environment is attained by labor, its effect is blunted by another and more dominant goal of society as a whole. This leads to legal restraints.

Legal Environment

Special legal institutions have been devised within which some labor-management negotiations in transportation must operate. These apply to railway and airline labor negotiations, although not to Teamster or maritime contracts. This fairly complicated set of legal machinery has been substituted for the usual procedure of settling labor-management differences with the intent of preventing work stoppages and the use of the ultimate weapon — the strike. The idea is to delay. Both sides must go through time-consuming procedures. With delay, issues are often more refined, tempers cooled, and time for careful reconsideration is allowed. Society hopes to avoid the consequences of work stoppages by the device of legalized delay.

MECHANICS OF LABOR-MANAGEMENT CONFLICT SETTLEMENT

The complicated legal mechanics of the settlement of labor-management disputes assume that a normal collective bargaining attempt will be made

by carriers and their employees. The mechanics are an addition to traditional methods of collective bargaining and are designed to come into
play only if and when traditional methods of settlement fail. Unfortunately, the existence of these legal procedures and mechanics sometimes may
tend to hasten the breakdown of the traditional methods of bargaining.

Background

The set of complicated legal procedures and mechanics surrounding the
transportation labor-management relationship has an interesting background. These procedures, devised by society in an attempt to avoid
service stoppages, evolved in the area of railway labor relations. This is
not surprising as railroad labor was organized at an early date and the
carriers had an even earlier history of acting in concert on other matters
of mutual concern.

Five laws serve as background to the Railway Labor Act of 1926
which, as amended, is the present applicable procedure. In 1888, labor
unrest on the railroads led to the Arbitration Act, which provided for
voluntary arbitration and investigation of disputes. This act was used but
once and was unsuccessful in dealing with the Pullman strike of 1894 and
the American Railway Union led by Eugene Debs. In 1898, the Erdman
Act allowed either party to a dispute to request the chairman of the ICC
and the commissioner of the Department of Labor to act as mediators. If
this mediation failed, these officials were to attempt to get voluntary
agreement to arbitration with a decision to be binding on both parties for
one year. This procedure was amended by the Newlands Act of 1913
which provided for a permanent commissioner of mediation and conciliation and two other persons, all appointed by the president, who would act
as the United States Board of Mediation and Conciliation. This board
could act without waiting for a request for its services and was obligated
to hand down a nonbinding arbitration award within thirty days. A
number of disputes were handled by this procedure.

During the federal operation of railways from 1917 to 1920, the federal
government dealt directly with unions and set up several advisory boards
to assist the director general of the railroads. Also during this wartime
period, the Adamson Act providing for the eight-hour day for railroad
workers, with no reduction in pay, was applied. This act had been passed
in 1916, but was under legal challenge before the courts as well as under
investigation by a special commission at the time.

When the rail carriers were returned to private control by the Transportation Act of 1920, two labor-management procedures that had grown
out of wartime experiences were provided. One, regional railroad boards

of labor adjustment with both labor and management members could be set up to handle minor disputes arising from grievances, working conditions, and rules interpretations. Two, a permanent Railroad Labor Board of nine members — three representing labor, three representing management, and three representing the public — was established. This group was to settle wage disputes and to act as an appeal board from adjustment board decisions. This solution was not successful.

Railway Labor Act of 1926

To some degree, the Railway Labor Act of 1926 drew upon the experiences of previous attempts to solve labor-management problems in transportation. The act was amended in 1934 and was extended to cover the employees of interstate air carriers in 1936. This discussion is of the act as amended. It should be emphasized that only rail and air transportation labor-management relations are involved.

Although each step under the Railway Labor Act is not clearly defined or provided under the law, there are five steps in the mechanics of labor-management conflict settlement. These are conference and collective bargaining, boards of adjustment or mediation, voluntary arbitration, emergency boards, and presidential or congressional action. These steps are illustrated in Figure 27.1.

Conference and Collective Bargaining

The mechanics of settlement, as noted above, assume that normally contracts will be reached by use of the traditional methods of free collective bargaining. Disputes over contracts, interpretations, and grievances, it is assumed, will usually be settled by conferences between carriers and employees. These two devices, it is hoped, will handle the majority of the problems occurring and no other procedure will be necessary. Unfortunately, sometimes the mere existence of additional procedures seems to jeopardize the effectiveness of earlier steps, and neither side makes any great effort to settle issues at the lower levels.

Boards of Adjustment or Mediation

Drawing upon previous experience, the Railway Labor Act set up two boards with jurisdiction to act in two broad areas. These are the National Railroad Adjustment Board and the National Board of Mediation.

Figure 27.1 Settlement Procedures Under Railway Labor Act

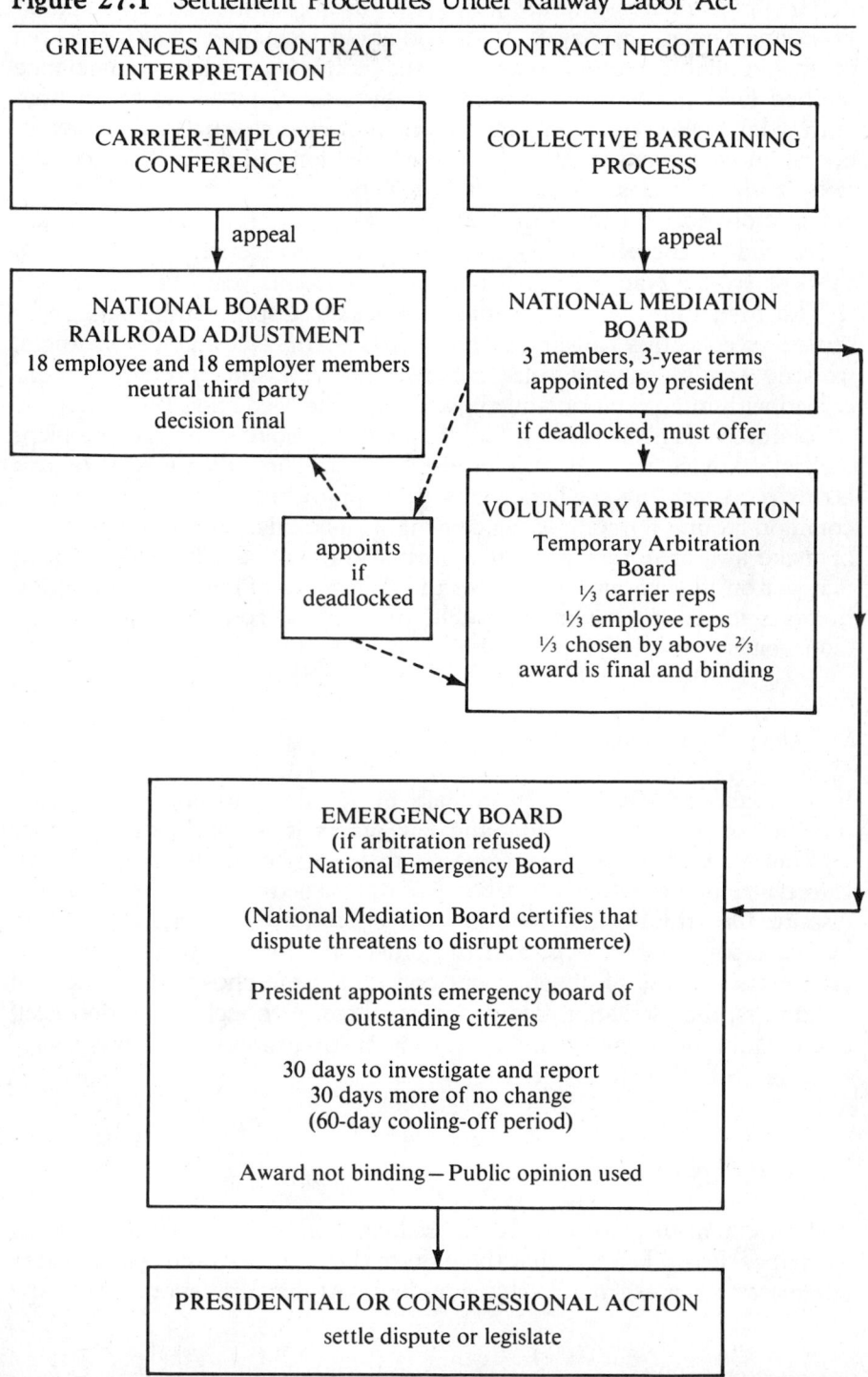

The Adjustment Board has jurisdiction over grievances and interpretation of agreements on pay, working conditions, and rules. This is the area of the conference noted above. If the employer-employee conference method fails, the board (composed of thirty-six members, eighteen from each side) makes an interpretation which is binding on both parties. In operation, the board is divided into four divisions, each with jurisdiction over a separate class of labor. If a deadlock occurs in a consideration before a division, a neutral third party is selected to serve until a decision is reached. If there is no agreement upon the selection of the neutral third party, the National Mediation Board appoints one.

The Mediation Board has jurisdiction over disputes that cannot be settled by collective bargaining. This involves contract changes in wages, working conditions, and rules (whereas the Adjustment Board is concerned with interpretation and application). The Mediation Board is made up of three members serving for three years appointed by the president with the advice and consent of the Senate. The primary task of this board is to institute mediation and attempt to help both parties find a common ground for contract agreement. The board does not decide issues or make awards. Either party may invoke the services of the board or it may act on its own motion. Unlike the Adjustment Board, the Mediation Board is made up of impartial public officials not connected with either management or labor.

Voluntary Arbitration

If the National Mediation Board fails in its efforts to bring the parties together on common ground, the law orders it to work for voluntary arbitration. Both sides must agree to abide by the results of arbitration before a temporary arbitration board is established to hear the particular dispute. One-third of the arbitrators are chosen by the carriers, one-third by the labor organizations, and the other one-third by the carrier-labor arbitrators. In case of disagreement concerning the choice of the neutral arbitrators, the Mediation Board chooses them. Although arbitration itself is voluntary, once the parties agree to it the arbitration decision is legally binding on both parties.

Emergency Boards

Arbitration may, of course, be refused. In such a case, if the National Mediation Board believes that the dispute threatens to interrupt interstate commerce, it must notify the president. At his discretion, then, the president may create a special emergency board charged with investigating the dispute. This emergency board has thirty days in which to investigate and report, and during that time no change may take place in the conditions that led to the dispute unless by agreement.

Actually, emergency boards make recommended awards or settlements in their reports, but this action is not binding. It is hoped, however, that the power of public opinion will induce acceptance of the findings of the emergency board. If the recommendation of the emergency board is refused, another thirty days must elapse before any change or action can commence. Hence, it is often said that the appointment of an emergency board postpones any work stoppage for a sixty-day cooling-off period.

While well over two hundred emergency boards have been created since 1926, it should be understood that the law states that the president *may* appoint a national emergency board *at his discretion.* This matter of discretion was forcibly brought to attention when President George Bush declined to appoint an emergency board in the Eastern Airlines dispute in 1989 and thus allowed a strike at Eastern which caused its bankruptcy.

Presidential or Congressional Action

If all the foregoing efforts fail and the power of public opinion does not induce a settlement, the president himself may act to avoid disruption of commerce. This step is not included in the Railway Labor Act, but it is a real possibility. On several occasions, the president has "seized" the railroads, and on several occasions, he has recommended immediate congressional action to avoid a nationwide rail strike.

In the so-called featherbedding issue, President Kennedy during the summer of 1962 requested that Congress pass a special law prohibiting a threatened strike and setting up compulsory arbitration. Congress responded, and an issue that had been in active bargaining for more than five years and that had gone through all the preliminary steps described above plus a special Presidential Railroad Commission investigation was solved only by presidential and congressional action. In the spring of 1964, President Johnson averted a nationwide rail strike by personally mediating and negotiating a settlement. The president used his considerable personal and official prestige and persuasive powers to force a settlement and avoid a nationwide work stoppage. Again, only the last step of presidential action, this time by bringing the negotiators to the White House itself, saved the nation from a crippling disruption of commerce. More recently, Congress has acted to prevent stoppages on numerous occasions by passing special legislation. Another recent incident was emergency congressional action to restore rail service in the fall of

1982 when a dispute with the Engineers Brotherhood brought the railroads to a halt.

PUBLIC EMPLOYEE STRIKES

As we noted in Chapter 8, public ownership of transportation facilities is considerable, particularly in local transit systems. Likewise, the FAA employees operating the airways are public employees. Here the matter of continuity of service is equally as important as in the private transportation sector.

The federal government and most state governments prohibit strikes by public employees. Some laws specify various mediation or arbitration procedures for labor-management disputes in this area. Potential work stoppages by police, firefighters, and sanitation workers invoke strong emotions and are quite complex. Almost all labor contracts in this area as well as transit contain no-strike provisions.

The problem of public sector employee labor relations was forcibly brought to the attention of the whole nation when the Professional Air Traffic Controllers Organization (PATCO) engaged in a work stoppage in August 1981. There had been previous illegal strikes in this area in 1970 and 1978 and a series of illegal work stoppages in transit in various cities in the past. However, in the PATCO strike, the Reagan administration took the strongest possible action and fired all striking employees. This gave a new dimension to public employee strikes and the action had considerable repercussions on the air transportation system. A similar illegal strike by the Boston Carmen's Union against the Massachusetts Bay Transportation Authority in April 1982 brought the threat of immediate firing. While the study of public employee strikes is a separate area of industrial relations, it seems clear that transportation workers in the public sector do not have the right to strike.

JOB PROTECTION

In addition to the publicly imposed procedural steps noted above, the federal government has promoted job protection in the transportation industries in various ways.

Job protection legislation developed primarily in the railroad industry. In the provisions of the Transportation Act of 1940 dealing with mergers and consolidations, Congress directed the ICC to approve only mergers in which the carriers agreed that no employee would be placed in a worse position because of the mergers for a period of four years. If employees had to be laid off because of the merger in the first four years, a cash settlement was usually involved. In the late 1960s, this provision cost the Penn Central consolidation $78 million.

When the Railway Passenger Service Act of 1970 created Amtrak, employee protection was extended to six years. Amtrak was literally forced to continue with the former employees of the railroads joining it or pay six years' wages. Job protection was continued in the 3-R Act of 1973 as noted in Chapter 12, and Congress appropriated $250 million to federally finance a job guarantee plan while the Northeast Railroad reorganization was under way. In the 1976 4-R Act setting up Conrail, Title V guaranteed all employees with five or more years' service their 1974 salaries for life. In 1981, Conrail was paying $4 million a month to displaced employees under the provisions of the 4-R Act. In that year, Congress passed the Northeast Rail Services Act, which rescinded the lifetime guarantee for displaced Conrail workers and substituted a three-year guarantee from the date of the act (1981). This change was an important factor in the subsequent attainment of profitability for Conrail (and its ultimate sale as a privately owned carrier). In the Milwaukee Railroad and Rock Island Line abandonment and reorganization, Congress allocated $75 million in the Staggers Rail Act to guarantee displaced workers 80 percent of their salary for three years and set up preferential hiring plans for labor.

Preferential hiring plans that provide that displaced workers must be given preference for job openings were included in both the Airline Deregulation Act of 1978 and the Bus Regulatory Reform Act of 1982. The air deregulation act further provided that if employment was reduced 7.5 percent or more because of deregulation, eligible employees with four years' service who were deprived of their jobs would receive monthly assistance payments for seventy-two months or until they were rehired. No funds were allocated for this provision as it was not anticipated that job protection would be activated. Controversy arose in 1981 and 1982 relative to how much reduction in airline labor was due to deregulation and how much was due to the recession.

No other industries have job protection plans similar to these, and in no other industry does the government allocate money for displaced workers. Job protection is just another illustration that labor-management relations in transportation exist in a unique environment.

THE EFFECT OF DEREGULATION ON LABOR

As we noted in Chapter 14 (Consequences of Deregulation), the deregulation movement has affected almost every aspect of transportation. Labor is no exception to that statement. For years management had been able to go before the regulatory authorities for increased rates when the labor bargain raised costs. With deregulation and more competition due to freer entry, this avenue of shifting labor costs into higher rates was effectively closed. What has been the effect of deregulation on labor-management relations?

First, almost all the new carriers entering air, motor, and rail transportation have been nonunion. As noted in Chapter 14, the Teamsters Union lost 116,633 jobs from 1980 to 1987. In air transportation, most new carriers were nonunion and were paid considerably lower wages. For example, unionized captains with ten years' experience received $108,000 annually, but at Continental Airlines (when it reentered the market as a nonunion carrier following its bankruptcy in 1983) an airline captain with the same ten years' experience was paid $52,500. In 1986, the average unionized airline pilot earned $80,000, but the Air Line Pilots Association reported that new-hire nonunion pilots averaged $21,000. Lower nonunion wages are one reason why many new airlines were able to offer such discount airfares. Also, as mentioned in Chapter 14, almost all of the "short-line" railroads were nonunion.

Second, in the face of increased competition from new carriers, management in trucking and air transportation was able to convince unions to allow a two-tier wage system. Under this system, beginning workers were hired at substantially lower wage levels than existing unionized workers. After a period of time (itself a controversial issue in bargaining) the "B scale" workers, as they are called, reach the level of the existing workers. The unions were often forced to accept this arrangement, even though it violated the historical "equal pay for equal work" union concept, in order to retain jobs.

Third, with free entry in trucking, many unionized carriers organized subsidiaries that were nonunion. This is known as "double breasting," like a man's suit. Sales personnel would solicit freight at regular rates but if unable to get traffic that way would offer lower rates in the nonunion subsidiary from the inside pocket of his or her double-breasted suit. The Teamsters have unsuccessfully attempted to write prohibitions of double breasting into their contract.

Fourth, in rail transportation the nonunion short lines which have increased substantially in number under deregulation as noted in Chapter 14 have been able to avoid costly work rules that were included in union contracts over the years. Instead of paying on the basis of mileage (110 miles equals a day's pay as noted above), most short-line railroads pay by the hour. Also, instead of four- or five-man crews (both male and female), the short lines operate a freight train with a two-man crew. Likewise, maintenance personnel are not restricted as to the type of mechanical work they can do by jurisdictional rules. Some changes in work rules have even begun to appear in union contracts in railroading under the pressure of deregulation.

Fifth, there has been an increase in local and regional bargaining rather than the prior pattern of industry-wide bargaining in trucking. In spite of the unions' goals of no pay differentials across the entire country, many carriers have been forced by competition to avoid such things as the National Motor Freight Agreements (bargained by representatives of the major motor carriers and the Teamsters on a nationwide basis). The alternative for local unions is to keep jobs, since entry and exit is so open in motor transportation. Many more local and regional contracts are now written and differentials in wages and conditions of work now vary widely.

Finally, there has been a growth of employee stock ownership plans (ESOPs). In 1974 Senator Russell Long pushed through Congress the first legislation promoting ESOPs. Since that time, more than twenty pieces of legislation have increased the appeal of these devices. The idea is to promote worker ownership and give workers more of a vested interest in their employers. Productivity is supposed to increase, along with better quality control, better cost control, and less acrimonious bargaining. A trust is established to hold stock in the corporation in the name of the employees, and the trust borrows funds to accomplish this. Lenders are taxed on only 50 percent of the income from such loans (making them eager to lend to ESOPs), dividends paid to an ESOP are not taxed, and there is a tax break on principal repayments. Also, corporate pension plans can be less generous since the ESOP will pay employees upon retirement. Many major U.S. firms such as Proctor and Gamble, Polaroid, Texaco, J. C. Penney, and Anheuser-Busch have ESOPs.

ESOPs were organized by many transportation firms in the early 1980s for all of the above reasons plus another important factor: survival. Many carriers were faced with the need to reduce costs but union contracts prevented this. Thus an ESOP was offered in place of a pay raise or as an offset to a pay decrease. Often workers were offered an ESOP in return for taking a 15 or 20 percent cut in pay. Sometimes this meant continuation of the carrier and avoidance of bankruptcy. For the workers, it was sometimes a choice between an ESOP and potential future payments from company profits or no job. Some transportation firms were successful and remained competitive and in business in the face of new entrants using ESOPs; some failed in spite of ESOPs.

One interesting aspect was that ESOPs made unions and workers a factor of importance in mergers and takeovers and bankruptcies since they now had an ownership position in the carrier. Another interesting development was where Avis advertised extensively that its customers were "dealing with the owners" due to an ESOP. Along the same line,

American West Airline requires that all employees own stock up to 20 percent of their annual salary (and help finance ownership with loans) as a condition of employment. Employee ownership either directly or through ESOPs is now found in transportation.

In summary, deregulation has changed many aspects of transportation labor-management relations. Unions have lost power, two-tiered wage systems are now used, double breasting continues, work rules are under pressure, regional and local bargaining is more common, and ESOPs are found in transportation.

ALTERNATIVE SOLUTIONS

There has been concern that the settlement procedures under the Railway Labor Act of 1926 actually impede traditional collective bargaining. The question is: Why bargain sincerely when you know that a settlement will be reached under the legal procedures at a later date? This has also made the settlement process very long. For example, in the 1989 Eastern Airlines strike and subsequent bankruptcy, bargaining and mediation had taken fifteen months before a strike was actually accomplished. Also, in recent times, presidential and congressional action has caused many persons to ask what alternatives exist. It is obvious that neither the president nor Congress can settle every labor-management dispute in transportation. Indeed, there is a real question whether they should be called upon to settle any specific labor-management dispute. Many have suggested that the mechanics of conflict settlement in this area have broken down and that the institutional structure of transportation labor-management relations must be reconstituted. This was one of the conclusions of the special Presidential Railroad Commission in its report on the featherbedding issue in 1962 and was one of the several suggestions made by President Kennedy in his precedent-making transportation message of April 1962.

There are several alternative solutions to this problem: work stoppage, reconstitution of the labor market, compulsory arbitration, government ownership, and private transportation.

Work Stoppage

One approach is to allow labor-management disputes to run their full course, including work stoppages, as they may do in other parts of the economy. This is hardly a possible alternative, however. General work stoppages on our railroads or airlines are unthinkable. Our economy is so dependent upon transportation that a work stoppage of even a few days, especially on the railroads, would paralyze all economic activity. No responsible government would or could permit this. A nationwide transportation strike, at least one involving a major mode, has become an industrial "hydrogen bomb," a weapon too destructive to use.

Reconstitution of the Labor Market

Another approach would be to abandon industry-wide bargaining in favor of bargaining between local and single companies or between national unions and single companies. Although this would avoid a nationwide strike, it would not settle the problem. At best, it only segments it. The effect upon commerce would still be severe, even if only on one geographic segment at a time, and our geographic regions are closely interconnected and highly interdependent.

There is some indication that the railroad brotherhoods have decided to pursue this alternative. They now seem to wish to bargain as national unions with a single railroad at a time. They do not, as yet, wish to have local unions bargaining with single companies. Their strength would be greatly dissipated by such a move.

The recent use of "selected strikes" in railroads, truck lines, and airlines seems to indicate that transportation labor now realizes that nationwide work stoppages will call forth government intervention. Under these tactics, unions do not strike all carriers but rather specific carriers or specific geographic regions. These strikes are much less likely to cause government intervention.

In spite of this apparent recent change in tactics by the unions, there are real disadvantages to such an approach. Differentials in wages and conditions may easily arise under such segmentation. Solidarity is lost, and the chance of having to settle at less than the national pattern with some carriers is a real one. It is not easy to give up the ideal of unionism and turn back the pages of time.

There is some question as to whether or not carrier management desires a segmented labor market. By bargaining as individual carriers, they lay themselves open to "whipsaw" tactics, where the union can play one carrier off against another. The airlines recognized this possibility, and as a result six of the trunk lines entered into a mutual aid pact in 1958. Under this agreement, all members pledge to pay to an airline suffering a service stoppage because of a strike an amount equal to the increased revenue, minus expenses, resulting from the increased business going to the nonstruck lines. This allows the carriers at least partial protection from successive work stoppages designed to force settlement on successive lines by the whipsaw device. After CAB approval, these mutual aid pacts were extended to cover all carriers.

Under the Airline Deregulation Act of 1978, Congress moved to blunt the power of mutual aid pacts in the airlines. Under Section 29 of that act, no airline could receive payments from a mutual aid pact during the first thirty days of a work stoppage, no carrier could receive payments in excess of 60 percent of its operating expenses during the strike period, no payments from a mutual aid plan could exceed eight weeks in duration, and carriers had to agree to binding arbitration if employees requested it. In effect, these provisions made mutual aid pacts much less desirable and their use in airlines has practically ceased.

Finally, it is highly questionable whether Congress could or would pass a statute forbidding industry-wide bargaining even if both labor and management agreed to such an approach.

Compulsory Arbitration

In 1963, Congress used the compulsory arbitration approach in the featherbedding issue. Various other schemes using this approach have been attempted, primarily at the state level and primarily involving public utilities whose services are considered equally essential. Special boards of arbitrators, special courts of industrial relations, or special awards of public officials have all been suggested or tried. None has been satisfactory. Certainly neither party was satisfied with the solution imposed in the 1963 experience. The major advantage of this approach is that service stoppages are avoided.

There are at least four disadvantages to this alternative. First, no workable plan has been set forth. In the utilities, all efforts to sustain service by forcing arbitration have proved either unworkable or have been declared illegal. People cannot be forced to work against their will. Second, the whole process of compulsory arbitration subverts collective bargaining. There is little incentive to do more than go through the motions of bargaining if both sides know that if they are dissatisfied they can force a board or an official to settle the issue. Bargaining is looked upon as wasted effort since the final positions of both sides will eventually have to be stated to the arbitrators; thus no effort is made in the bargaining process to find a settlement without resorting to this ultimate decision. To some degree, this is now true with presidential action as a step.

Third, labor feels that compulsory arbitration imposes second-class citizenship upon it. The ultimate weapon of the strike is denied, and a group of arbitrators determines labor's fate. Intelligent labor leaders wish to avoid compulsory arbitration if for no other reason than because it replaces the need for bargainers or even unions.

Fourth, compulsion goes against our traditional idea of what is right. Democracy is based on the idea of free people persuading others in open debate. Compulsory arbitration not only tends toward "involuntary servitude" by labor, but smacks of authoritarianism. The alternative of compulsory arbitration is not at all a realistic alternative.

Government Ownership

Some have proposed that the government should own the carriers, thereby obviating work stoppages. The whole question of government ownership has been debated for many years and involves aspects other than labor-management relations. There is real doubt that government ownership would solve the labor-management issue, however, and this alternative seems like a rather harsh and probably unworkable solution. Public employees do strike on occasion, and there is little reason to suspect that making transportation labor into public employees would make them any less interested in wages, working rules, and conditions of labor. Besides, most observers would agree that other problems brought on by government ownership would be too great a price to pay for labor-management peace even if public ownership would bring such peace.

Private Transportation

The final alternative approach might be to change the structure of the transportation industry itself. Where private transportation is possible, mainly in motor and water carriage, work stoppages have sometimes been avoided by producers providing their own transportation on a nonunion basis. At the very best, this is but a partial solution. It assumes no unions, a condition that would be most difficult to impose, and it assumes no common carriers, an equally unrealistic assumption. Extensive private transportation by rail, air, or pipeline would be virtually impossible. Who can own their own railroad or how many air travelers can afford their own plane? Even if such a move were possible, it would call for major traffic shifts and a complete technological, economic, and legal reorganization of the transportation industry. Although some large producers owning their own trucks and barges are partially insulated from national labor-management disputes, this certainly is not a practical solution.

Amended Procedures

A final alternative, which has received some support, is amended procedures with more presidential options. Proposals have varied, but generally the idea is that some further action should be available once an emergency board has reported and the sixty-day cooling-off period has elapsed. Various options, such as submission of best offers to employee votes, automatic government seizure, and enforced periods of extended operation, have been proposed. Congress has not yet seen fit to adopt any of these proposals, however.

SUMMARY

This chapter has noted the conflicting goals of the carriers, employees, and the public and has emphasized that in transportation *continuity of service* is the overwhelming public goal which colors all attempts to solve labor-management relations by legalistic means. The historical nature, the economic and technical aspects, the employment characteristics, carrier costs, process characteristics, substitutability of capital for labor, and changes in employment were all discussed as background to the nature of the problem. Next the mechanics of labor-management conflict settlement under the Railway Act of 1926, which applies to both railroad and air transportation, was detailed. The problem of public employee work stoppages was discussed, as well as job protection and the effects of deregulation. Finally, suggestions for alternatives were discussed, but none was found to be satisfactory. Perhaps our grandchildren will have to muddle through from crisis to crisis just as our grandparents did. Not every problem has a solution.

ADDITIONAL READINGS

Bohlander, George W., and Martin T. Farris, "Collective Bargaining in Trucking — The Effect of Deregulation," *The Logistics and Transportation Review*, 20, No. 3 (September 1984), 223–38.

Curtis, Ellen Foster, and Michael Crum, "Transportation Labor Relations: Contemporary Developments, Challenges and Strategies," *Transportation Journal*, 42, No. 3 (July 1988), 359–75.

Davis, Grant M., Martin T. Farris, and Jack J. Holder, Jr., *Management of Transportation Carriers*, New York: Praeger Publishers, 1975.
    Chapter 14, "Labor Relations and Collective Bargaining," pp. 247–59.

Davis, Grant M., William H. Holley, and A. G. Sullenberger, "The Railroad Industry: A Case for Final Offer Selection Arbitration," *Transportation Journal* (Summer 1978), 73–85.

Davis, Grant M., Charles S. Sherwood, and Richard W. Jones, "An Estimate of Labor Protection Cost in Selected Railway Consolidations," *I.C.C. Practitioners' Journal* (November-December 1975), 56–71.

Davis, Grant M., Norman Weintraub, and William H. Holley, Jr., "Employee Stock Ownership Programs and Their Use in Trucking: Capital Formation, Employee Participation or Survival?" *The Logistics and Transportation Review* 23, No. 3 (August 1987), 243–63.

Fair, Marvin L., and Ernest W. Williams, Jr., *Transportation and Logistics*, Rev. ed., Plano, Texas: Business Publications, 1981.
Chapter 15, "Management, Labor, and the Efficiency of Operations," pp. 253–76.

Hille, Stanley J., and Richard F. Poist, Jr., "Striking Transportation Matters," *Transportation: Principles and Perspectives*, Danville, Ill.: Interstate Printers and Publishers, 1974, pp. 331–38.

Levine, Marvin J., "The Railroad Crew Size Controversy Revisited," *Transportation: Principles and Perspectives*, Danville, Ill.: Interstate Printers and Publishers, 1974, pp. 317–30.

Lieb, Robert C., "A Review of the Federal Role in Transportation Labor Protection," *I.C.C. Practitioners' Journal* (March-April 1978), 333–41.

_____ , "The Changing Nature of Labor/Management Relations in Transportation," *Transportation Journal* (Spring 1984), 4–14.

_____ , *Labor in the Transportation Industry*, New York: Praeger Publishers, 1974.

_____ , *Transportation*, 3rd ed., Reston, Va.: Reston Publishing Co., 1985.
Chapter 17, "Labor in Transportation Industries," pp. 357–81.

Lieb, Robert C., and James F. Molloy, "The Major Airlines: Labor Relations in Transition," *Transportation Journal*, 26, No. 3 (Spring 1987), 17–29.

McCabe, Douglas M., "The Railroad Industry's Labor Relations Environment; Implications for Railroad Managers," *I.C.C. Practitioners' Journal* (September-October 1982), 592–608.

McMullen, B. Starr, "Employee Protection After Airline Deregulation," *Transportation Journal*, 25, No. 3 (Spring 1986), 20–34.

Pegrum, Dudley F., *Transportation: Economics and Public Policy*, 3rd ed., Homewood, Ill.: Richard D. Irwin, 1973.
Chapter 20, "The Special Problem of Labor," pp. 474–90.

Rich, Stuart, "Changing Railway Technology in the U.S. and Its Impact Upon Railroad Employment Since 1945," *Transportation Journal*, 25, No. 4 (Summer 1986), 55–65.

Taff, Charles A., *Commercial Motor Transportation*, 7th ed., Centreville, Md.: Cornell Maritime Press, 1986.
Chapter 10, "Labor Relations," pp. 224–40.

CHAPTER 28

PUBLIC AIDS
AND PROMOTIONS
OF TRANSPORTATION

NATURE OF THE PROBLEM

One of the special problems of domestic transportation is the matter of public aids and promotions. As noted earlier, Congress established as a goal in the Declaration of National Transportation Policy in 1940 the "fair and impartial regulation of all modes of transportation . . . so administered as to recognize and preserve the inherent advantages of each." This goal continues in the Declaration of National Transportation Policy even though it has been amended and lengthened in the Motor Carrier Act of 1980 and the Bus Regulatory Reform Act of 1982.

Inequality of public aid, investment, and promotion clouds the determination of the inherent advantage of each mode. The regulation of intermodal competition is particularly difficult when all modes do not need to meet their respective total costs of service.

Public aids and promotions are also a problem from the point of view of social policy. At any time, society can afford to invest only a portion of its resources in any one economic undertaking whether that investment be private or public. How much development of a particular type of transportation is needed in our economic system at any one time is a most challenging problem. Not only is the matter of timing involved, but also the amount of investment.

If a free market existed and competition and the private profit motive were allowed to operate fully in this field, the allocation problem would be much simpler. The particular allocation of resources to transportation would be decided according to which showed the greatest dollar return after cost. This would be true both between transportation and nontransportation undertakings and among the various modes of transportation. As long as the acquisitive spirit existed and was allowed to operate freely, we could expect the free market to allocate resources of all types to the most profitable undertaking.

But the completely free market does not exist, and for several reasons it does not determine the allocation of resources in transportation. These reasons may be summarized as historical, technological, economic, and social.

Historical

From the very first, transportation has been aided and promoted by various governmental levels in our society. An improved domestic transportation system was so important to the economic, political, and social development of our nation that internal improvement schemes comprised some of the first congressional problems after the attainment of independence. Even though our country was firmly committed to private enterprise, it was recognized that government had an obligation to assist in the creation of an environment conducive to economic development. A transportation system is akin to law and order, coinage, inviolability of contract, and other essentials of commercial enterprise.

Additionally, there is real question whether a privately owned transportation system would have been possible. Not only was the necessary investment overwhelming, but by its very nature, transportation used public resources such as rivers and harbors, roadways and streets, and airspace. A system of privately owned highways, waterways, or airways, even if such a thing were legally possible, would be unthinkable. Transportation agencies have no choice but to use public facilities in many cases.

Our society did not arise full grown. There existed a long history in Europe, particularly England, of the common carrier operating by sanction of the sovereign. This service, which was to be provided to all comers under common-law regulation, was transplanted to this continent by the early colonizers. No free market existed in the common-carrier tradition. Common carriers could not pick among customers and serve only the most profitable, nor was free entry or exit of firms allowed. Common carriers could never charge whatever they desired, raising fees to certain customers or at certain times and lowering them at other times or for other customers. In other words, the free market and competitive nature mandatory for the market type of allocation did not exist in the society that provided the historical background for our domestic transportation system.

Although the current transportation scene is more competitive — both intramodally and intermodally — than it has been for a long time, the idea of the *common carrier* still remains the underlying tradition in transportation. Society seems destined to exercise control over transportation; the question is what sort of control and in what form. Public aid and promotion is one of those forms.

Technological

The various modes of transportation developed at different periods of time. Technologically, of course, it was not possible to have some of the newer modes of transportation until recently. The invention of the internal combustion engine and the conquest of space by flight are but two illustrations of technological developments that were the outgrowth of competing transportation modes. The existence of choice and competition among several modes, then, was simply not a technological possibility until recently. Hence, the use of individual choice to allocate among modes was not feasible.

Technology has played a role in transportation aids and promotions in another way. It is often a drawn-out and expensive matter to develop technological breakthroughs. Even after the means are technologically available, periods of testing and gaining public confidence are long and expensive. Often some if not all of the expense of testing, acceptance, development, and research has been carried on with public aid. Americans have always been fascinated by new developments. It is not surprising, then, that society has been willing to sponsor research, development, and technology that ultimately lead to transportation choice. As will be noted shortly, a great deal of the research and development of air transportation is the direct result of governmental aid. This is one example that shows that part of the costs of some modes of transportation are paid for by society.

Economic

Another reason the free market and competitive structure have not existed in transportation, making allocation based completely on competition possible, is the economic structure of transportation itself. By nature, some types of transportation are monopolistic. In order for a rail system to exist, it must be a monopoly. The power of eminent domain, itself a type of governmental aid, was necessary in order to acquire rights of way. The huge amounts of capital necessary could not be attracted unless there was assurance that the service had a monopolistic element. During the developmental period of rail building, cities and towns were eager to grant monopoly privileges in order to get the desired rail service. The same was true of early canals and, to some degree, of pipelines.

The large capital investment necessary for a rail or pipeline system gives rise to a high degree of fixed costs. When high fixed costs exist, competition may lower prices drastically. Under such circumstances, it is not unusual for prices to fall below total costs, almost to the level of variable costs. Competing means of transportation without similar cost structures found they were unable to continue in the face of drastic price cutting. In order for them to exist at all in the face of such competition, it was necessary to have public aids or promotions of various types. An example of this situation is the popular justification of expenditures on waterways as a "way to keep rail rates low."

Likewise, highways and streets are extremely expensive, and although carriers using these facilities are considerably more competitive than railroads or pipelines, it would be almost impossible for an individual firm to build and own its own road. To be sure, some large businesses own their own railroads, usually short lines servicing their plants or production facilities, and some large lumber companies own their own forest roads or railroads. Also, there have been a few private/public toll roads and bridges where investor groups furnish capital and charge tolls for their use. However, highway and air carriers depend upon publicly owned ways and thereby the public assumes the fixed cost of these facilities and sometimes collects a user fee. In turn, these ways are available for use by everybody, since they are part of the public infrastructure.

Social Policy

Various social policies of the United States have provided a part of the cost of some modes of transportation and not of others. The provision of the way for motor carriers, air carriers, and water carriers are examples. In many cases, carriers were the fortuitous gainers of public aids whose goal was divorced from for-hire transportation and the inequality of transportation competition.

For example, interest in conservation has led to stream development for purposes of flood control, erosion control, irrigation, and water conservation. These goals also provide waterways upon which inland water carriers may operate. One of the justifications for federal expenditures on highways was to provide for free rural delivery of mail in order to bring educational and informational materials to rural America. However, improved roads used for mail delivery are equally available to commercial vehicles. The country's defense also calls forth public expenditures for airports and airways. Trained aviation personnel need to be available in case of wartime emergency. Equipment used on commercial airline operations can and does play a vital role in the defense plans of our society. Here again is a rationalization for an aid to transportation that is divorced from competitive considerations. Finally, it has been our social policy to encourage mobility of our population. Through mobility, it is assumed that individuals can seek their own fortune where they please or take their pleasure in their own fashion. There is also an educational aspect in encouraging travel in our society. The slogan "See America First" illustrates this point. Again, much of the rationalization for highway expenditures has been in terms of other than transportation competition.

In all these cases, the means of transportation have been provided publicly or have been publicly aided because of a social policy unrelated to transportation competition. Regardless of the social objectives involved, facilities have been made available to various modes of transportation. Part of the cost has been absorbed by the public for some modes and not for others. Even though the carriers may pay a portion of the cost of the facilities through user charges (taxes), their burden of immediate investment in the way has been lifted. Additionally, the users are not asked to pay taxes on the public investment or interest on the funds committed as under a privately owned way. True competition, with each competitor paying all its own costs and the traffic going to the low-cost bidder, is simply not possible under such an arrangement. The same reasoning holds for types of public aid other than provision of the way.

It is necessary to conclude, then, that a free market with completely competitive relationships has never existed in transportation. A market allocation of resources has been impossible because of historical, technological, economic, and social policy impediments. Allocation of transportation resources has always been affected by public aids of various types.

The problem, then, becomes a matter of evaluating the goals of public aid, the methods of carrying them out, and their effects on transportation. Only by understanding and carefully evaluating these points can intelligent choices be made by society. In evaluating goals, methods, and effects of public aid to transportation, as in other social decisions, readers should keep clearly in mind that conclusions concerning desirability or undesirability must be based in considerable part upon subjective value judgments. Rational economic analysis may tell us what happens under various conditions, but whether a result is good or bad usually depends upon an individual's or a society's philosophy, and philosophies may change from time to time.

GOALS OF PUBLIC AIDS

The goals of public aids and promotions in transportation are not always easy to ascertain because they are so interwoven with broad social objectives. These goals represent a consensus of opinion at any one time. As a consensus, they represent the desires of various groups in our economy, and these desires are not always the same over time. Public policy on transportation aids and promotions is not only hard to define, but has changed as transportation has developed. However, it seems possible to generalize that the broad goals of society in this matter are developmental and competitive.

Developmental Goals

During its first 100 years as a separate nation, America faced the major problem of developing its resources and physically settling the continent. Much domestic transportation policy was affected by this task. The problem certainly existed prior to the establishment of the nation as an independent country, and it continues to exist at present insofar as all areas of the nation are not equally developed. The developmental goal of public aids and promotions in transportation, therefore, is as important today as it was yesterday, and may be a future policy goal as well.

From the historical viewpoint, a great many of the internal improvement plans of Congress and the states were aimed at settling the country. The rationale behind the railroad land-grant movement, a type of public aid, was that railroads would open up the country. Promotion of canals by states and the building of the National Pike by the federal government are other historical examples of public aids and promotions with a developmental goal. Although it may seem that most of our country now has an adequate transportation system, the plea is still heard for improved transportation to develop the country. A substantial amount of the economic and social development program for Appalachia is for road building. In the mountainous areas of the nation, the need for forest roads is often justified as a method of economic development.

Pleas for improvement of transportation systems as an aid to commerce and industry are still heard, even though initial development has been completed in many areas. Technology moves ahead and old facilities become obsolete. Wider and more direct highways are needed, better waterways are called for, and safer airways become a necessity as development progresses. The rationale of helping commerce and industry develop applies to all levels of government aid. It is argued that with highly developed industry or commerce, more income is generated, more people are employed, and more taxes are collected. Although the actual productivity of public investment in transportation facilities is difficult to measure, it is generally believed that such expenditures lead to a worthwhile development of industry and commerce.

The matter of timing is implicit in this developmental goal. It is sometimes said that facilities would be built without special programs and aids if only society would wait. Perhaps this is true, and over time the profit potential might have caused railroads to expand and state and local governments to recognize the productivity of public investment in roads and airports and inland harbors. But the American people do not like to wait. Thus the main goal of these programs has not just been to develop facilities but to develop them faster than they would have come about had they not been promoted. Hence it is said that land grants caused the West to be settled sooner, the highway program opened up off-rail points faster, and the airways program hastened the development of air transportation.

Competitive Goals

In addition to the idea of providing a means of developing the country, there has been a broad competitive goal to much of our aid and promotion activity in transportation. Being constantly interested in improving ourselves and our society, the goal of our aids and promotions has sometimes been to provide new means of transportation. Certainly much of our program in air transportation has been related to this goal. Aid to helicopters, rail rapid transit, and local-service airlines are examples of the desire to have new transportation means.

Improvement in one area of transport ought to force improvement in competitive modes. Programs to induce waterways to compete with railroads illustrate this. The desire to supplement and replace regulation with transportation competition has also been a goal. There has always been concern, sometimes not always defined as such, that regulation is not working. Suspicion that the regulated and the regulators were somehow in collusion is often heard, hence the desire to have competition as the natural regulator. Even when regulation is trusted as a protector of the public interest, promotion of competitive transportation is justified as a supplement to regulation. Competition provided by public aid as a backstop to regulation has sometimes been sought.

Recognition of the differences in economic structure of the different modes has led to the sponsoring of competitive means of transportation in an attempt to equalize competition. Proposals have sometimes been made for aid programs based solely on the differences in cost of the various modes. Subsidies to help the economically weak compete with the financially strong are sometimes proposed. The evening-up process is also seen in proposals that user charges be used to equalize competitive advantage, although this is the opposite of subsidies and aids. In all these proposals, the rationale, whether recognized or not, is that competition and choice are the most desirable social policy regardless of the cost involved.

The goals of public aids, then, have been developmental and competitive. They overlap considerably and are sometimes hard to distinguish among other social goals, but they exist nevertheless.

MEANING OF THE TERM *SUBSIDIES*

The term *subsidy* is often used when discussing public aids, and many understand that to mean some sort of cash payment. Actually subsidies have many meanings. Basically, there are two types of subsidies: those that are external and direct or indirect, and those that are internal and indirect.

There are six types of external and direct or indirect subsidies as noted in Table 28.1. The most obvious is direct payments by various levels of government to transportation carriers. We shall detail these various subsidy schemes shortly. However, historically various governments have also made direct gifts to carriers. Also governments have often rendered services to the carriers at no charge, which is also a direct subsidy, and examples of this type will also be noted. Indirect subsidies may also be possible in the sale or purchasing functions. These are noted as types 4 and 5 in Table 28.1. Finally the exemption process can be an indirect subsidy, particularly if not everyone using governmental services is not exempted.

Internal subsidies are usually indirect, and some claim that this type of subsidization is widespread in transportation. The term *price discrimination* is widely used here, although actually the form may well be "price

Table 28.1 Types of External Subsidies (Direct and Indirect)

1. Cash payments by government	Direct
2. Outright gifts by government	Direct
3. Services by government rendered at no charge	Direct
4. Government sale of goods and services at less than market value	Indirect
5. Government purchases of goods and services at more than market value	Indirect
6. Exempting certain operations from taxes others must pay	Indirect

differentiation." Price differentiation means charging different prices to different customers for the same product or service. Transportation rates are a common form of price differentiation as noted in Part IV. Rates per 100 pounds are typically less for truckload shipments than for less-than-truckload shipments. If one considers the unit of output in transportation the movement of 100 pounds, then these rates, which are less for a greater volume of shipment, are a form of price differentiation.

"Price discrimination" is a somewhat more subtle concept. However, this term means charging different prices to different customers for the same services *not reflecting costs*. If it costs the carrier less per 100 pounds to move 20,000 pounds than it costs per 100 pounds to move 1,000 pounds and the difference in rates reflects this cost savings, no price discrimination is evident. However, if differences in rates do not reflect differences in costs, then price discrimination is present. The key here is *cost* and whether cost differences are reflected in rate differences.

Why is the existence of price differentials and price discrimination important in a discussion of subsidies? Because it is commonly said that one type of freight which pays a high rate per 100 pounds is subsidizing other freight that pays a lower rate per 100 pounds (a type of internal and indirect subsidy). This may or may not be true — it depends on the carrier's costs to move the respective commodities. Thus, internal subsidies turn on costs of providing the service, not only on the difference in rates per 100 pounds. Are there internal and indirect subsidies in the transportation rate system? Probably there are, but without an analysis of carrier costs, one cannot say definitively that a "cross subsidy" between various classes of freight exists.

The charge of "cross subsidization" in transportation is very hard to document and depends on individual costs. External and direct subsidies are much easier to document and will be our main concern here.

AMOUNT OF PUBLIC AID

As noted above, public aids to transportation have existed for a very long time. The amount of such aids (and external subsidies) has been substantial. We shall give some indication of the historical amounts in the next section. However, dollars paid by governments for the benefit of transportation have been substantial in recent times as well as historically. Some idea of the number of dollars paid out by governments recently is contained in Table 28.2.

It should be noted that some modes have received more dollars or public aid than others and that public aids vary over time (even in the

Table 28.2 Amounts of Federal and State/Local Governmental Expenditures for Transportation Facilities and Services — Selected Years 1950–1987 (Millions of Dollars)

	Airways	Airports	Highways	River/Harbor	Railroad	Transit	Maritime	Total
1950 Federal	115	44	503	189	—	—	N/A	851
State/Local	—	101	3,652	136	—	—	N/A	3,889
Total	115	145	4,155	325	—	—	—	4,740
1960 Federal	429	79	2,753	287	—	—	167	3,715
State/Local	—	342	7,407	237	—	—	—	7,986
Total	429	421	10,160	524	—	—	167	11,701
1970 Federal	965	111	5,181	376	40	133	300	7,106
State/Local	—	969	14,321	444	—	345	—	16,079
Total	965	1,080	19,502	820	40	478	300	23,185
1980 Federal	2,135	656	12,036	1,156	1,064	3,881	606	21,534
State/Local	—	2,501	27,152	1,168	—	3,308	—	34,129
Total	2,135	3,157	39,188	2,324	1,064	7,189	606	55,663
1985 Federal	2,263	879	15,092	1,189	917	3,491	356	24,187
State/Local	—	3,744	40,623	1,495	—	6,890	—	52,752
Total	2,263	4,623	55,715	2,684	917	10,381	356	76,939
1987 Federal	3,236	1,001	14,155	1,043	619	3,387	227	23,668
State/Local	—	4,538	48,217	1,800	—	7,226	—	61,781
Total	3,236	5,539	62,372	2,843	619	10,613	227	85,449

Source: Transportation Policy Associates, *Transportation in America*, 6th ed., Washington, D.C., March 1988, p. 26, and U.S. Department of Transportation, *Maritime Administration Annual Reports*, selected years, Appendix I, "Maritime Subsidies."

post–World War II period). Note that railroads and transit did not receive public aid until 1970. Actually, transit aid started in 1965 and had grown to be the second largest recipient of public aid by 1987 at $10.6 billion. We detailed some of these problems in Chapter 8. Public expenditures for highways and streets is by far the largest amount at $62.4 billion in 1987 — much of which comes from user charges.

It should also be noted that Table 28.2 separates the source of public aid between the federal government and state/local governments. Some programs are federal only (airways, maritime, and railroads) while others are a combination of federal and state/local. Notice also that state/local is usually larger than federal where both federal and state/local aid is given. This is partially due to the various user charge programs which we shall discuss below.

Total amounts of public aid (both federal and state/local) by mode (Table 28.2 is for specific selected years) from 1970 to 1987 are: airways, $34.650 billion; airports, $50.009 billion; highways, $649.226 billion; rivers/harbors, $33.673 billion; railroads, $15.645 billion (including Amtrak and Northeast Corridor Project); transit, $264.550 billion; and maritime, $8.274 billion. Various programs or methods of public aid will be noted next.

METHODS OF PUBLIC AIDS

Public aids and promotions in transportation have taken many forms. Each program has its own distinguishing features. One meaningful approach is to consider the methods or means of aids to transportation according to the tasks they are designed to accomplish rather than by mode. Briefly, four methods are used in public aid programs. These are financing the way, operating the way, financing operating costs, and providing research and development.

Financing the Way

Perhaps the predominant method of public aid is financing the way upon which carriers operate. This has not only been historically the most important aid program, but it remains today the best example of promoting transportation. The public is called upon to invest in the way or part of the way of nearly all modes of transportation. Among the for-hire modes of transportation, pipelines alone are the only ones that have not received some public aid through public investment in the way.

Railroad Land Grants and Aids

Many programs assisted in financing the railway during the developmental period of the railroads. Some of these have been mentioned in Chapter 2. All levels of government participated in these programs, and the major purpose of all was the building of the way.

The exact measurement of the amount and type of these aids during the construction period is quite difficult. Some of the aid was in the form of loans, part of which was repaid and part of which was not. Disputes as to the dollar value of such loans is understandable, because some of the aid was in the form of apparent donations and gifts about which poor records exist. Another form of aid was the guaranteeing of railroad bonds, which thereby permitted them to be sold at lower rates of interest than if they were solely based on railroad credit. Some outright gifts of securities by cities and counties were made to entice railroads to build. Again the problem of measurement is evident. Considerable amounts of land were also involved in land grants and gifts. Here the dispute centers around the value of the land not immediately sold.

One study by the federal coordinator of transportation concluded that federal aid to railroads amounted to $1.4 billion up to 1938. This included Depression loans during the 1930s, expenses of federal railway surveys, remission of import duties on railway iron, a figure for banking privileges granted by the states, guarantees of bonds, a value for streets vacated and occupied by railroads, a figure for railroad bonds subscribed to by cities and counties, and many other figures. An equally authoritative source, the Board of Investigation and Research set up under the Transportation Act of 1940, calculated the amount of aid at $627 million. The BIR study concentrated on land grants, direct loans, street vacations, and expenses of surveys and calculated values in a somewhat different fashion. About the only thing the two studies agreed upon was that the railroads had net proceeds of between $434 and $440 million from the sale of land grants.

State and local assistance to early railroads involved substantial stock and bond subscriptions, some loan guarantees and land grants, and many millions of dollars in outright gifts of cash or negotiable securities.

Perhaps the best-known aid program was land grants. Although states granted large blocks of land to a few railroads, it was principally the federal government that gave land to western railroads to aid in their construction. The total acreage involved approaches 10 percent of the country's area. Starting in 1850 with a grant to the Illinois Central, the program, which closed in 1871, included some seventy-five grants of land. The BIR study notes that the aggregate acreage was 179 million, of which more than 48 million acres were state grants. It also notes that 95 percent of this land was granted to the predecessors of only fourteen of the 1940 railroad companies.

In return for these land grants, railroads agreed to haul government passengers and freight at reduced rates. Practically all railroads extended these reduced rates (even though many received no land grants) in order to share in governmental traffic. The value of these reduced rates, which were not completely removed until 1945, has been estimated by the Board of Investigation and Research at $580 million up to 1943. The sharp increase in movement of troops and government property during World War II increased the value of these concessions immensely. Since the railroads realized somewhat less than this figure from the sale of the land, it is generally held that the land-grant rate concessions more than compensated the federal government for its grants.

In any event, the amount of public aid in providing the way for the rail carriers was substantial. Some contend that since the programs were instituted more than a century ago and a good part of the state aid in the South was subsequently destroyed by the Civil War, railroad aid should not be a factor in current policy. Certainly the money is long spent, and current policy should concern itself with current programs. Nevertheless, aid programs assisting the development of rail carriers are no different in their goals than current programs of aid to other carriers. The method may vary, but the goal is the same. The experience of rate concessions is worth noting for current policy.

The 4-R Act of 1976 established the Railroad Rehabilitation and Improvement Fund, with $1 billion in loan guarantees and $600 million for government loans on redeemable preference stock for railroads applying for aid to restore their roadbeds. Other federal funds were set up for Amtrak and Conrail (prior to its privatization). The Northeast Corridor Project Act has been noted before, and Table 28.2 shows that in 1987 $619 million was spent by the federal government on these current programs. While much of the aid to railroads was in the nineteenth century, public aids and promotions for railroads started again in 1970 and have been in excess of $15 billion from 1970 to 1987.

The Highway Program

The highway program is perhaps the most expensive and comprehensive program of public investment in the way. Public investment in the highway system is also one of the oldest types of transportation aid. As noted earlier, the federal government entered into highway building with the authorization of the National Pike (or Cumberland Road) in 1806.

Total cost of this project, including maintenance, was $6.8 million. Other expenditures for roads were made by federal, state, and local governments.

It was not until 1916, however, that large federal expenditures for highways began again, although local units of government had continued to spend money on roads between the early period of highway improvement and the revival of highway promotion in the twentieth century. Various types of state aid programs were in existence beginning in the 1890s as well, as noted in Chapter 2. It is because all units of government have been involved and the expenditures have been continuous that measurement is difficult. Many scholars, therefore, measure highway expenditures from 1921 when the federal government entered the highway aid program on a large scale.

The Highway Act of 1916 set the pattern of federal aid, but it was not until 1921 that the federal aid primary system was established. This system, originally limited to 7 percent of the total road mileage, is made up of approximately 303,000 miles of roads and was supported on a 50-50 federal-state basis historically. Originally, only rural mileage was included, but in 1944 urban extensions of the primary system were brought under the federal aid program. Approximately 146,000 of the miles in the federal aid system are city streets. Table 28.3 gives the mileage of these various systems.

The federal aid secondary system, originated during the Depression, is concerned with less heavily traveled roads. Approximately 398,000 miles, designated as secondary aid roads, also receive matching aid from the federal government. These secondary roads along with the primary and urban systems are known as the ABC aid program. Federal aid now is generally limited to 75 percent of the expenditures on the ABC system.

The most important road system from the point of view of both commerce and aid is the National System of Interstate and Defense Highways. This system, authorized in 1944, is made up of 43,500 miles of the most heavily traveled highways in the primary system. The system is currently 98 percent complete. Financing of this system was not undertaken until 1956 when it became known as the Interstate System. After extended debate, Congress decided that expenditures for this system should be on a pay-as-we-go basis. Consequently, revenues from the federal gasoline tax and other federal transportation excise taxes are put into a Highway Trust Fund used to finance these roads. The basic aid formula on the Interstate System is 90 percent federal and 10 percent state, with a federal maximum of 95 percent under some circumstances. The 1956 act authorized the federal government to spend $46.2 billion over sixteen years to build this system to the very highest highway standards. In a real sense, this has been a crash program of providing

Table 28.3 Highway Mileage in the United States by Type of Control and Federal-Aid Highway System, 1986 (In Thousands of Miles)

Federal-Aid Highway System

Primary		303
Interstate (part of Primary)	44	
Urban		146
Secondary		398
Total Federal-Aid Systems		847

Type of Control

Urban Mileage		701
Under State Control	94	
Under Local Control	606	
Rural Mileage		3,178
Under State Control	704	
Under Local Control	2,243	
Under Federal Control	231	
Total Mileage		3,880

Source: U.S. Department of Commerce, *Statistical Abstracts of U.S. 1989*, Washington, D.C., p. 591.

high-speed, limited-access highways for commerce and defense. However, construction has been slower than anticipated and costs have been larger than planned. The Interstate System will not be completed until the 1990s and will cost at least $150 billion.

In the 1970s the federal government was spending over $7 billion a year on the nation's highways, much of it on the Interstate System. Due to inflation, the need to reconstruct and rehabilitate federal aid highways constructed at an earlier period, and the need to get the Interstate System finally completed, federal highway expenditures exceeded $10 billion a year in the 1980s. In 1987, federal expenditures were more than $14 billion, as shown in Table 28.2. The ABC system continues to receive federal aid as well as the Interstate System (which is part of the primary system).

As noted above, the federal aid system provides only a portion of the cost and state and local funds pay the remainder based on various "matching" formulas (generally 75 percent federal and 25 percent state on the ABC system and 90 percent federal and 10 percent state on the Interstate System). However, note in Table 28.3 that the federal aid system is only 847,000 miles of the 3,880,000 miles of streets and highways. The vast majority of U.S. streets and highways, over 3 million miles, are supported by state and local governmental revenues. As shown in Table 28.3, rural road mileage, which is mostly under state or local control, makes up the vast majority of the highway mileage in the country. Table 28.2 has already indicated that in 1987 state and local highway expenditures exceeded $48 billion. It has been estimated that from 1970 to 1987 almost $650 billion was spent on highways by both federal and state/local governments combined.

It must be emphasized that while various levels of government have spent vast sums on highways and streets, much of these funds came from user charges. Mention has already been made of the Highway Trust Fund established in 1956 to finance the Interstate System by imposing a 4 cent per gallon user charge plus other related highway user charges on tires, rubber, vehicles, and other items. In 1982 the gasoline tax was raised to 9 cents per gallon (with 1 cent reserved for transit as we noted in Chapters 7 and 8) and in 1984 a special 15.5 cent per gallon diesel tax was imposed. Likewise, states levy gasoline and fuel user taxes, registration fees, and various mileage taxes to support street and highway expenditures. Local governments in some cases have additional gasoline taxes, but property taxes and sales taxes are important sources of local revenue for streets. We shall return to a discussion of user charges directly, but the point is that many of the dollars noted above are derived from the user of the streets and highways, not the general revenue funds of the various governments.

It should be pointed out that much of these highway expenditures have a defense goal and a general policy goal of mobility and safety of our population as well as of assisting commerce and industry with an improved transportation system. Very little of the public investment in highways has been explicitly justified on the basis of providing the way for motor carriers, although this certainly is a result.

This tremendous investment in highways carries with it responsibility for repayment by the users to some degree just as land grants were repaid by rate concessions. Distribution of the highway tax burden among classes of payers, then, becomes important as a policy matter. Likewise, distribution of the user tax portion of the burden among various classes of vehicles is of equal importance. These two policy matters, both basically concerning the allocation of the burden of public investment, will be considered later. At this point, our primary purpose is to point out that public investment in highways has been large, continuous, and comprehensive.

Airways and Airports

Airways, like highways and waterways, are publicly owned and operated. Programs of public investment in this area, though relatively new, are not small. During a recent year, the Federal Aviation Administration had jurisdiction over 381,000 miles of airways.

Airways are not as expensive as highways, of course. Marking and navigational aids are the most important items. (Airports, to be discussed later, are another matter.) Expenditures for airways have continued since the middle 1920s; and while measurement is difficult, it has been estimated that around $20 billion was expended on the establishment of airways between 1925 and 1976. The cost of their maintenance and operation has been several times larger.

Before 1933, airports were financed almost wholly by local funds. During the Depression, however, airport construction was included in various public works programs. Upon passage of the Civil Aeronautics Act of 1938, the Civil Aeronautics Authority was ordered to draw up a plan of airport development and make recommendations on the desirability of federal aid for airport construction. The agency reported in 1939, and Congress made appropriations for this purpose in the early 1940s. In 1946, Congress passed the Federal Airport Act, authorizing the expenditure of $520 million over seven years in the form of federal aid to local governments for airport construction. The time limit on this act was later extended.

As noted in Chapter 12, Congress instituted an airport and airway improvement program in 1970 with specific user charges earmarked for the Aviation Trust Fund. The largest revenue source for this program was the 8 percent tax on passenger tickets and the 5 percent tax on air freight waybills. Under this program, almost $4 billion was expended in grants to state and local governments for airport development between 1970 and 1980. Considerable sums were also spent on upgrading the airway itself.

In 1982 Congress reinstituted the Airport and Airway Improvement Act for another five years. Higher user fees were levied on jet fuel (14 cents per gallon) and aviation gas (12 cents per gallon), the 8 percent passenger ticket tax and the 5 percent air freight tax were continued, as well as a registration fee for aircraft, a head tax ($3) on international passengers, and an excise tax on aircraft tires and tubes. From 1982 to 1987, this program spent $4.7 billion for airport improvement grants, $6.3 billion for improving the airway system, and $7.4 billion for operation and maintenance of the airway (previously not taken from the Aviation Trust Fund) and provided money for the weather bureau and research and development. The total appropriated in this new program exceeded $19 billion for the five years. No funds from the Aviation Trust Fund can be used to pay FAA expenses of administration. In 1987 this program was extended for another five years with the same user charges. As noted in Table 28.2, federal expenditures in 1987 for airways (mostly out of the Aviation Trust Fund) was over $3 billion, and over $1 billion was made available for airport grants.

Airports are owned and operated by local or state agencies (sometimes a combination of local agencies organized as port authorities) with the exception of the airports in the nation's capital (National and Dulles). Federal aid to airports is on a grant basis and depends on the passengers enplaned by each airport. For smaller airports, federal aid is generally 90 percent of the cost of approved facilities. For larger airports, the federal ratio is 75 percent. The remaining portions come from local funds, as does money for construction of terminals and other facilities not included in the federal aid program. Note in Table 28.2 that in 1987 state and local expenditures on airports were over $4.5 billion.

Landing fees and lease charges for space, parking lots, and so forth make up the main source of local airport revenue. Many airports do not generate enough income to cover their total costs and are dependent on the general revenues of the city owning the airport. Some airports do not even cover their operating expenses, let alone repay the capital costs involved. No charge is made by the federal government for the airway, although some repayment is made by way of the 8 percent excise tax on airline tickets collected by the airlines on behalf of the Aviation Trust Fund and other taxes flowing into the fund as previously noted.

As far as public investment in airways and airports is concerned, it is possible to say that from 1970 to 1987 over $34 billion was spent on airways (a portion of which was for operation of the airways by the FAA) and over $50 billion was spent on airports, that it involves several levels of government, and that in all likelihood it will increase in the future especially with the current airport and airways improvement program.

Waterways

One of the oldest types of public investment is that in waterways. Again, all levels of government have been involved and the amount of public investment has been sizable. The history of public aid in this area is most interesting. The Board of Investigation and Research, studying public aids during the early 1940s, noted that Boston erected a town wharf in the 1630s, colonial governments built at least twelve lighthouses, and the state of Virginia began a short canal in 1785.

Some of our very first transportation policy regulation was related to waterways. The Treaty of Paris in 1763 guaranteed that the Mississippi River would be free and open to use from its source to the seas without discrimination as to nationality. The peace treaty at the end of the American Revolution contained the significant provision that the Mississippi would be "forever free." Article Four of the Northwest Ordinance of 1787 declared the navigable waters leading into the Mississippi and St. Lawrence rivers to be "common highways, and forever free" of "any tax, impost, or duty" to citizens of the United States. There is some question, of course, as to whether this "freedom" of use should be extended to cover expensive improvements to natural waterways. It is well established that Congress has complete power over navigable waterways of the nation (U.S. v. Appalachian Electric Co., 311 U.S. 377, 1940).

In connection with some necessary improvements in the upper Mississippi River waterway system, Congress levied a user fee on the waterways for the first time in 1978. This move was controversial, but ultimately a compromise was struck. With these actions, users paid a 4 cent per gallon fuel tax from 1978 to 1980, 6 cents per gallon from 1980 to 1986, and 10 cents per gallon after 1986. These revenues will not cover all the government costs of the waterways but will recoup a portion of the expense.

The experiences of the states during the canal era have been noted in Chapter 2. The exact amount of this state aid is hard to measure, but Professor Locklin states that between 1820 and 1840 nearly $200 million in state indebtedness was incurred, presumably mostly for canals. The provision of terminals and other facilities by local governments in modern times has also been substantial.

On the federal level, the BIR study notes that $2.7 billion was spent on rivers and harbors from 1791 to 1940. In the modern period, the Doyle report shows that $2.991 billion was spent by the Corps of Engineers for navigational improvements during the period 1917 to 1960. It is obvious that public investment in waterways has accelerated in recent times. One estimate places the amount spent at $11.8 billion up to 1976, and as we noted in Table 28.2, in the year 1987 the federal government spent over $1 billion and state and local governments spent $1.8 billion on rivers and harbors. From 1970 to 1987 total expenditures were over $33 billion for rivers and harbors improvement by all levels of government.

Provision of the way for water carriers has been almost entirely for assisting commerce and industry or for competitive purposes. Until very recently, the use of waterways by pleasure craft was negligible. Nontransportation policy has come into the picture insofar as some of the cost of multiple-purpose resource projects has been assigned to navigation.

Tolls have always been charged on the Saint Lawrence Seaway and fuel user taxes are now in effect on other waterways. Until 1978, inland waterway policy was a clear case of the public making the entire investment in the way for one means of transportation, whereas other modes provided their own ways or at least paid a portion of their costs by user charges (tolls or user taxes). This is no longer completely true.

Urban Transportation Systems

Portions of the grants made by the Urban Mass Transportation Administration (UMTA) under the Urban Mass Transportation Assistance Act of 1964 and its amendments have gone to finance rapid-rail mass transit systems. These grants were on a two-thirds federal, one-third local matching basis from 1964 to 1974. The National Mass Transportation Assistance Act of 1974 changed the matching formula to 80 percent federal and 20 percent local funds for capital grants.

Capital grants in urban transportation are partially based on population size and density and hence go primarily to the larger cities. Between 1965 and 1980, the UMTA granted $15.2 billion in capital grants to cities for urban transportation projects. A portion of this money — $2.9 billion — came from the Highway Trust Fund after such diversions were allowed in 1973. It should be noted that 1 cent of the 1982 increase in the federal fuel tax noted above is earmarked for urban projects. These highway user fees will yield over $1 billion a year for urban transportation in addition to the regular UMTA programs authorized by Congress. The 1987 act continues this program of using 1 cent of highway user fees for transit.

The amount of federal funds used for rail mass transit systems varies from city to city. Such projects typically are very expensive and often cost far more than originally estimated. Some projects such as BART (Bay Area Rapid Transit) in California have had very little federal assistance. Others such as MARTA (Metropolitan Atlanta Rapid Transit Administration) have received federal grants for a much larger portion of their total costs. The METRO in Washington, D.C., still under construction, is completely federally financed, as it is part of the nation's capital. METRO's total costs are unknown at this time but have been estimated to be as high as $5 billion ($70 million per mile).

During the 1970s, massive amounts were spent by both federal and local governments on urban systems. Only a part of these sums was spent directly for the way, of course — purchases of equipment as well as the financing of operating costs (50-50 federal-local match since 1974) absorbed large amounts of the funds. As noted in Table 28.2, over $3.3 billion was spent by federal sources and $7.2 billion by state and local governments on transit in 1987. As Chapter 8 pointed out (Table 8.2), from 1965 to 1987 federal capital grants totaled $34.7 billion and federal operating grants totaled $10.5 billion.

Operating the Way

Another method of public aids or promotion of transportation is operating the way. Actual public investment in the way is the major aid, to be sure, but physical operation and maintenance of the way are often a substantial program. Again, inequality exists insofar as one mode must operate and keep up its own way, whereas its competitor has its way operated for it.

Perhaps the most substantial example of the public operating a way and hence absorbing a portion of the cost of transportation is the airways. The FAA employs a considerable number of highly trained personnel to operate federal airways and spent more than $1 billion for these operations during a recent year. The cost of operating the airways is many times the investment in airway facilities. Although a portion of these funds is spent for general aviation, it is obvious that the majority of the expenditures assist commercial aviation. Under the 1982 Airport and Airways Improvement Act, a portion of these operating expenses come from the Aviation Trust Fund as noted above.

Waterways are also operated and maintained with government aid, and this is also expensive. It has been reported that more than $3 billion was spent by the Corps of Engineers in operating, maintaining, and administering inland waterways under its jurisdiction between 1917 and 1960 and that the Tennessee Valley Authority has spent more than $1 million a year since 1946 on operating, maintaining, and administering the navigation improvements on the Tennessee River (Doyle report). Since 1978, a portion of the cost of operating the waterways was to come from the waterway fuel tax but no funds have been expended to date.

A final type of this kind of aid relates to highways. Under the highway policy of our nation, the states own, operate, and maintain highways. Each state has a highway department which both lets contracts for the construction of highways in the state and operates and maintains these highways. As indicated in Chapter 1, highway expenditures amount to billions of dollars annually. A substantial amount of this is for maintenance and operation, which benefits highway carriers as well as motorists.

In all these instances, the operation of the way is another method of public aid.

Financing Operating Costs

A third method used in public aid is a direct operating subsidy or the financing of operating costs in some way. Although this method has been used infrequently, it is a good illustration of the developmental goal of assisting the early growth of new means of transportation.

A well-known example of this type of aid is the federal government's direct payments to certain air carriers. Generally these substantial aids have been in the form of mail payments. The Doyle report estimates that $723.7 million was expended on air mail subsidies from 1929 to 1960.

The actual amount of airline subsidy is not easy to determine. Prior to 1951, the CAB established mail rates on the basis of carrier revenue needs. Since 1951, there has been a separation of air mail payments and public service revenues (subsidies). In this way, the U.S. Postal Service is not burdened with the entire task of financing the development of air transportation. As far as domestic trunk-line air carriers are concerned, public service revenues to all but one of these ceased in 1956 and stopped entirely in 1960. At this point the cash subsidy for air carriers (called "public service revenues") was shifted to the local service and feeder lines. From 1956 to 1978 sums in the $100–$400 million a year range were paid to allow these carriers to serve points not able to be served economically on the basis of passenger and mail revenues. The concept was to assist smaller cities in their development. This program ceased with the Airline Deregulation Act of 1978. However, as noted in Chapter 13, a portion of this deregulation act set up a ten-year program of "essential air service" payments on selected routes to continue assistance to smaller communities. Also, a loan guarantee program for small-sized aircraft was included in this act. The essential air service provisions were extended for another five years in December 1987.

It will be recalled that under the Transportation Act of 1958, the Regional Rail Reorganization Act of 1973, and the 4-R Act of 1976, the federal government guarantees some loans made by private lenders to railroads. Similar loan guarantees are provided for Amtrak and under the maritime improvement program noted in Chapter 12. Guarantees, it was hoped, would aid carriers in borrowing and in updating their plants. But insofar as operating capital has been obtained in this manner, an indirect subsidy of operating costs is involved.

Operating subsidies to Amtrak, discussed in Chapter 12, have been used for operating deficits as well as for equipment and track upgrading. Conrail also incurred operating deficits and received aid for track rehabilitation before its privatization in 1986. Approximately $7 billion in federal funds were spent to rehabilitate Conrail and keep it in operation from 1975 to 1985. Amtrak has received operating subsidies and capital grants (mostly for new equipment and for the Northeast Corridor Project) since its inception in 1971. Between 1971 and 1988 over $4 billion was invested by Congress in continuing Amtrak. The Reagan administration set a goal for Amtrak to cover 50 percent of its operating costs out of fares, which was achieved in 1982. By 1988 Amtrak revenue covered 65 percent of operating costs, a considerable improvement over earlier years such as 1978 when Amtrak covered only 38 percent of operating costs by revenues. However, Amtrak continues to receive operating grants.

Another example of financing operating costs is found in the public transit area. Beginning with the National Mass Transportation Assistance Act of 1974, the federal government began making grants to cities to help operate urban transportation systems. These were based on a 50-50 matching formula and have been continued in every mass transportation act since that date. The total amounts going to operating deficits have not been small, and as noted above and detailed by year in Table 8.2 (Chapter 8), federal operating assistance grants to transit from 1965 to 1987 totaled $10.5 billion. One of the goals of the Reagan administration was to reduce these operating assistance grants, but Congress continues to fund this form of transportation aid.

A final type of financing operating costs is found in the maritime program. While it is true that we are primarily concerned with domestic transportation here, these maritime programs have a direct impact on domestic transportation. Also, as mentioned above, society can afford to invest only a portion of its resources in any one economic undertaking at a given time. Therefore, various transportation aids and promotion schemes compete with one another.

Various public aid programs have been used in maritime transportation over time. Perhaps the best known is the direct subsidy program involving the operating differential subsidy (ODS) and the capital differential subsidy (CDS). In order to attempt to make U.S. flag shipping competitive with ocean shipping in other countries, Congress began these programs in the Merchant Marine Act of 1935. The idea was to make cash payments by the federal government which would offset lower operating costs (often due to lower maritime wages) and lower capital costs (in the purchase of ships) of our competitors. Hence, ocean shipping companies qualifying for this program (U.S. flag and citizen crews) received a subsidy calculated to equal the differential in operating costs. This program was continued in the Merchant Marine Act of 1970 and continues today. In 1988 the ODS program cost $233 million for that year and since 1935 almost $8.5 billion has been expended on ODS. The CDS program was phased out after 1982 but from 1935 to 1988 about $3.8 billion was expended on subsidies for the purchase of U.S.-built ships. In effect, CDS was a subsidy to U.S. shipyards although it was paid to ocean shipping firms as they purchased new ships (which by law had to be built in U.S. shipyards).

Whether it be direct operating subsidies to airlines, urban transit, or maritime firms, or loan guarantees to railroads and airlines, or direct capital grants for equipment to Amtrak, Conrail, cities in the transit program, or maritime operators — all are examples of public aid financing operating costs.

Research and Development

A fourth method of public aid is the provision of research and development benefiting carriers. When governmental agencies do research and development for some modes of transportation and not for others, another type of inequality is involved. It should be emphasized again that much development of a military or defense nature applies to domestic transportation. Many advances in the designs of bomber planes, for example, have subsequently been adopted in commercial planes. Indeed, some types of commercial jetliners were originally developed as military aircraft. In these cases, the carriers benefit although the goal is most certainly a nontransportation one.

Measurement of research and development aids is extremely difficult. Carryover of military aircraft design advances to civil aircraft is an example of this difficulty. However, insofar as research and development funds are separately listed, some type of measurement is possible. The Doyle report notes that $137.8 million was spent by the FAA and CAA in research and development from 1939 to 1960; the majority of this was in later years.

It should be noted that the 1982 Airport and Airways Improvement Act appropriated $1.2 billion from user fees for research and development in air transportation between 1982 and 1987.

Air transportation has not been alone in receiving such assistance. Substantial research and development is undertaken by DOT in fields other than air transportation. Grants are made by almost every office in DOT for various types of research. Highway research is extremely extensive, and DOT maintains a large rail research center in Colorado for testing purposes. Research in urban transportation is also a function of UMTA. A portion of DOT research grants goes to universities.

For many years, the federal government owned and operated an inland waterway barge line. From 1920 to 1953, when it was sold, this barge line was operated "to demonstrate the practicability of barge operations." In a sense, this is research and development. Professor Locklin notes that this line operated at a profit during only twelve years of its twenty-nine-year corporate existence. Likewise, a great amount of research and development funds is spent by state governments on highway design. Again, these are almost impossible to measure.

Summary of Methods of Public Aid

From the above discussion, it is obvious that the four methods of aid programs are not used equally nor are they of equal importance. The provision of the way is by far the most important method we have used to obtain our public aid goals. Although operating the way, financing carrier operating costs, and financing research and development are secondary methods, a substantial amount is involved in each of these lesser programs and they serve the same goals.

The federal government alone spent more than $30 billion on various types of direct transportation aid programs from 1917 to 1960 (from figures given in the Doyle report). The Association of American Railroads estimates all governmental expenditures for highway, water, and air transport development at more than $436 billion from 1952 to 1976. As we have noted above, data on the years 1970 to 1987 for both federal and state/local aid combined (estimates of Transportation Policy Associates) total $34.6 billion for airways, $50 billion for airports, $649.2 billion for highways, $33.7 billion for rivers/harbors, $15.6 billion for railroads, $264.5 billion for transit, and $8.3 billion for maritime — for a grand total of over $1 trillion. Although various estimates of this kind can be debated, the totals give at least some idea of the magnitude of aid programs.

EFFECTS OF PUBLIC AIDS

Now that the goals and methods of public aids to transportation have been discussed, we can consider their effects. Two levels of approach to this may be used: the macro and the micro. By *macro* we mean the broad, overall, or general approach. *Micro* means the individualistic, singular, or specific view.

Macro Considerations

If transportation as a whole is considered, analysis of the effect of a public aid program is simple. It means merely that the general public assumes a portion of the cost of transportation rather than the users of the facilities paying the complete cost. When the goal of the program is a general one, such as developing the country or settling the West, such a program may be easily justified. The rationale of broad aid to transportation is that everyone benefits from improved transportation and everyone should share its costs.

Even when transportation is considered as a whole, which is an artificial distinction, to be sure, the matter of economic allocation again arises. Since unlimited public funds are not available, economics dictate that these monies should be spent where they make the greatest return to the whole of society. However, as has been pointed out above, it is almost impossible to measure the productivity of public investment, whether it is in transportation facilities, post offices, government power plants, schools, or armaments. About all that can be said on the macro level is that transportation is a necessary prerequisite for economic, social, and cultural development and that our society has decided that spending its public funds in partial support of transportation is a worthwhile undertaking. Sometimes this has been a political decision, sometimes an emotional decision, sometimes a military decision, and sometimes an economic decision. But regardless of motivation, decisions to aid transportation have been made in the past and will probably continue to be made in the future.

Micro Considerations

A more practical approach might be to consider public aids from an individualistic micro viewpoint. It might be argued that there is no such thing as transportation in the broad sense. Individual transportation modes and firms are too diverse, play too many separate as well as complementary and competitive roles, have too many startlingly different economic structures, and are otherwise too dissimilar for realistic consideration as a single entity. Certainly our discussion of public aids, as well as the material in Part II of this book, have amply illustrated this.

The matter of timing is also involved. As noted earlier, society has seen fit to aid and promote some modes at one time and other modes at other times. Aids have helped certain modes to develop, therefore, while penalizing other modes by sponsoring competition. Sometimes massive programs have been necessary when one mode has lagged badly behind the need for its services, as noted in Chapter 12. To be sure, transportation as a whole has grown larger by such action, but at the same time, some modes have played a relatively smaller role in that growth because, partially at least, of public aids to their competitors.

It seems evident that the major effect of public aids, considered from an individualistic viewpoint, has been an inequality of treatment. All modes have not been treated alike at any given time. To some degree, as noted at the beginning of this chapter, equality of treatment would have been an impossibility solely because of the vagaries of technology. Society obviously could not treat all modes equally when some modes did not exist because they were not then technologically feasible. We have also noted that equality of treatment is virtually impossible since some modes, by their very nature, must make use of public facilities, whereas others can be privately owned. Likewise, the intermingling of aids to transportation with nontransportation programs such as defense, water resource policy, general policy toward mobility, and other social programs has been mentioned.

To note the reasons for inequalities and how they have arisen does not excuse their existence or mitigate their effects. Understanding the rationale, the goals, and the methods of public aids and promotions is only a first step. Establishing the effects of public aids and promotions is the second step. Finally, social policy to ameliorate the inequality that results is the last step.

Importance of User Charges

Society has from time to time tried to mitigate the effects of public aids by the devices of user charges and rate concessions. These devices also may be used to recoup a part of public investment. Both of these techniques deserve serious consideration. They have two principal objectives: first, to place the cost of public investment on the user of the facility who benefits from it, and second, to recoup as much of the public investment as seems reasonable and fair in view of national or social objectives.

As frequently noted above, various types of user charges are now levied in highway, air, and water transportation. These user charges take various forms, with fuel taxes being important in highway user charges at both the federal and the state level. Other forms of taxes such as excise taxes and registration fees are also used in the highway user charges area. In air, these forms are supplemented by a passenger ticket tax and air freight waybill tax. Water charges are imposed solely on fuel.

The amount of these user charges is not small. Table 28.4 shows both federal and state user charges in selected years between 1960 and 1985. First, note the growth of the amounts here — from $9.7 billion in 1960 to $39.2 billion in 1985. Part of this is due to changes in the various programs, such as the increase in the federal gas tax from 4 cents per gallon to 9 cents per gallon in 1982, the new diesel fuel tax at the federal

Table 28.4 Federal and State Transportation User Taxes and Fees, Selected Years (in Millions of Dollars)

	1960	1970	1980	1985
Federal Taxes and Fees				
Air Transportation (Total)	263	366	1,877	2,643
Freight Shipments	2	11	92	137
Passenger Travel	261	350	1,693	2,402
Aircraft Parts	—	—	22	—
Aviation Fuel	—	5	70	104
Motor Vehicles (Total)	4,384	6,773	6,419	12,251
Gasoline	2,186	3,347	3,970	7,801
Diesel/Special Fuels	82	265	518	2,453
Large Truck User Tax	45	141	260	533
Lubricating Oils	45	57	77	—
Automobiles, Excise Tax	1,327	1,694	—	—
Trucks/Trailers/Buses	253	639	736	1,144
Tires & Tubes	258	545	634	320
Parts & Accessories	188	85	224	—
Inland Waterways (Total)	—	—	5	42
Total Federal	4,647	7,139	8,301	14,936
State Taxes/Fees				
Motor Fuels	3,396	6,435	9,486	14,742
Registration/License	1,696	3,196	5,732	9,484
Total State	5,092	9,631	15,218	24,226
Total Federal/State	9,739	16,770	23,519	39,162

Source: Transportation Policy Associates, *Transportation in America*, 6th ed., Washington, D.C., March 1988, p. 27.

level of 15.5 cents per gallon in 1984, the imposition of a fuel tax on inland water transportation in 1980, and the new fuel tax on general aviation in 1980. Also, states have generally raised their fuel taxes and registration/license fees during this period. However, the major cause for this increase in revenues has been the growth of transportation over the period involved — there are more vehicles that buy fuel and more passengers who travel and more freight which moves.

Second, some programs have been discontinued during this period, the largest being the federal excise tax on new automobiles. This was a World War II consumption tax that was not repealed until 1970. The tax on aircraft parts imposed in 1975 was not discontinued until 1983, along with the excise tax on automobile parts and accessories the same year.

Finally, Table 28.4 also shows that state taxes and fees have consistently raised more money than federal programs. Indeed, state user taxes and fees were 52 percent of all transportation user fees in 1960 and 61 percent of total transportation user fees by 1985. While federal user tax programs are better known, state user taxes and fees, known in each state only, generate greater sums.

No attempt is made here to match user charges against public expenditures. However, it should be noted that user charges are not applied to all modes and means of transportation. Transit carriers or users pay no user charges, for example. Indeed, as we have noted in Chapter 7, the farebox generates only 37 percent of the cost of urban transit on average — the rest comes from various levels of government. In this case, it is deemed desirable as a general social policy to subsidize urban transit operations. Likewise, both inland water and maritime transportation pay little or no user charges for the use of the harbors of the nation. The small fuel tax on inland waterway operators provides but a small portion of the expenditures of governments on rivers and canals. Also, railroads pay no user charges since they own their own right of way. And the various subsidies to Amtrak (and Conrail prior to privatization) were not recouped by user charges and were considered desirable from an overall social viewpoint. None of this detracts, however, from the fact that user charges are sizable and have been increasingly used in the post–World War II era to recoup a portion of the cost of public aids to transportation.

User charges and rate concessions, however, have many inherent problems. Additional inequality is easily possible if rate concessions continue long past the point of recouping investment or if user charges are ill-conceived and poorly planned. User charges are especially prone to abuse. For highways, for example, how much benefit is properly chargeable to land owners who gain access and increased property values and incomes because of the highways and how much to the actual highway user? Or between classes of user, how much of the cost of an improved highway should be charged to a heavy vehicle using the highway for profit and how much to a motorist using the highway for pleasure? Logic might hold that heavy vehicles should pay at least the additional cost of building the highway to standards suitable to serve their peculiar needs. How much of the airway user charges should be paid by commercial aviation, and how much by general (private) aviation? Although various approaches and formulas of cost allocation and benefit measurement are possible, there is little unanimity on how costs should be allocated. The analysis of these and similar problems is beyond the scope of this book, but we do want to point out that user charges have many problems inherent within them and are subject to possible abuse. Of course, it should be realized that user charges are not applied to all modes of transportation. This is another source of inequality.

Insofar as one mode is given more advantages in public aid than another, overcapacity may arise. The favored mode may expand further than it would have if all costs had been charged to users. If one mode is promoted while another is not, the mode without aid eventually may develop overcapacity because of a greater decrease in its traffic than in its plant. This is especially possible when two modes develop at different times. Some scholars feel that our railroads are overdeveloped in this sense. Certainly rail overcapacity seems to exist, and the railroad plant continues to decrease yearly.

Insofar as the national policy of preserving the inherent advantage of each mode (the stated policy of Congress) is concerned, public aids and promotions unequally applied subvert this goal. User charges to equalize modal advantage are simply not possible, although the goal of assessing some of the fixed costs of the infrastructure furnished by the public to the user is a laudable one. Inequality of treatment among modes under public aid programs is almost a given.

SUMMARY

Public aids and promotions in transportation have existed for a very long time. The public has invested in transportation infrastructure from its earliest history. This has led to many inequalities in the treatment of various modes — much of which is unavoidable because of timing, technology, and our social policy of developing new modes of transportation. Two goals — developmental and competitive — characterize public aid programs. The term *subsidy* has various meanings, as does *discrimination* and *cross subsidization*. The amount of public aid is considerable and public aid is not given equally to all modes. There are four methods of public aid: financing the way, operating the way, financing operating costs, and providing research and development. A number of programs involving several modes of transportation have been discussed as illustrations of these methods. The macro consequence of these programs is to raise the cost of transportation and the micro consequence is inequality. User charges and fees have been used to recoup a portion of the cost of these programs but they cause issues of inequality of treatment. Society continues to struggle to find its proper role in promoting transportation.

ADDITIONAL READINGS

Bess, H. David, and Martin T. Farris, U.S. Maritime Policy: History and Prospects, New York: Praeger Special Studies, 1981.
    Chapter 4, "Policy Foundations: The Merchant Marine Act of 1936," pp. 56–67.
    Chapter 6, "The Merchant Marine Act of 1970," pp. 101–13.
Carroll, Joseph L., and Srikant Rao, "Economics of Public Investment in Inland Navigation: Unanswered Questions," Transportation Journal, 17, No. 3 (Spring 1978), 27–54.
Conant, Michael, Railroad Mergers and Abandonments, Berkeley, Calif.: University of California Press, 1964.
    Chapter 1, "Route Capacity, Excess Capacity and Overinvestment," pp. 1–24.
Davis, Grant M., ed., Transportation Regulation: A Pragmatic Assessment, Danville, Ill.: Interstate Printers and Publishers, 1976.
    Farris, Martin T., and Ronald D. Scott, "Airline Subsidies in the United States," pp. 122–34.
Due, John F., "Government versus Private Financing of the Railroad Industry," Transportation Journal (Spring 1982), 16–21.
Fair, Marvin L., and Ernest W. Williams, Jr., Transportation and Logistics, Rev. ed., Plano, Texas: Business Publications, 1981.
    Chapter 23, "Government Provision of Transportation Facilities," pp. 460–82.
Farris, Martin T., and Paul T. McElhiney, eds., Modern Transportation: Selective Readings, 2nd ed., Boston: Houghton Mifflin Co., 1973.
    Nelson, James C., "Government's Role Toward Transportation," pp. 416–24.
Harper, Donald V., Transportation in America: Users, Carriers, Government, 2nd ed., Englewood Cliffs, N.J.: Prentice-Hall, 1982.
    Chapter 16, "Rationale of Government Promotion of Transportation: Government Promotion of Railroad and Highway Transportation," pp. 371–408.
    Chapter 17, "Government Promotion of Water, Oil Pipeline, and Air Transportation," pp. 409–35.
Jantscher, Gerald R., Bread Upon the Waters: Federal Aids to the Maritime Industries, Washington, D.C.: The Brookings Institution, 1975.
Johnson, James C., and Donald L. Berger, "Waterway User-Charges: An Economic and Political Dilemma," Transportation Journal, 16, No. 4 (Summer 1977), 20–29.
Locklin, D. Philip, Economics of Transportation, 7th ed., Homewood, Ill.: Richard D. Irwin, 1972.
    Chapter 6, "The Era of Railroad Building," pp. 109–41.
Pegrum, Dudley F., Transportation: Economics and Public Policy, 3rd ed., Homewood, Ill.: Richard D. Irwin, 1973.
    Chapter 19, "Financing Transportation," pp. 441–73.
Rao, Kant, and Thomas D. Larson, "Capital Investment, Performance, and Pricing in Highways," Transportation Journal (Spring 1982), 22–33.
Spychalski, John C., "Diversion of Motor Vehicle–Related Tax Revenues to Urban Mass Transportation: A Critique of Its Economic Tenability," Transportation Journal, 9, No. 3 (Spring 1970), 44–50.
Taff, Charles A., Commercial Motor Transportation, 7th ed., Centreville, Md.: Cornell Maritime Press, 1986.
    Chapter 3, "Highway Financing," pp. 52–79.

CHAPTER 29

NATIONAL TRANSPORTATION POLICY IN TRANSITION

The last three chapters have discussed specific transportation problems, all of which have policy implications. Specifically, transportation market structure, transportation labor-management relations, and public aids and promotions in transportation are problems as well as illustrations of specific transportation policy in the nation. However, transportation policy can also be discussed on a much broader and more comprehensive level. This chapter considers such a level — national transportation policy.

IDENTIFICATION OF NATIONAL TRANSPORTATION POLICY

The task of identifying national transportation policy is not as easy as it might at first appear. At any one time, there are always conflicts and inconsistencies in policy. Indeed, it has been suggested that at many times, the United States has not really had a national transportation policy at all! Rather, a series of goals and policies have existed — sometimes one for each mode of transportation — and very little consistent or explicit *national* transportation policy can be found.

This problem of identification arises because of two factors. First, for many years there has been a formal statutory policy on one hand and an informal institutional policy on the other. For example, it is the obligation of Congress to determine and establish transportation policy. This is done by various statutes and legislative actions over time. However, it is the task of regulatory commissions such as the ICC and executive offices such as DOT to administer transportation policy and make it work. Further, it is the task of the judiciary to pass upon the legality of these administrative acts as well as adjudicate disputes. This three-way structure has already been noted in Chapter 15.

Almost by definition, conflicts and inconsistencies arise with such a scheme. Sometimes congressional pronouncements cannot be turned into specific administrative actions. Sometimes the ICC (and the CAB up to 1984) and DOT conflict in their views on various policy matters. Sometimes Congress itself is inconsistent — taking one route on a given statute and another route on a later statute. Sometimes the courts interpret legislative statutes in a manner entirely different from what Congress intended or from what the ICC or DOT desires. Conflicts and inconsistencies are almost inevitable.

The second factor is that policies and goals change over time. Our discussion in Part III clearly illustrates this. During the past 100 years, the goal of transportation policy from 1887 to 1920 was clearly to regulate and control transportation monopoly. Concern here was with maximum rates and discriminatory action by the railroads and, after 1906, the pipelines. From 1920 to the 1970s, the goal of transportation policy was to provide an adequate transportation system. This was accomplished by regulating almost all modes of transportation and dealing with control of intermodal competitive relationships as well as with the economic health of the carriers. Major matters of concern were minimum rate levels, overcapitalization and mergers, and the role of each mode. In recent times, the goal of national transportation policy has shifted once again. Since the mid-1970s, our goal has seemed to be to stimulate competition among the carriers and to modify or remove the restraints of regulation whenever possible. Most recent action seems to be aimed at removing earlier regulatory restrictions and allowing the widest possible role for the actions of the competitive marketplace.

Further, statutory and administrative actions in pursuit of these shifting goals never occurred at one time nor were they completely consistent. Hence, the goal of regulating transportation monopoly evolved and was perfected by a whole series of statutes and administrative acts between 1887 and about 1916. Likewise, the goal of providing an adequate transportation system and controlling intermodal competitive relationships was pursued by a series of statutes and administrative actions from 1920 to about 1970. Finally, in recent times, the shift to stimulating competition among carriers and removing the restraints of regulation is still being implemented and perfected. In a word, U.S. national transportation policy is in transition.

Statutory National Transportation Policy

As noted in Chapter 15, one of the functions of the legislative process is to establish policy. This is often done by making a policy statement in the introduction or first section of a statute. Hence, one way to identify national transportation policy is to see what Congress has said.

The formal statement of national transportation policy (Section 10101, Revised Interstate Commerce Act) in its current form is:

It is hereby declared to be the National Transportation Policy of the Congress to provide for fair and impartial regulation of all modes of transportation subject to the provisions of the act, and —

(1) in regulating those modes — (A) to recognize and preserve the inherent advantage of each mode of transportation; (B) to promote safe, adequate, economical, and efficient transportation; (C) to encourage sound economic conditions in transportation, including sound economic conditions among carriers; (D) to encourage the establishment and maintenance of reasonable rates for transportation, without unreasonable discrimination or unfair or destructive competitive practices; (E) to cooperate with each State and the officials of each State on transportation matters; and (F) to encourage fair wages and working conditions in the transportation industry;

(2) in regulating transportation by motor carrier, to promote competitive and efficient transportation services in order to (A) meet the needs of shippers, receivers, passengers, and consumers; (B) allow a variety of quality and price options to meet changing market demands and the diverse requirements of the shipping and traveling public; (C) allow the most productive use of equipment and energy resources; (D) enable efficient and well-managed carriers to earn adequate profits, attract capital, and maintain fair wages and working conditions; (E) provide and maintain service to small communities and small shippers and intrastate bus services; (F) provide and maintain commuter bus operations; (G) improve and maintain a sound, safe, and competitive privately owned motor carrier system; (H) promote greater participation by minorities in the motor carrier system; and (I) promote intermodal transportation; and

(3) in regulating transportation by motor carrier of passengers (A) to cooperate with the States on transportation matters for the purpose of encouraging the States to exercise intrastate regulatory jurisdiction in accordance with the objectives of this subtitle; (B) to provide Federal procedures which ensure that intrastate regulation is exercised in accordance with this subtitle; and (C) to ensure that Federal reform initiatives enacted by the Bus Regulatory Reform Act of 1982 are not nullified by State regulatory actions.

The careful reader will recognize that the national transportation policy under (1) is essentially the same as the 1940 Statement of National Transportation Policy discussed in Chapter 11. The policy under (2) was added by the Motor Carrier Act of 1980 and amended by the Bus Regulatory Reform Act of 1982. Paragraph (3) was added by the Bus Regulatory Reform Act of 1982. Because of the manner in which the formal statement of national transportation policy evolved, paragraph (1) is the broadest in scope and applies to all transportation modes. Paragraph (2) applies only to motor carriers, both truck and bus, and paragraph (3) is a special policy statement applying only to buses.

Internal Inconsistencies

Internal inconsistencies and ambiguities are almost inevitable in any broad policy statement. However, these inconsistencies seem particularly striking in the formal national transportation policy statement. First, while the statement sounds general and national, it does not include air transportation or private or exempt transportation, even though reference is made to "all modes" and "transportation matters."

Second, "to encourage and preserve the inherent advantage of each mode of transportation," although commendable as a goal, is very difficult to implement as long as all modes are not treated equally and the costs of some modes are fully or partially subsidized. Although there has certainly been a move to more reliance on user fees as noted in Chapter 28, all modes are not treated equally, and there is a considerable element of public subsidy for some.

Third, the goal "to promote safe, adequate, economical, and efficient transportation" and "to encourage sound economic conditions in transportation, including sound economic conditions among carriers" all seem laudable. However, the fact that some of these goals may conflict with one another is not recognized. That is, "safe and adequate" may not always be "economical and efficient." Safety costs money, and adequacy presupposes excess capacity to cover peak demands, whereas "economical" connotes least cost and "efficient" might be interpreted as being only enough capacity to handle average needs. The meaning of "sound economic conditions" is vague and may mean whatever the person using the phrase wants it to mean at the time.

Fourth, the statement says that Congress should "encourage the establishment and maintenance of reasonable rates for transportation, without unreasonable discrimination or unfair or destructive competitive practices." This sounds much like the historic goal of control of monopoly practices coupled with minimum rate control. This goal is further emphasized by the phrase to "enable efficient and well-managed carriers to earn adequate profits, attract capital, and maintain fair wages and working conditions." However, the general thrust of the series of deregulatory acts has been to promote competition among carriers and remove the restraints of regulation. How can a policy promote reasonable rates without discrimination or unfair or destructive competitive practices without some sort of rate control? And if some sort of rate control exists, is the general goal of freedom of competition among carriers and removal of the restraints of regulation accomplished? Or how can there be a policy "to enable . . . carriers to earn adequate profits, attract capital and maintain fair wages and working conditions" without some type of control over carrier earnings and rates? How can the ICC control earnings and rates while at the same time promoting free competition and removing the restraints of regulation?

Fifth, Congress orders the ICC to "allow a variety of quality and price options," which implies some type of rate control once more in conflict with the general goal of more reliance on the market mechanism to set price and less reliance on the restraints of regulation.

Sixth, Congress recognized an obligation toward labor and stated it would "encourage fair wages and working conditions." "Fair wages and working conditions" has many meanings and could be interpreted many ways. Can a carrier "maintain fair wages and working conditions" without some assurance of "adequate profits"? Again, does this mean rate control and earnings control?

Seventh, Congress set a goal "to cooperate with each State and the officials of each State on transportation matters" in paragraph (1). But in paragraph (3) Congress states that it will specify state regulatory procedures and approaches. Indeed, the final phrase of the statement says that it wishes "to ensure that Federal reform initiatives . . . are not nullified by State regulatory actions." Does "cooperate" mean "dictate"?

Finally, Congress wishes policy to "provide and maintain service to small communities and small shippers and intrastate bus service." This matter of small community and small shipper service has always been a problem because it is high cost and equipment is not utilized to its fullest. Yet in the same paragraph, the goal of "the most productive use of equipment and energy resources" and "competitive and efficient transportation services" with "adequate profits" are also enumerated. The small community and small shipper problem thus remains unresolved.

In summary, the formal statutory national transportation policy, although upholding many high-sounding and laudable goals, is contradictory, vague, and indefinable.

Informal Institutional Policy

If the formal statutory transportation policy is vague, ambiguous, and self-contradictory even though written down and enacted by Congress, informal institutional policy is even less specific. Informal institutional policy comes out of practice and repetition by Congress in various laws as well as certain general economic beliefs and positions. Another important aspect of informal institutional policy derives from the actions and decisions of the regulatory agencies. Of particular importance has been the case law coming from the administration of the acts of Congress by the Interstate Commerce Commission, Federal Maritime Commission, Federal Energy Regulatory Commission, and until recently, the Civil Aeronautics Board — all discussed in Chapter 15. A final important institutional policy comes from the actions of the agencies in the executive branch of government. Of these, the most important is, of course, the Department of Transportation discussed in Chapters 13 and 15. However, the Department of Agriculture, Department of Commerce, Department of Defense, Department of Energy, Department of Justice, Department of Labor, and Department of State all have transportation responsibilities as noted in Table 29.1.

With so many entities involved, it is inevitable that policy conflicts will arise. However, it is possible to summarize informal policy in transportation into four groups or concepts: the ownership concept, the public investment concept, the common-carrier concept, and the exemption concept.

Table 29.1 Cabinet Offices with Transportation Responsibility (Other Than the Department of Transportation)

President	Rules on matters relating to *international air transport* by U.S. and foreign carriers. Nominates (Senate confirms) members, and appoints the chair of the FERC, FMC, and ICC.
Agriculture	*Office of Transportation* is responsible for developing USDA transport policies for agriculture and rural development and for representing their interests before federal and state regulatory agencies with respect to rates, charges, tariffs, and services of transport carriers.
Commerce	*U.S. Travel Service* plans and carries out a comprehensive program designed to stimulate and encourage travel to the United States by foreign residents. Accomplishes a quinquennial *census of transportation,* including "Truck Inventory and Use Survey" and "Commodity Transport Survey."
Defense	*Military Sealift Command* provides ocean transportation for DOD cargo and personnel and, as directed, for other U.S. agencies and departments; and operates ships in support of other U.S. agency programs.

Military Airlift Command provides air transportation for DOD cargo and personnel on a worldwide basis; and furnishes weather, rescue, and audiovisual services for the U.S. Air Force.

Military Traffic Management and Terminal Service directs military traffic management, land transportation, and common-user ocean terminal service within the United States and for worldwide traffic management of DOD's household goods moving and storage program. Provides for procurement of commercial freight and passenger transport services.

Corps of Engineers constructs, improves, and maintains river, harbor, and port facilities; administers laws for the protection and preservation of navigable waters and related wetlands. Compiles and publishes statistical data on domestic/foreign waterborne commerce.

Energy   Develops and implements national energy policies; administers petroleum and natural gas pricing, allocation, and import/export controls; assures energy supplies; and performs regulatory functions over oil and gas pipelines not assigned to FERC.

Justice   Performs a key role in ensuring strong competition in transportation under the U.S. free-enterprise system — such responsibilities becoming more pronounced as a result of recent laws sharply reducing transportation regulation, especially as they relate to antitrust issues.

Labor   Administers and enforces laws relating to wage earners, their working conditions, and employment opportunities, including court actions under the Longshoremen's and Harbor Workers' Compensation Act and the Employee Retirement Income Security Act (ERISA).

State   Develops policy recommendations and approves broad policy programs concerning *international aviation and maritime transportation,* especially as they affect U.S. foreign relations; e.g., bilateral pacts.

Source: Transportation Policy Associates, *Transportation in America,* 6th ed., Washington, D.C., 1988, p. 30.

Ownership Concept

Domestic transportation policy is firmly committed to the concept of private ownership. Although ownership of the means of transportation by the federal government has been widespread in other areas of the world, the United States has studiously avoided this path even though the opportunity for government ownership has arisen many times. During World War I, the federal government seized and operated the railroads. Labor strife has caused other seizures. Defense needs over the years have closely linked the government to all modes of transportation, especially air transportation. In attempting to solve both the inter-city rail passenger problems and the restructuring of the northeastern railroads, Congress came very close to nationalization. Both Amtrak and Conrail, however, were set up as semipublic corporations and are not part of the federal government. Both are supposed to become profitable eventually; however, both have been heavily subsidized by federal funds over the years. As previously noted, parts of Conrail passenger service have been transferred to state or regional government units, and, as Conrail became profitable, it was sold to private ownership. One innovative ownership pattern was employee ownership of a part of Conrail.

The rationale for federal government ownership has often existed, yet the strong preference for private ownership has always won out. It seems safe to say, then, that one of the informal institutional policies is private ownership of the transportation modes.

Public Investment Concept

Public investment in transportation, however, is another matter. As already noted in Chapter 28, the public has committed itself to providing a portion of the way, to operating the way, to financing some of the operating costs, and to providing some research and development funds for carriers. These types of investment by the public presently are concentrated in the highways, waterways, urban transportation, regional railways, and airways. Although federal ownership is avoided, public investment most certainly is not. The national policy on transportation rests on continuing public investment even though no law or statute so states it.

At the same time, public investment is accompanied by various user charges designed to recoup a portion of the investment. The importance of user charges has already been noted in Chapter 28, and all the public investment in transportation is not recouped. Likewise, all modes do not pay user charges and all users do not pay the same charges. Even so, the coupling of user charges to public investment seems to be one of the basic informal institutional policies in transportation.

Common-Carrier Concept

Third, the common-carrier concept is important in informal institutional transportation policy. The idea that the common carrier is the backbone of the national transportation system is implicitly assumed in practically all policy statements and discussions, even though one would be hard put to find a statutory pronouncement to that effect.

Exemption Concept

Modifying the common-carrier concept is the exemptions concept. Informally, national transportation policy has embraced the idea that certain types of transportation should be exempt from economic regulation. Individuals should be able to move their own goods relatively free from restrictions, for example. Certain types of goods such as agricultural commodities moving by truck and rail or bulk commodities moving by barge have been exempt from regulation for various reasons. Some groups, such as agricultural marketing cooperatives, newspaper carriers, and local operators, are also exempt. Air freight is exempt from economic regulation. Air passenger service is regulated only as to safety. The ICC has administratively exempted TOFC, or piggyback rail service, much of the rail carload traffic, and rail-owned truck operations. Although all these exemptions are explicitly stated in the law or arise from regulatory interpretation of the law, the concept that some groups, commodities, or types of transportation will be treated differently than others is an informal institutional policy.

These informal policies based on private ownership, public investment, common carriage, and exemption shape national transportation policy just as surely as the formal statutory policy. Both must be considered in order to understand national transportation policy. Indeed, these informal policies coupled with the ambiguous and vague formal policies lead to numerous conflicts.

KINDS OF CONFLICTS

Mention has been made of the self-contradictory nature of the formal, statutory, national transportation policy pronouncements, and conflicts among the informal and the formal policies are self-evident. Added to these conflicts, however, are three broad areas of conflict within national transportation policy. These are philosophical conflicts, regulatory conflicts, and administrative conflicts.

Philosophical Conflicts

The major philosophical conflict in national transportation policy is between the concept of a regulated transportation industry based on the common-carrier concept and the philosophy of free competition. This problem of regulation versus competition is not a new one, although, as noted in Chapter 13, there has been renewed interest in this subject because of various recent deregulation acts.

The prevailing policy of the United States has been based on the common-carrier idea. Here the transportation firm must hold itself out to serve all customers at all reasonable times and in a nondiscriminatory manner. This is thought to better serve society's needs since transportation is so basic to our economy.

Historically, the decision to base our transportation system on the common carrier is a very old one. Scholars of economic and business history indicate that many of the common-carrier concepts came with the merchant law of the late medieval period, and some scholars find evidence of something akin to the common carrier in the commerce of the ancient world. This evidence is based upon the laws of liability where the goods of another person are carried for pay.

The concept of common carriage, however, implies regulation of some type. Common carriers have always operated under various regulations, and the liability provisions noted above are really regulations applied by society to the conduct of those who undertake a public trust. Regulation of charges (rates) by the king or other sovereign and control over the number of firms holding themselves out to serve (entry controls) are also implied by the idea of common carriage.

Equally old is the tradition of competition, the philosophy that individual entrepreneurs should compete or strive against one another to serve the consumer and the general public. While elements of competition can be found in the earliest commercial undertakings, it was not until modern times that this policy pervaded all economic undertakings. This came with the development of the laissez-faire philosophy of minimum regulation or control in the eighteenth century.

Applied to transportation, the philosophy of competition and free enterprise holds that everybody should have the right to start any business they please. Entry should not be restricted. Once started, entrepreneurs should be allowed to conduct their business affairs in any way they please so long as they do not violate the rights of others. No authority should tell them what to charge for their service or when to serve it. If they see an opportunity for gain, they should be allowed to exploit it. By the very act of exploiting these opportunities, they will attract competition, and in the struggle, society will be better served than if competition had been controlled. It is obvious that the philosophy of competition and free enterprise is diametrically opposed to the philosophy of regulated common carriers.

The conflict, then, lies in determining the proper role of competition and the proper role of regulation. It is really a matter of degree rather than a matter of absolutes. The transportation system is neither fully regulated nor fully free enterprise. Given the importance of transportation to the economy as a whole, society will always provide some rules and regulations. The question is: How much regulation and how much competition?

Without doubt, the recent deregulatory acts have moved transportation policy closer to free competition than previously. Yet regulation of various types remains; only a small part of transportation actually operates in a fully unregulated competitive market and even it is subject to safety regulation.

To illustrate this, Table 29.2 considers seven regulatory policy matters and shows the difference between the previously fully regulated transportation scene and present-day regulation of competition in transportation.

It is readily apparent that the issue is not regulation versus nonregulation; rather it is a matter of the degree of regulation. The table also illustrates how national transportation policy has been in transition.

Regulatory Conflicts

Once it is determined that regulation has a role to play, the matter of public policy conflicts must be faced. Within regulation itself at least three conflicts exist. These are conflicts over comprehensiveness, jurisdiction, and procedure.

Comprehensiveness of Regulation

Since deregulation has decreased the role of regulatory bodies such as the ICC and since some of the previous powers of the CAB have been transferred to other agencies, there have been suggestions that a single regulatory agency would be desirable. Although consistency might well call for such an approach, those opposed to a single regulatory agency with comprehensive powers have pointed out that some modes developed more recently or are still developing. The argument is also heard that regulatory concepts designed for railroads hardly apply to an entirely different industry such as motor transportation. The same point could be, and sometimes is, made relative to motor and water transportation, both regulated by the ICC. Thus there is a question of consistency even within those modes now regulated by the ICC, for it is true that the economic and market characteristics of the ICC-regulated firms vary considerably.

There are also conflicts over the comprehensiveness of regulation of transportation as it now exists and the many nonregulatory aspects of transportation. Public aid programs greatly affect transportation, especially in highways, airways, urban systems, and waterways. Certain policies of the Postal Service also play a role in the effectiveness of transportation regulation, and military considerations have had a considerable effect.

For many years, transportation matters have been segmented among various governmental agencies without any real coordination. The Department of Transportation, as noted previously, brought many of these transportation agencies of the federal government under one head. But unfortunately the act creating DOT was less comprehensive in coverage than originally proposed. The new department is a start toward coordination of transportation functions, but only a start.

A most notable omission from the Department of Transportation is the whole matter of water transportation, both inland and maritime. Also proposed, but omitted from the final congressional action establishing DOT, was the authority to develop "standards and criteria for the formulation and economic evaluation of all proposals for the investment of federal funds in transportation facilities and equipment." Both of these omissions prevent the Department of Transportation from fully coordinating all transportation functions at the federal level. Congress was unwilling to delegate these kinds of powers to an executive agency.

In summary, even though problems of comprehensiveness of regulation and nonregulatory transportation matters exist, Congress has not yet seen fit to bring all transportation regulation under one regulatory agency or to give the Department of Transportation strong direct policy powers.

Jurisdiction

There has long been a conflict over which governmental level shall regulate common carriers. As noted in Chapter 10, the states initiated comprehensive regulation in this country. Regulation under the common law preceded state regulation, but is was far from comprehensive. The federal government was forced into transportation regulation by the *Wabash* decision of the Supreme Court in 1886. Since that time, the proper roles of the federal and the state governments have been in conflict.

Table 29.2 Degrees of Regulation and Competition

Fully Regulated Transportation	Regulation of Competition in Transportation
1. Concern with carrier earnings and an economically sound transportation system that does not exploit through high earnings.	Less concern with earnings — let carriers fail. Unconcern about level of earnings — let market adjust.
2. Concern with minimum rates, maximum rates, and exact rates. Avoidance of discrimination in pricing. Same price for all under similar circumstances and conditions.	Less concern with rates. Concern only with extremes of rates — too high or too low. Use of zone of rate freedom and allowance of flexibility in pricing. Concern only with predatory pricing.
3. Concern with entry and mergers so that degree of competition is controlled and carriers give adequate service.	Minimum concern with amount of competition. Concern mainly with safety. Handling of mergers left to market. Acceptance of relatively easy entry with antitrust laws applying.
4. Concern with service levels. Full application of common-carrier concept of serving all within capabilities according to certificate of public convenience and necessity.	Less concern with level of service as long as entry is easy. Concern mostly with service to small communities and small shippers.
5. Concern with overall system of adequacy to fulfill needs of commerce, defense, and postal system. Willingness to interfere to attain adequacy.	Less concern with overall adequacy; unwillingness to interfere to attain it. Needs of commerce, defense, and postal system left to market mechanisms.
6. Concern with miscellaneous controls, accounts, rate rules, finances, and securities so regulatory system is consistent.	Minimum concern with miscellaneous controls. Minimum level of regulatory rules.
7. Concern with promotion on an overall transportation policy matter.	Promotion generally on a modal basis with more user charges. Promotion only when market does not seem to work; for example, urban transportation.

It is easy to say that the federal government should regulate interstate commerce and that state governments should regulate intrastate commerce, but it is hard to define these terms. The courts have been called upon again and again to decide when interstate commerce (and hence federal regulation) is involved. The concept of interstate commerce has been an evolving one that over time has increased in scope to the point where many feel there is no room left for state regulation. Some movements wholly within a single state are in interstate commerce, depending on how the order for the goods was placed, the intent of the shipper, and the like. With the further extension of the *Shreveport* principle in the Transportation Act of 1958 so that it is no longer necessary to segregate intrastate movement and expenses when ascertaining if intrastate rates burden interstate commerce, the role of state regulation has become less clear. Likewise, the Bus Regulatory Reform Act of 1982 represents a further shift of regulatory jurisdiction to the federal government. Finally, some states have seen fit to follow the lead of Congress and deregulate motor transportation on the intrastate level, whereas other states have retained intrastate regulation.

It is not necessary here to trace the long and interesting history of legal conflict in this area of federal versus state jurisdiction. It is enough merely to point out that conflict as to jurisdiction exists and probably will continue.

Procedural Conflicts

Finally, there is a procedural conflict inherent in regulation. As discussed earlier, regulatory boards and commissions have substantial powers of fact finding and, in administering congressional policy, great powers of interpretation and definition. Indeed, they are often referred to as independent regulatory commissions since they establish their own precedents, maintain their own bar, have their own procedures, and make economic determinations with a minimum of judicial or executive interference.

As noted earlier, too, commissions have a peculiar procedure by which they act in the role of the prosecutor in representing the public, act as the judge in holding hearings before their bar, and finally act as jury in rendering a decision. Many have questioned whether one body can be all three — prosecutor, judge, and jury — no matter how objective and expert it may be.

Rather careful checks and balances are established and the whole commission, at least in the case of the ICC, often operates primarily as an appeal board. Procedure before commissions is rigid and minutely specified with many opportunities for appeal and reconsideration. However, by the very fact that procedure is rigid and specified, a conflict arises. Procedures tend to become institutionalized and are followed for the sake of procedure itself rather than because they lead to better decisions. Hence regulatory matters may at times be decided more on whether the procedure or ritual was observed than on the justice of the matter. This tendency has reinforced doubts about the efficiency of regulation.

One of the advantages of regulation over competition is that it expedites decisions. Yet long time lags are built into institutionalized regulatory procedures. Although rights of appeal are necessary and just, some time lag develops because the procedure forces it, not because it is needed. Much has been made of the time lag in commission decisions and the necessity of following outdated procedures at a time when speedy justice is required. Thus, some criticize the ironic fossilization and institutionalization of regulatory procedures over time when regulation was initially developed as a speedier and more certain method of control than the competitive marketplace. Certainly this institutionalization, which seems to come with age and acceptance, is one of the inherent conflicts of regulation, even though Congress has attempted to speed up decision making by the recent deregulation acts.

Administrative Conflicts

In addition to the philosophical and procedural conflicts inherent in regulation, there is a third area of administrative conflicts arising from regulation. This comes from a lack of coordination of two types: lack of coordination of nonregulatory agencies with regulatory agencies, and lack of coordination of nonregulatory agencies with other nonregulatory agencies involved with transportation.

Nonregulatory vs. Regulatory Conflicts

We have already mentioned the role of the Department of Transportation in attempting to coordinate all federal transportation activities. But even with this excellent start toward coordination, administrative conflicts between regulatory and nonregulatory agencies are common. Four examples of these types of administrative conflicts will illustrate this point.

The ICC is charged with regulating domestic water transportation. The Tennessee Valley Authority is charged with promoting water transportation on the Tennessee River as part of the comprehensive area-development plan of the authority. Promotion and regulation are not easily reconciled; and when two separate agencies are involved, administrative conflict is inevitable.

The ICC is charged with regulating rates in such a way as to maintain an adequate and nondiscriminatory transportation system. At the same time, the General Services Administration is charged with minimizing governmental expenditures as much as possible. The largest single purchaser of transportation is the U.S. government. The GSA wants the lowest possible rate and is not concerned with the ICC's struggle for adequacy. Special rate privileges (Section 22 rates, discussed in Chapter 17) are sought and used by the government and by the GSA. Although Congress declares that transportation may not discriminate among shippers, it explicitly makes provision for discriminatory low rates for the movement of government goods under these rates. Discrimination is illegal, it seems, unless it is done in favor of the U.S. government. Certainly this is an administrative conflict.

The aims of the antitrust laws and beliefs of our nation are in conflict with the ICC's attempts to promote an adequate transportation system by controlling consolidation and merger. Mergers that might add to the efficiency of the national transportation system do not always promote the goals of competition and antitrust. Hence, this is another area where administrative conflict between nonregulatory and regulatory policy exists.

The ICC controls all interstate movement of freight by motor vehicles except certain exempt goods, notably agricultural items. The Department of Agriculture, representing farm interests, has been most militant in seeing to it that this exemption is maintained and extended. Truck common carriers of agricultural goods are exempt from ICC regulation, as are the vehicles of agricultural marketing cooperatives where certified by the secretary of agriculture. Again, inconsistency is involved and administrative conflict between regulatory and nonregulatory agencies comes about.

Enough has been said to illustrate that little coordination between regulatory and nonregulatory agencies exists in transportation matters. This administrative conflict is one of the shortcomings of regulation.

Nonregulatory Interagency Conflicts

Administrative inconsistency and lack of coordination also exist between nonregulatory agencies where transportation is concerned. There is, for instance, no common purchasing policy applied to all governmental agencies purchasing transportation. Although some progress has been made by the military after many years of effort and a common military purchasing policy finally exists, similar coordination has not been achieved for nonmilitary agencies. Each agency proceeds independently of others in transportation matters, and often inefficiencies are involved.

Perhaps more important is the lack of coordination relative to public aid to transportation. No comprehensive plan or agency is involved, and the attempt to give the Department of Transportation powers to coordinate in this area was defeated. For many years, substantial aid and development of highways went on with little or no coordination with other agencies, either regulatory or nonregulatory. Even now that this portion of transportation has come under DOT, coordination is proving difficult in practice. Waterway improvement is quite divorced from transportation needs and often is undertaken for reasons of conservation (or as pork-barrel projects) with little regard to its effects on overall transportation.

The recent interest in the effects of transportation on our environment, discussed in Chapter 3, should give even greater impetus to the need for comprehensive planning and a reduction of nonregulatory conflicts. Actually, there does seem to be more concern for comprehensive thinking about transportation today than ever before. It remains to be seen if these conflicts can be reduced and a more overall view taken.

In general, then, conflicts of many types exist in national transportation policy. It is possible to delineate at least three types of conflicts: philosophical conflicts inherent in competition versus regulation; regulatory conflicts over comprehensiveness, jurisdiction, and the procedure of regulation; and administrative conflicts developing because of lack of coordination between regulatory and nonregulatory governmental agencies and among nonregulatory agencies.

SUMMARY

This discussion has emphasized the difficulties of identifying both statutory and institutional national transportation policy, the internal inconsistencies of policy, and the conflicts that arise in the application of national transportation policy. However, it should be pointed out that transportation policy has grown and developed over time and continues to evolve. Recent shifts in regulatory philosophy and the deregulation acts of Congress plus administrative action and proposals have all caused national transportation policy to shift more toward reliance upon competition than upon regulation. The effects of this shift are still being worked out.

The general goal of national transportation policy should be to promote an economical, efficient, and productive transportation system for the national economy. Present policy is in a state of transition, and it can only be hoped that this general goal will indeed be attained.

ADDITIONAL READINGS

Coyle, John J., Edward J. Bardi, and Joseph L. Cavinato, *Transportation*, 2nd ed., St. Paul, Minn.: West Publishing Co., 1986.
  Chapter 17, "National Transportation Policy," pp. 349–72.
Davis, Grant M., and Jack J. Holder, Jr., "Does the United States Have a Cohesive National Transportation Policy — An Analysis," *I.C.C. Practitioners' Journal*, 41, No. 3 (1974), 332–49.
Dearing, C. L., and Wilfred Owen, *National Transportation Policy*, Washington, D.C.: Brookings Institution, 1949, pp. 1–440.
Fair, Marvin L., and Ernest W. Williams, Jr., *Transportation and Logistics*, Rev. ed., Plano, Texas: Business Publications, 1981.
  Chapter 24, "National Transportation Policy," pp. 483–502.
Farris, Martin T., "Definitional Inconsistencies in the National Transportation Policy," *I.C.C. Practitioners' Journal* (November-December 1967), 25–33.
Harper, Donald V., *Transportation in America: Users, Carriers, Government*, 2nd ed., Englewood Cliffs, N.J.: Prentice-Hall, 1982.
  Chapter 25, "Evaluation of Government Regulation of Transportation," pp. 615–33.
Hazard, John L., *Managing National Transportation Policy*, Westport, Conn.: The Eno Foundation for Transportation, Inc., 1988.
  _____ , "National Transportation Policy Administration (Transitional Lessons from Home and Abroad)," *Transportation Journal* (Summer 1977), 4–19.
  _____ , "Transitional Administration of National Transportation Policy," *Transportation Journal* (Spring 1981), 5–23.
Johnson, James C., "Section 22: Panacea or Parasite?" *Transportation Journal* (Summer 1974), 34–40.
Kennedy, John F., *The Transportation System of Our Nation*, Message from the President of the United States, April 5, 1962, House of Representatives, Document No. 384, 87th Congress, 2nd Session.
Kneafsey, James T., *The Economics of the Transportation Firm*, Lexington, Mass.: D. C. Heath, 1974.
  Chapter 5, "National Transportation Policy and the Transportation Firm," pp. 89–94.
  _____ , *Transportation Economic Analysis*, Lexington, Mass.: D. C. Heath, 1975.
  Chapter 36, "Perspectives on National Transportation Policy," pp. 383–94.
Levine, Harvey, *National Transportation Policy: A Study of Studies*, Lexington, Mass.: Lexington Books, 1978.
Lieb, Robert C., *Transportation: The Domestic System*, 2nd ed., Reston, Va.: Reston Publishing Co., 1981.
  Chapter 20, "Policy Trends and Considerations in Intercity Transportation," pp. 350–59.
Mertins, Herman, Jr., *National Transportation Policy in Transition*, Lexington, Mass.: D. C. Heath, 1972.
  Chapter 3, "Modern Currents of Federal Transportation Policy," pp. 47–76.
National Transportation Policy Study Commission, *National Transportation Policies Through the Year 2000*, Washington, D.C.: Government Printing Office, June 1979.

Norton, Hugh S., *National Transportation Policy: Formation and Implementation*, Berkeley, Calif.: McCutchan, 1966.
Part 3, "Evaluation and Prospects," pp. 209–43.
Talley, Wayne Kenneth, *Introduction to Transportation*, Cincinnati, Ohio: South-Western Publishing Co., 1983.
Chapter 20, "U.S. Transportation and the Future," pp. 374–89.
Williams, Ernest W., Jr., "The National Transportation Policy Study Commission and Its Final Report: A Review," *Transportation Journal* (Spring 1980), 5–19.
Wilson, George W., *Essays on Some Unsettled Questions in the Economics of Transportation*, Bloomington, Ind.: Foundation for Economics and Business Studies, 1962.
Chapter 1, "The Concept of Inherent Advantage," pp. 5–30.
Chapter 3, "Inherent Advantage of Rail and Truck," pp. 79–122.

PART VIII
SUMMARY AND PREVIEW

What is past is prologue.
William Shakespeare

CHAPTER 30

THE FUTURE OF DOMESTIC TRANSPORTATION

Where we are today and where we will be tomorrow are, in considerable part, determined by where we were yesterday. We can no more escape our past than we can avoid our future. Although our primary goal in this chapter is to peer into the future, we must do this in the context of the past and the present.

A GLANCE AT THE PAST

Transportation always has been important to mankind. Civilization has advanced as transport has advanced. Rudyard Kipling once said that transportation *is* civilization.

Like development in other arts and sciences, progress in transportation has been relatively slow when viewed in terms of humanity's entire historical perspective. The human leg has been our primary motive power during most of our existence. The first revolution in transportation occurred when somewhere, by accident or design, someone discovered that animals could be domesticated and made to carry burdens or draw primitive vehicles and that crude sails could be used to propel floating craft capable of carrying persons and cargoes. Apparently a little later, that marvelous invention, the wheel, vastly multiplied transportation capacity just as it multiplied productive capacity.

The first revolution occurred only a few thousand years ago — relatively speaking, only moments ago on civilization's calendar. The next revolution, however, did not occur until around six hundred years ago. This was marked by improvements in the design and size of ships and sails combined with navigational aids and arts that permitted Western European peoples to break away from sight-of-land sea voyages and spread their culture and commerce to almost all parts of the planet. No other era in history has witnessed such tremendous social and economic changes brought about during such a short period of time by improved transport facilities.

The most recent transportation revolution, which is still in process, was ushered in by the substitution of mechanical power for the power of animals and winds. Imaginative persons from the mythical Icarus to the very real Leonardo da Vinci dreamed of, and sometimes even designed, "modern" transportation vehicles throughout the ages. But it was not until the development of a practical steam engine patented by James Watt in 1769 that modern transportation could get under way. Steamboats were operating within a generation afterward, and steam railroads and steamships a little later.

Steam power made the Industrial Revolution possible both by greatly increasing productive capacity and by enabling raw materials to be assembled and products distributed on a mass basis. The second transportation revolution had led to the discovery of the New World. The third permitted the United States to be settled and economically developed within a remarkably short time. Only sixty years after the first steam railroad was operated in this country, the U.S. Census Bureau officially declared that the frontier had ceased to exist.

Technological refinements of the third transportation revolution have progressed rapidly. Within little more than a century after the first practical steam engine, the internal combustion engine was invented and the oil industry began to develop. This made possible automobiles, buses, trucks, and airplanes. Oil replaced coal as fuel for ocean vessels, and following World War II, the coal-burning railroad steam locomotives were rapidly superseded by diesels. Power refinements during recent years have included jet propulsion (used by squids for millions of years) and rockets (whose principles were known by the Chinese two thousand years ago). And atomic power, especially in the area of ocean transportation, seems to have a niche in certain types of services.

We may be on the threshold of a fourth transportation revolution — transportation in space. The space programs of both the United States and the Soviet Union have progressed to the point where the technology of space travel seems proven. The recently developed space shuttle opens up a new type of transportation frontier — one that is no longer tied to the effects of gravity and forces of this planet. We are not suggesting that Star Wars, The Empire Strikes Back, and Return of the Jedi are the same as the dreams of Leonardo da Vinci, but they may be just as prophetic.

Of course, the cost of space transportation is very high. It has been estimated that it would cost $5,000 a pound to launch and recover a space shuttle for trips to a space station or space platform. Still, some products that are better manufactured in a zero-gravity atmosphere could absorb the high cost. For example, some pharmaceuticals are worth up to $22 million per pound, and gallium arsenide, used in semiconductor materials, is worth $50,000 per pound.

In summary, motive power has been the major technological key to transportation development. Vehicles, ways, and institutions have been developed to take advantage of each power breakthrough. Humanity has seen as least three great transportation revolutions, each consisting of a major change in motive power followed by a long period of refinements. But whereas several thousand years passed between the first and second revolutions, only a few hundred years separated the second and third. The rate of change has been much more rapid following the third revolution and seems to be accelerating. We draw upon all the accumulated body of knowledge and experience of the past, and as this body increases, so does our pace of new ideas and practices.

Transportation developments, of course, do not force corresponding economic and social developments, but changes in transport do permit changes in these other areas, and limitations of transport limit developments elsewhere. For example, we hear a great deal today about the population explosion, but without the earlier transportation explosion, a population explosion would not have been possible.

A VIEW OF THE PRESENT

This book has been primarily concerned with the domestic transportation system of the United States. Despite this system's weaknesses and problems, many of which have been mentioned, it is the finest fruit of transportation progress to date. By any criteria, we are blessed with the world's most efficient system of transportation and physical distribution.

Why is this so? In part, perhaps, our strength in transportation can be explained by our apparent knack for technology and organization, by geography, and by the resources that have contributed so much to the wealth of our nation. But this is not all. Institutional factors have played a vital role in our transportation development just as they have in other areas of development.

Our political and economic institutions have permitted and encouraged profit-seeking entrepreneurs and managers to exploit technological, organizational, and managerial innovations with relative freedom. The result has been what might be described as a "multicircuit" system of transportation. That is, we have available many competing alternate routes, modes, and firms from which users can choose. This flexibility of design permits carriage with the least expenditure of operational resources and energy, and with the least likelihood of a blockage of traffic flow arising from a breakdown in some component of the system. We benefit by not having all our eggs in one basket.

It is true that the excess capacity inherent in a multicircuit transport system in contrast with a single-circuit system requires a considerably greater initial investment of resources. But when this investment has been made, and we have made it, the benefits of flexibility and of price and service competition continue indefinitely. Even when additional investment is necessary, it is not necessarily true that expansion should occur only in that mode of carriage that is deemed most efficient in the overall sense. Efficiency must be viewed at the margin rather than as an average. The principle of diminishing returns is as important as the principle of economies of scale. Under some conditions, greater use of a so-called less efficient form of transport may be economically preferable.

One important part of our present-day regulatory policy is concerned with preserving the inherent advantages of competing modes of transportation. Critics sometimes allege that in reality this usually means simply maintaining the status quo. In moments of frustration, one may be tempted to believe that if our current regulation had been in effect in 1860, we would today have Pony Express riders competing with jet airplanes in moving mail between California and the East.

Most students of transportation agree that some economic regulation of the industry is desirable. No one can deny, however, that too much regulation or that particularly inflexible regulation tends to stifle experimentation and innovation. Attempts to impose static institutions on dynamic societies inevitably lead to conflict, with resulting disaster either for the institutions or the societies. A key problem in our present transportation regulation, then, is to keep our regulatory institutions reasonably flexible and dynamic. Only by doing this can we continue to enjoy the fruits of advancing technology and managerial ability.

A MURKY GLIMPSE AT MARVELS OF THE FUTURE

The past is history, interesting for what it can explain about the present or lead us to expect in the future. The present is only an instant of time, a transition between past and future, which disappears as we contemplate it. The future is all-important. Those thought to have the gift of foreseeing the future have been universally respected since time immemorial.

Forecasting, however, is an inexact and hazardous act. Crystal balls are better for looking backward than forward, and the further one gazes into the future, the more murky the image becomes. But we cannot escape forecasts and their consequences. All future economic planning, like all present economic activity, is necessarily based on forecasts, either explicit or implicit. All of us, whether we realize it or not, are constantly engaged in forecasting and planning our future activities according to our forecasts.

The authors, therefore, are willing to set forth some of their views of the future. We will not attempt to peer 1,000 years or even 100 years into the future, however. Instead, we will confine ourselves to the next two or three decades, a time during which present-day university students may be expected to approach their peak levels of activity in their chosen business and professional careers.

Our predictions are based only upon the continuation of presently existing visible trends in technology, organization, regulation, and physical distribution management. One can speculate but not forecast in a vacuum. For example, we think it highly probable (assuming that hydrogen bombs or other disasters do not destroy the human race) that new transportation revolutions based upon new forms of motive power will come. What this motive power will be — solar energy, antigravity or similar "wild" science-fiction power sources, or even undreamed-of sources — no one can say. These new sources may be harnessed within 5 years or 5,000 years. Who knows? What person in 1900 could have predicted that humans would be circling the earth in missiles at a height of several hundred miles and actually traveling to the moon during the 1960s? Yet this would have been easier to predict than a revolutionary motive power source.

Future Technology

Today's travelers and shippers are interested in speed. It seems fairly certain, therefore, that considerable refinements and improvements designed to move people and goods more rapidly will be made. Supersonic jets and jet buses capable of carrying hundreds of persons or many tons of cargo will be used more widely. The so-called X-30 with a speed twenty-five times the speed of sound, traveling from California to New York in less than an hour, using scramjets and carrying 150 passengers, is already on the drawing boards, and $1.5 billion has been spent on its development. Rocket-powered missiles and space shuttles may be used to a limited extent for transporting special types of cargo on the earth as well as for travel to orbiting space stations or the moon.

On the ground, intelligent vehicle-highway systems have already been designed. These use automatic vehicle control systems permitting greater speed and more intensive use of the highway by using computers to control vehicles. Advanced driver information systems indicating highway congestion and best routes are already available, as well as satellites for control of freight vehicles. Separate ways for freight and people are not inconceivable. Railroad trains can be, and probably will be, operated without crews on board. Automatic rail marshaling or assembling yards and centralized traffic control will be greatly improved and expanded. Mechanized loading and unloading will be stepped up, and containerization will continue to grow. These various techniques, of course, will result in modifications of vehicle design.

Continued rapid improvements in pipeline technology can be expected. Although used now mainly for carrying petroleum and its products, a considerable number of items can be transported by pipeline — crushed coal or ores, wood chips, and grain, for example. Technology in this field is already known and is past the experimental stage. Several kinds of nonpetroleum commodities are already being pipelined in some countries. Only one coal slurry pipeline exists in the United States at this time; however, more can be expected.

Mass rapid transportation within major metropolitan areas and between adjacent population centers must and will be improved and expanded. We cannot let automobiles continue to proliferate as they have in the past; if they do, city traffic will completely choke itself. Fast commuter trains or trainlike vehicles utilizing subways and elevated rails in the most congested areas seem to be the only present solution to the plight of many of our larger cities. High-speed train systems, such as the Japanese Bullet train and the French high-speed rail corridor, are already in use. Magnetic-levitation trains will increase intercity speeds and comfort in the future. Endless-belt-type conveyer sidewalks may be used in central business districts and to bring people downtown from outlying commuter stations and parking lots.

Hydrofoil vessels, now being used to a slight extent, promise to provide a fast and flexible form of passenger and specialized freight service on inland and protected waterways. The hovercraft or surface-effect vehicle riding on a cushion of air promises even more in the way of versatility. It may be used on water, rails, highways, or even over terrain where no roads exist.

Much of the hard physical labor will be removed from transportation and distribution, but this is not all. Routine clerical and minor administrative tasks will be handled more and more by electronic computers. Rate clerks already dial a computer for classification, rates, and routes. The computerization of traffic documents will progress markedly, and electronic data interchange (EDI) already allows shippers' computers to "converse" directly with carriers' computers and feed out their agreements to their respective masters.

All these developments and others are within the capabilities of presently existing technology. The limiting factor is cost. Even though we may be able to do something new and different, the old way may be less expensive. But the old ways are becoming increasingly expensive while technological refinements are bringing down the costs of newer techniques. We will adopt the newer methods when they become more profitable — less costly than the older ones.

Higher fuel costs and fuel scarcities will result in more freight moving by rail and more people moving by public transport than would otherwise occur. The use of alternative fuels in over a million new automobiles each year in the 1990s has already been proposed by President Bush as an attempt to clean up the atmosphere. These changes are not likely to be startling in the short run, however, unless the fuel situation becomes more serious than it now appears. The very fact of higher fuel costs, though, will encourage the modification of existing transport technology and the search for new technologies, as well as a search for new energy sources. Cost is the spur of efficiency.

Broader social costs and resources must be included among the costs of transportation along with individual carrier and customer costs. One important social resource whose consumption results in social costs is space — space for living, working, and recreation.

In our large and relatively thinly populated country, we have been little concerned with space to date. But the supply of land is fixed, and not all land is suitable for agriculture, building, or recreation. Population, on the other hand, continues to increase. There is a physical and economic limit to the amount of land we can set aside for transportation. This limit shrinks while the need for additional transportation expands each time a baby is born.

It is clear that we cannot continue building surface ways over our most desirable lands indefinitely. Neither can we take to the air where the saturation point is already dangerously close in many areas. We can, and no doubt will, postpone the inevitable somewhat by the costly expedient of building underground and elevated ways and by constructing ways across our less desirable lands. But before this, or along with it, economic and social pressures will force us to make maximum utilization of existing ways and facilities.

It appears that more and more of our additional mass commuter traffic and our long- and intermediate-haul freight movement must be handled by railroads, the mode most capable of doing this efficiently and with minimum space utilization. We are not predicting that highways and airports will not still be built a generation hence or that Sunday afternoon or rush-hour automobile driving will be less hectic. We are suggesting, however, that cost factors and a frustrated citizenry will see to it that proportionately more traffic moves by rail within the next generation. In fact, we may expect to see rail capacity almost fully utilized again and perhaps even expanded.

Future Transport Organization and Management

There is little doubt that for-hire transportation companies will become considerably fewer but much larger during the coming generation. Many of these for-hire firms, by one device or another, will evolve into true multimodal transportation companies rather than continuing to exist as railroad, truck, air, water, or pipeline firms. More managerial flexibility, more sophisticated management control techniques, and improved technologies will bring increased transport efficiency.

Private transportation will continue to play an important role in our economy, but probably will not grow as rapidly as for-hire transport. Increasingly, the diseconomies of small-unit operation, plus regulatory and user-charge restrictions purposely designed to limit the proliferation of privately operated vehicles, combined with relatively more efficient for-hire transport, will dampen the growth of private carriage.

Overall, the demand for transportation services will continue to keep pace with, or perhaps even exceed, the growth of our gross national product. This means that the demand for qualified and versatile transportation managers, professional employees, and skilled technicians will remain strong in the transportation industry, even though the relative numbers of manual and semiskilled workers in transport may decline.

Future Regulation and Policy

Regulatory institutions, like other social institutions, tend to lag behind environmental changes. Regulations and policies are adopted to deal with present (or past) problem situations. When the problems change, the regulations and policies remain or change very slowly.

Despite lag and slowness, however, institutions do change. During recent years, a general awareness of the need for some changes in transportation policy has developed. The deregulation movement was the result, and we foresee that more changes will occur.

We do not predict a completely free competitive transportation system, however. Rather, we foresee some additional loosening of the restraints on competition within the general framework of existing regulation. Unification, integration, coordination, and cooperation will receive more encouragement and perhaps even some prodding. Various kinds of public aids and promotions will not cease, but will become more selective and will be designed to achieve more specific goals. The application of regulation and policy will not be based completely upon economic and social rationality, but it will be more so than at present.

Regulatory and policy changes of this type will provide a better climate for the utilization and growth of presently known technology and for the birth of new technologies. Transportation and other resources will be better allocated and transport facilities more fully and profitably utilized. The scope of management decision making will be expanded, thus making good management even more crucial than it is now. The environmental and social impacts of transportation will be more widely recognized by the public, regulators, and management.

This brave new transportation world will not be accomplished without tribulations, however. Institutional change is never easy. Someone always is hurt. Competitors lose business, communities lose services or prestige, labor loses jobs, and politicians lose votes. But just as the past tells us that better technologies always supersede inferior ones, so it tells us that urgently needed institutional changes cannot be withstood. Fighting change is futile, and ignoring it is worse. We must expect change, try to anticipate its direction and extent, and attempt to adapt to it and minimize its adverse effects.

Future Managers of Transportation and Physical Distribution

We can anticipate with considerable certainty that the world of tomorrow, in transportation as well as in other areas of endeavor, will be more complex than the world of today. We believe that the role of transportation in tomorrow's world will be equally as important as today and that top management will become increasingly aware of this importance. We trust that transportation will remain free and unnationalized, and we expect that common carriers will continue to be the backbone of our transport system, that railroads will become relatively more important for many kinds of movements, that operating and materials-handling techniques will be more efficient, and that more interagency coordination and intra-agency cooperation will exist. Transport firms will be fewer but larger, and regulation will be less restrictive.

We foresee, too, a spreading and increased emphasis upon the total-cost approach to physical distribution. Management will use more electronic processing, operations research, linear programming, and sophisticated market research techniques. Also, although this book has been concerned mostly with domestic transportation, we feel that international business will grow and that some knowledge of ocean and foreign transportation problems will become increasingly important to the traffic manager or physical distribution manager.

What kind of education should young persons seek to prepare themselves for careers in transportation management, industrial traffic, or physical distribution management? Clearly, they must continue to be specialists and technicians in part, but they must also be generalists and managers. Opportunities for making great savings for a company by hammering through rate reductions are not as great as formerly, and many time-consuming necessary routine chores can be done more efficiently by computers.

Managers of the future must have a well-balanced knowledge of all forms of transportation. They should know a great deal about economics and business administration in general, and in their industry and firm in particular. They should have a good understanding of the social, political, and economic environments within which businesses operate, and they must be able to adapt to rapid change.

What college courses should our potential managers take? Instead of confining themselves to the basic required courses in economics and business administration plus the minimum of required science, social science, and humanities courses and instead of narrowly specializing in transportation, physical distribution, and traffic-management courses, we are firmly convinced that they should broaden themselves with a variety of business and nonbusiness courses beyond the introductory level. Mathematics, statistics, computerology, the behavioral sciences, international law, and similar topics should be seriously considered.

As teachers of transportation and at the risk of upsetting old friends in the field of transportation and traffic management, we are willing to go even further. We can dream of the time when a considerable number of graduates in our field, in addition to their professional tool kits, may be equipped with an above-average acquaintance with such areas as the physical and engineering sciences, American and world history, comparative economic and political systems, art and music, and languages other than English. Everyone is entitled to dreams, and sometimes they come true. As a matter of fact, noticeable changes in this direction have occurred since the first edition of this book was published, and we heartily applaud this trend.

We end on this optimistic note. We hope that the challenge of the future will inspire our readers to prepare themselves for adapting to, and influencing, the shape of future events so that a better transportation and physical distribution system in a more livable environment will contribute to a more satisfying life for all.

ADDITIONAL READINGS

Ballou, Ronald H., and James E. Piercy, "A Survey of Current Status and Trends in Transportation and Logistics Education," *Transportation Journal* (Winter 1974), 27–36.

Barriger, John Walker, *Super-Railroads for a Dynamic Economy*, New York: Simmons-Boardman, 1955, pp. xi, 91.

Becht, J. Edwin, *A Geography of Transportation and Business Logistics*, Dubuque, Iowa: Wm. C. Brown, 1970.
Chapter 6, "Summary/Conclusion — An Evolving National Transportation and Business Logistics Pattern," pp. 82–92.

Beier, Frederick J., "The Educational Challenge Facing Logistics and Physical Distribution Management," *Transportation Journal* (Summer 1972), 40–47.

Berkman, Herman G., "Some Perspectives on Transportation in the Next Decade," *Traffic Quarterly*, 34, No. 1 (January 1980), 143–54.

Berry, William L., "Dimensions and Directions of Education in Business Logistics and Transportation," *Proceedings: Transportation Research Forum*, 16 (1975), 195–202.

Bowersox, Donald J., Pat J. Calabro, and George D. Wagenheim, *Introduction to Transportation*, New York: Macmillan Publishing Co., 1981.
Chapter 18, "Future of Transportation," pp. 356–72.

Brewer, Stanley H., "The Dynamic Nature of Transportation Education," *Transportation Journal* (Summer 1963), 10–15.

Coyle, John J., Edward J. Bardi, and Joseph L. Cavinato, *Transportation*, 2nd ed., St. Paul, Minn.: West Publishing Co., 1986.
Chapter 23, "The Future Direction of Transportation," pp. 469–95.

Farmer, Richard N., "Transportation's Future in the Universities Revisited," *Transportation Journal* (Summer 1963), 23–27.

Farris, Martin T., Douglas C. Cochran, Grant M. Davis, and David R. Gourley, "Transportation Education — An Inter-Disciplinary Approach,'" *Transportation Journal* (Fall 1969), 33–44.

Harper, Donald V., "What Next for Transportation Education?" *Transportation Journal* (Spring 1965), 21–28.

Heskett, J. L., Nicholas A. Glaskowsky, Jr., and Robert M. Ivie, *Business Logistics*, 2nd ed., New York: Ronald Press, 1973.
Chapter 22, "A Look to the Future," pp. 733–58.

Maister, D. H., "Expanding the Role of Transportation Studies in Business Schools — An Example," *Proceedings: Transportation Research Forum*, 16 (1975), 203–11.

McElhiney, Paul T., "Transportation: A Developing Profession?" *Transportation Journal* (Fall 1964), 14–21.

Mundy, Ray A., C. John Langley, Jr., and Thomas E. Gibson, "Industry Evaluation of a Transportation/Logistics Curriculum," *Transportation Journal* (Fall 1977), 33–39.

National Transportation Policy Study Commission, *National Transportation Policy Through the Year 2000*, Washington, D.C., U.S. Government Printing Office, June 1979.

Plowman, E. Grosvenor, "The Intermodality and Cybernetics Keys to Profitable Computerization in Transportation," *Transportation Journal* (Spring 1969), 51–55.

Sampson, Roy J., "Transportation's Future in the Universities," *Transportation Journal* (Spring 1963), 7–11.

Stephenson, Frederick J., Jr., *Transportation USA*, Reading, Mass.: Addison-Wesley Publishing Co., 1987.
Chapter 20, "Transportation's Greatest Challenges," pp. 553–65.

Szent-Miklosy, Balint, "A Personalized Public Circulation System Applicable to a Four-Dimensional City of the Twenty-First Century," *Proceedings: Transportation Research Forum*, 14 (1973), 243–60.

Talley, Wayne Kenneth, *Introduction to Transportation*, Cincinnati, Ohio: South-Western Publishing Co., 1983.
  Chapter 20, "U.S. Transportation and the Future," pp. 374–90.

Vellenga, David B., and John E. Ettlie, "Technology Transfer in Transportation: Problems and Research Questions," *Proceedings: Transportation Research Forum*, 16 (1975), 165–68.

Wood, Donald F., and James C. Johnson, *Contemporary Transportation*, 2nd ed., Tulsa Okla.: PennWell Publishing Co., 1983.
  Chapter 15, "Future Issues and Prospects," pp. 685–726.

NAME INDEX

Allen, Benjamin J., 636
Altrogge, Phyllis E., 416
Applebaum, William, 468

Babcock, Michael, 334
Bagley, John W., 416, 572
Bailey, Elizabeth E., 334
Ballou, Ronald H., 469, 549, 590, 725
Bardi, Edward J., 19, 75, 95, 120, 152, 182, 229, 259, 281, 305, 387, 416, 469, 522, 549, 572, 710, 725
Barrett, Colin, 635
Barriger, John W., 725
Baumel, C. Phillip, 636
Baumol, William S., 387
Becht, J. Edwin, 204, 725
Beier, Frederick J., 306, 725
Bellock, Richard, 334
Berger, Donald L., 692
Berkman, Herman G., 725
Berry, William L., 725
Bess, H. David, 120, 281, 692
Bigham, Truman C., 436
Blackwell, Richard B., 416
Bohlander, George W., 660
Boisjuly, Russel P., 636
Bowersox, Donald J., 19, 44, 75, 94, 281, 362, 387, 498, 522, 549, 591, 725
Brenner, Melvin A., 334
Brewer, Stanley H., 725
Brown, Anthony E., 334
Brown, Stephen W., 362
Brown, Terrrance A., 572

Calabro, Pat J., 19, 44, 75, 94, 281, 362, 387, 498, 522, 725
Callson, Oliver G., 416, 498, 572
Calmus, Thomas W., 387
Carroll, Joseph L., 692

Carter, John P., 427, 436
Cavinato, Joseph L., 19, 75, 95, 120, 152, 282, 229, 259, 281, 305, 387, 416, 437, 522, 572, 710, 725
Cheslow, Melvyn, 56
Closs, David J., 549, 591
Cochran, Douglas L., 725
Conant, Michael, 636, 692
Converse, Paul D., 469
Corsi, Thomas M., 334, 636
Coyle, John J., 19, 75, 95, 120, 152, 182, 229, 259, 281, 305, 387, 416, 469, 522, 549, 572, 710, 725
Crum, Michael R., 636, 660
Curtis, Ellen Foster, 660

Daggett, Stuart, 204, 427, 436, 469, 498
Daley, James M., 636
Daniel, Norman E., 305
Davis, Grant M., 19, 281, 305, 335, 362, 522, 660, 661, 692, 710, 725
Dean, Joel, 387
Dearing, C. L., 710
Dempsey, Paul Stephen, 636
Due, John F., 636, 692

Eilsworth, T. P., 636
Elis, Charles R., 335, 637
Ettlie, John E., 726
Evans, James R., 416, 572

Fair, Marvin L., 152, 182, 229, 259, 281, 305, 387, 416, 469, 498, 523, 636, 661, 692, 710
Fanara, Phillip, Jr., 334
Farmer, Richard N., 725
Farris, Martin T., 19, 56, 120, 152, 183, 281, 305, 469, 498, 522, 636, 660, 692, 710, 725

727

SUBJECT INDEX